Lecture Notes in Computer Science　　10611

Commenced Publication in 1973
Founding and Former Series Editors:
Gerhard Goos, Juris Hartmanis, and Jan van Leeuwen

Editorial Board

David Hutchison
　Lancaster University, Lancaster, UK
Takeo Kanade
　Carnegie Mellon University, Pittsburgh, PA, USA
Josef Kittler
　University of Surrey, Guildford, UK
Jon M. Kleinberg
　Cornell University, Ithaca, NY, USA
Friedemann Mattern
　ETH Zurich, Zurich, Switzerland
John C. Mitchell
　Stanford University, Stanford, CA, USA
Moni Naor
　Weizmann Institute of Science, Rehovot, Israel
C. Pandu Rangan
　Indian Institute of Technology, Madras, India
Bernhard Steffen
　TU Dortmund University, Dortmund, Germany
Demetri Terzopoulos
　University of California, Los Angeles, CA, USA
Doug Tygar
　University of California, Berkeley, CA, USA
Gerhard Weikum
　Max Planck Institute for Informatics, Saarbrücken, Germany

More information about this series at http://www.springer.com/series/7408

Michael Felderer · Daniel Méndez Fernández
Burak Turhan · Marcos Kalinowski
Federica Sarro · Dietmar Winkler (Eds.)

Product-Focused Software Process Improvement

18th International Conference, PROFES 2017
Innsbruck, Austria, November 29 – December 1, 2017
Proceedings

Springer

Editors
Michael Felderer (ID)
University of Innsbruck
Innsbruck
Austria

Daniel Méndez Fernández (ID)
Technical University Munich
Garching
Germany

Burak Turhan (ID)
Brunel University London
Uxbridge
UK

Marcos Kalinowski (ID)
Pontifical Catholic University of Rio de
Rio de Janeiro
Brazil

Federica Sarro (ID)
University College London
London
UK

Dietmar Winkler (ID)
Vienna University of Technology
Vienna
Austria

ISSN 0302-9743   ISSN 1611-3349   (electronic)
Lecture Notes in Computer Science
ISBN 978-3-319-69925-7   ISBN 978-3-319-69926-4   (eBook)
https://doi.org/10.1007/978-3-319-69926-4

Library of Congress Control Number: 2017957552

LNCS Sublibrary: SL2 – Programming and Software Engineering

© Springer International Publishing AG 2017, corrected publication 2017
This work is subject to copyright. All rights are reserved by the Publisher, whether the whole or part of the material is concerned, specifically the rights of translation, reprinting, reuse of illustrations, recitation, broadcasting, reproduction on microfilms or in any other physical way, and transmission or information storage and retrieval, electronic adaptation, computer software, or by similar or dissimilar methodology now known or hereafter developed.
The use of general descriptive names, registered names, trademarks, service marks, etc. in this publication does not imply, even in the absence of a specific statement, that such names are exempt from the relevant protective laws and regulations and therefore free for general use.
The publisher, the authors and the editors are safe to assume that the advice and information in this book are believed to be true and accurate at the date of publication. Neither the publisher nor the authors or the editors give a warranty, express or implied, with respect to the material contained herein or for any errors or omissions that may have been made. The publisher remains neutral with regard to jurisdictional claims in published maps and institutional affiliations.

Printed on acid-free paper

This Springer imprint is published by Springer Nature
The registered company is Springer International Publishing AG
The registered company address is: Gewerbestrasse 11, 6330 Cham, Switzerland

Preface

The 18th International Conference on Product-Focused Software Process Improvement (PROFES 2017) brought together software researchers and industrial practitioners to Innsbruck in Austria, from November 29 to December 1, 2017. The hosting institution was the University of Innsbruck (UIBK) in Austria. In the spirit of the PROFES conference series, PROFES 2017 provided a premier forum for practitioners, researchers, and educators to present and discuss experiences, ideas, innovations, as well as concerns related to professional software process improvement motivated by product and service quality needs.

PROFES 2017 established an international committee of well-known experts in software quality and process improvement to peer review the scientific submissions. This year, we received 72 submissions of which 17 were selected as full papers and ten as short papers. The scientific contributions were strictly scrutinized by members of our international Program Committee. Scientific papers in the PROFES conference received three reviews each and passed through an additional quality assurance via a fourth meta-review.

As a novelty for conferences in our field, we have committed ourselves to making the first steps in establishing an open science policy for all accepted papers. This way, we support increasing the accessibility, reproducibility, and replicability of the research outcomes in PROFES. The steering principle is that all research output should be accessible to the public and that empirical studies should be reproducible. This open science initiative encompassed two key aspects: open access, and open data and open source. The first was achieved by supporting authors of accepted papers in making their preprint copies available to the public. The latter concerned papers that relied on empirical data. In such cases, we asked the authors to – and supported them in doing so – disclose the anonymized and curated data within the limits of existing non-disclosure agreements to increase the reproducibility and the replicability of their studies. To support the authors in such, often complicated, endeavors – sharing data comes with great effort and often with legal concerns and questions – we have established an open science chair to support the authors. Given that the open science initiative was newly introduced to our community, the conformance to the policy was not a mandatory prerequisite for paper acceptance, but overall the initiative was very well perceived and can serve as a model for other (empirical) software engineering conferences.

A further observation from this year's PROFES conference is that certain topics seem to manifest themselves as constantly relevant in the community, reflecting also the needs of the industrial community. This became evident in discussions and presentations, workshops, and tutorials. The topics included (1) software process models in general and agile software development in particular, (2) quality and quality assurance, (3) human factors and user-centric engineering, and (4) data analytics topics. Besides the open space events, there were three workshops and four tutorials given in these areas, many by researchers from industry or industry-close institutions. The tutorials in particular attracted additional participants from local industry and fostered discussion and knowledge exchange between industry and academia.

The keynote talks this year were once again of high quality. Marcus Ciolkowski is a principal IT consultant at QAWare in Munich, Germany, and has an excellent reputation in the field of software quality management and empirical software engineering. Barbara Weber is full professor at the Technical University of Denmark. Moreover, she holds an associate professor position at the University of Innsbruck (Austria), where she leads the research cluster on business processes and workflows. Her research is on, inter alia, human and cognitive aspects of software and information systems engineering.

We are thankful for having had the opportunity to organize PROFES 2017 in Innsbruck. The Program Committee members and additional reviewers provided excellent support in reviewing the papers. We are also grateful to all speakers, authors, and session chairs for their time and effort that made PROFES 2017 a success. We are especially thankful to our sponsors, the Economic Chamber of Tyrol, the Province of the Tyrol, and the University of Innsbruck. We would also like to thank the PROFES Steering Committee members for the guidance and support in the organization process.

Finally, we would like to thank everyone in the organization team as well as the UIBK's student and staff volunteers for making PROFES 2017 an experience that will live in the memory of the participants for years to come.

November/December 2017

Michael Felderer
Daniel Méndez Fernández
Burak Turhan
Marcos Kalinowski
Federica Sarro
Dietmar Winkler

Organization

Organizing Committee

General Chair

Michael Felderer — University of Innsbruck, Austria

Program Co-chairs

Daniel Mendez — Technical University of Munich, Germany
Burak Turhan — Brunel University London, UK

Short Paper Co-chairs

Federica Sarro — University College London, UK
Marcos Kalinowski — Pontifical Catholic University of Rio de Janeiro, Brazil

Workshop and Tutorial Co-chairs

Dietmar Pfahl — University of Tartu, Estonia
Rudolf Ramler — Software Competence Center Hagenberg, Austria

Posters and Tool Demos Co-chairs

Ayse Tosun — Istanbul Technical University, Turkey
Sousuke Amasaki — Okayama Prefectural University, Japan

Proceedings Chair

Dietmar Winkler — Vienna University of Technology, Austria

Open Science Chair

Daniel Graziotin — University of Stuttgart, Germany

Social Media and Publicity Chairs

Martin Solari — Universidad ORT, Uruguay
Davide Fucci — University of Hamburg, Germany
Masateru Tsunoda — Kindai University, Japan

Local Organization Chairs/Web Chairs

Ilona Zaremba — University of Innsbruck, Austria
Boban Celebic — University of Innsbruck, Austria

Program Committee

Silvia Abrahão	Universitat Politecnica de Valencia, Spain
Sousuke Amasaki	Okayama Prefectural University, Japan
David Ameller	Universitat Politècnica de Catalunya, Spain
Maria Teresa Baldassarre	University of Bari, Italy
Monalessa Barcellos	UFES, Brazil
Kristian Beckers	Siemens, Germany
Sarah Beecham	Lero - the Irish Software Engineering Research Centre, Ireland
Stefan Biffl	Vienna University of Technology, Austria
Andreas Birk	SWPM, Germany
David Bowes	Science and Technology Research Institute, University of Hertfordshire, UK
Luigi Buglione	Engineering IT/ETS, Italy
Andrea Burattin	University of Innsbruck, Austria
Marcus Ciolkowski	QAware GmbH, Germany
Steve Counsell	Brunel University, UK
Maya Daneva	University of Twente, The Netherlands
Jose Luis de La Vara	Carlos III University of Madrid, Spain
Sergio Di Martino	University of Naples Federico II, Italy
Oscar Dieste	Universidad Politecnica de Madrid, Spain
Michal Dolezel	MSD IT Global Innovation Center, Prague, Czech Republic
Christof Ebert	Vector, Germany
Fabian Fagerholm	University of Helsinki, Finland
Davide Falessi	Cal Poly, USA
Michael Felderer	University of Innsbruck, Austria
Filomena Ferrucci	Università di Salerno, Italy
Xavier Franch	Universitat Politècnica de Catalunya, Spain
Davide Fucci	University of Oulu, Finland
Vahid Garousi	University of Luxembourg, Luxembourg
Carmine Gravino	University of Salerno, Italy
Daniel Graziotin	University of Stuttgart, Germany
Noriko Hanakawa	Hannan University, Japan
Jens Heidrich	Fraunhofer IESE, Germany
Yoshiki Higo	Osaka University, Japan
Frank Houdek	Daimler AG, Germany
Andrea Janes	Free University of Bolzano, Italy
Janne Järvinen	F-Secure, Finland
Andreas Jedlitschka	Fraunhofer IESE, Germany
Petri Kettunen	University of Helsinki, Finland
Martin Kropp	University of Applied Sciences Northwestern Switzerland, Switzerland
Marco Kuhrmann	Clausthal University of Technology, Germany

Jingyue Li	Norwegian University of Science and Technology (NTNU), Trondheim, Norway
Stephen MacDonell	University of Otago, New Zealand
Lech Madeyski	Wroclaw University of Science and Technology, Poland
Ivano Malavolta	Vrije Universiteit Amsterdam, The Netherlands
Tomi Männistö	University of Helsinki, Finland
Mika Mäntylä	University of Oulu, Finland
Beatriz Marín	Universidad Diego Portales, Chile
Jouni Markkula	University of Oulu, Finland
Kenichi Matsumoto	Nara Institute of Science and Technology (NAIST), Japan
Maurizio Morisio	Politecnico di Torino, Italy
Jürgen Münch	Reutlingen University, Germany
Risto Nevalainen	Spinet Oy, Finland
Anh Nguyen Duc	NTNU, Norway
John Noll	Lero, the Irish Software Engineering Research Centre, Ireland
Renato Novais	Instituto Federal da Bahia, Brazil
Markku Oivo	University of Oulu, Finland
Paolo Panaroni	INTECS, Italy
Oscar Pastor Lopez	Universitat Politecnica de Valencia, Spain
Birgit Penzenstadler	California State University Long Beach, USA
Dietmar Pfahl	University of Tartu, Estonia
Rudolf Ramler	Software Competence Center Hagenberg, Austria
Michele Risi	University of Salerno, Italy
Daniel Rodriguez	The University of Alcalá, Spain
Bruno Rossi	Masaryk University, Czech Republic
Gleison Santos	UNIRIO, Brazil
Giuseppe Scanniello	University of Basilicata, Italy
Kláus Schmid	University of Hildesheim, Germany
Kurt Schneider	Leibniz Universität Hannover, Germany
Kari Smolander	Aalto University, Finland
Martin Solari	Universidad ORT Uruguay, Uruguay
Rodrigo Spinola	Unifacs, Brazil
Klaas-Jan Stol	Lero, University College Cork, Ireland
Michael Stupperich	Daimler, Germany
Marco Torchiano	Politecnico di Torino, Italy
Ayse Tosun	Istanbul Technical University, Turkey
Guilherme Travassos	COPPE/UFRJ, Brazil
Rini Van Solingen	Delft University of Technology, The Netherlands
Antonio Vetrò	Nexa Center for Internet and Society (DAUIN, Politecnico di Torino), Italy
Andreas Vogelsang	Technische Universität Berlin, Germany
Stefan Wagner	University of Stuttgart, Germany
Xiaofeng Wang	Free University of Bozen-Bolzano, Italy
Hironori Washizaki	Waseda University, Japan
Dietmar Winkler	Vienna University of Technology, Austria

Contents

Industry Relevant Qualitative Research

User and Value Centric Approaches

Software Startups

Scrum

Software Testing

Workshop: HELENA 2017

Workshop: QuASD 2017

Posters and Tool Demonstration Papers

Tutorials

Agile Software Development

Is Task Board Customization Beneficial?
An Eye Tracking Study

Oliver Karras[✉], Jil Klünder, and Kurt Schneider

Software Engineering Group, Leibniz Universität Hannover,
30167 Hannover, Germany
{oliver.karras,jil.kluender,kurt.schneider}@inf.uni-hannover.de

Abstract. The task board is an essential artifact in many agile development approaches. It provides a good overview of the project status. Teams often customize their task boards according to the team members' needs. They modify the structure of boards, define colored codings for different purposes, and introduce different card sizes. Although the customizations are intended to improve the task board's usability and effectiveness, they may also complicate its comprehension and use. The increased effort impedes the work of both the team and team externals. Hence, task board customization is in conflict with the agile practice of fast and easy overview for everyone.

In an eye tracking study with 30 participants, we compared an original task board design with three customized ones to investigate which design shortened the required time to identify a particular story card. Our findings yield that only the customized task board design with modified structures reduces the required time. The original task board design is more beneficial than individual colored codings and changed card sizes.

According to our findings, agile teams should rethink their current task board design. They may be better served by focusing on the original task board design and by applying only carefully selected adjustments. In case of customization, a task board's structure should be adjusted since this is the only beneficial kind of customization, that additionally complies more precisely with the concept of fast and easy project overview.

Keywords: Agile development · Task board · Customization · Eye tracking

1 Introduction

Agile software development is a general term for a set of development approaches which focus on social aspects. These approaches aim at increasing the developers' productivity, delivering working software in time and minimizing the risk of failure within software projects [27]. The core concept of agile development is based on fundamental values which are concretized by defined principles that are in turn fulfilled by certain practices [6].

© Springer International Publishing AG 2017
M. Felderer et al. (Eds.): PROFES 2017, LNCS 10611, pp. 3–18, 2017.
https://doi.org/10.1007/978-3-319-69926-4_1

eXtreme programming (XP) [5] and Scrum [24] are the most commonly used and combined agile approaches [3,20]. One practice of XP is the *informative workspace*. According to Beck and Andres, this practice is about how to "make your workspace about your work. An interested observer should be able to walk into the team space and get a general idea of how the project is going within 15 s" [5, p. 39f.]. Cockburn [8] provides a similar concept of the so-called *information radiator*. "An information radiator displays information in a place where passerby can see it" [8, p. 114]. An information radiator has to fulfill two features – representing information that changes over time, and requiring very little effort to view the display. In total, an implementation of these two concepts must be easy-to-use and offer a fast overview with minimal effort [22].

One implementation of both concepts is the *task board* [25]. It is one key artifact of agile development [3,14] which serves a dual purpose of supporting a team's work organization and constituting at a glance how much work is left [10,18]. Additionally, a task board allows communication and collaboration since it tracks and visualizes the software development process and thus simplifies its accessibility for everyone [17,20].

Although the original task board design of Cohn [10] provides a clear overview, teams tend to customize their own [26]. Sharp et al. [27] analyzed six different mature XP teams and their task boards. They identified that the teams' task boards were consistent in terms of usage, but not regarding a particular design. The different task board designs resulted from combinations of various customizations like modified structures, individual colored codings and changed card sizes. Customization itself is not serious since a task board can be easily and flexibly adjusted due to its physical nature [13,26]. Additionally, agile approaches involve customization by offering corresponding degrees of freedom [20,28]. Furthermore, any adjustment of a task board by an agile team according to its needs is plausible since the team members work with it every day [26].

However, multiple combined customizations complicated the maintenance and comprehensibility of a task board. In particular, the increased effort impedes the work of a team as well as team externals with a customized task board [13,15,27]. Thus, the underlying practice of a task board as an *informative workspace* for fast and easy project overview for everyone gets lost.

While the tight social and technical cohesion found in mature agile teams are not disputed, the effect of single practices like the informative workspace is little understood [27]. Berczuk emphasizes that "any team is best served by following the rules of the agile method with as few adjustments as possible" [7, p. 6]. Corresponding to Pikkarainen et al. [20], adoption and change of agile practices are aspects of future studies. Therefore, we investigated whether specific single task board customizations contribute to a task board's usage in comparison with an original task board design. As an example, we focused on the identification of a particular story card as one main task of using a task board.

We conducted an eye tracking study to compare an original task board design corresponding to literature [10,17] with three customized ones. Each customized task board differs exactly in one single aspect from the original one, such as modified structures, individual colored codings, or changed card sizes. Each modification could contribute to achieving a better overview of a task board in order to identify a particular story card faster. In our study, we observe whether a particular task board customization improves the work with a task board. These results identify whether specific kinds of customization are beneficial or not for a task board's usage. Our findings can help agile teams to rethink their current task board design in order to improve it.

The contribution of this paper is the insight that modified structures are the only kind of customization that shortens time to identify a particular story card. Individual colored codings and changed card sizes even have detrimental effects on the performance. Agile teams should reconsider their current task board designs. They may be better served by focusing on the original task board design and applying carefully selected adjustments. A task board's structure should be adjusted since this kind of customization is beneficial and complies with the agile practice *informative workspace*.

This paper is structured as follows: Sect. 2 discusses related work. We describe the task board and its major kinds of customization in Sect. 3. In Sect. 4, we report our eye tracking study and document its findings, which we discuss in Sect. 5. Section 6 concludes the paper.

2 Related Work

2.1 Task Board: Key Artifact of Agile Software Development

Several researchers investigated the task board's usage and role in the agile software development process.

Sharp et al. [25] systematically consider the use and role of story cards and a task board in one mature XP team. Based on story cards and the task board, the authors analyze the team's collaborative work by using the distributed cognition framework. Thus, the information flows in, around and within the XP team can be substantiated to answer "what if" questions regarding changes to the story cards' and task board's form to illustrate consequences for the teamwork. Sharp and Robinson [26] extend the previously mentioned study on three mature XP teams. Their results show significant similarities between the teams' usage of story cards and task board, but not in their particular designs. After discussing the importance of a physical representation of both artifacts, the authors highlight important aspects that need to be taken into account for technological tool-support of agile development. In a further study, Sharp et al. [27] investigate the role of story cards and a task board from two complementary perspectives: a notational and a social one. Based on both perspectives, they explain that these two physical artifacts are important key properties of successful teams. Any attempt to replace these artifacts with technological support needs to take into account the complex relationships between both perspectives and the artifacts. Petre et al. [18] consider the use of public visualizations, i.e. story cards and task boards, in different software development teams. In a number of empirical studies, the authors observe differences in the use of paper and whiteboards between traditional and agile teams. The findings are used to identify possible implications of these differences for software development in general. Liskin et al. [15] explore the use and role of story cards and task board within a Kanban project. Their findings reveal that despite a task board for requirements visualization and communication some requirements are still too implicit and caused misunderstandings. Katsma et al. [14] investigate the usage of software- and paper-based task boards in globally distributed agile development teams. They conclude that paper-based task boards currently offer many advantages compared to its software-based solutions. By applying the media synchronicity theory, Katsma et al. [14] explain the current use and future development of software tools to support globally distributed agile development teams. Perry [17] reports his experiences about transparency problems in agile teams due to difficulties in the transition from a physical to electronic task board. He discusses the advantages and disadvantages of physical and electronic task boards. Based on his observation, he concludes that both task board types have their place in team collaboration. However, the simple power and utility of physical task boards should not be neglected. Hajratwala [13] observes the creation and evolution of various task boards over time in different projects. He explains the reasons why the task boards evolved, and recommends key attributes that a task board should have.

The previous investigations focus on both the usage and role of story cards and task boards in agile software development. The main focus is on the general work with a task board and its importance for agile development. Additionally, different task board designs and their evolution over time are presented. Although differences in the designs were recognized, none of the researchers considered its possible impact on work with this artifact. Our paper addresses this topic by investigating whether task board customization is beneficial or not.

2.2 Viewers' Consideration of Software Development Artifacts

There are already several researchers who used eye tracking to investigate a viewer's consideration of a respective software development artifact.

Ahrens et al. [1] conducted an eye tracking study to analyze how software specifications are read. They identified similar patterns between paper- and screen-based reading. The results contribute awareness by considering readers' interests based on how they use a specification. Gross and Doerr [11] performed an explorative eye tracking study to investigate software architects' information needs and expectations from a requirements specification. The results allow first insights into the relevance of certain artifact types and their notational representations. Gross et al. [12] extended their previously mentioned eye tracking study by analyzing information needs and expectations of usability experts. Based on the findings, the authors introduced the idea of a view-based requirements specification to fulfill needs of different roles in software development. Santos et al. [23] evaluated the effect of layout guidelines for i^* goal models on novice stakeholders' ability to understand and review such models. They identified no statistically significant differences in success, time taken or perceived complexity between tasks conducted with well and badly designed model layouts. Ali et al. [2] applied eye tracking to the verification of requirements traceability links. Their data analysis allowed the identification and ranking of developers' preferred source code entities. Thus, the authors defined two weighting schemes to recover traceability links combined with information retrieval techniques.

All previous studies apply eye tracking to analyze how specific software development artifacts are read by persons with different functions. We follow this approach by using eye tracking to investigate the work with a task board. Our study specifically focuses on the impact of different task board customizations on a task board's usage by team externals respectively new team members.

3   Task Board: Structure and Content

The task board's origins are the *informative workspace* practice of Beck and Andres [5] as well as the concept of *information radiator* by Cockburn [8]. They present first ideas of story cards pinned on a wall or whiteboard. In their books, they offer possible implementations of these concepts.

Cohn [10] describes a first concrete task board design in his book *"Agile Estimating and Planning"*. According to his definition, a task board consists of up to seven columns to track and visualize a team's progress in development. The seven columns are:

1. *Stories*: A backlog of all story cards
2. *To Do*: All task cards to implement particular story cards
3. *Tests Ready*: Status of a story cards' acceptance tests
4. *In Process*: Task cards developers have signed up for
5. *To Verify*: Implemented task cards that need to be verified
6. *Hours*: Total working hours remaining for particular story cards
7. *Done*: All implemented and verified task cards

Furthermore, Cohn [10] defines that a task board includes one row for each story card. Each row contains all task cards that are related to the corresponding story card. According to Cohn [10], the columns *Tests Ready*, *To Verify*, *Hours* and *Done* are optional.

3.1   Task Board Customizations

Based on the previously mentioned findings in literature, we considered further research papers about the design and content of task boards. Additionally, we analyzed different task boards with respect to their design in online galleries of team spaces [4,19,29]. Thus, we identified three major kinds of customization: *modified structures, individual colored codings*, and *changed card sizes*.

Modified structures are changes regarding the amount and usage of a task board's rows and columns. Petre et al. [18] describe a task board as a vertical surface for story cards. This task board has a codified structure to indicate a story card's status. Other researchers [17,21,22] report in greater detail about this codified structure. Pries-Heje and Pries-Heje [21] focus on a task board for Scrum, which consists of the four columns *Backlog*, *Task in Progress*, *Done*, and *Done Done* corresponding to their description. A similar task board structure is mentioned by Rubart and Freykamp [22]. The columns of this task board are named *Selected Product Backlog*, *Tasks To Do*, *Work In Progress*, and *Done*. Perry [17] also reports that a simple task board has four columns called *Story*, *To Do*, *In Progress*, and *Complete*.

All descriptions have in common that the task board structure consists of the same four columns with only slightly different labels. However, none of these researchers mentions the use of rows on a task board. We could identify two variants for the use of rows based on our consideration of team spaces in online galleries. The first variant uses one row for each story card, which corresponds to Cohn's definition [10]. The second one uses rows in specific columns like *To Do* and *Work In Progress* to visualize the assignment of developers to story cards. The comparison of these insights with Cohn's original task board structure [10] shows clear differences regarding the amount and use of a task board's rows and columns between theory and practice.

Individual colored codings are colored cards and markers with arbitrary meaning which need to be memorized. Several researchers report the widespread individual use of colored codings on task boards. Katsma et al. [14] describe the use of different colored cards to indicate various card types, e.g. red for bugs cards. Liskin et al. [15] mention colored markers on cards to represent assigned developers. Sharp et al. [25–27] observe the use of colored markers and cards as status indicators and card types in four mature XP teams. These findings correspond to our observations of the task boards presented in the online galleries. Even though we cannot clarify the exact meanings of the used colored codings, we observe that their use is widely scattered.

Changed card sizes consider the size of story cards which are used to write down user stories and display them on the task board. The size of story cards has a wide range. Azizyan et al. [3] as well as Katsma et al. [14] report about story cards the size of sticky notes or post-its. In contrast, Perry [17] and Sharp et al. [27] state that a story card's size can be up to an index card of 5×7 in. These insights coincide with our observations of the online galleries. We identified the same range of card sizes from post-its up to index cards.

3.2 Task Board Designs

In consideration of the previously described findings, we developed four task board designs for our eye tracking study. These designs are based on a dataset of real story cards from a completed software project. While one task board design is similar to Cohn's initial definition of a task board design [10], each of the other designs takes one of the three major customizations into account.

During the design development, we took into account that all task boards represent the same content, except for exactly one specific difference according to the customizations. Figure 1 represents an overview of our four task board

designs. All task boards have four columns, labeled with *Stories, Task To Do,
W.I.P* (Work In Progress), and *Done*. These labels are adopted from the original
task board of the completed software project whose story cards were used. We
decided to change as little as possible from the original dataset. Therefore, we
retain the labels of the task board since they are similar to the previously mentioned ones. Furthermore, these four columns cover all three obligatory columns
corresponding to Cohn's definition [10].

Figure 1a presents the task board with an original design which is similar to
Cohn's definition [10]. This task board does not have Cohn's row structure [10]
since the used dataset of real story cards did not consider this aspect. Therefore,
the story cards could not be grouped to achieve a reasonable row structure.

Figure 1b shows the task board with modified structures. We decided to use
the second variant of additional rows over specific columns since Cohn's row
structure [10] was not applicable to the used dataset. We did not add additional
columns to change only one structural aspect. Thus, we added rows over the
columns *Task To Do* and *W.I.P.* to visualize the assignment of developers to
story cards. Each row starts with a letter that represents one developer.

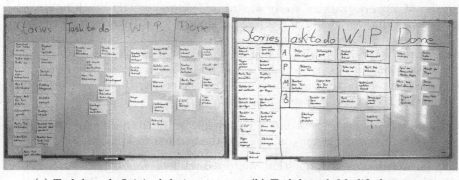

(a) Task board: Original design   (b) Task board: Modified structures

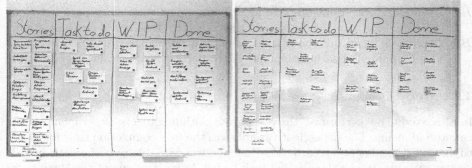

(c) Task board: Individual colored codings   (d) Task board: Changed card sizes

Fig. 1. Task board designs. (Color figure online)

Figure 1c represents the task board with individual colored codings. In accordance with literature [15,25], we added colored markers on the right lower corner of the story cards. Each of the three colors (green, orange and blue) represents one developer and his assignment to the corresponding story card.

Figure 1d illustrates the task board with changed card sizes. We decided to minimize the story cards to sticky note size (ca. 4×6 in.), since story cards have originally index card size (ca. 5×7 in.).

All task boards have the same amount of handwritten story cards whose content is based on the real dataset. The first three task boards (see Fig. 1a, b, and c) contain 40 story cards of index card size. The last task board (see Fig. 1d) contains 40 story cards of post-it note size. While the amount and general position of the story cards are the same in each column and task board, we shuffled the story cards before placing them on the task boards. Thus, we achieved a random placement regarding the story cards' content and no task board equals exactly any other.

4 Eye Tracking Study

The aim of our eye tracking study was to understand whether task board customization facilitates identifying a particular story card faster compared to an original task board design. We proceeded to achieve this aim by comparing the original task board design with each of the three task board customizations. Such an investigation enables us to judge whether the original task board design or the respective task board customization should be preferred. We were interested in answering the following research question:

RQ: Does the respective task board customization facilitate identifying a particular story card faster compared to the original task board design?

To answer the research question, we tested the following hypotheses for each of the three task board customizations:

H_0: There is no speed difference in identifying a particular story card between the original task board design and the respective task board customization.

H_1: There is a speed difference in identifying a particular story card between the original task board design and the respective task board customization.

4.1 Study Design

In this study, we performed three separate within-subjects experiments with counterbalancing. The dependent variable was the task completion time for identifying a particular story card. The independent variable was the task board design with two levels: the original task board design and one of the three task board customizations. We measured the task completion time by observing the participants with the *SMI Eye Tracking Glasses*[1]. Each experiment represents a

[1] https://www.smivision.com/eye-tracking/product/eye-tracking-glasses/.

scenario in which the participant joins an ongoing development project as a new team member who has to work with the existing task board. We decided to focus on the perspective of a new team member since a task board should support a fast and easy project overview for everyone, i.e. the team and team externals respectively new team members. If a new team member already benefits from a customization, a whole team should also benefit from it.

We analyzed task completion times with a two-tailed paired samples t-test at a significance level of $p = 0.05$. This allows us to determine whether the respective task board customization leads to a statistically significant speed difference in identifying a particular story card compared to the original task board design. Thus, we can identify whether a particular task board customization is beneficial for a task board's usage. An existing speed difference would allow us to reject H_0, while a missing one would not allow such a rejection.

4.2 Study Procedure

The eye tracking study was carried out with 30 participants consisting of 10 undergraduate and 20 graduate students of computer science. All participants had basic knowledge about agile software development and were close to the next step in graduation. Thus, they represent potential new team members in a software development team, which corresponds to our target population.

All in all, the whole eye tracking study with all three experiments was carried out within three months. Each experiment compared the original task board design with one of the three major task board customizations. We randomly assigned each participant to one of the three experiments. In each experiment, we conducted 10 separate sessions each with one of the 10 assigned participants. Each session included an introduction to the experiment with its task of considering two task boards. In this context, we explained the basic concept of a task board. Depending on the experiment, we assigned the letter "J" (see Fig. 1b) respectively the color "green" (see Fig. 1c) to the participant since the task boards with modified structures respectively individual colored codings required the assignment of a row or color to the participant. After the calibration of the *SMI Eye Tracking Glasses* for the participant, we captured their examination of the task board. We repeated the same process for the second task board design.

4.3 Analysis and Results

Table 1 shows the measured task completion times of each participant for the particular experiment and respective task board design. The first five subjects of each experiment (see Table 1, *Group* 1) received the original task board design first and then the customized one. The other five subjects of each experiment (see Table 1, *Group* 2) received the designs in reversed order. For each experiment, we verified that the data is normally distributed by applying the *Shapiro-Wilk* test. Subsequently, we performed the two-tailed paired samples t-tests at a significance level of $p = 0.05$. Thus, we can determine whether an observed difference exists due to the test conditions or by chance. Additionally, we calculate Cohen's d

which is the most common type of effect size for t-tests that indicates whether or not the difference between two groups' mean is large enough to have practical relevance independently from statistical significance.

In Table 2, we present the results of our conducted two-tailed paired samples t-tests and their effect size d.

The analysis of the first experiment yields a significant difference in the task completion times for the original task board design ($M = 15.0$ s, $SD = 3.6$ s) and the modified structures ($M = 9.8$ s, $SD = 3.9$ s); $t(9) = -2.39, p = 0.04$. Hence, H_0 can be rejected for the first experiment. Modified structures shorten time to identify a particular story card compared to the original task board design. The value of Cohen's d is 0.76, which is close to the threshold of 0.8 for a large effect [9]. Hence, the identified difference has almost large practical relevance.

The t-test of the second experiment shows a significant difference between the task completion times for the original task board design ($M = 11.7$ s, $SD = 3.2$ s) and the individual colored codings ($M = 14.3$ s, $SD = 4.7$ s); $t(9) = 2.86, p = 0.02$. The null hypothesis H_0 can be rejected for the second experiment.

Table 1. Experiment results – task completion time [s]

| Subj. | Experiment 1 | | Subj. | Experiment 2 | | Subj. | Experiment 3 | |
	Original	Structures		Original	Codings		Original	Cards
P1	16	10	P3	16	15	P4	10	11
P2	18	4	P14	16	22	P5	13	27
P11	16	11	P15	11	12	P24	30	36
P12	12	9	P16	10	9	P25	4	19
P13	19	4	P17	13	16	P26	19	18
P6	18	10	P18	12	20	P23	22	12
P7	8	16	P19	13	16	P27	9	19
P8	12	9	P20	11	13	P28	19	28
P9	13	15	P21	5	6	P29	17	27
P10	18	10	P22	10	14	P30	12	16
Mean	15.0	9.8	Mean	11.7	14.3	Mean	15.5	21.3
SD	3.6	3.9	SD	3.2	4.7	SD	7.5	7.9

(Group 1 = P1–P13 rows; Group 2 = P6–P10 rows)

Table 2. Two-tailed paired samples t-test

Experiment	1	2	3
Calculated t-value	-2.39	2.86	2.41
t-value from table ($df = 9, \alpha = 0.05$)		2.26	
Calculated p-value	0.04	0.02	0.04
Result (p-value ≤ 0.05?)	Significant	Significant	Significant
Cohen's d	0.76	0.90	0.76

Consequently, the original task board design allows to identify a particular story card faster compared to the individual colored codings. Cohen's d is 0.90 and thus greater than the threshold of 0.8 for a large effect [9]. The determined difference between the individual colored codings and the original task board design has large practical relevance.

The results of the third experiment also show a significant difference in the task completion time for the original task board design ($M = 15.5$ s, $SD = 7.5$ s) and the changed card sizes ($M = 21.3$ s, $SD = 7.9$ s); $t(9) = 2.41, p = 0.04$. Consequently, we can reject H_0. This leads to the insight that changed card sizes increase the required time for identifying a particular story card compared to the original task board. The calculated effect size d is 0.76 and thus close to the threshold of 0.8. We identified a difference between changed card sizes and the original task board design that has almost large practical relevance.

4.4   Interpretation

Our findings provide insights with respect to the influence of task board customizations in comparison with an original task board design. Whereas modified structures shorten time to identify a particular story card, individual colored codings and changed card sizes increase the required time.

The performed t-tests substantiate that there is a statistically significant difference between the respective task board customization and the original task board design. Our results indicate that customizing a task board's structure supports its usage. In case of customization, agile teams should focus on adjusting the structure of a task board according to their needs. Since this customization supports the work of new team members who are unfamiliar with the task board, we assume that a whole team will also benefit from it. Such a customized task board provides a fast and easy project overview for everyone, i.e. the team and team externals respectively new team members. Thus, the task board complies more precisely with the agile practice *informative workspace*.

However, according to our results, not every customization is beneficial for a task board's usage. Adjustments on story cards such as individual colored codings or changed card sizes lead to an increased amount of time to identify a particular story card. Even though these two kinds of customization do not necessarily support a task board's usage, they are extensively applied in practice by agile teams [15, 25–27]. Therefore, our findings are in conflict with the observed widely distributed use of these customizations.

In total, we identified a statistically significant difference in each of the three experiments. Each difference indicates that one of the two compared task board designs (customized vs. original) allows identifying a particular story card faster. All findings have an almost large effect size d that emphasizes their practical relevance. According to our results, modified structures should be preferred compared to the original task board design, which is, in turn, preferable to individual colored codings and changed card sizes. Hence, the original task board design is a good solution. In case of customization, however, agile teams may be better served by adjusting their task board's structure instead of its story cards. As an answer to our research question, we can summarize:

A: We identified that only the modified structures allow identifying a particular story card faster compared to the original task board design. Both of the other customizations result in an increased amount of time. Hence, adjusting a task board's structure is the only beneficial option of all investigated customizations.

4.5   Threats to Validity

In the presented eye tracking study, we considered threats to construct, external, internal and conclusion validity corresponding to Wohlin et al. [30].

Construct validity: We selected the content for the story cards from a completed software project. All task boards (see Fig. 1) were based on this content. Thus, we have a mono-operation bias since we only use one dataset for the task boards' content. As a consequence, the constructed task boards do not convey a comprehensive overview of the task boards' complexity in practice. However, we expected that the amount of 40 handwritten story cards and their different arrangement on each task board result in sufficient realistic complexity for the participants. Another threat to validity was the participants falsely reporting having finished. Our experiments required the exact measuring of the task completion time. However, people are afraid of being evaluated and they are inclined to convey the impression of being better than they really are. Therefore, this human tendency endangered the outcome of our experiment. We counteracted this threat by using eye tracking combined with an additional acoustical statement of the participants when they identified the particular story card. Thus, we could determine the exact task completion time of each participant beyond doubt. The single use of eye tracking is a further threat to validity. This mono-method bias is problematic since it only allows a restricted explanation of our findings. However, we focused on an objective measure instead of a subjective one since objective measures can be reproduced more easily and are thus more reliable. The given task of identifying a particular story card caused an interaction of testing and treatment. The comparison of task boards with the given task could imply to find the story card as fast as possible. Even though we did not mention to measure task completion time, the participants could be aware of the time as a factor. Instead of understanding the task board designs, they could only have tried to be as fast as possible. We mitigated this threat to validity by using eye tracking. Thus, we could observe how the participants examine the task boards and make sure that all of them took the respective design into account.

External validity: The choice of involving almost graduated students as participants, and the use of data from a completed software project produced a good level of realism. At the same time, the experimental setting endangered the external validity since the environment was different from the real world. None of the task boards had true pragmatic value for the participants since none of them had a genuine working task with the task board. Future evaluation should be done on real industry projects with team members that truly work with the task board.

Internal validity: In our eye tracking study, the three experiments were distributed over three months altogether. This large period of time could have an effect on the participants' motivation to contribute to our study. However, we could not compare all task board designs within one experiment due to the use of eye tracking, which is time-consuming as well as exhausting for the participants. A single session with one participant required as much as 25 min for the comparison of two task board designs. Additionally, we could mitigate possible learning effects since all task board designs equaled one another except for exactly one specific difference with respect to the corresponding customization.

Conclusion validity: We decided to use eye tracking to improve the reliability of our results since an objective measuring is easier to reproduce and it is more reliable than a subjective one. Additionally, we only selected students as participants who were close to their graduation. Hence, they form a more homogeneous group which counteracts the threat of erroneous conclusions. Therefore, we mitigated the risk that the variation due to the subjects' random heterogeneity is larger than due to the investigated task board designs.

5 Discussion

This presented work investigates the *task board* as one implementation of the agile practice *informative workspace* and the benefit of task board customization.

Although agile teams use task boards in a similar manner, they tend to customize their task boards according to their needs. Combined customizations such as modified structures, individual colored codings, and changed card sizes lead to complexity, which impedes a task board's maintenance and comprehensibility. The increased effort is in conflict with a task board's underlying agile practice of fast and easy project overview for everyone, i.e. the team and team externals respectively new team members. We performed an eye tracking study to analyze whether there is a significant speed difference in the time required to identify a particular story card between the original task board design and the respective task board customization.

We contribute the insight that only modified structures improve a task board's usage. In contrast, individual colored codings and changed card sizes did not improve performance beyond the original design.

The modified structures are the only beneficial customization. We assume that the additional rows improve the arrangement of the story cards. Spatially close object seems to be grouped since they are perceived as belonging to each other. This effect is called *law of proximity*, which is part the *Gestalt Principles* [16]. The additional rows influence the story card's visual appearance by position without further support. The story cards' improved proximity simplifies a viewer's consideration of the task board. This finding can help agile teams to rethink their task board in order to improve it. They may be better served by focusing on the original task board design and by only adjusting its structure according to their needs. Thus, they can create a task board which complies more precisely with the concept of fast and easy project overview for everyone.

In contrast, individual colored codings and changed card sizes are not beneficial. The missing benefit of individual colored codings is caused by a counteracting effect of combined laws of the *Gestalt Principles*. According to the *law of similarity*, using colors for similar objects supports the visual appearance of belonging together. At the same time, the story cards' spatial arrangement complies with the *law of proximity*. The colored markers are more difficult to perceive since the *law of proximity* dominates the *law of similarity*. Therefore, individual colored codings do not provide a benefit for customizing a task board. The changed card sizes are not an improving task board customization, either. According to our results, a viewer's effort increases by considering and recognizing smaller story cards to identify a particular one. Smaller story cards are more difficult to perceive and read, which complicates a task board's clarity. Thus, changed card sizes provide no benefit, either.

The impact of the different task board designs on the performance of a single team is low. Even if a team member identifies 120 times a day a story card with an average saving of 5 s per identification, his total saving would only be 10 min per workday. The benefit of our results is the finding that the original design of a task board by Cohn [10] with its underlying agile practices constitutes already a good solution for a single team to be productive. Even though agile approaches offer corresponding degrees of freedom for customization, in the worst case each team of a company has its own specific task board design. Due to the wide variety of customization options, the individual task boards complicate the collaboration across teams and the work of team externals. Thus, the collaboration performance of multiple teams, as well as the work of team externals, can be improved by focusing on one consistent and beneficial task board design.

All in all, we can conclude that not each kind of task board customization is beneficial. Based on our findings, we agree with Berczuk [7]: Teams are better served by adjusting their task boards as little as possible. As a consequence, agile teams should rethink their current task board design with respect to the applied customizations. The original task board design (see Fig. 1a) is already a good solution. However, if customization is desired, teams should focus on adjusting a task board's structure since only this kind of customization improves the use of a task board according to our results.

6   Conclusion

This work contributes the insight that not every kind of task board customization is beneficial. Agile teams tend to extensively customize their task boards according to their needs [27]. However, the use of modified structures, individual colored codings, and changed card sizes impede work with a task board. Thus, task board customization is in conflict with the agile practice of fast and easy project overview for everyone, i.e. the team and team externals.

We performed an eye tracking study consisting of three separate experiments comparing an original task board design with each of three identified major task board customizations. Based on these results, we identified statistically significant differences in all three experiments. These findings show that modified structures such as additional rows support a task board's usage with respect to the used exemplary main task of identifying a particular story card. In contrast, individual colored codings and changed card sizes do not improve performance beyond the original design.

Our work points to the conclusion that agile teams should rethink their current task board design. They may be better served by focusing on the original task board design and applying carefully selected adjustments. In case of customization, teams should adjust the task board's structure since this is the only beneficial kind of customization. Additionally, such a customized task board design complies more precisely with its implemented agile practice.

Acknowledgment. This work was supported by the German Research Foundation (DFG) under ViViReq (2017–2019). We follow ethical guidelines of the Central Ethics Commission of our university. They regulate subject information and rights. Since recognizable persons should not be visible on distributed video, our data is archived internally for future reference.

References

1. Ahrens, M., Schneider, K., Kiesling, S.: How do we read specifications? Experiences from an eye tracking study. In: Daneva, M., Pastor, O. (eds.) REFSQ 2016. LNCS, vol. 9619, pp. 301–317. Springer, Cham (2016). doi:10.1007/978-3-319-30282-9_21
2. Ali, N., Sharafl, Z., Gueheneuc, Y.G., Antoniol, G.: An empirical study on requirements traceability using eye-tracking. In: 28th IEEE International Conference on Software Maintenance. IEEE, Piscataway, NJ (2012)
3. Azizyan, G., Magarian, M.K., Kajko-Matsson, M.: Survey of agile tool usage and needs. In: Agile Conference. IEEE, Piscataway, NJ (2011)
4. Babik, L., Sheridan, R.: Breaking down walls, building bridges, and Takin' out the trash, https://www.infoq.com/articles/agile-team-spaces
5. Beck, K., Andres, C.: Extreme Programming Explained: Embrace Change, 2nd edn. Addison-Wesley, Boston (2007)
6. Beck, K., Beedle, M., Van Bennekum, A., Cockburn, A., Cunningham, W., Fowler, M., Grenning, J., Highsmith, J., Hunt, A., Jeffries, R., et al.: Manifesto for Agile Software Development (2001)
7. Berczuk, S.: Back to basics: the role of agile principles in success with an distributed scrum team. In: Agile Conference. IEEE, Los Alamitos, Calif (2007)
8. Cockburn, A.: Agile Software Development: The Cooperative Game, 2nd edn. Addison-Wesley, Upper Saddle River (2009)
9. Cohen, J.: A power primer. Psychol. Bull. **112**(1), 155–159 (1992)
10. Cohn, M.: Agile Estimating and Planning, 12th edn. Prentice Hall PTR, Upper Saddle River (2012)
11. Gross, A., Doerr, J.: What do software architects expect from requirements specifications? Results of initial explorative studies. In: 1st IEEE International Workshop on the Twin Peaks of Requirements and Architecture. IEEE, Piscataway, NJ (2012)

12. Gross, A., Doerr, J.: What you need is what you get!: The vision of view-based requirements specifications. In: 20th IEEE International Requirements Engineering Conference. IEEE, Piscataway, NJ (2012)
13. Hajratwala, N.: Task board evolution. In: Agile Conference. IEEE, Piscataway, NJ (2012)
14. Katsma, C., Amrit, C., Hillegersberg, J., Sikkel, K.: Can agile software tools bring the benefits of a task board to globally distributed teams? In: Oshri, I., Kotlarsky, J., Willcocks, L.P. (eds.) Global Sourcing 2013. LNBIP, vol. 163, pp. 163–179. Springer, Heidelberg (2013). doi:10.1007/978-3-642-40951-6_10
15. Liskin, O., Schneider, K., Fagerholm, F., Münch, J.: Understanding the role of requirements artifacts in Kanban. In: 7th International Workshop on Cooperative and Human Aspects of Software Engineering. Association for Computing Machinery Inc., New York, NY (2014)
16. Palmer, S.E.: Vision Science: Photons to Phenomenology. MIT Press, Cambridge (1999)
17. Perry, T.: Drifting toward invisibility: the transition to the electronic task board. In: Agile Conference. IEEE, Los Alamitos, Calif (2008)
18. Petre, M., Sharp, H., Freudenberg, S.: The mystery of the writing that isn't on the wall: differences in public representations in traditional and agile software development. In: 5th International Workshop on Cooperative and Human Aspects of Software Engineering. IEEE, Piscataway, NJ (2012)
19. Pietri, W.: An XP team room. http://scissor.com/resources/teamroom/
20. Pikkarainen, M., Haikara, J., Salo, O., Abrahamsson, P., Still, J.: The impact of agile practices on communication in software development. Empir. Softw. Eng. 13(3), 303–337 (2008)
21. Pries-Heje, L., Pries-Heje, J.: Why scrum works: a case study from an agile distributed project in Denmark and India. In: Agile Conference. IEEE, Piscataway, NJ (2011)
22. Rubart, J., Freykamp, F.: Supporting daily scrum meetings with change structure. In: Proceedings of the 20th ACM Conference on Hypertext and Hypermedia, NY. ACM, New York (2009)
23. Santos, M., Gralha, C., Goulão, M., Araújo, J., Moreira, A., Cambeiro, J.: What is the impact of bad layout in the understandability of social goal models? In: IEEE 24th International Requirements Engineering Conference (2016)
24. Schwaber, K., Beedle, M.: Agile Software Development with Scrum. Prentice Hall, Upper Saddle River (2002)
25. Sharp, H., Robinson, H., Segal, J., Furniss, D.: The role of story cards and the wall in XP teams: a distributed cognition perspective. In: Agile Conference. IEEE, Los Alamitos, Calif (2006)
26. Sharp, H., Robinson, H.: Collaboration and co-ordination in mature eXtreme programming teams. Int. J. Hum Comput Stud. 66(7), 506–518 (2008)
27. Sharp, H., Robinson, H., Petre, M.: The role of physical artefacts in agile software development: two complementary perspectives. Interact. Comput. 21(1–2), 108–116 (2009)
28. Sutherland, J., Downey, S., Granvik, B.: Shock therapy: a bootstrap for hyperproductive scrum. In: Agile Conference. IEEE, Piscataway, NJ (2009)
29. Wake, B.: A gallery of team rooms and charts. http://xp.123.com/articles/a-gallery-of-team-rooms-and-charts/
30. Wohlin, C., Runeson, P., Höst, M., Ohlsson, M.C., Regnell, B., Wesslén, A.: Experimentation in Software Engineering. Springer, Berlin (2012). doi:10.1007/978-3-642-29044-2

Influence of Software Product Management Maturity on Usage of Artefacts in Agile Software Development

Gerard Wagenaar[1(✉)], Sietse Overbeek[2], Garm Lucassen[2],
Sjaak Brinkkemper[2], and Kurt Schneider[3]

[1] Avans University of Applied Sciences, Breda, The Netherlands
g.wagenaar@avans.nl
[2] Utrecht University, Utrecht, The Netherlands
{s.j.overbeek,g.lucassen,s.brinkkemper}@uu.nl
[3] Leibniz Universität Hannover, Hanover, Germany
kurt.schneider@inf.uni-hannover.de

Abstract. *Context*: Agile software development (ASD) uses 'agile' artefacts such as user stories and product backlogs as well as 'non-agile' artefacts, for instance designs and test plans. Rationales for incorporating especially non-agile artefacts by an agile team mainly remain unknown territory. *Goal*: We start off to explore influences on artefacts usage, and state our research question as: To what extent does maturity relate to the usage of artefacts in ASD in software product organizations? *Method*: In our multiple case study 14 software product organizations were visited where software product management maturity was rated and their artefacts usage listed. *Results*: We found maturity to be negatively correlated with the non-agile/all artefacts ratio. In other words, the more mature software product management is, the fewer non-agile artefacts are used in ASD. *Conclusions*: This suggests that an organizational factor influences an agile team in its artefacts usage, contradictory to the concept of self-organizing agile teams.

Keywords: Agile · Artefacts · Maturity · Software product management

1 Introduction

Agile software development (ASD) has been introduced in the domain of product software development [1, 2], with product software defined as: *"A packaged configuration of software components or a software-based service, with auxiliary materials, which is released for and traded in a specific market"* [3, *p. 534*], where auxiliary materials consist of software documentation, user material and the like. Product software differs from tailor-made software in, among other aspects, the importance of architecture [3]. The necessity of auxiliary materials and the requirement of a future-proof architecture are indicative for the use of documentation artefacts in the product software development lifecycle. Research in ASD has devoted attention to the usage of artefacts, where a distinction can be made between 'agile' and 'non-agile' artefacts. Agile artefacts are artefacts which are inherent to an ASD (for instance user

© Springer International Publishing AG 2017
M. Felderer et al. (Eds.): PROFES 2017, LNCS 10611, pp. 19–27, 2017.
https://doi.org/10.1007/978-3-319-69926-4_2

stories or a backlog); all other artefacts are considered to be non-agile (for instance architectures or designs). In agile product software development, software product organizations (SPOs) as manufacturers of such software could be expected to use non-agile artefacts precisely because of their needs with regard to architecture and auxiliary materials. In this research we explore one influencing factor on the decision to use, especially non-agile, artefacts. To this extent we assume that artefacts usage is a quality consideration and relates to the quality of software product management (SPM) in an SPO, where software product management is the discipline and role, which governs a product from its inception to the market/customer delivery in order to generate biggest possible value to the business [4]. In the Capability Maturity Model Integration for Development (CMMI-DEV), documentation artefacts, for instance architecture documentation and design data, are explicitly mentioned and they contribute to achieving higher maturity levels [5].

To explore influencing factors we formulate our research question as: *To what extent does SPM maturity relate to the usage of artefacts in ASD?*

Fourteen organizations were visited as part of a multiple case study. Our findings show a negative correlation between SPM maturity and the usage of non-agile artefacts. Altogether our findings contribute to a better understanding of factors that influence an agile team in its artefacts usage, an area in which research is scarce. From a practitioner's perspective one of the principles behind the agile manifesto, "The best architectures, requirements, and designs emerge from self-organizing teams" [6], is put to the test if an organizational factor can be shown to relate to artefacts usage.

The remainder of this paper is organized as follows. In Sect. 2 we outline the theoretical background with an overview of research on the usage of artefacts in ASD (Sect. 2.1), and SPM in general and a method to establish its maturity in particular (Sect. 2.2). In Sect. 3 we present our research method, a multiple case study, including data collection and coding, leading to our findings. Section 4 discusses our conclusions, which may be summarized as a new insight in the relation between SPM maturity in SPOs and the usage of non-agile artefacts in ASD in SPOs.

2 Theoretical Background

2.1 Artefacts in Agile Software Development

An artefact (in ASD) is defined as a tangible deliverable produced during software development [7]. In ASD artefacts, such as architectures, requirements, and designs, are used as a decision of the self-organizing ASD team [6], dependent on the value it attaches to them. ASD practitioners perceive their internal documentation as especially important but feel that too little of it is available [8]. A decision on usage of artefacts is in fact a decision on 'non-agile' artefacts, because agile artefacts already are part of an ASD method itself. Previous research shows the dilemma of the optimal level of agile and non-agile artefacts in ASD. Gröber [9] constructed an (agile) artefact class diagram with artefacts and relationships between them as result of a systematic literature study on the usage of artefacts in agile methods. Based on this research and adding findings from three case studies Wagenaar et al. [7] developed a Scrum artefact model, distinguishing product from process artefacts and Scrum from non-Scrum artefacts. In a study on large-scale offshore software development programmes Bass [10] identified 25 artefacts on five levels of abstraction: Programme governance, Product, Release, Sprint, and Feature.

In summary, various models show a mixture of agile and non-agile artefacts, although based on different viewpoints varying from agile or Scrum development to offshore software development. The models classify both agile and non-agile artefacts, but, with one exception, do not explicitly address the distinction between the two. This precludes, as one consequence, insight in reasons for using them.

2.2 Software Product Management Maturity

Assessing maturity of software development processes and thus contributing to their improvement has led to several maturity models. General ones, like CMM [11], or ISO/IEC 15504 [12] and more specialized agile models are all composed of hierarchical maturity levels, but are otherwise quite different in their domains, backgrounds, structures, and contents [13]. However, because of our focus on SPM a more dedicated model, but similar in its constitution, is available, which describes the SPM process as consisting of four business functions: Portfolio management, Product planning, Release planning, and Requirements management [14, 15]. Each business function is in turn divided into focus areas. In case of the business function Requirements management, these are: Requirements gathering, Requirements identification, and Requirements organizing. The model has an associated method, the Situational Assessment Method (SAM), which can be used to measure a maturity level specifically for SPM [15]. To this extent the SAM provides a matrix with an overview of capabilities at different levels that need to be implemented to reach a full-grown maturity. The matrix is used in a bottom up way. Maturity is ranked per focus area, and then aggregated to SPM maturity on a scale from 0–10.

3   Research Method

To investigate our research problem, we used a multiple case study, which is an accustomed way to investigate phenomena in a context where events cannot be controlled and where the focus is on contemporary events [16]. Data collection took place through single-site case studies following Yin's widely accepted guidelines for case studies [16]. We first collected basic data on artefacts and maturity on basis of a protocol including: (1) SPM theory and research, (2) interview instructions, and (3) reporting guidelines. We found 14 organizations willing to participate, all using ASD[1]. The organizations develop product software (1) for a broad range of domains, from (semi-)government to software development, (2) with five to over hundred employees (organization as a whole), and (3) for ten to several thousands of customers.

---

[1] A description of the organizations is available at https://osf.io/dez9k/?view_only=3171388053194c 549f09b22fe4fbcfc0.

In case a SPO produced more than one product, one of them was selected. In Sect. 3.4 we discuss threats to external validity regarding our participating organizations.

3.1 Data Collection

Data collection was the same for all organizations. Interviews were held, ranging from one interview through one interview with two interviewees to two or more interviews with several interviewees. Interviewees were in general product manager or owner, although some Scrum masters were also included. Interviews lasted on average one hour. They were semi-structured to allow interviewees to speak freely and to be able to ask follow-up questions. The interview instructions concerned two tasks: (a) Determine SPM maturity, and (b) Describe artefacts during ASD[2].

For the establishment of maturity, a description of capabilities required to achieve a certain maturity level is already provided in the SAM [14]. For each capability the organization being assessed has to answer the question *"Have you implemented this capability within your organization?"* with either Yes or No, for example: *"Can stakeholders submit requirements directly to the central database?"*.

For the listing of artefacts the interview guidelines were based on the life cycle of a user story or a requirement, starting with the SPM's pre-development stage (portfolio management, product planning). Then they continued with questions about the activities in ASD, often starting with user stories in a product backlog and ending with the production of source code. Finally, post-development activities were identified, such as bugs, again leading to requirements. For the description of this life cycle a common vocabulary was established by using the FLOW modelling technique [17, 18]. FLOW's emphasis on information and its distinction between solid and fluid information makes it suitable for the representation of artefacts. Documented information is called solid information if it is long term accessible, repeatedly readable, and comprehensive for third parties. In contrast, undocumented or fluid information is information that violates any one of the above criteria.

3.2 Coding

Data on maturity needed no further coding, because answers to questions from the SAM directly translate to a maturity level for each focus area (see Sect. 2.2).

Data analysis for artefacts started by extracting solid information as artefacts from the FLOW models, identifying 201 artefacts. Because of differences in SPO's terminology this initial list was subject to: (1) lexical analysis, and (2) semantic analysis [20]. In lexical analysis we removed distinctions in singular and plural forms, for instance 'Bug report' (listed 5 times) and 'Bug reports' (1 appearance). We removed adjectives, for instance mapped both 'Product roadmap' and 'Company annual roadmap' on 'Roadmap', and we unified words having the same lexical roots, for instance 'Acceptance criteria' and 'Acceptation criteria'. This reduced the number of 201 to 123

---

[2] Interview instructions are available at https://osf.io/dez9k/?view_only=3171388053194c549f09b2 2fe4fbcfc0.

artefacts. In further semantic analysis we used the description of solid information in the FLOW model to identify similarities and differences in artefacts. Based on this description and also guided by the artefact model [7] and the artefact list [10] we further pruned our list. For instance, 'Application' with description "*Code implemented by developers based on the release and sprint plan*" and 'Code', "*A (set of) implemented and unit-tested product feature(s)*", were mapped.

Finally we excluded a number of artefacts, since not all artefacts in our findings are artefacts directly related to ASD. Since our interviews used the pre-development stage as starting point we identified some 'Business Artefacts': Business case, Business plan, Market intelligence, Market requirement, Strategy, and Roadmap. An SPO's strategy certainly influences decisions with an impact on ASD, but it is not an ASD artefact. Business artefacts are important SPM artefacts, but are neither produced nor used directly by an agile team.

3.3 Findings

We aggregated maturity in a maturity level per business function where this maturity is calculated as the average maturity of underlying focus areas (Table 1)[3]. For example, the focus areas 'Gathering', 'Identification', and 'Organizing' within the business function 'Requirements management', scored 7, 9, and 10 respectively for organization A. This results in (7 + 9 + 10)/3 = 8.7 for 'Requirements management' for organization A. The last row shows the overall SPM maturity as the average of the four business functions.

Table 1. Maturity of SPM

	SPO	A	B	C	D	E	F	G	H	I	J	K	L	M	N
Maturity	Requirements management	8.7	4.3	5.0	7.3	4.3	5.7	7.0	5.7	4.7	5.3	4.7	4.7	4.7	10.0
	Release planning	6.3	3.8	9.0	5.8	5.3	6.5	8.5	7.2	5.3	7.5	3.7	7.3	6.0	7.2
	Product planning	5.0	3.7	5.3	6.7	6.7	8.3	10.0	6.0	7.0	6.7	5.3	4.0	8.0	5.7
	Portfolio management	5.0	5.0	7.0	8.0	8.7	8.3	8.7	7.0	7.0	4.3	5.3	4.3	5.7	7.3
	Overall SPM maturity	6.25	4.21	6.58	6.96	6.25	7.21	8.54	6.46	6.00	5.96	4.75	5.08	6.09	7.54

We found a total of eighteen artefacts, which were mentioned by at least two organizations (Table 2). The one but last row in Table 2 lists the number of artefacts (per organization) which were mentioned by that organization only. Since they tend to be rather organization-specific we have aggregated them in this way.

---

[3] Scores per focus area are available at: https://osf.io/dez9k/?view_only=3171388053194c549f09b22fe4fbcfc0.

Table 2. Artefacts per SPO

Artefact	A	B	C	D	E	F	G	H	I	J	K	L	M	N
User story	v	v	v			v	v		v	v	v	v	v	v
Code	v	v		v	v	v	v		v	v	v			
Sprint backlog		v	v	v		v	v	v	v				v	v
Epic	v		v			v							v	v
Product backlog		v	v	v		v		v						v
Definition of done	v	v				v		v					v	
Estimated user story		v		v							v			
Agile artefacts	*4*	*6*	*4*	*4*	*1*	*6*	*3*	*3*	*3*	*2*	*3*	*1*	*4*	*4*
Product requirement	v		v			v			v	v	v		v	v
Bug report	v		v		v				v	v	v			
Release note		v			v		v		v		v		v	
Test deliverables		v			v		v		v			v		
Request for change		v			v	v							v	
Acceptance criteria	v				v						v	v		
Release	v				v					v				
Functional design		v										v		
Release plan					v				v					
Technical design		v									v			
User documentation			v				v							
Non-agile artefacts	*4*	*5*	*3*	*0*	*7*	*2*	*3*	*0*	*5*	*3*	*5*	*3*	*3*	*1*
Organization-specific	*5*	*2*	*3*	*2*	*1*	*2*	*1*	*0*	*1*	*0*	*0*	*6*	*2*	*0*
Non-agile ratio	*0.69*	*0.54*	*0.60*	*0.33*	*0.89*	*0.40*	*0.57*	*0.00*	*0.67*	*0.60*	*0.63*	*0.90*	*0.56*	*0.20*

Artefacts in Table 2 are also classified in one of two categories: (1) Agile artefacts, and (2) Non-agile artefacts, since we are especially interested in the usage of additional, non-agile artefacts. We identified 'Agile artefacts' as: Product backlog, Sprint backlog, Code, User story, Epic, Definition of done, and Estimated user stories, because those are explicitly part of agile practices [20, 21]. Various artefacts all are non-agile artefacts. To be able to compare between organizations we calculated the ratio of non-agile artefacts compared to the total number of artefacts.

Our research question was: To what extent does SPM maturity relate to the usage of artefacts in ASD? We identified both SPM maturity (Table 1) and the usage of ASD artefacts (Table 2). A measure of correlation dependency between two variables is the Pearson correlation coefficient [22]. We calculated it between SPM maturity and non-agile artefacts ratio as $\rho(14) = -0.3576$. This outcome is considered to be of a weak to moderate strength. The answer to our research question thus is: SPM maturity is negatively correlated with the non-agile/all artefacts ratio. In other words, the more mature SPM is, the fewer non-agile artefacts are used in ASD.

3.4 Validity

Validity of our research depends on four criteria: Construct validity, internal and external validity, and reliability [16]. To enhance construct validity we: (1) had interviewees comment on results of interviews, (2) complemented viewpoints in the interviews with more than one interviewee, and (3) followed a strict procedure in interpreting an interview, by means of the FLOW modelling technique as well as in applying the SAM. Nevertheless, organizations were not visited by one and the same interviewer, so interpretation may have influenced especially the listing of artefacts. Additionally, the maturity level is based on self-assessment, which may introduce bias. Internal validity is mainly a concern for explanatory case studies, but we did apply pattern matching in translating solid information in the models through lexical and semantic analysis to our artefacts listing. External validity benefits from using a multiple case study on the basis of a common procedure. It has to be noted however, that our results only show a weak to moderate correlation. Furthermore, we visited SPOs, which was also reflected in our choice for measuring maturity. Generalizability to non-SPOs is therefore limited. From our findings organizations E and L show remarkable ratios, using (far) more non-agile artefacts than agile ones. This may be reason to question their application of indeed an ASD method. Finally, reliability increases because of our use of a procedure with interview instructions and the use of a case study database.

4   Conclusions and Future Research

We rated SPM maturity for 14 organizations and listed their artefact usage. We found evidence for SPM maturity to be negatively correlated with the non-agile/all artefacts ratio. A possible explanation could be that a 'mature' SPO' has organized its software product management already in such a way that additional documentation during ASD is hardly required, but further research should be carried out to prove this. Although a causal relationship has not been proven, our evidence suggests that an organizational factor – maturity in SPM – influences an agile team in its usage of artefacts. This would be quite contradictory to self-organizing teams, from which the best architectures, requirements, and designs emerge. Our research goes beyond the sole modelling of artefacts and provides initial knowledge about factors that influence agile teams in their artefacts usage.

Our research also strengthens empirical evidence with regard to the usage of artefacts in ASD. Our current findings confirm both artefacts that appeared in the artefact list [9], but not in the Scrum artefact model [7], as well as vice versa. The relatively small yield of 'new' artefacts, proves an already high degree of coverage in the research on the existence of artefacts in ASD.

Further research is necessary, not only to prove a causal relationship between (SPM) maturity and artefacts usage, but also to identify other factors influencing agile teams in their choice for (non-agile) artefacts. Candidates are team composition (size, experience), project characteristics or explicit team decisions as opposed to maturity of an organization as a whole. This would provide an answer to the question whether, especially non-agile, artefacts emerge from an agile team or are used for reasons which originate from outside the team. More general, how does an agile team reach a balance between agile and non-agile artefacts?

Acknowledgements. The authors express their gratitude to the students and organizations involved in this research; the first author also expresses his gratitude to Avans University of Applied Sciences for facilitating and supporting this research.

References

1. Dzamashvili Fogelström, N., Gorschek, T., Svahnberg, M., Olsson, P.: The impact of agile principles on market-driven software product development. J. Softw. Maint. Evol. Res. Pract. **22**(1), 53–80 (2010)
2. Vlaanderen, K., Jansen, S., Brinkkemper, S., Jaspers, E.: The agile requirements refinery: applying SCRUM principles to software product management. Inf. Softw. Tech. **53**(1), 58–70 (2011)
3. Xu, L., Brinkkemper, S.: Concepts of product software. Eur. J. Inf. Syst. **16**(5), 531–541 (2007)
4. Ebert, C.: The impacts of software product management. J. Syst. Softw. **80**(6), 850–861 (2007)
5. CMMI Product Team: CMMI for development, version 1.3. resources.sei.cmu.edu/library/asset-view.cfm?assetID=9661 (2010). Accessed 04 Sept 2016
6. Beck, K., Beedle, M., Van Bennekum, A., Cockburn, A., Cunningham, W., et al.: Agile Manifesto. agilemanifesto.org/principles (2001). Accessed 24 Sept 2012
7. Wagenaar, G., Helms, R., Damian, D., Brinkkemper, S.: Artefacts in agile software development. In: Abrahamsson, P., Corral, L., Oivo, M., Russo, B. (eds.) PROFES 2015. LNCS, vol. 9459, pp. 133–148. Springer, Cham (2015). doi:10.1007/978-3-319-26844-6_10
8. Stettina, C.J., Heijstek, W.: Necessary and neglected? An empirical study of internal documentation in agile software development teams. In: Proceedings SIGDOC, pp. 159–166. ACM, New York (2011)
9. Gröber, M.: Investigation of the usage of artifacts in agile methods. www4.in.tum.de/~kuhrmann/studworks/mg-thesis.pdf (2013). Accessed 23 May 2016
10. Bass, J.M.: Artefacts and agile method tailoring in large-scale offshore software development programmes. Inf. Softw. Tech. **75**, 1–16 (2016)
11. Paulk, M.C., Curtis, B., Chrissis, M.B., Weber, C.V.: Capability maturity model SM for software, version 1.1. sei.cmu.edu/reports/93tr024.pdf (1993). Accessed 24 June 2013
12. ISO/IEC 33002:2015. iso.org/standard/54176.html (2015). Accessed 11 Aug 2016
13. Leppänen, M.: A Comparative Analysis of Agile Maturity Models. In: Pooley, R., Coady, J., Schneider, C., Linger, H., Barry, C., Lang, M. (eds.) Information Systems Development, pp. 219–230. Springer, New York (2013). doi:10.1007/978-1-4614-4951-5_27
14. Bekkers, W., Brinkkemper, S., van den Bemd, L., Mijnhardt, F., Wagner, C., Van de Weerd, I.: Evaluating the software product management maturity matrix. In: Proceedings RE, pp. 51–60. IEEE (2012)
15. Bekkers, W., Spruit, M., Van de Weerd, I., van Vliet, R., Mahieu, A.: A situational assessment method for software product management. In: Proceedings ECIS, paper 22 (2010)
16. Yin, R.K.: Case Study Research: Design and Methods, 4th edn. Sage Publications, Thousand Oaks (2009)
17. Stapel, K., Knauss, E., Schneider, K.: Using FLOW to improve communication of requirements in globally distributed software projects. In: Proceedings CIRCUS, pp. 5–14. IEEE (2009)

18. Stapel, K., Schneider, K.: Managing knowledge on communication and information flow in global software projects. Expert Syst. **31**(3), 234–252 (2014)
19. Jurafsky, D., Martin, J.H.: Speech and Language Processing, 2nd edn. Prentice Hall, Englewood Cliffs (2008)
20. Schwaber, K., Sutherland, J.: The Scrum guide™. www.scrumguides.org/scrum-guide.html (2016). Accessed 25 May 2017
21. Cohn, M.: User Stories Applied for Agile Software Development. Addison Wesley, Boston (2004)
22. Wohlin, C., Runeson, P., Höst, M., Ohlsson, M.C., Regnell, B., Wesslén, A.: Experimentation in Software Engineering. Springer, Heidelberg (2012). doi:10.1007/978-3-642-29044-2

Real-Life Challenges on Agile Software Product Lines in Automotive

Philipp Hohl[1]([✉]), Jürgen Münch[2], Kurt Schneider[3], and Michael Stupperich[1]

[1] Daimler AG, Research and Development, Ulm, Germany
{philipp.hohl,michael.stupperich}@daimler.com
[2] Reutlingen University, Reutlingen, Germany
juergen.muench@reutlingen-university.de
[3] Leibniz Universität Hannover, Hanover, Germany
kurt.schneider@inf.uni-hannover.de

Abstract. Context: The current situation and future scenarios of the automotive domain require a new strategy to develop high quality software in a fast pace. In the automotive domain, it is assumed that a combination of agile development practices and software product lines is beneficial, in order to be capable to handle high frequency of improvements. This assumption is based on the understanding that agile methods introduce more flexibility in short development intervals. Software product lines help to manage the high amount of variants and to improve quality by reuse of software for long term development.

Goal: This study derives a better understanding of the expected benefits for a combination. Furthermore, it identifies the automotive specific challenges that prevent the adoption of agile methods within the software product line.

Method: Survey based on 16 semi-structured interviews from the automotive domain, an internal workshop with 40 participants and a discussion round on ESE congress 2016. The results are analyzed by means of thematic coding.

Results: Two main expected benefits of merging agile practices and product line development are pushing the change in software development for future proof agile automotive organizations. Challenges that prevent agile adoption within software product lines are mainly of organizational, technical and social nature. Key challenges are related to transforming organizational structures and culture, achieving faster software release cycles without loss of quality, appropriate quality assurance measures for software variants, and the collaboration with suppliers and other disciplines such as mechanics.

Conclusion: Significant challenges are imposed by specific characteristics of the automotive domain such as high quality requirements and many interfaces to surrounding rigid and inflexible processes.

Keywords: Automotive · Agile software development · Software product line

© Springer International Publishing AG 2017
M. Felderer et al. (Eds.): PROFES 2017, LNCS 10611, pp. 28–36, 2017.
https://doi.org/10.1007/978-3-319-69926-4_3

1   Introduction

The automotive domain is recently in a disruptive change. High-frequent changes due to innovations and new technology confront the automotive domain. Several possible future scenarios are becoming apparent. One scenario comprises the changeover from the internal combustion engine to electric and hydrogen fuel cell cars [1]. New competitors entering the market, pushing the traditional car manufactures to react on the changing market situation. The situation is further exacerbated by political agenda, e.g., german politics requests for 1 million electric cars within 2020[1]. The plan is now abandoned because at present it is considered unrealistic[2]. Nevertheless, a lot of suppliers are very active in this development area, encourage the traditional car manufactures to make more effort to achieve at least the same development pace. It is seen as a necessity to be competitive in future. Another scenario comprises self-driving, community owned cars. This will be a further disruptive change in the domain, because car-sharing has a direct impact on the ownership of private cars. The scenario implies that anyone can order a car wherever and whenever it is needed. Several challenges arise with this form of car-sharing, like challenges in high-precise navigation and autonomous driving. The solution of these challenges will all be addressed in software. The described scenarios are likely to exist in parallel. This does not solely affect the entire car transportation system, but the automotive software development as well.

The software development must consider deep integration between hardware and software, strong focus development processes, strong supplier involvement, and safety-critical functionality. In this context, it is challenging to develop and distribute high-quality software at a high pace. Furthermore, the amount of software in the car increased exponentially the last decades [2]. To handle the increased complexity and the high amount of variations, a Software Product Line (SPL) was and is used. The SPL helps to handle changes, coordinates the software development worldwide and increases the software quality by reuse. However, increasing market pressure and fast changing requirements are challenging the existing solution with SPL. Agile Software Development (ASD) methods are a promising solution to keep pace with the market. The combination of ASD and SPL development is assumed to be difficult [3]. Agile development uses short development cycles and only a few Product Owners (PO), whereas SPL comprises several POs and a scoping process that hinders short iterations. This publication presents expected benefits and challenges for the integration of ASD into existing automotive SPL development. In summary, our contributions are as follows:

– Identify the expected benefits for the combination of ASD and SPL in the automotive domain.

---

[1] www.bundesregierung.de/Webs/Breg/DE/Themen/Energiewende/Mobilitaet/pod-cast/_node.html.

[2] http://www.elektronikpraxis.vogel.de/elektromobil/articles/608627/.

– Analyze the real-life challenges on Agile Software Product Lines in the automotive domain.

2   Related Work

To investigate the topic and find all the related work, we conducted a literature review to search for the Common Ground of Automotive Agile Software Product Lines [4]. The literature review revealed that there is no approach specifically tailored to the automotive domain handling the combination of ASD and SPLs. As presented in the study, it is therefore necessary to take the related research areas into account. Three major challenges for related research areas are identified, like the competitive pressure and the need to shorten development cycles (1) [5–9], different development cycle-times for related development systems (2) [9–11], and unclear management of software reuse and agile development (3) [5, 10, 12].

3   Study Approach

The goal of this study is to gain a better understanding of the expected benefits for a combination of ASD and SPLs. Furthermore, it identifies the automotive specific challenges that prevent the adoption of ASD within existing SPLs.

3.1   Research Questions

RQ 01: What are the expected benefits for the combination of ASD and SPL in the automotive domain?
RQ 02: Which real-life challenges hinder the adoption of Agile Software Product Lines in the automotive domain?

3.2   Research Design

The research reported in this paper builds on on-going research in collaboration with Daimler AG[3]. This study is based on a qualitative survey we conducted 2016 [13], the outcome of an internal expert workshop on Automotive Agile Software Product Lines with 40 participants as well as a discussion round on the ESE Congress 2016[4] in Stuttgart with 60 participants.

The interview study [13] took place between May and June 2016. The interviews were designed as exploratory semi-structured interviews to gain insights into the examined topic. For the semi-structured interviews an interview guide was implemented and tested in a pilot interview. We held an internal workshop with automotive experts at the Daimler AG. We let the participants vote on different statements to confirm the findings from the interview study. Furthermore, we presented these findings on the ESE Congress and repeated the voting.

---

[3] www.daimler.com.
[4] https://www.ese-kongress.de/.

3.3   Data Collection and Analysis

Research Sites and Participants. The interview participants are employees of an OEM and one automotive consultant. The interviewee selection was based on two criteria: First, the interviewee should have a work experience of at least two years. The length of employment varied from 3 to 20 years, with an average working experience of 16 years. Second, the interviewee should already use agile practices with intent on implementing a software reuse strategy or vice versa. The following participants were selected: Two managers, five process owners, two system architects, six software developers and one automotive consultant for agile development processes. The interviews were conducted by the primary researcher from May to June 2016. In an internal workshop, 40 participants discussed the challenges in adopting agile practices to existing development processes. All participants were explicitly invited and from the automotive domain or related research institutes from universities. Furthermore, the workshop searched for requirements for the combination of ASD and SPL. The findings from the workshop were verified on the ESE Congress 2016 in Stuttgart, within a discussion round in the automotive agile session.

Interviews. The interviews consist of 14 face-to-face interviews and one group interview with two participants. In consent with the interviewee, the interview was recorded and transcribed verbatim for detailed analysis. All transcribed interviews notes were managed using the reference management program Citavi.

Analysis. The analysis used the coding concepts of Straussian Grounded Theory, based on the classification of Stol et al. [14]. We used the three coding phases of Straussian Grounded Theory: open coding, axial coding, and selective coding [14]. The interpretive process of open coding breaks down the data analytically and generates categories and concepts. The concepts were grouped together and related to their subcategories in the axial coding. In the selective coding the central categories were defined.

3.4   Threat to Validity

This section treats the identified threats to the validity.

Interview and Interview Guide. The possibility of misunderstandings between interviewees and the researcher is a threat to validity. To minimize the threat, the study goal was explained to the participants prior to the interview. Steps taken to improve the reliability of the interview guide included a review and a pilot test.

Research Sites and Participants. It is possible that the selection of the participants biased the outcome. For the internal workshop, it could be that the identified challenges are only in-house challenges. We validated the outcome on the ESE Congress 2016 to be sure that the challenges are not only in-house.

Researcher Bias. Data extraction and coding was done by Researcher 1. This could introduce bias due to misunderstanding and misinterpretation on the researcher side. To minimize the risk, the interviews were recorded and transcribed.

4 Results

The study reveals that the combination of ASD and SPL is a desired way of managing the software development in the future. There are several aspects why a combination is seen as beneficial.

4.1 Research Question 1

The study reveals two areas in which the participants identified a benefit.

Customer Collaboration. All participants mentioned that it is required for future success, to react on customer expectations faster. This ensures that customer-oriented products or features can be rapidly launched in the market with profit. One participant mentioned that with a rapid customer feedback the software development will be more effective. Not accepted solutions by the customer are identified in an early stage and could be dropped before they are further developed. The development capacity is better and more efficiently used. Trends in the customers behavior could be recognized and developed towards customer satisfaction.

Improvement of Development. The main expected benefit is an improved software development process. The development process benefits from several improvements, which could be categorized as: Transparency (1), collaboration within the development team (2), efficiency in development (3), flexibility (4), software quality (5), development speed (6), cost of delay (7), and a better verification and reuse strategy (8).

With the introduction of agile development, an agile mindset is presumed to be introduced as well. Most interviewees mentioned that transparency (1) in work will be resulting from the new way of collaborative working (2). With the consequential distribution of knowledge within the software development team, it is expected to be an open and genuine cooperation between employees (2). The developers mentioned that work could be more effective (3) by granting more responsibility to lower hierarchy levels. This results in less coordination for management approval. A possible solution is the resolving of too many levels in the hierarchy into flat hierarchies with self-organizing teams.

However, some participants are still critical about this proposed way of working. They mentioned that some developers do not want to change their working behavior and it is not possible to force a mindset change. Furthermore, the change need time and is not always necessary. A mixture of employees specialized in a specific field, and more general employees is necessary. With the right mixture, the development could benefit from in deep knowledge and flexibility (4) in the development. This flexibility is explicitly mentioned by the managers as a need to react on customer needs. For developers, the customer satisfaction is of secondary importance compared to software quality (5). They assumed that with a combination of ASD and SPLs it will be possible to deliver high quality software (5) at the required faster pace (6), due to increased software reuse and shorter release cycles. They further emphasized that it is important to bundle the competence in-house, to deliver software faster and react on changing requirements. With faster in-house communication channels, one participant mentioned that this will be beneficial considering the cost of development and cost of delay (7). The developers mentioned that a good reuse strategy and SPL (8) is necessary to use parts of the software more often and save further money. All participants emphasized that an agile development speeds up the development to get a high quality software, whereas the existing SPL helps to ensure that already verified software is reused within a mature reuse strategy.

4.2 Research Question 2

Real-life challenges are evaluated, in order to combine ASD and SPLs in the automotive domain to handle agile development and software product lines. We focus on the development process, as the process must change and adopted to verify a smooth development in an agile way. The challenges could be categorized into organizational challenges (1), worldwide development (2), management (3), dependencies (4), synchronization processes (5), validation (6), release (7), and the software development process itself (8).

Organization. All participants mentioned that coordination is a challenge for introducing agile elements to the existing SPL. The existing hierarchy is changing slowly towards an open minded agile development. However, the existing processes are not bad and still valid. Special milestones in the processes verify worldwide coordination and planning, like scoping, to decide which features are relevant for implementation. By introducing agile development into the processes, it is seen that the coordination of the software development hinders a faster pace. The pace is influenced by coordination among the SPL. One challenge is to prevent a decomposition of the SPL. With many software variants and a faster development pace, it is the risk that the common software part becomes stunted. Therefore, it is important to consider synchronization points between software variants, several development processes like hardware and software, as well as supplier and in-house development.

Worldwide Distribution of the Development Team. A major challenge is the collaboration with suppliers and a worldwide distribution of the development team. Different cultures and different mindset are likely hindering an agile development. In addition, the purchase department is often interfering an agile collaboration with suppliers. This challenges are important to consider, while setting up the development team. Furthermore, the worldwide distribution of the development team leads to challenges in the team communication. Different time-zones, no face-to-face conversation and mistakes in translation represent big dangers. Furthermore, the process to maintain and scope the common software parts requires a lot of communication between all participants. This is seen as slowing down the development because of slow communication channels. A lot of planning and coordination is necessary to maintain the SPL. A participant mentioned that it is necessary that the communication is not only top-down, but in both directions.

Management. It is mentioned that the management does not want to give up any responsibility. With less responsibility on management level, scheduling of the development and reporting will be challenging. It is unclear for the managers how the agile software product line could be planned and features are scoped. Planning although is of high importance in an automotive development.

Dependencies and Synchronization. The automotive software development is a worldwide development with a lot of dependencies, like many included technical systems, test and verification steps and other developments domains like hardware and mechanical. A dynamic coordination is seen as necessity to introduce agile development practices into SPL development. The development process across several domains must be synchronized. Challenging is the fact, if just parts of the organization are working in an agile way and others not. Interfaces between those departments must be well organized and set up.

Validation and Release. Maintaining the compliance to standards while developing a lot of different software variants is seen as highly challenging. On the one hand, the development speed is increased but on the other hand, it is necessary to validate the software to maintain standards like ISO 26262 and other restrictions given by the law. It is a challenge to scale the test framework to test all variants within the SPL. It is unclear how far the automation of test could help in the process. Testing strategy must be context specific and scalable. With the use of the SPL already validated software parts could be reused. One participant mentioned the use of composable certification to be always compliant in all software variants. This form of certification is far from being legally allowed. New ways of certification and releasing software must be considered to maintain the development pace.

Software Development. One major challenge is the software development itself. Here is a lot potential for improvement. The identified challenges in the software development are clustered as technical issues (1), costs (2), requirements management (3), software architecture (4), software quality (5), safety regulations (6) and the use of SPL and variants (7).

As mentioned by the participants, the automotive domain is a cost-driven business. Therefore often the smallest possible hardware is selected to meet the requirements whereas this does not mean that there is a reduction of quality or functionality. But it leads to the unpleasant effect that in some cases, different variants of software are compiled separately to fit on the hardware. To get such a high modularity, it is necessary that the architecture is well chosen. One challenge is now, to maintain a good shaped architecture but have the possibility to integrate not foreseen features into the software. Furthermore it is necessary that all adoptions are always in relation to the selected hardware target. The developers mentioned that a benefit of the agile development is to re-prioritize features. The downside of this is that it is challenging to freeze the functionality for different variants of the SPL, because of late or incomplete requirements. The developers mentioned that it is important to analyze and prioritize the features to prevent chaos. This is even more important when developing within a SPL.

Scoping must always be considered to check for the affected variants. All variants must be validated to work as expected and defined by standards. The challenges in the software development are hard to tackle, but worth to consider.

5   Discussion and Conclusion

The identified challenges in the related work, such as the difficult management of software reuse and agile development [5,10,12] are valid for the automotive domain as well. A major finding of the study is that the use of agile elements in combination with software product lines require a precise analysis of dependencies to surrounding processes and organizational structures. For example, dependencies between departments and suppliers must be taken into account. It is also important to consider processes that are necessary to meet legal requirements. In the automotive sector global coordination is taking place due to global development. The currently typical form of coordination across several hierarchical levels (for example, to identify common components) is considered too slow and difficult to combine with the agile mindset. Dependencies between departments and compliance with rigid development processes are seen as an obstacle. It was important to all participants that the advantages of the software product line cannot be replaced by a more agile development. Particularly with regard to legal requirements and the verification and certification of software components, it is necessary to reuse software parts. This is particularly important in the automotive domain, as legal requirements require long-term certifications.

For future work, we plan to create and evaluate an Agile Software Product Line Automotive - Model (ASPLA-Model) for the adoption of ASD in the context of existing automotive SPL development. Next step will be deriving requirements for the ASPLA-Model based on the challenges reported herein.

References

1. Samuelsen, S.: The automotive future belongs to fuel cells range, adaptability, and refueling time will ultimately put hydrogen fuel cells ahead of batteries. IEEE Spectr. **54**(2), 38–43 (2017)
2. Broy, M., Krüger, I.H., Pretschner, A., Salzmann, C.: Engineering automotive software. Proc. IEEE **95**(2), 356–373 (2007)
3. Pohjalainen, P.: Bottom-up modeling for a software product line: an experience report on agile modeling of governmental mobile networks. In: Proceedings of 15th SPLC, pp. 323–332 (2011)
4. Hohl, P., Ghofrani, J., Münch, J., Stupperich, M., Schneider, K.: Searching for common ground: Existing literature on automotive agile software product lines. In: Proceedings of ICSSP 2017 (2017)
5. Babar, M.A., Ihme, T., Pikkarainen, M.: An industrial case of exploiting product line architecturesin agile software development. In: Proceedings of 13th SPLC (2009)
6. Farahani, F., Ramsin, R.: Methodologies for agile product line engineering: a survey and evaluation. In: Conference on 13th SOMET (2014)

7. Noor, M.A., Rabiser, R., Grünbacher, P.: Agile product line planning: a collaborative approach and a case study. J. Syst. Softw. **81**(6), 68–882 (2008)
8. O'Leary, P., McCaffery, F., Thiel, S., Richardson, I.: An agile process model for product derivation in software product line engineering. J. Softw. Evol. Process **24**(5), 561–571 (2012)
9. Olsson, H.H., Bosch, J., Alahyari, H.: Towards R&D as innovation experiment systems: a framework for moving beyond agile software development. In: Proceedings of IASTED (2013)
10. Díaz, J., Pérez, J., Alarcón, P.P., Garbajosa, J.: Agile product line engineering-a systematic literature review. Softw. Pract. Exp. **41**(8), 921–941 (2011)
11. Eklund, U., Olsson, H.H., Strøm, N.J.: Industrial challenges of scaling agile in mass-produced embedded systems. In: Dingsøyr, T., Moe, N.B., Tonelli, R., Counsell, S., Gencel, C., Petersen, K. (eds.) XP 2014. LNBIP, vol. 199, pp. 30–42. Springer, Cham (2014). doi:10.1007/978-3-319-14358-3_4
12. Ghanam, Y., Maurer, F.: Extreme product line engineering: managing variability and traceability via executable specifications. In: Agile 2009 (2009)
13. Hohl, P., Münch, J., Schneider, K., Stupperich, M.: Forces that prevent agile adoption in the automotive domain. In: Abrahamsson, P., Jedlitschka, A., Nguyen Duc, A., Felderer, M., Amasaki, S., Mikkonen, T. (eds.) PROFES 2016. LNCS, vol. 10027, pp. 468–476. Springer, Cham (2016). doi:10.1007/978-3-319-49094-6_32
14. Stol, K.-J., Ralph, P., Fitzgerald, B.: Grounded theory in software engineering research. In: Proceedings of 38th ICSE (2016)

Measuring Team Innovativeness: A Multiple Case Study of Agile and Lean Software Developing Companies

Richard Berntsson Svensson[✉]

Department of Computer Science and Engineering,
Chalmers University of Gothenburg, Gothenburg, Sweden
richard@cse.gu.se

Abstract. **[Context/Background]** Innovation is seen as the basis of competitive economy and measuring the innovation process is important for organizations. In the literature, focus has been on innovation and innovation capabilities on an organizational level, while few studies has been placed on innovation at team level. Furthermore, organizations tend to focus on the measurement of innovation to input and outputs of the innovation process and ignoring the process in-between. **[Goal]** This paper explores how a team's innovation capability is measured, and can be measured in practice in agile and lean software developing companies. **[Method]** It is based on data collected through semi-structured interviews with 28 practitioners from 11 software developing companies. **[Results]** The contribution of this study is twofold: First, it characterizes which metrics are used in industry to measure a team's innovation capability. Second, it identifies which metrics that could be used in practice to measure a team's innovation capability. **[Conclusions]** Measuring the performance of the innovation process is not seen as important during product planning and development.

Keywords: Innovation · Measurement · Agile · Case study · Empirical

1 Introduction

Innovation is widely seen as the basis of a competitive economy [21] and has resulted in a multidisciplinary body of knowledge. This multidisciplinary body of knowledge shows that an organizations competitive ability is dependent upon successful management of the innovation process [4, 8, 13]. However, for many organizations, evaluating the innovation competence is a complex task. For an organization to optimally manage the innovation process, an important challenge lies in measuring the performance of the process.

In the innovation literature, measures of aspects of innovation management are frequently proposed. For example, the literature stresses the importance to measure factors such as innovation strategy, ideas, customer and market, and organizational culture [1, 11]. However, while there has been much focus on innovation and innovation capabilities on an organizational level in the literature, less focus has been placed on a team level. Moreover, according to Adams et al. [1], many organizations

© Springer International Publishing AG 2017
M. Felderer et al. (Eds.): PROFES 2017, LNCS 10611, pp. 37–51, 2017.
https://doi.org/10.1007/978-3-319-69926-4_4

tend to focus on the measurement of innovation to inputs and outputs of the innovation process, but ignore the process in-between.

Innovation is complex and unpredictable [18, 19], which makes measuring the innovation process particular challenging. In particular since practitioners have problems to understand what to measure. That is, to identify the right metrics in order to evaluate the efficiency of the innovation process [1, 7, 24]. One reason for the difficulties of measuring innovation is that important factors of innovation, e.g. knowledge and ideas, cannot be measured directly due to their intangible characteristics [14, 24]. This has led to that organizations rarely track the needed information to evaluate and assess the innovation process in a systematic way. Adams et al. [1] point to the need for both practitioners and academics to measure innovation, and stress the absence of frameworks for innovation management measurements as well as that there are relatively few empirical studies of innovation measurement in practice.

What are the aspects of the innovation process that can be measured in practice? The aim of this paper is to contribute to the measurement theory and practice beyond the focus on measuring inputs and outputs of the innovation process by investigating the process in-between at agile software developing companies. This paper presents the results of an empirical study that includes data collected through in-depth interviews with 28 practitioners from 11 companies in Sweden of which six are multinational. The study focuses on how innovation can be measured in practice, and what metrics can be used to measure a team's innovation capability. This exploratory study can be seen as a study of state-of-practice in industry, but also an investigation as to what extent state-of-the-art in research, in terms of innovation measurement metrics, has penetrated industry practice.

The remainder of this paper is organized as follows. Section 2 presents related work. In Sect. 3 presents the research methodology and discusses the limitations of the study. The results are presented and discussed in Sect. 4, while Sect. 5 gives a summary of the main conclusions.

2 Related Work

The amount of literature on innovation is vast and goes back many years. However, while there has been much focus on innovation and innovation capabilities on an organizational level i.e. innovation processes, as well as on the individual level i.e. entrepreneurship or corporate entrepreneurship, less focus has been placed on a team level. The same accounts for measurement and assessment methods of innovation and innovation capabilities. Furthermore, a majority of innovation metrics focuses on product or process performance and are of a post-hoc character i.e. when products or processes are put on the market or implemented. Popular performance innovation metrics in industry are percent of revenue from new products (NPs), percent of growths in NPs, overall profits generated by NPs [9]. Other popular metrics include number of patents and number of ideas generated in various suggestion facilities.

Measuring climate for work group innovation is something that Anderson and West [3] address. They present a multidimensional measure of facet-specific climate for innovation in group called Team Climate Inventory and pinpoint that *"most previous measures of [innovative] climate have evaluated organizations as a whole"* [3]. They conclude that by focusing on specific aspect of climate and specific group level out- comes the predictive accuracy is high.

Other sources provide different aspects and dimensions to innovation measurement and assessment. One of the most comprehensive sources is Adams et al. [1] review on innovation management measurements. Based on their review a framework of seven areas for measurement of innovation is provided. They point to the need for both practitioners and academics to measure innovation and stress the absence of frame- works for innovation management measurements as well as *"the relatively small number of empirical studies on measurement in practice"* [1]. Griffin and Page [16] argue that a firm can assess failure or success of development projects by using appropriate sets of measures with alignment to project and innovation strategies. The framework presented by Griffin and Page [16] is relevant when products are placed on the market i.e. post hoc measures (e.g. customer acceptance, market share goals, competitive advantage) and provides mostly insights for innovation on the organiza- tional (firm) level. The same measurement focus can be found in Huang et al. [17] i.e. on firm level and on post-hoc measures. Based on their study on the measurement of new product success in Australian small and medium sized enterprises, it is concluded that firms should use multiple criteria when measuring new product success. The most contributing factors to customer success were in their study found to be customer satisfaction and customer acceptance, hence post-hoc measures.

Davila et al. [12] present another view, based on a business model for innovation with appropriate measures based on four phases; input, process, output, and outcome. For each of these phases they present a plethora of measures. They also define three roles of measurement systems; plan, involving designing and monitoring strategy; monitor, tracking of execution efforts and performance evaluation; and learn, in order to identify new opportunities. Chiesa et al. [6] present a framework for technical innovation audit. Their framework consisting of four core processes: (1) the identifi- cation of new product concepts; (2) taking the innovation from concept to launch; (3) the development of innovation in production; and (4) the development and man- agement of technology per se. However, the focus in both [6, 12] is mostly on an organizational (firm) level, hence team-level innovation measurement on climate, processes and performance is not addressed explicitly.

Other literature on measurement of innovation extends the mainstream focus on product and technology by addressing other innovation areas such as service innova- tion, aesthetic innovation and the measurement thereof. For example, Alcaide-Marzal and Tortajada-Esparza [2] approach innovation and the assessment thereof in industries that are not focused on technological innovation but instead aesthetic innovation. In their review of innovation surveys they especially investigate the occurrence of the following aspects; goals of innovation, inputs to innovation, outputs of innovation, innovation diffusion, and aesthetic design.

While creativity and customer requirements have been addressed in a number of publications how to measure innovation is rather absent in software related literature. Couger [10] uses the work environment inventory to measure the climate for creativity in information systems focused organizations. The MINT framework [22] is, to the best of our knowledge, the only framework that focuses on team level and measurement of innovation in Software Engineering. The MINT framework [22] consists of four major innovation areas, (1) innovation elicitation, (2) project selection, (3) ways-of-working, and (4) impact of innovation. Each of the four areas consists of a number of factors of how to measure innovation.

3   Research Methodology

The purpose of this study is to gain in-depth understanding of how agile software developing companies measure team level innovation capability, and what metrics could be used, in practice, to measure a teams innovation capability. Innovation is both complex and unpredictable, hence, a qualitative multiple case study approach was chosen because it allows the researcher to understand the studied phenomenon and its context in more depth [25]. According to Burns [5], case studies are an appropriate and often used approach to qualitative research, in particular when the objective of the research is the further understanding of a particular phenomenon that has not been investigated fully, as in this study. The two research questions that provided the focus for the empirical investigation are:

- **RQ1:** How do agile software developing companies measure team level innovation capability?
- **RQ2:** What metrics can be used in agile software development practice to measure team level innovation capability?

3.1   Sample Selection

The sampling strategy used was a combination of maximum variation sampling [20] and convenience sampling [20] within our industrial collaboration network. The researcher contacted a "gate-keeper" at each company who identified subjects that he/she thought were the most suitable to participate in this study. Twenty-eight subjects from 11 agile software-developing companies participated (see Table 1 for number of subjects per company). According to the contacted "gate-keepers", and the 28 subjects, all 11 companies use an agile software development approach in a market-driven software development context. The companies themselves vary in respect to size, type of products, type of customers, and application domain, a characterization can be seen in Table 1 (more details are not revealed for confidentiality reasons).

3.2   Data Collection

The research investigation was carried out using a semi-structured interview strategy [23]. We decided to use interviews over doing a large survey as the concepts of creativity, innovation, and innovation capability are treated very differently in industry, what might be considered creativity in one company is simply adherence to innovation in another. For this reason it was important to have a presence when gathering the data making it possible to elaborate on what we were looking for and compensate for those differences in naming. Moreover, due to the potential richness and diversity of the data

Table 1. Company characteristics

ID	Type of customer	# of employees	Domain	# of interviews
A	B2B	70	Information and technology service	3
B	B2B	3	Data migration	1
C	B2B	100	Control systems	3
D	B2B	24	Wireless connectivity	1
E	B2B	110	Telecom	3
F	B2B	850	Telecom	4
G	B2B	1300	Telecom	3
H	B2B	3000	Telecom	3
I	B2C	5000	Telecom	4
J	B2C	35	Information and technology devices	2
K	B2B	600	Control systems	1

that could be collected, semi-structured interviews would best meet the objectives of this study. Semi-structured interviews help to ensure common information on pre-determined areas is collected, but allow the interviewer to probe deeper where required. In addition, the interviewer had the chance to validate the questions with the interviewee lessening changes of misunderstandings. That is, the interviewer went back to the interviewee to validate the interviewers interpretation of the results to minimize misinterpretations and to validate the results.

The research instrument (see Table 2) used in this study was designed with respect to innovation, innovation capability, and innovation metrics. One interviewee and one interviewer attended all interviews. During the interviews, the purpose of the study and explanations of innovation were presented to the interviewee, followed by questions about innovation, innovation capability, and metrics were discussed in detail. Several times we had to put five to ten minutes of explanation what we were investigating, what is innovation (the introduction of a product/feature/service, or production/delivery method including software development processes and practices, that is new or significantly improved with respect to its characteristics or intended uses) and innovation capability (the overall capability/capacity encompassing the ability to absorb, adapt, and transform ideas into new products/processes/features/systems) before the interview subject understood and we could proceed. This was done in order to make sure that the interviewees and we had the same understanding of the key concepts of the study. For all interviews, varying in length from 40 to 60 min, we took records in the form of written extensive notes in order to facilitate and improve the analysis process. Due to confidentiality reasons, and non-disclosure agreements with all participating companies and participants, the data (that is, the written extensive notes) cannot be disclosed.

Table 2. Interview instrument

Characterization	Tell us about the company
	Tell us about the company's products
	Tell us about your role at the company
Innovation	How do you know that you and your team are innovative?
	Do you measure the innovation capabilities of a team? If so, how and what metrics are used?
	According to you, what aspects of innovation capability can be measured?
	What aspects of innovation can be helpful in industry?
Final question	Can you think of anything else that we have not covered that you think we should have asked?

3.3   Data Analysis

In the data analysis phase, the data from the written extensive notes was analyzed using content analysis [23] based on the interview instrument. Content analysis is a method for analyzing and interpreting data [23]. The focus of content analysis is to gather information and generate findings. The gathered information (content) can be any written information and different categories containing content are constructed for analysis. The content analysis involved marking and discussing interesting sections in the written extensive notes. The chunks of text from the written extensive notes were placed within the relevant sections (corresponding to a team's innovativeness, innovation capability and innovation measurements). These were numbered and relationships were captured by identifying dependencies to and from each category.

Based on the results from the content analysis, three main categories of innovation emerged, namely: (1) *How ideas are created and/or found*; (2) *prioritization of new ideas*; and (3) *innovation efforts*, which includes more 'traditional' innovation measurements such as patents and return on investment. The meaning of, and the results related to these three categories are reported in Sect. 4.

3.4   Limitations

For this study, as for any empirical study, there are limitations to discuss and address. The threats to description and interpretation validity and steps taken to mitigate them are reported herein, and the generalizability of the results is discussed. The limitations are described based on guidelines for flexible designs provided by Robson [23].

Description validity: The two main threats to description validity is the risk of participants not freely expressing their views during the interviews and the risk of misinterpreting what is said. To mitigate the risk of participants not freely sharing their opinions each participant was guaranteed company internal and external anonymity. Concerning the risk of misinterpretations, written extensive notes were taken during the interviews. These notes were used when making transcriptions of the interviews and were sent back to the participants to check that they correctly reflect what was said at the interviews.

Interpretation validity: The main threat to providing a valid interpretation is that of imposing a framework or meaning on what is happening rather than this emerging from what is learnt during the involvement with the setting. However, this does not preclude starting with a set of predefined categories, but these categories must be subjected to checking of their appropriateness, with possible modification. In this study, the threat of interpretation was managed by discussing the researcher's final interpretation of the interviewee's answers with each of the 28 interviewees.

Generalizability: Considering generalizability, the results are limited to the included case companies. However, qualitative studies rarely attempt to generalize beyond the actual setting since it is more concerned with characterizing, explaining and understanding the phenomena under study. The nature of qualitative designs also makes it impossible to replicate since identical circumstances cannot be recreated. However, the development of a theory can help in understanding other cases and situations. The fact that more than one participant and company acknowledge several of the discovered results and challenges increases the possibility of transferring the results to other situations. The large number of companies and contexts also contributes to generalizability. To avoid the interaction of selection and treatment, interviewees were selected by a gate-keeper at each company, hence the researchers did not select the subjects themselves. Moreover, companies were selected from different geographical locations.

4   Results and Analysis

Innovation management measurement is an important discipline for practitioners. An organizations capacity to innovate is determined by several factors, both relating to their own internal organization as well as to their market environment. The task of generating, and then, converting creative ideas into usable marketable products requires high levels of inter-functional coordination and integration.

An overview of the results from the interviews is shown in Table 3. In Table 3, we have mapped the empirical findings from each participant from each company (A-K in Table 3) to three main categories of innovation measurements at team level based on, how do the practitioners know if a team is innovative ('*How to know*' in Table 3), how do the practitioners' companies and teams measure their team's innovation capability today ('*Currently measuring*' in Table 3), and what metrics do the practitioners think could be used in practice to measure a team's innovation capability ('*Could be measured*' in Table 3). The three main categories of innovation that we identified are: (1) *How ideas are created and/or found*, which includes if the ideas internally and/or externally collected and generated; (2) *prioritization of new ideas*, which focus on the prioritization of the newly generated/created/discovered ideas into actual projects; and (3) *innovation efforts*, which includes more 'traditional' innovation measurements such as patents and return on investment.

If a company has an 'X' in both the category "currently measuring" and in "Could be measured" in Table 3, that means that one interviewee stated that they currently measure this, while another interviewee stated that this could be measured. That is, the interviewees from the same company had different understandings of what they

Table 3. Overview of how to know if a team is innovative, what is currently measured, and what metrics could be used to measure a team's innovation capability

	Companies											#
	A	B	C	D	E	F	G	H	I	J	K	
How to know												
How ideas are created and/or found	X		X		X	X		X	X		X	18
Prioritization of new ideas												0
Innovation efforts			X	X			X	X		X	X	11
Currently measuring												
How ideas are created and/or found					X	X	X	X				11
Prioritization of new ideas			X									3
Innovation efforts			X	X		X	X	X	X	X	X	17
Could be measured												
How ideas are created and/or found	X	X	X		X	X	X	X	X	X	X	24
Prioritization of new ideas			X									2
Innovation efforts			X	X	X	X	X	X	X	X	X	10

currently measure. The second main category, *prioritization of new ideas*, was only identified among the interviewees for what they currently measure and what they believe could be measured. Hence, the reason for the count of "0" under **How to know** in Table 3. The reason for including this category under **How to know** was to show that none of the interviewees stated that prioritization of new ideas can be used to know if a team is innovative or not. The column '#' in Table 3 shows how many of the 28 participants that identified a measurement in each category. A more detailed description of each of the categories is presented in the following sub-sections.

In Table 3, we can see that Company A can identify a team's innovation capability by measuring factors related to how the ideas from the team are created and found, Company E currently measure factors in relation to how ideas and created and/or found to identify a team's innovation capability, while the participants from Company F believes that metrics related to innovation effort could be used to measure a team's innovation capability.

Looking into how to know if a team is innovative or not, seven companies, and 18 out of 28 participants, identified factors related to how ideas are created and/or found, six companies, and 11 participants, in the innovation effort category, while only two companies (Companies C and H) and four participants identified both how ideas are created and/or found and innovation efforts. That how ideas are created and/or found was seen as a possible way to measure a team's innovation capability is not surprising since measuring the performance (i.e. how ell they perform an activity/task) of the organization – regardless of which level (project/product/company) – has been identified in previous studies (e.g. [1, 2, 6, 12, 22]) as a measurement of innovation.

The following two sub-sections present and discuss one research question each, corresponding to the research questions in Sect. 3.

4.1   Measure Team Level Innovation Capability (RQ1)

Looking into how agile software developing companies currently measure a team's innovation capability, 18 participants from six companies stated that they currently use number of granted patents to measure a team's innovation capability, while four participants from three companies mentioned number of submitted patent applications, as illustrated in Table 4. This result is in line with the findings from Adams et al. [1] and Crossan and Apaydin [11]. Although several interviewees from several companies mentioned number of granted patents and number of patents applications, none of the participants believe that patents is a good measure for a team's innovation capability, or that the number of patents tell the whole truth about a team's innovation capability.

One participant from Company F explained that *"number of patents could give some indications, but it does not tell the whole truth. We have several innovations in our products that are not patented"*. Another participant (Company H) explained, *"number of granted patents and patent applications may be a decent start, but there are many companies that come up with innovative products that are not patented"*. Besides not taking patents on new innovations, the patent process itself may be a hinder for creativity and new innovations. One participant from Company G explained that the patent process is a hinder for innovations. The participant further explained, *"I had a new idea that I found extremely interesting and we decided to write a patent application. The whole process of rewriting the idea with a patent engineer made my idea so generalized that I did not recognize it anymore. After this experience I lost my ambition to come up with new innovative ideas"*.

That Company B does not measure innovation capability by number of granted patents or number of patent applications, nor sees it as potential metrics that could be used to measure a team's innovation capability (see Table 5 in Sect. 4.2) is not surprising since the patent application process is both expensive and time consuming, which was supported by the participant. Another participant shared the same view, *"the whole process of writing a patent application took so much time that I felt it is not worth it anymore"*.

Looking into Table 4, we see that three companies (E, H and I) use number of collected ideas from key stakeholders to measure a team's innovation capability (for Company H and I, in combination with number of granted patents), while two companies (F and G) use number of generated ideas by the team. To measure number of generated ideas by the team, the participants from the to companies mentioned three different ways of encouraging the teams to generate new ideas. First, encouraging the employees to generate new innovative ideas for an internal or local innovation competition. For each year, both of the companies participate in innovation competitions and then it is possible to measure number of submitted ideas to the competition from each team. Second, both companies mentioned that they measure number of generated ideas by the team in general. Third, one company use the metrics of number of new solutions to existing problems to measure a team's innovation capability.

Company G is the only company that currently uses number of generated ideas from third party (i.e. sub-contractors, eco-systems, and open innovation) to measure their team's innovation capability. In addition, Company G is the only company that

Table 4. Detailed view on what is measured today

	A	B	C	D	E	F	G	H	I	J	K	#
How to know												
Number of collected ideas from key stakeholders			X		X	X						9
Number of generated ideas by the team					X	X						3
Number of generated ideas from/based on third party	X		X		X	X		X	X		X	14
When a feature is wanted by the customer									X	X		3
Number of granted patents			X	X		X	X					8
Number of patents applications			X	X		X	X					8
Currently measuring												
Number of collected ideas from key stakeholders					X			X	X			4
Number of generated ideas by the team						X	X					4
Number of generated ideas from/based on third party							X					1
When a feature is wanted by the customer									X	X		3
Return on Investment			X									3
Number of granted patents			X	X		X	X	X	X			18
Number of patents applications			X	X			X					4

Table 5. Detailed view of what could be measured

	A	B	C	D	E	F	G	H	I	J	K	#
Could be measured												
Number of collected ideas from key stakeholders	X	X	X									7
Number of generated ideas by the team					X	X	X	X	X			7
Number of generated ideas from/based on third party					X	X	X	X	X	X	X	20
When a feature is wanted by the customer									X	X		3
Return on Investment			X									3
How much each team's features/products sell for									X	X		3
Pre-release to key customers	X	X	X									7
History of number of innovations					X		X	X				6
History of number of generated ideas that led to new innovations					X	X					X	5
'Gut-feeling'	X	X	X		X	X	X	X	X	X	X	26

uses more than two (they use four metrics, see Table 4) metrics today. No further elaboration was given of why they used four metrics.

When a customer wants a released feature is used by two companies (J and K) as a metric (how many times this happens) to measure a team's innovation capability. One participant from Company J explained that "*it is difficult to measure before a product is released. You are measured in comparison to your competitors – if you have a new feature or enter the market first with something new, then you have proof for innovation*".

To our surprise, only companies (E, F, G, H, and I) from the telecom and mobile domains, which is all of the companies in the telecom and mobile domain, are currently using any metrics from the category '*How ideas are created and/or found*' (see Table 3) to measure a team's innovation capability. One explanation may be that this way of measuring a team's innovation capability is domain related. However, another more likely explanation may be related to the size of the company. The five telecom and mobile companies are the largest companies, in terms of number of employees, among the participating companies in this study.

One interesting finding in what is currently used to measure innovation capability is that Company C is the only company that uses any factor from the category '*prioritization of new ideas*' (see Table 3). The metric being used by Company C in the *prioritization of new ideas* area is estimated return on investment, which is in line with the popular performance innovation metrics in industry identified by Cooper et al. [9]. No further elaboration was given of how and why estimated return on investment is used to measure a team's innovation capability.

The results show that Companies A and B do not measure a team's innovation capability at all. The reason for Company A not to measure innovation was explained by all three participants, "*it is not possible to measure innovation and measurement frameworks do not provide an overall picture of our innovation capability*". For Company B, one participant explained, "*no, we do not do this, but perhaps it is possible. However, I think it is too complex and it will not give us an overall picture. In addition, it takes too much time and since it will not give us a true picture, it is not worth it*". The time aspect is important in agile software developing companies due to the short sprints where a company should deliver a working software product within 2–4 weeks. Another possible explanation of why Company B does not measure innovation capability could be that it is a small company with only three employees. The complexity of measuring innovation capability that is described by companies A and B is in line with the findings in McCarthy et al. [18] and Murray and Blackman [19].

In summary, to answer RQ1, the results show that seven metrics are currently used in practice to measure a team's innovation capability. The seven metrics that are used in practice today are:

- Number of ideas from key stakeholders
- Number of ideas generated by the team
- Number of ideas generated from third parties
- When a feature is wanted by the customers
- Return on investment
- Number of granted patents
- Number of patent applications

Currently, 6 of the 11 companies use number of granted patents to measure a team's innovation capability, which makes this metric the most used ones in practice. To use number of patents to measure the innovation process is in line with previous findings from Adams et al. [1] and Crossan and Apaydin [11]. However, none of the participants believed that number of patents are particular useful in determining a team's innovation capability.

4.2   What Could Be Measured (RQ2)

In analyzing research question 2, what metrics could be used in practice to determine a team's innovation capability, we see that the most frequently mentioned "metric" was 'gut-feeling', which was mentioned by 10 out of 11 companies, and by 26 out of 28 participants (see Table 5). Several of the interviewees explained that measuring innovation, in particular at team level, is highly subjective and that the output from an innovation measurement framework, or most of the other innovation metrics would be highly uncertain. Therefore, using ones 'gut-feeling' to determine a team's innovation capability was considered more reliable than most 'hard' metrics. This result may be related to the result of RQ1 (see Sect. 4.1), where the participants expressed that measuring innovation, and a team's innovation capability is very difficult, if not impossible. This result is not in line with any previous studies in innovation measurement in general, nor in studies focusing on innovation in software engineering (see Sect. 2 for example of previous studies in the field). One possible explanation for why 'gut-feeling' was considered the most useful metric may be related to that measuring the performance of a team's innovation capability is not seen as important during product development.

Looking at Table 5, we see that the participants from companies (E-I) in the Telecom and Mobile domains believe that the number of ideas generated by the teams is a good metric to use. Moreover, the five companies (E-I) from the Telecom and Mobile domain together with two other companies (J and K) believe that number of generated ideas from/based on third party is a good metric to use when measuring a team's innovation capability. With third party, some participants referred to sub-contractors, a few mentioned ideas that were generated from the use of Open Source Software, but most of the participants (14 our of 20, see Table 5) explicitly mentioned Open Innovation. That is, most of the participants believe that a good way to measure the innovation capability is to count the number of ideas that have been generated due to participation in Open Innovation.

Using number of generated ideas as a way to measure innovation is in line with the finings from Adams et al. [1], Crossan and Apaydin [11], and Regnell et al. [22]. However, using Open Innovation as part of measuring innovation capability in general, and particularly at team level has not been reported in previous studies. On the other hand, the participants from companies A, B, and C believe that number of collected ideas from key stakeholders, and pre-release to key customers could be measured to determine a team's innovation capability. One hypothesis may be related to the market and type of customers. For the companies in the Telecom and Mobile domains, the market and the customers may be pushing for new innovations and therefore externally generated ideas could be used to measure the innovation capability. Moreover, if the market "pushes" the companies to generate new innovative products and features, this may stimulate the employees to internally generate new ideas, hence it could be used to measure the innovation capability.

Two interesting metrics for measure innovation are using the history of a team's number of innovations (companies E, G, and H), and to use the history of how many of the generated ideas actually led to real innovations (companies E, F, and K). One participant explained, *"if a team has generated 20 ideas, of these 20 ideas, 10 led to the creation of prototypes/mockups, while only 1 of these 10 prototypes/mockups actually became an innovation, then we can use this data to measure each team's innovation capability"*. The participant further explained the benefits of measuring these kinds of metrics, *"this provides the managers with some indications of how many ideas each team must generate to get one new innovation"*.

For Company D, no metrics were identified that could be used to measure a team's innovation capability. Although the participant from Company D believes that number of patents could, to some extent, be useful for other things, the participant believes that it is not possible to measure the innovation capability in general, nor by using number of patents. The participant explained, *"to measure number of patent applications could give some indications to some things, but it does not tell the truth about innovation or innovation capability. A team's innovation capability is based on very subjective measures and therefore it is not a very reliable measure. It is not worth the effort considering how unreliable the measurement will be. Therefore, I do not believe that there are any metrics that you can use so it would be useful in practice"*.

None of the 11 companies mentioned any metrics or possible way of measure a team's innovation capability that could be mapped to 'ways-of-working', that is related to the process of innovation, organizational abilities, the innovation climate, or continuous process improvement. Although, for example, organizational climate factors have been shown to be important for creating an innovative organization [15], these factors can only stimulate creativity and innovation, but may not be able to measure how innovative a team is.

None of the participants mentioned granted patents, or number of patent application as metrics that could be used to measure the innovation capability. This result is in line with the participants view (see RQ1 in Sect. 4.1) on that patents are not a good metrics to use to determine the innovation capability.

In summary, the results show that the participants believe that some metrics can be used in practice to measure a team's innovation capability. The most frequently mentioned metric was 'gut-feeling', followed by number generated ideas from third parties, especially number of ideas that have been received from participating in Open Innovation.

5 Conclusions

In conclusion, this paper presents the results of an empirical study that examines how a team's innovation capability in agile software developing companies is currently measured, and what metrics could be used in practice to measure the innovation capability. Data are collected from 28 participants at 11 agile software developing companies.

In relation to RQ1, what metrics are currently used in practice to measure a team's innovation capability, the overall result indicates that relatively few metrics are used in practice to measure the performance of the innovation process at team level. The two most used metrics in practice are number of granted patents and number of patent applications; however, none of the participants believed that patents could be used to measure a team's innovation capability. In addition to patent, the only other metrics used in practice are, number of ideas from key stakeholders, number of ideas generated by the team, number of ideas generated from third parties, when a feature is wanted by the customers, and return on investment.

The relatively few metrics used in practice to measure a team's innovation capability may be an indication that innovation is complex and unpredictable; hence, it is difficult to get a reliable measure of a team's innovation capability. Another possible explanation may be that innovation is not prioritized in practice, which may be because of the agile development process. That is, the short sprints with a focus on delivering a working product may force the practitioners to solely focus on implementing features that the market wants and that their competitors already have implemented, hence the companies are more focused on following others rather than inventing new ideas to gain competitive advantage.

In relation to RQ2, what metrics could be used to measure a team's innovation capability, the findings reveal that 'gut-feeling' is the most frequently mentioned metric. 'Gut-feeling' is seen as at least as reliable as any other innovation measurement frameworks. The second most frequently mentioned metric was number of generated ideas from/based on third parties, where generated ideas from participating in Open Innovation was the most frequently mentioned one.

The main problem is that measuring the performance of the innovation process are not seen as important during product planning and development, making the realization of new innovative products/features a reactive (i.e. identify competitors new innovations and follow them) rather than a proactive effort to gain competitive advantage. The companies may thus not be able to rely on the innovation capacity to achieve competitive economy.

Further research is encouraged to investigate other industries in order to establish how innovation capabilities are measured. Furthermore, based on the results from our study, a broad survey, involving more companies from different parts of the world could also provide interesting if the pattern found in this study is similar in the wider scope of software based companies.

References

1. Adams, R., Bessant, J., Phelps, R.: Innovation management measurement: a review. Int. J. Manag. Rev. **8**, 21–47 (2006)
2. Alcaide-Marzal, J., Tortajada-Esparza, E.: Innovation assessment in traditional industries, a proposal of aesthetic innovation indicators. Scientometrics **72**, 33–57 (2007)
3. Anderson, N.R., West, M.A.: Measuring climate for work group innovation: development and validation of the team climate inventory. J. Organ. Behav. **19**, 235–258 (1998)

4. Balachandra, R., Friar, J.: Factors for success in R&D projects and new product innovation: a contextual framework. IEEE Trans. Eng. Manag. **44**, 276–287 (1997)
5. Burns, R.B.: Introduction to research methods, 4th edn. Pearson Education, Sydney (2000)
6. Chiesa, V., Coughlan, P., Voss, C.A.: Development of a technical innovation audit. J. Prod. Innov. Manag. **13**, 105–136 (1996)
7. Christensen, C.M., Kaufman, S.P., Shih, W.C.: Innovation killers: how financial tools destroy your capacity to do new things. Harvard Bus. Rev. **86**(1), 98–105 (2008)
8. Cooper, R.G.: The dimensions of industrial new product success and failure. J. Mark. **44**, 93–103 (1979)
9. Cooper, R., Edgett, S., Kleinschmidt, E.: Benchmarking best NPD practices. Res. Technol. Manag. **47**, 31–43 (2004)
10. Cougar, J.D.: Measurement of the climate for creativity in IS organisations. Creat. Innov. Manag. **5**(4), 273–279 (1996)
11. Crossan, M.M., Apaydin, M.: A multi-dimensional framework of organizational innovation: a systematic review of the literature. J. Manag. Stud. **47**, 1154–1191 (2010)
12. Davila, T., Epstein, M.J., Shelton, R.: Making Innovation Work: How to Manage it, Measure it, and Profit From it. Wharton School Publishing, NJ (2006)
13. Di Benedetto, C.A.: Identifying the key success factors in new product launch. J. Prod. Innov. Manag. **16**, 530–544 (1996)
14. Edvinsson, L., Dvir, R., Roth, N., Pasher, E.: Innovations: the new unit of analysis in the knowledge era: the quest and context for innovation efficiency and management of IC. J. Intellect. Cap. **5**(1), 40–58 (2004)
15. Ekvall, G.: Organizational climate for creativity and innovation. Eur. J. Work Organ. Psychol. **5**, 105–123 (1996)
16. Griffin, A., Page, A.L.: PDMA Success measurement project: recommended measures for product development success and failure. J. Prod. Innov. Manag. **13**, 478–496 (1996)
17. Huang, X., Soutar, G.N., Brown, A.: Measuring new product success: an empirical investigation of Australian SMEs. Ind. Mark. Manag. **33**, 117–123 (2004)
18. McCarthy, I.P., Tsinopoulos, C., Allen, P., Rose-Anderssen, C.: New product development as a complex adaptive system of decisions. J. Prod. Innov. Manag. **23**(5), 437–456 (2006)
19. Murray, P., Blackman, D.: Managing innovation through social architecture, learning, and competencies: a new conceptual approach. Knowl. Process Manag. **13**(3), 132–143 (2006)
20. Patton, M.Q.: Qualitative Research and Evaluation Methods. Sage Publications, California (2002)
21. Porter, M.E., Ketels, C.H.M.: UK Competitiveness: Moving to the next stage. DTI Economics Paper No 3, URN 03/899 (2003)
22. Regnell, B., Höst, M., Nilsson, F., Bengtsson, H.: A measurement framework for team level assessment of innovation capability in early requirements engineering. In: Bomarius, F., Oivo, M., Jaring, P., Abrahamsson, P. (eds.) PROFES 2009. LNBIP, vol. 32, pp. 71–86. Springer, Heidelberg (2009). doi:10.1007/978-3-642-02152-7_7
23. Robson, C.: Real World Research, 2nd edn. Blackwell, Oxford (2002)
24. Smith, K.M.: Measuring Innovation. The Oxford Handbook of Innovation. Oxford University Press, New York (2005)
25. Yin, R.K.: Case Study Research: Design and Methods, 3rd edn. Sage, London (2003)

Data Science and Analytics

What Can Be Learnt from Experienced Data Scientists? A Case Study

Leah Riungu-Kalliosaari[1], Marjo Kauppinen[2], and Tomi Männistö[1(✉)]

[1] University of Helsinki, Helsinki, Finland
{leah.riungu-kalliosaari,tomi.mannisto}@helsinki.fi
[2] Aalto University, Espoo, Finland
marjo.kauppinen@aalto.fi

Abstract. Data science has the potential to create value and deep customer insight for service and software engineering. Companies are increasingly applying data science to support their service and software development practices. The goal of our research was to investigate how data science can be applied in software development organisations. We conducted a qualitative case study with an industrial partner. We collected data through a workshop, focus group interview and feedback session. This paper presents the data science process recommended by experienced data scientists and describes the key characteristics of the process, i.e., agility and continuous learning. We also report the challenges experienced while applying the data science process in customer projects. For example, the data scientists highlighted that it is challenging to identify an essential problem and ensure that the results will be utilised. Our findings indicate that it is important to put in place an agile, iterative data science process that supports continuous learning while focusing on a real business problem to be solved. In addition, the application of data science can be demanding and requires skills for addressing human and organisational issues.

Keywords: Data science · Software development · Service engineering

1 Introduction

Data science is defined as "a new interdisciplinary field that synthesises and builds on statistics, informatics, computing, communication, management and sociology to study data and its environments (including domains and other contextual aspects, such as organizational and social aspects) in order to transform data to insights and decisions by following a data-to-knowledge-to-wisdom thinking and methodology" [4]. The interdisciplinary nature implies that knowledge from different fields is needed in order to ensure successful outcomes, making data scientists valued members of teams in many different fields. In particular, there is a growth in the application of data science in software engineering [3]. For example, in 2015, Microsoft grew its 'data and applied science' discipline

© Springer International Publishing AG 2017
M. Felderer et al. (Eds.): PROFES 2017, LNCS 10611, pp. 55–70, 2017.
https://doi.org/10.1007/978-3-319-69926-4_5

to over six hundred people and more than 1600 people were interested in data science work and signed up to data science related mailing lists [10].

Five years ago, Davenport and Patil [7] described the data scientist position as the sexiest job of the 21st century. In the recent past, the data scientist role has grown in both popularity and demand. However, there is a wide shortage of data scientist despite an increasing need for them across many fields [7]. In order to fill the growing gap, education institutions are also making efforts in educating future data scientists [14].

In order for data scientists to add the most value, they must be part of a team that encourages them to 'innovate with customer-facing products and services and not just to create reports and presentations' [7]. As part of a large Finnish research programme Need for Speed[1], we wanted to understand how data science can enable organizations to gain deep customer insight. We conducted a case study with one of the project partners whose data science team was involved in service and software development projects. We wanted to understand the activities involved in the data science projects along with the challenges associated with them. Hence, we focused on these research questions: (1) What are the key characteristics of the data science process applied in service and software development projects? and (2) What are the challenges of applying the data science process in the projects?

We present the results of the study in this paper. We found the data science process to be an agile, end-to-end and continuous learning process. We classified the challenges into three groups: (1) the demanding problems, e.g., difficulties in identifying relevant problems and measuring the impact of the results; (2) moderate problems e.g. unrealistic customer expectations; (3) mild problems such as poor data quality and differences in modelling and production technologies.

The rest of the paper is as follows: Sect. 2 takes a look at related research; Sect. 3 presents the research process; Sect. 4 presents the results as lessons learnt; Sect. 5 discusses the results and Sect. 6 concludes the paper.

2   Related Work

As data science continues to gain more prevalence in software engineering, so does the role of data scientists within organisations. The role and job titles of data scientists can vary greatly in practice. Kandel et al. [9] conducted interviews with 35 data analysts from 25 organisations, and they identified three analyst archetypes: hackers, scripters and application users. *Hackers* were proficient programmers and comfortable manipulating data. *Scripters* were experts in modeling and producing visualizations with software packages such as R and Matlab. *Application users* worked with smaller data sets using application such as SAS and SPSS.

---

[1] http://n4s.fi.

More recently, Kim et al. [10] identified five emerging roles of data scientists in software development teams:

(1) *"Insight Providers*, who work with engineers to collect the data needed to inform decisions that managers make;"
(2) *"Modelling Specialists*, who use their machine learning expertise to build predictive models";
(3) *"Platform Builders*, who create data platforms, balancing both engineering and data analysis concerns;"
(4) *"Polymaths*, who do all data science activities themselves;"
(5) *"Team Leaders*, who run teams of data scientists and spread best practices."

Data science has the potential to improve software engineering in many ways. Begel and Zimmermann [1] surveyed the areas in which software engineers desired input from data scientists. They found 12 potential areas where data science could be applied namely, bug measurements, development practices, development best practices, testing practices, evaluating quality, services related to cloud computing and continuous delivery, customers and requirements, software development lifecycle, software development process, productivity, teams and collaboration, and reuse and shared components.

Handling of data and producing results involves different activities. These may include tasks such as discovering the data for analysis, wrangling or manipulating the data into an appropriate format, profiling data to ensure its quality and suitability for analysis, modelling the data, and reporting the results of the analysis [9]. Similarly, according to Fisher et al. [8], the analysis process may include five activities, i.e., acquiring data, choosing an architecture, shaping the data into the architecture, writing an editing code, and reflecting and iterating on the results. All these activities have challenges that can make data analysis an exhausting process.

Some of the existing challenges include data access restrictions, data quality issues, i.e., missing, incorrect or inconsistent data values, difficulties with identifying data sources and integrating data from multiple sources, problems with inferring the most important data while creating models and visualizations, and communication issues, e.g., while presenting the results [8,9].

The presence of data everywhere has led to a rapid growth of the data science field. Data-driven decision making is becoming increasingly critical while addressing different information needs in the software domain [3]. Critical and careful analysis of the problems should be practised in order to effectively apply data science interventions. As the goal in such interventions is not primarily to analyse data, but make the data useful for decision-making in relation to the business processes. It is of importance to consider the problems from a wider perspective than, e.g., data analytics only. Hence, our focus is on the data science process, i.e., the activities and tasks carried out while analysing data to produce actionable insights and outcomes.

3   Research Process

We conducted a qualitative study with experienced data scientists to understand their data science process along with its challenges (see Table 1 for an overview of our research process). We use the term 'experienced data scientist' because the participants had each been involved in data science or analytics type of work for 4–12 years (see Table 2). Despite the experience of the data scientists themselves, the team in question was new and worked on newly started data science projects. The data scientists were employees of an industrial partner Reaktor[2] in the Need for Speed programme. The industrial partner has 400 employees spread out in 4 offices across 3 continents. The company provides consultancy services in different areas with a connection to digital products and services. The data science team was composed of seven people.

At the beginning of the Need for Speed programme, the industrial partner hosted a workshop where its data science process was presented and discussed (Phase I, Table 1). After the workshop, collaboration between the researchers and the company was agreed upon. In addition, the presentation material was compared and linked with the findings from the focus group interview.

Our primary unit of analysis was the data science team. The work of the team was concretely characterised by examples from case projects. In addition, the informants also described the work of the team beyond the case projects.

Table 1. Research process

Phase	Theme	Method	Data	Informants
I	Overview of data science process	Workshop: presentations, discussions	5 slidesets	DS1, DS3, DS4
II	Characteristics and challenges related to data science process	Focus group interview	Audio recording, Post-it pictures	DS1, DS2, DS3, DS4
III	Validation of analytic interpretations (for Phase II), current situation	Feedback session, group interview	Slides, audio recording	DS1, DS4, Research manager

Next, we carried out a focus group interview (Phase II, Table 1). We chose the focus group method because it is suitable for gathering experiences and discovering new insights as well as allowing an in-depth discussion within a reasonable period of time [11,12]. The goal of the focus group was to know more about the data science process in the organization. The themes of the focus group included individual introductions, the company, the data science team,

---

[2] http://reaktor.com.

skills of a good data scientist, example projects, and lessons learnt (including challenges and success factors). Four researchers and four data scientists were present during the focus group interview. One researcher acted as the moderator and the others took notes and asked clarifying questions. The focus group was audio recorded and later transcribed for analysis. Details of the data scientists and the projects they had worked or were working on are shown in Table 2.

Table 2. Details of focus group participants

Participant	Background	Experience (years)	Examples of customer projects
DS1	Theoretical physics, data mining	12	Personalisation, optimisation; make predictions
DS2	Machine learning, CS, statistics	4	Change detection, make recommendations, produce more tailored advertisements
DS3	Machine learning, statistics	8	Marketing campaigns, make recommendations, location analysis
DS4	Psychology, IS, machine learning	11	Segmentation; make recommendations, improve revenue and user experience

The data scientists were given post-it notes where they wrote notes related to the discussed themes. The post-it notes were collected, placed on a white board and a picture was taken that would be used to support the analysis.

After the analysis, we held a two-hour feedback workshop session (Phase III, Table 1). Regarding the research process and its validation strategy, the feedback session also acted as member checking [5]. The goal was to present the results of the analysis from the focus group session and get feedback from the data scientists. The company's research manager, two most experienced data scientists (DS1 and DS4), and three researchers were present during the feedback session. The feedback session was also audio recorded and transcribed for analysis.

We analysed the data iteratively using the thematic analysis approach [6]. To guide our analysis, we used the pre-existing themes of interest discussed in the focus group interview, i.e., key characteristics of the data science process, challenges, success factors, example projects, and skills of a good data scientist. We iterated and refined the codes as we discussed with each other during the analysis as well as after the feedback session. We also used material obtained from the company to supplement our analysis, e.g., presentation slides. In this paper, we present the analysed themes related to the data science process, its characteristics and challenges.

4   Lessons Learnt

4.1   Data Science Process

The organisation had defined a data science process. During a Need for Speed programme workshop, the organisation presented the data science process on a high abstraction level. During the focus group and feedback sessions, the study participants provided more details about the process composed of six steps (Fig. 1): conceptualization, problem definition, data collection and preparation, modelling, evaluation and validation, and deployment and utilization of results.

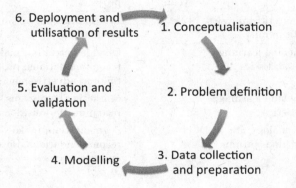

Fig. 1. Overall data science process of the case company.

Conceptualization: The main focus of this activity is the business problem. This involves interacting with the customer in order to assess the customer's understanding of (1) the business problem and (2) data science as a solution to the business problem. The business problem should be described clearly, putting the business targets and constraints into consideration, so as to develop the appropriate solution. The data scientists stressed the importance of knowing the customer's understanding of data science because it helped in preparing to address different customer expectations. One participant emphasised this:

It's important [for the customer] to understand the possibilities and limitations, really understanding what you are able to do and not do with data science. [DS3]

Problem definition: This activity focuses on the data science solution to the identified business problem. The business problem is formalised into an analytically solvable problem. One data scientists explained that many customers needed help to *'translate the [business] problem into a computational or mathematical problem'* [DS1]. Successful problem definition therefore calls for a lot of interaction between the customer and the data scientist.

A good data science solution starts by understanding who the customer or end-user is. This helps to know how the data science solution will be applied.

With this knowledge, the data scientists said that it was the best way to provide an optimum solution.

Data collection and preparation: The end result is determined by the data at hand. Hence, this makes collecting the data and preparing it for efficient use a vital aspect. In order to make this a fruitful endeavour, the data scientists wished that not only would the data be handed over to them, but that they would also be granted access to the actual data collection process. This would grant them the opportunity to improve the data collection process which they believed would have significant impact on the results.

Modelling: When the data is in good shape for analysis, the data scientists then manipulate the data using different data analysis and modelling techniques. Depending on the problem, modelling aims at describing what has happened, diagnosing why something has happened, predicting what will happen or providing guidance on how to make something happen. Often, the models are demonstrated using visualisations.

Evaluation and validation: The data scientists need to provide results that are reliable and relevant to the business problem. The participants were very interested in knowing the effectiveness of their results and therefore desired to obtain feedback from the real end users, not just from the business stakeholders or domain experts.

Deployment and utilization of results: It is essential that the results are put into use so as to assess their impact. Continuous and consistent monitoring is imperative along with a feedback loop that enables the end users to communicate their thoughts about the results. One participant [DS1] emphasised that *tight collaboration with the end result user* was very important.

4.2   Characteristics of the Data Science Process

Agility: Data science projects are exploratory and iterative in nature. Following an agile approach helps to manage customers? expectations and produce useful results. The data scientists said that their way of working resonates well with the agile approach.

There's a lot in common that you can really apply...Like always [in software development], do the MVP ["Minimum Viable Product"]...start iterating quick and try to have lots of communication and have the end user involved. [DS4]

...agility fits very well [with our] approach because we have to start with something and then actually try to produce as quickly as possible some kind of insight or results and then learn from those results and build on top of that. [We also] learn the environment that the customer has. Then actually I think it?s more visible also to the customer [that] we are producing something useful. [DS3]

Data science problems have to deal with a degree of uncertainty. The agile approach provides the opportunity to address the unexpected changes along the way.

Continuous learning process: The agile approach supports continuous learning throughout a project. It is important that both the data science team and the customer have the opportunity to learn during the process. The data scientists want to work with domain experts in order to gain good understanding of the application domain and the problem to be solved. The customer can learn what kind of results can be gained from the application of data science and how to utilize the results. It should be everyone's aim to 'learn by doing' [DS1] and use the new knowledge to improve the end results and possibly 'inspire some other ideas' [DS1].

End to end process: This means that the data scientists start the project by first understanding the customer and the customer's problem. This entails evaluating the relevance of the business problem. It also important that end-users are willing to utilize the solution. This calls for understanding the problem from the end-user?s point of view in order to provide the appropriate solution.

...we have sort of tried to formulate our way of getting into projects that go on and we really want to put an emphasis on the starting point or the end usage point, of who is going to use this result and how. And we start from there and then go backwards and do what we can and then try to improve it always...really start from the end user. [DS1]

4.3   Challenges

We present the challenges as they were experienced by the data scientists in different phases of the data science process. Table 3 shows an overview of the challenges.

Table 3. Overview of the challenges

Data Science Process Phase	Challenges
Conceptualization	Unrealistic customer expectations, communicating uncertainty
Problem definition	Identifying the right problem, limited interaction with domain experts, preference for tools as a solution
Data collection and preparation	Limited access to the data collection process, poor data quality, lack of cooperation from all required parties
Modelling	Lack of the required computational resources, differences in modelling and production technologies
Evaluation and validation	Lack of feedback from the end user
Deployment and utilization of results	The results are not utilised, what is the impact of the results?

Conceptualization. The challenges of this activity had to do with unrealistic customer expectations and communicating uncertainty.

Unrealistic customer expectations: The participants found that most customers did not have a realistic view of data science and its capabilities. In order to sell their solutions, tool vendors had propagated a tools-driven approach in the market. Hence, the customers expected quick solutions, mostly in the form of tools or systems but not recommendations or guidelines to aid in decision making. This led to a tendency to acquire tools without clearly knowing the initial problem for which to use the tools.

...people have need for data science but they don't understand it...then the other thing is that the market is kind of saturated by vendors who don't really sell data science in the sense that we understand it. [DS4]

If customers did not understand data science well, it made it difficult for them to view the problem correctly, hence hindering how well they could conceptualise the problem. The participants strongly advocated for a data-driven approach and had to employ some effort in getting the customer to gain the appropriate focus on the problem.

Communicating uncertainty: Due to the exploratory nature of data science, it is not always easy to predict the results. The conceptualization process also involved getting the customer to have an open mind towards what the results might imply. It was difficult for the participants to get the customer to understand and accept the inherent uncertainty of the outcome. This resulted in prolonged initial negotiations that were not always fruitful in closing the deals.

...often times, it is that you [i.e., the data scientist] really cannot say beforehand that—okay this is the result and that is what you will get. Basically because the outcome is very vague. You [i.e., the customer] use the money and you don?t know what you are investing [in]. [DS1]

Problem Definition. The main challenge here was identification of an essential problem to be addressed. The other issues were the limited interaction with the domain experts and the customers' overemphasis on tools.

Identifying an essential problem: A correct problem should·be one that is solved by the obtained results. The participants had a great desire to produce useful results. However, it was often that the customers could not clearly explicate the problem in the first place.

...in many cases, you notice that your customer has collected data, but what to do with the data is unclear. And then there are lots of things we can actually calculate from the data but, all of them are not useful ones. So you really should find the useful thing and then concentrate on that. Then we would try to make the point that okay—in a way such data collection is not enough but you really need to find the correct problem that you actually need to solve. [DS3]

Limited interaction with domain experts: In most cases, the domain experts would be the ones to evaluate and sometimes use the data science results.

When defining the problem, the participants expressed that it was important to have input from the customers' domain experts. The domain experts know the problem best and are able to describe it very well—but their input was not readily available.

We might have a communication problem with the customer since we're not experts on the domain. We don't know what their problems are. And on the other hand they might not be aware of what we could do. [DS1]

The other one [i.e., problem] is how much we can actually communicate with the domain expert. [DS2]

Preference for tools as a solution: The participants found that there was a general bias towards tools and products in the market. Tools were seen as easy solutions to the problems as they were easy to acquire, were well-defined, easy to start using, and were perceived with less uncertainty. This hindered the customers' attitudes towards more thorough problem solving that data science requires.

I think many times the products are preferred to in a way because if you don't know the field then you actually think [of a product]. Because it's a product you can teach anybody to use it. But that's not really the case because if you don't know what you are doing or you don't know what the problem you are solving is, you put rubbish [in] and get rubbish out. I think it goes for why [the] typical thinking [is] okay, we buy a tool and then everybody can use it. [DS3]

Data Collection and Preparation. The challenges encountered during this activity are as follows.

Limited access to the data collection process: The participants were uncomfortable with being seen as magicians that could unravel wonderful discoveries from any sort of data without knowing its context. Not only did the participants want to have access to the data, but they also felt that understanding the process through which the data was collected would be useful in evaluating the problem and achieving the desired results.

...data is produced by some process. And, what we really need to do is understand the process or, preferably intervene with the process so that we get measurements that we really are after. Not so that there's some shadow on the wall [and] we try to deduce from that—we want to set up the whole thing. [DS4]

Poor data quality: There were several factors that compromised the data quality, such as the data being random and subpar, incorrect formatting and missing attributes, values and information. One participant gave an example:

But just as a practical example, it was not a data science project per se but in one project they had this legacy database of users where they only had one field for name. And then you had one to three first names and then several different variations of surnames and then we spent two weeks to build the engine that parsed the names to extract a surname. And even after two weeks, we got like two per cent of errors. [Research manager]

The way the data was gathered might also have had a negative effect, especially if it was collected without knowledge or intention of its use in the future.

...the data is originally not for the use that we [intend] but it has been collected for other purposes, maybe as log [data] and it's a side product of a process, and it's supposed to be somehow, [a] gold mine of insights. Or useful for some specific purpose. [DS2]

The data is often scattered around the organizations, the quality is poor. [DS1]

During the feedback session, the participants said that the data quality problem was improving. This was mainly because the market was becoming more informed about data science, hence investing effort and resources to collect meaningful data that could be utilised in the future and for different purposes.

Lack of cooperation from all required parties: We observed that some customer organizations had internal issues that hindered the participants' involvement in the projects. The issues mainly stemmed from the lack of a shared vision for the data science project amongst different departments in the customer organizations. This made it especially difficult to gather or have access to the required data.

One thing is that often the processes are lateral in the organization so that they [spread across] different branches of the organization. So there's IT and marketing and someone else involved and it's often hard to get [them] working [together]. [DS4]

Modelling. There were a couple of challenges related to this activity.

Lack of the required computational resources: During the focus group interview, the participants mentioned having difficulties with getting access to the IT resources and computational environments that they needed for modelling the results, particularly if the data could not be moved from the company premises.

More than so, it?s difficult to get the IT resources, both the data and the computational environment that we need. Often it?s difficult to get either of them or at least one of them. [DS1]

During the feedback session, the participants pointed out that the situation had improved due to cloud solutions becoming readily acceptable and accessible.

Differences in modelling and production technologies: Sometimes, there was a difference between the modelling technology and the one in which the results are applied. This led to difficulties with integrating the results in the customer's environment and required more time, effort and money. In the end, this would limit the impact of the results.

Evaluation and Validation. The main challenge here was an apparent gap between the data scientists and the end users of the results. The people who ordered the project and thus got the results, e.g., the business experts, were not necessarily the actual end users acting on or using the results.

Lack of feedback from the end user: There is a difference between the feedback received from the business or domain experts working in the customer company, and the real end users of the results. If the real end users are not connected to the data scientists, it makes hard for the data scientists to actually assess the progress of their results.

This is actually the number one [problem], [lack of] tight collaboration with the end result user. [DS1]

Deployment and Utilization of Results. The data scientists were sometimes frustrated by how the customers handled the project outcomes. Sometimes, the results were not put into use which meant that the participants would never know the real impact of the results.

The results are not utilised: Sometimes, the results were not applied. This was due to factors, such as (1) lack of cooperation between different departments, e.g., marketing and IT, (2) the business stakeholders failed to facilitate the utilization of the results if they did not understand, were not fully convinced or they did not feel confident about the results.

...I think most of the failures that we [have] had are because the results are just never [used]. They are ready and nobody ever uses them for anything...like I said, most of the time the problem is really to get the results into use. [DS1]

What is the impact of the results? As a result of the outcomes not being utilised, the participants found it difficult to know, measure or observe the effectiveness of the results.

For the results to be useful, they [i.e., customers] have to accept that—well—things are how they are, not how people thought they would like them to be. [DS4]

On the other hand, the participant quoted above [DS4] pointed out the fact that in order to effectively measure the impact, one would require an experimental setup which is usually *'expensive and technically heavy'* to put in place. This means some considerations have to made with respect to investments towards experimentation.

Summary of the Challenges. The challenges we have presented above reflect the complications of applying data science in software and service engineering as experienced by the study participants. We classified the challenges into three groups, i.e., difficult, moderate, and mild problems. The groups were according to the perceived ability to solve them, as observed during the analysis. Table 4 summarises the challenges.

The difficult problems were those considered hard to solve. They comprised of human and organisational aspects which are always not easy to resolve. These problems also seemed to be more out of the participants' control, even though the participants considered them to be very important. The moderate problems were seen as somewhat solvable with some persistent intervention from the participants. The mild problems, such as those related to data quality, computational resources, and modelling issues, were seen as clear and easily solvable.

Table 4. Summary of the challenges

Problem Group	Challenges
Difficult	Communicating uncertainty, identifying essential problems, lack of cooperation from all required parties, lack of feedback from the end user, the results are not utilised, what is the impact of the results?
Moderate	Unrealistic customer expectations, limited interaction with domain experts, preference for tools as a solution, limited access to the data collection process
Mild	Poor data quality, lack of required computational resources, differences in modelling and production technologies

The human and organisational nature of the difficult problems is an indication of immature markets, which have spread extremely fast to many new application domains. Some of these problems can be expected to fade with time as the misconceptions about data science get clearer and data scientists become integrated as members of software and service development teams.

5   Discussion

The goal of this study was to gain understanding on how data science can be applied in software development organisations. The results are based on a qualitative case study approach. This paper presents the process that the experienced data science team of the case study company recommends to be used with customers. The paper also describes the key characteristics of the process and challenges encountered in practice when data science projects were conducted with customers.

The recommended data science process consists of six activities. The first activity focuses on understanding customers? business problem and their expectations for the project. The second step is to translate the business problem into a computational or mathematical problem. The following two activities cover data collection and modelling tasks. During the fifth activity of the data science process, the results are evaluated and validated with the customers and end users. Finally, it is essential to ensure that the results are put into use and their impacts are assessed. Some of the activities of this process are similar to activities mentioned in other data science analysis processes, i.e., discovering the data [8,9], modelling the data [8,9], and reflecting and iterating on the results [8].

Based on the interview study of 16 data scientists, Kim et al. [10] found that data scientists at Microsoft worked on three activities: (1) data collection, (2) data analysis, and (3) data use and dissemination. The authors also point out that this list is not complete, but an overview of the activities they identified from their study. When comparing the list of the three activities with the data science process described in this paper, the main difference is that the data scientists of our case study highlighted especially the importance of identifying a real business problem that can be translated into a computational problem.

According to the experienced data scientists of our case study, identifying essential problems to be solved by data science is one of the most difficult challenges in their work. Similarly, Zhang et al. [15] report that it is often easy to start from some datasets, apply certain data analysis techniques and make some observations that actually do not help practitioners. One of the main lessons Zhang et al. learned was that it is important to first identify essential problems and then obtain the right dataset to help solve the problems.

Another difficult challenge that data scientists can face in practice is that it is not easy to communicate and get the customer to understand the uncertainty of outcomes from data science projects. According to the experienced data scientists, it is often so that they cannot state precisely at the beginning of the project what results the customer will get. In order to solve this challenge and also other challenges, such as identifying essential problems and managing unrealistic customer expectations, the experienced data scientists recommended the agile and iterative data science process. This lesson from our case study supports the lesson learned by Zhang et al. [15]. Based on a case study conducted at Microsoft, they report that creating software analytics solutions for real-world problems is an iterative process. They also point out that it is important to work in an agile way to build a quick feedback loop with practitioners and to identify essential problems early.

From the perspective of research, the main contribution of this paper is that it describes a rather large set of challenges that are based on the experiences of the data scientists who have worked in customer projects. An increasing number of companies are interested in applying data science. Therefore, it is important that software engineering and data science researchers can develop solutions to these challenges in close collaboration with practitioners. It is also important that challenges related to the application of data science in software development projects will be investigated in different kinds of companies and contexts. For example, Kim et al. [10] plan to conduct a large-scale survey to quantify data science tasks identified in their interview study and describe the challenges associated with data science work. It will be interesting to compare the results of the survey with the results of our case study.

From the perspective of practice, the paper offers an overview of the six data science activities. The results also suggest that the data science process should be an agile, continuous learning and end-to-end process. Continuous learning means that data scientists need to gain iteratively a good understanding about the business problem and application domain. In addition, customers need to learn what kind of insights can be gained from the application of data science and what these insights mean in practice. The end-to-end process means that it starts from the discovery of relevant problem and covers the activity where the results from the application of data sciences are actually used and their impacts are evaluated.

Threats to Validity. As this study is a case study and descriptive in nature, there is little evidence to support any causal relationships, thus the internal validity is not the main concern of this study. However, the results do include knowledge constructs that could be interpreted having some causal characteristics, such as the claims from the informants that iterative approach to design science process would help to overcome certain challenges. These are clearly the views of the informants and thus to be taken with appropriate caution if interpreted as guidelines to follow. On the other hand, however, the informants were data science experts, who have encountered the challenges in their work and thought for the possible solutions beyond the interview sessions of this study, so their claims may be more valid and justified than random opinions.

In terms of construct validity, the richness of the data from multiple interviewees and member checking the results with the informants significantly reduce the risk that major issues would have been misunderstood by the researchers. However, one issue on construct validity may rise from the varied definitions or understandings of the term data science, particularly as its interpretation beyond this study may differ from the semantics captured between the informants and the researchers, which is broader than, e.g., data collection and analytics only (see Fig. 1). To build a basis for the credibility [13], the interviews were audio recorded, transcribed and analysed using Atlas.ti as the tool.

Our study is conducted with the case company only, although through their customer projects, the results cover data science challenges beyond the case company only. The external validity or transferability of the results beyond the case would be based on the assumption that the informants would have encountered challenges that are not particular or stemming from the context of the case company only. That is, it is very much possible that the challenges identified have relevance beyond the case as well as the ideas proposed by the informants for alleviating the challenges. However, it is clear that the potential application of the results in other cases essentially expects a knowledgeable person or persons with good expertise in their own domain in order to interpret and apply the results in their context.

6   Conclusions

This study contributes to the growing interest in data science across different disciplines, specifically service and software engineering. It helps both researchers and practitioners to understand the applicability of data science in service and software development and be informed about some of the impending challenges.

The difficult problems identified comprised of human and organisational aspects, whereas the problems such as poor data quality and modelling issues were not seen as primary concerns for the data science process. Our results also indicate that it is important to establish an agile and lightweight data science process that supports continuous learning while focusing on a real business problem. The experienced data scientists highlighted that it is not enough to focus on data collection and modelling. Instead, you really need to find the relevant problem that you actually need to solve and can be solved by applying data science.

Our future work will focus on the factors influencing the successful application of data science in service and software development projects. In addition, we are interested in investigating how customers experience the application of data science in service and software development projects.

Acknowledgments. This work was supported by TEKES as part of the N4S Program of DIMECC (Digital, Internet, Materials & Engineering Co-Creation). We would also like to thank the case company Reaktor for the possibility to conduct this research.

References

1. Begel, A., Zimmermann, T.: Analyze this! 145 questions for data scientists in software engineering. In: ICSE, pp. 12–22 (2014)
2. Bener, A., Misirli, A.T., Caglayan, B., Kocaguneli, E., Calikli, G.: Lessons learned from software analytics in practice. In: The Art and Science of Analyzing Software Data, pp. 453–489 (2015)
3. Bird, C., Menzies, T., Zimmermann, T.: Past, present, and future of analyzing software data. In: The Art and Science of Analyzing Software Data, 1st edn., pp. 1–13 (2015)
4. Cao, L., Science, D.: A comprehensive overview. ACM Comput. Surv. 59(3) (2017). Article No 43
5. Creswell, J.W.: Research Design-Qualitative, Quantitative, and Mixed-Methods Approaches, 4th edn. SAGE, California (2014)
6. Cruzes, D., Dyba, T.: Recommended steps for thematic synthesis in software engineering. In: International Symposium on Empirical Software Engineering and Measurement (ESEM), pp. 275–284 (2011)
7. Davenport, T.H., Patil, D.J., Scientist, D.: The Sexiest Job of the 21st Century, Harvard Business Review, pp. 70–76 (2012)
8. Fisher, D., DeLine, R., Czerwinski, M., Drucker, S.: Interactions with big data analytics. Int. Mag. **19**(3), 50–59 (2012)
9. Kandel, S., Paepcke, A., Hellerstein, J.M., Heer, J.: Enterprise data analysis and visualization: an interview study. IEEE Trans. Vis. Comput. Graph. **18**(12), 2917–2926 (2012)
10. Kim, M., Zimmmermann, T., DeLine, R., Begel, A.: The emerging role of data scientists on software development teams. In: ICSE, pp. 96–107 (2016)
11. Kontio, J., Lehtola, L., Bragge, J.: Using the focus group method in software engineering: obtaining practitioner and user experiences. In: ISESE, pp. 271–280 (2004)
12. Liamputtong, P.: Focus Group Methodology-Principles and Practices. SAGE, California (2011)
13. Patton, M.Q.: Qualitative Research & Evaluation Methods, 3rd edn. SAGE, California (2002)
14. Strawn, G.: Data Scientist, IT Pro, pp. 55–57. Computer.org
15. Zhang, D., Han, S., Dang, Y., Lou, J.-G., Zhang, H., Xie, T.: Software analytics in practice. IEEE Softw. **30**(5), 30–37 (2013)

A Virtual Study of Moving Windows for Software Effort Estimation Using Finnish Datasets

Sousuke Amasaki[1(✉)] and Chris Lokan[2]

[1] Okayama Prefectural University, Department of Systems Engineering, Soja, Japan
amasaki@cse.oka-pu.ac.jp
[2] School of Engineering and Information Technology,
UNSW Canberra, Canberra, Australia
c.lokan@adfa.edu.au

Abstract. CONTEXT: Studies have shown contradictory results on the effectiveness of using a moving window of only the most recent projects for effort estimation, compared to using the full history of past data. Moving windows improved the accuracy of effort estimates for a single-company subset of the ISBSG dataset (www.isbsg.org), but not for three single-company subsets of the Finnish dataset (www.4sumpartners. com). The contradiction may be caused by different characteristics of the data sets: in particular, they differ noticeably in heterogeneity of industry sector. **GOAL:** To investigate the effect on estimation accuracy of differences in the characteristics of the data sets. **METHOD:** Conduct an experiment with a virtual data set, composed from the three subsets of the Finnish dataset. The composite data set is similar to the ISBSG subset in that it includes data from multiple industry sectors; the largest group of projects in both data sets comes from the same industry sector; and in both data sets the projects are concentrated in a similar number of years. **RESULTS:** The conclusions is the same as in the past study using the individual Finnish subsets: in the composite data set, moving windows are of no help. **CONCLUSIONS:** In this instance, increased heterogeneity of projects does not explain the contradiction. It is still not clear when windows may be helpful. Practitioners and researchers should not assume automatically that only the most recent data is best for effort estimation.

1 Introduction

A software effort estimation model is developed from past project data. The set of past project data grows as projects finish. When estimating the effort for a new project, an estimator must choose whether the estimate should be based on the whole set of past data. It may make intuitive sense to discount older projects, as they may be less representative of an organization's current practices.

Lokan and Mendes [7] examined whether using only recent projects improves estimation accuracy. They used a window to limit the amount of training data so

© Springer International Publishing AG 2017
M. Felderer et al. (Eds.): PROFES 2017, LNCS 10611, pp. 71–79, 2017.
https://doi.org/10.1007/978-3-319-69926-4_6

that an effort estimation model used only the most recently-completed projects. As data from a newly-completed project is added to a repository of data from past projects, the window moves forward so that the oldest one drops out. The results supported the advantage of the windowing approach, on one company's project data. A series of studies has also explored the use of windows over various effort estimation models and window policies [2,4,8] with the same dataset.

Studies using other datasets [3,9,10] have given contradictory results: the use of moving windows did not improve the accuracy of effort estimates, or even made it worse. The question arises: what is different about the datasets, or the organizations and projects from which the data were collected, that may explain the different results? Some possible causes were suggested in [10].

To attempt to answer this question requires replicating the experiments with further datasets. As obtaining project data with dates is a difficult task, combining existing datasets of past project data is a realistic approach for replication.

This paper replicates previous experiments [7,10], using a dataset composed from the three datasets used in [10]. The composite dataset varies more in time density, size, and industry sector than the three individual subsets; in this sense it is more similar to the dataset studied in [7]. The aim is to investigate whether these changes in the characteristics of the dataset affect estimation accuracy.

Using the combined dataset, we revisit the same research questions of [7,10]:

RQ1: Is there a difference between the accuracy of estimates using prediction models that are built using all available data in a training set, and the accuracy of estimates using prediction models that are built using only the N most recently-completed projects in the training set?

RQ2: Can insights be gained by observing trends in estimation accuracy as N varies?

2   Related Work

The first detailed studies on the effect of using moving windows were conducted by Lokan and Mendes [6,7]. They used linear regression (LR) models, and a single-company data set from the ISBSG repository. Training sets were defined to be the N most recently completed projects. They found that the use of a window could affect accuracy significantly, predictive accuracy was better with larger windows, and some window sizes were particularly effective.

Further studies have investigated the use of moving windows, considering different effort estimation models (Estimation by Analogy [2], and CART [1,4]), windows whose size was based on a fixed duration instead of a fixed number of projects [9], and giving more weight to more recent training projects in a window of the most recent projects [3].

Several studies used the single-company ISBSG data set studied originally in [7], finding that the use of moving windows was effective when using a suitable window size. Recent studies have considered other data sets, drawn from the Finnish data set, to further investigate the effectiveness of moving windows.

The Finnish data set contains three substantial subsets, which come from different organizations. Lokan and Mendes [10] found that with these data sets, the use of windows was never beneficial, and with some window sizes was significantly harmful, to estimation accuracy.

Some notable differences between the ISBSG subset and the three Finnish subsets are in homogeneity of industry sector, sample sizes, and time span. These differences can be reduced by combining the three Finnish organizations' data sets: the combined data set is more like the ISBSG data set by being larger and more heterogeneous than the individual subset; the same industry sector (Insurance) contributes the most projects to both; most of the projects in the combined data set cover a time span of the same length as the ISBSG subset. This study focuses on examining the effects of those factors by using the combined data set.

3   Research Method

3.1   Description of Combined Datasets

This study uses a composite data set, combining data from the three single-company subsets of the Finnish dataset that were analyzed in [10]. The fundamental variables are size, effort, and four basic project classifiers: development type, hardware platform, development language, and business sector. The combined dataset contains 398 projects, implemented from 1982 to 2007.

Table 1. Basic statistics for ratio-scaled variables of the combined Finnish dataset

Variable	Mean	Median	St. Dev.	Min.	Max.
Size (FP)	466	261	790	6	6294
Effort (hours)	2992	1305	5583	42	67576
Duration (months)	8.8	6.5	9.6	0.8	105.1
PDR (hours/FP)	7.5	6.6	5.0	0.4	47.8

Table 1 summarizes the ratio-scaled variables for the combined dataset. Some temporal tendencies were also observed as follows:

- Size, Effort, and Duration are higher in the earlier projects.
- PDR (project delivery rates; defined as effort divided by size) declines to begin with, but thereafter increases with time.
- New developments dominate the earlier projects, but decline as enhancement and maintenance projects increase.
- 3rd Generation Languages always dominate, even more so in the later projects.
- Multi-platform and mainframe projects are always dominant.

Even in the combined dataset, projects are sparse to begin with (15 projects in the first 10 years). By start date, the first 20% of completed projects span 20 years; the next four groups of 20% of projects in chronological order span about 4.5, 4.3, 2.8, and 3 years.

3.2   Modeling Technique

This study follows previous studies [7, 10] by using linear regression to form estimation models, with some procedures for feature selection and outlier detection, Its procedure includes the following treatments:

- Size and Effort metrics were log-transformed, as in the original study and as is common in this research field [5].
- Independent variables whose values were not known for a target project were not considered for inclusion in the estimation model.
- Every model included $log(Size)$ as an independent variable.
- Outliers were determined by Cook's distance and removed after examining its effects.
- Models constructed in our experiment can be different for every project.

Full details are as described in [10].

3.3   Effort Estimation with Chronologically Ordered Projects

This study evaluated the effects of moving windows of several sizes along with a timeline of projects' history. The effects were measured by performance comparisons between moving windows and a growing portfolio.

For a window of N projects, this evaluation was performed as follows:

1. Sort all projects by starting date.
2. For a given window size N, find the earliest project p_0 for which at least $N + 1$ projects were completed prior to the start of p_0 (projects from p_0 onwards are the ones whose training set is affected by using a window, so they form the set of evaluation projects for this window size. For example, with a window of 20 projects at least 21 projects must have finished for the window to differ from the growing portfolio; in this data set 373 projects had yet to start when the 21st project finished.)
3. For every project p_i in chronological sequence, starting from p_0, form estimates using moving windows and the growing portfolio (all completed projects). For moving windows, the training set is the N most recent projects that finished before p_i started. If multiple projects finished at the same date, all of them are included. For the growing approach, the training set is all projects that finished before p_i started.
4. Evaluate estimation results.

We explored window sizes from 20 to 240 projects. The minimum size was that used in [7]. As the size of the combined data set is approximately twice that used in [7], the maximum size was set as twice the maximum size of that study.

3.4   Performance Measures

We used Mean Absolute Error (MAE) as the performance measure, as it is not biased towards either under- or over-estimates. Effect size was used for quantitative comparison. Effect size is considered to be small below ≈ 0.2, medium at ≈ 0.5, and large at ≈ 0.8 or above [11]. To test for statistically significant differences between accuracy measures, we used the two-sided Wilcoxon signed-rank test for paired samples, setting $\alpha = 0.05$. As this study uses multiple related tests, the p-values of the tests must be controlled. We used the Holm-Bonferroni correction.

4   Results

Table 2 shows the effect of moving windows of different sizes on MAE[1]. The first column shows window sizes. The second column shows the total number of projects used as testing projects with the corresponding window size: the larger the window size, the smaller the number of testing projects. The third and fourth columns show accuracy measures for the growing portfolio and moving windows for the corresponding window sizes. The fifth column shows the difference in percentages. The sixth column shows the p-value from statistical tests on accuracy measures between the growing portfolio and moving windows. The last column shows the effect size compared to using the growing portfolio. Positive values mean a preference for the growing portfolio.

Table 2. Mean absolute residuals with different window sizes

Window size (N)	Testing projects	Growing portfolio	Moving windows	Diff. (%)	p-value	Effect size
20	373	1346.8	1472.3	9.32	0.78	0.04
40	340	1227.0	1323.0	7.82	0.45	0.04
60	319	1239.6	1289.2	4.00	0.58	0.02
80	281	1162.6	1237.5	6.44	0.08	0.03
100	277	1173.6	1228.6	4.69	0.23	0.02
120	253	1128.9	1161.7	2.90	0.64	0.01
140	232	1103.8	1114.1	0.94	0.79	0.00
160	202	926.2	939.4	1.42	0.86	0.01
180	176	918.9	942.4	2.56	0.08	0.01
200	160	948.9	977.8	3.05	0.00	0.02
220	142	861.5	884.1	2.63	0.04	0.01
240	132	777.0	812.0	4.50	0.02	0.03

---

[1] The results are graphed for all window sizes. The tables only show every twentieth window size, due to space limitations. This is sufficient to show the essential trends.

Figure 1 plots the difference in mean absolute error against window sizes. The x-axis is the size of the window, and the y-axis is the subtraction of the accuracy measure value with the growing approach from that with the window at the given x-value. Moving windows are advantageous on average when the line is below 0, and disadvantageous when the line is above 0.

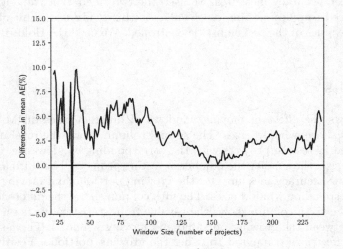

Fig. 1. Difference in MAE between growing portfolio and moving windows

Figure 1 shows that MAE is always better (the line is above 0), except for a single spike at $N = 35$, when all past data is used to train an estimation model rather than a moving window of the most recent projects. The advantage is up to 10%, compared to using windows. Although the sixth column in Table 2 has some p-values below 0.05, with the Holm-Bonferroni correction no difference remains statistically significant.

In summary, for this virtual organization, there is no reason to use a window instead of the growing portfolio. Effect sizes are very small, and there is no window size that produces a statistically significant difference in accuracy.

5   Discussion

5.1   Answer to RQ1

The first question is whether the use of moving windows affects the accuracy of effort estimates, in the combined dataset.

The use of moving windows did not improve the accuracy of estimates, for any window size. With this composite dataset, as in the three subsets from which it is composed, it is always better to retain all past data when building an estimation model. Heterogeneity in industry sector does not change the result.

5.2 Answer to RQ2

The second question is whether insights can be gained by observing trends in estimation accuracy as the window size varies.

The line in Fig. 1 is always above zero (meaning that windows are detrimental), except for a single spike. It is well above zero for smaller window sizes: estimation accuracy is 2.5–10% worse with the window, averaging about 5% worse, for windows of up to about 100 projects. With larger windows, the loss of accuracy averages around 3%. The loss of accuracy with small window sizes agrees with previous studies. It suggests that small windows do not contain enough training projects to learn an accurate effort estimation model.

It may be arguable that experiments with a data set similar to the single-company ISBSG data set could result in a similar trend. The heterogeneity could be a possible factor for instability (and lower performance) of models with small training datasets.

Doubling the range of window sizes does not reveal a window size that improves estimation accuracy.

In summary, in this virtual organization, the use of moving windows does not improve the accuracy of effort estimates. It is better to use all past projects as training data for effort estimation.

5.3 Comparison to Previous Studies

Moving windows were able to improve estimation accuracy in [7], but not in [10].

The contribution of this study is that none of heterogeneity in industry sector, a wider range of window sizes, nor more training and testing projects at each window size was found to be related to the different results concerning the effectiveness of moving windows. This reinforces the previous result that moving windows are not always useful. Also, it implies a need for exploring other factors relating to the potential effectiveness of using windows.

6 Threats to Validity

First, the data sets we used are convenience samples, and may not be representative of software projects in general. Thus, the results might not be generalizable beyond these data sets; this is true of all studies based on convenience samples.

Next, this study combines data sets from multiple companies, and may not represent any real company. In a sense this is an arbitrary combination. However, we think it is a reasonable approach for our purpose, because this treatment creates a data set with characteristics more similar to the subset from ISBSG.

All the models employed in this study were built automatically. The validity of our results depends on the automated process being suitable for model-building using linear regression. Based on our experience building models manually, we believe that the automated process is appropriate.

7   Conclusion

This study investigated a possible cause of contradictory results regarding the effectiveness of moving windows for effort estimation. An experiment was conducted with a virtual dataset, comprising three subsets of the Finnish dataset, which retains characteristics of those subsets but is more similar to the subset of ISBSG. The results show that moving windows do not improve the accuracy of estimates with this dataset, compared to using the growing portfolio.

Contradictory results from past studies could not be explained by the differences in the data that were considered here. In particular, this study suggests that differences in the heterogeneity of industry sector do not account for the different results found in [7,10].

For practitioners, the value of this research is that it reinforces that recency of data is not necessarily a dominant factor of representativeness. Using recent data as a basis for estimation seems intuitively attractive, but keeping in mind what can be learned from both recent data and older data can be beneficial.

Exploring the effects of other differences between the data sets is a future research direction.

Acknowledgment. This work was supported by JSPS KAKENHI Grant #15K15975.

References

1. Amasaki, S., Lokan, C.: The effect of moving windows on software effort estimation: comparative study with CART. In: Proceedings of IWESEP 2014, pp. 1–6. IEEE (2014)
2. Amasaki, S., Lokan, C.: A Replication of comparative study of moving windows on linear regression and estimation by analogy. In: Proceedings of PROMISE 2015, pp. 1–10. ACM, New York, October 2015
3. Amasaki, S., Lokan, C.: On the effectiveness of weighted moving windows: experiment on linear regression based software effort estimation. J. Softw. Evol. Process **27**(7), 488–507 (2015)
4. Amasaki, S., Lokan, C.: Evaluation of moving window policies with CART. In: Proceedings of IWESEP 2016, pp. 24–29. IEEE (2016)
5. Kitchenham, B.A., Mendes, E.: Why comparative effort prediction studies may be invalid. In: Proceedings of PROMISE 2009, p. 4. ACM (2009)
6. Lokan, C., Mendes, E.: Investigating the use of chronological splitting to compare software cross-company and single-company effort predictions. In: Proceedings of EASE 2008 (2008)
7. Lokan, C., Mendes, E.: Applying moving windows to software effort estimation. In: Proceedings of ESEM 2009, pp. 111–122 (2009)
8. Lokan, C., Mendes, E.: Investigating the use of duration-based moving windows to improve software effort prediction. In: Proceedings of APSEC 2012, pp. 818–827 (2012)
9. Lokan, C., Mendes, E.: Investigating the use of duration-based moving windows to improve software effort prediction: a replicated study. Inf. Softw. Technol. **56**(9), 1063–1075 (2014)

10. Lokan, C., Mendes, E.: Investigating the use of moving windows to improve software effort prediction: a replicated study. Empir. Softw. Eng. **22**(2), 1–52 (2016)
11. Shepperd, M., MacDonell, S.: Evaluating prediction systems in software project estimation. Inf. Softw. Technol. **54**(8), 820–827 (2012)

A Survival Analysis of Source Files Modified by New Developers

Hirohisa Aman[1(✉)], Sousuke Amasaki[2], Tomoyuki Yokogawa[2], and Minoru Kawahara[1]

[1] Ehime University, Matsuyama, Ehime 790–8577, Japan
aman@ehime-u.ac.jp
[2] Okayama Prefectural University, Soja, Okayama 719–1197, Japan

Abstract. This paper proposes an application of the survival analysis to bug-fix events occurred in source files. When a source file is modified, it has a risk of creating a bug (fault). In this paper, such a risk is analyzed from a viewpoint of the survival time—the time that the source file can survive without any bug fix. Through an empirical study with 100 open source software (OSS) projects, the following findings are reported: (1) Source files modified by new developers have about 26% shorter survival time than the others. (2) The above tendency may be inverted if the OSS project has more developers relative to the total number of source files.

Keywords: Open source development · Survival analysis · Time to bug fix

1 Introduction

Open source software (OSS) products have been more and more popular in the IT world. Many users and companies have utilized in their social life or business. As an OSS product has more users or stakeholders, post-release failures occurred in the product have larger impacts [4]. Hence, the quality management of OSS products has gotten a lot of attention recently. A software product usually evolves through its functional enhancements and bug (fault) fixes. Although it is ideal that developers never create any bugs, the bug-free evolution would be hard in reality; some code modifications are also creations of new bugs [6,8]. Nonetheless, frequent bug fixes are always undesirable in software development.

There have been many studies in regard to bug-fix prediction in the past. Rahman et al. [11] reported the trend that recently-bug-fixed source files are likely to be fixed again. Google utilized their results and released the prediction tool working on Git repositories [5]. Bird et al. [3] and Posnett et al. [10] focused on the ownership of source files and reported that a source file having lower ownership is likely to be more fault-prone; low ownership of a source file means that the file has not been developed and maintained by specific core developer(s), i.e., the file has been modified by various developers.

© Springer International Publishing AG 2017
M. Felderer et al. (Eds.): PROFES 2017, LNCS 10611, pp. 80–88, 2017.
https://doi.org/10.1007/978-3-319-69926-4_7

According to the previous work, the change history and ownership of source files are promising data for analyzing the occurrence of bug fixes. However, most previous studies focused on the number of bug fixes or the bug-fix rate; we consider that the time to bug fix would be yet another noteworthy feature to be analyzed. For example, suppose bug fixes were made in two files f_A and f_B. If f_A was modified "one day" ago and f_B was done "one year" ago, we should preferentially examine the precedent modification of f_A than f_B. In order to analyze such a difference, we will focus on the survival analysis [12]. The survival analysis is popular in the medical field, which analyzes the survival rate and the survival time of patients who were received specific treatments. In this paper, we propose an application of the survival analysis to the bug-fix survival time—the time to bug fix. The key contributions of this paper are as follows:

1. An application of the survival analysis to the bug-fix events in source files: To the best of our knowledge, although there have been studies utilizing the survival analysis to the substantivity of OSS projects [2,14], there have not been a study applying it to the time to bug fix.
2. An empirical report with many OSS projects: We collected data from 100 OSS projects, and report the results of the bug-fix survival analysis.

2 Survival Analysis and Its Application to Bug Fix

2.1 Survival Analysis

The survival analysis is a statistical method for analyzing the time to the occurrence of an event (e.g., a patient death in a clinical site).

Let t be the elapsed time from the start of our observation, and $S(t)$ be the probability that the event of interest had not been occurred until t, i.e., a subject survives at t. $S(t)$ is a monotonically decreasing function and called the survival rate function. The expected survival time μ_t is computed as:

$$\mu_t = - \int t \; dS(t). \tag{1}$$

That is to say, μ_t is the area under $S(t)$ (see Fig. 1).

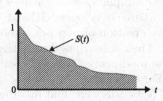

Fig. 1. Example of $S(t)$ and μ_t (area of the hatched part).

Needless to say, there may be a subject which has survived after the end of our event observation. Such a subject is called a "censor sample." If we have a censor sample, we cannot get true $S(t)$. However, when our event occurrence time is discrete type ($t = t_1, t_2, \ldots, t_i, \ldots$), we can estimate it by using the Kaplan-Meier (KM) method (see [7] for the details). The KM method is a popular non-parametric method for estimating $S(t)$ using the cumulative hazard as:

$$S(t_i) = \prod_{k=1}^{i} \{1 - \lambda(t_i)\}, \tag{2}$$

where $\lambda(t_i)$ is the hazard at t_i and $\lambda(t_i) = e_i/n_i$; n_i is the number of subjects which have survived at least just before t_i and e_i is the number of subjects which died (encountered the event) at t_i, respectively.

2.2 Application of Survival Analysis to Bug Fix

Now we consider another survival analysis in which a subject and an event are a source file and a bug fix, respectively. Then, we can develop a model of the time to bug fix in a source file. While many studies have been done for predicting bug fixes in the past, most of them focused on the number of bug fixes or the occurrence rate. We will focus on yet another point of view in this paper. According to the previous work regarding the file ownership [3,10], modifications made by new developers may have higher risks of causing future bug fixes. By analyzing the survival time to bug fix, we will evaluate such risks. We describe the survival analysis of the time to bug fix in the remainder of this section.

Let f be a source file, and t_E be the time when the observation was finished, respectively. Then, let $t_M(<t_E)$ be the time when f was finally modified (or created) but the modification was not a bug fix. If a bug is fixed in f at t_B, the life time of f to the bug fix; $L(f)$, is computed as $L(f) = t_B - t_M$. If bug fixes occurred in f twice or more, use the oldest bug-fix time as t_B; if no bug fix was observed until t_E, f is a censor sample. Then, we define $L(f) = t_E - t_M$.

Next, we check the developer who made the modification at t_M, and examine whether he/she is a new developer who has never been involved in f before t_M. Then, we categorize f into two types, NEW and CONV—if f is modified by a new developer at t_M, we consider f to be Type NEW; otherwise, f is Type CONV which means that the modification is made by a conventional developer.

Table 1 presents a simple example where eight files f_1, f_2, $\cdots$, f_8 have been developed and maintained by three developers (ID = 1, 2, 3). Symbols "A," "M" and "B" in the table signify a creation of new file, a modification of a file, and a bug fix of a file, respectively. Their subscripts denote the developer ID who made those work. For each file, the modification (or the creation) according to its t_M is marked with an asterisk. For example, f_1, f_4 and f_5 are modified by developer 1 at $t = 21$. f_1 is Type NEW because its final modification at $t = 26$ is made by developer 2 and it is the first time for developer 2 to modify f_1 at that time. Similarly, f_5 is Type CONV since its final modification before the bug fix (at $t = 21$) is made by developer 1 and he/she had already been involved in f_5. Since f_1, f_4, f_6 and f_8 have no bug fix within the observation duration ($0 \leq t \leq t_E$), they are censor samples and their life times are computed as $L(f_i) = t_E - t_M$. The remaining files' life times are obtained as $L(f_i) = t_B - t_M$.

Table 1. Example of source file development history.

file	t											t_E	type	t_B	t_M	$L(f_i)$
	0	5	12	15	18	20	21	25	26	30	31	35				
f_1	A_1	M_1					M_1		M_2^*				NEW	—	26	9
f_2		A_1			M_2^*			B_2					NEW	25	20	5
f_3		A_1	M_2^*	B_1									NEW	18	15	3
f_4				A_2			M_1				M_3^*		NEW	—	31	4
f_5		A_1					M_1^*	B_2					CONV	25	21	4
f_6	A_1		M_2	M_2^*									CONV	—	15	20
f_7			A_2^*					B_2					CONV	25	12	13
f_8										A_3^*			CONV	—	30	5

The KM method can estimates the survival rate function $S(t)$ with Eq. (2). Figure 2 shows the estimated $S(t)$ of each type. We can see that NEW has a shorter life time to bug fix than CONV. The expected survival time of NEW and CONV are 6 and 13.375, respectively[1]. While both type have the same bug-fix rate (50%), they have remarkable differences in terms of expected survival time—6 vs. 13.375: the expected survival time of Type NEW is shorter than the half of Type CONV's survival time.

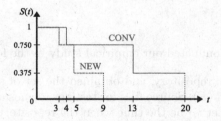

Fig. 2. Estimated $S(t)$'s for NEW and CONV types in Table 1.

3 Empirical Study

3.1 Dataset

We collected 100 local copies of OSS projects' repositories which are available on the GitHub, and obtained data to be analyzed from those repositories. Our subject projects consist of 50 Java projects and 50 C++ ones. The main reason why we selected these projects is their popularities; we believe that a finding derived

---

[1] NEW: $1 \times 3 + 0.750 \times (5 - 3) + 0.375 \times (9 - 5) = 6$; CONV: $1 \times 4 + 0.750 \times (13 - 4) + 0375 \times (20 - 13) = 13.375$.

Table 2. Analyzed OSS projects (in decreasing order of "stars").

Java projects	C++ projects
RxJava, elasticsearch, retrofit, okhttp, java-design-patterns, guava, leakcanary, zxing, libgdx, interviews, fastjson, dubbo, Android-CleanArchitecture, realm-java, MaterialDrawer, ExoPlayer, deeplearning4j, BottomBar, spark, vert.x, dagger, presto, junit4, Android-Bootstrap, dropwizard, UltimateRecyclerView, uCrop, jedis, auto, guice, mybatis-3, jadx, metrics, mockito, HikariCP, webmagic, buck, j2objc, jsoup, lombok, rebound, swagger-core, pinpoint, scribejava, okio, android-classyshark, async-http-client, mosby, CoreNLP, dex2jar	folly, imgui, json, libphonenumber, openFrameworks, Catch, proxygen, capnproto, rapidjson, libzmq, libsass, muduo, crow, tiny-dnn, ppsspp, dlib, spdlog, Cpp-Primer, openpose, pybind11, GamePlay, re2, concurrentqueue, envoy, oclint, zopfli, nghttp2, cpprestsdk, websocketpp, osrm-backend, BansheeEngine, swig, i2cdevlib, algorithms, AtomicGameEngine, mlpack, thrust, iaito, glog, cpr, cpp-ethereum, magnum, cppcheck, gosu, phxpaxos, deepdetect, actor-framework, cereal, oryol, cling

from more popular projects is more attractive for more researches and practitioners. These projects have high "stars" scores at GitHub: We performed project searches sorted by "most stars" option, where the search keywords were "Java" and "C++," respectively. Table 2 presents the names of collected projects.

3.2 Procedure

For each project, we conducted our empirical study in the following four steps.

1. Made a copy of the repository, and obtained the set of source files included in the latest version (F). Source files for testings, demos and documents were excluded from F. Let t_E be the time when the repository was copied.
2. For each $f \in F$, extracted its change history from the commit logs, and decided t_B: if the commit message of f contained a bug fix-related keyword, we considered that a bug fix was performed in f at the commit [13].
3. For each $f \in F$, determined t_M and and f's type—NEW or CONV. The identification of developer was performed in accordance with the following rules [1]: if two developers had the same name or the same e-mail address, we considered that they are the same developer.
4. Estimated the survival rate function $S(t)$ for each types, NEW and CONV, using the KM method. Then, computed the expected survival time with Equation (1): let μ_N and μ_C be the expected survival time in NEW and CONV, respectively. To compare their differences across projects, define the following criterion, $\Delta\mu$:

$$\Delta\mu = \frac{\mu_C - \mu_N}{\mu_C}. \tag{3}$$

If $\Delta\mu$ has a larger positive value, Type NEW files have shorter expected survival times than Type CONV ones. While "$\mu_C - \mu_N$" directly shows the difference of two survival times, we considered it is better to normalize the difference with using one of those times because there would be dispersions of survival times among projects; such a raw difference would not be suitable for comparing different projects.

3.3 Results

Table 3 and Fig. 3 show distributions of $\Delta\mu$ values. The median and the average (mean) of $\Delta\mu$ in the 100 OSS products are 0.394 and 0.258, respectively (see Table 3). Moreover, a majority of projects show $\Delta\mu > 0$ (see Fig. 3). In other words, the expected survival times of Type NEW source files tend to be about 26% shorter than that of Type CONV on average.

Table 3. Distribution of $\Delta\mu$ values in analyzed OSS projects.

Min.	25%	Median	Mean	75%	Max.
−1.675	0.048	0.394	0.258	0.628	0.997

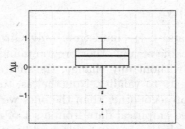

Fig. 3. Boxplot of $\Delta\mu$ values in analyzed OSS projects.

3.4 Discussions

Through the survival analysis, we have understood a major trend of time to bug fix in many OSS projects—how long time a source file tends to take until a bug fix, rather than whether a bug fix would occur or not. A source file modified by a new developer (Type NEW) would have a higher risk of a latent bug and the time to bug fix would be about 26% shorter than another type of source file (Type CONV). This trend seems to support the previous work regarding the file ownership [3,10].

While the above results show an overall trend, some projects had small $\Delta\mu$ values or the opposite trends. To examine if there is a statistically significant difference between NEW and CONV in terms of $S(t)$, we performed the log-rank test [9] (at a 5% significance level). The test results were as follows: there seem to be significant differences in 65 products (does not in 35 products); in 56 out of 65 products, Type NEW tends to have a shorter survival time (denote it by "NEW < CONV"); the remaining 9 products show the opposite tendency ("CONV < NEW").

To explore a difference between two cases "(a) NEW < CONV" and "(b) CONV < NEW," we examined the numbers of developers ($=n_d$) and source files ($=n_f$) in those projects, and calculated the ratio between them: $r = n_d/n_f$. While the average of r values in case (a) is about 0.079, that in case (b) is 0.246. That is to say, r in case (b) is about 3 times larger than case (a); furthermore, the average r of the outliers shown in Fig. 3 is 3.93 which is about 50 times larger than case (a). Hence, case (b) tends to have more variety in terms of developers relative to the number of source files to be maintained, and they would be projects which more new developers can actively contribute to. We would like to do a further analysis from such a viewpoint as our future work.

Now, we have to notice that we have checked bug "fixing" events but not bug (fault) "inducing" ones. In other words, even if a bug fix occurred after a new developer's commit, it is not always true that the corresponding fault was induced by the new developer. We need to perform a further analysis of fault-inducing commits in the future for an enhanced discussion.

3.5   Threats to Validity

We collected only Java and C++ data from only Git repositories. Since our analysis method is applicable to any other programming languages and version control systems (VCSs) without any change, the limitations of language and VCS are not serious threats to validity. Nonetheless, there is a risk of getting different results in OSS projects other than the ones we examined. To mitigate such a threat, we collected empirical data from a set of many popular projects.

While we focused on whether a source file modification was made by a new developer or not, we did not examine his/her experience of maintaining other source files and expertise. Since our findings in this paper are derived from a lot of samples, impacts of individuals on our results might not be serious threats. A further analysis on individuals is our important future work.

We decided whether a commit is a bug fix or not, by using a keyword matching method [13], and it is a popular way of detecting bug-fix commits in the mining software repository community. However, our analysis was based on the assumption that all commit messages provided proper information in regard to their code changes. The assumption can be a threat to validity. For example, some bug-fix commits might be missed in our dataset because some developers might not appropriately describe their commit messages even if they performed bug fixes. The development of a more accurate detection method is one of our future challenges.

4   Conclusion

For a bug fix of a source file in an OSS development, we focused on the developer who made the last modification of the file before the bug fix—whether the developer had an experience of modifying the file at the time or not. In accordance with the above developer type, we categorized source files into the following two types, NEW and CONV: if a source file's last modification before its bug fix (or the end of our observation) was made by a new developer who had never modified that file, the source file is Type NEW; otherwise, it is Type CONV. Then, we considered to compare these two types in terms of the time to bug fix through a survival analysis, and conducted an empirical study with 100 OSS projects which are available on the GitHub. The empirical results showed that the expected survival time of Type NEW source files is about 26% shorter than that of Type CONV ones. That is to say, when a source file is modified by a new developer who had not been involved in the maintenance of the file, that file is likely to require a bug fix sooner. In such a case, a more careful review would be useful to prevent a quality degradation.

On the other hand, if a project has more developers relative to the total number of source files, the project tends to produce the opposite tendency: Type NEW has a longer expected survival time. Such a project may be easier for more new developers to contribute. A further analysis on those points of view is our future work. Moreover, we plan to take into account the degree of a developer's familiarity with a file and to perform a further analysis toward a just-in-time defect prediction.

Acknowledgment. This work was supported by JSPS KAKENHI #16K00099. The authors would like to thank the anonymous reviewers for their helpful comments.

References

1. Bird, C., Gourley, A., Devanbu, P., Gertz, M., Swaminathan, A.: Mining email social networks. In: Proceedings of International Workshop Mining Software Repositories, pp. 137–143 (2006)
2. Bird, C., Gourley, A., Devanbu, P., Swaminathan, A., Hsu, G.: Open borders? Immigration in open source projects. In: Proceedings of 4th International Workshop Mining Software Repositories (2007)
3. Bird, C., Nagappan, N., Murphy, B., Gall, H., Devanbu, P.: Don't touch my code!: examining the effects of ownership on software quality. In: Proceedings of 19th ACM SIGSOFT Symposium and 13th European Conference Foundations of Software Engineering, pp. 4–14 (2011)
4. Duck, B.: The 2017 open source 360° survey (2017). https://www.blackducksoft ware.com/about/news-events/releases/open-source-360-organizations-increase-reliance-open-source
5. Google: Bugspots (2011). https://github.com/igrigorik/bugspots
6. Jones, C.: Applied Software Measurement: Global Analysis of Productivity and Quality, 3rd edn. McGraw-Hill, New York (2008)

7. Kaplan, E.L., Meier, P.: Nonparametric estimation from incomplete observations. J. Am. Stat. Assoc. **53**(282), 457–481 (1958)
8. Li, Y., Li, D., Huang, F., Lee, S.Y., Ai, J.: An exploratory analysis on software developers' bug-introducing tendency over time. In: Proceedings of International Conference Software Analysis, Testing and Evolution, pp. 12–17 (2016)
9. Peto, R., Peto, J.: Asymptotically efficient rank invariant test procedures. J. Roy. Stat. Soc. Ser. A (Gen.) **135**(2), 185–207 (1972)
10. Posnett, D., D'Souza, R., Devanbu, P., Filkov, V.: Dual ecological measures of focus in software development. In: Proceedings of International Conference on Software Engineering, pp. 452–461 (2013)
11. Rahman, F., Posnett, D., Hindle, A., Barr, E., Devanbu, P.: Bugcache for inspections: hit or miss? In: Proceedings of 19th ACM SIGSOFT Symposium and 13th European Conference on Foundations of Software Engineering, pp. 322–331 (2011)
12. Rupert, G., Miller, J.: Survival Analysis. John Wiley & Sons, Hoboken, NJ (2011)
13. Śliwerski, J., Zimmermann, T., Zeller, A.: When do changes induce fixes?. In: Proceedings of International Workshop Mining Software Repositories, pp. 1–5 (2005)
14. Samoladas, I., Angelis, L., Stamelos, I.: Survival analysis on the duration of open source projects. Inf. Softw. Technol. **52**, 902–922 (2010)

Top Management Support for Software Cost Estimation
A Case Study of the Current Practice and Impacts

Jurka Rahikkala[1], Sami Hyrynsalmi[2(✉)], Ville Leppänen[1], Tommi Mikkonen[3], and Johannes Holvitie[1]

[1] University of Turku, Turku, Finland
{juperah,ville.leppanen,jjholv}@utu.fi
[2] Tampere University of Technology, Tampere, Finland
sami.hyrynsalmi@tut.fi
[3] University of Helsinki, Helsinki, Finland
tommi.mikkonen@helsinki.fi

Abstract. *Context:* Despite decades of research in software cost estimation (SCE), the task remains difficult and software project overruns are common. Many researchers and practitioners agree that organisational issues and methodologies are equally important for successful SCE. Regardless of this recent development, SCE research is revolving heavily around methodologies. At the same time project management research has undergone a major shift towards managerial issues, and it found that top management support can be the most important success factor for projects.

Goal: This study sheds light on top management's role in SCE by identifying real-life practices for top management participation in SCE, as well as related organisational effects. Also, the impact of top management actions on project success is examined.

Method: The study takes a qualitative and explorative case study based approach. In total, 18 semi-structured interviews facilitated examination of three projects in three organisations.

Results: The results show that top management takes no, or very little, direct actions to participate in SCE. However, projects can conclude successfully regardless of the low extent of participation.

Conclusions: Top management actions may also induce bias in estimation, influencing project success negatively. This implies that senior managers must recognise the importance of seeking realism and avoid influencing the estimation.

Keywords: Senior management · Software cost estimation · Project management

1 Introduction

The global software spending is growing rapidly [12]. Especially R&D spending on software has increased by 65% between 2010 and 2015 [43], driven by

© Springer International Publishing AG 2017
M. Felderer et al. (Eds.): PROFES 2017, LNCS 10611, pp. 89–107, 2017.
https://doi.org/10.1007/978-3-319-69926-4_8

innovations depending more and more on electronics and software [13]. While software has become increasingly important for companies, estimating the cost of software is difficult. The annual losses from software projects are measured in billions of euros [11,36], and software project overruns are common [9,14,16].

Software cost estimation (SCE) and project management (PM) are both inseparable parts of a software project, and project management should always consider estimation [17]. Therefore the reasons for overruns may also reside in SCE, PM, or other project areas [6,24,35,38]. Considering the gravity of the problem and the known positive effect of using methodologies on project success [52], both SCE and PM professionals have developed a plethora of methodologies to aid in guiding the project to a planned conclusion. In the area of SCE, hundreds of estimation methodologies have been developed [22,34], some of which have been proven to produce accurate results, when used properly [40,42]. Yet, overruns are common [9,14,16].

Recent studies show that there are severe deficiencies in applying SCE methodologies in organisations [3,20,30,33,45], although the problems have been known for decades [15,27]. The situation is significantly better in the area of PM, where 95% of the projects report using PM methodologies [50]. This difference in the extent of use of methodologies is surprising, because SCE research is methodology heavy, having 84% of the studies focusing on methodologies [22]. At the same time PM research has undergone a major shift towards topics like management and business, having only 16% of the recent articles focusing on methodologies [25]. Especially Top Management Support (TMS) has been an important topic for PM research, and it has been found to be even the most important success factor for projects [50]. The body of knowledge regarding top management support in PM is extensive, and contains clear advice for top management for how to support projects, including *refreshing project procedures and appropriate project management assignment* [53].

Considering the previous, the estimation related problems are not connected only to methodologies, but also to how these methodologies are applied in organisations. Although SCE research is still mainly focusing on methodologies, recently topics like estimation bias [18–20], organisational inhibitors and distortions [30,33], and top management participation [45], have become focus of the research. This paper continues on this highly relevant path of examining other than technical factors in SCE.

The research objective of this paper is to address the role of top management in SCE, and to answer the following unanswered questions:

RQ1 What are the real life top management support practices for SCE and how do they appear in an organisation?

RQ2 How much effort top management invests in participating in SCE?

RQ3 Which persons or items are affected by top management actions?

RQ4 What is the impact of TMS for SCE on project success?

In the scope of our study, when a reference to top management is made, we refer to the highest up manager, who is aware of the estimate on the basis on their responsibilities related to the studied projects. This paper provides in-depth findings from three projects in three case companies. Based on the study of 18 interviews[1], the paper contributes to the scientific literature by reporting on the current practice of top management participation in software cost estimation, and the effects of this participation in organisations. Additionally, the impact of top management participation in SCE on project success is addressed. Understanding the role of top management in SCE may better justify project managers, other software professionals and researchers to pay more attention to top management's role in software cost estimation.

The remainder of the study is structured as follows. Section 2 presents the background and related work of software cost estimation and top management support for project management. Section 3 describes the case study subject and research design. It is followed by the presentation of findings in Sect. 4. Section 5 discusses the results and Sect. 6 concludes the study.

2   Background

The purpose of software cost estimation, or effort estimation, is to provide the management and project leadership a clear enough view of the project to make good decisions about how to control the project to hit its targets [34]. SCE has already been studied for over half of a century, c.f. [37], and hundreds of different estimation methods have been developed [5,22]. Still, despite of the long and extensive work on the area of SCE, many software projects fail to meet estimates.

Software cost estimation research has heavily focused on estimation methodologies; leaving organisational issues with relatively little attention. According to Jørgensen's and Shepperd's [22] systematic literature review, organisational issues have been discussed only in 16% of the reviewed articles (Table 1). Furthermore, the interest towards organisational issues is decreasing. The recent study of SCE research trends shows also that the research focus has remained consistently on estimation methodologies and techniques between 1996 and 2016 [48].

The previous may be problematic, because the SCE challenge seems to reside elsewhere than in estimation methodologies. Researchers and practitioners largely agree on this point [22,27,30,34], getting support from recent studies [30,44,45]. Also, major industrial software development frameworks, such as CMMI [1], ITIL v3 [2] and PRINCE2[2], continue along the same lines, emphasising the importance of estimation, without giving specific advice, which estimation techniques to use. Thus, while the estimation problems seem to reside on the application of the methodologies in an organisation, the research is still focusing on the methodologies themselves, leaving a gap between the actual problem and the means to fix it.

---

[1] Due to the non-disclosure agreements, the raw data cannot be disclosed.
[2] https://www.axelos.com/qualifications/prince2-qualifications.

Much of the work performed in organisations is organised as projects which is understandable because the results of projects are critical for organisations [7,49]. Considering the importance of PM, also PM has been intensively studied for over decades which has resulted into an extensive body of knowledge. However, whereas the SCE research is still focusing on methodologies as its primary line of research, the PM research has undergone a significant shift from methodologies towards other topics, such as leadership and business. According to Kolltveit et al. [25] (Table 2), PM research related to Task and Transaction perspectives, representing technical methodologies, has decreased from 68% to 18% over the time, measured in the number of published articles. This shift of focus seems natural, since organisational issues are reported to be even more important factors in project success than technical ones [10,29,52]. Also, top management's interest in PM is increasing along with the number of PM related articles published in top management and business journals [26].

Table 1. Distribution of published SCE articles among research topics [22].

Perspective	-1989	1990–1999	2000–2004	Total
Estimation method	73 %	59 %	58 %	61 %
Size measures	12 %	24 %	16 %	20 %
Organisational issues	22 %	15 %	14 %	16 %
Uncertainty assessment	5 %	6 %	13 %	8 %
Calibration of models	7 %	8 %	4 %	7 %
Production function	20 %	4 %	3 %	6 %
Measures of estimation performance	5 %	5 %	6 %	5 %
Data set properties	0 %	1 %	2 %	1 %
Other	0 %	2 %	1 %	1 %

Regardless of the methodology heavy mainstream of the SCE research, some of the recent research has also been attending to non-technical problems, such as human bias, organisational inhibitors and distortions, as well as top management participation. Jørgensen et al. have conducted a broad and widely cited work on human bias, originating from different sources. Their studies have covered e.g. the impact of the first impression [19], customer expectations [23], irrelevant or misleading information [18], and wording [21] on the estimate. Magazinius et al. have published their results regarding intentional distortions [30–32] and organisation inhibitors [33] in SCE. Additionally, among the studies of organisational factors, Rahikkala et al. [44,45] have studies top management participation in SCE, and Ahonen et al. [3] have found problems in the reporting effort in projects.

To summarise, although both SCE and PM are inseparable parts of a software project [17], only PM research takes a holistic view, and examines the organisational context of the respective area to any great extent. SCE continues

Table 2. The distribution of published PM articles among different perspectives [25].

Perspective	1983–1987	1988–1992	1993–1997	1998–2002	2003–2004	Total
Task	49%	34%	32%	23%	12%	29%
Leadership	8%	16%	25%	28%	33%	23%
System	23%	25%	18%	19%	15%	20%
Stakeholder	1%	3%	1%	5%	6%	3%
Transaction	19%	9%	6%	10%	6%	10%
Business	0%	13%	17%	15%	29%	15%

to focus on methodological problems. This is a noteworthy observation, because the problems for software project overruns reside both in SCE and PM [6,35,38]. Understanding the organisational context of SCE may better help to overcome many organisational problems related to SCE, and to eliminate related sources of estimation error. This paper continues examining the organisational context of SCE, and addresses specifically the top management's role, which has been found to be of critical importance in PM.

3   Research Process

3.1   Research Approach

The study is based on three anonymous case companies and projects. For each company, we interviewed stakeholders involved in the projects (Table 3) and analysed 18 documents related to the project, including project plans, design documents, and minutes of meetings.

This study is based on a qualitative research approach [8]. We use a case study research strategy and interviews as the main tools of inquiry. The qualitative research approach was selected to allow us to get an in-depth understanding about the phenomenon under the study lens. The case study research strategy was used as the researchers have no control over the study subject [51]. As Patton [39] states, case studies are well capable of shedding light on phenomena occurring in the context of real-life. This study is of exploratory type, finding out what is happening, seeking new ideas, and generating hypotheses and ideas for new research [46]. The research uses a multiple case study design following a replication logic [51]. The unit of analysis is a single software cost estimate. The study is focused on the experiences gained during the preparation of the cost estimate. The conceptual framework of the study assisting in answering the research questions is presented in Fig. 1. Additionally, we have employed the list of 16 top management support practices suggested by Rahikkala et al. [45] for studying top management participation practices.

An interview protocol consisting of questions related to top management participation in SCE was created, following the guidelines by Runeson and Höst [47]. The one hour interviews were conducted as semi-structured [46] by

Table 3. Interviewees of the research.

Small Global	Large Multinational	Tech Giant
Product Owner (KI)	Project Manager (KI)	Program Manager (KI)
Senior Business Manager	Business Manager	Line Manager
	Testing Manager	Senior Manager
Senior Technology Manager	Requirements Engineer	Requirements Engineer
Project Manager	Software Developer	Head of Product Management
		Head of Programs

KI = Key informant for the study, interviewed twice

two researchers, and the discussion was recorded. The recordings were transcripted and sent to the interviewees for review. All case subjects participated in the study voluntarily and anonymously, and the collected data was treated as confidential.

For the analysis of data, we used nVivo 10. All transcripted interviews, notes done during the interviews, in addition to the auxiliary materials, were imported into the software. The analysis was conducted in a series of steps [46]. First the texts were coded by the researchers, whereafter iteration followed, until conclusions were reached.

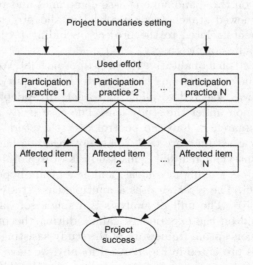

Fig. 1. The conceptual model of this research.

3.2   Case Companies and Projects

'*Small Global*' is a software producing firm of about 100 persons. The company's line of business consists of selling consultancy and support services in addition to software products to businesses. The company is global; it has customers and offices in several countries. The selected project, referred to as *Developer Tool* (DT), was about producing a visual design tool for developing applications. The end-result is a commercial product. The project followed a waterfall-style software engineering method, but the actual development work was divided into sprints. The estimation was done by using work breakdown structure (WBS) and expert estimation.

The DT project started with a prototype where technical challenges were studied. After the prototype project, a project aiming at the release of version 1.0 was planned. The product owner crafted a design document for the product, and based on that document, the project manager created a project plan with time and effort estimates. Initially, the project was estimated to take three months with a team of four people. The project completed nine months after the deadline with a team of approximately six persons.

'*Large Multinational*' produces software and consultancy for a wide area of business sectors. The company has tens of thousands of employees around the world. The selected project, referred to as *Operational Control System* (OCS), is a business intelligence reporting system for following certain control activities. The software was ordered by a long-term customer of the company.

Also this project followed a waterfall-like software development process. The estimation was done by the developers using expert estimation, whereafter the values were filled into a structured sheet. The project manager prepared the final estimates based on the results from expert estimation. The OCS project was planned according to certain preconditions: the customer had a fixed budget and schedule for development. The project lasted 10 months, and the size of the project was approximately 30 man-months. The project concluded successfully on time and budget.

'*Tech Giant*' is selling products with software to global business-to-business markets. The company has tens of thousands of employees around the world. We studied the *Network Management Product* (NSP) project of Tech Giant. The project produced a new release of a tool for managing the network. The project produced a new release of the system. The NSP has been in use for several years.

The project was part of a continuous development cycle involving just under 100 people. A new release of the system is developed every three months. The development methodology it used was based on Scrum with two week sprints. The development teams were distributed over several locations. The cost estimation was conducted in two phases: firstly, rough planning for the whole three month release in the product management function. Secondly, the backlog items were estimated in the scrum teams, the main responsible being the program manager. The backlog items were estimated using expert estimation. The project concluded successfully and delivered over 85% of the planned scope, which is the goal for all releases.

4   Findings and Results

This section presents the findings identified during the analysis of the data as described in the research methodology section. The findings are grouped into the following five categories according to the conceptual framework (c.f. Fig. 1): (1) Project boundaries, (2) Participation practices, (3) Participation effort, (4) Practical impacts, and (5) Impact on project success. The Project boundaries were separated clearly from the participation practices because, from this study's point of view, they are related to creating prerequisites for the estimation and the project rather than directly to the estimation itself.

4.1   Project Boundaries: Scope, Cost and Schedule

Software cost estimation is fundamentally about estimating the size of the software for a given scope. The size is then converted into a schedule and budget, based on different factors, like the composition of the development team. However, there are usually boundaries for an acceptable scope, cost or schedule, originating from the business environment. Based on these boundaries, the decision makers, project management and estimators try to find an optimal balance between the previously mentioned three dimensions. This section summarises boundaries for the studied projects and estimation.

At Tech Giant, who operates in a three month release cycle, the schedule was fixed. Also the cost (resources) was fixed to a great extent, although there were some additional resources available for situations, where overruns seemed probable. Large Multinational reported that their customer also operated under a predefined system update cycle and budget framework, also fixing the schedule and cost. At Small Global, the Senior Business Manager and other team members reported that the schedule was fixed. The Senior Business Manager also reported that the planned scope was a minimum viable and nothing could not have been dropped out, making also the scope of the project fixed. Thus, for Tech Giant and Large Multinational, the only variable element was the scope, and for Small Global the resources. Additionally, the senior managers monitored the progress of the projects against the estimate regularly, and made adjusting decisions based on the situation, where deemed necessary.

4.2   Participation Practices

First of all, top management did not exercise seven of the sixteen studied support practices at all, as shown in Table 4. Practices 1–16 are adapted from [45]. Additionally, the presence of three practices, 'TM ensures the involvement of the project manager during the estimation stage', 'TM ensures ongoing estimation

Table 4. Exercised top management support practices.

	Practice	Tech Giant	Large Multinational	Small Global
1.	TM ensures existence of estimation procedures			
2.	TM ensures that the estimator has adequate skills			
3.	TM ensures improving estimation procedures			
4.	TM ensures the involvement of the project manager during the estimation stage	+++	+++	+++
5.	TM ensures good communication between the estimator and the organisation			
6.	TM ensures that there are criteria for evaluating the meaningfulness of the estimate			
7.	TM ensures ongoing estimation skills training programmes	+	+	
8.	TM requires re-estimating during the project to get more accurate estimates			
9.	TM ensures that the estimate relies on documented facts rather than guessing and intuition			
10.	The IT executive studies and approves the estimate			
11	TM recognizes that estimates are critical to this organization's success	+++	+++	++
12.	TM is knowledgeable of estimation procedures		+++	
13.	TM understands the consequences of an erroneous estimate to the project success	+++	+++	+/-
14.	TM can distinguish between estimates, targets and commitments	+++	+++	-
15.	TM recognizes that the estimates are inaccurate in the beginning of the project	N/A	+	+
16	TM takes the output of an estimate as given without debate	+++	+++	+++
17.	NEW: TM studies and approves the estimate	+++	+++	+++
18	NEW: TM ensures adequate resources for estimation	+++	+++	+++

(+) signs and (−) signs indicate evidence of assumed positive and negative presence, respectively. N/A signs for not available.

skills training programmes' and 'TM recognizes that the estimates are inaccurate in the beginning of the project', was indirect, meaning that the presence of the practices could not be tracked back to any specific TM actions related to the studied projects. 'TM recognizes that the estimates are inaccurate in the beginning of the project' was not relevant for Tech Giant, as they are in a continuous three month release cycle, and the delivered scope must be constantly at least 85% of the planned scope. Large Multinational and Small Global had improved the accuracy with a specification phase, but this was a standard practice in both companies, like the involvement of the project manager during the estimation phase was for all three companies. Large Multinational and Tech Giant had arranged training for SCE earlier, but there were no ongoing training programs during the studied projects.

In all projects the senior managers reported that they had studied and approved the estimates. At Small Global, the Senior Business Manager studied the estimate in detail, as part of the project plan, while at Large Multinational and Tech Giant, the senior managers studied the estimates only on a summary level. Certain items in the estimates were also challenged by the senior managers in the OCS and NSP projects, which resulted in better estimates for the items in question. Considering the list of predefined 16 practices at hand, studying the estimates is close to 'TM ensures that the estimate relies on documented facts rather than guessing and intuition' and 'IT executive studies and approves the estimate'. However, as studying and approving the estimates does not fit precisely under either of the previous, we decided to report it as a new TM support practice for SCE, 'TM studies and approves the estimate'. 'TM is knowledgeable of estimation procedures' was present in the OCS project, where the Business Manager reported having been well aware of the estimation practices. This was, according to the Business Manager, coincidental rather than a result of planned actions. The presence of the four remaining support practices was strong in all case projects. The interviewees reported that the management considered the estimates having a high importance. However, none of the interviewees specified concrete examples of how the importance was demonstrated during the case projects, which means that the importance has most likely been established before these particular projects. At Large Multinational, the estimate was used for preparing an offer for a customer, who made the order decision based on it. At Tech Giant, a business plan, product roadmap and customer commitments were made based on the estimates. At Small Global, a GO/NOGO decision of the project was made based on the estimate. However, the Senior Business Manager at Small Global reported that the decision of making the product was practically made, and the estimate was used for reassuring that the scope was small or minimum viable, and that the delivery was possible in the targeted schedule. Thus, the estimate was connected to significant financial interests at Tech Giant and Large Multinational, and for making important planning decisions at Small Global.

When asked, all interviewees reported that realism and accuracy were always sought during the estimation. Furthermore, each interviewee also concluded that there was no push from the management to make the estimates smaller, and the management did not try to negotiate the estimate smaller. The Line Manager from Tech Giant says that estimates are accepted as facts, and the scope is reduced, if necessary. The Business Manager from Large Multinational says that the price can be negotiated with the customer, but not the estimate itself. However, although all interviewees at Small Global report that there was no push from the management, they also say that there was still a pressure to make the estimate smaller, conveyed by the Senior Business Manager in form of a strict deadline. The Project Manager, who was responsible for making the estimate, says that he experienced a high pressure and started to doubt his own estimates and eventually made them smaller.

As described earlier in this section, all of the projects had clear targets, or business goals, consisting of the scope, budget, and schedule. In the OCS and NSP projects the estimates were also accepted as facts which steered the planning. However, in the DT project, the Project Manager described that he made the estimate smaller because of the perceived pressure. The Senior Business Manager also told that the purpose of the estimate was to verify that the fixed scope was possible to be delivered within the target schedule, with higher resources, if necessary. The decision of executing the project was practically done. The previous signals that, in addition to creating estimates, the management seem to have expected the estimation to result into a plan, how to hit the targets, even though this seems not to have been consciously understood and intended.

In the NSP project, there was a continuous commitment to deliver at least 85% of the target scope, and at Large Multinational the normal practice was to use the estimate also as a commitment. At Small Global, the Project Manager says having been committed to the estimate in the beginning, but during the re-estimations in the later phases of the project he describes as having been afraid of giving estimates, because the estimates were taken literally by the management. Thus, estimates seem to have been implicitly taken as commitments by the management, although there was no explicit agreement on this.

In addition to the findings related to the 17 support practices reviewed earlier, resource provisioning for SCE emerged from the discussions. According to the interviewees' subjective perception, all projects had enough time and resources for preparing the estimates. At Small Global and Large Multinational, there was a separate specification phase prior to the actual implementation phase. The requirements engineer at Tech Giant reports that pre-studies are conducted, when necessary, to gain adequate understanding of the features. However, also this support practice was indirect of nature, and could not be attributed to any top management actions specific for the studied projects.

4.3   Participation Effort

According to the evidence discovered during the interviews and review of the documents, top management's effort for participating in SCE was low in all case projects. In terms of time and effort, the most significant contribution was the follow-up of the progress against the estimate. This, however, is primarily connected to project management, and not to SCE. Additionally, the senior managers studied the estimate in all projects. However, as an investment of time and effort, this was relatively small. The effort related to all other participation practices could not be attributed to the studied project in particular. The practices had emerged in a longer period of time and become established routines, which do not need attention for each new project. The interviewees in all projects also confirmed that the top management did not participate directly in the estimation.

4.4   Affected Items

As concluded earlier, top management sets boundaries for the project and estimation in form of budget, schedule and scope. This, however, is not influencing the estimation itself. Furthermore, the indirect support practices 'TM ensures the involvement of the project manager during the estimation stage', 'TM recognizes that the estimates are inaccurate in the beginning of the project', 'TM ensures ongoing estimation skills training programmes', 'TM ensures adequate resources for estimation' and 'TM is knowledgeable of estimation procedures' did not have any direct effects on estimation, which could have been attributed to the studied projects.

The awareness related practices, 'TM recognizes that estimates are critical to this organization's success', 'TM understands the consequences of an erroneous estimate to the project success', 'TM can distinguish between estimates, targets and commitments' and 'TM takes the output of an estimate as given without debate' did not have any tangible effects either in their positive occurrences. However, in the DT project the Project Manager reported that he had made the estimates smaller, because of the awareness of the target schedule. Furthermore, he reported that his willingness to give re-estimates during the project had decreased and he had started to give upper bound estimates, because the estimates were taken literally and interpreted as commitments. So, the awareness related support practices seem to have tangible effects on people or SCE related artefacts only, when the effects are harmful.

'TM studies and approves the estimate' was the only support practice that had direct positive impacts on estimation as a result of top management actions. After studying the estimates, managers challenged some parts of the estimate in the OCS and NSP projects. This lead to re-estimation, and improved the effort estimates for those particular functionalities.

4.5   Impact on Project Success

Cost estimation is an inseparable part of any software project [41], thus the cause of an overrun may reside in SCE, PM or other areas [6,35,38]. Not even the best project management can control a project if it has to meet unrealistic goals, while chaotic project control will usually overshoot set limits, making cost estimation meaningless. In this study our aim was to find evidence from the real-life experiences of how management's actions impact SCE, which further influences project success. Of the studied projects, two, OCS and NSP, delivered on time, scope and budget, and one project, DT, suffered from significant cost and schedule overruns.

In the two successful projects, top management's participation in SCE has been minimal, and we found very little evidence of their actions' impact on persons or artefacts during the estimation. On the other hand, top management seemed to have understood well that a realistic and unbiased estimate is critical for the success of a project and organisation. We found plenty of evidence of this understanding in both projects, although this understanding did not manifest into any concrete actions. For example, the software developer in the OCS project told that top management did not try to negotiate the estimate in any direction, customer agreements and offers are depending on the estimates. The requirements engineer in the NSP project said that top management was seeking realistic estimates—nobody wants to betray themselves, and everybody understands that without realistic estimates things will fail.

Top management's efforts for participating in SCE were equally low in the studied runaway project. But where the senior managers refrained themselves from any interference in SCE in the two successful projects, top management seemed to have influenced the estimation results by emphasising the importance of the targeted release date, and that the scope was small or minimum viable. The project manager reported having made the estimates smaller under this pressure. Additionally, implicitly interpreting estimates as commitments influenced the project manager's willingness to give estimates, and he reported having given upper bound estimates after noticing this. Although the reasons for the experienced project overruns may have been many, one of the reasons seem to have been top management induced pressure to make the estimate conform to the target delivery date. The Senior Business Manager of Small Global also attributes the overrun both to SCE and project execution.

5   Discussion

5.1   Implications for Practice

Our study clearly shows that a project can conclude successfully with no, or with very little, direct top management participation in software cost estimation. On the other hand, this study presents evidence that top management's incautious interference may lead to undesired outcomes, and influence the project success negatively. The most important distinctive factor between a positive and negative top management participation seems to be to not create bias. Not creating bias manifests through understanding the negative impact of poor estimates on project and organisation success, and therefore avoiding influencing the estimation to any direction.

Previous studies have found plenty of evidence about the negative effects emerging from influencing estimation. Magazinovic and Pernstål [33] have found that management goals affect the results of estimation. Furthermore, Magazinius et al. [30] found that personal agenda, management pressure and attempt to avoid re-estimation may affect an estimate. The previous studies also show that cognitive bias may affect estimators: e.g. high or low expectations influence even experienced estimators [4], first impression may dictate a significant part of the estimation result [19], and even the wording may have a significant impact on the estimate [21]. The estimators may not even notice the influence of the expectations, or consider it to be very low [23]. The findings from the studied runaway project show, in accordance with the above mentioned studies, that it is indeed easy for top management to influence the estimation and project success in a negative way. Thus, in the light of our findings and previous studies, it seems advisable for top management to stay outside of estimation to minimise any biasing effect they may induce.

The most tangible top management participation practice in SCE was 'TM studies and approves the estimate'. Although the general recommendation seems to be staying outside of the estimation, we cannot reject the potential importance of this support practice. Studying the estimate may be a necessary action to ensure that the estimate is prepared professionally and with due care. Some other studies support the potential importance of studying the estimate: e.g. Rahikkala et al. [45] report that the extent of use for 'Top management ensures that the estimate relies on documented facts rather than guessing and intuition' correlates positively with project success, and Lederer and Prasad [28] recommend that computing management should study and approve the estimate.

The remaining three top management support practices that were present during the estimation, 'TM ensures the involvement of the project manager during the estimation stage', 'Top management ensures adequate resources for estimation' and 'Top management ensures ongoing estimation skills training programmes', are indirect of nature, and were not directly related to any of the studied projects. Additionally, none of these practices could be tracked back to any specific top management actions, implying that these practices were among the presumably many results of top management actions to create an overall framework for software development. Thus, because of the lack of direct top management participation, these practices cannot be considered as top management support practices for SCE, and do not seem to justify for top management's attention during SCE.

Finally, this study shows that top management invests very little time in SCE. In light of the previous findings this was expected, and even recommended, because the successful conclusion of a project did not need significant participation from top management. As is natural considering the low extent of top management participation, the footprint of their actions is also low. The results of top management actions tend to have a negative impact on project success, which was the case in the studied runaway project. The only exception for this was studying the estimate, which triggered re-estimation of certain items in the two successful projects, resulting in more accurate estimates.

5.2   Implications for Theory

The current SCE literature sparsely contains studies addressing management aspects of software cost estimation [22], and, to our best knowledge, this is among the first studies to report on experiences related to top management participation practices in SCE. This paper contributes to the body of knowledge by showing that no, or very little, direct actions are required from senior management for a successful project delivery. On the contrary, the results indicate that top management must understand SCE's delicate nature prone to bias, and stay outside of the estimation to avoid any negative effects they may induce. This study also shows, from the perspective of top management that many known negative effects from biasing the estimation can also be caused by firms' top management.

Furthermore, our results show that the time top management invests in SCE is low, as well as the footprint that their actions leave on SCE related artefacts and actors. Considering the previous, the responsibility of improving SCE seems to move back towards project management and technical experts. However, as the literature has shown, methodologies are not a silver bullet, and a holistic view considering techniques, people and procedures is needed for producing more useful estimates.

5.3   Validity, Limitations and Further Research

The qualitative case study methodology involves the researchers themselves as the instrument of the research, which poses a risk that the results are biased by the researchers' subjective opinions. As countermeasures to the validity threats, we have employed six strategies outlined by Robson [46]: prolonged involvement, triangulation, peer debriefing, member checking, negative case analysis and audit trail. Additionally, we have tried to maximise the richness of the data set by selecting different case companies and projects, improving the transferability of the results. However, as this study is explorative of nature and has not been widely examined prior to this study, generalisation of the results must be done with caution.

Overall, this study provides evidence that top management participation in SCE is low and that their participation is not needed for successful estimation. Although we believe that the results of this study can be transferred to similar settings, the situation can still vary from context to context. For example, we may have overlooked the role of some company properties, like size or maturity. Therefore, further studies in different project and company contexts are needed to see if the same phenomena are repeated, or new phenomena discovered. Quantitative studies would also provide certainty in how commonly the reported phenomena are repeated in organisations. The importance of top management studying and approving the estimate was also left unanswered in this study.

6   Conclusions

This study examined top management support for SCE by using a case study approach and interviewing 15 experts involved in three software projects in three organisations. Top management support practices for SCE were studied by employing a list of 16 predefined practices. The results show that 8 from the 16 studied practices were not present in any of the projects, and that 'Top management studies and approves the estimate' was the only tangible practice present (RQ1). This study also found evidence that the time and effort top management invested in SCE was low (RQ2), and the items or persons affected by their actions were only a few (RQ3). However, the results show further that some of the top management actions induced undesired bias on estimation, and affected project success negatively (RQ4).

The main implications from the results for managers, software experts, project managers and academia are the following:

1. No, or very little, direct top management participation in software cost estimation is required for the successful conclusion of a project.
2. 'Top management studies and approves the estimate' was the only concrete top management participation practice.
3. Top management actions may induce undesired bias on estimation, and affect project success negatively.
4. Senior managers must recognize the importance of seeking realism in estimation, and avoid inducing accidental bias in cost estimation.

Finally, the aforementioned also serve as a good starting point for further research.

Acknowledgment. The authors gratefully acknowledge Tekes – the Finnish Funding Agency for Innovation, DIMECC Oy and Need for Speed research program for their support.

References

1. CMMI for development, V1.3. Technical report CMU/SEI-2010-TR-0336, Carnegie Mellon (2010)
2. Adams, S.: ITIL V3 Foundation Handbook, vol. 1. The Stationery Office, Norwich (2009)
3. Ahonen, J.J., Savolainen, P., Merikoski, H., Nevalainen, J.: Reported project management effort, project size, and contract type. J. Syst. Softw. **109**, 205–213 (2015)
4. Aranda, J., Easterbrook, S.: Anchoring and adjustment in software estimation. In: Proceedings of the 10th European Software Engineering Conference, pp. 346–355. ACM (2005)
5. Briand, L.C., Wieczorek, I.: Resource Estimation in Software Engineering. Encyclopedia of Software Engineering. Wiley, New York (2002)
6. Cerpa, N., Verner, J.M.: Why did your project fail? Commun. ACM **52**(12), 130–134 (2009)

7. Cleland, D.I.: The strategic context of projects. In: Project portfolio management - selecting and prioritizing projects for competitive advantage. CBP, PA, USA (1999)
8. Creswell, J.W.: Research Design: Qualitative and Quantitative and Mixed Methods Approaches. SAGE Publications Inc., Thousand Oaks (2003)
9. Dwivedi, Y.K., Wastell, D., Laumer, S., Henriksen, H.Z., Myers, M.D., Bunker, D., Elbanna, A., Ravishankar, M., Srivastava, S.C.: Research on information systems failures and successes: status update and future directions. Inf. Syst. Front. **17**(1), 143–157 (2015)
10. Fortune, J., White, D.: Framing of project critical success factors by a systems model. Int. J. Proj. Manag. **24**(1), 53–65 (2006)
11. Galorath, D.: Software project failure costs billions. In: Better Estimation & Planning Can Help (2012). http://www.galorath.com/wp/software-project-failure-costs-billions-betterestimationplanning-can-help.php
12. Gartner, I.: Gartner says global it spending to reach $3.5 trillion in 2017 (2016). http://www.gartner.com/newsroom/id/3482917
13. Grimm, K.: Software technology in an automotive company: major challenges. In: Proceedings of the 25th international conference on Software Engineering, pp. 498–503. IEEE (2003)
14. Halkjelsvik, T., Jørgensen, M.: From origami to software development: a review of studies on judgment-based predictions of performance time. Psychol. Bull. **138**(2), 238 (2012)
15. Hihn, J., Habib-agahi, H.: Cost estimation of software intensive projects: a survey of current practices. In: Proceedings of the 13th ICSE, pp. 276–287. IEEE Computer (1991)
16. Hughes, D.L., Dwivedi, Y.K., Simintiras, A.C., Rana, N.P.: Success and Failure of IS/IT Projects: A State of the Art Analysis and Future Directions. Springer, Heidelberg (2015). doi:10.1007/978-3-319-23000-9
17. PMI: a guide to the project management body of knowledge. PMBOK® Guide Series, Project Management Institute (2013)
18. Jørgensen, M., Grimstad, S.: The impact of irrelevant and misleading information on software development effort estimates: a randomized controlled field experiment. IEEE Trans. Softw. Eng. **37**(5), 695–707 (2011)
19. Jørgensen, M., Løhre, E.: First impressions in software development effort estimation: easy to create and difficult to neutralize. In: Proceedings of EASE 2012, pp. 216–222 (2012)
20. Jørgensen, M.: Communication of software cost estimates. In: Proceedings of EASE 2014, pp. 28:1–25:5. ACM (2014)
21. Jørgensen, M., Grimstad, S.: Avoiding irrelevant and misleading information when estimating development effort. IEEE Softw. **25**(3), 78–83 (2008)
22. Jørgensen, M., Shepperd, M.: A systematic review of software development cost estimation studies. IEEE Trans. Softw. Eng. **33**(1), 33–53 (2007)
23. Jørgensen, M., Sjøberg, D.I.: The impact of customer expectation on software development effort estimates. Int. J. Proj. Manag. **22**(4), 317–325 (2004)
24. Keil, M., Rai, A., Mann, J.E.C., Zhang, G.P.: Why software projects escalate: the importance of project management constructs. IEEE Trans. Eng. Manag. **50**(3), 251–261 (2003)
25. Kolltveit, B.J., Karlsen, J.T., Grønhaug, K.: Perspectives on project management. Int. J. Proj. Manag. **25**(1), 3–9 (2007)
26. Kwak, Y., Anbari, F.: Analyzing project management research: perspectives from top management journals. Int. J. Proj. Manag. **27**(5), 435–446 (2009)

27. Lederer, A.L., Prasad, J.: Causes of inaccurate software development cost estimates. J. Syst. Softw. **31**(2), 125–134 (1995)
28. Lederer, A.L., Prasad, J.: Software management and cost estimating error. J. Syst. Softw. **50**(1), 33–42 (2000)
29. Luna-Reyes, L., Zhang, J., Gil-García, J., Cresswell, A.: Software developments development as emergent socio-technical change: a practice approach. Eur. J. Softw. Dev. **14**(1), 93–105 (2005)
30. Magazinius, A., Börjesson, S., Feldt, R.: Investigating intentional distortions in software cost estimation – an exploratory study. J. Syst. Softw. **85**(8), 1770–1781 (2012)
31. Magazinius, A., Feldt, R.: Exploring the human and organizational aspects of software cost estimation. In: Proceedings of the 2010 ICSE Workshop on Cooperative and Human Aspects of Software Engineering, pp. 92–95. ACM (2010)
32. Magazinius, A., Feldt, R.: Confirming distortional behaviors in software cost estimation practice. In: 2011 37th EUROMICRO Conference on Software Engineering and Advanced Applications (SEAA), pp. 411–418. IEEE (2011)
33. Magazinovic, A., Pernstål, J.: Any other cost estimation inhibitors?. In: Proceedings of the 2nd ACM-IEEE International Symposium on Empirical Software Engineering and Measurement, pp. 233–242. ACM (2008)
34. McConnell, S.: Software Estimation: Demystifying the Black Art. Microsoft Press, Redmond (2006)
35. McLeod, L., MacDonell, S.G.: Factors that affect software systems development project outcomes: a survey of research. ACM Comput. Surv. **43**(4), 24 (2011)
36. McManus, J., Wood-Harper, T.: A Study in Project Failure. BCS (2008). www.bcs.org/content/ConWebDoc/19584
37. Nanus, B., Farr, L.: Some cost contributors to large-scale programs. In: Proceedings of the Spring Joint Computer Conference 1964, AFIPS 1964, pp. 239–248. ACM, New York (1964)
38. Nasir, M.H.N., Sahibuddin, S.: Critical success factors for software projects: a comparative study. Sci. Res. Essays **6**(10), 2174–2186 (2011)
39. Patton, M.: Qualitative Research and Evaluation Method. SAGE Publications, Thousand Oaks (2001)
40. Pitterman, B.: Telcordia technologies: the journey to high maturity. IEEE Softw. **17**(4), 89–96 (2000)
41. PMI: A Guide to the Project Management Body of Knowledge (PMBOK), 5th edn. Project Management Institute, Newtown Square (2012)
42. Putnam, L., Myers, W.: Five Core Metrics: The Intelligence Behind Successful Software Management. Dorset House Publishing, New York (2003)
43. PwC: Companies shifting more R&D spending away from physical products to software and services: 2016 global innovation 1000 study (2016). http://www.pwc.com/us/en/press-releases/2016/pwc-2016-global-innovation-1000-study-press-release.html
44. Rahikkala, J., Hyrynsalmi, S., Leppänen, V.: Accounting testing in software cost estimation: a case study of the current practice and impacts. In: Proceedings of 14th Symposium on Programming Languages and Software Tools, Tampere, Finland, pp. 64–75 (2015)
45. Rahikkala, J., Leppänen, V., Ruohonen, J., Holvitie, J.: Top management support in software cost estimation: a study of attitudes and practice in Finland. Int. J. Manag. Proj. Bus. **8**(3), 513–532 (2015)
46. Robson, C.: Real World Research: A Resource for Social Scientists and Practitioner-Researchers, 2nd edn. Blackwell Publishing, Oxford (2002)

47. Runeson, P., Höst, M.: Guidelines for conducting and reporting case study research in software engineering. Empirical Softw. Eng. **14**, 131–164 (2009)

48. Sehra, S.K., Brar, Y.S., Kaur, N., Sehra, S.S.: Research patterns and trends in software effort estimation. In: Information and Software Technology. Elsevier, Amsterdam (2017)

49. Turner, R.: The Handbook of Project Based Management, 2nd edn. McGraw-Hill, New York (1999)

50. White, D., Fortune, J.: Current practice in project management-an empirical study. Int. J. Proj. Manag. **20**(1), 1–11 (2002)

51. Yin, R.K.: Case Study Research: Design and Methods, 3rd edn. SAGE Publications Inc., Thousands Oaks (2003)

52. Zwikael, O.: Top management involvement in project management: a cross country study of the software industry. Int. J. Manag. Proj. Bus. **1**(4), 498–511 (2008)

53. Zwikael, O.: Top management involvement in project management: exclusive support practices for different project scenarios. Int. J. Manag. Proj. Bus. **1**(3), 387–403 (2008)

Software Engineering Processes
and Frameworks

The Choice of Code Review Process: A Survey on the State of the Practice

Tobias Baum[(✉)] , Hendrik Leßmann, and Kurt Schneider

FG Software Engineering, Leibniz Universität Hannover, Hannover, Germany
{tobias.baum,hendrik.lessmann,kurt.schneider}@inf.uni-hannover.de

Abstract. Code review has been known to be an effective quality assurance technique for decades. In the last years, industrial code review practices were observed to converge towards "change-based/modern code review", but with a lot of variation in the details of the processes. Recent research also proposed hypotheses on factors that influence the choice of process. However, all current research in this area is based on small and largely non-random samples of cases. Therefore, we set out to assess the current state of the practice and to test some of these hypotheses with a survey among commercial software development teams. We received responses from 240 teams. They support many of the stated hypotheses, e.g., that change-based code review is the dominating style of code review in the industry, and that teams doing change-based code review have a lower risk that review use fades away. However, other hypotheses could not be confirmed, mainly that the balance of effects a team tries to reach with code reviews acts as a mediator in determining the details of the review process. Apart from these findings, we contribute the survey data set as a foundation for future research.

Keywords: Code reviews · Code inspections and walkthroughs · Change-based code review · Modern code review · Empirical software engineering

1 Introduction

Code review is a well-established method of software quality assurance. Several researchers noted that, in recent years, change-based review[1] has become the dominant style of code review in practice [8,24]. The main characteristic of change-based review is the use of code changes performed in a unit of work, e.g., a user story, to determine the scope of the review. This is often combined with the replacement of management intervention through conventions or rules for many decisions [8], making a review planning phase [22] largely obsolete.

However, recent quantitative information on the use of different review practices in the industry is largely missing. Furthermore, it is important for

---

[1] Also called "modern code review", "differential code review" or "patch review" in other publications.

© Springer International Publishing AG 2017
M. Felderer et al. (Eds.): PROFES 2017, LNCS 10611, pp. 111–127, 2017.
https://doi.org/10.1007/978-3-319-69926-4_9

researchers trying to improve development processes to know what mechanisms influence process choices in practice. Although previous research has put forward hypotheses on the benefits of change-based code review and reasons for the choice of a review process, these have not yet been verified on a larger sample. Consequently, the purpose of this article is to test hypotheses on industrial code review use and the use of change-based code review in particular and to provide further empirical data on current review practices.

Specifically, we selected three research questions based on hypotheses put forward in our and others' earlier research, all relating to how review processes are shaped in the industry and why they are shaped that way:

RQ1 How prevalent is change-based review in the industry? (based on [8,24])

RQ2 Does the chance that code review remains in use increase if code review is embedded into the process (and its supporting tools) so that it does not require a conscious decision to do a review? (based on [9])

RQ3 Are the intended and acceptable levels of review effects a mediator in determining the code review process? (based on [9])

To answer these questions, we conducted an online survey among commercial software development teams. We will further concretize the questions and derive testable sub-hypotheses in Sects. 4.1, 4.2 and 4.3. In addition to answering the research questions, we give some descriptive statistics from the survey and we note some findings on review process characteristics and the use of reading techniques in Sects. 4.4 and 4.5. A secondary contribution of the study is the questionnaire instrument used to assess a team's review process, which we publish along with the full survey data for reuse in future research [7].

2   Related Work

As described in the previous section, the hypotheses we test in the current article stem from earlier research, mainly the summary of converging code review practices by Rigby and Bird [24] and the Grounded Theory study on code review use by parts of the current article's authors and others (Baum et al. [8,9]).

The most recent academic survey on the state of review practices we are aware of was published by Ciolkowski, Laitenberger, and Biffl in 2003 [13], with partial results also published in a technical report [21]. This survey targeted not only code review, but also reviews in other lifecycle phases. Its authors found a share of 28% of the 226 respondents using code reviews. We will discuss some similarities and differences between their and our survey in Sect. 6.

Bacchelli and Bird [2] surveyed expectations regarding code review at Microsoft and found a set of intended effects similar to the ones we are using. A recent survey on software testing practices by Winter et al. [30] briefly touches upon reviews and notes that 52% of the respondents often or always perform reviews for source code.

Looking beyond the academic literature, there are some more recent surveys that contain information on code review practices. A whitepaper written in 2010 by Forrester Consulting [15] for Klocwork, a company selling a code review tool, notes that 25% of the 159 survey respondents use a review process that we would describe as "regular, change-based code review" [8].

A survey performed in 2015 by Smartbear [26], another company selling code review software, contains information on code review practices and perceptions on code quality from about 600 respondents. Like the Forrester study, it contains very little information on the sampling method and possible biases. It states that 63% of their respondents are doing tool-based code review.

Compared to the small number of surveys, there is a lot more qualitative and case study research on code review practices and we can just name a few here. Baker [3] gave an early description of a change-based code review process in the industry and Bernhart et al. [11] describe its use (under the term "continuous differential code review") in airport operations software. Other small-scale studies of code review and inspection practices in the industry have been performed by Harjumaa et al. [17] and by Kollanus and Koskinen [19].

A survey by Bosu and Carver studied the impact of code review on peer impression in open source projects [12]. Peer review practices in open source software development have been studied intensively in the last decade, with further contributions for example by Asundi and Jayant [1], Rigby and Storey [25], Wang et al. [29], Thongtanunam et al. [28] and Baysal et al. [10].

3   Methodology

Our goal was to reach out to a large number of commercial software development teams. We used (online) survey research as our main vehicle. In the following, we describe details of the planning, execution, and analysis of the survey.

3.1   Participant Selection

Our research questions deal with the code review practices and context of commercial software development teams. Consequently, our target population consists of all commercial software development teams.

As there is no repository of all software development teams, a controlled random sampling of participants was not possible. Instead, we relied on a number of communication channels to reach possible participants: We directly contacted 32 people belonging to the target population from our personal networks. We further asked 23 people outside the target population from our networks to advertise the survey. We posted the survey invitation to several online communities, on Twitter, Xing, and Facebook; and also advertised the survey at a German software engineering conference. Finally, we posted the invitation on some mailing lists. Probably the most important single channel was a post on the mailing list of the German software craftsmanship communities ("Softwerkskammer"), reaching out to roughly 1400 people. When selecting channels, we took care to avoid introducing bias on the type of review process used. Specifically, we decided against sampling GitHub users, and we turned down an offer to spread our invitation to a mailing list of former participants of a series of review courses. In Sect. 5, we discuss the remaining risk of sampling bias.

Since we were not able to exactly control who was answering the survey, we included a filter question at the start of the survey and excluded participants not working in a commercial software development team. Our intended granularity of sampling was teams. As our survey was conducted anonymously, we could not tell whether two respondents come from the same or different teams. We told survey participants that we only want one response per team and asked them to only forward the invitation to people in other teams or companies. When inviting participants directly, we took care to only invite one person per company. Nevertheless, there is a risk that the sample includes several respondents from the same team.

3.2 Questionnaire Creation and Pilot Tests

Most parts of the survey were created based on existing qualitative empirical research, mainly the classification scheme for change-based code review processes by Baum et al. [8] and the collection of contextual factors influencing review process choices by the same authors [9].

The process of survey creation followed established guidelines [18,27]. To ease answering and analyzing the survey, we mainly used multiple choice and numerical questions. Many questions contained an "Other" option to allow participants to specify missing options in free-text. The instrument was self-contained and it included all relevant information, for example by giving a definition of code review (from [8]) when asking for the use of code review in the team.

Based on our sampling strategy, we expected the main share of participants to come from Germany and a mix of other countries for the remaining share. Therefore, we decided to create a German as well as an English version of the survey, following the rationale that it is better to have a consistent, pre-tested translation instead of demanding translation effort from each participant.

Following guidelines for survey research [27], we tried to reuse questions from existing surveys, but only a limited number of questions from the first version of the HELENA survey [20] could be reused after some adjustments.

To ensure that the survey questions were comprehensible and valid with respect to the study constructs, we iteratively tested and refined the questionnaire. Initial testing of the research and survey questions was performed among the authors of this article. We used a checklist distilled from existing guidelines to check each survey question. This was followed by 6 rounds of pre-tests, 4 of these with members of the target population and 2 with members of our lab. During each pre-test, a participant completed the survey, followed by a discussion about possible problems and misunderstandings. For two of these pre-tests, we had detailed knowledge about the process used by the team and could, therefore, compare answers to our expectations. The final survey also allowed the participants to enter feedback on the survey, which we checked for possible problems.

The review process classification scheme [8] we used as a foundation consists of 20 process facets, and we identified 16 potentially relevant contextual factors in our previous research [9]. It became evident early during questionnaire creation that even if we restricted the survey to these two groups of questions, it would become too long for the intended audience. Therefore, we limited the questionnaire to a subset of the contextual factors and split the remaining questions into a main part and an optional extension part. Answering the main part took around 15 min and answering the extension part additional 8 min in our pre-tests. The exact number of questions differed depending on the answers of a respondent, e.g., it was shorter for teams that have never used code reviews.

3.3 Data Collection and Instrument

We started data collection on February 22nd, 2017, and closed the survey on March 20th, 2017. Invitations were sent out gradually during the first weeks. The questionnaire was implemented using LimeSurvey, hosted by our university.

The survey questions can be roughly classified into four groups: (1) Demographics or filter questions (e.g., on the country, role of the participant or the use of reviews), (2) questions on the context of the review process (e.g., product, development process, team characteristics,...) (3) questions on the used review process (based on [8]) and (4) ranking questions to assess the relative importance of intended and unintended review effects. The full instrument can be found in our online material [7]. Most parts of the survey were confirmatory or descriptive, but it also contained some exploratory parts, mainly on the non-use of reviews. In the current article, we focus on the former.

We offered respondents the chance to leave an email address if they were interested in the results of the survey. All participants that did this have been informed about preliminary results some weeks after the survey closed.

3.4 Data Analysis

Our data analysis constitutes a mix of descriptive and inferential statistics. We will describe the detailed analyses for the research questions in the respective subsections of Sect. 4.

Multiple-choice questions that contained an "other" option with free-text answers were coded for analysis. The free-text answers were either converted to new categories or classified as belonging to one of the existing categories.

All but the filter questions were optional, to avoid forcing participants to answer. We handled the resulting missing data by "pairwise deletion" (also called "available case analysis"), i.e., we excluded participants only from those analyses where data was missing for at least one of the needed questions. Consequently, the total number of respondents taken into account differs between analyses.

Most statistical tests performed during analysis checked for a dependence between two dichotomous variables. Unless otherwise noted, these 2×2 contingency tables were checked using Fisher's exact test and statistical significance was tested at the 5% level. We perform Bonferroni correction when there are multiple tests for a research question (i.e., for *RQ3*), but not between research questions. When we give confidence intervals for proportions, they will be 95% confidence intervals calculated using the Clopper-Pearson method. All percentages will be presented rounded to the nearest integer.

The raw data of the survey, descriptive statistics for all questions, and the source code used for data analysis is available in the study's online material [7].

4   Results

In total, 240 respondents from the target population answered the survey.[2] 130 participants went on to answer the extension part after finishing the main part. Due to our sampling method, we are not able to give a response rate, but we will describe some characteristics of the sample in the following.

The respondents are working in 19 different countries. The majority of respondents, 170 (76%), is from Germany. 33 respondents (15%) work in other European countries, 11 (5%) in Asia (including the Middle East) and 11 (5%) in Northern America.[3] We distributed the survey invitation through various channels and asked the respondents how they heard about the survey. 19 respondents (10%) were invited directly by one of the researchers, 30 (16%) were indirectly invited by other people, 104 (55%) heard about the survey on a mailing list, 24 (13%) in an online forum and 13 (7%) named some other channel. When asked about their role, 154 respondents (67%) said they mainly work as a developer, 50 (22%) work as architects, 14 (6%) as managers and 11 (5%) gave other roles.

The target population of this survey is teams in commercial software development. Quite unsurprisingly, the large majority (94%, 215 teams) of the responding teams works on closed source software. The remaining share (14 teams) said their team mainly works on an open source project. The teams work in companies of vastly differing sizes, from less than 10 to more than 10,000 employees; Fig. 1 shows the detailed distribution of company sizes. 68% (148 of 217) of the participants work in collocated (as opposed to distributed) teams.

We asked teams whether they are currently using code reviews. Teams not using code reviews were subdivided further: Have they never used reviews before, and if so have they never thought about it or did they explicitly decide against review use? Or did they stop using reviews in the past, and if so was this an explicit decision or did the review use "fade away" (i.e., end without an explicit decision, just becoming less and less frequent over time)? Figure 2 shows the results: With a share of 78% (186 teams), the majority of teams is currently

---

[2] More precisely, 240 respondents answered at least the questions about being part of the target population and about their team's review use, which were the only obligatory questions in the survey.

[3] The remaining 15 did not answer this question. Unless otherwise noted, we only include respondents that answered the respective questions in our analyses; consequently, the total sum of respondents will differ between analyses.

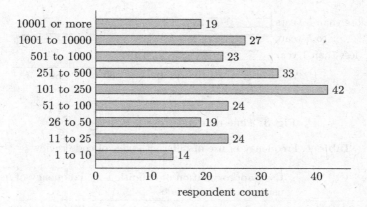

Fig. 1. Company sizes (number of employees)

using code reviews.[4] 38 teams (16%) have never used code reviews so far, 8 of them because there was an explicit decision against their use. In 16 teams (7%), the use of code reviews ended, but in only one of those teams this was an explicit decision. For teams that currently use code reviews, we asked how much time ago they started using them. The results are shown in Fig. 3.

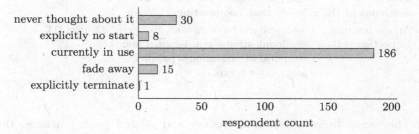

Fig. 2. Use of reviews

4.1 The Dominance of Change-Based Code Review (RQ1)

A number of recent articles postulate that code review based on code changes/patches is dominating in industrial as well as open-source practice [8,24]. In this section, we provide quantitative empirical support for this claim (RQ1) and study the prevalence of several more specific review styles.

To answer RQ1, we asked our participants how the review scope is determined: Based on changes, based on architectural properties of the software (whole module/package/class) or in some other way (with free text for further details). With a share of 90% (146/163; confidence interval 84–94%) of the teams doing code reviews, a change-based review scope is indeed dominating.

---

[4] This number is likely biased, see Sect. 5.

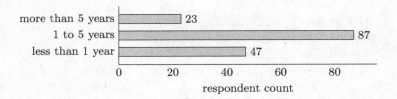

Fig. 3. Time that code review is in use

Table 1. Frequency of use of different styles of code review

Style	Used approximation of definition using survey constructs	Frequency of use
Review based on code-changes	scope = changes	90% (146/163)
Regular, change-based code review [8]	scope = changes and trigger = rules	60% (96/160)
Contemporary code review [24]	scope = changes and publicness = pre-commit and unit-of-work ≤ user-story	46% (61/133)
Pull-based software development [16]	scope = changes and trigger = rules and publicness = pre-commit and interaction = no-meeting	22% (29/134)
Approximating Inspection [14]	interaction = meeting and communication = oral + stored and temporal-arrangement = parallel and trigger = explicit	2% (3/141)

In the recent literature on code review and related work practices, there are slightly differing definitions and descriptions of sub-styles of change-based code review. Table 1 shows the frequency of use for "modern/contemporary code review" [24], "regular, change-based review" [8] and "pull-based software development" [16]. As not all of these sub-styles are concisely defined in the respective publications, the table also shows how the definitions/descriptions were approximated in terms of constructs used in the survey. We will not discuss every detail of the table, but want to note that most of the teams that do not fall under Rigby and Bird's description of contemporary code review do so because they do not use pre-commit reviews (pre-commit: 46%, 61 teams; post-commit: 54%, 72 teams). There is only one respondent whose team uses a review scope that is larger than a user story/requirement.

We did not focus on Fagan-style Inspection [14] in our survey and therefore cannot completely tell whether a team uses a fully-fledged Inspection process to review code. To estimate an upper bound on the number of teams doing Inspection, we combined a number of necessary conditions that we would expect to hold for those teams (see Table 1). Only 2% (3/141; confidence interval 0–6%) of the teams have a process that approximates Inspection in that way.

Because much existing research on modern/change-based code review is based on open-source development or agile teams, we also checked whether there is a difference in the use of change-based review between open-source and closed-source products and between agile and classic development processes. We did not find a statistically significant difference in either case.

4.2   Change-Based Code Review and the Fading of Review Use (RQ2)

This section mainly deals with Baum et al.'s hypothesis *"Code review is most likely to remain in use if it is embedded into the process (and its supporting tools) so that it does not require a conscious decision to do a review."* [9]. More specifically, we tested a subset of this hypothesis:

H2 The risk that code review use fades away depends on the mechanism that is used to determine that a review shall take place: This risk is lower when rules or conventions are used instead of ad-hoc decisions.

To test this hypothesis, we compare two sub-samples: Teams currently doing code reviews, and teams where review use faded away. We also asked how it was decided whether a review should take place: By fixed rules or conventions, or ad-hoc on a case-by-case basis. For the ad-hoc triggers, we further distinguished triggering by the reviewer, the author or a manager. There was the possibility for respondents to select "other" and enter a free-text description.

Of 12 teams where review use faded away, 3 used rules or conventions and the remaining 9 used ad-hoc decisions. For the 162 teams currently doing reviews, the relation was 103 with rules/conventions compared to 59 without. Put differently, the risk to be in the "fade away" subsample increases from 2.8% with rule triggers to 13.2% with ad-hoc triggers, a risk ratio of 4.7. The exact Fisher test of the corresponding 2×2 contingency table results in a p-value of 0.01237, therefore the difference is statistically significant at the 5% level. Table 2 shows the detailed numbers for the different review triggers. An interesting side-note is that having managers trigger reviews seems to be especially prone to discontinuation.

Another possible explanation for the higher share of teams with ad-hoc triggers in the "fade away" subsample is a generation effect: Teams that introduced reviews more recently could use rule triggers more often. Therefore, we compared teams that have used reviews for less than a year with those that used them for two years or more. Of 45 teams with brief review use, 25 use rules. For teams with long review use, the share is 49 of 75. This higher share of rule-use for longer review use supports *H2* and opposes the stated generation effect.

Table 2. Review triggers vs. review continuation

Trigger	Reviews in use	Review use faded away
Manager	7	3 (30%)
Reviewer	14	2 (13%)
Author	38	4 (10%)
Rules/conventions	103	3 (3%)

4.3 Rankings of Review Effects as a Mediator in Determining the Review Process (RQ3)

In this section, we deal with another of Baum et al.'s [9] hypotheses: *"The intended and acceptable levels of review effects are a mediator in determining the code review process."* (H3) More specifically, Baum et al. state that "Many process variants are expected to promote certain effects, and often also to impair others. . . . Consequently, the chosen review process is heavily influenced by the combination of intended effects. Some effects are seen as more important than others, while others are seen as secondary or not pursued at all. This is used to perform trade-offs while designing the review process." [9] Intended review effects are for example "better code quality", "finding defects" and "learning of the reviewer". Unintended effects are "[increased] staff effort", "increased cycle time" and "offending the author/social problems". Following *H3*, we would expect to find that the relative ranking of review effects influences the chosen variant for some of the review process facets, that the team's context influences the relative ranking of review effects, and that this indirect effect is in most cases stronger than the direct influence of context on review process facets.

Based on the addendum to Baum et al.'s article [6], we systematically checked each of the listed combinations of review effect and process facet.[5] For intended review effects, none of the checked interactions were statistically significant, even at the 10% level and without Bonferroni correction. For the relative ranking of undesired effects, some of the predicted effects had p-values smaller than 0.05:

- When "increased staff effort" is most unintended this makes a "very small review scope" (i.e., more overhead due to a higher number of small reviews) less likely: Risk ratio = 2.2; p = 0.034. The detailed contingency table can be found in Table 3.
- When "increased staff effort" is most unintended this makes "pull or mixed reviewer to review assignment" more likely: Risk ratio = 1.6; p = 0.037. The detailed contingency table can be found in Table 4.
- When "increased cycle time" is most unintended this makes "review meetings" less likely: Risk ratio = 2.8; p = 0.006. The detailed contingency table can be found in Table 5.

---

[5] I.e. we did not check every possible combination, but only those where the prior research gave reason to expect an influence.

Table 3. Contingency table: staff effort most undesired vs. small review scope

	Small review scope	Medium to large review scope (≥Task)	Total
Increased staff effort most undesired	5	19	24
Something else most undesired	36	43	103
Total	41	62	103

Table 4. Contingency table: staff effort most undesired vs. review assignment

	Push assignment	Pull or mixed assignment	Total
Increased staff effort most undesired	12	20	32
Something else most undesired	52	34	86
Total	64	54	118

Table 5. Contingency table: increased cycle time most undesired vs. review meetings

	Meetings	No meetings	Total
Increased cycle time most undesired	6	40	46
Something else most undesired	27	46	73
Total	33	86	119

Those three interactions are also those with the highest risk ratio (i.e., effect size). Even though they have p-values smaller than 0.05, none of them is statistically significant after Bonferroni correction. A complete list of all tested interactions can be found in the study's online material [7].

Summing up, only 3 of 30 cases give some support for the expected relationship. Therefore, there is little evidence that the intended and acceptable levels of review effects influence the code review process, except in some narrow areas. Consequently, they cannot be mediators, and we cannot support hypothesis *H3*.

4.4 Further Convergence in Review Practices?

Apart from their description of a change-based review process that we referred to in Sect. 4.1, Rigby and Bird consolidated three further convergent review practices, cited in the following. In this section, we analyze to what degree these practices can also be observed in the survey's sample.

"Contemporary review usually involves two reviewers. However, the number of reviewers is not fixed and can vary to accommodate other factors, such as

the complexity of a change." [24]: Our results support the finding that the usual number of reviewers is low, indeed our numbers are even lower than Rigby and Bird's.[6] The average usual number of reviewers in our sample is 1.57, the median is 1 reviewer. With regard to the accommodation of other factors when determining the number of reviewers, 51% of the teams (47 of 92) named at least one rule that they use to adjust the number of reviewers in certain situations. The most commonly used rule is to decrease the number of reviewers or to skip code review completely when the code change was implemented using pair programming: Such a rule is used in 36% of the teams.

"Contemporary reviewers prefers [sic] discussion and fixing code over reporting defects." [24]: Fig. 4 shows how the surveyed teams usually interact during a review. Depending on how many of the teams discuss code during review meetings, between 55% and 81% of the teams have a review process that includes discussion of the code. Regarding fixing the code, 54% (84 of 157) of the respondents indicate that reviewers sometimes or often fix code during a review. This pragmatic attitude towards the classic boundaries of code review also shows up when 76% (69 of 91) of the respondents state that the reviewer executes the code for testing during review at least occasionally.

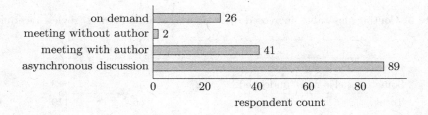

Fig. 4. Interaction during reviews

"Tool supported review provides the benefits of traceability, when compared to email based review, and can record implicit measures, when compared to traditional inspection. The rise in adoption of review tools provides an indicator of success." [24]: In our sample, 59% of the teams (96 of 163) use at least one specialized review tool. 33% (33 of 163) use only general software development tools, like ticket system and version control system, for review. 13 respondents indicated no tool use.[7] The ability of specialized review tools to record implicit measures might be one of their benefits, but it is seldom used in practice. Only 5% (4 of 88) of the teams systematically analyze review metrics.

---

[6] The numbers are not fully comparable: Rigby and Bird looked at the actual number of reviewers in a large sample of reviews, whereas we asked our participants for the usual number of reviewers in a review.

[7] A weakness in the used questionnaire is that there was no explicit "We do not use any tool" choice available. Therefore, the distinction between non-response and non-use of tools cannot be reliably made.

4.5   Some Notes on the Use of Reading Techniques

Research on Inspection has resulted in a number of different "reading techniques" to guide the reviewer during review [4]. We looked at the spread of some reading techniques in the survey, albeit not in much detail, and will describe the corresponding results in the following.

It is sometimes claimed that "checklist-based reading" is the prevalent reading technique in practice. Our results do not support this claim: Only 23% (22 of 94) of the respondents state that they use a checklist during reviews.

Another family of reading techniques uses different roles/perspectives to focus the reviewers (e.g., perspective-based reading [5]). 7% (6 of 90) of the respondents state that they explicitly assign distinct roles to the different reviewers. 72% (63 of 88) use neither checklists nor roles.

5   Limitations

This section discusses the addressed and unaddressed threats to validity.

The primary threat to internal validity in this study is sampling bias, given that we distributed the survey over various channels and could not control who answered. Consequently, our participants likely differ systematically from the population of all developers, and they do so not only in their geographical distribution: They are probably more interested in code reviews and/or in process improvement or software quality in general. People who introduced code reviews just recently are probably more interested in learning more about them, which could explain the high share of participants that introduced reviews less than a year ago. The tendency to have participants with a higher than average quality orientation was probably further amplified by using the software craftsmanship mailing list to advertise the survey. Due to this bias, the share of teams using code review that we observed in the survey should be regarded as an upper limit rather than as an estimate of the real proportion. Apart from this bias, we actively tried to avoid favoring certain types of code review processes in the sample.

A general problem of online surveys is that there is little control over the quality of responses. We included filter questions to check whether participants belong to the target population. We also screened free-text answers for obviously nonsensical responses. These checks, and the fact that there was no financial reward and therefore little incentive to participate without giving honest answers make us believe that this threat is under control. Another threat with long online surveys is survey fatigue. As 209 of 240 participants reached the end of the main part, there is no indication of major fatigue effects.

The survey was anonymous, and most of the questions did not touch upon sensitive topics. However, the results of some questions might be influenced by social desirability bias, e.g., by stating that the team is using reviews just because it is desirable to do. Again, this might have influenced the descriptive parts but we do not see a major influence on the confirmatory parts of the current article.

An important input for the testing of *H3* was the ranking of intended and unintended review effects. We used LimeSurvey's ranking widget for these questions, and we observed some usability problems with it that might have increased noise in the results or lowered the response rate.

To reduce the threat of participants misunderstanding a question, we spent approximately four months carefully designing the survey during which we performed several rounds of quality control and pre-testing. Furthermore, our questions were based on a qualitative study, which increases our confidence in their ecological validity. To further reduce threats to construct validity, we used randomization where appropriate, and we provided definitions for key terms.

Although the total sample contains 240 respondents, some of our conclusions might be affected by threats due to a small sample size. The test of *H3* demanded the comparison of many imbalanced and therefore small sub-samples. Consequently, the power of these statistical tests was largely low.

A weakness of our method of data collection, i.e., of cross-sectional observational studies, is that they cannot be used to distinguish between correlation and causation. Therefore we cannot reliably exclude other explanations for *H2*.

The coding of free-text answers might be affected by subjectivity. For most questions, the proportion of free-text "other" answers was low. Exceptions were generally easy to code, e.g., country or review tool. An unexpectedly high number of free-text answers was given for the review trigger question: We regard "a review has to be performed for every task/story" as a special kind of rule, but many participants selected "other" instead of "rule" in this case. Details on how the free-text answers were coded can be found in the study's online material [7].

6   Conclusion

To conclude, we relate our findings to other studies and outline future work.

Comparing our results to those of Ciolkowski et al. [13], the raw numbers indicate a large increase in the use of code reviews in the last 15 years. We already noted that the proportion observed in our survey is probably biased, but even when taking the much smaller number from Winter et al. [30] as a comparison, there was a significant increase. The systematic use of review metrics, on the other hand, seems to have decreased, as has the use of review meetings. We cannot reliably decide whether this is really due to a change in practices or due to differences between the studies.

By answering our first research question, we provided quantitative evidence that change-based review is indeed dominating in practice and that there is still a lot of variation in the details. Many researchers have begun to study and improve change-based code review, and our results should encourage them further.

By strengthening the evidence that using rules or conventions to trigger code reviews helps to keep code review use from fading away, we provide a partial explanation for the dominance observed in RQ1. As a more abstract consequence for future software engineering research, we believe this finding strengthens the case for software engineering techniques that not only work in isolation but are also able to "survive" in the environment of a software development team. The low number of teams using perspective-based reading or a similar technique for code review could be an example for such a mismatch: There is little use in perspectives when there is only one reviewer.

Due to the low statistical power and multiple threats, the analysis of RQ3 is problematic. Assuming that our non-finding is not caused by flaws in the data collection and analysis, we see two explanations: (1) There is an effect, but we checked the wrong sub-hypotheses, or (2) the intended effects determine a team's review process only to a small degree. The second explanation is in line with Ciolkowski, Laitenberger, and Biffl's conclusion that many companies use reviews unsystematically [13]. It would also mean that satisficing [23] and orientation along experiences from peers and processes used by review tools are even more important than noted by Baum et al. [9]. There remains a lot of research to be done, both to find out which process variants are best in a given situation, and to find ways to bring these results into practical use.

Finally, we hope that by making the questionnaire and the survey data available [7], independent researchers can profit and build upon our efforts.

Acknowledgments. The authors would like to thank all pre-testers and all participants of the survey for the time and effort they donated. We would further like to thank Philipp Diebold and Paul Clarke for providing questions from their surveys for reuse.

References

1. Asundi, J., Jayant, R.: Patch review processes in open source software development communities: a comparative case study. In: 40th Annual Hawaii International Conference on System Sciences, HICSS 2007, p. 166c. IEEE (2007)
2. Bacchelli, A., Bird, C.: Expectations, outcomes, and challenges of modern code review. In: Proceedings of the 2013 International Conference on Software Engineering, pp. 712–721. IEEE (2013)
3. Baker Jr., R.A.: Code reviews enhance software quality. In: Proceedings of the 19th International Conference on Software Engineering, pp. 570–571. ACM (1997)
4. Basili, V., Caldiera, G., Lanubile, F., Shull, F.: Studies on reading techniques. In: Proceedings of the Twenty-First Annual Software Engineering Workshop, vol. 96, p. 002 (1996)
5. Basili, V.R., Green, S., Laitenberger, O., Lanubile, F., Shull, F., Sørumgård, S., Zelkowitz, M.V.: The empirical investigation of perspective-based reading. Empirical Softw. Eng. 1(2), 133–164 (1996)
6. Baum, T.: Detailed table with review effects (team level) and their connections to contextual factors and process variants for "factors influencing code review processes in industry" (2016). http://dx.doi.org/10.6084/m9.figshare.5104111
7. Baum, T., Leßmann, H., Schneider, K.: Online material for survey on code review use. http://dx.doi.org/10.6084/m9.figshare.5104249
8. Baum, T., Liskin, O., Niklas, K., Schneider, K.: A faceted classification scheme for change-based industrial code review processes. In: 2016 IEEE International Conference on Software Quality, Reliability and Security (QRS). IEEE, Vienna (2016)

9. Baum, T., Liskin, O., Niklas, K., Schneider, K.: Factors influencing code review processes in industry. In: Proceedings of the ACM SIGSOFT 24th International Symposium on the Foundations of Software Engineering. ACM, Seattle (2016)

10. Baysal, O., Kononenko, O., Holmes, R., Godfrey, M.W.: Investigating technical and non-technical factors influencing modern code review. Empirical Softw. Eng. **21**, 932–959 (2016)

11. Bernhart, M., Strobl, S., Mauczka, A., Grechenig, T.: Applying continuous code reviews in airport operations software. In: 2012 12th International Conference on Quality Software (QSIC), pp. 214–219. IEEE (2012)

12. Bosu, A., Carver, J.C.: Impact of peer code review on peer impression formation: a survey. In: 2013 ACM/IEEE International Symposium on Empirical Software Engineering and Measurement, pp. 133–142. IEEE (2013)

13. Ciolkowski, M., Laitenberger, O., Biffl, S.: Software reviews: the state of the practice. IEEE Softw. **20**(6), 46–51 (2003)

14. Fagan, M.E.: Design and code inspections to reduce errors in program development. IBM Syst. J. **15**(3), 182–211 (1976)

15. Forrester Research Inc.: The value and importance of code reviews, March 2010. http://embedded-computing.com/white-papers/white-paper-value-importance-code-reviews/. Accessed 13 June 2017

16. Gousios, G., Pinzger, M., Deursen, A.V.: An exploratory study of the pull-based software development model. In: Proceedings of the 36th International Conference on Software Engineering, pp. 345–355. ACM, Hyderabad (2014)

17. Harjumaa, L., Tervonen, I., Huttunen, A.: Peer reviews in real life-motivators and demotivators. In: Fifth International Conference on Quality Software (QSIC 2005). IEEE (2005)

18. Jacob, R., Heinz, A., Décieux, J.P.: Umfrage: Einführung in die Methoden der Umfrageforschung. Walter de Gruyter (2013)

19. Kollanus, S., Koskinen, J.: Software inspections in practice: six case studies. In: Münch, J., Vierimaa, M. (eds.) PROFES 2006. LNCS, vol. 4034, pp. 377–382. Springer, Heidelberg (2006). doi:10.1007/11767718_31

20. Kuhrmann, M., Diebold, P., Münch, J., Tell, P., Garousi, V., Felderer, M., Trektere, K., Linssen, O., Hanser, E., Prause, C.R.: Hybrid software and system development in practice: waterfall, scrum, and beyond. In: ICSSP 2017 (2017)

21. Laitenberger, O., Vegas, S., Ciolkowski, M.: The state of the practice of review and review technologies in Germany. Tech. report 011.02, Virtual Softw. Eng. Competence Center (VISEK) (2002)

22. Laitenberger, O., DeBaud, J.M.: An encompassing life cycle centric survey of software inspection. J. Syst. Softw. **50**(1), 5–31 (2000)

23. March, J.G., Simon, H.A.: Organizations. Wiley, London (1958)

24. Rigby, P.C., Bird, C.: Convergent contemporary software peer review practices. In: Proceedings of the 2013 9th Joint Meeting on Foundations of Software Engineering, pp. 202–212. ACM, Saint Petersburg (2013)

25. Rigby, P.C., Storey, M.A.: Understanding broadcast based peer review on open source software projects. In: Proceedings of the 33rd International Conference on Software Engineering, pp. 541–550. ACM (2011)

26. SmartBear: The state of code quality 2016. https://smartbear.com/resources/ebooks/state-of-code-quality-2016/. Accessed 13 June 2017

27. Sudman, S., Bradburn, N.M.: Asking Questions: A Practical Guide to Questionnaire Design. Jossey-Bass Publishers, San Francisco (1982)

28. Thongtanunam, P., McIntosh, S., Hassan, A.E., Iida, H.: Investigating code review practices in defective files: an empirical study of the QT system. In: Proceedings of the 12th Working Conference on Mining Software Repositories, MSR 2015 (2015)
29. Wang, J., Shih, P.C., Wu, Y., Carroll, J.M.: Comparative case studies of open source software peer review practices. Inf. Softw. Technol. **67**, 1–12 (2015)
30. Winter, M., Vosseberg, K., Spillner, A.: Umfrage 2016 "Softwaretest in Praxis und Forschung". dpunkt.verlag (2016)

Unwasted DASE: Lean Architecture Evaluation

Antti-Pekka Tuovinen[1(✉)], Simo Mäkinen[1], Marko Leppänen[2,3],
Outi Sievi-Korte[2], Samuel Lahtinen[2], and Tomi Männistö[1]

[1] Department of Computer Science, University of Helsinki, Helsinki, Finland
antti-pekka.tuovinen@helsinki.fi
[2] Department of Pervasive Computing,
Tampere University of Technology, Tampere, Finland
[3] Ministry of Education and Culture, Helsinki, Finland

Abstract. A software architecture evaluation is a way to assess the quality of the technical design of a product. It is also a prime opportunity to discuss the business goals of the product and how the design bears on them. But architecture evaluation methods are seen as hard to learn and costly to use. We present DASE, a compact approach that combines carefully selected key parts of two existing architecture evaluation methods while making evaluation lean and fast. We have applied DASE in three industrial cases and the early results show that even a one-day evaluation workshop yields valuable results at a modest cost.

Keywords: Software architecture evaluation · Product development

1 Introduction

The purpose of *architecture evaluation* is to analyze how well a software system will satisfy its quality requirements, uncover the key architectural decisions, and identify risks. The effectiveness of architecture evaluation has been proven many times after the introduction of the first methods in the late 1990's [1–4].

An evaluation is an *expert review* that requires the key technical persons and other stakeholders to meet in person and contribute their knowledge. Usually, this entails a deep discussion about the mission of the product and about the possibilities created by technology. This strengthens common understanding of the goals but provides also a golden chance to share experiences, knowledge, and the rationale behind the design decisions [3] [2, p. 6]. These 'soft effects' may in practice be even more valuable than the hard technical results [5].

However, architecture evaluation is still not yet a common practice in the industry [5–7]. There is a learning curve, a general perception of high cost, and problems in quantifying results for decision making, which make companies reluctant to adopt them [1,3,8]. Industrial use is reported, e.g., in [1,3–5,7].

An architecture evaluation is typically a staged review process. Depending on the method, the different stages produce outputs that are not necessarily used later on. For example in some scenario-based methods, due to time pressure and

© Springer International Publishing AG 2017
M. Felderer et al. (Eds.): PROFES 2017, LNCS 10611, pp. 128–136, 2017.
https://doi.org/10.1007/978-3-319-69926-4_10

set priorities, half of the created and elaborated scenarios may not be used at all [1], which is considerable waste. Also, a perceived dependency on explicit architecture design may alienate agile developers. They fear that "big design up-front" incurs waste because if the design assumptions are incorrect or out-of-date, it leads to inability to cope with change and to expensive rework [9].

In this paper we present our architecture evaluation approach called DASE, short for decision and scenario based architecture evaluation. Our goal is to make architecture evaluation more attractive to practitioners: First, based on our own experiences, we have carefully selected from well-known scenario-based and decision-centric methods the elements that we know to work best. Second, we aim at minimizing the calendar time and the resources needed for an architecture evaluation by concentrating the main effort in a one-day workshop and by keeping the learning curve low. Third, we keep the evaluation focused on the most important things from both business and technology viewpoints.

In Sect. 2, we discuss existing architecture evaluation methods and our own experiences. Section 3 describes the DASE approach. We describe three industrial case studies of using DASE and the results, observations, and feedback in Sect. 4. Section 5 presents the conclusions and outlines future work.

2   Background

2.1   Architecture Evaluation Methods

The idea of scenario-based methods, like ATAM [10,11], is to evaluate an architecture through *scenarios* elicited from all *stakeholders* in workshops. Typically, a scenario focuses on one quality aspect from a quality tree (defined in the process) and specifies a situation and a stimulus that test the response of the system and its architecture. The scenarios are evaluated to determine the system's response and to identify risks. To be useful, scenarios need to be concrete, clear and prioritized. The results of properly executed assessments are valuable and usually well received [1,3]. Scenarios are a powerful tool for assessing the adequacy of the system under evaluation and also for making the technical people aware of the needs of the business and for making the business people aware of the technical opportunities and challenges [1,3].

Instead of scenarios, the Decision-Centric Architecture Review method DCAR [5] focuses on identifying *architectural design decisions*, their rationale, and their interrelationships. The decisions are ranked based on importance. In the evaluation part, the participants discuss the forces affecting the decisions and their consequences (pros and cons) and vote whether each decision is good or needs to be reconsidered. The importance of identifying and analyzing the key design decisions is also emphasized by others [7]. Because of their emphasis on design and its consequences, these kind of methods could be characterized as bottom-up or inside-out as opposed to scenario-based methods that emphasize requirements.

Other approaches include, e.g., the TARA method [7] that is a light-weight expert review where a single assessor does the evaluation (consulting others) according to a specific focus of interest. At the other end of the spectrum is the comprehensive RATE approach [1,2] that recognizes different types of assessments based on their purpose and employs several analysis and evaluation methods including ATAM, as needed.

On the down side, an architecture evaluation typically requires several meetings, couple of weeks of calendar time, and tens of person hours (sometimes hundreds) [1]. Understandably, organizations may be reluctant to make this investment [7]. Also, there is a certain learning curve [3,7]. For example, the construction of the quality tree and the formulation and prioritization of the quality attribute scenarios in ATAM can be challenging [1,3,12]. The results can sometimes be hard to quantify for decision makers [1].

2.2   Our Architecture Evaluation Experience

Tampere University of Technology has a lot of experience in architecture evaluation [3,8]. At TUT, the third author facilitated about ten evaluations carried out in the local industry, using either ATAM [11] or DCAR [5]. The first author has over ten years of experience in architecture work in mobile device industry including architecture evaluations. Several of the authors have also experience in teaching the methods. The evaluations have brought a lot of insights. First, companies are rarely willing to invest in an evaluation – except in the engineering domain, where architecture is valued and changes are slow [3]. Second, the most valuable outcome was information transfer: both the stakeholders and the architect gained valuable knowledge. For example, scenario creation was often turned into an ad hoc requirements elicitation workshop. Last, but not least, the architects felt that they had been designing the system on their own and the evaluation provided an opportunity to challenge their decisions. Usually, the architect was the 'defendant' and had to explain the rationale of a decision. Even if the other participants did not have the expertise to really challenge it, the questions posed and the process of explaining the decision deepened understanding and forced the architect to see the problem from different perspectives. So, the assessment acted as a form of 'rubber duck debugging' [13, p. 95].

3   Decision and Scenario-Based Architecture Evaluation

The DASE approach picks and combines parts of architectural design decision review from DCAR [5] and parts of scenario analysis from ATAM [11]. The idea is to work faster by involving less people and by focusing on key issues. There are two phases: First, in the pre-work (preparation) phase, technical and business information is collected and processed into a list of decisions and scenarios. Second, the decisions and scenarios are used to evaluate the architecture in a one day workshop (the main phase). Figure 1 shows an overview.

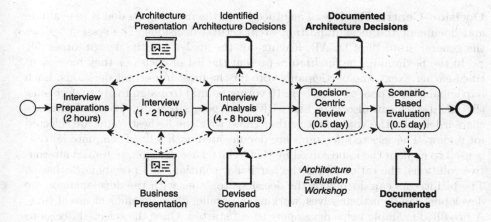

Fig. 1. Phases in the decision and scenario-based architecture evaluation (DASE)

3.1   Pre-work

The pre-work phase is centered around an interview (1–2 h) where the *product owner* presents the mission and the business objectives of the product and the *architect* presents the technical solution. The interview is lead by the *facilitators*, a team of two to three people who facilitate and guide the evaluation process from start to finish.

Based on the presentations, their notes (and possible recordings), the facilitators identify and list significant design decisions (described in a few words). In this point the design starts to become visible, if it wasn't so before. The architect is asked to check the list. Together with the architectural information, the business objectives are then used to devise a number of scenarios that reflect the interests and topical issues that came up in the interview. Good scenarios are relevant to the stated business objectives and challenge the architecture in some way, by targeting potentially problematic areas or by focusing on architectural hot spots that could affect system responses. The facilitators have an important role in identifying the key issues because there is no extensive scenario collection and elaboration phase involving multiple stakeholders. The scenarios are reviewed in the next phase and can be adjusted, if needed.

3.2   Architecture Evaluation Workshop

The one-day architecture evaluation workshop is split into two sessions: the first (morning) is for the decision-centric review and the second (afternoon) for the scenario based evaluation. The order is important because the design is then fresh in mind when evaluating the scenarios. In addition to the *facilitators*, the morning session requires the presence of the *architect* and other technical people (who know the design) and *business stakeholders* are required for the afternoon session. The presence of the *product owner* is good also for the morning session.

Decision-Centric Review. The objective of the morning session is to evaluate and document the most important architectural decisions. The session follows the general protocol of DCAR, leaving out the analysis of the design forces [5].

In the beginning, the *facilitators* present the list of decisions they have identified earlier. Next, the participants[1] vote for the most important decisions. Each participant has a pool of votes (e.g. 10 voting points) to assign freely to decisions; the facilitators can also vote but with fewer points (e.g. 5). The decisions are then ordered by the vote count so that those with the highest count are selected for review. The selected decisions are documented with a fixed template [5] that is used to explain the issue solved by the architecture decision, potential alternative solutions, the rationale for the particular solution, and possible drawbacks. The facilitators can document the decisions together with the developers or the developers can do it themselves, working in parallel for more efficient use of time. A pre-filled example helps developers to get started. Once the selected decisions have been documented, each decision is discussed together. The discussion ends with another vote where the participants are asked whether the decision can be considered a good one, neutral, or risky. The number of decisions documented depends on the number of people working on them, typically it is three to five.

Scenario-Based Evaluation. The afternoon session focuses on the scenarios. The scenarios have been defined using the ATAM [11] template that includes a descriptive name, the related quality attributes, an environment description, the stimulus triggering the scenario, and the expected response.

First, the facilitators present an overview of the devised scenarios in order to assess their feasibility and to make any adjustments. Each scenario is then evaluated so that the participants will try to explain what would happen when the triggering event happens, given the conditions, and whether the expected outcome (system response) would be achieved. The facilitators add the explanation to the scenario's description. The architectural decisions affecting the outcome are also noted and listed. The decisions have just been reviewed, which helps in this. The workshop ends when all relevant scenarios are covered or when time runs out. At this point, the facilitators wrap up the workshop and ask for immediate feedback. The facilitators supply a report of the *documented decisions* and *scenarios* to the participants after some final editing. These reports are the concrete outcome of the evaluation.

4   Applying the Method

The DASE method has been tested in three Finnish companies during 2015–2017. The companies were selected by convenience and based on their own interest. Two of the companies, A and B, were participants of the Finnish software research program Need for Speed[1]. Each architecture evaluation focused on a single project. The first, second and third author were the facilitators in cases A and C, and the first, second, and fourth author in B.

---

[1] http://www.n4s.fi/en.

As general results, in all cases the company representatives found the evaluations useful and they appreciated the concise schedule. Below, we describe the cases and the findings that are specific for them. The number of decisions and scenarios in each case are listed in Table 1. The amount of covered scenarios in all cases was about 10 (same as reported, e.g., in [14]).

Case A was a mid-sized software company working in business software solutions. The evaluated project was a large and mature accounting product. Architecturally, they needed to take into account multiple customers sharing same server-side data resources and many external dependencies (banks, tax office).

Table 1. Number of decisions and scenarios in evaluation cases

	A	B	C
Decisions identified	20	16	9
Decisions receiving votes	15	11	6
Decisions documented	4	3	3
Scenarios devised	10	15	10
Scenarios evaluated	10	13	8
Scenario waste ratio	0%	13%	20%

The four documented decisions concerned the customer database design (single-tenancy), the nature of transactions in the services, the requirements for strong authentication in many system functions, and the technical infrastructure of the application hosting servers and database servers. The scenarios touched on quality attributes such as maintainability, availability, and scalability of the system that were affected by the design decisions on data management.

The participants of the evaluation workshop found the scenarios mostly relevant but thought that some of the scenarios were too exploratory and unlikely in the near future. A new employee was present in the workshop and he thought it was good training for him.

Case B was a small company developing an on-demand video broadcasting application for different devices. The product was not very big but there were several versions of it, and it was already in the market. The architecture of the product had been just restructured to be more modular and flexible to enable parallel development of features. There were also real-time requirements.

The three documented decisions defined the key aspects of the new plug-in architecture that promoted separation of concerns and made testing easier, for instance. Modifiability and testing were the main themes in scenarios. Scalability did not concern company B because the customer is responsible for the infrastructure. Two new scenarios were created on the fly in the afternoon session.

The mixing of 'bottom-up' (decisions) and 'top-down' (scenarios) analysis was appreciated, and the order of the sessions was considered good. However, even better scenarios could have been devised if the facilitators could have used the product first. It was seen helpful to have architecture decision templates with concrete examples in order to get started with documenting the decisions.

Case C was a mid-sized company closely associated with the public sector in Finland. The product evaluated was a recently launched user authentication solution meant for educational on-line services for primary schools. The product was developed by a single person. Company C wanted to utilize and maintain an open-source based solution for its product in an environment where there are many authentication providers and learning service providers.

The three documented decisions concerned the use of an open source authentication framework as a basis for the solution, storing of client configurations in databases, and a specific dependency to legacy code that added extra complexity to the overall architecture. The scenarios touched on the central role of the company acting as a hub and a connection point for authentication and service providers. Interoperability and maintainability were important quality attributes as well as the ability to integrate new providers. Being able to monitor the responsiveness of the authentication providers was also important.

The architect would have liked the facilitators to more strongly challenge the solution and provide alternatives. Doing evaluations regularly as part of development was considered possible but it was seen important to get an external viewpoint. Reporting and making the outcome of the scenario analysis actionable was also raised as a topic as people were uncertain what to do with the scenarios after the evaluation. One suggestion was that the evaluation report could include options and recommendations for addressing a particular concern.

5 Conclusions

We have presented the DASE approach that combines selected activities from two best of breed architecture evaluation methods into a compact process. DASE has been validated in three commercial projects, and the results show that at a modest use of resources (two days per facilitator and one day per other participant) an architecture can be successfully evaluated in a one-day workshop. The participants saw the evaluations as useful in general and appreciated the broad perspective to architecture they gained through design decisions and scenarios. The facilitators do need to understand design decision analysis and scenario evaluation enough to guide the process, but templates and pre-filled examples help participants to get quickly on board. The facilitators have a key role in preparing for the main evaluation workshop and in keeping it focused on key issues. However, based on our earlier experiences, the facilitators have even more coaching and guiding to do when doing an ATAM-evaluation, for example.

As criticism and improvements, some participants asked for more actionable results that would guide further development. They asked for challenging the design stronger and for suggesting alternative solutions. This implies that the goals of an evaluation need to be openly discussed and that relevant expertise must be available, e.g. an internal consultant from another team. We observed also the risk that because the participants select the decisions to document, there may be a tendency to select only 'good' decisions. In the three cases, none of the documented decisions were considered problematic. The situation might be different for a system in an early phase of development.

As further work, it would be important to study how the approach scales up for really big systems. Also, the consequences of the fact that the number of documented design decisions seems to be constant need to be understood better.

Acknowledgments. This work was supported by the Finnish Funding Agency for Innovation (Tekes) as part of the N4S Program of DIMECC (http://www.dimecc. com/).

References

1. Knodel, J., Naab, M.: Software architecture evaluation in practice: retrospective on more than 50 architecture evaluations in industry. In: 2014 IEEE/IFIP Conference on Software Architecture (WICSA), pp. 115–124, April 2014
2. Knodel, J., Naab, M.: Pragmatic Evaluation of Software Architectures. The Fraunhofer IESE Series on Software and Systems Engineering. Springer, Cham (2016). doi:10.1007/978-3-319-34177-4
3. Reijonen, V., Koskinen, J., Haikala, I.: Experiences from scenario-based architecture evaluations with ATAM. In: Babar, M.A., Gorton, I. (eds.) ECSA 2010. LNCS, vol. 6285, pp. 214–229. Springer, Heidelberg (2010). doi:10.1007/978-3-642-15114-9_17
4. Bellomo, S., Gorton, I., Kazman, R.: Toward agile architecture: insights from 15 years of ATAM data. IEEE Softw. **5**, 38–45 (2015)
5. van Heesch, U., Eloranta, V.P., Avgeriou, P., Koskimies, K., Harrison, N.: Decision-centric architecture reviews. IEEE Softw. **31**(1), 69–76 (2014)
6. Bass, L., Nord, R.: Understanding the context of architecture evaluation methods. In: 2012 Joint Working IEEE/IFIP Conference on Software Architecture (WICSA) and European Conference on Software Architecture (ECSA), pp. 277–281, August 2012
7. Woods, E.: Industrial architectural assessment using TARA. J. Syst. Softw. **85**(9), 2034–2047 (2012)
8. Eloranta, V.P., Koskimies, K.: Lightweight architecture knowledge management for agile software development. In: Ali Babar, M., Brown, A.W., Mistrik, I. (eds.) Agile Software Architecture, pp. 189–213. Morgan Kaufmann, Boston (2014)
9. Sedano, T., Ralph, P., Péraire, C.: Software development waste. In: Proceedings of the 39th International Conference on Software Engineering, ICSE 2017, pp. 130–140. IEEE Press (2017)
10. Kazman, R., Klein, M., Barbacci, M., Longstaff, T., Lipson, H., Carriere, J.: The architecture tradeoff analysis method. In: Proceedings of the Fourth IEEE International Conference on Engineering of Complex Computer Systems, ICECCS 1998, pp. 68–78 (1998)
11. Kazman, R., Klein, M., Clements, P.: ATAM: method for architecture evaluation. Technical Report CMU/SEI-2000-TR-004, Carnegie Mellon Sw. Eng. Inst. (2000)
12. Boucké, N., Weyns, D., Schelfthout, K., Holvoet, T.: Applying the ATAM to an architecture for decentralized control of a transportation system. In: Hofmeister, C., Crnkovic, I., Reussner, R. (eds.) QoSA 2006. LNCS, vol. 4214, pp. 180–198. Springer, Heidelberg (2006). doi:10.1007/11921998_16

13. Hunt, A., Thomas, D.: The Pragmatic Programmer: From Journeyman to Master. Addison-Wesley, Boston (1999)
14. Del Rosso, C.: Continuous evolution through software architecture evaluation: a case study. J. Softw. Maintenance Evol. Res. Pract. **18**(5), 351–383 (2006)

Towards a Usability Model for Software Development Process and Practice

Diego Fontdevila[1(✉)], Marcela Genero[2], and Alejandro Oliveros[1]

[1] Universidad Nacional de Tres de Febrero, Caseros, Argentina
{dfontdevila, aoliveros}@untref.edu.ar
[2] University of Castilla-La Mancha, Ciudad Real, Spain
marcela.genero@uclm.es

Abstract. Context/Background: Process and practice adoption is a key element in modern software process improvement initiatives, and many of them fail. Goal: This paper presents a preliminary version of a usability model for software development process and practice. Method: This model integrates different perspectives, the ISO Standard on Systems and Software Quality Models (ISO 25010) and classic usability literature. For illustrating the feasibility of the model, two experts applied it to Scrum. Results: Metrics values were mostly positive and consistent between evaluators. Conclusions: We find the model feasible to use and potentially beneficial.

Keywords: Usability · Process and practice · Adoption · Model

1 Introduction

Process and practice adoption is a key element in modern software process improvement initiatives, and it has become a central issue for organizations trying to become more agile. Many of these initiatives fail to accomplish their objectives [1, 2], producing negative impact on costs, productivity and motivation for future improvements. On the other hand, there is evidence that human factors like emotion influence productivity, turnover, and job satisfaction in software development [3].

Processes and practices are tools that people use to coordinate and define their activities [4]; and adoption success may depend on the interactions between people as users of the process, and the process itself [5, 6]. Since usability characterizes good interactions between users and tools that are appropriate and satisfactory to use [7], we propose that applying usability concepts to process and practice might improve adoption strategies. That is to say, focusing on process and practice usability might improve the probability of success of any process improvement, culture transformation or practice adoption initiative.

We initially defined process and practice usability as "how easy it is to follow a process or practice, including the effort needed to learn, the probability of making mistakes, the cost of such mistakes and the overall satisfaction and motivation promoted by following the practice or process" [8]. To operationalize this definition, our main contribution is the definition of a process and practice usability model composed of a set of sub-characteristics and metrics. Our model integrates three different sources,

© Springer International Publishing AG 2017
M. Felderer et al. (Eds.): PROFES 2017, LNCS 10611, pp. 137–145, 2017.
https://doi.org/10.1007/978-3-319-69926-4_11

the work of Kroeger et al. [5], the ISO Standard on Systems and Software Quality Models [7] and classic usability literature as well.

This model should help practitioners and process improvement specialists to better plan improvement initiatives, methodologists to better design new ways of working, and researchers to better understand adoption challenges. Adoption initiatives might increase their probability of success by adapting processes and practices to make them more usable, or at least by refining adoption strategies to take usability challenges into account. As an example, in the practice of Test Driven Development [9] the name of the practice suggests a testing practice but is actually about designing and coding software. Unclear naming is a typical usability issue [10].

The objective of this paper is to present a preliminary version of this model, and its application to Scrum as a feasibility study.

The rest of this paper is organized as follows: Sect. 2 presents related work, Sect. 3 describes our research method, Sect. 4 presents the preliminary version of the Usability Model for Software Development Process and Practice, Sect. 5 presents how we applied the model to Scrum, Sect. 6 analyzes threats to validity and Sect. 7 outlines the conclusions and future work.

2 Related Work

Very few studies consider people users of their processes or even mention process usability: Feiler and Humphrey mention process usability in the introduction to their work, but do not include it in their list of process quality attributes [11]. Culver-Lozo discusses usability but in terms of process documentation usability [12]. Kroeger et al. have published significant research on the subject [5]. As an example of methodology analysis in terms of its relationship with its practitioners, Alistair Cockburn has reflected on the concept of high-discipline methodologies [13], which he defines as those that might probably be abandoned if a mechanism to keep them up is not put in place (an example of such mechanism is the Coach role in XP).

Kroeger et al. [5] built their model from the concepts that they identified as quality attributes for software development processes. These quality attributes, in turn, the researchers grouped into 4 groups: Suitability, Usability, Manageability and Evolvability. They arrived at Usability as a grouping of: Learnability, Understandability, Accessibility and Adaptability. The ISO 25010 Standard on Systems and software quality models presents a product-oriented perspective on usability. Considering process to be like a software product is an analogy that other researchers have already used [11]. Since there is no Software Development Process Quality Standard, using the product standard seemed the right complement to the study by Kroeger et al. [5].

The classic literature on usability represented by the work of Norman [10] and Nielsen [14] brought into the model very specific and rich terminology. An example of this is the generalization of the concept of appropriateness Recognizability from ISO 25010, aligned with the principle of affordance from Norman [10], into Self-evident Purpose.

3   Research Method

Our research includes the following activities: review the state of the art for software development process and practice usability; define a usability model for software development process and practice; perform a feasibility study to determine preliminary viability; refine the model and perform model validation.

To define the model we first identified the source literature related to process and practice usability. We conducted unstructured interviews with expert researchers on the subject[1] to identify candidate sources. From references provided by some of the experts we established three source types: process and practice usability, classic product usability literature, and product usability standards. We chose the study by Kroeger et al. [5] as the reference source for process usability, and three reference sources on product usability [7, 10, 14]. Then, for each of the sources we added all elements to an initial candidate list of sub-characteristics. We proceeded to identify and group similar concepts, and then to purge the ones that did not seem to fit. We then refined or changed names in specific cases, mainly for clarification purposes. Finally, we added candidate metrics, some inspired from metrics defined in the sources, but mainly based in our experience with software process and practice adoption. The main author defined the model as described, and both other authors acted as reviewers of the model. We then performed a feasibility study on Scrum as described in Sect. 5. At this point we are planning further model refinement and validation (See more details in Appendix A, Sects. 1 to 4).

4   A Usability Model for Software Development Process and Practice

In this section we present an analysis of the sources and then describe the Process and Practice Usability Model.

4.1   Analysis of Model Sources

We based our model in the following sources: the study by Kroeger et al. [5]; ISO 25010 [7], a standard for quality of systems and software products; and the classic works by Norman [10] and Nielsen [14].

Kroeger et al. [5] have developed a model for improving software development processes from the perspective of the people involved. Their model is a generic quality model. Beyond its wider scope and its sound research methodology, their model has limitations regarding usability: although they define Process Usability as "ease with which a software engineering process can be *interpreted* and *performed* by practitioners" (the highlight is ours), its quality sub-attributes have little relationship with

---

[1] Personal interviews with Eduardo Miranda, Laurie Williams and Mario Piatinni.

actual process performance. Specifically, understandability, learnability and accessibility are related to the interpretation of the process, and adaptability to is modification, which leaves no attribute to characterize process performance. Their definition of accessibility is "ease with which a process user is able to find information about a software engineering process" [5], which is focused in what we consider today a comparatively minor issue, information acquisition, as opposed to the traditional definition of "access for users with different capabilities" [7]. From our perspective, the most significant interactions are those between the people involved and the actual process, not between the people and the process definition documentation.

ISO 25010 [7] is a systems and software products quality standard, it has a comprehensive usability perspective that includes "soft" sub-characteristics like user satisfaction and user interface aesthetics. It defines usability as "degree to which a product or system can be used by specified users to achieve specified goals with effectiveness, efficiency and satisfaction in a specified context of use". It provided our work with a more modern perspective on usability (i.e. more related to user experience). It also defines three of the four sub-characteristics that Kroeger et al. [5] consider for usability (learnability, adaptability and accessibility), although in the case of accessibility, with a very different meaning; and adaptability is considered a sub-characteristic of maintainability, not usability.

The classic usability literature [10, 14] provided the first elements for the earliest forms of the model, starting with Feedback [10] and Tolerate mistakes [14]. It also provided some of the more nuanced sub-characteristics, like Affordance, which the ISO 25010 standard [7] confirmed with its own Appropriateness recognizability sub-characteristic. We later renamed affordance to Self-evident purpose, to increase model understandability since early discussions with expert practitioners[2] showed affordance as a term that was hard to apprehend.

4.2   The Model

The model is composed of nine sub-characteristics, which are aligned with our definition and emerged from the study of our model sources. In building the model we made sure that none of the concerns identified in the sources were left out, except accessibility as explained in Sect. 4.1, and avoid modes [14], which seemed inapplicable.

The model has several sub-characteristics that support process performance, in particular: visibility, that characterizes how transparent the status of a process and its intermediate products are to its stakeholders; controllability, that describes how easy it is for different stakeholders to control a process or practice during execution; and user satisfaction, which is a by-product of the experience of using the process or practice.

---

[2] Mary and Tom Poppendieck, Alistair Cockburn, Tobias Mayer and Brian Marick.

For each sub-characteristic we present a name, a definition and explain the rationale behind the inclusion of that sub-characteristic. We also present a set of candidate metrics for each sub-characteristic. The sub-characteristics are presented in Table 1 and the candidate metrics in Table 2.

Table 1. Process and practice usability sub-characteristics.

Sub-characteristic	Definition	Rationale
Self-evident purpose	Degree to which users can recognize what a process or practice is for	Purpose is a key motivator
		Newcomers to a process or practice need to be able to make sense of it
Learnability	"Ease with which a process user is able to learn how to perform the activities of a software engineering process" [5]	Difficulty to learn a new process or practice is a basic barrier for adoption
Understandability	"Ease with which a process user is able to understand whether a software engineering process is relevant and how it can be used to achieve desired results" [5]	Understandability applies to process and practice selection before adoption, and also during process performance
Error tolerance	Degree to which the process is safe for its users, preventing errors or limiting their impact	Error tolerance supports efficiency and effectiveness, and it also makes a process or practice easier to learn "on the job"
Visibility	Degree to which process structure, activities, status and information inputs and outputs are visible to stakeholders of the process in a specified context of use	Visibility allows stakeholders to know the status of a process or practice and take early corrective action when necessary. It also helps set realistic expectations early
Controllability	Degree to which a process or practice has attributes that make it easy to control	Decisions need to be made at the appropriate time and impact the results effectively
Adaptability	"Ease with which a process user is able to adapt a software engineering process for use in different situations" [5]	Adaptability is about a process or practice supporting different contexts and users. This allows better fit and a higher reuse rate
Attractiveness	Degree to which users of the process or practice find it attractive or resonate with its form or structure	Attractiveness characterizes the appeal to newcomers. It might impact the desire to learn and adopt
User satisfaction	Degree to which user needs are satisfied when using a process or practice	Satisfaction is a key element for positive feedback and impacts the creation of new habits

To improve model application consistency and make it easier to use, we defined an evaluation process based on the ISO 25040 [15]. Table 2 describes model metrics.

Table 2. Candidate metrics.

Sub-characteristic	Candidate metric	Definition	Values	Type
Self-evident purpose	Appropriateness of name	Measures how appropriate the name is for describing the purpose of the process or practice	Deceiving, Ambiguous, Partial, Appropriate, Accurate	Nominal
Self-evident purpose	Purpose alignment for stakeholders	Measures the alignment of purpose for all stakeholders	None, Low, Medium, High, Complete	Ordinal
Learnability	Volume of information of introductory material	Measures the size of introductory material as defined by authoritative sources, e.g. for an authoritative introductory course	Number of words	Absolute
Learnability	Standard introductory course duration	Measures standard course duration in hours, as defined by authoritative sources	Number of hours	Absolute
Understandability	# of elements	Measures how many components make up the definition of the process or practice	Number of elements	Absolute
Understandability	Conceptual model correspondence	Measures the level of correspondence between the user's conceptual model of an activity and the conceptual model of that same activity that the process or practice implies	Low, Medium, High	Ordinal
Understandability	Data model complexity index	Measures the subjective complexity of the data model	Low, Medium, High	Ordinal
Error tolerance	Cost of error	Measures the cost of error as overall impact	Low, Medium, High	Ordinal
Error tolerance	Safety perception	Measures how safe is it to use the process or practice	Low, Medium, High	Ordinal
Error tolerance	Use of restraining functions	Measures whether the process or practice provides hard restrictions to prevent risk materialization	Yes/No	Nominal
Visibility	# of indicators	Measures how many standard indicators the process or practice defines	Number of indicators	Absolute

(continued)

Table 2. (*continued*)

Sub-characteristic	Candidate metric	Definition	Values	Type
Visibility	Use of information radiators	Measures whether information radiators are used in the process or practice. Information radiators display information regardless of user action	Yes/No	Nominal
Visibility	Audience alignment for information	Measures whether information is presented in the same way to all stakeholders	Yes/No	Nominal
Controllability	Degree of control concentration by role	Measures how concentrated control is among the roles defined	Low, Medium, High	Ordinal
Controllability	Level of autonomy	Measures the level of autonomy users have in making decisions related to the process or practice	Low, Medium, High	Ordinal
Controllability	Control granularity	Measures the control granularity of the process or practice	Fine, Medium, Coarse	Ordinal
Adaptability	# of adaptation points	Measures how many adaptation points the process or practice defines	Number of adaptation points	Absolute
Adaptability	Ratio of roles allowed to adapt	Measures how many roles are allowed to adapt the process or practice out of the total number of roles	0 to 1	Ratio
Attractiveness	User attractiveness rating	Measures how attractive the process or practice is to prospective users (i.e. those lacking experience)	1 to 5	Ordinal
User satisfaction	User experience rating	Measures the subjective experience of using the process or practice	1 to 5	Ordinal

5 Applying the Model to Scrum

In this section we describe how we applied the model to Scrum to evaluate its feasibility. We limited evaluation to standard Scrum implementations [16]. First, one of the authors performed an evaluation, and then we proceeded to select two external Scrum experts[3] with more than 10 years of experience with Scrum. We provided them with introductory training to understand the model and the evaluation process, and also specific clarifications when required. For each model sub-characteristic, the evaluators assigned values to the model's candidate metrics, and added qualitative comments.

Evaluation results show that almost all metric values are in the middle or positive spectrum for that metric (see details in Appendix A, Sect. 5). This is consistent with Scrum's popularity, simplicity and its focus on visibility and risk mitigation.

After the evaluation, informal feedback from the external evaluators provided interesting insights: granularity of the object of evaluation might be an issue (scrum vs. retrospective); differences between correct and incorrect implementations (one of the evaluators made a related distinction when evaluating Cost of error); distinguish standard from typical implementations (this emerged in the case of the Use of information radiators metric); evaluation is context sensitive (the Safety perception metric yielded two different values but with coherent underlying explanations); there are definitions that need to be improved. Overall, the results of both evaluators were highly consistent (see details in Appendix A, Sects. 5 and 6).

Finally, external evaluators were able to use the model effectively and produce qualitative comments that are aligned with model concepts. Thus, this provides initial confirmation that the model is understandable and feasible to apply.

6 Threats to Validity

Our work, being still on its early stages, presents issues that need to be addressed: lacks completeness validation, there is not enough confirmation of theoretical saturation; we cannot yet assess applicability to other processes or to specific practices; sample of evaluations is very limited, we have only two external evaluations; evaluators trained only with informal material (verbal explanations from the authors and access to the model in its current version); validation is limited, we need to improve on issues like consistency in evaluations by different evaluators and model accuracy in describing real life processes and practices.

7 Conclusions and Future Work

In this paper we presented our process and practice usability model, defining its sub-characteristics and candidate metrics. Through an initial application of the model to Scrum by one author and two external evaluators, we found the model feasible to use and potentially beneficial.

Next steps include model and evaluation process refinement, including adding details, improving unclear definitions and metrics, defining how to compose metrics, and a user guide and training material; further validation with experts; application to

---

[3] Juan Gabardini and Alan Cyment.

other software development processes and practices to increase representativeness of the study; and empirical studies in industry.

Appendix A

Supplementary data available at https://doi.org/10.6084/m9.figshare.5296276.v1.

References

1. Ambler, S.: Agile practices survey results, July 2009. http://www.ambysoft.com/surveys/practices2009.html. Accessed 24 Jan 2017
2. Paez, N., Fontdevila, D., Oliveros, A.: Characterizing technical and organizational practices in the agile community. In: Proceedings of CONAIISI, Salta, Argentina (2016)
3. Graziotin, D., Wang, X., Abrahamsson, P.: Software developers, moods, emotions, and performance. IEEE Softw. **31**, 24–27 (2014)
4. Cockburn, A.: What the Agile Toolbox Contains, Crosstalk Magazine, November 2004
5. Kroeger, T.A., Davidson, N.J., Cook, S.C.: Understanding the characteristics of quality for software engineering processes: a grounded theory investigation. Inf. Softw. Technol. **56**, 252–271 (2014)
6. Brown, J.S., Duguid, P.: The Social Life of Information. Harvard Business Press, Boston (2000)
7. International Organization for Standardization: ISO/IEC 25010 Systems and Software Engineering - Systems and Software Quality Requirements and Evaluation (SQuaRE) - System and Software Quality Models, Geneva, Switzerland (2011)
8. Fontdevila, D.: A tool evaluation framework based on fitness to process and practice. In: International Conference on Software Engineering Advances, ICSEA, Nice, France (2014)
9. Beck, K.: Test Driven Development by Example. Addison-Wesley, Boston (2002)
10. Norman, D.A.: The Design of Everyday Things. Basic books, New York (1988)
11. Feiler, P., Humphrey, W.: Software process development and enactment: concepts and definitions. Software Engineering Institute, CMU/SEI-92-TR- 004 (1992)
12. Culver-Lozo, K.: The software process from the developer's perspective: a case study on improving process usability. In: Proceedings of Ninth International Software Process Workshop, Airlie, VA, pp. 67–69 (1994). doi:10.1109/ISPW.1994.512766
13. Cockburn, A.: Agile Software Development: The Cooperative Game. Pearson Education, London (2006)
14. Nielsen, J.: Usability Engineering. Elsevier, Amsterdam (1994)
15. International Organization for Standardization: ISO/IEC 25040 Systems and Software Engineering – System and software Quality Requirements and Evaluation (SQuaRE) – Evaluation process, Geneva, Switzerland (2011)
16. Kchwaber, K., Sutherland, J.: Scrum Guide. http://www.scrumguides.org/scrum-guide.html. Accessed 24 Jan 2017

More for Less: Automated Experimentation in Software-Intensive Systems

David Issa Mattos[1]([⊠]) [iD], Jan Bosch[1] [iD],
and Helena Holmström Olsson[2] [iD]

[1] Department of Computer Science and Engineering,
Chalmers University of Technology, Hörselgången 11,
412 96 Gothenburg, Sweden
{davidis,jan.bosch}@chalmers.se
[2] Department of Computer Science and Media Technology, Malmö University,
Östra Varvsgatan 11, 205 06 Malmö, Sweden
helena.holmstrom.olsson@mah.se

Abstract. Companies developing autonomous and software-intensive systems show an increasing need to adopt experimentation and data-driven strategies in their development process. With the growing complexity of the systems, companies are increasing their data analytic and experimentation teams to support data-driven development. However, organizations cannot increase in size at the same pace as the system complexity grows. Experimentation teams could run a larger number of experiments by letting the system itself to coordinate its own experiments, instead of the humans. This process is called automated experimentation. However, currently, no tools or frameworks address the challenge of running automated experiments.

This paper discusses, through a set of architectural design decisions, the development of an architecture framework that supports automated continuous experiments. The contribution of this paper is twofold. First, it presents, through a set of architectural design decisions, an architecture framework for automated experimentation. Second, it evaluates the architecture framework experimentally in the context of a human-robot interaction proxemics distance problem. This automated experimentation framework aims to deliver more value from the experiments while using fewer R&D resources.

Keywords: Continuous experimentation · Automated experimentation · Architectural design decisions

1 Introduction

During the development of a system, existing or new features are expected to add value to the systems, e.g. increase the number of users, improved security, better battery performance. Features that deliver low or negative value can have a negative impact on the system and maintenance cost [1]. However, often deployed features to customers fail to deliver the desired value or these features are rarely used [2]. The development of a full feature from conception to user deployment can result in losses, or at least opportunity cost if it does not deliver the expected value. The decisions in companies

© Springer International Publishing AG 2017
M. Felderer et al. (Eds.): PROFES 2017, LNCS 10611, pp. 146–161, 2017.
https://doi.org/10.1007/978-3-319-69926-4_12

sometimes are based on the Highest Paid Person's Opinion (HiPPO) and not actual data [3]. Data-driven companies rely on data provided by running experiments with their system in the field and from customer feedback.

Continuous Experimentation can be seen as the evaluation of different alternatives decisions formulated and evaluated with hypothesis testing. Continuous Experimentation does not refer to verification and validation of the system functionality. It rather represents techniques to evaluate alternatives captured in the hypothesis. Some examples of continuous experimentation in industry context can be seen in [4].

Many web-facing companies continuously report the use of experiments in their data-driven decision process [5, 6]. However, there are a number of challenges associated with manual experimentation. The first challenge appears when the experiments go beyond simple user interface changes with traditional metrics. Running experiments in the whole system and the system's infrastructure, challenge R&D departments to develop a scalable experimentation system able to handle a large amount of experiments [5].

The second challenge arises with the growing complexity of the systems. Companies are increasing their data analytic and experimentation teams to support data-driven development. However, it is unfeasible to grow the size of R&D teams with this increasing demand. To address this second challenge, in [7], it is proposed a conceptual solution where the R&D teams build part of the functionality, set guardrails and let the system autonomously experiment its functionality. These large companies report automation in part of their experiments. However, most experiments are still manually developed, conducted and analyzed.

Automated continuous experimentation refers to a set of experimental techniques that allows the system to test variants, generate new variants and learn continuously from the field experiments [8]. Automated experimentation offers a significant return on investment as it allows systems to run experiments with significantly less R&D effort. Moreover, generating new variants allows the system to converge to an optimal state faster compared to manually conducted experiments [8].

Works on experimentation focus on experimentation algorithms, metrics and machine learning techniques to analyze the data [6, 9]. However, to the best of our knowledge, there is no research that addresses from a software engineering perspective the architecture of an experimentation system that employs automated experimentation.

This research paper investigates the design decisions, the problem constraints and their implication in the development of an architecture framework to support automated experimentation. The presented architecture is based on decisions, evaluation and experiences based on different research and industrial frameworks as described in this paper and in previous work [8].

In this context, we propose an approach that combines manual and automated experimentation in an integral framework. We present an architecture framework that facilitates automated experiments in a system. The benefits of using this architecture framework are shown in a human-robot interaction problem.

The contribution of this paper is twofold. First, it presents, through a set of architectural design decisions [10], an architecture framework for automated continuous experimentation. Second, it evaluates the architecture framework experimentally in the context of a human-robot interaction proxemics distance problem. This evaluation suggests a more effective way to develop a system, as compared to traditional manual experiments. This automated experimentation framework aims to deliver more value from the experiments while using fewer R&D resources.

The rest of this paper is organized as follows. Section 2 provides a background and related works in controlled experiments, in automated experiments and describes the research process. Section 3 discusses the context, requirements, the architectural design decisions and the architecture framework. Section 4 presents the human-robot inter-action (HRI) proxemics distance problem, discusses the framework instantiation, and shows some experimental results. Section 5 concludes this paper and discusses future works and research challenges.

2 Related Work and Research Process

2.1 Controlled Experiments in Software Systems

Controlled experiments use the scientific method to establish a causal relationship between changes and their influence on the observed behavior [3]. Controlled experiments (A/B tests, split tests, multivariable tests among others) are a central part of the development process in web-facing companies [11]. In the most basic form, A/B tests, users are randomly assigned to one of two variations (also known as a challenger). With a large number of interactions (high statistical power) with the two variations, it is possible to measure the difference in the behavior and establish a causal relationship to the variations. Randomized experiments are not restricted to web-companies and are present in several fields, such as Social Sciences, Medicine, Marketing and Behavioral Economics. Online software systems have the advantage of being able to introduce variations on the system without significant engineering cost and expose these variations to a high number of users. Data-driven companies use controlled experiments to optimize their systems, to iterate more frequently by validating hypotheses and to support the design and decision-making processes throughout the product lifecycle [4].

Industry software engineering research provide a techniques, tools and guidelines on how to run effectively controlled experiments on online systems [3, 5, 11, 12]. However, companies still struggle on how to guide the R&D activities towards experiments and evolve the organization to data-driven at [4]. The work presented in [4] shows how Microsoft teams evolve from few experimentation to continuous experimentation in large scale in their development, from the technical, organizational and business perspective.

Although experimentation is gaining traction not only in web systems, the available commercial platforms for A/B experiments focus only in web-systems (websites, mobile apps and Facebook web pages) and are guided towards GUI changes.

2.2 Automated Experiments

Successful data-driven companies such as Microsoft, Google, Facebook, LinkedIn and Booking continuously report an exponential growth in experimentation over time [5, 11, 12]. The exponential growth in the number of experiments is accompanied by an increased growth in the R&D team and the need for new tools to address new problems, such as overlapping experiments [12]. However, it is unfeasible to grow the size of R&D teams at the same rate. R&D organizations do not increase productivity linearly with the size of the teams [7]. In [7], the need for automated experimentation is also discussed in large extent. This discussion includes not only some of technical needs but also organizational changes.

Running experiments for system optimization is common practice in web companies. However, the optimization process requires, through the experimentation process, a high number of users for a number of days. As the systems and the organizations grow in size each team reaches a maximum number of experiments they can run in parallel.

Automated continuous experimentation refers to a set of experimental techniques that allows the system to test variants, generate new variants and learn continuously from the field experiments. Automated experiments aim to alleviate some of the burdens of running experiments for optimization and transferring it to the system. Work in automated experimentation is under development by different research groups and companies. However, no companies report the use of automated experiments in their operational side, but rather only from a research perspective [8].

To the best of our knowledge, no research exists that addresses the architecture of an experimentation system that employs automated and continuous experimentation. To address this research gap, our on-going research [8] started analyzing several frameworks and architectures for experimentation and adaptation. In [8], we focus on the analysis of research and industrial architectures to automated experimentation, while in this paper we focus on the design decisions to develop an architecture framework. Also in [8], we identified software architectures qualities to support automated experimentation. These qualities together with the functional requirements, described in Sect. 4, consist the structure of our design decisions. The identified qualities are listed below, in order of relevance.

External experiment control: it allows separation between the application logic from the experimentation part. This implies the use of an external manager, that interacts with the system through sensors and effectors interfaces. This facilitates adding experiments to existing features and also removing it for features that have reached a static loop (the system under experimentation converges to a unique solution) [7].

Data collection as an integral part of the architecture: collecting experiment data, from both the system and the environment should be an integral part of the architecture. The collected data can be processed to provide insightful information and allow development data-driven software. A systematic approach to data collection allows the scalability of automated experimentation from one to several features.

Performance reflection: performance here does not mean the ability to meet timing requirements. Performance reflection consists of the system evaluating the current system behavior due to the variant and according to an expected value.

Explicit representation of the learning component: learning techniques can be used to help the system to achieve an optimal solution. Machine learning techniques such as multi-armed bandits and reinforcement learning can leverage the experiment speed. However, not all controlled experiment problems support all kinds of algorithms and the experiment designer needs the ability to replace the learning component to a more suitable one.

Decentralized experimentation framework: this refers to the use of different instances of an experimentation manager in contrast with using only one manager for the whole system. This allows experimentation in feature-level while maintaining scalability.

Knowledge exchange: experimentation can happen in different scenarios with one or several systems. In the case where several systems are deployed, one system can share information and the learning process with other systems. This knowledge exchange can help several systems collaboratively optimize their behavior.

2.3   Research Process

This research follows the design-science process and the guidelines described by Hevner [13]. The correspondence process of this research to the design-science method are listed below:

Design as an artifact: this research produces an architecture framework for automated experimentation as the artifact.

Problem relevance: the relevance of this problem is discussed in the introduction and background session. A more in-depth discussion can be found in [7] and in [8].

Design evaluation: the architecture framework developed is instantiated in a human-robot interaction problem and evaluated experimentally in both simulation with artificial data and in a real-world scenario. In this step, it was collected experimental data from the interaction of the robot with the participant. The experimental setup deals with the optimization for one participant without knowledge of the system. This experimental setup does not aim to determine the best proxemics distance for a population, but rather investigate the use of the framework in such case.

Research contributions: this research breaks down the design decision process and the tradeoffs of different configurations of an architecture that supports automated experimentation.

Research rigor: foundations in controlled experiments and architectures for adaptation guided the design decisions for the architecture framework. A previous literature review identified relevant software qualities and evaluated existing architectures alternatives and how they implement solutions for their domain-specific problems [8].

Design as a search process: the architecture framework was developed in an iteration process. The different versions were evaluated against the experimental and descriptive scenarios and updated by the design decisions.

3   Architecture Framework Design Decisions

The introduction and background sections provided the motivation for the development of this architecture framework. We assume the system is already developed using a particular set of technologies and following a specific software architecture. The automated experimentation architecture framework will enhance the system capabilities using the existing system infrastructure. The system under experimentation (SuE) refers to the part of the system that is being experimented. For simplification, we divide a system into three levels: system, subsystems and components. Although we envision to automated experimentation in different levels of a system, we started the development of an automated experimentation architecture framework in the component level only.

3.1 Functional Requirements

Below we describe the functional requirements of the experimentation system. These requirements were obtained by analyzing the automated experimentation problem [7, 8], the descriptive scenario presented in [7] and the attributes needed to support it in a family of systems.

- The experimentation system allows the system under experimentation to run experiments, measure its own behavior and learn from this process. Based on predefined metrics the system under experimentation will improve its behavior aided by the experimentation system.
- The architecture framework should support different learning algorithms and not be restricted to one in particular.
- If the system under experimentation is part of a family of systems It should be able to learn and share learned solutions with the other systems.
- More than one feature can be experimenting at the same time. Confounding factors associated with multivariable experiments should be considered.
- The system should support manually predefined variations, as well as an automatically generator of new variations.
- The system should keep track of some guardrails metrics [7] while experimenting. If the system is not in the experiment boundaries, a predefined safe version should be active.

3.2 Problems, Potential Solutions and Decision

We describe the design decisions using a set of {problem, potential solutions, decision}. Some of these problems are recognized from research literature or industry challenges in both the controlled experimentation, software architecture and adaptive systems.

1. Type of experimentation

Problem: the experimentation can be integrated into the application logic or developed as a separate part of the application logic. **Motivation**: several systems that can benefit from experimentation are built using different architectures, frameworks and technologies.

Potential solutions

External experimentation manager. Description: this solution creates an external manager to the system. This separates the experimentation logic from the application logic. **Design rules:** the experimentation manager interacts with the system through its interfaces. The system should continue to work even if the experimentation manager is removed. **Design constraints:** the manager should only interact with the system through its interfaces. **Consequences:** the becomes loosely coupled with the system. **Pros:** maintainability of both the system and the experiment. **Cons:** reduced timing performance of the system. Additional complexity as it introduces a communication layer and new interfaces.

Internal to the application logic. Description: this solution incorporates the experiment into the application logic, combining into one system. **Design rules:** the experiment design is incorporated into the development workflow of the systems. **Design constraints:** the feature developments should handle the experiment design. **Consequences:** the correct functionality of the system becomes dependent on the experiment logic. Difficult to reuse code between similar experiments. **Pros:** integrated with the current development workflow. Better timing performance compared to an external manager. **Cons:** reduced maintainability. If there is a need to change the experiment/learning algorithms or the application functionality, affects both the application and experiment logic.

Decision

The decision is made to use the external experimentation manager solution, which decreases maintainability, facilitates changes and new algorithms and increases the reliability of the system. This decision is also acknowledged in the manually controlled experimentation [11] and in adaptation architectures [9].

2. The degree of decentralization

Problem: the external experimentation manager can be integrated with the systems in different degrees of decentralization. **Motivation:** the degree of decentralization of the system impacts both performance, maintainability and scalability.

Potential solutions

Centralized experimentation manager. Description: in this solution, the system has only one manager coordinating all experiments. **Design rules:** the experimentation manager is responsible for getting all the system data and coordinating the experiment at all levels, from sub-systems and component to feature-level. **Design constraints:** only one instantiation of the manager. the manager should be able to control independent experiments and different algorithms. **Consequences:** each experiment is controlled in only one central place. **Pros:** only one place to keep track of the experiments. Easier to coordinate different experiments and avoid confounding factors. **Cons:** a single point of failure, experiments not related to each other can be influenced by the manager performance. Scalability might be affected when dealing with several experiments at the same time.

Decentralized experimentation at feature-level. Description: in this solution, several experimentation managers are deployed in feature-level. **Design rules:** each manager is responsible only for the feature it is interacting with. **Design constraints:** a feature experiment should not alter other features experiments. The managers should not share resources with each other. **Consequences:** several instances of experiment managers are deployed. **Pros:** provides a way to scale the system and a failure in one manager does not affect the other experiments. Customization of the manager for a particular experiment does not imply changes in a larger manager. **Cons:** different software versions of a manager might be running at the same time, reducing maintainability. In this approach, lack of synchronization between the managers can introduce confounding factors between the experiments.

Decision

The decision is made to use a decentralized approach. Data-driven companies experimenting at large scale report using decentralized tools to run experiments, segmenting the system to allow concurrent experiments [11, 12]. Although, in simple cases a single manager might be easier, in systems where the software is distributed in different computational nodes (such as robotics, automotive and other embedded systems) a single manager is not an alternative. This approach allows to experiment at different levels of the system hierarchy. Moreover, parts of the system can be isolated (e.g. security) from each other and a single manager in those parts might break other architectural rules of the application logic.

3. Confounding factors

Problem: different experiments can influence the same aspect of the system behavior. In this scenario, it is hard to correctly interpret which experiment lead to the correct change (confounding factors). **Motivation:** in a decentralized architecture, lack of synchronization on the on-going experiments can lead to confounding factors.

Potential solutions

Centralized experiment coordinator. Description: the system has only one experiment coordinator to manage all the experiments. The other parts of the architecture would remain decentralized. **Design rules:** all the decentralized components communicate and coordinate the experiments with a central coordinator. **Design constraints:** each decentralized component does not have full autonomy to run the experiment. They should receive permission from the central coordinator. **Consequences:** every new experiment should register and communicate with the central coordinator. **Pros:** simplify the coordination process in a single instance. **Cons:** reduces the reliability of the system by having a single point of failure. Changes in the experiment coordinator can affect all experiments. Changing the coordinator with running experiments can insert bias in the sample and possibly affect all running experiments (in the order of hundreds in large data-driven companies [12]).

Decentralized conflict manager. Description: each experiment instantiation has its own experiment coordinator and a conflict manager. The conflict manager is responsible for keeping track of the current experiments in the system and the experiment coordinator is independent of other experiments. **Design rules:** the conflict manager signals when starting an experiment and it is notified when other experiments start or stop. This allows the experimenting feature to keep track of potential confounding factors. **Design constraints:** experiments should be independent of each other and communication happens decentralized. **Consequences:** each experiment system is contained, not depending on the other experiments. **Pros:** independent experiments reduce the risk of one experiment failure increasing the risk of failures in all experiments, facilitates the scalability of the number of concurrent experiments. **Cons:** introduces an extra layer of complexity when running the experiments or create decentralized communication infrastructure between features.

Decision

The decision is made to use a decentralized conflict manager. Although this solution introduces an extra layer of complexity, it is the solution used in open source tools from companies that experiment in large scale [11, 12]. The extra complexity comes in the designing of the experiment inside the organization. Experiments in the system can be divided between different teams in a way that there is no overlapping. Google divides different experiments in a layer model [12]. Facebook uses namespaces mapped to independent segments of users [11]. Sometimes experiments go through several iterations until the result can be considered valid and the cost to affect several on-going experiments might be prohibited for an organization.

4. Information exchange

Problem: The learning behavior can take a long time to converge in a system isolated. Moreover, the learning process might converge to a specific context where the system is inserted. This situation can reduce the value that the system is delivering. **Motivation:** In the case of several systems being deployed, one system can help the learning process of the other systems. A system initializing with more advanced versions can converge quicker to a solution or initialize with a pre-defined solution.

Potential solutions

Central server. Description: in this solution, the system sends experiment data back to the development team and to other systems through a central server. This data can be used to initialize new learning processes in other systems and be integrated into future developments by the R&D team. **Design rules:** the system needs an infrastructure to communicate with the other systems and the R&D when it learns. A central server infrastructure is necessary to coordinate the information flow. **Design constraints:** the system should have access to a reliable and secure network. Communication directly between systems is not allowed. Control over quality and origin of the information is transferred to the central server. **Consequences:** The system is constantly sharing information with a central server. This solution requires a backend infrastructure. **Pros:** the company behind the system has control of the information flow and the information quality. **Cons:** a central server introduces a point of failure in the system. If the server is down communication between systems is compromised.

Peer-to-peer. Description: this solution equips the system the ability to handle communication directly between systems. **Design rules:** each system should be able to discover other systems and manage the communication and information flow. **Design constraints:** control over the quality and origin of the information is constrained to each system. **Consequences:** this solution can use the same network infrastructure as the central server solution. However, each system should be able to discover other systems, authenticate and verify the quality of information. **Pros:** reduces the dependency on a central server, eliminating a possible point of failure. This also facilitates communication directly between the systems. **Cons:** this solution introduces an overhead to verify the source and quality of information in each system. Systems producing incomplete or faulty information become harder to detect. The research and development team does not have access to the full information shared between systems.

Decision

The decision is made to use a central server to coordinate information exchange. Knowledge, tools and solutions for running central servers and handling communication are largely available. This solution also provides a way to control the information flow concerning user's private usage data, quality and origin of the information. Moreover, it allows sharing data with the R&D team.

5. Guardrails

Problem: experiments should happen in predefined boundaries and conditions. Running experiments outside the experiments boundaries can decrease the performance, deteriorate systems metrics or business goals, and generate invalid experiment results. **Motivation:** systems experimenting outside their experiment boundaries can lead to situations that put the user or the system safety in risk, or deteriorate metrics that were not considered when designing the experiment.

Potential solutions

Restrict when the system can experiment. Description: in this solution, the R&D team only allows experiments in systems that fulfill the experiment criteria in advance. **Design rules:** the experimentation framework is not responsible for selecting when the system can experiment. This is done by the R&D team. **Design constraints:** the system does not keep track of the boundaries or the experiment context. **Consequences:** if the system or the user change context, an experiment might be running outside boundaries. Unless the R&D teams take action, the system will continue running the experiment. **Pros:** this solution is easier to implement when experimenting a low number of features in a small user base. The system does not need to monitor the context of the experiment. **Cons:** this solution can introduce bias in the experiments, because of the population selection process. Depending on the experiment this solution might require a large user base. Moreover, this solution might not scalable with a large number of experiments in parallel.

Measure and keep track of the experiment conditions. Description: in this solution, the experimentation manager feature decides if the systems can experiment or not. **Design rules:** the experimentation manager needs to keep track of the context and determine the current state of the system. **Design constraints:** the system is not allowed to experiment without determining complying with the experiment boundaries. **Consequences:** this requires the system a capability of keeping track of its context and business goals. Incomplete or wrong information of the context leads to experiments running outside its boundaries. **Pros:** each experiment is independent. The experimentation manager can stop the experiment if the system is running out of the experiment boundaries. **Cons:** the system needs to instrument several context variables to correctly induce the current state. This can create a large overhead for the first experiments in an organization that is not data-driven.

Decision

The decision is made to measure and keep track of the experiment conditions. In dynamic systems and in uncertain environments the system there are no guarantees that the system will stay in its initial experiment boundaries. Traditional controlled experiments systems rely on the R&D teams to check the conditions of the experiment.

Manually keeping track of the experiments limits the number of experiments the R&D team can run in parallel.

3.3   The Architecture

The architecture framework for automated experimentation is represented in Fig. 1. This architecture is the result of the design decisions over several iteration processes and inspired by solutions already developed in frameworks for controlled experimentation and architectures for adaptation [8]. The architecture is presented in a general way. Implementation and instantiation of it for a particular domain would require a new set of design decisions linked to both the domain as to the technologies of the system itself. These decisions are linked to the framework in the different components. The design decision 2 affects the architecture framework as a whole. The architecture components are described next:

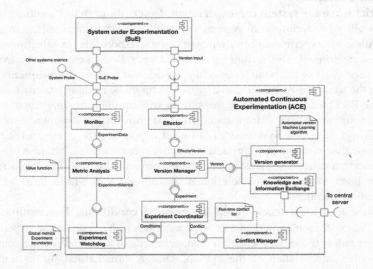

Fig. 1. The architecture framework for automated continuous experimentation

Monitor. This component implements the data collection. The both local and global behavior of the system. This component is directly related to the data collection in the discussed qualities. This component does not represent only a stream of raw data into the experimentation architecture framework, it represents data processed that add information to experimentation framework system. This component is linked to the design decision 1.

Experiment Coordinator. This component is responsible for running the experiment and coordinating with the version manager. This component controls only the specific SuE, other experiments have their own experiment coordinator components. The experiment coordinator can control experiments such as A/A, A/B/n, explore/exploitation and crossover experiments. This component keeps track on when to experiment, the number of experiments that should be run, which solution is more significant. This component receives inputs from the conflict-list manager if it is allowed to run an experiment or not. It also receives inputs from the experiment watchdog component, if the system is deteriorating any global metrics, if it went out of boundaries or if it still needs to perform more experiments. This component is linked to the design decision 3.

Version Manager. This component is responsible for managing and generating different versions (or variations) to experiment. This can be acting in parameters or replacing whole sub-component models. The version generator keeps a list of the versions used and accepts versions inputs from the Knowledge Exchange component and the Version Generator. This allows the experimentation system to use both automatically generated versions, as well as manual versions crafted by the R&D team. Although this component is not directly connected to a one of the design decision listed, this component is linked to both the functional and quality requirements.

Version Generator. This component can accommodate different artificial intelligence algorithms that we might want to test. The generation algorithm is not specified, but it could include machine learning algorithms, such as reinforcement learning algorithms, genetic algorithms, parameter scheduling or randomized versions. This component is directly connected to the learning quality.

Experiment Watchdog. This component checks the conditions that the system can run the experiments, such as when the system should continue experimenting and when it should stop. If the system goes out the predefined boundaries or if there is deterioration in global metrics this component can stop the experiment and return the system to the "safe" version. Having a stop condition for global metrics prevents the system improving a local metric, but degrading a global metric. If any of the stop conditions is reached this component signals to the experiment coordinator to stop the experimentation process or to roll back to a safe version. This component is linked to the design decision 5.

Conflict Manager. This component keeps track in run-time of components that are being experimented with and which factors it affects. This manager keeps track of those systems in order to avoid confounding variables in the experiment. This is directly related to the decentralized experimentation manager decision. Different alternatives can be used for implementing this component, such as the use layers [12] or namespaces management [11]. This component is linked to the design decision 3.

Effector. This component is responsible for interfacing with the managed system. Besides the monitor, it is the only point of contact with the rest of the experimentation framework. This component requires that the managed system expose interfaces for interaction with the system. This concept of not intermixing the experimentation logic and the application is directly related to the external experimentation quality. The same observations made to the monitor component are valid for the effector. This block is linked to the design decision 1.

Metric Analysis. This component is responsible for keeping track of the managed system behavior and the value function. This component analyzes and guides the experimentation through by checking the delivered value of all variants. In this component, we insert the value function or overall evaluation criteria [3] and we run our statistical analysis. This component is directly related to the performance reflection quality.

Knowledge and Information Exchange. This component exchange information with the external world. This component is responsible for sharing discovered solutions in the experimentation process and also for sharing and learning the validated solutions from the experiment through a central server infrastructure. This also represents a way in which the R&D can interact with the system, either helping in the analysis step or proposing different versions not generating by the version manager, for example, testing different algorithms. This component is directly related to the Knowledge Exchange quality and linked to the design decision 4.

4 Evaluation of the Architecture Framework

Human interaction is based on several unwritten and subjective rules. One example is respecting other people's personal space. In human-human relations, several social factors play an important role in this interaction. Not conforming to these rules may cause miscommunication and discomfort. Different works recognize some base distances and how they are influenced depending on a change of factor. However, this is still an open problem. The development of new robots and the deployment of these robots in very different contexts (e.g. different countries) require new experiments to validate and optimize the proxemics distance as seen in [14].

4.1 Instantiation of the Framework

The framework was instantiated in a research mobile robot Turtlebot 2^1 using the Robot Operating System (ROS) middleware[2]. The source code for the full automated experimentation framework implementation is available at https://github.com/davidissamattos/david_ws. Each of the component blocks represented in Fig. 1 were implemented as a separate Python process communicating through publish-subscribe messages. In this instantiation, the conflict manager and information exchange components were not implemented as the system is only running one experiment using only one platform robot.

Feedback Monitor: this component listens to events implemented in the robot such as distance to a person, audio feedback and battery level.

Metric Analysis: this component keeps track of the user satisfaction with the robot approach. It summarizes the event input in an evaluation criteria similar to the OEC [3]. We expect our user to be satisfied at least 70% of the approaches in the long run or an increase of absolute 20% in our 50% baseline [8].

Experiment Watchdog: this component verifies the current state of the system and the boundaries of our problem. For this system, we defined some boundaries such as, human safety distance (minimum of 20 cm), restrict experiment in the case of low

---

[1] www.turtlebot.com.

[2] www.ros.org.

battery and deterioration of our business metrics, e.g. if the experiment is performing poorly (e.g. less than 30% of the cases) we roll back to the baseline variation.

Experiment Coordinator: this component is responsible for implementing traditional A/B experiments control and multi-armed bandit algorithms. We are using a heuristic algorithm for the k-armed bandit optimization problem.

Version Manager: the version manager component receives input from the experiment coordinator regarding which experiment is running. The version manager generates these versions either by static input (manual experiments) or by calling a learning component to generate it (e.g. calling the machine learning component).

Machine Learning: the version manager requests new versions to the machine learning component. This component uses the K-means clustering algorithm with the k-means++ initialization algorithm implemented in the scikit-learn Python library.

Effector: this component changes the system behavior using a parameter server, similar to remote configuration libraries for mobile development.

This system was evaluated against a user in an office environment. The baseline distance was 1.5 meters. The framework took 37 samples to converge to an optimal solution for a user (0.92 m). This solution can be then validated with traditional A/B experiments against the baseline variation (Fig. 2).

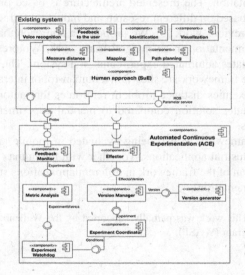

Fig. 2. Instantiation of the automated continuous experimentation framework in the human-robot proxemics distance problem.

4.2   Cost-Effectiveness

Kohavi [3] provides guidelines on a minimum number of samples when running A/B experiments. Using these guidelines, the optimization of the proxemics distance for one individual requires at least 96 samples for each variation (assuming a baseline of 50% with a minimum detectable effect of 20%, with a statistical power of ß = 80% and significance level of $\alpha = 95\%$) [3]. Considering a grid of 1 m per sample in a range of 1 m to 5 m, it results in 480 samples. Using the automated continuous experimentation framework, the system converged to a distance in 37 samples. Integrating this result with a traditional A/B experiment results in a total of 133 samples to achieve statistical validity in the optimization process. Although this result was not generalized, it already suggests a more effective way to run experiments.

5   Conclusion

Data-driven companies employ controlled experiments as an essential mechanism to evaluate ideas and optimize their systems [3, 5, 11, 12]. Research in this area emphasize the algorithms and building blocks for manual experimentation. However, as the number of experiments grows, organizations face challenges in both the scalability of their experiments as well as the complexity. Automated continuous experimentation addresses the problem of the ever-growing number of the R&D organization to support experimentation.

This research paper investigates different design solutions, the problem constraints and their implication in the development of an architecture framework to support automated experimentation. The presented architecture is based on decisions, evaluation and experiences based on different research and industrial frameworks as described in this paper and in previous work [8]. We propose an approach that combines manual and automated experimentation in an integral framework. We present an architecture framework that facilitates automated experiments in a system. The use and benefits of using this architecture framework are shown in a human-robot interaction problem. The evaluation in the proxemics distance problem reinforces that automated experimentation can lead to a better solution compared to manual experimentation while using fewer R&D resources.

Currently, this framework is also being evaluated in mobile and web systems, in both research and industrial applications. Together with the human proxemics distance problem, the evaluation of the framework in different applications strengths the benefits of automated experimentation.

Acknowledgements. This work was partially supported by the Wallenberg Autonomous Systems and Software Program (WASP).

References

1. Fabijan, A., Olsson, H.H., Bosch, J.: Time to say 'good bye': feature lifecycle. In: 2016 42th Euromicro Conference on Software Engineering and Advanced Applications (SEAA), pp. 9–16 (2016)
2. Olsson, H.H., Bosch, J.: From opinions to data-driven software R&D: a multi-case study on how to close the 'open loop' problem. In: Proceedings of 40th EUROMICRO Conference on Software Engineering and Advanced Applications (SEAA), SEAA 2014, pp. 9–16 (2014)
3. Kohavi, R., Longbotham, R., Sommerfield, D., Henne, R.M.: Controlled experiments on the web: survey and practical guide. Data Mining Knowl. Discov. **18**(1), 140–181 (2009)

 4. Fabijan, A., Dmitriev, P., Olsson, H.H., Bosch, J.: The evolution of continuous experimentation in software product development. In: Proceedings of the 39th International Conference on Software Engineering, ICSE 2017 (2017)
 5. Kohavi, R., Deng, A., Frasca, B., Walker, T., Xu, Y., Pohlmann, N.: Online controlled experiments at large scale. In: Proceedings of the 19th ACM SIGKDD international conference on Knowledge discovery and data mining - KDD 2013, p. 1168 (2013)
 6. Li, L., Chu, W., Langford, J., Schapire, R.E.: A contextual-bandit approach to personalized news article recommendation. WWW **2010**, 10 (2010)
 7. Bosch, J., Olsson, H.H.: Data-driven continuous evolution of smart systems. In: Proceedings of the 11th International Workshop on Software Engineering for Adaptive and Self-Managing Systems - SEAMS 2016, pp. 28–34 (2016)
 8. Mattos, D.I., Bosch, J., Olsson, H.H.: Your system gets better every day you use it: towards automated continuous experimentation. In: 2017 43th Euromicro Conference on Software Engineering and Advanced Applications (SEAA) (2017)
 9. Kohavi, R., Deng, A., Frasca, B., Walker, T.: Online controlled experiments at large scale. In: Proceedings of the 19th ACM SIGKDD international conference on Knowledge discovery and data mining, KDD 2013, pp. 1–9 (2013)
10. Jansen, A., Bosch, J.: Software architecture as a set of architectural design decisions. In: 5th Working IEEE/IFIP Conference on Software Architecture (WICSA 2005), vol. 2005, pp. 109–120 (2005)
11. Bakshy, E., Eckles, D., Bernstein, M.S.: Designing and deploying online field experiments. In: Proceedings of 23rd International Conference on World wide web - WWW 2014, pp. 283–292, September 2014
12. Tang, D., Agarwal, A., O'Brien, D., Meyer, M.: Overlapping experiment infrastructure. In: Proceedings of the 16th ACM SIGKDD International Conference on Knowledge Discovery and Data Mining - KDD 2010, p. 17 (2010)
13. Hevner, A.R., March, S.T., Park, J., Ram, S.: Design science in information systems research. MIS Q. **28**(1), 75–105 (2004)
14. Oskoei, M.A., Walters, M.L., Dautenhahn, K.: An autonomous proxemic system for a mobile companion robot. In: Proceedings of Second International Symposium on New Frontier Human-Robot Interaction, pp. 9–15, April 2010

Industry Relevant Qualitative Research

The Evolution of Design Pattern Grime: An Industrial Case Study

Daniel Feitosa[1](✉) ⓘ, Paris Avgeriou[1] ⓘ,
Apostolos Ampatzoglou[1] ⓘ, and Elisa Yumi Nakagawa[2]

[1] Department of Mathematics and Computer Science, University of Groningen,
Groningen, The Netherlands
{d.feitosa, a.ampatzoglou}@rug.nl, paris@cs.rug.nl
[2] Department of Computer Systems, University of São Paulo, São Carlos, Brazil
elisa@icmc.usp.br

Abstract. *Context:* GoF design patterns are popular among both researchers and practitioners, in the sense that software can be largely comprised of pattern instances. However, there are concerns regarding the efficacy with which software engineers maintain pattern instances, which tend to decay over the software lifetime if no special emphasis is placed on them. Pattern grime (i.e., degradation of the instance due to buildup of unrelated artifacts) has been pointed out as one recurrent reason for the decay of GoF pattern instances. *Goal:* Seeking to explore this issue, we investigate the existence of relations between the accumulation of grime in pattern instances and various related factors: (a) projects, (b) pattern types, (c) developers, and (d) the structural characteristics of the pattern participating classes. *Method:* For that, we empirically assessed these relations through an industrial exploratory case study involving five projects (approx. 260,000 lines of code). *Results:* Our findings suggest a linear accumulation of pattern grime, which may depend on pattern type and developer. Moreover, we present and discuss a series of correlations between the accumulation of pattern grime and structural characteristics. *Conclusions:* The outcome of our study can benefit both researchers and practitioners, as it points to interesting future work opportunities and also implications relevant to the refinement of best practices, the raise awareness among developers, and the monitoring of pattern grime accumulation.

Keywords: Design patterns · Pattern grime · Industrial case study

1 Introduction

The most popular catalogue of design patterns among practitioners consists of the 23 GoF design patterns (from the Gang of Four—Gamma, Johnson, Helm, and Vlissides) [1]. In Java applications, it has been reported that the number of classes that participate in GoF pattern occurrences can vary from 15% to 65% (e.g., in software libraries) [2, 3], leading to a significant influence on the overall quality of the system. However, the effect of patterns on quality is not uniform [4]; the same pattern can have both a positive and a negative effect on the quality of a software product. Therefore, gaining more

© Springer International Publishing AG 2017
M. Felderer et al. (Eds.): PROFES 2017, LNCS 10611, pp. 165–181, 2017.
https://doi.org/10.1007/978-3-319-69926-4_13

insights on how exactly patterns have an impact on quality is of paramount importance. A significant parameter that determines how pattern instances affect quality is the amount of artifacts (e.g., methods and attributes) that exist in the pattern-participant classes, which however, are not compliant to the original pattern definition [5]. Izurieta and Bieman [5] named this phenomenon **pattern grime** and defined it as *the degradation of design pattern instance due to buildup of unrelated artifacts in pattern instances*. For example, grime can be introduced to a Template Method pattern instance by adding public methods that are not invoked inside the template method. Similarly, grime is introduced to a concrete state class of a State pattern instantiation when adding public methods other than those defined in the state interface. For both the aforementioned examples, such changes would lead to a reduced cohesion for the specific class, as well as reduced levels of source code understanding. Thus, the accumulation of grime can certainly be harmful to the quality of pattern instances and the overall system [5–7].

Despite the potential effect of pattern grime on software quality, there is currently a lack of studies that investigate factors related to the accumulation of pattern grime. Therefore, in this study, we take a first step by exploring two types of factors related to the accumulation of pattern grime, i.e., different: *projects, pattern types, developers*, and *structural characteristics of pattern-participating classes* (e.g., coupling and lack of cohesion). To this end, we performed an industrial case study, in which we analyzed five projects (that sum up to approx. 260,000 source lines of code) containing eight different GoF pattern types and implemented by 16 developers. To measure grime, we provide an open-source tool that automates the assessment of several pattern grime metrics. The outcome of this study sheds light on the factors that influence the accumulation of grime in pattern instances. Our results can be used by architects and designers to develop best practices while using design patterns, but also to monitor the evolution of grime and its respective effect on software quality.

The remainder of this paper is organized as follows. In Sect. 2, we present work related to ours. The design of the case study is presented in Sect. 3, reported according to the guidelines of Runeson et al. [8], i.e., the Linear Analytic Structure. In Sects. 4 and 5 we present the results of our study and discuss the most important findings, respectively. We report on the identified threats to validity and actions taken to mitigate them in Sect. 6. Finally, in Sect. 7 we conclude the paper and present some interesting extensions for this study.

2 Related Work

In this section, we present work reporting on empirical studies on the evolution of grime and/or its relation to other characteristics of software pattern instances (e.g., quality attributes and metrics).

Izurieta and Bieman [9] investigated the evolution of various design pattern instances from an open-source project to understand how patterns decay. The results suggest that the main reason for pattern instances to decay is due to grime. Schanz and Izurieta [10] proposed a taxonomy for subtypes of modular grime (one type of grime) and performed a pilot study on nine pattern instances evolving throughout eight versions of one industrial software. The study validated the proposed classification, as well as suggested an increase of pattern grime. Regarding how the accumulation of grime correlates to other characteristics of the system, Griffith and Izurieta [11] proposed a taxonomy for one type of grime, class grime, and performed a pilot study on randomly selected pattern instances from open-source projects to investigate the effects of class grime on design pattern understandability, and found this quality attribute to be negatively affected by the accumulation of class grime. In another study, Izurieta and Bieman [6] evaluated the testability of design pattern instances from three different patterns and found that as grime is accumulated, other issues such as code smells also appears, and the testability of the pattern instances decreases.

Izurieta and Bieman [5] studied the accumulation of grime and rot (another form of pattern decay, due to deterioration of the structural or functional integrity) during the evolution of pattern instances of three open-source systems. The study also correlated grime to testability, adaptability and pattern instability. The results are similar to those observed in the aforementioned studies, including increase of pattern grime and negative correlation with testability and adaptability. The authors also reported that they could not identify rot of pattern instances nor correlation between grime and pattern instability. Dale and Izurieta [7] reported an experiment to study the correlation between three subtypes of modular grime and technical debt. Pattern instances of three example systems were used and modular grime was systematically injected in the instances. The results suggest that one subtype of modular grime (i.e., strength) is more strongly correlated to technical debt, in the sense that strong coupling (through class attributes) is correlated with stable grime, while weak coupling (other kinds of coupling) is correlated to increased technical debt.

In comparison to related work, we contribute the following: (a) we studied five industrial non-trivial projects that collectively provided 36,571 units of analysis (i.e., editions to pattern instances' source code, see Sect. 3). Therefore, we can compare our results with those obtained from the analysis of open-source projects and toy examples; (b) among other facets, we investigated how pattern grime is accumulated by different developers (16 in total), which has not been considered in previous studies; and (c) we studied the correlation between pattern grime and multiple structural metrics of pattern instances, which has not been thoroughly explored in previous studies.

3   Study Design

Objectives and Research Questions (RQs): The goal of this study, described using the Goal-Question-Metric (GQM) approach [12], is formulated as follows: "*analyze* instances of GoF design patterns *for the purpose of* investigating the factors of project, pattern type, developers and structural characteristics of pattern participants *with respect to* their relationship with pattern grime, *from the point of view of* software designers *in the context of* industrial software development". Based on this goal, we defined the following research questions—RQs:

> **RQ₁: How does grime accumulate in pattern instances?**
> **RQ_{1.1}: Are there differences in accumulated grime among different projects?**
> **RQ_{1.2}: Are there differences in accumulated grime among different pattern types?**
> **RQ_{1.3}: Are there differences in accumulated grime among different developers?**

RQ₁ aims at assessing pattern grime within the five projects and exploring differences across three different factors: projects, types of pattern (e.g., Observer, Template Method) and developers. We chose these factors as they may potentially influence the accumulation of grime: the projects vary in requirements, design, size, scope etc. and may thus influence grime accumulation; the types of patterns exhibit different solutions and may allow or inhibit the accumulation of grime; the developers have diverse backgrounds and experience thus knowingly or inadvertently accumulating grime differently.

> **RQ₂: Are structural characteristics of the pattern participants related to the accumulation of grime?**

RQ₂ aims at investigating the relationship between levels of grime and a different type of factor: the structural characteristics of pattern-participating classes. This helps to further understand the details of how the structure of the pattern itself relates to accumulating grime, and can thus inform best practices on the usage of design patterns.

Case Selection, Unit of Analysis, and Subjects: To answer the research questions, we designed an exploratory case study [8], in which we analyze five industrial projects from one company in the domain of web and mobile applications development. Two projects were developed by two independent teams, whereas the remaining three projects were developed by a third team. We selected an industrial case study, since there is a lack of empirical studies on pattern grime for such projects; *most of the previous studies have been performed on toy examples or open-source projects.*

As cases, we used the pattern instances of the explored projects. From each case, we recorded multiple units of analysis, based on the evolution of the specific instance. In particular, we recorded a unit of analysis for every change in the instance (i.e., pair of successive commits). We decided to focus on pairs of commits to *isolate and assess events (changes to pattern instances) performed by a single developer*. This allows to investigate developers as a potential factor influencing grime (see RQ1.3).

Variables and Data Collection: To answer the research questions, we extracted four groups of variables:

(1) *Identification of unit of analysis (commit, developer).* To identify every unit of analysis, we queried the git repository and extracted the author information and files that were changed for every commit. We ignored merge commits, as they do not provide new information regarding changes to files. In addition, we considered only changes to java classes that participate in a pattern instance.

(2) *Pattern information (instance-id, pattern).* The collection of the pattern instances is a time-consuming task. For that reason, we used two tools, namely SSA (Similarity Score Analysis, v4.12) [13] and SSA+ (v1.0.0), to detect pattern instances and performed a series of validations. In short, these tools allow us to detect pattern instances of 12 types: Adapter/Command, Composite, Decorator, Factory Method, Observer, Prototype, Singleton, State/Strategy, Template Method, and Visitor. Due to space limitations, we do not elaborate on the SSA tool nor its validation. However, we used a similar design setup to detect patterns in a previous study [14], in which all relevant information can be found. We note that we manually verified various (randomly selected) outputs. Regarding SSA+, it detects 10 extended pattern-participant classes, i.e., that participate in the pattern but it is not part of the main pattern structure (e.g., Concrete State/Strategy). The full list of detected extended pattern participants is available in the tool's website[1]. To validate SSA+, we also manually verified randomly selected outputs.

(3) *Assessment of grime change (cg-*, mg-*, og-*) between a pair of successive commits.* According to Izurieta and Bieman [9], there are three types of grime, which can be assessed independently: class, modular and organizational. To measure these types, we selected six metrics, as shown in Table 1. Each metric is estimated based on diverse design elements of pattern-participating classes: (a) class grime metrics are based on attributes and public methods; (b) modular grime metrics are based on incoming and outgoing dependencies; and (c) organization grime metrics are based on package and their dependencies. Due to space limitations, we do not elaborate further on the metrics, which are calculated as described by Izurieta and Bieman [9]. We chose these metrics because they allow us to assess different aspects of each type of grime, and they were previously used and validated to assess pattern grime in non-trivial systems [5]. To automate the calculation of the metrics, we created an open-source tool, *spoon-pttgrime*[2] (v0.1.0), available online as a public repository, which also contains further information on how the metrics are calculated. To validate the tool, we manually verified the output for 20 pattern instances (randomly selected) over five consecutive commits. Bugs were fixed and additional verification rounds showed no errors. As we are interested in assessing the change of grime in pattern instances for a pair of commits, we subtracted the grime estimation at the current commit (identified by the unit of analysis) from the estimation of the immediate previous commit (i.e., its parent).

(4) *Assessment of structural change (s-*) between a pair of successive commits.* To assess structural change, we selected three sets of metrics, proposed by Chidamber and Kemerer [15], Li and Henry [16], and Bansiya and Davis [17], accounting for the 21 metrics presented in Table 1. We selected these metrics because they allow us to investigate many characteristics of the structure of pattern participants, and because they are well-known by both researchers and practitioners. To calculate the metrics, we used Percerons Client, i.e., a tool developed in our research group

---

[1] https://github.com/search-rug/ssap.

[2] https://github.com/search-rug/spoon-pttgrime.

that automates the assessment of these metrics for Java classes. Percerons is a software engineering platform [18] to facilitate empirical research in software engineering and has been used for similar reasons in [11, 19].

Presented in Table 1, these variables are recorded for each unit of analysis (i.e., change to pattern instance). The entire process of identifying and measuring the units of analysis culminates in the creation of a dataset of all extracted variables for each unit. This dataset is recorded as a table in which the columns correspond to collected variables. We clarify that due to a non-disclosure agreement signed with the company in this case study we cannot share the created dataset.

Analysis Procedure: To answer RQ_1, we analyze the descriptive statistics of the variables for unit identification, pattern information, and assessment of grime change. As our study comprises several projects/subjects and encompasses several GoF patterns, we derive data subsets, so as to group the units of analysis based on the different analyzed factors (i.e., project, pattern and developer). When necessary we also perform linear regressions and parametric or non-parametric tests [20] in order to devise trends and test differences between groups. To answer RQ_2, we first analyze whether the distribution of all measurements for each metric is normally distributed. If true, we can select the Pearson correlation method [20], otherwise the Spearman's rank correlation method [20]. For each pattern grime metric, we perform the analysis as follows: first we calculate the correlation between the grime metric and all structural metrics; next, we identify strong correlations (>0.8) that are statistically significant, and discuss the results from the perspective of grime accumulation.

Table 1. List of collected variables

Group	Variable	Description
Unit information	project	Project from which the pattern instance was extracted
	commit	Hash of the commit in the git repository
	dev	Developer author of the commit
Pattern information	inst_id	ID of the pattern instance the class belongs to
	pattern	GoF design pattern of the instance
Assessment of grime change	cg-npm	Difference in the total number of alien public methods in all classes of the pattern instance (Class grime)
	cg-na	Difference in the total number of alien attributes in all classes of the pattern instance (Class grime)
	mg-ca	Difference in the pattern instance afferent coupling (Modular grime)
	mg-ce	Difference in the pattern instance efferent coupling (Modular grime)
	og-np	Difference in the number of packages within the pattern instance (Organizational grime)
	og-ca	Difference in the fan-in at the package level (Organizational grime)

(*continued*)

Table 1. (*continued*)

Group	Variable	Description
Assessment of structural change	s-wmc	Difference in the average weighted methods per class
	s-dit	Difference in the maximum depth of inheritance tree
	s-noc	Difference in the average number of children
	s-cbo	Difference in the average coupling between object classes
	s-rfc	Difference in the average response for a class
	s-lcom	Difference in the average lack of cohesion in methods
	s-nom	Difference in the average number of methods
	s-mpc	Difference in the average message-passing coupling
	s-dac	Difference in the average data abstraction coupling
	s-size1	Difference in the lines of code
	s-size2	Difference in the number of properties
	s-dsc	Difference in the design size in classes
	s-noh	Difference in the number of hierarchies
	s-ana	Difference in the average number of ancestors
	s-dam	Difference in the data access metric
	s-camc	Difference in the cohesion among methods of class
	s-moa	Difference in the measure of aggregation
	s-mfa	Difference in the measure of functional abstraction
	s-nop	Difference in the number of polymorphic methods
	s-cis	Difference in the class interface size
	s-fan-in	Difference in the afferent couplings

4 Results

In this section, first we briefly describe the collected data and subsequently address each research question independently. We note that we investigated six metrics for pattern grime, and therefore report the results for all metrics and highlight findings independently for each one, when this is relevant. We collected a total of 1,422 commits, from the five studied projects, that include the creation or modification of pattern-participating classes. From these commits, 94% (i.e., 1,341) include modifications to one or more pattern instances. We identified 2,349 pattern instances of eight different GoF patterns: (Object) Adapter-Command, Factory Method, Observer, Singleton, State-Strategy, and Template Method. Each pattern instance was created and then modified up to 178 times (i.e., the maximum number of modifications for a single instance). From the total number of pattern instances, 87% (i.e., 2,039) were modified at least once after being created, and 64% (i.e., 1,500) at least five times. The data collection resulted in the identification of 36,571 units of analysis (i.e., creation/modification of a pattern instance in a commit).

RQ1 - Accumulation of Grime: To study the differences. in accumulated grime among different projects, types of patterns and developers, we first present how the assessed pattern grime metrics change within the instances' evolution. Table 2 shows the following descriptive statistics for the six metrics (previously presented in Table 1): minimum and maximum values, mean value among all units of analysis and standard deviation (i.e., how much measurements vary from the mean value). Based on the Table 2, we notice that grime can either reduce (i.e., negative measurement) or increase. However, the data suggest that on average, grime in pattern instances tends to increase during the instance's evolution. Another observation is that the number of packages in a pattern instance (og-np) seems to be the grime indicator that is less likely to change, which is a probable sign of common design practices. Moreover, despite considerably higher maximum values, we notice that the measurements are consistently close to the mean, since the standard deviation is not much higher than the mean (especially compared to maximum values).

Table 2. Amount of grime accumulated per commit

Metric	Minimum	Maximum	Mean	Std. deviation
cg-npm	−1.00	15.00	0.28	0.64
cg-na	−1.50	9.50	0.12	0.45
mg-ca	−3.75	44.00	0.21	1.18
mg-ce	−10.00	85.00	1.61	4.53
og-np	−0.25	2.00	0.02	0.14
og-ca	−2.00	35.00	0.14	1.13

Next, we are interested in investigating how grime accumulated in different projects ($RQ_{1.1}$). Figure 1 depicts this information for the six metrics. P1 is the project with most collected commits (605), while P5 provided the least commits (76). The y-axis represents the mean amount of grime accumulated per modified instance in a given commit. The x-axis represents consecutive commits. We note that the x-axis does not represent the full history of commits. Our goal is to investigate the evolution of pattern instances and, thus, we considered only commits that include the modification of pattern-participant classes. By inspecting Fig. 1, we observe that every project individually reflects the trend of the population, i.e., pattern grime linearly increases during the project evolution. To verify this, we performed linear regression for every pair *<metric, project>* and assessed how well the calculated equation fits the data.

In Table 3, we present the results, which are all statistically significant. We notice that the vast majority of the equations are powerful descriptors, since R^2 (i.e., how close the data fit the regression line) is close to 1. The exceptions are the tuples *<og-np, P1>* , *<og-np, P5>* , and *<og-ca, P5>* , which regard metrics of organization grime. This is due to the drastic change in the accumulated grime observed for these tuples, which may reflect systematic changes in the design (e.g., package renaming).

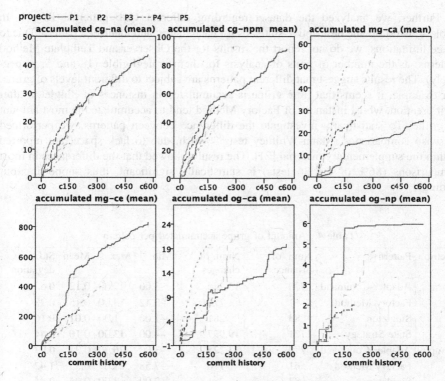

Fig. 1. Accumulation of grime per project for each grime metric

Table 3. Linear regression of pattern grime accumulation per project

Metric	Project	Equation	R^2	Metric	Project	Equation	R^2
cg-npm	P1	13.91 + 0.15x	0.91	cg-na	P1	5.47 + 0.07x	0.93
	P2	−0.28 + 0.19x	0.99		P2	−0.59 + 0.08x	0.92
	P3	−1.79 + 0.24x	0.99		P3	−0.51 + 0.11x	0.99
	P4	7.44 + 0.24x	0.95		P4	1.89 + 0.13x	0.95
	P5	5.32 + 0.37x	0.95		P5	3.44 + 0.17x	0.89
mg-ca	P1	2.27 + 0.04x	0.90	mg-ce	P1	129.84 + 1.40x	0.89
	P2	−1.72 + 0.34x	0.99		P2	−9.04 + 1.00x	0.99
	P3	−2.24 + 0.17x	0.93		P3	−15.42 + 1.34x	0.99
	P4	5.68 + 0.11x	0.92		P4	15.36 + 1.21x	0.96
	P5	0.71 + 0.04x	0.87		P5	26.47 + 1.20x	0.89
og-np	P1	2.00 + 0.01x	0.58	og-ca	P1	1.09 + 0.03x	0.92
	P2	−0.06 + 0.00x	0.82		P2	3.11 + 0.12x	0.95
	P3	−0.20 + 0.02x	0.96		P3	−3.86 + 0.08x	0.90
	P4	−0.02 + 0.01x	0.89		P4	2.61 + 0.03x	0.81
	P5	0.12 + 0.01x	0.61		P5	1.04 + 0.00x	0.64

Further, we analyzed the dataset regarding different GoF patterns ($RQ_{1.2}$). In Table 4, we show the descriptive statistics for each metric and identified pattern. Due to space limitations, we do not report the results for the Observer and Template Method patterns, as the number of units of analysis for them is negligible (18 and 5, respectively). The results suggest that different patterns are subject to different levels of grime. For example, it seems that little grime is accumulated in instances of Singleton after their creation, whilst instances of Factory Method tend to accumulate the most amount of grime. To statistically investigate the difference between patterns, we performed pairwise comparisons (Mann-Whitney tests), which, due to lack space, are reported within the supplementary material [21]. The results showed that the differences in most comparisons (86% of the 36 tests) is statistically significant, thus supporting our findings.

Table 4. Amount of grime accumulated per pattern

Metric	Pattern	Num. of instances	Num. of changes	Min.	Max.	Mean	Std. deviation
cg-na	Adapter-Command	770	13,225	−3.00	17.00	0.12	0.53
	Factory Method	61	776	−3.42	13.00	0.15	0.78
	Singleton	83	281	−1.00	1.00	0.01	0.16
	State-Strategy	1121	19,937	−4.00	13.00	0.10	0.44
cg-npm	Adapter-Command	770	13,225	−3.00	26.00	0.21	0.77
	Factory Method	61	776	−7.58	21.67	0.35	1.42
	Singleton	83	281	−2.00	4.00	0.06	0.44
	State-Strategy	1121	19,937	−8.00	21.33	0.21	0.80
mg-ca	Adapter-Command	770	13,225	−2.00	44.00	0.08	0.89
	Factory Method	61	776	−7.00	102.00	0.59	4.15
	Singleton	83	281	−1.00	7.00	0.49	0.96
	State-Strategy	1121	19,937	−15.00	44.00	0.12	0.87
mg-ce	Adapter-Command	770	13,225	−20.00	197.00	1.19	5.60
	Factory Method	61	776	−13.00	60.00	1.44	4.40
	Singleton	83	281	−4.00	17.00	0.47	1.85
	State-Strategy	1121	19,937	−30.00	159.00	1.23	5.66
og-ca	Adapter-Command	770	13,225	−2.00	35.00	0.06	0.75
	Factory Method	61	776	−36.00	36.00	0.17	2.32
	Singleton	83	281	−1.00	27.00	0.41	2.19
	State-Strategy	1121	19,937	−6.00	34.00	0.06	0.62
og-np	Adapter-Command	770	13,225	0.00	2.00	0.01	0.13
	Factory Method	61	776	−1.00	3.00	0.03	0.21
	Singleton	83	281	0.00	1.00	0.01	0.10
	State-Strategy	1121	19,937	−1.00	3.00	0.01	0.15

The last facet we investigated was how different developers accumulate grime ($RQ_{1.3}$). Due to space limitations, we do not report the complete descriptive statistics for each metric and developer, which are available within the supplementary material [21]. In Table 5, we present the number of pattern instances maintained by the 16 developers, changes to pattern instances and mean value of the grime metrics. By analyzing the results, we notice that some developers seem to consistently accumulate more grime than others (e.g., D7, D8 and D9), or less grime than others (e.g., D1 and D3), with respect to most metrics. Furthermore, we can observe that developers that changed pattern instances more often tend to accumulate less grime. Seeking to support our observations statistically, we compared pairs of developers based on every metric using the Mann-Whitney test. By observing the findings of the test, we suggest that 73% of the 396 tests are statistically significant, and that the non-significant tests regard mostly the number of packages (og-np). Due to lack space, detailed results are reported on the supplementary material [21].

Table 5. Average amount of grime accumulated per developer

Developer	Num. of instances	Num. of changes	cg-na	cg-npm	mg-ca	mg-ce	og-ca	og-np
D1	465	7,525	0.08	0.17	0.04	0.93	0.04	0.00
D2	1,132	6,232	0.12	0.34	0.20	1.25	0.05	0.00
D3	549	5,232	0.07	0.07	0.04	0.85	0.01	0.00
D4	837	5,141	0.10	0.14	0.13	0.96	0.04	0.01
D5	335	3,442	0.10	0.23	0.04	1.35	0.02	0.02
D6	469	1,554	0.13	0.24	0.14	2.28	0.24	0.00
D7	292	1,406	0.17	0.29	0.23	2.54	0.19	0.05
D8	326	1,346	0.20	0.26	0.21	1.72	0.18	0.02
D9	161	697	0.13	0.38	0.27	1.68	0.20	0.02
D10	225	636	0.07	0.37	0.24	1.05	0.27	0.01
D11	233	515	0.01	0.19	0.34	0.37	0.06	0.00
D12	170	431	0.23	0.28	0.06	1.89	0.00	0.00
D13	41	56	0.79	1.64	0.89	8.04	0.29	0.21
D14	13	17	0.00	0.00	0.00	2.06	0.00	0.00
D15	3	8	0.00	0.03	−0.25	0.00	0.38	0.00
D16	2	4	0.00	0.00	0.00	0.75	0.00	0.00

Summarizing the results for RQ_1, pattern grime: (a) *is likely to increase linearly over system evolution*; (b) *grows similarly across different projects*; (c) *accumulates at different paces depending on the pattern type and the individual developer*. The interpretation of all findings reported in this section, as well as their implications to researchers and practitioners are discussed in Sect. 5.

RQ2 - Structural Characteristics and Pattern Grime: To assess the correlation between pattern grime and structural metrics, we first verified whether all measurements for each metric are normally distributed. We found that not all are normally distributed and, thus, we decided to use a non-parametric method to study the metrics: Spearman's rank correlation. All assessed correlations are presented in Table 6, and are all statistically significant.

Table 6. Correlation between grime and structural metrics

	cg-npm	cg-na	mg-ca	mg-ce	og-np	og-ca
s-wmc	*0.86*	0.44	0.38	0.48	0.46	0.38
s-dit	0.44	0.53	0.55	0.43	*0.99*	0.71
s-noc	0.45	0.52	0.60	0.41	*0.99*	0.73
s-cbo	0.47	0.67	0.50	0.73	0.46	0.41
s-rfc	0.65	0.54	0.31	0.65	0.41	0.33
s-lcom	0.70	0.35	0.32	0.36	0.35	0.31
s-nom	*0.86*	0.44	0.38	0.48	0.46	0.38
s-mpc	0.43	0.44	0.22	0.55	0.35	0.27
s-dac	0.36	*0.87*	0.34	0.59	0.56	0.42
s-size1	0.69	0.53	0.31	0.58	0.41	0.35
s-size2	0.79	0.65	0.38	0.58	0.44	0.38
s-dsc	0.44	0.53	0.56	0.43	*0.99*	0.70
s-noh	0.38	0.43	0.50	0.35	0.77	0.60
s-ana	0.45	0.53	0.51	0.43	*0.93*	0.66
s-dam	0.34	0.56	0.42	0.43	0.76	0.54
s-camc	−0.14	0.16	0.17	0.03	0.45	0.30
s-moa	0.37	*0.90*	0.36	0.61	0.58	0.44
s-mfa	0.03	0.11	0.03	0.08	0.21	0.07
s-nop	0.71	0.35	0.48	0.34	0.51	0.43
s-cis	*0.97*	0.41	0.41	0.44	0.48	0.41
s-fan-in	0.46	0.42	*0.90*	0.36	0.70	0.63

Regarding the metrics for *class grime*, we make the following observations. The metric cg-npm is strongly correlated (>0.8) to s-wmc, s-nom, and s-cis. This may be an indication that when many methods are added to pattern-related classes it is common that a large portion of them are not related to the pattern realization. The metric cg-na is strongly correlated to s-dac and s-moa. This may be an indication that a considerable part of the pattern instance coupling is coming from added attributes. This may not be necessarily an alert for bad design, but it rather depends on how many attributes are added. Regarding *modular grime*, we notice that the metric mg-ca is strongly correlated to s-fan-in only, which is a metric that is similar to mg-ca, but at class level. This suggests that most of the pattern instance afferent coupling comes from regular afferent coupling of the pattern participants. This may indicate that pattern instances tend to evolve by adding functionality not related to the pattern. The metric mg-ce is not strongly correlated to any metrics, whereas the strongest correlations are with s-rfc and s-cbo. These moderate correlations also indicate that, to some extent, the introduction of coupling in pattern instances is also introducing grime. Finally, regarding *organizational grime*, the metric og-np is strongly correlated to s-dit, s-noc, s-dsc, and s-ana. Despite the strong correlations, this finding may be inconclusive as og-np rarely changes and this is probably the main reason for such high correlations. Finally, the metric og-ca is not strongly correlated to any metrics, whereas the strongest correlations are with s-noc, s-dit and s-dsc. These moderate correlations may indicate that, to some extent, the addition of new classes to the pattern instance is to serve a new purpose, i.e., serve a class not served before.

5 Discussion

In this section, we discuss the findings of our case study, as well as their implications. First, we interpret our findings, elaborating on explanations and consequences for the observed results. Next, we present how our findings can benefit both researchers and practitioners.

Interpretation of Results: In Sect. 4, we reported the raw findings of our case study, whereas in this section, we interpret them and compare them against the state-of-the-art. First, regarding the evolution of grime, we observed that *pattern grime is constantly increasing along the versions of a system*. This result can be considered intuitive as it aligns with Lehman's laws on software evolution: software quality deteriorates as the software becomes larger and more complex. However, there is an interesting aspect of this finding: the amount of grime that is accumulated in pattern instances clearly suggests that pattern-participating classes are not "closed to modifications", in the sense that they are continuously "polluted" with artifacts (e.g., methods, dependencies, etc.) that are not pattern-related. This pollution potentially influences how the application of design patterns affects quality attribute indicators of a system. Thus, pattern instantiation does not have a constant effect on quality, but it changes along evolution. This finding is in accordance to the literature, which suggests that the effect of GoF design patterns on product quality is not uniform along different pattern instances [4], and aligns with results of studies with similar setups [5–7]. In particular, Izurieta and Bieman [5] used the same pattern grime metrics and investigated some patterns in common (e.g., Singleton and Factory Method), but by inspecting open-source systems. The results of both studies agree on the increase of grime metrics.

Regarding the three parameters that were investigated in RQ_1 (i.e., grime in different projects, patterns, and developers), the results suggested that *the levels of grime are similar at the different projects of the same company despite the little overlap of developers among projects*. This outcome can be potentially explained by the fact that the developers were guided by the same practices, since they usually follow the same company process. Nevertheless, this finding needs to be further validated through a follow-up study conducted in different companies. Another finding is that *the levels of grime are different among pattern types*, which complies with the literature suggesting that different patterns have different effect on quality attributes (e.g., [3] on stability).

In particular, we noticed that instances of the Singleton pattern are the least likely to accumulate grime, whereas instances of Factory Method are the most grime-prone. The acknowledgement of certain good practices (e.g., avoid creation of God Classes) can lead to more "grime-free" Singleton instances. However, if not careful, developers may enlarge the responsibility of classes unnecessarily, as observed with Factory Method instances, which may include methods that suffer from the Feature Envy, Shotgun Surgery, or Divergent Change smells. Therefore, *we suggest monitoring pattern grime to identify spots of bad quality in the system*. Such a practice may support the preservation of quality indicators (such as understandability and testability) at acceptable levels and thus increase productivity. Moreover, in comparison with related work, Izurieta and Bieman [5] also show that Singleton pattern instances tend to accumulate less grime, whereas on the contrary Factory Method instances tend to accumulate grime faster than other investigated patterns. This observation further supports that open-source and industrial systems have similarities with regards to the accumulation of pattern grime.

From the last investigated parameter, we found that *the levels of grime also differ among developers*. Their tendency to accumulate grime likely depends on diverse factors. In particular, varied levels of programming skills, knowledge of the system and of GoF patterns can explain the different tendency to accumulate grime. This finding supports the belief that personalized quality assessments are required in industry [22]. Furthermore, we observed that developers that performed more changes are related to lower levels of accumulated grime, suggesting that most tasks (resulting in more changes) are assigned to more experienced developers, inclined to accumulate less grime. *We suggest using such information about developers in order to improve the software development process*. For example, since our industrial partner use agile methodologies, such information can be considered in daily Scrum meetings in which issues are assigned to individual developers. The personalization of software development and the effect on human factors in the quality of the software have been extensively studied in the last years, underlying the importance of such strategies.

Finally, regarding the relation of structural metrics with grime metrics, the results point out that some of the most established structural quality metrics are related to the grime metrics. For example, the fan-in metric is at least moderately correlated to all grime metrics. This finding may be explained by the fact that pattern grime is calculated at the detailed-design level. Since class dependencies consist one of the main elements of object-oriented design, it is intuitive to expect the obtained correlations, e.g., between two metrics that are calculated based on class dependencies. However, we note that the strength of the correlations varies among pattern instances, which shows that structural metrics can be adequate predictors of grime accumulation.

Implications to Researchers and Practitioners: *Researchers* can benefit from our results from several perspectives. We presented a thorough exploration of the accumulation of pattern grime and we identified several factors that influence how pattern grime grows during the evolution of pattern instances. This exploration not only reinforces the importance of investigating pattern grime, but also suggests several opportunities of future work, e.g., investigate characteristics of developers that tend to accumulate grime. In addition, the identified correlations between pattern grime and structural metrics help on understanding how pattern grime is introduced, as well as open further possibilities to investigate other relevant aspects of software systems and processes, for example technical debt. We also foresee benefits of our results to *practitioners*. Because we investigated five non-trivial projects, our findings can help practitioners improve best practices on the usage of design patterns, e.g., by warning developers to avoid accumulating grime on Singletons pattern instances. Moreover, the metrics and correlations that we present can be considered in processes for monitoring the evolution of the software systems, e.g., high levels of fan-in in pattern-participating classes may indicate that considerable grime is being inserted.

6 Threats to Validity

In this section, we discuss threats to construct validity (i.e., if the studied phenomenon is connected to the set objectives), reliability (if the study can be replicated), and external validity (i.e., generalizability). We do not analyze internal validity, as we do not try to establish causal relationships.

Concerning construct validity, the tool SSA is limited by its precision and recall: false positives and negatives may bias the presented results. However, to the best of our knowledge the used tool is among the most reputed in the community, and has adequate performance (see Sect. 3). For mitigating this threat, we verified its precision and recall manually by checking 30 random pattern instances for each GoF pattern that was detected (i.e., over 100 instances in total), which were all successful. Additionally, regarding SSA+ and spoon-pttgrime, we acknowledge that the tools may have bugs. However, we verified over 50 random outputs of each tool and, to the best of our knowledge, no bugs were found.

In order to mitigate reliability threats, two different researchers performed the collection and analysis, double-checking sample outputs. Besides that, we acknowledge that non-disclosure agreements do not allow us to share the collected dataset. However, all used tools are freely available and replication studies can be carried out. Finally, the external validity of our study is threatened by the fact that we analyzed projects of the same company, thus, our findings may not be generalizable to other projects nor teams. However, our results relate to those obtained in other studies with similar setup, e.g., we expected modular grime to be the main contributor for the pattern grime, and we found mg-ce to clearly grow at a faster pace. In addition, our results are bounded by our study design. Adding other GoF patterns, pattern grime metrics, or structural metrics could lead to adjustments in our findings.

7 Conclusion

In this paper, we presented an exploratory case study on how grime accumulates in pattern instances and its correlation to structural characteristics of the pattern participants. To this end, we investigated the evolution of 2,349 pattern instances of eight patterns, assessing six grime metrics of three types of grime (class, modular and organization), as well as 21 structural metrics. We explored how grime is distributed according to: (a) projects, pattern types, and developers, and (b) structural characteristics of pattern-participating classes. The results suggest that pattern grime tends to increase linearly, it is likely independent of project but depends on pattern type and developer. Moreover, we identified a series of correlations between metrics for pattern grime and structural characteristics, e.g., the coupling added to pattern participants tend to also introduce grime. Based on our results and observations, we envisage several opportunities for future work. First, some of the investigated facets on how pattern grime accumulates can and should be further explored, e.g., what factors may be related to developers that tend to accumulate more or less grime. Furthermore, our observations based on the correlation between pattern grime and structural metrics raised questions that can be investigated in confirmatory studies, e.g., whether most introduced afferent coupling is indeed resulting in the accumulation of grime.

Acknowledgements. The authors would like to thank the financial support from the Brazilian and Dutch agencies CAPES/Nuffic (Grant No.: 034/12), CNPq (Grant No.: 204607/2013-2), as well as INCT-SEC (Grant No.: 573963/2008-8 and 2008/57870-9).

References

1. Gamma, E., Helm, R., Johnson, R.E., Vlissides, J.: Design Patterns: Elements of Reusable Object-Oriented Software. Addison-Wesley Longman Publishing Co., Inc., Boston (1995)
2. Khomh, F., Gueheneuc, Y.-G., Antoniol, G.: Playing roles in design patterns: an empirical descriptive and analytic study. In: 25th IEEE International Conference on Software Maintenance, pp. 83–92. IEEE (2009)
3. Ampatzoglou, A., Chatzigeorgiou, A., Charalampidou, S., Avgeriou, P.: The effect of GoF design patterns on stability: a case study. IEEE Trans. Softw. Eng. **41**, 781–802 (2015)
4. Ampatzoglou, A., Charalampidou, S., Stamelos, I.: Research state of the art on GoF design patterns: a mapping study. J. Syst. Softw. **86**, 1945–1964 (2013)
5. Izurieta, C., Bieman, J.M.: A multiple case study of design pattern decay, grime, and rot in evolving software systems. Softw. Qual. J. **21**, 289–323 (2013)
6. Izurieta, C., Bieman, J.M.: Testing consequences of grime buildup in object oriented design patterns. In: First International Conference on Software Testing, Verification, and Validation, pp. 171–179. IEEE (2008)
7. Dale, M.R., Izurieta, C.: Impacts of design pattern decay on system quality. In: Eighth ACM/IEEE International Symposium on Empirical Software Engineering and Measurement, pp. 1–4. ACM Press, New York (2014)
8. Runeson, P., Host, M., Rainer, A., Regnell, B.: Case Study Research in Software Engineering: Guidelines and Examples. Wiley Blackwell, Hoboken (2012)
9. Izurieta, C., Bieman, J.M.: How software designs decay: a pilot study of pattern evolution. In: First International Symposium on Empirical Software Engineering and Measurement, pp. 449–451. IEEE (2007)
10. Schanz, T., Izurieta, C.: Object oriented design pattern decay. In: Fourth ACM/IEEE International Symposium on Empirical Software Engineering and Measurement, pp. 1–8. ACM Press, New York (2010)
11. Griffith, I., Izurieta, C.: Design pattern decay: the case for class grime. In: Eighth ACM/IEEE International Symposium on Empirical Software Engineering and Measurement, pp. 1–4. ACM Press, New York (2014)

12. Basili, V.R., Caldiera, G., Rombach, H.D.: Goal question metric paradigm. In: Encyclopedia of Software Engineering, pp. 528–532. Wiley (1994)
13. Tsantalis, N., Chatzigeorgiou, A., Stephanides, G., Halkidis, S.T.: Design pattern detection using similarity scoring. Softw. Eng. IEEE Trans. **32**, 896–909 (2006)
14. Feitosa, D., Alders, R., Ampatzoglou, A., Avgeriou, P., Nakagawa, E.Y.: Investigating the effect of design patterns on energy consumption. J. Softw. Evol. Process. **29**, e1851 (2017)
15. Chidamber, S.R., Kemerer, C.F.: A metrics suite for object oriented design. IEEE Trans. Softw. Eng. **20**, 476–493 (1994)
16. Li, W., Henry, S.: Object-oriented metrics that predict maintainability. J. Syst. Softw. **23**, 111–122 (1993)
17. Bansiya, J., Davis, C.G.: A hierarchical model for object-oriented design quality assessment. IEEE Trans. Softw. Eng. **28**, 4–17 (2002)
18. Ampatzoglou, A., Michou, O., Stamelos, I.: Building and mining a repository of design pattern instances: practical and research benefits. Entertain. Comput. **4**, 131–142 (2013)
19. Alhusain, S., Coupland, S., John, R., Kavanagh, M.: Towards machine learning based design pattern recognition. In: 13th UK Workshop on Computational Intelligence, pp. 244–251. IEEE (2013)
20. Field, A.: Discovering Statistics Using SPSS. SAGE Publications Ltd., Thousand Oaks (2009)
21. Feitosa, D., Avgeriou, P., Ampatzoglou, A., Nakagawa, E.Y.: Supplementary Material: "The Evolution of Design Pattern Grime: An Industrial Case Study." https://doi.org/10.5281/zenodo.806800
22. Amanatidis, T., Chatzigeorgiou, A., Ampatzoglou, A., Stamelos, I.: Who is producing more technical debt? A personalized assessment of TD principal. In: Nineth International Workshop on Managing Technical Debt, pp. 1–8. ACM (2017)

Should I Stay or Should I Go?

On Forces that Drive and Prevent MBSE Adoption in the Embedded Systems Industry

Andreas Vogelsang[1]([✉]), Tiago Amorim[1], Florian Pudlitz[1], Peter Gersing[2], and Jan Philipps[3]

[1] Technische Universität Berlin, Berlin, Germany
{andreas.vogelsang,buarquedeamorim,florian.pudlitz}@tu-berlin.de
[2] GPP Communication GmbH & Co. KG, Munich, Germany
p.gersing@gppag.de
[3] foqee GmbH, Munich, Germany
philipps@foqee.de

Abstract. [Context] Model-based Systems Engineering (MBSE) comprises a set of models and techniques that is often suggested as solution to cope with the challenges of engineering complex systems. Although many practitioners agree with the arguments on the potential benefits of the techniques, companies struggle with the adoption of MBSE. [Goal] In this paper, we investigate the forces that prevent or impede the adoption of MBSE in companies that develop embedded software systems. We contrast the hindering forces with issues and challenges that drive these companies towards introducing MBSE. [Method] Our results are based on 20 interviews with experts from 10 companies. Through exploratory research, we analyze the results by means of thematic coding. [Results] Forces that prevent MBSE adoption mainly relate to immature tooling, uncertainty about the return-on-investment, and fears on migrating existing data and processes. On the other hand, MBSE adoption also has strong drivers and participants have high expectations mainly with respect to managing complexity, adhering to new regulations, and reducing costs. [Conclusions] We conclude that bad experiences and frustration about MBSE adoption originate from false or too high expectations. Nevertheless, companies should not underestimate the necessary efforts for convincing employees and addressing their anxiety.

Keywords: System engineering · Model-based · Process improvement · Embedded systems · Interview study · Empirical research

1 Introduction

Model-based Systems Engineering (MBSE) describes the use of models and model-based techniques to develop complex systems, which are mainly driven by software [5]. MBSE tackles the complexity of those systems through an interrelated set of models, which connects development activities and provides comprehensive analyses. Many companies face problems with the increasing complexity

© Springer International Publishing AG 2017
M. Felderer et al. (Eds.): PROFES 2017, LNCS 10611, pp. 182–198, 2017.
https://doi.org/10.1007/978-3-319-69926-4_14

of software-intensive systems, their interdisciplinary development, and the huge amount of mainly text-based specifications. MBSE offers a solution to managing these problems and companies are attracted to its benefits.

Despite the envisioned MBSE benefits, companies are struggling with implementing it within the organization. Of course, organizational change is never easy [7], however other methodologies, such as agile practices, have been adopted much faster. So, what are the reasons and factors that prevent or impede companies from adopting MBSE?

In this paper, we investigate the forces that prevent or impede the adoption of MBSE in companies that develop embedded systems. We contrast forces that hinder its adoption with forces that drive companies towards introducing MBSE.

Our results are based on 20 interviews with experts from 10 organizations in Germany. We analyze the results by means of thematic coding and categorize the identified forces into inertia and anxiety forces, which prevent MBSE adoption, as well as push and pull forces, which drive the companies towards MBSE adoption. We frame the results with a coding of what the interviewees considered as MBSE. Our paper makes the following contributions:

- We present a set of hindering and fostering forces on MBSE adoption in industry. These results were extracted from interviews with 20 experts from 10 organizations located in Germany.
- We analyze these forces to differentiate between MBSE specific forces and forces inherent to any kind of methodological change.

Forces that prevent MBSE adoption mainly relate to immature tooling, uncertainty about the return-on-investment, and fears on migrating existing data and processes. On the other hand, MBSE adoption also has strong drivers and participants have high expectations mainly with respect to managing complexity, adhering to new regulations, and detecting bugs earlier. We observed that the hindering forces are much more concrete and MBSE-specific compared with the fostering forces, which are oftentimes very generic (e.g., increase in product quality, managing complexity, supporting reuse). Oftentimes, the interviewees could not even tell why or which part of MBSE contributes to the expected benefits.

From this, we conclude that bad experiences and frustration about MBSE adoption originate from false or too high expectations. Nevertheless, companies should not underestimate the necessary efforts for convincing employees and addressing their anxiety.

2   Background and Related Work

Model-based Systems Engineering (MBSE) is a methodology to develop systems with focus on models. Compared with traditional development, MBSE supports engineers with automation capabilities (e.g., code generation, document derivation) and enhanced analysis capabilities (e.g., behavioral analysis, performance analysis, simulation). INCOSE defines MBSE as the following [11]:
"MBSE is the formalized application of modeling to support system requirements,

design, analysis, verification and validation activities beginning in the conceptual design phase and continuing throughout development and later life cycle phases. "

UML and SysML are standardized graphical modeling languages for MBSE with capabilities to define different types of models, processes, procedures, and operations. While UML is predominantly used for software development, SysML encompasses also physical aspects of a system. The languages' graphical models are intended to cover all development phases of a system.

In some application domains, MBSE is widely used and is an integral part of development [4]. Large tool vendors, such as IBM, Oracle, Microsoft, or the Eclipse Foundation offer tooling solutions for MBSE.

Studies on MBSE Adoption. Bone and Cloutier [4] report on a survey conducted by the OMG, in which participants were asked about MBSE adoption within their organization. *Culture and general resistance to change* was identified in the study as the largest inhibitor for MBSE adoption. The study found that SysML is being used primarily for large-scale systems.

Motamedian [15] performed an applicability analysis for MBSE. Similar to the results of Bone and Cloutier, she found that MBSE is widely used in specific application areas. She reported that 50–80% of respondents who declared the use of MBSE in real programs or projects work in defense and aircraft industries. In contrast, over all responses, only 10% of participants claimed that they use MBSE in their organization. The study identified *lack of related knowledge and skills* as main barrier to MBSE introduction.

Mohagheghi et al. [14] collected data from four large companies that use *Model-Driven Engineering (MDE)* in different projects. Their study summarizes qualitative data from internal empirical studies, interviews, and a survey to investigate the state of the practice and adoption of MDE. All participants see advantages in *developing domain-specific solutions and modeling at different levels of abstraction*. None of the companies mentioned *shorter development time* or *improved quality of code* as main motivation. In addition, the integration with other tools is problematic and mature tools for complex models are missing. *Higher degree of automation and reuse* was considered the most important aspect to improve productivity in the long-term. Hutchinson et al. [10] describe the practices of three commercial organizations as they adopted MBSE. Later, they built a taxonomy of tool-related issues affecting the adoption of MBSE [24].

Kuhn et al. [12] focus on contextual forces and frictions of MBSE adoption in large companies. They found that *diffing in product lines*, *problem-specific languages and types*, *live modeling*, and *traceability between artifacts* are the main drivers for adopting MBSE. Aranda et al. [1] focus more on developers and infrastructure changes. They conclude that MBSE brings developers closer, disrupts organizational structures, and achieves improvements in productivity.

Besides these studies on MBSE adoption, several case studies exist on applying model-based techniques to complex systems in different domains (e.g., railway [3], automotive [22], maritime traffic [21]).

Summary. Related studies report on successful applications of MBSE in several cases but also mention challenges related to its adoption. MBSE techniques are widely used in some industries, however, the majority of companies do not apply MBSE. The goal of our study is to identify reasons and forces that prevent companies from adopting MBSE and contrast them with the envisioned benefits that drive the companies towards MBSE.

3   Study Approach

3.1   Research Questions

We structure our research by two research questions that focus on hindering and fostering forces of MBSE adoption.

- RQ1: What are perceived forces that prevent MBSE adoption in industry?
  - RQ1.1: What are habits and inertia that prevent MBSE adoption?
  - RQ1.2: What are anxiety factors that prevent MBSE adoption?
- RQ2: What are perceived forces that foster MBSE adoption in industry?
  - RQ2.1: What are perceived issues that push industry towards MBSE?
  - RQ2.2: What MBSE benefits are perceived as most attractive?

3.2   Research Design

This is an *exploratory research* [20] based on semi-structured interviews. The method provides insights into the examined topic and gives essential information to understand the phenomenon in its real context [8,18]. We developed an interview guide [6] that was structured along a funnel model [18] starting with general questions about the participant's context and the understanding of MBSE and afterwards going into detail about specific topics such as employee training, MBSE integration, or experiences in the past.

3.3   Data Collection and Analysis

Study Participants. The interview participants were selected from personal contacts of the authors and industrial partners that participate in a German research project[1] that has a focus on MBSE adoption in practice. The interviewee selection was based on two criteria: First, the interviewee should have a work experience of several years. Second, the interviewee should work in an environment where MBSE adoption is a realistic option. In our case, we therefore restricted the group of interviewees to people working on embedded systems or in the context of embedded systems. It was not necessary that interviewees have adopted MBSE in their context, however, 13 of the 20 interviewees stated that they already have experiences in adopting MBSE. Table 1 provides an overview of the participants and their context. The interviews were conducted by two of the authors from May to December 2016.

---

[1] https://spedit.in.tum.de/.

Table 1. Study participants

ID	Industry sector	Type of company	Role of participant	MBSE attitude
P1	Tool vendor	OEM	Technical Sales	Neutral
P2	Tool vendor	Academic	Professor	Neutral
P3	R&D services	SME	Manager	Neutral
P4	Automotive	OEM	Head of Development	Positive
P5	Automotive	OEM	Systems Engineer	Neutral
P6	Medical	SME	Head of SW Development	Positive
P7	Medical	SME	Head of QA	Positive
P8	Automotive	Supplier	Function Architect	Negative
P9	Automotive	OEM	SW Architect	Neutral
P10	Automotive	OEM	Function Architect	Positive
P11	Research	Academic	Professor	Negative
P12	Avionics	Supplier	Technical Project Manager	Neutral
P13	Automotive	Supplier	Developer	Positive
P14	Avionics	OEM	SW Developer	Neutral
P15	Avionics	Supplier	SW Developer	Negative
P16	Avionics	OEM	Team Lead	Neutral
P17	Electronics	OEM	Head of SW Development	Neutral
P18	Avionics	SME	Head of System Engineering	Negative
P19	Robotics	OEM	Team Lead	Positive
P20	Automotive	OEM	Research and Development	Negative

Interviews. There were 20 fact-to-face interviews. Every interview took around one hour. In consent with the interviewee, the interviewer took notes for detailed analysis. All interview notes were managed using the qualitative data analysis tool ATLAS.ti[2].

Analysis. Three researchers analyzed the interviews using *qualitative coding* [16]. Neither of them participated in the interview phase. The study was framed using the framework of *Forces on MBSE Adoption* (see Sect. 4.2) with the following codes: {Push, Pull, Inertia, Anxiety}. The analysis started with all three researchers working on the same five interviews. The results were later discussed and merged in a meeting. The discussions helped to homogenize the understanding of the codes among the researchers [23] (i.e., what/how to look for on each force). The remaining 15 interviews were tackled in a cross-analysis fashion. The interviews were divided equally into three groups (A, B, C) and each researcher coded the interview transcripts of two groups (i.e., AB, BC, or AC) individually the same way as before. Then, each researcher merged the results

---

[2] http://atlasti.com.

and judged existing conflicts of the group he did not work on (a researcher coding interviews of groups AB merged the results of interviews of group C). In a round with all three researchers, the unresolved conflicts were ironed out. Finally, the codes were divided into three groups {Pull, Inertia, (Anxiety, Push)} and each researcher worked on the quotations of codes of a group individually, performing open coding to create second level codes. We present the results in Sect. 4 by reporting the codes with the number of related quotations and the number of interviews in which the code appeared. The number of quotations indicates the significance of a code over all interviews and the number of interviews indicates the pervasiveness of the code within the interviews.

Availability of Data. Due to unreasonable effort necessary for anonymizing the interview transcripts, we do not disclose them. However, we disclose the interview guide and the codebook.[3]

4   Results

4.1   Overview and Definition of MBSE

As depicted in Table 1, we had a balanced set of participants with respect to MBSE attitude. For 9 out of the 20 interviews, we coded a similar number of fostering and hindering forces (i.e., neutral attitude). In 6 interviews, the fostering forces dominated (i.e., positive attitude) and in 5 interviews, the hindering forces dominated (i.e., negative attitude). In the interviews, we did not refer to any specific MBSE approach. We did this on purpose to identify forces independent from any concrete technique or tooling. Additionally, comparing the results would have been much harder due to the large variety of MBSE approaches and flavors. Nevertheless, we asked the interviewees to define MBSE. The result can be seen in Fig. 1, where a word cloud representation of terms mentioned more than 2 times is depicted.

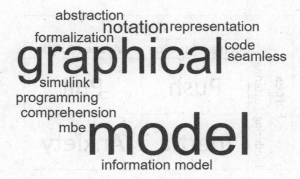

Fig. 1. Word cloud of MBSE descriptions

[3] https://doi.org/10.6084/m9.figshare.5368453.

The word cloud shows the close association of MBSE with graphical models. Especially graphical descriptions of architectures and processes were mentioned several times. However, some interviewees mentioned that *"graphical representation is only a part of MBSE, not everything" (P12)* and others pointed out that MBSE should not be deformed to *graphical programming*. The only reference to a specific instance of MBSE in the word cloud is given by *Simulink*. Simulink[4] is a widely used tool in the embedded systems domain for modeling, simulating, and analyzing dynamic systems. Interestingly, the interviewees mentioned that using Simulink is *not* considered as doing MBSE (e.g., P4: *"Pure implementation with Simulink is graphical programming, not MBSE."*, P16: *"Simulink is model-based engineering but not model-based* systems *engineering"*). UML/SysML, which we expected to appear more often in the characterization of MBSE, was only mentioned rarely, however, *notation* was mentioned several times. The term *information model* was used a few times as important part of an MBSE approach. P7: *"A core topic of MBSE is the information model that specifies and relates all development artifacts."* Apart from that, the interviewees frequently mentioned several well-known properties related to MBSE such as *abstraction, formalization, and comprehension.* In summary, the results show that our interviewees were not biased by a specific MBSE flavor or approach that they previously had in mind when answering our questions. However, the variety of answers also shows that the term MBSE is still far away from common understanding.

4.2   Forces on MBSE Adoption

Inspired by the categorization of Hohl et al. [9], we defined a quadrant-wise framework for categories of forces on MBSE adoption (see Fig. 2). The categorization aims to better understand the different aspects of the transition process from traditional to MBSE practices. We designed the framework to identify *Forces* that work towards *Hindering* or *Fostering* the adoption of MBSE and their origin. These forces have different origins or *Triggers* and are classified

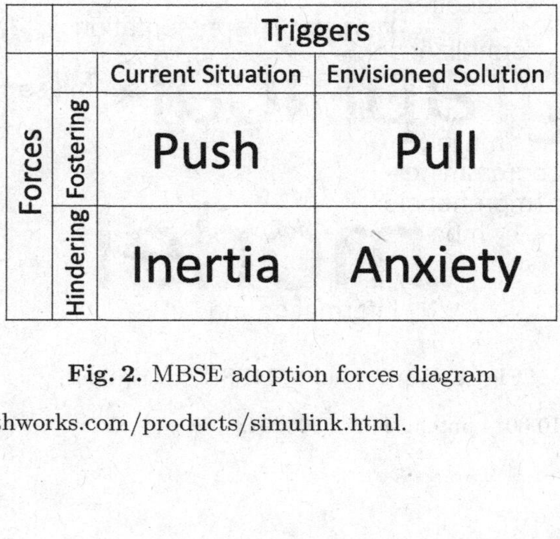

		Triggers	
		Current Situation	Envisioned Solution
Forces	Fostering	Push	Pull
	Hindering	Inertia	Anxiety

Fig. 2. MBSE adoption forces diagram

4 https://de.mathworks.com/products/simulink.html.

either into shortcomings of the *Current Situation* or expected benefits of the *Envisioned Solution* (MBSE in our case). We distinguish between *Push* and *Pull* as forces that foster MBSE adoption. The former is triggered by issues or demands that the current situation cannot address, the latter is triggered by the "to-be harvested" benefits of the new solution. In contrast, we define *Inertia* and *Anxiety* as forces that hinder MBSE adoption. The former is triggered by the feeling that the current solution is "good enough" and habits that keep people from trying out something new. The latter is triggered by fears that MBSE introduction will not pay-off, mainly caused by uncertainties and perception flaws. According to Hohl et al. [9], this classification is inspired by the Customer Forces Diagram by Maurya[5] that itself is inspired by the Forces Diagram by Moesta and Spiek from the Jobs-to-be-done framework[6]. All four forces are present within an organization at the same time.

Fig. 3. Number of quotations related to MBSE adoption forces

In total, we coded 242 quotations. Their distribution between the forces can be seen in Fig. 3. The fostering (131 times) and hindering (111) forces were mentioned to a similar amount. Quotations categorized as pull (94) are almost triple of push (37). Comparing both (pull and push), 72% of the fostering quotations were driven by the benefits of MBSE, while problems in their in-house processes represented 28%. This can be compared to the number of quotations on inertia (51). Pull forces were coded most, representing 39% of all quotations. To analyze the general attitude of a participant towards MBSE adoption, we divided the number of coded quotations related to fostering forces (push and pull) by the total number of quotations coded for that participant. We considered a participant to have a positive attitude when the ratio of fostering forces was higher than 60%, a neutral attitude for ratios between 60% and 40%, and a negative attitude

---

[5] https://leanstack.com/science-of-how-customers-buy/.
[6] http://jobstobedone.org.

for a ratio smaller than 40%. This can be seen in Table 1. The results of the last step of the coding process generated similar codes in different categories (e.g., *Tooling Shortcomings* from Anxiety category and *Immature tooling* or *Incompatibility with existing tools*, both from Inertia category). Although similar names, these codes encompasses disjoint characteristics and their coexistence serves a purpose. All codes created during the analysis can be seen in Fig. 4.

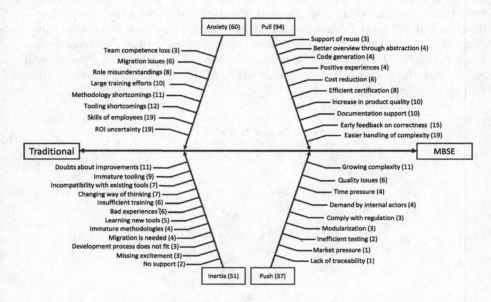

Fig. 4. Overview of MBSE adoption forces

In the following, the preventing forces found in the study are subsequently described and explained using the information from the interview transcripts and the interpretations from coding and analysis.

4.3 Hindering Force: Inertia

With 51 distinct quotations, *inertia* forces were mentioned fewer times compared with forces related to anxiety (60 quotations). We structured the inertia related quotations with respect to four inertia topics.

Tooling Inertia (21 coded quotations from 15 interviews). With 21 quotations, tooling inertia was the most frequently mentioned inertia force. Tooling inertia describes phenomena of the current in-house tooling environment that made our participants refrain from adopting MBSE. Tooling inertia includes resistance against *learning new tools* as well as potential *incompatibilities of MBSE tools* with current tools. *"People preferred using Excel instead of the new*

MBSE tool" (P8), "Especially elderly employees who are used to textual specifi-cations have difficulties with drawing tools" (P15), "It's not possible to connect/trace the models with artifacts in other tools." (P5)

Apart from the resistance of learning and integrating new tools, our partici-pants reported on resistance of employees if *MBSE tools are immature.* Especially tools with bad user experience, low stability, and missing basic features are a major factor why employees resist MBSE adoption. *"Tool is not user friendly. Things are distributed over several menus; you have to look for everything." (P5), "We are working in teams. That's why we need a tool with fine-grained access rights and control." (P10)*

We classified *immature tooling* as inertia force because the expectation that tools are missing important features makes the current situation look not so bad. Tooling issues were also mentioned in the context of anxiety. In that cases, interviewees feared that the available tools cannot fulfill the promises of MBSE.

Context Inertia (18 quotations, 13 interviews). A second inertia force mentioned quite often was context inertia, which describes people refraining from MBSE adoption because they believe it does not fit their current business situation. The most mentioned in this category was doubts about whether MBSE would really improve the current situation. *"It needs a huge emergency to justify the costs of introducing an MBSE tool." (P7), "Currently, problems are not so urgent yet. Therefore, there is not much willingness to act." (P20)* Another aspect of the context that make people refrain from MBSE adoption is the potential need to migrate old data or legacy systems or when it seems that the current development process does not fit MBSE techniques. *"Legacy problems are a huge hurdle because, in general, the old way of working must further be maintained and supported." (P20), "MBSE adoption would have caused changes in our development process. Therefore, we didn't do it." (P2)*

Personal Inertia (16 quotations, 9 interviews). Personal inertia captures forces related to an individual's personality and experiences that hold him/her back from adopting MBSE. In our study, these forces were led by the resistance against learning a new way of thinking. *"MBSE is not just about changing the notation; it's about changing the way of how I think about systems" (P2), "Abstractions in MBSE are not easy to comprehend." (P12)* Similarly, if people had bad experiences with MBSE or related techniques, they have a personal reluctance against adopting MBSE in their current situation.

Maturity Inertia (12 quotations, 8 interviews). Maturity inertia was least mentioned in our interviews. Participants were critical about a potential MBSE adoption if they had the impression that the MBSE methodology is not mature enough, there has not been sufficient training before, and there is no support by experts. *"We first need a common terminology between employees of different departments" (P7), "The support for debugging problems is very limited" (P9)*

4.4 Hindering Force: Anxiety

Anxiety is a force related to expectations and fears that make MBSE adoption less appealing. These expectations originate from uncertainties that are still to be clarified or a false perception of reality. We structured the anxiety related quotations into the following topics:

ROI Uncertainty (19 quotations, 12 interviews). Return on investment (ROI) is the benefit resulting from an investment. Introducing MBSE will incur cost spread in several factors such as training, tooling, migration, or lower productivity. Many interviewees were concerned that the investments on introducing MBSE will not pay off. *"[It will costs us] A large sum in the million range" (P7)*, *"Coaching on the job is very important, but it costs a lot" (P2)*

Skills of Employees (19 quotations, 11 interviews). Some interviewees fear that (some of) the employees in their company may lack the necessary skills to efficiently adopt MBSE. This can negatively influence the introduction of MBSE in two different ways: Either those employees do not adopt MBSE or they apply them incorrectly. *"Mechanical engineers know CAD modeling but don't know modeling of behavior" (P1)*, *"Modeling should not be an end in itself" (P16)*

Tooling Shortcomings (12 quotations, 8 interviews). The interviewees perceived problems with tooling as a reason for not introducing MBSE. The interviewees fear that current tool solutions do not address a significant part of the development process and the envisioned benefits of MBSE. Thus, extra work would be necessary to fill the gaps (e.g., migration of data between MBSE tools and current tools). *"Everything in one tool? Nobody wants that" (P5)*, *"Performance of the tools [is a challenge for introducing MBSE]" (P7)*

Methodology Shortcomings (11 quotations, 6 interviews). Many interviewees emphasized the lack of maturity on the current MBSE methodology. This category can be interpreted in two ways. Either the methodology really is incomplete or the knowledge of practitioners is immature. In addition, concerns about the lack of tailored approaches for MBSE introduction were pointed out. *"A consistent methodology is lacking, resulting in uncertainties" (P1)*, *"There are no process models that integrate MBSE properly." (P11)*

Large Training Efforts (10 quotations, 5 interviews). This category groups perceived potential problems related to training the team on using MBSE and its respective tools. Some of the codes were related to the costs of training and had intersections with *ROI uncertainty*. Other codes were related to the fear of unsuccessful training. *"Training is necessary: How do I bring my employees to the same level as the experts?" (P7)*, *"Employees will not accept MBSE if no training is provided before." (P7)*

Besides these major categories, interviewees also mentioned potential *team competence loss* (3 quotations, 3 interviews) and new responsibilities in the team that could cause *role misunderstandings* (8 quotations, 5 interviews). The interviewees perceived *migration issues* (6 quotations, 6 interviews) of projects that started with traditional development method to MBSE.

4.5 Fostering Force: Push

With 37 distinct quotations, *push* was the force with the smallest number of quotations. We structured push forces within three categories:

Product Push (20 quotations, 10 interviews). We grouped here codes related to product-oriented push forces. *Growing complexity* (11 quotations/8 interviews) of the software was the code with most quotations within the push forces. As systems become more software-intensive, tackling the growing complexity is currently a real challenge, thus, organizations feel the need to shift to better solutions. *"Increasing complexity of products [pushes us towards MBSE]" (P1)*, *"Complex software, especially with concurrency [pushes us towards MBSE]" (P3)* Further codes were *quality issues* (6/3) within the product or its specification and the need for *modularization* (3/3) in order to make certification and reuse more efficient.

Stakeholder Enforcement (8 quotations, 4 interviews). Some interviewees mentioned that they are forced or at least pushed towards MBSE by recommendations or requests from stakeholders. *Demands by internal actors* (4/3) such as developers or management push companies towards MBSE adoption as well as legal requirements to *comply with regulations* (3/1). *Market pressure* (1) was mentioned with respect to issues with acquiring talented employees: *"We have to be modern, otherwise we will not get good people anymore" (P2)*

Process Push (7 quotations, 4 interviews). Deficiencies of the current process were only mentioned a few times as forces that push companies towards MBSE. The codes were *time pressure* (4/3), *inefficient testing* (2/2), and *lack of traceability* (1). *"We have no idea what happens when something changes" (P5)*, *"[We have] Large amounts of requirements; how can the tester handle this?" (P5)*.

In summary, interviewees provided more push forces related to issues with the product instead of issues with the process.

4.6 Fostering Force: Pull

We identified several factors of envisioned benefits that drive companies towards MBSE adoption. A majority of the responses given by the interviewees is related to envisioned improvements of the development process. This is interesting since process issues were only mentioned a few times as push factors.

Easier Handling of Complexity (19 quotations, 12 interviews). With each new function to integrate, the complexity of software increases. Managing the different software components gets more and more complicated. The interviewees see great opportunities in MBSE to support this challenge. Due to a large number of possible variants of products, complexity of software increases in many companies. *"[MBSE will help us to] understand highly complex issues or illustrate something" (P15)*, *"[MBSE will support the] management of product line and variability" (P1)*

Early Feedback on Correctness (15 quotations, 10 interviews). The desire for early feedback and front-loading was also a strong pull factor. Especially early verification on higher levels of development were mentioned to improve the development process and finally also the product. *"Early verification and simulation saves time in the end" (P7), "[MBSE will provide] better quality due to early fault detection" (P4), "[MBSE will] Enable automatic verification" (P6)*

Documentation Support (10 quotations, 7 interviews). The interviewees expect support to create and manage documentation. The increasing complexity of software development has complicated the management of requirement documents. *"[MBSE will provide] better documentation" (P13), "[MBSE will] generate documentation and code" (P12)*

Increase in Product Quality (10 quotations, 5 interviews). The interviewees expect better products by introducing MBSE. This includes the final product as well as intermediate development artifacts. *"[MBSE will] improve the quality of requirement documents" (P10)*

Efficient Certification (8 quotations, 5 interviews). Some interviewees envision that MBSE will make it easier to certify software-intensive products. Some interviewees specifically mentioned that MBSE would enable a modular certification, where only parts of the product are certified and not the entire product. *"[MBSE is] necessary to comply with regulatory requirements" (P6), "[MBSE will enable] modular certification and parallel development" (P6)*

Additional, less frequently mentioned, pull factors include *cost reduction* (6 coded quotations), *positive experiences* (4), *code generation* (4), *better overview through abstraction* (4), and *support of reuse* (3).

5   Discussion

The results show that people from industry have high hopes and expectations for MBSE. However, there are also several hurdles that need to be addressed when adopting MBSE, some of which are very generic. These problems are sometimes even part of the human nature and its natural resistance to change in general.

Relation to Existing Evidence. When comparing our results to related studies on forces of adopting development methodologies in industry, we can identify some general patterns. Hohl et al. [9] report on forces that prevent the adoption of agile development in the automotive domain. They also report on forces of inertia and anxiety resisting a necessary change of mind-set, or limited acceptance for organizational restructuring. Additionally, the current development process was perceived as good-enough. The same forces also appeared in our study. Riungu-Kalliosaari et al. [17] performed a case study on the adoption of DevOps in industry, where they identified five high-level adoption challenges. Three of these challenges were also mentioned as inertia or anxiety factors in our study, namely *deep-seated company culture*, *industry constraints and feasibility*, and *unclear methodology*. Parallels can also be found in the work of Bauer and Vetrò [2] with respect to the adoption of structured reuse approaches in industry.

Similarly, we also found common and generic goals (i.e., pull forces) that are in the focus of many process improvement activities. Schmitt and Diebold [19] have analyzed common improvement goals that are usually considered when improving the development process. The pull factors that we extracted in our study are part of the main goals elicited by them (e.g., quality and time-to-market).

When focusing on the forces specific to MBSE that did not appear (so strongly) in the related studies, some factors remain. Incompatibility of MBSE tools with existing tools is a specific inertia force that prevent MBSE adoption. A second force of inertia that was specifically reported for MBSE adoption is the need to adopt a new way of thinking, especially with respect to abstractions. The anxiety forces that we identified were rather generic such that we did not identify any MBSE specific anxiety forces. Interestingly, loss of competences or loss of power, which is a typical anxiety factor, was not mentioned very often.

Impact for Industry. MBSE streamlines the activities in all phases of the software lifecycle. It replaces document-based systems engineering and automates several tasks (e.g., code generation). An organization doing the transition from document-based to model-based will require changes in all software development stages, including tools, processes, artifacts, and developing paradigms.

Our interviewees focused more on push forces related to the product and not so much on the process. One might infer that engineers recognize the growing complexity of their products but they cannot link it to the shortcomings of the current processes. Perhaps, inside their mind, the processes are OK since it has been functioning properly until now and the problem is the product that is getting more difficult to develop.

The results support decision-making and are an initial step towards efficiently introducing MBSE in companies. Implementing change is always a hassle, therefore companies should manage expectations by setting concrete improvement goals, relating them to concrete MBSE techniques, and making changes step-by-step. Many interviewees mentioned that MBSE adoption should best be piloted in small projects with a clear scope.

Impact for Academia. MBSE complexity raises uncertainties towards effort and success of its introduction. These uncertainties can be mitigated by knowledge building. Misunderstandings of MBSE, its tools, and processes were quoted many times, which means research is not properly reaching practitioners. This problem is not limited to the MBSE domain but to research in general. With a clear idea of the forces fostering and hindering MBSE introduction, the next step is to understand how to manage those factors, mitigating them when necessary, or strengthen the ones that contribute to successful MBSE introduction. The results provide promising research directions based on real industry needs.

5.1   Threats to Validity

The validity of our results is subject to the following threats:

Subject Selection Bias. Since this is an exploratory study, we selected a convenience sample of project partners and personal contacts as study subjects. Although we selected participants from a broad spectrum of companies and industrial domains, the results may be influenced by the fact that all study participants work in Germany. Additionally, the interviewees were selected from an environment where MBSE adoption is a realistic option.

Researcher Bias. Our study was carried out in the context of a project on transferring MBSE into practice, which means that the authors have a positive attitude towards MBSE in general. Additionally, some of the interviewees are also partners in this project, however, we also interviewed people from companies not involved in the project. To reduce researcher bias, the interviews were conducted by two researchers who took notes independently.

Research Method. Validity is threatened by the possibility of misunderstandings between interviewees and the researchers. To minimize this risk, the study goal was explained to the participants prior to the interview. Steps taken to improve the reliability of the interview guide included a review and a pilot test. We followed several strategies proposed by Maxwell [13] to mitigate threats. The interviews were conducted as part of a larger project, where we established a *long-term involvement* of the study subjects. As part of this, we presented our study in the context of the project, where the results were reviewed by the project partners. We substantiate our assertions by providing *quasi-statistics* on the frequency of codes occurrences in the interview data. To validate our results, we *compared* them with existing studies on development methodology adoption.

External Validity. We expect that our results are representative for the German embedded systems industry, however, we cannot generalize the results to other countries or other types of systems engineering.

6   Conclusions

Organizational change is never easy, especially when trying to introduce complex approaches such as MBSE. In this research, we look for the reasons and factors that prevent or impede companies from adopting MBSE. For this means, we created a forces framework that we used to analyze the information from the verbatim of 20 interviews. We identified forces that hinder and foster MBSE adoption in organizations. We coded the interviews within several discussion rounds. Based on our results, practitioners may challenge their decision processes and adoption strategies. Researchers may study our results and find evidence to quantify and detail the considerations of practitioners. We conclude that bad experiences and frustration about MBSE adoption originate from false or too high expectations. Nevertheless, companies should not underestimate the necessary efforts for convincing employees and addressing their anxiety.

As future work, we plan to analyze the data to investigate correlations between roles and identified categories as well as dependencies between the forces. Additionally, the research community may create mechanisms to identify the forces within the organization in a more effective and systematic way, analyze how hindering forces can be mitigated, understand how to harvest forces synergy, and figure out which tools and techniques have the highest ROI.

Acknowledgements. This work was partly funded by the German Federal Ministry of Education and Research (BMBF), grant "SPEDiT, 01IS15058".

References

1. Aranda, J., Damian, D., Borici, A.: Transition to model-driven engineering. In: France, R.B., Kazmeier, J., Breu, R., Atkinson, C. (eds.) MODELS 2012. LNCS, vol. 7590, pp. 692–708. Springer, Heidelberg (2012). doi:10.1007/978-3-642-33666-9_44
2. Bauer, V., Vetrò, A.: Comparing reuse practices in two large software-producing companies. J. Syst. Soft. **117**, 545–582 (2016)
3. Böhm, W., Junker, M., Vogelsang, A., Teufl, S., Pinger, R., Rahn, K.: A formal systems engineering approach in practice: an experience report. In: International Workshop on Software Engineering Research and Industrial Practices (SER&IPs) (2014). doi:10.1145/2593850.2593856
4. Bone, M., Cloutier, R.: The current state of model based systems engineering: results from the OMG SysML request for information 2009. In: CSER (2010)
5. Broy, M., Damm, W., Henkler, S., Pohl, K., Vogelsang, A., Weyer, T.: Introduction to the SPES modeling framework. In: Pohl, K., Hönninger, H., Achatz, R., Broy, M. (eds.) Model-Based Engineering of Embedded Systems, pp. 31–49. Springer, Heidelberg (2012)
6. Bryman, A.: Social Research Methods. Oxford University Press, Oxford (2015)
7. Conner, D.R.: Managing at the Speed of Change. Random House, New York (1993)
8. Dresch, A., Lacerda, D.P., Antunes, J.A.V.: Design Science Research. Springer, Cham (2015)
9. Hohl, P., Münch, J., Schneider, K., Stupperich, M.: Forces that prevent agile adoption in the automotive domain. In: Abrahamsson, P., Jedlitschka, A., Nguyen Duc, A., Felderer, M., Amasaki, S., Mikkonen, T. (eds.) PROFES 2016. LNCS, vol. 10027, pp. 468–476. Springer, Cham (2016). doi:10.1007/978-3-319-49094-6_32
10. Hutchinson, J., Rouncefield, M., Whittle, J.: Model-driven engineering practices in industry. In: ICSE (2011)
11. INCOSE: Systems engineering vision 2020 (2007)
12. Kuhn, A., Murphy, G.C., Thompson, C.A.: An exploratory study of forces and frictions affecting large-scale model-driven development. In: France, R.B., Kazmeier, J., Breu, R., Atkinson, C. (eds.) MODELS 2012. LNCS, vol. 7590, pp. 352–367. Springer, Heidelberg (2012). doi:10.1007/978-3-642-33666-9_23
13. Maxwell, J.A.: Qualitative Research Design: An Interactive Approach, vol. 41. Sage publications, Thousand Oaks (2012)
14. Mohagheghi, P., Gilani, W., Stefanescu, A., Fernandez, M.A.: An empirical study of the state of the practice and acceptance of model-driven engineering in four industrial cases. Empirical Soft. Eng. **18**(1), 89–116 (2013)
15. Motamedian, B.: MBSE applicability analysis. Int. J. Sci. Eng. Res. **4**(2) (2013)

16. Neuman, W.: Social Research Methods: Qualitative and Quantitative Approaches, 7th edn. Alpha Books, New York (2010)
17. Riungu-Kalliosaari, L., Mäkinen, S., Lwakatare, L.E., Tiihonen, J., Männistö, T.: DevOps adoption benefits and challenges in practice: a case study. In: Abrahamsson, P., Jedlitschka, A., Nguyen Duc, A., Felderer, M., Amasaki, S., Mikkonen, T. (eds.) PROFES 2016. LNCS, vol. 10027, pp. 590–597. Springer, Cham (2016). doi:10.1007/978-3-319-49094-6_44
18. Runeson, P., Höst, M.: Guidelines for conducting and reporting case study research in software engineering. Empirical Soft. Eng. **14**(2), 131–164 (2008)
19. Schmitt, A., Diebold, P.: Why do we do software process improvement? In: Abrahamsson, P., Jedlitschka, A., Nguyen Duc, A., Felderer, M., Amasaki, S., Mikkonen, T. (eds.) PROFES 2016. LNCS, vol. 10027, pp. 360–367. Springer, Cham (2016). doi:10.1007/978-3-319-49094-6_23
20. Shields, P., Rangarjan, N.: A Playbook for Research Methods: Integrating Conceptual Frameworks and Project Management. New Forums, Stillwater (2013)
21. Vogelsang, A., Eder, S., Hackenberg, G., Junker, M., Teufl, S.: Supporting concurrent development of requirements and architecture: a model-based approach. In: MODELSWARD (2014)
22. Vogelsang, A., Femmer, H., Winkler, C.: Systematic elicitation of mode models for multifunctional systems. In: International Requirements Engineering Conference (RE) (2015). doi:10.1109/RE.2015.7320447
23. Weston, C., Gandell, T., Beauchamp, J., McAlpine, L., Wiseman, C., Beauchamp, C.: Analyzing interview data: the development and evolution of a coding system. Qual. Sociol. **24**(3), 381–400 (2001)
24. Whittle, J., Hutchinson, J., Rouncefield, M., Burden, H., Heldal, R.: A taxonomy of tool-related issues affecting the adoption of model-driven engineering. Soft. Syst. Model. **16**(2), 313–331 (2017)

How *Accountability* is Implemented and Understood in Research Tools
A Systematic Mapping Study

Severin Kacianka[1]([✉]), Kristian Beckers[2], Florian Kelbert[3],
and Prachi Kumari[4]

[1] Technical University of Munich, Munich, Germany
kacianka@in.tum.de
[2] Siemens, Munich, Germany
kristian.beckers@siemens.com
[3] Imperial College London, London, England
f.kelbert@imperial.ac.uk
[4] Munich, Germany
prachi.kumari@tum.de

Abstract. [**Context/Background**]: With the increasing use of cyber-physical systems in complex socio-technical setups, mechanisms that hold specific entities accountable for safety and security incidents are needed. Although there exist models that try to capture and formalize accountability concepts, many of these lack practical implementations. We hence know little about how accountability mechanisms work in practice and how specific entities could be held responsible for incidents. [**Goal**]: As a step towards the practical implementation of providing accountability, this systematic mapping study investigates existing implementations of accountability concepts with the goal to (1) identify a common definition of accountability and (2) identify the general trend of practical research. [**Method**]: To survey the literature for existing implementations, we conducted a systematic mapping study. [**Results**]: We thus contribute by providing a systematic overview of current accountability realizations and requirements for future accountability approaches. [**Conclusions**]: We find that existing practical accountability research lacks a common definition of accountability in the first place. The research field seems rather scattered with no generally accepted architecture and/or set of requirements. While most accountability implementations focus on privacy and security, no safety-related approaches seem to exist. Furthermore, we did not find excessive references to relevant and related concepts such as reasoning, log analysis and causality.

Keywords: Accountability · Tools · Literature review · Survey · Systematic mapping study

---

The original version of this chapter was revised. Modifications have made to Table 3. For detailed information please see Erratum. The erratum to this publication is available online at https://doi.org/10.1007/978-3-319-69926-4_56
P. Kumari was formerly at TU Munich, Munich, Germany.

© Springer International Publishing AG 2017
M. Felderer et al. (Eds.): PROFES 2017, LNCS 10611, pp. 199–218, 2017.
https://doi.org/10.1007/978-3-319-69926-4_15

1   Introduction

Traditionally, IT practitioners have aimed to avoid safety and security incidents using preventive measures. In complex systems, however, it is often hard to enumerate and plan for possible contingencies. Besides, preventive measures generally require many additional resources and are expensive to implement [17]. As a consequence, the focus of research has shifted towards alternative ideas like detective security [23] or root cause analysis [24]. Detective security is inspired by how law enforcement works in the real world [26]: Speeding violations are not prevented by technical means, e.g. by limiting the maximum speed of the car, but by punishment if caught exceeding the speed limit.

To develop a broad and structured understanding of these and related issues and research undertakings, we designed a mapping study with a focus on *accountability* in the context of privacy, safety, and security. We thus survey the literature of practical accountability implementations that address violations of safety, security, and privacy requirements with the goal to identify the set of existing methods and approaches. Our focus is on the post-mortem analysis of unwanted events.

In terms of related work, Xiao et al. [30] investigate accountability in computer networks and distributed systems. In contrast to their work, we focus on implementations and do not restrict our study to computer networks. While Papanikolaou and Pearson [19] give a cross-discipline overview of the term accountability, they focus on theoretical definitions and do not consider applications.

Our **contribution** is a systematic mapping study on accountability in the context of privacy, safety, and security requirements. We identify which contributions were made over time, the various application domains, layers of abstraction, technologies and protocols in implementing accountability in socio-technical systems. We find that even though there exist very few tools for accountability, it is a growing area of research in different domains. All **raw data** of our study can be found online [16]; see https://acc.in.tum.de/accountability_2016/ for a more interactive viewer of the data.

2   Methodology

We followed the five-step methodology laid out by Petersen et al. [21]: (1) definition of research questions (Sect. 2.1), (2) conduct search (Sect. 2.2), (3) screening of papers (Sect. 2.3), (4) keywording using abstracts (Sect. 2.4), and (5) data

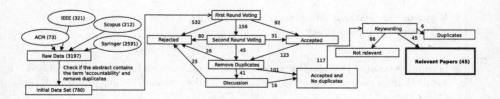

Fig. 1. The "sieving" process

extraction and mapping process (Sect. 2.5). This section describes our instantiation of this methodology. All steps were conducted jointly by the four authors of this paper. The later stages (screening, keywording and mapping) were conducted using a custom written web tool, that offered all authors a unified interface and functioned as a review tool. Figure 1 illustrates our process.

2.1 Definition of Research Questions

We were interested in answering the following research questions:

RQ1 What types of research papers have been published over the years?
RQ2 Which application domains have seen most implementations?
RQ3 Which underlying techniques/protocols are implemented by these tools, at which layers of abstraction are these tools deployed and is there a trend?
RQ4 What do the underlying definitions of accountability have in common?
RQ5 Are prominent contributors recognizable? How are they related to each other?

2.2 Paper Search

In accordance with our research questions, we constructed the search string *accountability AND (privacy OR safety OR security) AND (tool OR implementation OR application)* and adapted it to the idiosyncrasies of each digital library. We limited our search to those technical domains, because we know that accountability is a focus in those fields and because otherwise the result set balloons, encompassing mostly papers covering (non-technical) management and governance problems.

We obtained a basic set of publications from ACM [1] (73 results), IEEE [2] (321), Scopus [3] (212) and Springer [4] (2591), as shown in Table 1, column 'Raw'. As a first step, we stored the search results as CSV files. For this, IEEE and Scopus provided CSV export functionalities, comprising authors, titles, and abstracts. Springer's export functionality did not include abstracts, hence we used a simple script to access the abstracts from the publication's URL. To extract this information from ACM, we used the Zotero tool [5].

Table 1. Dataset overview

Source	Raw	Cleanup	Relevant
ACM	73	45	5
IEEE	321	201	25
Scopus	212	212	5
Springer	2591	322	10
Total	**3197**	**780**	**45**

Due to the comparatively large amount of results returned by Springer, we performed an initial screening step for all Springer results. We realized that a large amount of those results did not feature the term "accountability" within their abstract. We thus randomly selected 40 publications that did not refer to accountability in their abstract. As it turned out that none of these publications were indeed related to our study subject, we removed all Springer publications that did not feature the term accountability in their abstract. For consistency, we also did this check for the other sources, but had to remove no papers for that reason. Further, Scopus is a meta-search engine that searches, amongst other sources, also the three primary libraries. Scopus thus introduced duplicates. After an additional screening for duplicates and removing them, we obtained the dataset shown in Table 1, column 'Cleanup'. To be consistent in the removal process, we always kept the Scopus version of a paper. Hence for Scopus the number of papers is the same in the columns 'Raw' and 'Cleanup'.

2.3   Screening

We used a custom collaborative web tool to further screen the remaining 780 papers based on their title, keywords and abstract. In this step, we excluded all publications that (i) did not report a tool, implementation or application, (ii) were not related to privacy, safety, or security, or that (iii) reported only an idea, formalism or abstract framework. To ensure consistent decisions from all reviewers, we had frequent meetings. The first meeting was scheduled after every reviewer completed approximately 10 reviews, follow up meetings were held after approximately 50 reviews per authors. The frequency of meeting slowly decreased after the reviewers got more familiar with the screening process.

In practice, our web tool presented each paper randomly to two (out of four) researchers, who then read the abstract and decided whether to include or exclude the paper based on the above criteria. If the researchers' decision was unanimous, the paper was accepted (92 papers) or rejected (532 papers) accordingly. In a second round, all 156 papers with disagreements were presented to two additional researchers. Upon a clear majority of 3–1, the paper was accepted (31 papers) or rejected (80 papers). After this phase, we manually identified and removed 26 more duplicates.

In the following round, the 41 papers that had received a 2–2 draw were discussed in the presence of all researchers and a final verdict was reached. In this phase 25 papers were rejected. Overall, 117 papers proceeded to the next phase of keywording.

2.4   Keywording

In the keywording phase, we classified the remaining 117 papers. For this, we initialized our custom web tool with an intuitive set of keywords agreed upon by discussion among the authors (e.g., security, monitoring, or cloud). These keywords emerged from the authors' experience during the initial screening phase. We also added some keywords under the category of "sanity check" to further

[31] Ahmed and Ahamad (2014)	[32] Alexiou et al. (2013)	[33] Ali and Moreau (2013)
[34] Ali et al. (2014)	[35] Ali et al. (2013)	[36] Asokan et al. (2013)
[37] Brzuska et al. (2014)	[38] Cherrueau and Sudholt (2014)	[39] Choi et al. (2005)
[40] Clifton and Fernandez (1988)	[41] Dailianas et al. (2000)	[42] De Oliveira et al. (2013)
[43] Fahl et al. (2014)	[44] Flegel (2002)	[45] Fugkeaw et al. (2007)
[46] Fugkeaw et al. (2009)	[47] Haidar et al.(2010)	[48] Jedrzejczyk et al. (2010)
[49] Kang et al. (2014)	[50] Khalasi et al. (2012)	[51] Ko et al. (2011)
[52] Ko and Will (2014)	[53] Kuacharoen (2012)	[54] Langheinrich (2002)
[55] Wonjun et al. (2009)	[56] Lin and Chang (2009)	[57] Masmoudi et al. (2014)
[58] Michalas and Komninos (2014)	[59] Mivule et al. (2014)	[60] Mortimer and Cook (2010)
[61] Naessens et al. (2005)	[62] Pato et al. (2011)	[63] Pearce et al. (2005)
[64] Pearson et al. (2009)	[65] Popa et al. (2011)	[66] Rubin (1995)
[67] Ruth et al. (2004)	[68] Sriram et al. (2007)	[69] Such et al. (2012)
[70] Such et al. (2013)	[71] Chun et al. (2013)	[72] Kang et al. (2010)
[73] Yang et al. (2010)	[74] Gang et al. (2012)	[75] Zhou et al. (2010)

Fig. 2. All papers part of this study. The full citations can be found online: https:// acc.in.tum.de/accountability_2016/study_papers.pdf

exclude irrelevant papers. These keyword-categories were: "No implementation", "Not about accountability", "Full text not available" (was never used) and "I am not sure, I need help". The last category was used if an author was not sure and wanted to discuss the paper with another author. Each paper was then keyworded by one author. Apart from the above initial keywords, each author was able to create new ones on the fly. To ensure a common understanding of the keywords, we again held regular meetings to discuss the keywords.

Despite the previous screening step, 66 papers had to be removed because they (i) did not describe an implementation or (ii) were not about accountability. This is because in the initial screening process we were only deciding on the basis of the papers' titles, abstracts, and provided keywords. Since on this basis it was often not clear whether a paper described an implementation or not, we decided to accept papers if in doubt. After this process, 45 relevant research papers where subject to our study as shown in Table 1, column 'Relevant', and Fig. 2.

2.5 Mapping

During the mapping process, our web tool randomly and equally assigned the 45 accepted papers to the four researchers. Each researcher screened the full text, categorized the paper, and gave a short rationale for the categorization. If the paper did not fit into any existing categories, the researcher could create new categories. All of the categories were shared by all researchers in a "tag-cloud" (for example: *Security*, *Efficiency*, or *Health Care*) that was managed by our collaborative web tool. During the process we had several meetings to discuss new categories and unclear publications.

3 Findings

Types of research papers and distribution over the years (RQ1). Our classification of the contributions is based on the classification scheme by Wieringa et al. [28] which was applied to systematic mapping studies by Peterson et al. [21]. We classify the selected papers strictly according to their criteria, which are: Validation Research, Evaluation Research, Solution Proposal, Philosophical Papers, Opinion Papers and Experience Papers. Table 2 maps the selected papers according to these criteria. We realize that all papers focus on solutions and their evaluations. Note that our mapping study focuses on papers that report on techniques that are actually implemented; we excluded meta studies. Hence, we find no papers in the categories experience paper, opinion paper, or philosophical paper.

Table 2. Paper categorisation into research type facets; grouped by publisher

Category	ACM	IEEE	Springer	Others
Validation research	[43]			
Evaluation research	[32, 35, 65, 75]	[31, 34, 38, 46, 51, 52, 55, 57, 71, 73]	[37, 39, 44, 61]	[70]
Solution proposal	[48, 50]	[33, 40–42, 45, 47, 49, 58, 60, 62, 64, 66, 68, 72, 74]	[36, 53, 54, 56, 63, 67, 69]	[59]

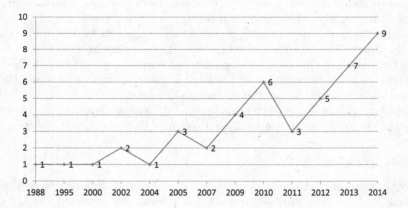

Fig. 3. Number of papers over the years

To identify how the number of contributions developed over time, we analyzed the papers according to their year of publication. Figure 3 shows the graph of the distribution from 1988 to 2014, revealing that accountability implementations started gaining interest in 1988 beginning with the work of [40]. For the first few years until the year 2000, this area did not attract much attention with only three papers in 12 years. There are several crests and troughs starting in the year 2000, but the overall interest of the research community has been increasing. In fact, as shown in Fig. 3, every trough is at a higher level than the previous one. Since

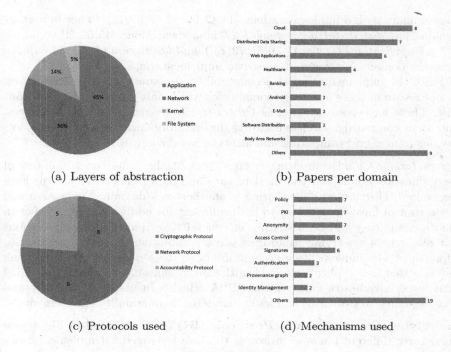

(a) Layers of abstraction

(b) Papers per domain

(c) Protocols used

(d) Mechanisms used

Fig. 4. Findings

2011, there has been a consistent growth in the number of implementations. It is also notable that after the publication of the influential paper by Weitzner et al. [26] (which, as a theoretical paper, is not subject of our study) in 2008, we see relevant publications in every consecutive year.

Interpretation: The research types in the field of implemented accountability approaches are validation, evaluation and solution approaches. It is no surprise that the field started with solution approaches and moved over time to evaluation approaches. The majority of publications in the years 2013 and 2014 are of that type. We have seen only one validation approach. We assume over time the focus of research will go towards evaluation approaches and ultimately validation approaches. Hence, the field evolves towards evaluation research, while we see a clear gap in validation research. Though the initial work on implementing accountability is by [40] in the year 1988, the field of accountability implementations started growing only from the year 2000, as shown in Fig. 3. In summary, contributions over the years indicate that accountability is (1) not yet a mature field as indicated by the low number of tools and implementations, and (2) a growing field of research with a consistent increase in the number of tools over the last decade.

Application Domains (RQ2). To answer the second research question, we classified the papers according to the targeted application domains. As shown in Fig. 4b, accountability concepts have been mostly implemented for the *cloud* domain with 8 implementations [33,42,50–52,57,60,71]. Other important domains are *distributed data sharing* (7 implementations [45,52,59,60,63,67, 68]), *webapplications* (6; [38,47,49,58,72,74]), and *health care* (4; [31,34,35,59]). For other domains we found at most two implementations.

Since the implementation of accountability mechanisms is a relatively new area of research, there are many domains for which only single implementations exist. These have been grouped as *Others* in Fig. 4b and include web services, ubiquitous computing, wireless networks, business organization, ecommerce, lottery, insurance, grid computing and location based services.

Interpretation: Cloud computing is en vogue. At the same time, it is one of the application domains where most privacy and data protection concerns have been raised. Distributed data sharing is another such domain. Encryption and access control have been shown to be insufficient for addressing these issues in remote computing and data sharing in general [26]. Hence, it is only obvious that researchers are trying to address privacy and security issues by detective enforcement viz. implementing accountability in these domains. An interesting finding is that web applications and health care domains have not attracted equal focus, especially health care where HIPPA (Health Insurance Portability and Accountability Act of 1996) explicitly mandates accountability enforcements.

Underlying Techniques and Protocols (RQ3). As depicted in Fig. 4c, we found three different kinds of protocols that are leveraged by implementations to achieve accountability.

Eight papers use *network protocols* [39,41,42,58,72–75] or *cryptographic protocols* [32,34,37,39,58,63,68,74], while five papers make use of *accountability protocols* [35,36,61,63,74]. Contrary to our expectation, data provenance protocols are not commonly used for accountability implementations.

Since accountability is the focus of this study, we took a more detailed look at the accountability protocols: [35] uses fingerprinting of wireless connection in body area networks to later proof communication between two parties. [36] describes a system for friends to share resources and uses accountability to prevent abuse. They use internet connection sharing as a use case. [61] treats a similar problem, considering an anonymous e-mail service and providing accountability in case a user abuses the system to commit criminal acts. [63] describes a protocol to resolve disputes about transactions in e-commerce systems. [74] proposes the term "accountable anonymity" and uses an encryption scheme to build an accountable and anonymous internet proxy.

Furthermore, we investigated which mechanisms and techniques are used to implement accountability. As detailed in Fig. 4d, we found that most solutions are concerned with *enforcement of policies* (7 solutions [33,38,46,50,54,55,62]), *public key encryption schemes* (7; [32,37,43,46,47,63,66]), *anonymity* (7; [32,44, 58,61,63,65,74]), *access control* (6; [33,36,45,46,55,62]), and *digital signatures* (6; [34,37,42,43,67,68]). Some tools also use *authentication* (3; [45–47]), *provenance graphs* (2; [67,71]), and *identity management* (2; [55,69]) to hold entities accountable in systems. 19 further mechanisms appeared in only one implementation each. These are represented as "Others" in Fig. 4d and include certificates, traces, pseudonyms, pseudonymity, log tamper resistance, time synchronization, reputation systems, unlinkability, accountable anonymity, OLAP, questionnaire and report generation, key management, resource description framework (RDF), job-flow tracking, fault detection, monitoring, onion routing, decentralization, and Shamir's threshold scheme.

We further found that accountability mechanisms are mainly implemented at the *application layer* (10 instances; [37,46,50,59–62,65,69,72]) and the *network layer* (8; [34,39,47,52,58,63,72,74]), see Fig. 4a. Few solutions are implemented at the *kernel layer* (3; [40,52,71]) and the *file system layer* (1; [44]).

Interpretation: The underlying techniques in accountability implementations are dominated by cryptographic protocols and network protocols. We found only one implementation relying on data provenance and very few accountability-centric protocols which combine, e.g., anonymity with accountability. In addition, we observed three overall trends in mechanisms offered within accountability implementations. First, cryptography is dominating the field with, e.g., public key infrastructures, signature-based solutions, and certificates. Second, access control mechanisms are wide-spread. Either under the term access control or in supporting topics such as policy-based approaches, authentication mechanisms, or identity management. Third, privacy is a recurring theme in particular with respect to anonymity. Further privacy goals such as pseudonymity and unlinkability are supported as well, but to a lesser extend. We sparsely encountered further supporting mechanisms such as provenance and traceability.

Definitions of Accountability (RQ4). We scanned all 45 papers for the definition of accountability. To find the definition, we searched the documents for all occurrences of the term "accountability". We then read the text before and after the highlighted term and looked for a definition.

We found that 20 of the 45 papers provide no explicit definition of accountability. 17 papers provide their own definition, not taking other sources into account. These definitions define accountability in terms of responsibility/assigning blame (6), non-repudiation/integrity (3), a-posteriori enforcement (3), collect evidence (2), transparency (2), traceability (1).

Only 8 papers rely on a previously-published and peer-reviewed definition:

Anderson et al. [6] the "(...) ability to associate an action with the responsible entity."

Bhargav-Spantzel et al. [7] "(...) the ability of holding entities responsible for their actions."

Brzuska et al. [8] "A sanitizable signature scheme satisfies non-interactive public accountability, if and only if for a valid message/signature pair (m, σ), a third party can correctly decide whether (m, σ) originates from the signer or from the sanitizer without interacting with the signer or sanitizer."

Ko et al. [18] who rely on [20] and use the definition from the "The Best Practices Act of 2010" (we, however, could not find the formulation in the original source): "the obligation and/or willingness to demonstrate and take responsibility for performance in light of agreed-upon expectations."

Pearson [20] relies on Weitzner et al. [26] and extends the definition of the "Galway project": "Accountability is the obligation to act as a responsible steward of the personal information of others, to take responsibility for the protection and appropriate use of that information beyond mere legal requirements, and to be accountable for any misuse of that information."

Xiao [29] "Accountability implies that any entity should be held responsible for its own specific action or behavior so that the entity is part of larger chains of accountability. One of the goals of accountability is that once an event has transpired, the events that took place are traceable so that the causes can be determined afterward."

These definitions, like the 17 definitions provided by the other papers, are not peer-reviewed and rely on a common understanding of the (dictionary-)meaning[1] of accountability.

Interpretation: It was surprising that no clear and accepted definition of accountability emerged. We assume that the main reason for this is that it is a common English word and everyone has some intuitive understanding of the term. The lack of a clear definition and differentiation from other terms like "responsibility" or "detection" hinders the scientific discourse and the comparability of the approaches. We hope that in the future works will rely on a peer reviewed definition of accountability and that thus trends and relations among approaches will become more pronounced. Despite this, all definitions see accountability as some form of a-posteriori mechanism to provide evidence and ultimately assign blame or responsibility. It relies either on logs or some other form of monitor.

Contributors and Relationships (RQ5)

Collaboration Networks. We analyzed the author networks of the selected papers. First, we find that most authors feature only one publication on accountability implementations, as indicated by the size of the nodes in Fig. 5. 13 authors feature two publications, while only one author features three. For the authors with at least two publications, we found that the corresponding papers are closely related follow-up papers. As also indicated by Fig. 5, the analyzed author network is very scattered. The authors of accountability tools do not collaborate across research groups. Again, the only papers published by the same authors are [34, 35], [45, 46], and [51, 52, 71] all of which are a series of papers.

These results lead us to the conclusion and hypothesis that the field of accountability implementations would greatly benefit from more systematic collaborations and research among the identified researchers.

---

[1] The Oxford dictionary defines accountability as "The fact or condition of being accountable; responsibility". For a more detailed discussion see [19].

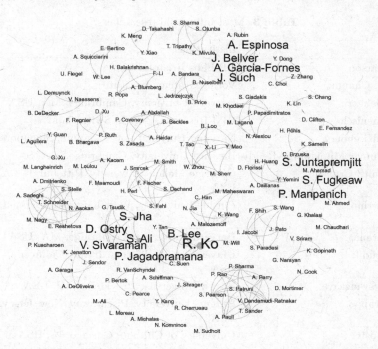

Fig. 5. Collaboration map. The size of nodes and author names corresponds with the author's number of papers (1–3) considered in this study.

Most Influential Researchers. We further analyzed the references of the 45 selected papers. Our goal was to find out whether they share common literature that is essential for the understanding and implementation of accountability mechanisms. Because some authors made heavy use of self citations, we decided to exclude any self references. We realized that there exist some researchers that are cited across many of the study papers. Table 3 shows those researchers that were cited at least seven times.

Interpretation: In contrast to the theoretical discussions of accountability, where we often find citations to papers like the one by Weitzner et al. [26] or Feigenbaum et al. [12], there are no especially noticeable contributors. We assume that there are more prominent works on topics related to (but not called) accountability, like fault localization or root cause analysis. This suggests that a clear and thorough overview of the whole field of computer science is needed. This should then yield to a clearer definition and taxonomy of the term accountability and its related concepts.

Table 3. Most influential researchers.

Name	Institution	Cit.
Siani Pearson	HP Labs Bristol, UK	16
David L. Chaum	Voting Systems Institute	14
Margo Seltzer	Harvard University, Cambridge, MA, USA	13
Jan Camenisch	IBM Research, Zurich, Switzerland	13
Markus Kirchberg	National University of Singapore, Singapore	11
Kiran Kumar Muniswamy-Reddy	Harvard University, Cambridge, MA, SA	9
Lorrie Faith Cranor	Carnegie Mellon University, Pittsburgh, PA, USA	9
Elisa Bertino	Purdue University, West Lafayette, Indiana, USA	8
Uri J. Braun	Harvard University, Cambridge, MA, USA	8
Gene Tsudik	University of California, Irvine, California, USA	8
Anna Lysyanskaya	Brown University, Providence, RI, USA	8
Wade Trappe	Rutgers University, Piscataway, New Jersey, USA	7
Ian T. Foster	University of Chicago, Chicago, IL, USA	7
Peter Macko	Harvard University, Cambridge, MA, USA	7
Susan Hohenberger	Johns Hopkins University, Baltimore, MD, USA	7

4   Synthesis

4.1   Definition of Accountability

One of the main motivation for us to conduct this mapping study was to come to a unified definition of accountability. We originally anticipated that most papers would agree on a specific definition; we assumed it would be the definition of *Information Accountability* as given by Weitzner et al. [26]. We did not expect that most papers would use the term without any definition or that so many papers would use ad-hoc definitions. Yet, this diversity of definitions also highlights the different facets of accountability and can serve as a basis for a more general definition. Analyzing all given definitions, we can identify five main themes:

1. Accountability should associate (or *link*) actions to entities (often individuals).
2. This link should then be used (often by a neutral third party) to hold the entity *responsible* for that action (often the terms blame and punish are used).
3. All definitions implicitly rely on some notion of *log* that is complete, tamper-proof and available to the neutral third party.

4. Another implicit assumption is that the log data can be used to *reason* about the events that have transpired.
5. All definitions only consider *single* systems. There is no notion of "distributed" accountability in those definitions.

Considering these aspects, we propose the following work-in-progress definition of accountability:

1. *Accountability* is a property of a system or a collection of systems and is ensured by an *Accountability Mechanism*.
2. An *Accountability Mechanism* is part of an *Accountable System* and reasons over a tamper-proof log to link effects of that system to entities.
3. An entity is (partially) *accountable* for a given effect if an *Accountability Mechanism* can prove a causal link between the entity's action and the given effect.
4. The set of entities *accountable* for a given effect is the set of all entities for which an *Accountability Mechanism* can prove a causal link between the entities' actions and the given effect.

4.2   Future Research Directions

We identified two main observations from the 45 study papers:

1. Preventing unwanted behavior is increasingly difficult in distributed and highly interconnected systems.
2. The impact of any unwanted behavior of computer systems increases with their adoption.

The first observation is corroborated by the domains that accountability mechanisms are mostly used in: cloud computing, distributed data sharing and web applications are all highly distributed systems. The use for accountability in a single user system is limited: as long as the system is not faulty, any effect is the result of its sole user's actions. Consequently, we expect a rising demand for accountability and its implementations in the fields of cyber-physical systems, smart systems, and similar fields where devices are only now being connected to form a wider Internet of Things. Indeed, a recent position paper by Datta et al. [11] calls for exactly such mechanisms to enhance the security of cyber-physical systems.

The second observation is best illustrated with the surprisingly high number of papers from the health care and medical domain. In our opinion, this can be explained with the legal risks and liabilities within the field. Medical devices are highly regulated and malfunctioning can be a serious threat to life and limb. If a pacemaker malfunctions, it is impossible to simply reboot the system or to restore the last backup. Similarly, computer systems already control cars, drones and hydro-dams. Any malfunctioning can have serious consequences and thus a high risk of legal action. In such a case the operator (and often also regulatory bodies) want a clear trace of accountability.

5   Threats to Validity

There are three main threats to validity of this mapping study: the selection of papers, our potential bias when reviewing and categorizing the papers, and the timeliness of the data.

Selection of papers. By limiting our study to the term "accountability", we might have missed papers that implement similar concepts but refer to them by different terms (e.g., "black box" or "root cause analysis"). We made our choice based on experiences of existing research. Petticrew and Roberts [22] highlight that the two main issues in conducting a literature survey are the sensitivity and specificity of the search. The sensitivity refers to the number of relevant publications of a search. Specificity describes the number of irrelevant studies of a search. The aim is to have a high sensitivity and a low specificity of a search. Synonyms may increase the sensitivity, but it also increases the specificity. Previous experiences of literature studies advocate simple search strings and limited synonyms to achieve an optimal trade-off between specificity and sensitivity [25].

Potential bias. It is possible that we collectively misclassified some papers. We countered this with a multi-staged voting process and took special care that every paper was reviewed by at least two different researchers. Furthermore, an inherent limitation of mapping studies is the superficial review of the source literature. Especially in the early stages we only looked at the abstract of a paper and not at its content. In the later stages, however, we examined each paper more carefully.

Timeliness of data. A well-known problem with literature reviews is that they are quickly outdated. The present data was gathered in 2015 and contains works up to the year 2015. This means that any more recent works are not part of our dataset. A recent (June 2017) manual check of the publishers' digital databases with study's search string returned one additional survey about accounting in content distribution networks [10] and some additional implementations in the field of e-health [13,14,27] and cloud computing [9,15]. While this search was not backed by a systematic process, we have not found any indication that our study's conclusions need revision. On the contrary, this cursory search seems to confirm our findings.

6   Conclusion and Future Work

Through this systematic mapping study, we establish the state of the art in accountability implementations and tools.

We have considered only those papers that describe an implementation. We did not consider contributions that described, even if in detail, how the ideas *could* be implemented. In this context, an interesting finding is that none of the papers have evaluated their tools for performance. This is important because one key factor that could limit the usefulness of accountability mechanisms is performance efficiency. The reason is that the origin of unwanted events is typically tracked using logging and analysis of "interesting" system events. Depending on the complexity of the analysis algorithm and the size of the logs, accountability implementations could be very expensive in terms of computation. It would help to get an insight into how the existing implementations perform and if the concepts can be reused in domains where real-time processing is needed, e.g., the automotive domain.

Another identified gap is the missing link between the high-level unwanted events that take place in an environment (e.g., personal and medical data is leaked in a Healthcare domain application) and the low-level unwanted events that are logged in the running technical systems (e.g., system calls reading from confidential files and writing to a socket in a network connection). It is important to establish this link because unwanted events are extracted from high-level requirements of privacy, security and safety properties and there is no universally agreed upon semantics of the relevant high-level events (e.g., data leak) in terms of low-level technical events (e.g., system calls writing to sockets). Though this gap has been filled in the context of preventive enforcement of usage control, it is not clear how this could be done for accountability.

One of our goals of this study was to identify which properties are often considered in combination with accountability. We found that security and privacy are most often considered along with accountability. Other important properties are integrity, provenance, trust, legal compliance, confidentiality, transparency, traceability, auditability and non-repudiation. While most papers consider more than one of these properties, an interesting finding is that none of the papers implement a safety property. This discovery points out a gap in the work on accountability for safety-critical systems.

We were also surprised that relevant concepts like reasoning, log analysis and causality did not feature prominently in the result set. Current accountability technologies focus mainly on preventive concepts (policies and access control) or authenticity/Non-repudiation (public key infrastructures, anonymity and signatures). At the high-level view of this mapping study we could not reliably identify an a-posteriori approach. We believe that this needs to change in the future: While it is feasible to manually analyze the logs (flight recorders) the few times a year an aircraft crashes, it becomes infeasible when multiple drones crash every day.

Our conclusion is that though accountability concepts have been around for quite some time, this area has not seen enough implementations, especially of a-posteriori approaches. At the technical level, there exists no generally accepted architecture and we did not come across contributions that give insights into acceptability issues like usability, scalability, etc. At the methodological level, there are no processes for deriving accountability-specific requirements. Thus, there is plenty of room for developing accountability infrastructures.

Acknowledgments. This work was funded in part by the Munich Center for Internet Research and the TUM Living Lab Connected Mobility (TUM LLCM) project which has been funded by the Bavarian Ministry of Economic Affairs and Media, Energy and Technology (StMWi) through the Center Digitisation. Bavaria, an initiative of the Bavarian State Government.

References

1. ACM digital library (2017). http://dl.acm.org/. Accessed 07 June 2017
2. IEEE Xplore (2017). http://ieeexplore.ieee.org. Accessed 07 June 2017
3. Scopus (2017). http://www.scopus.com. Accessed 07 June 2017
4. Springer (2017). http://link.springer.com. Accessed 07 June 2017
5. Zotero (2017). http://www.zotero.org. Accessed 07 June 2017
6. Andersen, D.G., Balakrishnan, H., Feamster, N., Koponen, T., Moon, D., Shenker, S.: Accountable internet protocol (AIP). ACM Comput. Commun. Rev. **38**, 339–350 (2008). ACM
7. Bhargav-Spantzel, A., Camenisch, J., Gross, T., Sommer, D.: User centricity: a taxonomy and open issues. J. Comput. Secur. **15**(5), 493–527 (2007)
8. Brzuska, C., Pöhls, H.C., Samelin, K.: Non-interactive public accountability for sanitizable signatures. In: De Capitani di Vimercati, S., Mitchell, C. (eds.) EuroPKI 2012. LNCS, vol. 7868, pp. 178–193. Springer, Heidelberg (2013). doi:10.1007/978-3-642-40012-4_12
9. Chen, H., Tu, S., Zhao, C., Huang, Y.: Provenance cloud security auditing system based on log analysis. In: 2016 IEEE International Conference of Online Analysis and Computing Science (ICOACS), pp. 155–159 (2016). doi:10.1109/ICOACS.2016.7563069
10. Coileáin, D.O., O'mahony, D.: Accounting and accountability in content distribution architectures: a survey. ACM Comput. Surv. **47**(4), 59:1–59:35 (2015). http://doi.acm.org/10.1145/2723701
11. Datta, A., Kar, S., Sinopoli, B., Weerakkody, S.: Accountability in cyber-physical systems. In: 2016 Science of Security for Cyber-Physical Systems Workshop (SOSCYPS), pp. 1–3 (2016). doi:10.1109/SOSCYPS.2016.7579998
12. Feigenbaum, J., Jaggard, A.D., Wright, R.N.: Towards a formal model of accountability. In: Workshop on New Security Paradigms Workshop, pp. 45–56. ACM (2011)
13. Grunwel, D., Sahama, T.: Delegation of access in an information accountability framework for ehealth. In: Proceedings of the Australasian Computer Science Week Multiconference, ACSW 2016, NY, USA, pp. 59:1–59:8. ACM, New York (2016). doi:10.1145/2843043.2843383
14. Grunwell, D., Batista, P., Campos, S., Sahama, T.: Managing and sharing health data through information accountability protocols. In: 2015 17th International Conference on E-health Networking, Application Services (HealthCom), pp. 200–204 (2015). doi:10.1109/HealthCom.2015.7454498
15. Jain, J.R., Asaduzzaman, A.: A novel data logging framework to enhance security of cloud computing. In: SoutheastCon 2016, pp. 1–6 (2016). doi:10.1109/SECON.2016.7506764
16. Kacianka, S., Beckers, K., Kelbert, F., Kumari, P.: Dataset: How Accountability is Understood and Realized (2017). https://doi.org/10.5281/zenodo.807129
17. Kelbert, F., Pretschner, A.: A fully decentralized data usage control enforcement infrastructure. In: Malkin, T., Kolesnikov, V., Lewko, A.B., Polychronakis, M. (eds.) ACNS 2015. LNCS, vol. 9092, pp. 409–430. Springer, Cham (2015). doi:10.1007/978-3-319-28166-7_20
18. Ko, R.K., Jagadpramana, P., Mowbray, M., Pearson, S., Kirchberg, M., Liang, Q., Lee, B.S.: Trustcloud: a framework for accountability and trust in cloud computing. In: IEEE World Congress on Services, pp. 584–588. IEEE (2011)

19. Papanikolaou, N., Pearson, S.: A cross-disciplinary review of the concept of accountability. In: Proceedings of the International Workshop on Trustworthiness, Accountability and Forensics in the Cloud (TAFC) (2011)
20. Pearson, S.: Toward accountability in the cloud. IEEE Internet Comput. **15**(4), 64 (2011)
21. Petersen, K., Feldt, R., Mujtaba, S., Mattsson, M.: Systematic mapping studies in software engineering. In: 12th International Conference on Evaluation and Assessment in Software Engineering, vol. 17 (2008)
22. Petticrew, M., Roberts, H.: Systematic Review in the Social Sciences: A Practical Guide. Blackwell Publishing, Oxford (2006)
23. Povey, D.: Optimistic security: a new access control paradigm. In: Proceedings of the 1999 Workshop on New Security Paradigms, pp. 40–45. ACM (2000)
24. Rooney, J.J., Heuvel, L.N.V.: Root cause analysis for beginners. Qual. Prog. **37**(7), 45–56 (2004)
25. Salleh, N., Mendes, E., Grundy, J.: Empirical studies of pair programming for CS/SE teaching in higher education: a systematic literature review. IEEE Trans. Softw. Eng. **37**(4), 509–525 (2011)
26. Weitzner, D.J., Abelson, H., Berners-Lee, T., Feigenbaum, J., Hendler, J., Sussman, G.J.: Information accountability. Commun. ACM **51**(6), 82–87 (2008)
27. Wickramage, C., Sahama, T., Fidge, C.: Anatomy of log files: implications for information accountability measures. In: Healthcom, pp. 1–6 (2016). doi:10.1109/HealthCom.2016.7749426
28. Wieringa, R., Maiden, N., Mead, N., Rolland, C.: Requirements engineering paper classification and evaluation criteria: a proposal and a discussion. Requir. Eng. **11**(1), 102–107 (2005)
29. Xiao, Y.: Flow-net methodology for accountability in wireless networks. IEEE Netw. **23**(5), 30–37 (2009)
30. Xiao, Z., Kathiresshan, N., Xiao, Y.: A survey of accountability in computer networks and distributed systems. Secur. Commun. Netw. **9**(4), 290–315 (2012)

Study Papers

31. Ahmed, M., Ahamad, M.: Combating abuse of health data in the age of eHealth exchange. In: IEEE International Conference on Healthcare Informatics, pp. 109–118 (2014)
32. Alexiou, N., Laganà, M., Gisdakis, S., Khodaei, M., Papadimitratos, P.: VeSPA: Vehicular Security and Privacy-preserving Architecture. In: 2nd ACM Workshop on Hot Topics on Wireless Network Security and Privacy, pp. 19–24. ACM (2013)
33. Ali, M., Moreau, L.: A provenance-aware policy language (cProvl) and a data traceability model (cProv) for the cloud. In: Third International Conference on Cloud and Green Computing, pp. 479–486 (2013)
34. Ali, S., Sivaraman, V., Ostry, D., Tsudik, G., Jha, S.: Securing first-hop data provenance for bodyworn devices using wireless link fingerprints. IEEE Trans. Inf. Forensics Secur. **9**(12), 2193–2204 (2014)
35. Ali, S.T., Sivaraman, V., Ostry, D., Jha, S.: Securing data provenance in body area networks using lightweight wireless link fingerprints. In: Proceedings of 3rd International Workshop on Trustworthy Embedded Devices, pp. 65–72. ACM (2013)
36. Asokan, N., Dmitrienko, A., Nagy, M., Reshetova, E., Sadeghi, A.-R., Schneider, T., Stelle, S.: CrowdShare: secure mobile resource sharing. In: Jacobson, M., Locasto, M., Mohassel, P., Safavi-Naini, R. (eds.) ACNS 2013. LNCS, vol. 7954, pp. 432–440. Springer, Heidelberg (2013). doi:10.1007/978-3-642-38980-1_27

37. Brzuska, C., Pöhls, H.C., Samelin, K.: Efficient and perfectly unlinkable sanitizable signatures without group signatures. In: Katsikas, S., Agudo, I. (eds.) EuroPKI 2013. LNCS, vol. 8341, pp. 12–30. Springer, Heidelberg (2014). doi:10. 1007/978-3-642-53997-8_2

38. Cherrueau, R.A., Sudholt, M.: Enforcing expressive accountability policies. In: IEEE 23rd International WETICE Conference, pp. 333–338 (2014)

39. Choi, C., Dong, Y., Zhang, Z.-L.: LIPS: Lightweight Internet Permit System for stopping unwanted packets. In: Boutaba, R., Almeroth, K., Puigjaner, R., Shen, S., Black, J.P. (eds.) NETWORKING 2005. LNCS, vol. 3462, pp. 178–190. Springer, Heidelberg (2005). doi:10.1007/11422778_15

40. Clifton, D., Fernandez, E.: A microprocessor design for multilevel security. In: Fourth Aerospace Computer Security Applications Conference, pp. 194–198 (1988)

41. Dailianas, A., Yemini, Y., Florissi, D., Huang, H.: MarketNet: market-based protection of network systems and services-an application to SNMP protection. In: Proceedings 19th Annual Joint Conference of the IEEE Computer and Communications Societies, vol. 3 (2000)

42. De Oliveira, A., Sendor, J., Garaga, A., Jenatton, K.: Monitoring personal data transfers in the cloud. In: IEEE 5th International Confernce on Cloud Computing Technology and Science, vol. 1, pp. 347–354 (2013)

43. Fahl, S., Dechand, S., Perl, H., Fischer, F., Smrcek, J., Smith, M.: Hey, NSA: stay away from my market! Future proofing app. Markets against powerful attackers. In: Proceedings of 2014 ACM Conference on Computer and Communications Security, pp. 1143–1155. ACM (2014)

44. Flegel, U.: Pseudonymizing unix log files. In: Davida, G., Frankel, Y., Rees, O. (eds.) InfraSec 2002. LNCS, vol. 2437, pp. 162–179. Springer, Heidelberg (2002). doi:10.1007/3-540-45831-X_12

45. Fugkeaw, S., Manpanpanich, P., Juntapremjitt, S.: AmTRUE: authentication management and trusted role-based authorization in multi-application and multi-user environment. In: The International Conference on Emerging Security Information, Systems, and Technologies, pp. 216–221 (2007)

46. Fugkeaw, S., Manpanpanich, P., Juntapremjitt, S.: A-COLD: access control of web OLAP over multi-data warehouse. In: International Conference on Availability, Reliability and Security, pp. 469–474 (2009)

47. Haidar, A., Zasada, S., Coveney, P., Abdallah, A., Beckles, B.: Audited credential delegation - a user-centric identity management solution for computational grid environments. In: Sixth International Confernce on Information Assurance and Security, pp. 222–227 (2010)

48. Jedrzejczyk, L., Price, B.A., Bandara, A.K., Nuseibeh, B.: On the impact of realtime feedback on users' behaviour in mobile location-sharing applications. In: Proceedings of Sixth Symposium on Usable Privacy and Security, pp. 14:1–14:12. ACM (2010)

49. Kang, Y., Schiffman, A., Shrager, J.: RAPPD: a language and prototype for recipient-accountable private personal data. In: IEEE Security and Privacy Workshops, pp. 49–56 (2014)

50. Khalasi, G., Chaudhari, M.: TrustGK monitor: 'Customer Trust As a Service' for the cloud. In: Proceedings of CUBE International Information Technology Conference, pp. 537–543. ACM (2012)

51. Ko, R., Jagadpramana, P., Lee, B.S.: Flogger: a file-centric logger for monitoring file access and transfers within cloud computing environments. In: IEEE 10th International Conference on Trust, Security and Privacy in Computing and Communications, pp. 765–771 (2011)

52. Ko, R., Will, M.: Progger: an efficient, tamper-evident kernel-space logger for cloud data provenance tracking. In: IEEE 7th International Conference on Cloud Computing, pp. 881–889 (2014)
53. Kuacharoen, P.: Design and implementation of a secure online lottery system. In: Papasratorn, B., Charoenkitkarn, N., Lavangnananda, K., Chutimaskul, W., Vanijja, V. (eds.) IAIT 2012. CCIS, vol. 344, pp. 94–105. Springer, Heidelberg (2012). doi:10.1007/978-3-642-35076-4_9
54. Langheinrich, M.: A privacy awareness system for ubiquitous computing environments. In: Borriello, G., Holmquist, L.E. (eds.) UbiComp 2002. LNCS, vol. 2498, pp. 237–245. Springer, Heidelberg (2002). doi:10.1007/3-540-45809-3_19
55. Lee, W., Squicciarini, A., Bertino, E.: The design and evaluation of accountable grid computing system. In: 29th IEEE International Conference on Distributed Computing Systems, pp. 145–154 (2009)
56. Lin, K.J., Chang, S.: A service accountability framework for QoS service management and engineering. Inf. Syst. e-Business Manag. **7**(4), 429–446 (2009)
57. Masmoudi, F., Loulou, M., Kacem, A.: Multi-tenant services monitoring for accountability in cloud computing. In: IEEE 6th International Conference on Cloud Computing Technology and Science, pp. 620–625 (2014)
58. Michalas, A., Komninos, N.: The lord of the sense: a privacy preserving reputation system for participatory sensing applications. In: IEEE Symposium on Computers and Communication, pp. 1–6 (2014)
59. Mivule, K., Otunba, S., Tripathy, T.: Implementation of data privacy and security in an online student health records system. Technical report, Department of Computer Science, Bowie State University (2014)
60. Mortimer, D., Cook, N.: Supporting accountable business to business document exchange in the cloud. In: IEEE International Conference on Service-Oriented Computing and Applications, pp. 1–8 (2010)
61. Naessens, V., De Decker, B., Demuynck, L.: Accountable anonymous E-mail. In: Sasaki, R., Qing, S., Okamoto, E., Yoshiura, H. (eds.) SEC 2005. IAICT, vol. 181, pp. 3–18. Springer, Boston (2005). doi:10.1007/0-387-25660-1_1
62. Pato, J., Paradesi, S., Jacobi, I., Shih, F., Wang, S.: Aintno: demonstration of information accountability on the web. In: IEEE 3rd International Conference on Privacy, Security, Risk and Trust and 2011 IEEE 3rd International Conference on Social Computing, pp. 1072–1080 (2011)
63. Pearce, C., Bertok, P., Van Schyndel, R.: Protecting consumer data in composite web services. In: Sasaki, R., Qing, S., Okamoto, E., Yoshiura, H. (eds.) SEC 2005. IAICT, vol. 181, pp. 19–34. Springer, Boston (2005). doi:10.1007/0-387-25660-1_2
64. Pearson, S., Rao, P., Sander, T., Parry, A., Paull, A., Patruni, S., Dandamudi-Ratnakar, V., Sharma, P.: Scalable, accountable privacy management for large organizations. In: 13th Enterprise Distributed Object Computing Conference Workshops, pp. 168–175 (2009)
65. Popa, R.A., Blumberg, A.J., Balakrishnan, H., Li, F.H.: Privacy and accountability for location-based aggregate statistics. In: Proceedings of 18th ACM Conference on Computer and Communications Security, pp. 653–666. ACM (2011)
66. Rubin, A.: Trusted distribution of software over the internet. In: Proceedings of Symposium on Network and Distributed System Security, pp. 47–53 (1995)
67. Ruth, P., Xu, D., Bhargava, B., Regnier, F.: E-notebook middleware for accountability and reputation based trust in distributed data sharing communities. In: Jensen, C., Poslad, S., Dimitrakos, T. (eds.) iTrust 2004. LNCS, vol. 2995, pp. 161–175. Springer, Heidelberg (2004). doi:10.1007/978-3-540-24747-0_13

68. Sriram, V., Narayan, G., Gopinath, K.: SAFIUS - a secure and accountable filesystem over untrusted storage. In: Fourth International IEEE Security in Storage Workshop, pp. 34–45 (2007)

69. Such, J.M., Espinosa, A., Garcia-Fornes, A.: An agent infrastructure for privacy-enhancing agent-based E-commerce applications. In: Dechesne, F., Hattori, H., ter Mors, A., Such, J.M., Weyns, D., Dignum, F. (eds.) AAMAS 2011. LNCS, vol. 7068, pp. 411–425. Springer, Heidelberg (2012). doi:10.1007/978-3-642-27216-5_31

70. Such, J.M., García-Fornes, A., Espinosa, A., Bellver, J.: Magentix2: a privacy-enhancing agent platform. Eng. Appl. Artif. Intell. **26**(1), 96–109 (2013)

71. Suen, C.H., Ko, R., Tan, Y.S., Jagadpramana, P., Lee, B.S.: S2Logger: end-to-end data tracking mechanism for cloud data provenance. In: 12th IEEE International Conference on Trust, Security and Privacy in Computing and Communications, pp. 594–602 (2013)

72. Wang, K., Malozemoff, A., Jia, N., Han, C., Maheswaran, M.: A social accountability framework for computer networks. In: IEEE Global Telecommunications Conference, pp. 1–6 (2010)

73. Xiao, Y., Meng, K., Takahashi, D.: Implementation and evaluation of accountability using flow-net in wireless networks. In: Military Communications Conference, pp. 7–12 (2010)

74. Xu, G., Aguilera, L., Guan, Y.: Accountable anonymity: a proxy re-encryption based anonymous communication system. In: IEEE 18th International Conference on Parallel and Distributed Systems, pp. 109–116 (2012)

75. Zhou, W., Sherr, M., Tao, T., Li, X., Loo, B.T., Mao, Y.: Efficient querying and maintenance of network provenance at internet-scale. In: Proceedings of 2010 ACM SIGMOD International Conference on Management of Data, pp. 615–626. ACM (2010)

User and Value Centric Approaches

Differentiating Feature Realization in Software Product Development

Aleksander Fabijan[1(✉)], Helena Holmström Olsson[1], and Jan Bosch[2]

[1] Faculty of Technology and Society, Malmö University,
Nordenskiöldsgatan 1, 211 19 Malmö, Sweden
{Aleksander.Fabijan,Helena.Holmstrom.Olsson}@mah.se
[2] Department of Computer Science and Engineering,
Chalmers University of Technology, Hörselgången 11,
412 96 Gothenburg, Sweden
Jan.Bosch@chalmers.se

Abstract. Context: Software is no longer only supporting mechanical and electrical products. Today, it is becoming the main competitive advantage and an enabler of innovation. Not all software, however, has an equal impact on customers. Companies still struggle to differentiate between the features that are regularly used, there to be for sale, differentiating and that add value to customers, or which are regarded commodity. **Goal:** The aim of this paper is to (1) identify the different types of software features that we can find in software products today, and (2) recommend how to prioritize the development activities for each of them. **Method:** In this paper, we conduct a case study with five large-scale software intensive companies. **Results:** Our main result is a model in which we differentiate between four fundamentally different types of features (e.g. 'Checkbox', 'Flow', 'Duty' and 'Wow'). **Conclusions:** Our model helps companies in (1) differentiating between the feature types, and (2) selecting an optimal methodology for their development (e.g. 'Output-Driven' vs. 'Outcome-Driven').

Keywords: Data · Feedback · Outcome-driven development · Data-driven development · Goal-oriented development

1 Introduction

Rapid delivery of value to customers is one of the core priorities of software companies [1–3]. Consequently, the amount of software added to products with attempts to deliver the value is rapidly increasing. At first, software functionality was predominately required in products to support tangible electrical, hardware and mechanical solutions without delivering any other perceptible value for the customers. Organizations developed the software as a necessary cost, leaving the prioritization part to the responsible engineering, hardware and mechanical departments, without exploring the value of software features as such. Today, products that were once built purely from hardware components such as e.g. cars and household appliances, contain functionality that allows them to connect to the Internet, exchange information and self-improve over

© Springer International Publishing AG 2017
M. Felderer et al. (Eds.): PROFES 2017, LNCS 10611, pp. 221–236, 2017.
https://doi.org/10.1007/978-3-319-69926-4_16

time. Software functionality is rapidly becoming the main competitive advantage of the product, and what delivers value to the customers [4].

However, the way in which software features are being developed, and how they are prioritized is still a challenge for many organizations. Often, and due to immaturity and lack of experience in software development, companies that transitioned in this way (e.g. from electrical to software companies) treat software features similarly to electronics or mechanics components. They risk being unable to identify what features are differentiating and that add value to customers, and what features are regarded commodity by customers. As a consequence of this, individual departments continue to prioritize what they find the most important and miss the opportunities to minimize and share the investments into commodity features [5, 6]. Companies that are becoming data-driven, are exploring this problem and trying to learn from the feedback that they collect to optimize the prioritization decisions. The focus of software companies and product team that recognized the benefits of being data-driven is to develop the product that delivers the most value for the customer [1–3]. For every feature being developed, the goal is to create clarity in what to develop (Value Identification), develop it to a correct extent (Value Realization), and accurately measure the progress (Value Validation).

In our work, we perform an exploratory case study in which we were interested in (1) identifying how companies differentiate between different types of features and (2) how they prioritize the development activities with respect to the type of the feature that they are developing. In this study, we identify that the lack of distinguishing between different types of features is the primary reason for inefficient resource allocation that, in the end, make innovation initiatives suffer. In our previous work [7], we confirmed that differentiating between the different levels of functionality is indeed a challenge that software companies face today. In this paper, however, we further detail the feature differentiation model and evaluate it in two additional case companies.

The contribution of this paper is twofold. First, we provide detailed guidelines on how to distinguish between different types of features that are being developed and we provide empirical evidence on the challenges and implications involved in this. Second, we detail a conceptual model to guide practitioners in prioritizing the development activities for each of the feature types identified in our differentiation model. We identify in our work that for the successful development of innovative 'Wow' and 'Flow' features, a different methodology is required. We label this methodology 'Outcome-Driven development' and demonstrate how it differs from 'Output-Driven approach'. With our contribution, companies can develop only the amount of feature that is required for commoditized functionality and, on the other hand, frees the resources to maximize their investments in innovative features that will deliver the most value.

2   Background

Software companies strive to become more effective in delivering value to their customers. Typically, they inherit the Agile principles on an individual development team level [8] and expand these practices across the product and other parts of the organization [9]. Next, they focus on various lean concepts such as eliminating waste [10, 11], removing constraints in the development pipeline [12], and advancing towards continuous integration and continuous deployment of software functionality [13]. Continuous deployment is characterized by a bidirectional channel that enables companies not only to deliver new updates to their customers in order to rapidly prototype with them [14], but also to collect feedback on how these products are used. By evaluating ideas with customers, companies learn about their preferences. In this process, the actual product instrumentation data (for example, features used in a session) has the potential to identify improvements and make the prioritization process of valuable features more accurate [15]. In fact, a wide range of different techniques is used to collect feedback, spanning from qualitative techniques capturing customer experiences and behaviors [16–18], to quantitative techniques capturing product performance and operation [19, 20]. However, this development of getting rapid feedback in real time is only possible today when software products are increasingly becoming connected to the internet. And as such data focuses on what customers do rather than what they say, it complements other types of feedback data [21] and improves the understanding of the value that the product provides [22]. For example, knowing which features are used in a certain context helps companies in identifying customer preferences and possible bottlenecks. The intuition of software development companies on customer preferences, can be as much as 90% of the time inaccurate [23–25]. In most companies, customer feedback is collected on a frequent basis in order to learn about how customers use products, what features they appreciate and what functionality they would like to see in new products [16]. This enables the companies to very quickly test new variants with the customers and explore how they perform with the respect to the metrics that are important. This concept is known as Continuous Experimentation [26] and its impact is extensive [27].

2.1 Business and Design Experimentation

Davenport [28] suggests the design of smart business experiments to emphasize the need to bridge business needs closer to software design and engineering. The importance of running experiments to learn more about customer behavior is one of the core principles of the Lean Startup methodology [14, 29]. This idea is emphasized also in the product management literature by Bosch [18] who propose the need of constant generation of new ideas that should be evaluated with customers. Fagerholm et al. [1] suggest the RIGHT model for continuous experimentation and support constant testing of ideas. In their view, this is essential to create the evaluation of product value as an integral part of the development process. The strength of experimentation is further accelerated with controlled experiments. In controlled experiments (also known as A/B test), users of a software product or a feature are randomly divided between the variants (e.g., the two different designs of a product interface) in a persistent manner (a user receives the same experience at multiple software uses). Users' interactions with the product are instrumented and key metrics are computed [30, 31]. Research contributions with practical guides on how to create controlled experiments in software product development have previously been published both by Microsoft [19, 32] and Google [33]. The Return on Investment (ROI) of controlled experiments has been demonstrated and discussed a number of times in the literature [31, 32].

2.2 Feature Differentiation

Already in 1984, Kano [34] has identified the need to differentiate between product attributes (e.g. attractiveness, satisfaction, must-be, indifferent and reverse attributes) based on their importance for the product and the stakeholders. One of the key characteristics of the Kano model itself is the notion of attribute drift (for example, an attribute such as camera resolution is expected to improve over time). Attribute drift is driven by customers' expectations and changes over time. In this context, Bosch [35] developed the 'Three Layer Product Model' (3LPM) on the idea that a return on innovation requires differentiation [36]. The model provides a high-level understanding of the three different layers of features, i.e. commodity, differentiating and innovative, and it has been constructed for the purpose of reducing architectural complexity. And although these models can be applied to an industrial context, they do not provide guidance on how to differentiate between the different types of features, neither how to prioritize software development activities based on the differentiation. At the same time, the pace at which we are becoming to be able to learn from the customers in the software industry is faster than anywhere else [16, 19]. The feedback that is available today (e.g. feature usage data while the product in the hands of the users) opens new possibilities for understanding and differentiating features in products. Using existing models (e.g. such as the Kano model or the 3LPM model) and accommodating new dimensions of learnings that we discussed above is challenging for software companies, and it blocks them from fully benefiting from the new possibilities [7, 20]. The implications of limited customer learning are substantive and can cause companies to inaccurately prioritize feature development by e.g. develop the software features to the wrong extend in either direction.

In our previous research [7], we developed a model in which four fundamentally different types of features are being developed. We name them "duty", "wow", "checkbox" and "flow" types of features. With "duty", we label the type of features that are needed in the products due to a policy or regulatory requirement. "Checkbox" features are the features that companies need to provide to be on par with the competition that provides similar functionality. With "wow", we label the differentiating features that are the deciding factor for buying a product. Finally, and with "flow", we label the features in the product that are regularly used.

In this paper, we address the new possibilities of learning from customers to (1) detail the differentiation of features for software products, and (2) to suggest on how to prioritize the development activities for each of them. Our model (1) helps companies in differentiating between the feature types, and (2) selecting a methodology for their development (e.g. 'Output-Driven' vs. 'Outcome-Driven' development).

3 Research Method

In this section, we describe our research method. This case study [37] builds on an ongoing work with five case companies and it was conducted between January 2015 and June 2017. The goal of this study was to identify a state-of-the-art differentiation of software features. Companies A–C were participating for the full period of the ongoing research while companies D–E joined in this research in April 2016.

We present the case companies in Table 1.

Table 1. Case company descriptions.

Company A is a manufacturer and supplier of transport solutions construction technology and vehicles for commercial use. The systems that they develop require stable and fine-defined operation with no margin for misunderstanding. Companies' portfolio is extensive and includes both products for B2B as well as B2C types of customers.
Company B is a provider of telecommunication systems and equipment, communications networks and multimedia solutions for mobile and fixed network operators. Companies' portfolio is extensive and primarily consists of products developed for B2B customers.
Company C is a software company specializing in navigational information, operations management and optimization solutions. Their portfolio includes products and services for the B2B market.
Company D develops software systems for several different domains, including healthcare, energy and infrastructure operations. Their portfolio is extensive and includes products and services for both B2B as well as B2C types of customers.
Company E produces software and hardware systems for various surveillance purposes. Their portfolio includes products mostly for B2B types of customers and it operates in many market segments such as transport, infrastructure, retail, banking, education, etc.

3.1   Data Collection

We collected our data using three types of data collection activities. First, we conducted **individual workshops** with the companies involved in this research. Second, we conducted **joint workshops** with participants from multiple companies discussing the focus of our research. Finally, we conducted semi structured **interviews** following a guide with pre-defined open-ended questions with participants from each of the companies for in-depth analysis. During the group workshops, we were always three researchers sharing the responsibility of asking questions and facilitating the group discussion. The data collection activities were conducted in English and lasted on average three hours (individual workshops and joint workshops), and one hour (interviews). Each of the data-collection activities was conducted with practitioners in different roles (software engineers, project/product managers, sales specialists, and line/portfolio managers). In total, we performed 14 individual workshops, 7 joint workshops and 45 interviews.

3.2   Data Analysis

During analysis, the workshop notes, interview transcriptions and graphical illustrations were used when coding the data. The data collected were analyzed following the conventional qualitative content analysis approach [38]. We read raw data word by word to derive codes. In this process, we first highlighted individual phrases that captured our attention in the transcriptions. We used color coding to highlight different topics that emerged during the analysis process. In this process, we reflected on the highlighted text several times and took notes. As this process continued for a few iterations (e.g. by analyzing the first few workshop notes and interviews), codes emerged from the highlights. In the next step, we sorted these codes into categories (e.g. grouping them by color). This type of design is appropriate when striving to describe a phenomenon where existing theory or research literature is limited. After we emerged with a few codes, we created definitions for those codes and continued to code the rest of the data using the definitions.

3.3   Threats to Validity

Internal Validity. As the participants were familiar with the research topic and expectations between the researchers and participants were well aligned, this can be a potential source of bias and thus a possible threat to internal validity. We mitigate this threat by providing unbiased overviews of the research area at the beginning of every data collection session, and avoiding suggestive interrogation during the workshops and leading questions during the interviews.

Construct Validity. To improve the study's construct validity, we used multiple techniques of data collection (e.g. workshops, interviews) and multiple sources of data collection (product managers, software engineers, sales representatives, managers, etc.). The complete meeting minutes from the workshops and interview transcriptions were independently assessed by two of the researchers. This process was overseen by the third researcher for quality control.

External Validity. Our results cannot directly translate to other companies. However, we believe that certain software companies could benefit from studying our results. Specifically, the results of this research are applicable for companies that are transitioning from mechanical or electrical towards software companies, which may experience similar issues in differentiating and prioritizing software features.

4   Empirical Findings

In this section, we present our empirical findings. First, and to understand the current development practices in our case companies to identify the type and the extent of the feature that they are developing, we outline the current customer data collection practices in the case companies. We recognize that the practices to collect customer data do not differ with respect to the feature being developed, but rather depend on the perceived need of information ad-hoc. Next, we identify the challenges that are associated with distinguishing between the different feature types. Finally, we explore their implications.

4.1   Current State of Feature Differentiation

In the case companies, products and features that are being developed are handed over from one development stage to another, together with their requirements and priorities. Although our case companies acknowledge that they are aware of the need for differencing between the types of features, i.e. commodity, differentiating and innovative, the information that would help them achieve that does not circulate with the requirements. The differentiation strategy is unclear to the practitioners developing the features. And consequently, setting the development investment level for a feature does not vary with respect to the type of the feature, allowing the prioritization strategy to be in favour of commodity features. We illustrate and describe the current state with description and quotes from our case companies below.

"Should we go into Maintenance budget? Or should it go to investment budget and we prioritize there?"   *- Product Strategist from Company C.*

"There is a lot of functionality that we probably would not need to focus on."
                                                      - Technology Specialist from Company C.

"Customer could be more involved in prioritization that we do in pre-development. Is this feature more important that the other one?"   *- Product Owner from Company B.*

4.2 Challenges with Feature Differentiation

The current state advocates a situation where features are not differentiated in the strategy between being innovative, differentiating or commodity and, consequently, development activities do not differ between the features. Based on our interviews, we see that there are several challenges associated with this situation. Our interviewees report that the collection of feedback, which serves as the base for developing a feature is conducted ad-hoc and not following the type of the feature being developed. Second, the directives to differentiate the feature on a granular level are incomprehensible for our practitioners. Therefore, it is very challenging for the R&D staff in our case companies to be effective in understanding which of the features are differentiating and innovative in the market.

"We want to understand what the customer wants to have and truly, what do they need."
                                                      -Product Manager from company A.

"Functionality is software basically and the features are more subjective opinions and things that we can't really... it is hard to collect data."   *–Function owner from Company C.*

"Those are the things that worry us the most. All of us, since it is so hard, you need to gamble a bit. If it turns out that you are wrong, then you are behind."

                                                      –Product Manager from Company A.

4.3 Implications

Due to an unclear differentiating strategy, our case companies experience several implications during the development process of a feature. The companies consider the stakeholders that the features are being developed for as a uniform group and not differentiating the development extent of the features based on the type of the feature and stakeholder. This leads to a situation where resources are used in developing and optimizing the features that might never get used by a customer to a similar extent as the ones that are regularly utilized. Consequently, commodity suppresses resources that could be better used to develop features in the innovation layer.

"If you are sitting in a team and then you talk to maybe 2 or 3 customers, then you see that this is the most important thing we need to do." -Product Manager from company A.

"We tend to focus on the wrong things. We need to look at the benefit for their customers."

"In our organization is difficult to sew everything together, to make it work. That requires funding that is almost non-existent." –Software engineer from Company A.

"We do also our own tests of competitors. We do feature roadmaps for [feature name] for example. And then we have a leading curve... We measure are we on track or not."

-Product Strategist from Company C.

4.4 Summary of Our Empirical Findings

Vague differentiating strategy results in challenges with the purpose of the feature being developed, implicating uniform treatment of features. Invariable investment levels into development activities results in incomprehensible directives, implicating arbitrary investments in development activities. Favoring commodity results in a challenge of identifying what innovation, implicating the suppression of the actual innovation and projecting competitors current state as the norm. We summarize them in Table 2.

Table 2. Mapping of the current state, challenges and implications.

Current state	Challenges	Implications
Vague differentiating strategy	Understanding the stakeholder and purpose of the feature	Stakeholders treated uniformly, not reflecting their differing business value
Invariable investment levels	Incomprehensible high-level directives	Arbitrary investments in development activities
Feature prioritization processes is in favor of commodity	Commodity functionality is internally considered to be innovative	Commodity suppresses innovation Projecting competitors current state is the norm

5 Differentiating Feature Realization

In this section, and as a response to the empirical data from our case companies, we present and detail our model for feature differentiation. The contribution of our model is threefold. First, it provides four different categories of features and their characteristics to give practitioners an ability to better differentiate between feature types. Second, and as a guide for practitioners after classifying a feature, we provide a summary of development activities that should be prioritized for every type of feature.

5.1 Feature Differentiation

In our model, four fundamentally different types of features are being developed. The differentiation is based on the characteristics in Table 3.

Table 3. Feature differentiation.

Stake-holder	We recognize four types of fundamentally different stakeholders that are targeted with new feature development. Product users, the competitor developing or already selling a similar feature, the customer purchasing and asking for a feature, or a regulatory entity imposing it.
Feature Engagement	This characteristic describes the level of engagement expected with the feature. Features are primarily used by the end-users and occasionally by the customers directly. The engagement with the features is therefore expected for these two groups. Regulators and competitors, however, typically do not use the features directly. Instead, and what we see in our case companies is that verify the documents or tests demonstrating the existence or compliance of the feature. The expected exposure to the feature for regulators and competitors is therefore low.
Feedback	Feedback data that is collected about features under development is of various types. For example, the "Flow" features' will be regularly used by users and should be equipped with automatic feedback collection mechanisms to retrieve customer data about feature usage. The "Checkbox" features source are the competitors that are being analysed for a similar offering. In the case of "Wow" features, the primary stakeholders are customers, whom companies study extensively through market analysis and available reports. Finally, and in the case of the regulation and standardization services (A), companies query regulation agencies for regulatory requirements.
Focus	"Flow" features focus on the user and maximizing user value. Practitioners, in this case, develop and iterate features that are validated with the users. For "Wow" features, practitioners use their own technical ability to maximize the technical outcome of the feature. Here, for example, companies use their simulators to test the speed of the software or its stability. For "Checkbox" features, practitioners compare the feature under development towards the ones from the competitors. In this case, the objective of the development organization is to develop a feature that is matching or improving the competitors' feature. Companies continuously compare towards competition and intentionally slows down if they are performing better as expected.
Sales Impact	The greatest influence on driving sales have the features that focus on the customer "Wow" features and features that focus on the user "Flow" features. Both types are differentiating or innovative. However, in B2B markets, the user of the product is different from the customer and hence "Flow" features are less of a deciding factor for potential customers. As an example, users communicate and show satisfaction with a product to their managers and departments that purchase the features and products. Their opinions have the possibility to indirectly influence the opinion of the customer. "Duty" and "Checkbox" features have very low or no impact at all for choosing a product over the one from a competitor.

By going through the process of articulating different views on the characteristics below, product teams can make the most of their collective insight on classifying them into **"duty"**, **"wow"**, **"checkbox"** or **"flow"** type. What is important for the practitioners, however, is how to optimally prioritize the development activities for each of the features types. We present this in the next section.

5.2   Activity Prioritization

In this his section, we present the activities that should be prioritized for each of the four feature types. We suggest how to set the extent of the feature that should be developed. Here, the extent of the feature can be either defined once (constant) or dynamically adjusted during development and operation (*floating* alternates, *following* follows the competitors *or open* no limitation). Second, the sources that contain the information required to set the development extent need to be defined. Next, we suggest the most important activities for feature realization. They are followed by the activities that do not deliver value and should be avoided. Finally, we suggest how to set the deployment frequency. For details see Table 4.

Table 4. Activity prioritization.

Duty Features	The development extent for this type of features is constant and defined by the regulators. To identify it, practitioners can use research institutions, standardization industries and industry publishers as a source of feedback to get access to various standardization reports, vendor communications and obtain the regulatory requirements. For this type of features, identifying regulatory requirements and developing them until they satisfy the requirements are the two main activities. UX optimization, investments in marketing activities developing infrastructure and other similar activities for this type of features should be minimized. Deployment of this type of features is single.
Wow Features	For this type of feature, development extent is dynamically set using the feedback from the market. Practitioners query social media, marketing agencies, customer reports, requests, and interviews to identify business cases and sentimental opinions about the product. The two most important activities of this type are the identification of technical selling points and selling characteristic of the product, and maximizing investments in the technical development of the feature and marketing it. The feature's quantifiable value should be maximized with periodically scheduled deployment increments.
Checkbox Features	This type of features should be developed following a "sliding bar" extent that follows the competitor's trend. Practitioners should guarantee to be on par with the indicative trend collected from industry test magazines and internal evaluation of customer products. It is essential to read articles in the media, consolidative question the customers, participate in customer events and perform trend analysis. Practitioners should perform competitor analysis to determine feature characteristics and develop the feature incrementally following the trend. Since features of this type will not be used extensively by the actual users, investments in improving user experience and interaction with the feature can be minimized. Deployment should be frequent and scheduled. Although products typically require this type of features to be even considered by the customers, they are not the decisive reason for customers to churn or select a product over a competitor.
Flow Features	With this type of features and the ambition to discover new and innovative concepts, practitioners should continuously deploy changes to their products, collect product feedback, analyse it, and perform A/B test to rank alternatives. The two most important activities for this type of feature are the defining of evaluation criteria and maximizing the ability to experiment with them. Interviewing the stakeholders or gathering qualitative information should be of secondary value and used for interpreting results. Also, and due to the continuous deployment, there is a high impact on the infrastructure.

6 Model Evaluation

We detailed our model and evaluated its feasibility with the five case companies in recent workshop and interview sessions. Our validation criteria were to identify whether companies identify the feature types that they develop (based on our model), and whether it helps them mitigate any challenges. Based on the evaluation, we identified that four of the five companies develop all types of features, whereas company E does not develop "duty" features. They do, however, acknowledge that they developed duty features in their early stages of building the key products.

Effortless Differentiation: One of the key challenges for companies is to identify whether a feature is a commodity, differentiating or innovative. With the feature differentiation model, practitioners felt empowered to perform this distinction based on the five key characteristics. By passing through the characteristics, practitioners can determine in which of the four quadrants their feature under development belongs to. We illustrate this with the two quotes next.

"Now we talk about these differentiators. This is known now, the wow features... One of the wow features, that we are selling is that we change rules and we demonstrate it in front of the customers."

– Product Owner from Company C

"We have a lot of checkbox features in our products that are only there because the competitors have them, but it is not directly the end user that wants them."

- Product Manager from Company E

Directive Comprehension: With the differentiation between the features ('Duty', 'Checkbox', 'Wow' and 'Flow') and the development process (Output-Driven vs. Outcome-Driven), we give practitioners in large software companies the ability to define the right ambition level for a certain type of the feature, the preferred methods of collecting customer feedback, and provide them with instructions on which development activities to focus on.

"More experimentation is done in outcome-driven development. Absolutely in the Flow type."

- Product Manager from Company E

"For Duty and Checkbox features you know what you need to do, and you just have to do enough. You need to say that you have it, but it does not need to work that nicely."

- Product Manager from Company E

Distinguishing Innovative Features: With a clear separation between different types of features, our model enables practitioners to prioritize innovative functionality and invest in relevant activities, e.g. running continuous controlled experiments with customers for "Flow" features, or prioritizing investments into identifying regulation requirements for "Duty" features.

"You define the outcomes and see what activities contribute to that."

- Product Owner from Company C

7 Output-Driven vs. Outcome-Driven Development

In the previous sections, we provided guidance on how to differentiate between the different types of features and which development activities to prioritize for each of them. In this section, we illustrate the differences in the development approaches (based on additional learnings during the validation sessions) for the three stages of feature development (Value Identification, Value Realization, and Value Validation). For each of the stages, we provide indications on what is beneficial and a drawback for this type of development. For example, in the Value Identification phase (illustrated with 1 in Fig. 1), we discuss requirements freedom (the extent to which feature teams can interpret and change requirements) of both approaches. Next, we contrast 'Value Realization' phase (illustrated with 2 in Fig. 1) by briefly presenting the differences in the autonomy of the development teams. In the Value Validation phase (illustrated with 3 in Fig. 1 below, we compare the extent to which a completion goal is known to a development team, and how distant they are from the customer data (e.g. feedback that can be used to validate how well the feature satisfies the objectives.

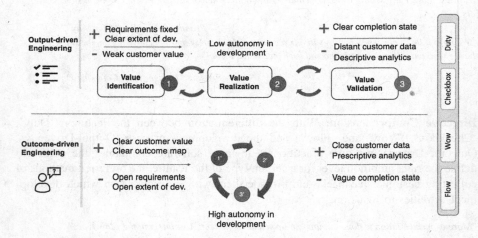

Fig. 1. Feature development in Output-Driven and Outcome-Driven development.

Output-Driven Development. Our findings indicate that 'Duty' and 'Checkbox' features development follows a common process. We select this label to emphasize the long-lasting tradition that our case companies followed in their transition from electronics to software companies. Companies that develop features in this way typically spend a considerable amount of time studying the requirements and/or competitors to determine what to develop in the Value Identification phase. Because of known policies, defined standards or competitor's development outcomes (for example, a feature that was realized), they fix the requirements on what they should develop and information to which extent is given (for example, a safety feature should activate under 10 ms). This enables teams in the Value Realization phase to focus on meeting the requirements and following the standards and sparing the team from customer representative roles. The teams that develop these types of features have limited autonomy and they do not re-prioritize development activities at execution. This is not necessarily a drawback. Certain approaches for feature development [39] reject the autonomy of teams and consider it an overhead. Minimizing the number and significance of the prioritization decisions that the development teams must do makes teams more focused on the development activity at hand. Generally, the development team should be deciding on feature priority only after the priorities of regulations, the business, and the customer have already been addressed. Because of the Stakeholder objectives, the teams in the 'Value Validation' phase can benefit from knowing what exactly satisfies the objectives. The resulting feedback used for evaluation, however, can be very distant. As described in the previous section, features developed in this way typically do not get instrumented with real-time feedback collection. This implies that development teams depend on the time distance of feature integration and deployment to the customer, and the time distance of feedback collection, which can be (and in several of features developed by our case companies is) significant. In this development process, our case companies define the following question and strive to answer it: "Are the customers using the system and how?" and answer it using typically qualitative feedback such as observations and interviews, and quantitative raw logs.

Outcome-Driven Development. We contrast the approach above by presenting how 'Wow' and 'Flow' features are being developed. In what we label 'Outcome-driven development' development teams work significantly more iteratively and autonomously. In the Value Identification phase, and due to the nature of 'Wow' and 'Flow' features, teams invest into identifying what customers and users expect as an outcome and outline a feature idea around this. As a result of studying the value as it will be experienced by the customer and not a requirement, it is very challenging to quantitatively describe the extent to which the feature should be developed. In the Value Realization phase, agile teams embed a customer representative within the development team and the customer representative determines the priorities for development. Therefore, the team has a high autonomy and ownership of the features that they are developing. This is, in principal different than traditional agile teams which follow the backlog items as defined and prioritized by a product owner. This is possible as the Value Validation phase is closely connected with the first two phases due to proximity to customer data. In this development process, our case companies define the following question that they try to answer: "Are the customers efficiently achieving desired outcomes with minimal blocking?" and measure their success with prescriptive analytics (for example experimentation) on customer value metrics (for example task success, time needed to result).

8 Conclusions

In this paper, based on case study research in five large software-intensive companies, we identify that companies struggle to differentiate between different types of features, i.e. they don't know what is innovation, differentiation or commodity, which is the main problem that causes poor allocation of R&D efforts and suppresses innovation. To address this challenge, we developed and detailed a model in which we depict the activities for differentiating and working with different types of features and stakeholders. Also, we evaluated the model with our case companies.

With our model, which differs from existing models and similar models (e.g. the Kano model [34]) in that it focuses on software products with rapid customer feedback capabilities, practitioners can (1) categorize the features that are under development into one of the four types and invest into activities that are relevant for that type, (2) maximize the resource allocation for innovative features that will deliver the most value, and (3) mitigate certain challenges related to feature differentiation.

Our model, however, still requires an in-depth validation on a larger scale to claim its general applicability. The current evaluation is based on qualitative impressions of the practitioners from our study, which is certainly a limitation. In future work, we plan to expand this model by studying how mature online companies differentiate between the different types of features that they develop, how their activities are prioritized, and validate the model using quantitative metrics (e.g. counting the number of features of individual type in each of the case companies).

References

1. Fagerholm, F., Guinea, A.S., Mäenpää, H., Münch, J.: The RIGHT model for continuous experimentation. J. Syst. Softw. **0**, 1–14 (2015)
2. Denne, M., Cleland-Huang, J.: The incremental funding method: data-driven software development. IEEE Softw. **21**, 39–47 (2004)
3. Boehm, B.: Value-based software engineering: reinventing. SIGSOFT Softw. Eng. Notes **28**, 3 (2003)
4. Khurum, M., Gorschek, T., Wilson, M.: The software value map - an exhaustive collection of value aspects for the development of software intensive products. J. Softw. Evol. Process. **25**, 711–741 (2013)
5. Lindgren, E., Münch, J.: Software development as an experiment system: a qualitative survey on the state of the practice. In: Lassenius, C., Dingsøyr, T., Paasivaara, M. (eds.) XP 2015. LNBIP, vol. 212, pp. 117–128. Springer, Cham (2015). doi:10.1007/978-3-319-18612-2_10
6. Olsson, H.H., Bosch, J.: Towards continuous customer validation: a conceptual model for combining qualitative customer feedback with quantitative customer observation. In: Fernandes, J.M., Machado, R.J., Wnuk, K. (eds.) ICSOB 2015. LNBIP, vol. 210, pp. 154–166. Springer, Cham (2015). doi:10.1007/978-3-319-19593-3_13
7. Fabijan, A., Olsson, H.H., Bosch, J.: Commodity eats innovation for breakfast: a model for differentiating feature realization. In: Abrahamsson, P., Jedlitschka, A., Nguyen Duc, A., Felderer, M., Amasaki, S., Mikkonen, T. (eds.) PROFES 2016. LNCS, vol. 10027, pp. 517–525. Springer, Cham (2016). doi:10.1007/978-3-319-49094-6_37
8. Martin, R.C.: Agile Software Development, Principles, Patterns, and Practices (2002)
9. Olsson, H.H., Alahyari, H., Bosch, J.: Climbing the "Stairway to heaven" - a multiple-case study exploring barriers in the transition from agile development towards continuous deployment of software. In: Proceedings of 38th EUROMICRO Conference on Software Engineering and Advanced Applications, SEAA 2012, pp. 392–399 (2012)

10. Mujtaba, S., Feldt, R., Petersen, K.: Waste and lead time reduction in a software product customization process with value stream maps. In: Proceedings of the Australian Software Engineering Conference, ASWEC, pp. 139–148 (2010)
11. Sedano, T., Ralph, P., Sedano, T.: Software development waste. In: Proceedings of the 39th International Conference on Software Engineering - ICSE 2017, pp. 130–140. IEEE Press, Buenos Aires (2017)
12. Goldratt, E.M., Cox, J.: The Goal: A Process of Ongoing Improvement. North River Press, Great Barrington (2004)
13. Rodríguez, P., Haghighatkhah, A., Lwakatare, L.E., Teppola, S., Suomalainen, T., Eskeli, J., Karvonen, T., Kuvaja, P., Verner, J.M., Oivo, M.: Continuous deployment of software intensive products and services: a systematic mapping study. J. Syst. Softw. **123**, 263–291 (2015)
14. Ries, E.: The Lean Startup: How Today's Entrepreneurs Use Continuous Innovation to Create Radically Successful Businesses. Crown Business, New York (2011)
15. Fabijan, A.: Developing the right features: the role and impact of customer and product data in software product development (2016). https://dspace.mah.se/handle/2043/21268
16. Fabijan, A., Olsson, H.H., Bosch, J.: Customer feedback and data collection techniques in software R&D: a literature review. In: Fernandes, J., Machado, R., Wnuk, K. (eds.) ICSOB 2015. LNBIP, vol. 210, pp. 139–153. Springer, Cham (2015). doi:10.1007/978-3-319-19593-3_12
17. Williams, L., Cockburn, A.: Introduction: Agile Software Development: Its About Feedback and Change (2003)
18. Bosch-Sijtsema, P., Bosch, J.: User involvement throughout the innovation process in high-tech industries. J. Prod. Innov. Manag. **32**, 1–36 (2014)
19. Kohavi, R., Deng, A., Frasca, B., Walker, T., Xu, Y., Pohlmann, N.: Online controlled experiments at large scale. In: Proceedings of the 19th ACM SIGKDD International Conference on Knowledge Discovery and Data Mining, pp. 1168–1176 (2013)
20. Lindgren, E., Münch, J.: Raising the odds of success: the current state of experimentation in product development. Inf. Softw. Technol. **77**, 80–91 (2015)
21. Cao, L., Ramesh, B.: Agile requirements engineering practices: an empirical study. IEEE Softw. **25**, 60–67 (2008)
22. Olsson, H.H., Bosch, J.: From opinions to data-driven software R&D: a multi-case study on how to close the "open loop" problem. In: Proceedings of 40th Euromicro Conference Series on Software Engineering and Advanced Applications, SEAA 2014, pp. 9–16. IEEE (2014)
23. Manzi, J.: Uncontrolled: The Surprising Payoff of Trial-and-Error for Business, Politics, and Society. Basic Books, New York (2012)
24. The Standish Group: The Standish Group Report. Chaos, vol. 49, pp. 1–8 (1995)
25. Castellion, G.: Do it wrong quickly: how the web changes the old marketing rules by Mike Moran. J. Prod. Innov. Manag. **25**, 633–635 (2008)
26. Fabijan, A., Dmitriev, P., Olsson, H.H., Bosch, J.: The evolution of continuous experimentation in software product development: from data to a data-driven organization at scale. In: 2017 IEEE/ACM 39th International Conference on Software Engineering (ICSE), pp. 770–780. IEEE, Buenos Aires (2017)
27. Fabijan, A., Dmitriev, P., Olsson, H.H., Bosch, J.: The benefits of controlled experimentation at scale. In: 43rd Euromicro Conference on Software Engineering and Advanced Applications (SEAA), Vienna, Austria. 30 August–1 September 2017. IEEE, Vienna (2017)
28. Davenport, T.H.: How to design smart business experiments (2009). https://hbr.org/2009/02/how-to-design-smart-business-experiments
29. Blank, S.: Why the lean start up changes everything. Harv. Bus. Rev. **91**, 64 (2013)

30. Kohavi, R., Longbotham, R.: Online controlled experiments and A/B tests. In: Encyclopedia of Machine Learning and Data Mining, pp. 1–11 (2015)
31. Siroker, D., Koomen, P.: A/B testing - the most powerful way to turn clicks into customers (2012)
32. Kohavi, R., Longbotham, R., Sommerfield, D., Henne, R.M.: Controlled experiments on the web: survey and practical guide. Data Min. Knowl. Discov. **18**, 140–181 (2009)
33. Tang, D., Agarwal, A., O'Brien, D., Meyer, M.: Overlapping experiment infrastructure. In: Proceedings of the 16th ACM SIGKDD International Conference on Knowledge Discovery and Data Mining, KDD 2010, p. 17. ACM Press, New York (2010)
34. Kano, N., Seraku, N., Takahashi, F., Tsuji, S.: Attractive quality and must-be quality. J. Jpn. Soc. Qual. Control. **14**, 39–48 (1984)
35. Bosch, J.: Achieving simplicity with the three-layer product model. Computer (Long Beach Calif.) **46**, 34–39 (2013)
36. Moore, G.A.: Dealing with Darwin: How Great Companies Innovate at Every Phase of their Evolution. Penguin, New York (2005)
37. Runeson, P., Höst, M.: Guidelines for conducting and reporting case study research in software engineering. Empirical Softw. Eng. **14**, 131–164 (2008)
38. Mayring, P.: Qualitative content analysis - research instrument or mode of interpretation. In: The Role of the Researcher in Qualitative Psychology, pp. 139–148 (2002)
39. Augustine, S., Payne, B., Sencindiver, F., Woodcock, S.: Agile project management: steering from the edges. Commun. ACM **48**, 85–89 (2005)

A Method to Transform Automatically Extracted Product Features into Inputs for Kano-Like Models

Huishi Yin[✉] and Dietmar Pfahl

Institute of Computer Science, University of Tartu,
J. Liivi 2, 50409 Tartu, Estonia
{huishi,dietmar.pfahl}@ut.ee

Abstract. Background: In the context of a larger research project, we plan to automatically extract user needs (i.e., functional requirements) from online open sources and classify them using the principles of the Kano model. In this paper, we present a two-step method for automatically transforming feature related text extracted from online open sources into inputs for Kano-like models. **Goal:** The problem we are facing is how to transform requirements and related sentiments extracted from raw texts collected from an online open source into the input format required by our Kano-like models. To solve this problem, we need a method that transforms requirements and related sentiments into a format that corresponds to answers that would be given to either the functional or dysfunctional question of the Kano method on a specific requirement. **Method:** We propose a method consisting of two steps. In the first step, we apply machine learning methods to decide whether a text line extracted from an online open source corresponds to an answer of the functional or dysfunctional question asked in the Kano method. In the second step, we use a dictionary-based method to classify the sentiment of each statement such that we can assign an answer value to each text line previously classified as functional or dysfunctional. We implemented our method in the R language. We evaluate the accuracy of the proposed method using simulation. **Result:** Based on the simulation results, we found the overall accuracy of our method is 65%. We also found that data sources such as app store reviews are better suited to our analysis than question/answer sources such as Stack Overflow. **Conclusion:** The method we proposed can be used to automatically transform feature-related text into inputs for Kano-like models but performance improvements are needed.

Keywords: Sentiment analysis · Kano model · Online source

1 Introduction

Noriaki Kano developed the Kano model in the 1980s [9]. It characterizes the relationship between user satisfaction and product features. The Kano model defines five categories[1] (O, A, M, I, R) of user needs having different effects on user satisfaction.

---

[1] O = One-dimensional Quality, A = Attractive Quality, M = Must-be Quality, I = Indifferent Quality, R = Reverse Quality.

© Springer International Publishing AG 2017
M. Felderer et al. (Eds.): PROFES 2017, LNCS 10611, pp. 237–254, 2017.
https://doi.org/10.1007/978-3-319-69926-4_17

Since it is possible to receive contradictory responses from customers, the Questionable (Q) category is also an option. To use the Kano model, the Kano questionnaire is necessary. It is composed of a pair of questions, i.e., a functional and a dysfunctional question, that a group of users has to answer for every feature that is to be categorized. In the software engineering domain, it is a well-known method to classify user preferences according to their importance, and by doing so support requirements prioritization [10].

To be able to apply the idea of the Kano model to categorize product features automatically extracted from online open sources one needs to find a way to simulate the answering of the paired Kano questions as usually such answers are not readily available. To be able to do so, in our previous work, we designed two modified Kano models, which we denote Kano-like models, to classify user needs [10]. In this paper, we describe and evaluate a two-step method using analysis to transform raw text related to user needs voiced in online open sources into inputs for Kano-like models.

2   Related Work

Mustasfa et al. [28] presented an example of classifying software requirements by using Kano model. Based on the Kano model, Nascimento et al. [29] proposed an approach of using the crowd for requirements classification. This approach extends the scope of a survey from a smaller range of existing users to the Internet-wide of people, all potential users are considered in the scope of the survey. As same as Nascimento's research, we use the Kano model as a basis, to survey the opinions from Internet-wide users. The different between their research and ours is that their research is based on an artificial survey, but our goal of the research is to achieve the classification and prioritization of software requirements automatically.

There exists quite a lot of research related to sentiment analysis. Sentiment analysis, also known as opinion extraction, opinion mining, or emotion mining, is a field of study that analyzes texts containing opinions, comments, and evaluations. While research on sentiments and opinions started in 2001 [1–5], the terms 'opinion mining' and 'sentiment analysis' appear the first time in 2003 [6–8]. In this paper, we use the terms 'sentiment analysis' and 'opinion mining' interchangeably.

Sentiment classification at the document and sentence levels classifies documents and sentences (e.g., product comments, reviews) with regards to their emotional bias towards either the positive or negative side [11–13]. Research that analyses the emotional bias of text related to a finer granular level either combine topic modeling with sentiment analysis [14, 15] or apply sentiment analysis directly at the level of product features. For example, Shah et al. [16] presented a method for automated feature-based opinion mining involving two steps: (1) extracting product features (e.g., "picture quality" and "battery life" in a camera review) and (2) finding orientations (positive, negative or neutral) of opinions expressed on the features by reviewers. There are also studies on discovering orientations of context dependent on opinion comparative words [17]. The main difference of our research compared to the mentioned studies is that, in addition, we need to classify the features and related sentiments extracted from online open sources into two classes corresponding to answers of the Kano paired questions, i.e., functional and dysfunctional, and within each of these classes, each feature related text must be classified into the classes very negative, negative, neutral, positive, and very positive.

3   Research Context and Goal

In the context of a larger research project, Open Innovation in Requirements Engineering (OIRE) [30], we plan to extract systematically user needs from online open sources to complement traditional approaches to elicit and prioritize software requirements. Figure 1 shows the four-main phases of our project. Currently, we focus on the second phase where we extract from raw data product features and related sentiments and format the extracted material such that it can serve as an input to a Kano-like model. The input to Kano-like models consists of two vectors, i.e., the functional and dysfunctional vectors, corresponding to answers that would be given to either the functional or dysfunctional question of the Kano method. Each vector contains numbers ranging from −2 to 2 which represent the sentiment classes very negative (−2), negative (−1), neutral (0), positive (1), and very positive (2).

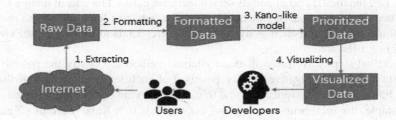

Fig. 1. Main phase of the OIRE model

The goal of the research presented in this paper is to transform the feature-related raw text collected from an online open source into the input format required by a Kano-like model. To achieve this goal, we need to analyze and transform the raw data into a format that corresponds to answers that would be given to either the functional or dysfunctional question of the Kano method.

4   Method

The method by which we tackle this goal consists of two steps. Figure 2 shows an example of how the two-step method transforms the text that relates to feature A is transformed into inputs for a Kano-like model. How the input text is extracted from open online sources is outside the scope of this study and will be described elsewhere. In Fig. 2, the program that will produce the feature-related text for us is labeled Feature Text Extraction Method.

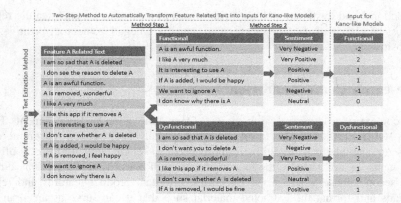

Fig. 2. Example illustrating the transformation of feature-related text into inputs for Kano-like models using our two-step method

In method step 1, since the input data of this step already contains only feature-related text, we use machine learning methods to classify the input text into two classes, i.e., functional (exist) and dysfunctional (not exist). The unit of analysis is one line of text. Text classified as functional corresponds to text lines stating the presence of a feature, and text classified as dysfunctional corresponds to text stating the absence (or lack) of a feature.

In method step 2, we use a dictionary-based method to classify the polarity of a sentiment (from very negative to very positive) of each text line in each of the two classes functional and dysfunctional and translate it into the corresponding Kano score. For example, the sentiment very negative corresponds to a Kano score of –2 and the sentiment very positive corresponds to a Kano score of +2.

4.1   Method Step 1

Figure 3 shows the process of classifying feature-related text lines into the functional and dysfunctional dimensions of the Kano model. We apply supervised machine learning in this step. The process consists of four sub-steps.

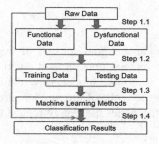

Fig. 3. The process of method step 1.

Step 1.1: To be able to select a suitable machine learning method for our classification task, we must analyze the performance of candidate machine learners. To do so, we need labeled training and test datasets.

Since our input is unlabeled, we either need to find such data sets or we need to create them by ourselves. If we cannot find suitable existing labeled data sets for our purpose, we must create such data sets manually. We can do this, for example, by taking a subset of the input data set and analyzing each text line relating to a feature as follows: If a text line contains words of affirmation or complaint about using/having a feature, it means the feature exists or is imagined as being present, and thus we label the related text line to be of the category functional. If a text line contains words that express affirmation or complaint about the lack of a feature, it means the related feature does not exist and thus we label the related text line to be of the category dysfunctional. However, when the subjunctive mood is used, we classify the text line according to the imagined or wished part of the text line. For example, when someone says, "I would be happy if you can add this feature", even though this means the feature is still missing, the text line expresses the feeling a person has imagined the feature exists. Hence, we will classify this text line to be of category functional.

The total size of the labeled dataset should be large enough to facilitate proper training and small enough to not be too time-consuming. We suggest a dataset size of 100–250 labeled text lines. Table 1 shows some example text lines that we labeled to be functional or dysfunctional.

Table 1. Examples of labeled text lines

	Examples
Functional	The plugin function is good. I have found that this method works. I use 'checkstyle' to analyze my code. I cannot figure out why people want this button here. I would be happy if you can add this feature.
Dysfunctional	I miss the hierarchical (frame-based) view. The link is not available now. Basically I'd like to avoid to do this in a js file. So far I've had no luck to use the Bespin one in Pydev. I would be sad if this feature be deleted.

Step 1.2: We split the set of labeled text lines into a test and a training dataset. The ratio of the lines of text of training dataset to it of the test dataset is 80:20.

Step 1.3: We use the training dataset to train the classification models and the test dataset to check the accuracy of the output of the models. We may select several supervised machine learning methods for comparison, e.g., Naïve Bayes, MaxEnt, Decision Trees, Support Vector Machines (SVM) and others.

We use a confusion matrix [18] to calculate the performance of each method. Table 2 shows the confusion matrix for our classification problem. Based on the predicted results of each model, we calculate the accuracy[2] of each trained classification model as well as FPV[3] (Functional predictive value), which shows the proportion of the functional text lines that are predicted correctly, and DPV[4] (Dysfunctional predictive value), which shows the proportion of the dysfunctional text lines that are predicted correctly.

Table 2. The confusion matrix used to assess the performance of supervised machine learners

		Predicted condition	
		Functional	*Dysfunctional*
True condition	*Functional*	True Functional (TF)	False Functional (FF)
	Dysfunctional	False Dysfunctional (FD)	True Dysfunctional (TD)

Step 1.4: We select the best performing classification model to our original input and classify each text line into either functional or dysfunctional.

4.2   Method Step 2

In the second step of our method, the purpose is to conduct opinion mining to attach sentiment scores to each of the labeled text lines. According to Reagan et al.'s study [19], sentiment detection methods can be one of the following types:

- Dictionary-based methods [20],
- Supervised learning methods [21],
- Unsupervised/Deep learning methods [22].

In this step, we need to classify text lines into five categories, i.e., very positive, positive, neutral, negative, and very negative. To do so, multiclass instead of binary classification methods are needed. However, the multiclass classification case is more intricate than solving binary classification problems [27]. In other words, using supervised learning methods is more costly. Since it is easy to implement, we decided to design a dictionary-based method to classify the polarity of sentiments contained in each of the labeled text lines received from step 1 of our method.

Step 2.1: We first create a special Emotional Dictionary consisting of seven corpuses, i.e., containing 'Positive Emotional Words' (PEW), 'Very Positive Emotional Words' (VEPW), 'Negative Emotional Words' (NEW), 'Very Negative Emotional Words'

---

[2] Accuracy = (TF + TD)/(TF + FF + FD + TD).

[3] FPV = TF/(TF + FF).

[4] DPV = TD/(FD + TD).

(VNEW), 'Adversative Words' (AW), 'Negative Words' (NW), and 'Intense Words' (IW), respectively.

The PEW and NEW corpuses of our Emotional Dictionary are created based on the sentiment dictionary consisting of two files provided by Minqing Hu and Bing Liu [23]. The two files contain 2041 positive words (file: positive-words.txt), and 4818 negative words (file: negative-words.txt), respectively. The IW corpus refers to the intense corpus file of the HowNet sentiment dictionary collected by Qiang Dong and Zhendong Dong [24]. The IW includes 71 words. To create VPEW, VNEW, AW, and NW, we use the world's largest and most trusted free online Synonyms dictionary, Thesaurus.com. We first find a keyword, for example, the word "amazing" as a keyword of VPEW, or the word "awful" as a keyword of VNEW. Then we search the synonyms of this keyword, next we manually check all the synonyms words suggested by the Synonyms dictionary, and finally we get word lists for the VPEW, VNEW, AW, and NW corpuses. We also remove those words listed in VPEW from 'positive-words.txt' (PEW) and very negative emotional words (listed in VNEW) from 'negative-words.txt' (NEW). Table 3 shows the total numbers of words and example words of each corpus of the Emotional Dictionary.

Table 3. Emotional Dictionary with example words.

	Corpus	No. of words	Examples
Emotional Dictionary	*PEW*	2013[a]	like, good, well, accept,
	NEW	4794[b]	bad, sad, cannot, delete,
	VPEW	28	amazing, love, brilliant,
	VNEW	24	awful, worst, terrible,
	IW	71	very, much, extremely,
	AW	9	but, however,
	NW	18	no, not, never, aren't,

[a] = 2041-28
[b] = 4818-24

Step 2.2: We split each labeled text line into words and search each word in the Emotional Dictionary to identify its sentiment polarity. When one word is confirmed included in one corpus of our Emotional Dictionary, we assign different sentiment score to this word according to the different corpuses it belongs to. For example, if one word is included in VPEW or in VNEW, the sentiment score of this word is 100 or −100. If this word is included in PEW or in NEW, the sentiment score of this word is 1 or −1.

Step 2.3: We calculate the total sentiment score of each text line and transfer it to Kano score (ranging from −2 to 2, i.e., very negative to very positive) which constitutes the input needed for the Kano-like models. Figure 4 uses a simplified algorithm to show the schematic process for automatically calculating the sentiment score when using our dictionary-based method. The real script is implemented in the R language with over 100 lines of code.

```
for each sentence in text:
        for each word in sentence:
                if word in PEW:
                        SentimentScore = (SentimentScore + 1)
                if word in VPEW:
                        SentimentScore = (SentimentScore + 100)
                if word in NEW:
                        SentimentScore = (SentimentScore - 1)
                if word in VNEW:
                        SentimentScore = (SentimentScore - 100
                if word in AW:
                        SentimentScore = SentimentScore * 0
                if word in NW:
                        SentimentScore = SentimentScore * (- 1)
                If word in IW:
                        SentimentScore = SentimentScore * 100;
        end for
end for
```

Fig. 4. The schematic process of calculating the sentiment score in the Dictionary-based method.

Instead of classifying sentiments into three categories, i.e., positive, negative, and neutral, like other researchers did, we need to classify functional and dysfunctional text lines into five categories, i.e., very positive (sentiment score >= 100), positive (0 < sentiment score < 100), neutral (sentiment score = 0), negative (-100 < sentiment score < 0), and very negative (sentiment score <= -100).

Table 4 shows examples of how to calculate the sentiment score and Kano score of text lines using the algorithm presented in Fig. 4. The words in different colors indicate the reference to different emotional corpuses as shown in Table 3. For example, words in red refer to corpus PEW.

Table 4. Examples of calculating the sentiment and Kano scores for text lines

Text line[a]	Sentiment Score	Polarity	Kano Score
i like (α) this function very much (β).	10000	Very positive	2
why cannot (γ) you delete (γ) this function	-2	Negative	-1
i hate (δ) this feature	-100	Very Negative	-2
this feature is not (ε) bad (γ)	1	Positive	1
the software allows user to open files automatically	0	Neural	0

[a] α = words from PEW, β = words from IW, γ = words from NEW, δ = words from VNEW, ε = words from NW.

5 Method Application Example

In this section, we demonstrate the applicability of our two-step method with an example (Sects. 5.1 and 5.2) and discuss its overall performance (Sect. 5.3). In addition, we discuss the suitability of different types of sources from which the input data to our method was extracted. We do this by comparing the outcomes of the sentiment analyses conducted in step 2 of our method applied to data retrieved from a question/answer web-page, i.e., Stack Overflow, and from an App store, i.e., a joint data set extracted from Google Play and Apple Store (Sect. 5.4).

5.1 Application Example for Method Step 1

Input: We used a dataset containing 1493 lines of text from an App store as input to our method. This dataset was derived from an original set of 92217 reviews which was cleaned to be appropriate for further processing. For example, we only used text lines from the reviews which correspond to one feature. In addition, we removed stop words (e.g. 'a', 'an', 'the', etc.) as well as punctuation and strange symbols. We also removed text lines contained in reviews containing less than 20 words, because we believe long reviews may be able to comprehensively express a reviewer's real thought.

Approach: In order to classify the input text lines and transform them into input for Kano-like models, we first created a 'functional-dysfunctional' corpus as training and test datasets for selecting machine learning methods. We followed the rules described in Sect. 4.1. We needed approximately 4 person-hours of effort to manually label 250 lines of text. The split between text lines labeled as functional and dysfunctional was 50:50.

We compared five frequently used machine learning methods, i.e., Naïve Bayes, MaxEnt, Decision Trees, Random Forest, and SVM. We used the confusion matrix (cf. Table 2) to calculate the performance of each method. To check whether the proposed ratio of 80:20 between training and test dataset really gets the best results, we vary the size of the training data set in the range from 50 to 200 with a fixed test dataset of size 50. Thus, we check for the ratios 50:50 (training dataset size = 50), 66:34 (training dataset size = 100), and 80:20 (training dataset size = 200). Table 5 shows the results of the experiment.

We can see from Table 5 that the Naive Bayes method achieved the highest average FPV (90%), and the SVM method achieved the highest average DPV (76.7%) and the highest average overall accuracy value (64.2%). For the training dataset containing 200 text lines, the methods MaxEnt and SVM have the highest accuracy (65%) and closest FPV and DPV values. In additional, the standard deviation of accuracy values of MaxEnt and SVM methods (0.006 and 0.014 respectively) from three tests are very small. This suggests that the performance of methods MaxEnt and SVM is stable and no further improvement can be expected for larger training datasets. However, although the accuracy values when using MaxEnt and SVM methods are the highest in Table 5, the absolute values (65% for both methods) are not very high. Thus, to improve accuracy further, we decided to use the training dataset of size 200, then implement both MaxEnt and SVM methods together, and then only keep those cases where the predictions of the two methods are consistent. According to the experiment

Table 5. Experiment results

Methods	Indicator	Size of training set (number of text lines)			Average Value	Standard Deviation (σ)
		50	100	200		
Naive Bayes	*FPV*	100%	100%	70%	90%	0.173
	DPV	0	0	45%	15%	0.260
	Accuracy	50%	50%	57.5%	52.5%	0.043
MaxEnt	*FPV*	45%	40%	60%	48.3%	0.161
	DPV	75%	80%	70%	73.3%	0.076
	Accuracy	60%	60%	65%	61%	0.006
Decision Trees	*FPV*	50%	40%	40%	43.3%	0.058
	DPV	55%	80%	80%	71.7%	0.144
	Accuracy	52.5%	60%	60%	57.5%	0.043
Random Forest	*FPV*	60%	70%	60%	63.3%	0.058
	DPV	35%	50%	45%	43.3%	0.076
	Accuracy	47.5%	60%	52.5%	53.3%	0.063
SVM	*FPV*	45%	45%	65%	51.7%	0.115
	DPV	80%	85%	65%	76.7%	0.104
	Accuracy	62.5%	65%	65%	64.2%	0.014

results, we found that the two methods yielded the same classifications for 44 out of 50 text lines in the test datasets. A further analysis showed that 15 out 22 text lines were accurately classified as functional (FPV = 68%) and 17 out of 22 text lines were accurately predicted as dysfunctional (DPV = 77%). This means that the overall accuracy increased to 73% from 68%. Hence, we decided to use MaxEnt together with SVM in our application example, and only keep those cases where the predictions of the two methods are consistent.

Result: After implementing the classification method of step 1, we found that 1151 out of 1493 lines of text were classified into the same categories when using both SVM and MaxEnt methods. 628 lines of text were classified as functional, and 523 were classified as dysfunctional.

To estimate the actual classification accuracy of method step 1, we used the Probability Proportional to Size (PPS) method [25]. We randomly chose 20% of the total number of classified text lines and then we manually checked the correctness of the classification of the text lines contained in this sample. The results of this performance check are shown in Table 6. We can see that the overall accuracy of method step 1

Table 6. Prediction accuracy of method step 1

	Lines of texts	Proportion	Samples	Correct classification
Functional	628	55%	126	116
Dysfunctional	523	45%	105	61
Total	1151	100%	231	173
FPV	92%			
DPV	58%			
Accuracy	75%			

is 75%. The accuracy of classifying text lines into category functional is very high (FPV = 92%), while the accuracy of classifying text lines into the category dysfunctional (DPV = 58%) is relatively low.

5.2 Application Example for Method Step 2

Input: The output of method step 1 contained two categorized files. One file has 628 lines of functional text, and another file has 523 lines of dysfunctional text. These two files were used as the input of method step 2. In the following, we use 'functional input' and 'dysfunctional input' when referring to these two files.

Approach: We ran the dictionary-based method as described in Sect. 4.2 to calculate the sentiment and Kano scores of each line of text in the functional and dysfunctional inputs separately. Then we used again the PPS method to check the performance for 20% of the text lines contained in each input. To be able to manually check the emotions expressed in the sampled text lines to verify the accuracy of classification, we used the guidelines presented in Table 7.

Table 7. Evaluation criteria for manually checking sentiment classifications

Sentiment Classi-fication	Evaluation Criterion
Very positive	When the content shows a very happy or excited mood or high satisfaction.
Positive	When the content shows a happy or excited mood or satisfaction without a very strong expression.
Neutral	When the content does not clearly show positive or negative emotions or the content has contradictory expression.
Negative	When the content shows an unhappy or disappointed mood without a very strong expression.
Very negative	When the content shows a very unhappy or disappointed mood.

Result: After implementing method in step 2, text lines were classified into five sentiment classes. The classification details as well as the corresponding accuracies for the samples drawn from each class are presented in Table 8.

Table 8. Prediction accuracy of method step 2

	Lines of text	Proportion	Samples	Correct classification	Accuracy
Very Positive	629	55%	127	118	93%
Positive	154	13%	31	18	58%
Neutral	135	12%	27	20	74%
Negative	146	13%	29	23	79%
Very Negative	87	7%	17	10	59%
Total	1151	100%	231	188	81%

We can see from Table 8, that the highest accuracy value (93%) was achieved for class Very Positive. 118 out of 127 text lines were accurately predicted. The lowest accuracy value (58%), was achieved for class Positive, closely followed by class Very Negative (59%). Nonetheless, due to the larger number of text classified as Very Positive (55% of 231) and a very high accuracy for this class, the overall accuracy of step 2 of our method reached 81%.

5.3   Overall Performance of the 2-Step Method

To see the combined accuracy of both steps of our proposed method, we consider those lines of text which are classified into correct categories both in method step 1 and method step 2 as final correct classifications. As described in Sects. 5.1 and 5.2, the analysis of classification accuracy was done manually based on a sample of 231 text lines (out of a total of 1151 classified text lines). The results of this analysis are shown in Tables 9 and 10, presenting the results for text lines classified in step 1 of the method as functional and dysfunctional, respectively. When comparing the results shown in Tables 9 and 10, we observe that the overall accuracy of text lines classified as functional (81%, i.e., 102 of 126 text lines in the sample) is much higher than the accuracy of text lines classified as dysfunctional (46%, i.e., 48 of 105 text lines in the sample). The overall weight average of accuracy of all 231 text lines of the sample is 65%.

Table 9. Accuracy of method steps 1 and 2 for text lines classified as functional in step 1

	Lines of text	Proportion	Analyzed samples	Method Step 1		Method Step 2		Overall	
				Correct classification	Accuracy	Correct classification	Accuracy	Correct classification	Accuracy
Very Positive	413	66%	83	77	93%	77	93%	76	92%
Positive	78	12%	16	14	88%	9	56%	9	56%
Neutral	52	8%	10	7	70%	9	90%	7	70%
Negative	50	8%	10	8	80%	7	70%	6	60%
Very Negative	35	6%	7	6	86%	4	57%	4	57%
Total	628	100%	126	116	92%	107	85%	102	81%

Table 10. Accuracy of method steps 1 and 2 for text lines classified as dysfunctional in step 1

	Lines of text	Proportion	Analyzed samples	Method Step 1		Method Step 2		Overall	
				Correct classification	Accuracy	Correct classification	Accuracy	Correct classification	Accuracy
Very Positive	216	41%	44	16	36%	41	93%	14	32%
Positive	76	15%	15	10	67%	9	60%	6	40%
Neutral	83	16%	17	11	65%	11	65%	8	47%
Negative	96	18%	19	16	84%	15	79%	14	74%
Very Negative	52	10%	10	7	70%	6	60%	6	60%
Total	523	100%	105	61	58%	85	81%	48	46%

When looking deeper into the details of Tables 9 and 10 we observe that classification correctness varies a lot. For example, the highest overall accuracy is 92% for text lines expressing very positive emotions about something existing (functional). On the other hand, the overall accuracy of dysfunctional text lines is very low, especially when expressing very positive (32%), positive (40%), and neutral (47%) emotions. While generally, the accuracy of text lines classified as functional is better than that of text lines classified as dysfunctional, those text lines classified as dysfunctional expressing negative and very negative emotions have higher accuracy (74% and 60%) than the corresponding text lines classified as functional (60% and 57%). We also observe that the main cause for low overall accuracy can be traced to both steps of the method depending on the sentiment classification. For example, the low overall accuracy of 32% for text lines classified as dysfunctional and expressing very positive emotion is mostly due to the low accuracy in method step 1 (36%). On the other hand, the relatively low overall accuracy of 56% for text lines classified as functional and expressing positive emotion is mostly due to low accuracy in method step 2 (56%).

When comparing the accuracies of the method steps 1 and 2, we observe that the lowest accuracy value for step 1 is 36%, which is the only value less than 65%, while the lowest accuracy values for step 2 are 56%, 57%, 60%, and 60%, respectively. The low accuracy values in step 2 relate to text lines classified as positive and very negative for both functional and dysfunctional categories.

5.4   Applicability of the Dictionary-Based Method for Sentiment Analysis

We ran a separate experiment to test the accuracy of the Dictionary-based Method. In that experiment, we used a small set of 250 user questions and comments collected from Stack Overflow as our test input 1. Meanwhile, we used another small set of 250 reviews collected from App stores Google Play and Apple Store as our test input 2. We manually labeled the test inputs by attaching a sentiment score to all 500 input text lines. To do so, we use the criteria shown in Table 7.

Tables 11 and 12 show the actual and predicted classifications of input 1 and input 2, respectively. Table cells with gray background show the numbers of those cases where input text lines were classified correctly by the Dictionary-based Method. We can see from Tables 11 and 12 that the overall prediction accuracies are very similar (71.6% and 78%). We also observe that the highest prediction accuracies for both inputs 1 and 2 were achieved for text lines expressing very positive emotions. However, when looking at other sentiment categories, we see that there are also several differences between input 1 and input 2. For example, the prediction accuracy of text lines expressing negative emotions is much higher for input 1 (72%) than for input 2 (47%).

Another observation we made is related to the distribution of sentiments in the two input sets. Input 1, which contains data collected from a question/answer web-page, contains considerably more text lines expressing neutral emotions than input 2, which contains data collected from app store reviews. Also, input 1 contains more text lines expressing positive or very positive emotions and less text lines expressing negative and very negative emotions than input 2. Based on that, we believe that inputs stemming from reviews (such as those found in app stores) are a more suitable data source for our purpose than question/answer web-pages. When people post a question, they

Table 11. Prediction accuracy based on input 1 (Stack Overflow)

		Predicted sentiment classification					Accurate prediction	Text lines	Accuracy
		Very positive	Positive	Neutral	Negative	Very negative			
Actual sentiment classification	Very positive	10	2	0	0	0	10	12	83%
	Positive	2	30	1	8	1	30	47	64%
	Neutral	1	15	61	9	1	61	87	70%
	Negative	1	12	14	68	0	68	95	72%
	Very negative	1	2	0	1	10	10	14	71%
Overall							179	250	71.6%

Table 12. Prediction accuracy based on input 2 (Google Play and Apple Store)

		Predicted sentiment classification					Accurate prediction	Text lines	Accuracy
		Very positive	Positive	Neutral	Negative	Very negative			
Actual sentiment classification	Very positive	86	3	2	1	1	86	93	92%
	Positive	8	30	2	4	2	30	46	65%
	Neutral	7	3	27	6	2	27	45	60%
	Negative	13	10	0	24	4	24	51	47%
	Very negative	5	0	0	0	10	10	15	67%
Overall							177	250	78%

usually describe problems, and they need answers, so most of the posts are written in an objective mode describing facts, rather than in a subjective mode expressing emotions. Even if someone wants to express feelings in a question/answer forum, it is difficult to have a positive feeling when someone has a problem. However, when writing an app review, sentiments expressed are often related to features and if a feature is good/bad, more positive/negative sentiments will be expressed. Thus, app reviews are potentially more comprehensive with regards to the expression of sentiments.

6   Threats to Validity

Threats to Internal Validity: The results of our performance analysis rely highly upon the nature of the input data. If the input data is not good, the accuracy will be affected. After analyzing the input data, we found that non-standard language is a problem.

There are three main types of non-standard language issues of the input text. In Table 13, we show some examples that we picked from the input data that we used.

Table 13. Main issues of non-standard language

Type of issues	Example
Spelling issues	"sssssssshhhhhhhhhooooccccccccckkkkkkkkkk wave" "awsome" "good bye"
Contradictory text	"terribly love it" "why cant android users disable last seen timestamp and iphone users can sort it out"
Unclear content	"its ma 1 of d fvrt app plz upload it n njoy wid uh frndzzz its just awesome bt still i hv prblm wid it" "this game needs to be better like really oh my gosh like i love lipstick and i put like it on in school like school is cool i get straight as like really do you dress nice i do really you should"

- Spelling issues: For example, when "goodbye" is spelled as "good bye", the dictionary-based method will detect a positive emotion ("good") instead of a neutral one.
- Contradictory text: For example, the text line "terribly (negative) love (positive) it" will be classified by the dictionary-based method as neutral although the sentence probably expresses a positive feeling.
- Unclear content: Whatever sentiment will be detected is meaningless.

Another threat is that during our experiment, only one person labeled all the training data and test data in method step 1. Due to the somewhat subjective flavor of the labeling task, there is a probability of occasional mislabeling. Similarly, the evaluation of the sentiment classification conducted in method step 2 was done manually by a single person. In order to mitigate this threat to validity, we created the guidelines for labeling and evaluation presented in Tables 1 and 7, respectively. Applying the guidelines standardizes the labeling and evaluation tasks to some degree and thus reduces the danger of mislabeling and misjudgment.

Threats to External Validity: In this paper, we only give one application example, which may not offer enough evidence to prove that our proposed two-step method is reliable (at least to the degree of accuracy that we reached in our application). However, given the size of our data set extracted from app reviews, we expect that our results are to some degree representative for data stemming from app stores such as Google Play and Apple Store. We also compared the input of app reviews with another type of input text collected from Stack Overflow in Sect. 5.4 and found that app reviews are a more suitable input data source for our method than question/answer web-pages.

7   Conclusions and Future Plan

In this paper, we have presented a method that helps analyze and classify text lines extracted from online open sources such as app stores into a format that can be further processed by Kano-like models in order to classify features. The proposed method is supported by R scripts[5] and thus can be performed to a large degree automatically. The value of this method is that product managers and other stakeholders who are developing software products can learn from feedback posted in online open sources with little effort.

We demonstrated the applicability of our method in an application example using real-world data extracted from two popular app stores.

Based on the results of our application experiment, we found the accuracy of the prediction of dysfunctional text lines, especially when these text lines express positive emotions, is low. Also, the accuracy of classifying the sentiments expressed in text lines into positive and negative classes when using our dictionary-based method is still too low for practical purposes. These two reasons affect the overall accuracy of our method negatively.

The overall accuracy of our two-step method is 65%. Compared with other research results, we think the performance of the method is acceptable. Hence, we think our proposed two-step method can already be used for transforming the feature related text into the inputs for Kano-like models.

As in all research endeavors, we see possibilities for improving our method, e.g., by optimizing the size and the quality of the training dataset in step 1 of our method and by refining the dictionary in step 2 of our method. We also plan to further investigate how certain characteristics of the input data (e.g., length of text lines, balance between dysfunctional and functional text lines, as well as the distribution of sentiments) affect the overall accuracy of our method. In addition, we also plan to experiment with deep learning approaches in step 2 of our method. For example, we plan to apply the Stanford Sentiment Analysis [26] approach which uses recursive deep models to analyze movie reviews.

Acknowledgement. The research was supported by the institutional research grant IUT20-55 of the Estonian Research Council. In addition, Huishi Yin was funded by the European Regional Development Fund for Higher Education.

References

1. Das, S., Chen, M.: Yahoo! for Amazon: extracting market sentiment from stock message boards. In: Proceedings of the Asia Pacific Finance Association Annual Conference (APFA), vol. 35, p. 43 (2001)
2. Morinaga, S., Yamanishi, K., Tateishi, K., et al.: Mining product reputations on the web. In: Proceedings of the Eighth ACM SIGKDD International Conference on Knowledge Discovery and Data Mining, pp. 341–349. ACM (2002)
3. Tong, R.M.: An operational system for detecting and tracking opinions in on-line discussion. In: Working Notes of the ACM SIGIR 2001 Workshop on Operational Text Classification, vol. 1, p. 6 (2001)
4. Wiebe, J.: Learning subjective adjectives from corpora. In: AAAI/IAAI, pp. 735–740 (2000)

---

[5] https://figshare.com/s/d13b6f16738190d7b935.

5. Pang, B., Lee, L., Vaithyanathan, S.: Thumbs up?: sentiment classification using machine learning techniques. In: Proceedings of the ACL-02 Conference on Empirical Methods in Natural Language Processing, vol. 1, pp. 79–86. Association for Computational Linguistics (2002)
6. Nasukawa, T., Yi, J.: Sentiment analysis: capturing favorability using natural language processing. In: Proceedings of the 2nd International Conference on Knowledge Capture, pp. 70–77. ACM (2003)
7. Dave, K., Lawrence, S., Pennock, D.M.: Mining the peanut gallery: opinion extraction and semantic classification of product reviews. In: Proceedings of the 12th International Conference on World Wide Web, pp. 519–528. ACM (2003)
8. Liu, B.: Sentiment Analysis and Opinion Mining. Morgan & Claypool Publishers, San Rafael (2012)
9. Kano, N., Seraku, N., Takahashi, F., et al.: Attractive quality and must-be quality. J. Jpn. Soc. Qual. Control **14**, 39–48 (1984)
10. Yin, H., Pfahl, D.: Evaluation of Kano-like models defined for using data extracted from online sources. In: Abrahamsson, P., Jedlitschka, A., Nguyen Duc, A., Felderer, M., Amasaki, S., Mikkonen, T. (eds.) PROFES 2016. LNCS, vol. 10027, pp. 539–549. Springer, Cham (2016). doi:10.1007/978-3-319-49094-6_39
11. Turney, P.D.: Thumbs up or thumbs down? Semantic orientation applied to unsupervised classification of reviews. In: Proceedings of the 40th Annual Meeting on Association for Computational Linguistics, pp. 417–424. Association for Computational Linguistics (2002)
12. Yu, H., Hatzivassiloglou, V.: Towards answering opinion questions: separating facts from opinions and identifying the polarity of opinion sentences. In: Proceedings of the 2003 Conference on Empirical Methods in Natural Language Processing, pp. 129–136. Association for Computational Linguistics (2003)
13. Wilson, T., Wiebe, J., Hwa, R.: Just how mad are you? Finding strong and weak opinion clauses. In: AAAI, vol. 4, pp. 761–769 (2004)
14. Lin, C., He, Y., Everson, R., et al.: Weakly supervised joint sentiment-topic detection from text. IEEE Trans. Knowl. Data Eng. **24**(6), 1134–1145 (2012)
15. Rao, Y., Li, Q., Mao, X., et al.: Sentiment topic models for social emotion mining. Inf. Sci. **266**(5), 90–100 (2014)
16. Shah, F.A., Sabanin, Y., Pfahl, D.: Feature-based evaluation of competing apps. In: Proceedings of the International Workshop on App Market Analytics, WAMA 2016, pp. 15–21. ACM, New York (2016)
17. Ganapathibhotla, M., Liu, B.: Mining opinions in comparative sentences. In: Proceedings of the 22nd International Conference on Computational Linguistics, vol. 1, pp. 241–248. Association for Computational Linguistics (2008)
18. Stehman, S.V.: Selecting and interpreting measures of thematic classification accuracy. Remote Sens. Environ. **62**(1), 77–89 (1997)
19. Reagan, A., Tivnan, B., Williams, J.R., et al.: Benchmarking sentiment analysis methods for large-scale texts: a case for using continuum-scored words and word shift graphs. Comput. Sci. (2015)
20. Ku, L.W., Wu, T.H., Lee, L.Y., et al.: Construction of an evaluation corpus for opinion extraction. In: NTCIR, pp. 513–520 (2005)

21. Dasgupta, S., Ng, V.: Mine the easy, classify the hard: a semi-supervised approach to automatic sentiment classification. In: Joint Conference of the, Meeting of the ACL and the, International Joint Conference on Natural Language Processing of the AFNLP: Volume, pp. 701–709. Association for Computational Linguistics (2009)

22. Socher, R., Perelygin, A., Wu, J.Y., et al.: Recursive deep models for semantic compositionality over a sentiment treebank. Proceedings of the conference on empirical methods in natural language processing (EMNLP). **1631**, 1642 (2013)

23. Hu, M., Liu, B.: Mining and summarizing customer reviews. In: Proceedings of the Tenth ACM SIGKDD International Conference on Knowledge Discovery and Data Mining, pp. 168–177. ACM (2004)

24. HowNet knowledge Database (2016). http://www.keenage.com/html/e_index.html. Accessed 2 Feb 2017

25. Skinner, C.J.: Probability proportional to size (PPS) sampling. In: Encyclopedia of Statistical Sciences (1983)

26. Recursive Neural Tensor Network (2017). http://nlp.stanford.edu/sentiment/index.html. Accessed 2 Feb 2017

27. Aly, M.: Survey on multiclass classification methods. Neural Netw., 1–9 (2005)

28. Mustasfa, B.A.: Classifying software requirements using Kano's model to optimize customer satisfaction. In: SoMeT, pp. 271–279 (2014)

29. Nascimento, P., Aguas, R., Schneider, D., et al.: An approach to requirements categorization using Kano's model and crowds. In: 2012 IEEE 16th International Conference on Computer Supported Cooperative Work in Design (CSCWD), pp. 387–392. IEEE (2012)

30. Yin, H.: A study plan: open innovation based on internet data mining in software engineering. In: Proceedings of the 2015 International Conference on Software and System Process. ACM (2015)

Feedback Gathering for Truck Parking Europe: A Pilot Study with the AppEcho Feedback Tool

Melanie Stade[1,2(✉)] and Holger Indervoort[3,4]

[1] Centre for Requirements Engineering (CeRE), University of Applied Sciences and Arts
Northwestern Switzerland (FHNW), Windisch, Switzerland
melanie.stade@fhnw.ch
[2] Cognitive Psychology and Cognitive Ergonomics, Berlin University of Technology (TUB),
Berlin, Germany
[3] PTV Planung Transport Verkehr AG, Karlsruhe, Germany
[4] PTV Truckparking BV, Utrecht, The Netherlands

Abstract. Feedback communication channels enable end-users to express their needs and problems when using a software system. This feedback can increase a software company's knowledge about real software usage and can positively affect software evolution and maintenance. However, research shows that gathering feedback can be cumbersome for software companies. In a pilot study with Truck Parking Europe, we explore how we can enable truckers to communicate feedback on an app for parking slots. Results of our pilot study, consisting of a small group of truckers, show that the truckers provided useful feedback through a dedicated, mobile, and screenshot-based feedback tool. As stated by the Truck Parking Europe team, the feedback received is understandable and relevant for improving the parking app. In our future work, we will investigate the extent to which an integrated feedback tool can allow many truckers to provide feedback simultaneously and the extent to which the gathered feedback can aid in improving software evolution and maintenance activities at Truck Parking Europe.

Keywords: Post-deployment end-user feedback · User involvement · User participation · Mobile application · Software evolution

1 Introduction

1.1 User Involvement for Software Evolution

User involvement can positively affect software development and evolution [1] as it increases a software company's knowledge about real software usage [2]. To engage end-users in software evolution and requirements elicitation activities, software companies can either solicit feedback or allow end-users to trigger the feedback communication process [3]. Both cases entail explicit feedback where end-users provide the input deliberately. In contrast, software usage data that is unintentionally provided by end-users is treated as implicit feedback [3]. Explicit feedback communication channels that allow end-users to remotely communicate their needs, opinions, and problems with a software

© Springer International Publishing AG 2017

M. Felderer et al. (Eds.): PROFES 2017, LNCS 10611, pp. 255–262, 2017.
https://doi.org/10.1007/978-3-319-69926-4_18

system can include public channels such as online forums, social media, and app stores as well as non-public channels like email, contact forms and phone. Research on dedicated tools that support gathering of end-user feedback has increased [4, 5], and there are various commercial service providers who offer feedback gathering solutions such as Usabilla (usabilla.com), Usersnap (usersnap.com), and UserVoice (uservoice.com). However, previous work shows that in several cases, software companies are not satisfied with the quantity and quality of the feedback received from their end-users [6]. Moreover, the characteristics of the feedback communication channels can contribute towards the end-users' willingness to provide feedback, along with the existing hurdles that discourage end-users from providing feedback [6, 7].

In our study, we focus on a specialized end-user group who are not easily accessible for user involvement activities in practice because they are working under time pressure and are constantly on the road, i.e., truckers.

1.2   Feedback Gathering for Truck Parking Europe and Study Goal

Truck Parking Europe (TPE) is the largest free European platform for truck parking facilities (truckparkingeurope.com). More than 25,000 parking spots are updated and assessed by a pan-European community of more than 500,000 truckers. The app that shares the same name (Fig. 1) helps truckers find the best truck parking space on their route across Europe based on their needs related to infrastructure, comfort, and security. Moreover, the TPE app can help to avoid overcrowded parking areas by supporting a better utilization of parking spaces. *PTV Planung Transport Verkehr AG*, the German company behind the idea of the app, supports the TPE project. The app is available for free for iOS and Android users.

Fig. 1.   Truck Parking Europe (TPE) app supports truckers to find the best parking slot. (Pictures: truckparkingeurope.com)

User involvement at TPE and PTV is an emerging topic. For the last few years, preliminary user involvement activities have been evolving, and both TPE and PTV are using several feedback communication channels (e.g., surveys, Facebook pages, app stores) to gather end-user feedback. However, TPE and PTV are not always satisfied with the quantity and quality of the feedback. Thus, they want to improve their feedback gathering process in the long run. To facilitate this, a comparison of current and new feedback channels is planned. New feedback channels like dedicated screenshot-based feedback tools are not just promising to support end-users to describe (with additional textual description) the *exact location* (e.g., button) and *context* (e.g., active page) of the feedback object but also allow the feedback receiver to understand the issue behind the feedback [8, 9]. However, before starting a complex study and providing such a feedback tool to all the truckers, we want to test whether a small sample of truckers can use the feedback tool at all during their daily work.

In particular, we explore *whether a dedicated, mobile, and screenshot-based push feedback tool enables truckers to express their feedback (RQ1), how satisfied the truckers are with this feedback gathering approach (RQ2)*, and *whether the feedback received is useful for the TPE team (RQ3)*.

2   Study Procedure and Data Collection

2.1   Our Criteria for the Feedback Tool

For our pilot study, we had two reasons for deliberately opting against an embedded feedback tool solution that is integrated in the TPE app. First, we would have to wait for the next release of the TPE app to start the pilot study. Second, we would have to convince the stakeholders that an integrated feedback tool would neither adversely influence the performance of the TPE app nor the end-users' opinion of it. Thus, we had to find a *dedicated*, *mobile push* feedback tool that is *standalone, but easy to access* [9]. Because commented and marked screenshots are very promising feedback formats (see previous section), the tool needs to support *text input* and annotations of a created or uploaded *screenshot*.

2.2   AppEcho – The Chosen Feedback Tool

By applying the aforementioned criteria, we conducted an unsystematic analysis of research tools and commercial service providers. The *AppEcho* app [5] was the only app that satisfied our criteria. The AppEcho Android app guides the end-user step by step in a wizard-like interface to document feedback on other applications and on the mobile platform in situ. When the trucker wants to communicate feedback on the TPE app, she takes a screenshot of the app and opens AppEcho by clicking on the feedback tool icon in the Notification Center. The latest screenshot is automatically inserted (Fig. 2a), but can be replaced by any other picture file (folder symbol at the top-right corner). The trucker can use two simple annotation functions: a marker to highlight elements and segments on the screenshot (Fig. 2b), and an eraser to void areas. The trucker can type a short text in the window that pops up after three seconds of user inactivity (Fig. 2c). In this study, we de-activated the option to provide an audio message (Play, Record, and Stop buttons shown in Fig. 2c), because we assumed that we would receive recordings with a lot of background noise and also estimated that we would have limited resources to transcribe verbal feedback. Finally, after clicking on the send button, the trucker receives a confirmation message, the AppEcho app closes automatically, and the latest active screen of the parking app is displayed. In contrast to other available mobile feedback tools, the trucker can get an overview of the sent feedback (not shown here). In our previous work, this was identified as an important feature [10].

Fig. 2. Main interaction steps in the English version of the mobile feedback tool, AppEcho [5], exemplified with an original feedback documented by a trucker (in German).

2.3 Sampling and Task Alignment

The truckers, who received an Amazon voucher of €20 as a monetary incentive for taking part in the study, were invited to the study by the TPE Facebook group, the TPE newsletter, and the TPE website. After their registration to the study, we briefly explained the study procedure via email, including their task to provide feedback whenever they had a positive or negative experience with the TPE app. Then, the truckers downloaded the AppEcho app from the app store on their smartphones. They used the app in German or English. The truckers viewed an illustration of all the functions of AppEcho through a short one-minute video and they were able to familiarize themselves with the feedback tool by sending a test feedback after the installation of AppEcho and prior to the study period. In total, nine truckers (one female, eight males, mean age = 46.9, SD = 7.4) participated in our study in the capacity of a feedback sender for a two-week period.

2.4 Feedback Sender's Questionnaire

After two weeks, the truckers completed a short online questionnaire on their experience with the AppEcho app. We were interested to know (i) whether they could imagine themselves giving feedback on the TPE app *again with the AppEcho app* (yes/no format), (ii) what they *liked about the AppEcho app*, (iii) how we should *improve the*

AppEcho app, and (iv) what would be the *best feedback communication channel* for them to provide feedback on the TPE app (ii-iv in free text format).

2.5 Feedback Receiver's Questionnaire and Discussion Session

We also wanted to explore how useful the feedback is for the TPE team. To answer this question, five TPE team members (Product Management, Marketing, Design, Usability Engineering; multiple roles possible) judged each feedback that was documented in the form of (annotated) screenshots and texts. For this, each representative rated the *understandability* and the *relevance* of a feedback entry on a 5-point scale (1 = not understandable/relevant, 2 = slightly understandable/relevant, 3 = moderately understandable/relevant, 4 = understandable/relevant, 5 = completely understandable/relevant). With understandability, we indicated how clearly the feedback was formulated and whether the feedback documentation included all the necessary information required to understand the issue being reported. Regarding relevance, we probed as to what extent did the feedback included information that helped the TPE team to ensure a high quality of the parking app. After completing the rating questionnaire individually, the academic author moderated a brief discussion with all the five representatives regarding the study procedure, results, and the next steps. The data was analyzed by the academic author. The ratings were aggregated among the raters and the feedback entries.

3 Results

3.1 Number and Characteristics of Feedback Entries (RQ1)

In total, nine truckers sent 40 feedback entries, referring to shortcomings (n = 27), followed by feature requests (n = 16), and praise (n = 3) (multiple categories possible). On average, each of the truckers provided 4.4 feedback entries (MIN = 1, MAX = 8). Interestingly, none of the truckers repeated the same feedback issue several times, and only one issue was communicated by two truckers (missing zoom function). The feedback entries had an average length of 19 words (SD = 11.1) with a minimum of one word ("sometimes") and maximum of up to 41 words. The eraser function was not used at all. In more than half of the cases, the marker was used. In 14 cases where the marking function was not used, the truckers referred to problems or feature requests that were valid for the TPE app in its entirety (e.g., request for a landscape mode) or when the feedback issue did not pertain to any object of the current view. The marker was not used exclusively to locate the object of the feedback by framing an object with a circle (n = 13) (Fig. 3a: wrong parking spot status) or to point to an object with an arrow (n = 6) (Fig. 3b: overlaying column of the list). The marking function was also used in three cases where the truckers communicated feedback regarding the entire TPE app or the visible screen. For this, they drew an exclamation point (Fig. 3c: missing option to add a parking slot on this screen). In addition, four truckers used free-hand drawing to sketch where a function or information should be located on the app screen. For example, the location for a zoom function was sketched (Fig. 3d) while another trucker indicated that additional characteristics of a parking slot should be represented as an icon (Fig. 3e).

Fig. 3. Original marked screenshots sent with the mobile feedback tool. Name and photo of the trucker have been blackened by the authors (e).

3.2 Feedback Sender's Experience (RQ2)

Seven of the eight truckers, who completed the questionnaire, could imagine themselves using the AppEcho app again to provide feedback on the TPE app. The truckers stated that it was simple to provide feedback as AppEcho was user-friendly. Improvement ideas included suggestions to make it possible to send feedback without a screenshot and to clearly mention the receiver of the feedback in the app. The truckers stated that email (n = 4), the AppEcho app (n = 3), a feedback screen that can be accessed within the TPE app (n = 2), and phone (n = 1; multiple answers possible) are the best communication channels for providing feedback on the TPE app. Interestingly, email was chosen as the best channel although it requires the trucker to open an external application, similar to the AppEcho app. One of the explanations for this could be that the information about the feedback receiver was not communicated in the AppEcho app (see improvement idea above), while it is obvious when writing an email to TPE.

3.3 Feedback Receiver's Experience (RQ3)

Most of the feedback entries rated by the five TPE members varied from understandable to completely understandable (Mean = 4.3, SD = 0.8) and from relevant to completely relevant (Mean = 4.2, SD = 0.6). They stated that the feedback helped them not only to confirm their presumptions about the weaknesses of the TPE app, but also to be aware of the unknown issues that were identified by the truckers. The team was pleasantly surprised regarding the low amount of effort needed for feedback gathering and about the relatively high number of feedback entries that were received in a short time-period from nine truckers – given that their end-users were usually unavailable for user involvement activities. Please note that we did not compare the results of the pilot study with the quantity and quality of feedback received from other feedback communication channels as we did not define a baseline yet.

4   Discussion

4.1   Threats to Validity

Regarding the feedback data collection process, the main limitation is that we cannot guarantee to what extent the truckers would use the AppEcho app over a *longer period* and without getting paid for study participation. Furthermore, our *sampling* might be biased due to self-selection of the truckers and advertising of the study not in the TPE app (where the advertisement would ideally reach all truckers) but on the TPE website, Facebook, and newsletter. These channels might not be used by all truckers.

Regarding data collection from the TPE team, the feedback quality ratings might be affected by the biased *selection of raters* as we chose availability as the only criterium. However, we assumed that the five raters represented the whole TPE team, including the development team's perspective. The *understandability* and the *relevance ratings* were averaged for all the raters and the feedback issues, without handling outliers and extremely divergent judgments. We assume that the presented ratings were underestimated because most of the divergences were caused by only one or two raters who gave low ratings. Unfortunately, as we had time restrictions and as the rating was paper-pencil based, we could not compare and discuss the values of the individual ratings in the session.

4.2   Conclusion and Next Steps

In this pilot study, we explored a tool-supported approach to enable truckers to communicate their problems and needs regarding a parking app. Together with TPE, we have shown that the nine truckers, who participated in our pilot study, could use a dedicated, mobile, and screenshot-based feedback tool to provide feedback on the TPE app (RQ1). Barring one exception, the truckers could imagine themselves using AppEcho again to provide feedback on the TPE app, and we received positive comments as well as improvement ideas regarding the AppEcho app (RQ2). Most of the 40 feedback entries that were received were rated by the TPE team as understandable and relevant for improving the TPE app (RQ3).

In our future work with TPE, we want to solve the limitations of our pilot study. First, we want to *scale* our study by involving more truckers for a longer duration. Second, we plan to use an *embedded* feedback gathering tool that was developed in the SUPERSEDE EU project [11]. In contrast to the AppEcho feedback app, this tool supports a wide range of feedback formats, such as advanced marking functions and customizable categories and ratings. We assume that the SUPERSEDE feedback tool supports the investigation of how to best assist truckers to provide feedback on the TPE app in their everyday work. Third, we will test the extent to which such a dedicated feedback tool can increase the feedback quality and quantity compared to feedback received from other feedback communication channels such as the app store or email. Fourth, we will trace the influence of a single feedback in the decision-making process of the TPE team, including, what feedback is finally considered in the TPE app evolution.

Finally, we will investigate the contribution of end-user feedback in improving TPE's software evolution and maintenance processes.

Acknowledgment. The authors thank Ronnie Schaniel, Norbert Seyff, the anonymous reviewers, the study participants, and the TPE team members. We also thank the Requirements Engineering Research Group at the University of Zurich who made the AppEcho app available for our study. This work was partially supported by the European Commission within the SUPERSEDE project (Agreement No. 644018) and by the UseTree project (Bundesministerium für Wirtschaft und Energie im Förderschwerpunkt Mittelstand Digital, Initiative Usability, Förderkennzeichen 01MU12022A).

References

1. Ko, A.J., Lee, M.J., Ferrari, V., Ip, S., Tran, C.: A case study of post-deployment user feedback triage. In: Proceedings of the 4th International Workshop on Cooperative and Human Aspects of Software Engineering, pp. 1–8 (2011)
2. Maalej, W., Pagano, D.: On the socialness of software. In: Proceedings of the 9th International Conference on Dependable, Autonomic and Secure Computing (DASC), pp. 864–871 (2011)
3. Maalej, W., Happel, H.-J., Rashid, A.: When users become collaborators: towards continuous and context-aware user input. In: Proceedings of the 24th Conference on Object-Oriented Programming, Systems, Languages, and Applications (OOPSLA), pp. 981–990 (2009)
4. Yetim, F., Draxler, S., Stevens, G., Wulf, V.: Fostering continuous user participation by embedding a communication support tool in user interfaces. AIS Trans. Hum. Comput. Interact. **4**(2), 153–168 (2012)
5. Seyff, N., Ollmann, G., Bortenschlager, M.: AppEcho: a user-driven, in situ feedback approach for mobile platforms and applications. In: Proceedings of the 1st International Conference on Mobile Software Engineering and Systems, pp. 99–108 (2014)
6. Stade, M., Fotrousi, F., Seyff, N., Albrecht, O.: Feedback gathering from an industrial point of view. In: Proceedings of the 25th International Requirements Engineering Conference (RE), pp. 63–71 (2017)
7. Almaliki, M., Ncube, C., Ali, R.: The design of adaptive acquisition of users feedback: an empirical study. In: Proceedings of the International Conference on Research Challenges in Information Science (RCIS), pp. 1–12 (2014)
8. Elling, S., Lentz, L., de Jong, M.: Users' abilities to review web site pages. J. Bus. Tech. Commun. **26**(2), 171–201 (2012)
9. Schneider, K.: Focusing spontaneous feedback to support system evolution. In: Proceedings of the 19th International Requirements Engineering Conference (RE), pp. 165–174 (2011)
10. Stade, M., Seyff, N.: Features for mobile feedback tools: applying the KANO method. In: Proceedings of Mensch und Computer (Human and Computer), pp. 171–180 (2017)
11. Stade, M., Oriol, M., Cabrera, O., Fotrousi, F., Schaniel, R., Seyff, N., Schmidt, O.: Providing a user forum is not enough: first experiences of a software company with CrowdRE. In: Proceedings of the 25th International Requirements Engineering Conference (RE), pp. 164–169 (2017)

Software Startups

Towards Understanding Startup Product Development as Effectual Entrepreneurial Behaviors

Anh Nguyen-Duc[1]([⌗]), Yngve Dahle[2], Martin Steinert[2], and Pekka Abrahamsson[3]

[1] University College of Southeast Norway, Bø, Norway
anh.nguyen.duc@usn.no
[2] Norwegian Univesrity of Science and Technology, Trondheim, Norway
[3] University of Jyväskylä, Jyväskylä, Finland
https://www.usn.no/

Abstract. With the rapid development of technology and competitiveness of IT sectors, the speed of learning and evolving is vital for success of software startups. However, software startups often face with multiple technical and business challenges, which lengthen the duration of their idea-to-launch process. Little is known about the relation of entrepreneurial characteristics of software startups and their product development. We conducted an empirical study on twenty software startups to understand their challenges that leads long idea-to-launch processes. Six engineering-related challenges were identified and interpreted via a lens of an entrepreneurial behavior theory. Our main finding is that the effectuation-based approach of developing a startup business is mismatched with the iterative, evolutionary-oriented approach of developing a startup product. Software startups search for local optimal solutions, emphasize on short-run feedback rather than long-run strategies, which results in vague prototype planning, paradox of demonstration and evolving throw-away prototypes.

Keywords: Effectuation · Entrepreneurial behavior theory · Software development · Prototyping · Empirical study

1 Introduction

The software industry has witnessed a growing trend, where software products are developed by small teams with limited resource and little operating history. This is especially visible in newly created companies with new kinds of business models. These companies are developing products and services to which potential customers can be quickly adopted. Slack, Spotify, Appsumo, Grasshopper and Github, to name a few, are examples of successful software startups with rapid user acquisitions and rapid growths.

With the advancement of software and hardware technology, it seems that everyone with a business idea, a website and a pitch can launch a new company. However, not so many business ideas are realized as concrete prototypes. Furthermore, even a smaller portion of prototypes is transformed into commercialized products. By engaging at multiple coarse-grained mockups and prototypes, startups refine the understanding about customers and market, while at the same time refining their business concepts. At a certain point in time, evolutionary prototypes are created, which will eventually turn

© Springer International Publishing AG 2017
M. Felderer et al. (Eds.): PROFES 2017, LNCS 10611, pp. 265–279, 2017.
https://doi.org/10.1007/978-3-319-69926-4_19

into the final products. Difference from practitioner's perception on quick learning [1] or "*learn fast, fail fast*" [2], our observation in a Norwegian incubator gives an impression that this launching process can be time-consuming. An entrepreneur might take a year or more to delivery the initial intended value to mass market.

The uncertainty in both market and product gives a basic understanding about the heterogeneity in journeys from ideas to launch. Startups travel iteratively though the space of market knowledge and product concept development in order to achieve product-market fit. We argue that there is a mismatch between the way startup evolving their business and the way their products are developed. Startups are different from established companies, from not only their dynamic and multiple-influenced environment, but also an entrepreneurial approach in decision-making and reaction to the situation. Prototyping and product development are not supported by entrepreneurial activities, which leads to the delay in the idea-to-launch journey.

The research community in Software Engineering (SE) and Information Systems (IS) has shown an increased interest in software startups from a procedural viewpoint. Some empirical research attempt to visualize the evolution of software startups in the form of models, processes and patterns [4–6]. Increasing number of studies attempt to combine the business aspect of startups in the product development. Nevertheless, there is very rare research that considers the specific entrepreneurial characteristics of startups in the context of software product development. Looking at software startups from the lens of entrepreneurial theory can be useful in relating the contextual factors of software startups and their product development, hence be able to better and more practically support software startups.

Our research objective is to understand the challenges software startups facing and through in the phases from ideas to launch and to look for possible explanation. The investigation of different challenges leading to the delay of startup launching was reported in an International Conference on Agile Software Development (XP2017) [3]. In the scope of this work, we focus on describing the typical startup idea-to-launch duration and discussing the influencing factors from entrepreneurship perspective. Our primary research questions are as follows:

RQ1: How long does it take to transform a business idea into a launching product in software startups?

RQ2: How can we explain for technical challenges occurred during the idea-to-launch journey of software startups?

The paper is organized as follows; firstly we will present related work about software startups, software development in startups and a behavior theory of entrepreneur firm (Sect. 2). Then, we described our research methodology (Sect. 3). After that, findings for RQs are presented (Sect. 4). Finally, we will discuss the threats to validity and conclude the paper (Sects. 5 and 6).

2 Background and Related Work

2.1 Software Startups

The fundamental differences between a startup and an established company can be described as in Table 1. While a startup often aim to grow fast, an established company focuses on doing stable business for years [24]. Another difference lies on product and market certainty. Established companies generally sell known products to known customers in known local markets. Rather than a formal organization, a software start-up is likely to be a task-oriented group. Entrepreneurs are central to the organization as a whole and they carry out most of tasks. In the scope of this work, we considered startup companies that adopt software technology as part of their core business value.

Table 1. Comparison between a startup and a SME

Elements	Startups	Established firms
Business goal	High growth	Stable business
Risk	High risk	Low risk
Organization structure	Various from agile team to more structured organization	A structured and stable group of employees
Funding	Often seek large-scale funding from venture capitalists or angel investors, IPO	Self-funded or financed from family, friends or a bank loan
Product	Unknown, often related to advanced technology	Often known, various
Customer	Unknown	Often known

2.2 Product Development in Early Stage Software Startups

From idea to launching, startups typically go through a significant amount of early-stage prototyping and product development. Empirical research yielding insights on early-stage activities in software startups are limited. Paternoster et al. performed a systematic mapping study of 43 primary studies about software development in startups [7]. The authors summarize that startups adopt fast releases to build a prototype in an evolutionary fashion and quickly learn from the users' feedback to address the uncertainty of the market. Teixeira et al. describe a case where mockup prototypes were used to support requirement engineering processes [8]. The author found that that a rapid and functional prototyping model can improve the effectiveness of the requirement elicitation of any software development. Fagerholm et al. investigate how a minimum viable product (MVP) is created and how a product hypothesis is tested in the context of university-industry collaboration [5]. Nguyen-Duc et al. conduct five case studies to explore usage scenarios of a MVP. The authors found that benefit from MVPs were not fully achieved in current prototyping practices [9].

A body of SE research reveal some development practices and techniques in software startup context [10–12]. Kordon et al. introduce the brief overview of rapid prototyping, suggested that prototyping-based development methodologies will increase in industry

[10]. Brandt et al. describe the concept of opportunistic programming in writing code to prototype [11]. By studying 20 web programmers, five prototyping traits are found: glue together high-level components, add functionality via copy-and-paste from the web, iterate rapidly, consider code impermanent, and face unique debugging challenges. Grevet et al. describe a rapid prototyping technique called piggyback prototyping [12]. The six-stage prototyping process is validated in a single startup case. While these studies provide knowledge on what are done in early stage software startups, they do not relate these engineering practices with technical challenges faced by startups. Furthermore, there is no attempt to explaining for these challenges.

2.3   Behavioral Theory of the Entrepreneurial Firm

Entrepreneurship research has long focused on understanding the formation, development and influencing factors to the succeed of startups. When reasoning about startups' activities and behaviours, an important assumption one can make is to consider a startup with causation or effectuation theory. In one hand, the causation process takes an outcome as given and focus on selecting between means to implement the outcome [23]. Particularly, the behavior theory of firms (BTF), authored by Cyert and March [14], propose that company decision making consists of finding a satisfactory solution (satisficing) rather than in evaluating the best possible alternative (optimization). Even though BTF was originally applied to large companies, recent work has paid attention in using the theory to explain for entrepreneurial learning [13]. In the other hand, effectuation processes take a set of means as given and focus on selecting between possible outcomes that can be realized [23]. Alternatively, entrepreneurial companies are seen as heterogeneous, bounded rational entities [13]. In the face of environmental uncertainty, therefore, these bounded rational firms form expectations based on available means and information.

Dew et al. proposed a behavioral theory of the entrepreneurial firm (BTEF), based on Cyert and March's idea. Assuming entrepreneurs as an effectual unit, Dew et al. [13] propose four constructs related to entrepreneurial decision-making (as shown in Fig. 1):

- Means-driven transformation: startup companies tend to be effectual, available means drive action. Effectual action involves transforming extant means into new possibilities, including new problems of interest. Transformation processes are actor-centric, as who comes on board determines goals, not vice versa. The transformation is appeared as a search activity, aiming at solving pressing problems rather than developing long-run strategies.
- Docility: conflict and difference among stakeholders is avoided through stakeholder docility, goals are residual of the process. Simon et al. defined docility as "*the tendency to depend on suggestions, recommendation, persuasion and information obtained through social channels, as a major basic of choice*" [20]. The decisions made by startups, for instance, can be done by cooperating other's ideas and not necessary to go through conflict resolution.
- Leveraging contingency: avoiding uncertainty by short run feedbacks. But also encouraging surprise; even 'bad' surprises can be leveraged to provide new means

and new opportunities. Actions emphasize commitment and contingency, not choice and determinacy.

- Technology of foolishness: insulation from learning sought through allowing experimental actions with regard to affordable lost. The technology of foolishness allows startups to relax the primacy of functional rationality, to temporarily suspend intentionality, and promote the openness to new actions, objectives and understandings.

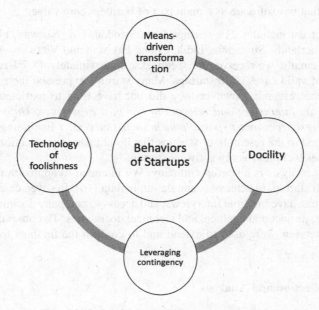

Fig. 1. Behaviour theory of entrepreneurial firm

3   Research Approach

3.1   Study Design

We conducted this study by using a multiple-case study design [15]. Exploratory case studies are suitable to explain the presumed causal links in real-life interventions [16]. The case designed was conducted by the first authors and reviewed by the fourth author. Different early-stage software startup companies were chosen to acquire a broad view of state-of-practices in startups. We tested the data collection instrument using two interviews, which is not included in this study. As stated by Yin [15], a case in a multiple-case study can be a typical case, a confirmatory case, a contrasting case, or a theoretically diverse case. We intended to have a small set of typical cases that we can have in-depth investigation, and remaining cases as confirmatory cases.

Contacts for startups were searched via four channels, (1) startups within professional networks of papers' authors, (2) startups in the same town with the authors, (3) startups listed in Startup Norway and Crunchbase database. We also include contacts we got from startups events, such as Norwegian Investment Forum, Startup Weekend and Hackathons. Case selection criteria include:

(1) a startup that has at least two full-time members, as we look at startups from an aspect of entrepreneurial team
(2) a startup that have already launched their product(s), so their experience can be relevant
(3) a startup that has software as a main part of business core value.

The contact list includes 219 startups from Sweden, UK, Norway, Finland, Italy, Germany, Netherlands, Singapore, India, China, Pakistan and Vietnam. After sending out invitation emails, we received 41 feedbacks, approximately 18.7% response rate. The final set of valid cases is 20 startups. Many startups expressed their interest with the result of the research, however they did not have time to participate, i.e. *"The research appears interesting and relevant to our past experience. Unfortunately, we don't have the resources/time to participate in such a survey..."* Excluding startups that are not interested in the research, or startups that do not pass our selection criteria, the final set of cases includes twenty software startups.

The unit of analysis is a startup company. We intended to approach multiple data sources in each startup, to achieve triangulation in data [16]. In seven cases (S01–S05, S07, S08), we can have multiple interviews, and access to company documents, such as data repository, project management and technical documents. The other thirteen cases with single interview were used to extend and to confirm the findings from the main cases.

3.2   Data Collection and Analysis

The data were collected in eleven months, from March 2015 to February 2016. Interviews were semi-structured to understand the engineering activities from the idea stage to the final product stage. The interviewees were asked questions about (1) realization of business idea (2) pivot practices (3) product design and development. The interview guideline is published online[1]. Methodological triangulation in data collection was done by data extracted from technical documents and participant observations. For piloting and refining interview guideline, we talked to software startups in coworking spaces and incubators in Trondheim to get familiar with startup scenes and their current issues.

We conducted 25 interviews from CEO or CTO of these twenty companies. Five companies allowed us to carry a follow up interview. Fifteen interviews (60% of total interview) were conducted via Skype. During each interview, the first authors also did note taking to mark important concepts coming up from the interview. Later on, all the interviews were transcribed by using a freelancing service[2]. The service was recommended by a researcher in our network and pilot test of the service was conducted before actual adoption. The total number of transcripts is 313 A4 pages.

---

[1] www.goo.gl/r9okCu.
[2] www.fiverr.com/debbierojonan.

We used thematic analysis to analyze the data, a common technique for identifying, analyzing, and reporting conceptual themes found from qualitative data [17]. We started by reading all interview transcripts and relevant documents, and coded them according to open coding [17]. We attempted to label all meaningful text segments with appropriate codes. To support the data analysis, we used a tool, NVivo 11[3], which enables classification and analysis of textual data and summary of extracted codes. To feed data to this study, we filtered the codes that are related to prototyping, technical implementation, and testing activities prior to product launching. By this bottom-up approach, statements from interviewee about challenges with technical implementation of software startups are revealed.

Collected code are grouped into higher-order representing different technical challenges when going from ideas to commercialized product. After that, all of the authors go through each challenge, one by one and attempt to use a theory to explain for the challenges [21]. Several theoretical frameworks were considered, such as Cynefin model [18], boundary spanning object theory [19] and theory about entrepreneurial firm behavior [13]. Considering the rationale behind startup decisions and activities, we found that entrepreneurial literature is the most relevant choice.

4   Results

4.1   RQ1: How Long Does It Take to Transform a Business Idea into a Launching Product in Software Startups?

Figure 2 describes the time of idea-to-launch duration in our cases at pre-startup, startup and scaling phases. The cases are classified based on their current stage (pre-startup, startup or scaling stage [22]) and the time-to-launch of their startup product. The time-to-launch is defined as the time between that the business idea appeared and was discussed relative to the time the first product version was released to the market. There are multiple prototypes created during the time-to-launch duration. It is noticed here that counting the starting time of a business idea is bases on the perception of the interviewee. The launching version, is also subjective, based on the interviewee's definition of "*public*" users. For instance, company S02 counted a product launched when it is publicly available in Apple store. Company S09 considered a launch of their product after they have more than 5000 users in the local region.

As described from Fig. 2, there is a diversity in terms of time-to-launch in pre-startup, startup and scaling companies. Successful startups (who scale) might take months to years to launch their products. One of the pre-startup teams are struggling to launch their product. However, their startup involved hardware development and long R&D processes.

In our startup sample, there are no startups that launch their products one month after initializing their ideas. There is only one startup launched their product after two months development. In this case, the CEO did spin off from a large company with the business idea to extend their existing product. He also had a group of customers lined up before

---

[3] www.fiverr.com/debbierojonan.

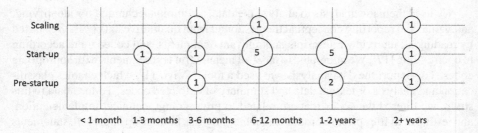

Fig. 2. Time idea-to-launch of startups

the product was developed. All the necessary team competence was onboard. The major time-to-market duration is between six months to two years. There are three companies, which took more than two years to conceptualize, prototype and launch their products. Interestingly, one of them surpassed startup level and became a successful company with more than 50 developers.

4.2 RQ2: How Can We Explain for Technical Challenges Occurred During the Idea-to-Launch Journey of Software Startups?

Figure 3 describes challenges that result in a delay or a longer-than-expected duration of prototyping and product development. We preliminarily map the issues that are found relating to software developer's work, i.e. task implementation and communication. Description of each challenge and our interpretation is given in the following sub-sections.

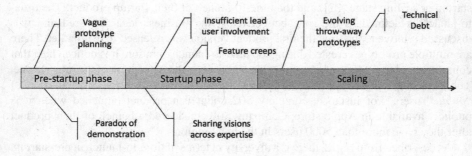

Fig. 3. A preliminary map of technical challenges during startup launch

4.2.1 Challenge 1: Vague Prototype Planning

Description: In early stage, defining and planning for prototypes is often overlooked. Designers expect a conception phase prior to a prototyping phase that provides a roadmap for the prototypes. However, rapid prototyping that involve a great deal of implementation are very difficult to sufficiently conceptualize in advance. When each of the prototypes turned out to be something else than envisioned, the following prototypes are often chosen in an ad-hoc manner, without considering the overall plan of how many prototypes are actually needed, what assessment criteria to use. The plan for acting against uncertainty drives the prototype costs and the timeline.

Illustration: Startup S05 develops a peer-to-peer platform for news publication. Their business roadmap aims at having a community of citizen reporters after five years. The ultimate goal is implemented via some milestones for both product development and community development. However, when realizing the general business ideas, many different alternative business cases appear, i.e. building an event sharing platform, building a hyper-local news sharing space, etc. The product roadmap is diverged from the initial business roadmap. Prototypes were created one after the other, little was reused and the prototypes was not designed in a detailed way before starting building them. This lead to a long (three to six months per prototype) and costly prototyping process.

Interpretation: According to BTEF theory, startups avoid uncertainty by emphasizing short-run reaction to short-run feedback rather than anticipation of long-run uncertain events [13]. Causal rationality with a pre-determined goal and existing resource, and seeks to identify the optimal product roadmap, is not the case of our startups [23]. Prototyping is encouraged to find suboptimal set of features or functionalities. Prototyping roadmap, which is to find the optimal product development plan, is not encouraged.

4.2.2   Challenge 2: Feature Creeps

Description: Startups operate under multiple influences, which introduces different, sometimes conflicting feature requests for a startup product. Feature prioritization is often performed during sprint planning. At a certain point in time, features from important customers or investors is prioritized over features from smaller customers or experimented features. Chasing customer requirements without a proper synchronization with the product development roadmap can lead to increased development costs and unnecessary business divergence.

Illustration: Startup S03 developed a mobile solution for managing the construction and maintenance of buildings. The startup was firstly funded by a large construction cooperation to develop a solution for some of their on-going construction projects. After that, the startup had few more customers, which require slightly different set of features, i.e. reporting, connecting to their existing databases, etc. The startup failed to balance the customer requests and consolidate a launching version to a mass market: *"We are adding features all the time. This is not a product that will ever stop evolving. We will always have a strong engineering team to develop the product forward. We are not talking about maintenance here. We are talking about this being the core of the company's competence"* (CEO of S03).

Interpretation: According to BTEF theory [13], startups tend to perform different experiments with technology, i.e. features, user experience etc. Many startup features are a good representation of technology of foolishness. A new feature might reasonably come from essential needs of customer, but also come from trying out variation of details, which are not certainly served for any pre-determined purpose. The technology of foolishness allows startups to relax the primacy of functional rationality, to temporarily suspend intentionality, and promote the openness to new actions, objectives and understandings.

4.2.3   Challenge 3: Paradox of Demonstration

Description: Highly influenced by funding sources and large customers, many startups have a discrete product development, synchronized with their funding stream. A software startup might pause technical activities at different phases of the project, waiting for adequate funding. In order to complete business development, prototypes need to be well-prepared and convincing in term of business concept and technical implementation. For such prototypes, it often require a reasonable amount of product development effort. However, an early stage prototype is rapidly developed to serve the learning propose tightly tied to a specific timing and budgeting constraints. Financial and time constraints are often a main barrier for carrying out the proper product development. The well-preparedness and rapidness of prototyping is therefore a paradox in early-stage software startups.

Illustration: Company S08 develops a platform promoting and selling event tickets. An angel investor wanted to see how the platform worked in practice and also how easy it was to use. The demonstration, planned to happen one week after the initial investor meeting, was critical for having the investor onboard. During this week, all development effort was focused on developing demonstrable features, work-around solutions for some components and fixing of some use case scenarios. After securing funding, the product was developed from scratch again. The series of high fidelity prototypes with little reuse lasted for more than 18 months before the actual product got launched.

Explanation: Startups operate based on mean-driven transformation [13]. Demonstrated prototypes were limited by the current means startups possess, including financial and human resources. Effort to reducing the gap between the reality of prototypes and the expectations of startup stakeholders, i.e. entrepreneurs, investors, and customers, leads to the paradox of demonstration.

4.2.4   Challenge 4: Sharing Visions Between Business and Technology

Description: Entrepreneurial teams typically consist of people with diverse skillsets and mindsets. Conceptualizing a business idea includes discussion and development of ideas. While prototypes are iteratively refined, derivations among team members, especially between the non-technical persons and software developers can lengthen the idea conceptualization. In one hand, communicating the product ideas and convincing the technical people about the product value can be time-consuming. In the other hand, the communication of technical difficulties is sometimes difficult.

Illustration: Startup S03 outsourced the development part to a software provider. Frequent meetings, sprint reviews and site visit were done to overcome the geographical distribution. However, there was still the gap on perceiving business value of the features. The communication between the development team and the CEO was time consuming, and sometimes lead to rework due to misunderstanding: *"She [the CEO] is very sharp about business and finance stuff, but it takes a long discussion to explain her about the importance of having flexible product design..."* (S03 team leader).

Interpretation: According to March's theory of firm, there can be internal inconsensus about firm's strategy and decision-making [14]. Not only different visions but also different ways to achieve the same vision creates the diverged opinions among startup team members. However, conflicts do not necessarily happen in startup context, as startup team members are both persuadable and persuasive to different degrees about different matters [13]. The duration of prototyping needs to account for amount of time to pursue different startup team members.

4.2.5 Challenge 5: Insufficient Involvement of Lead Users

Description: Not all users' input is equally valuable to product development. Finding a group of users that represents the market needs is essential for market-driven software products. These users are often referred as lead users [25]. In some cases, lead users can act as a market creator by their ability to adopt the proposed technology in the early phases. Getting access to lead users early in the prototyping process is not always a straight forward task for the entrepreneurs. In some startups, it may become a bottleneck in the prototype validation phases to find appropriate early lead users. Balancing the speed of learning (learning fast) and the relevancy (learning the right things) of learning is a challenging task for the founding team in a startup.

Illustration: Startup S12 develops an Internet of Thing (IoT) operating system (OS) with a target market of IoT application developers. Most of the features were invented by the CEO. The startup had problems when validating the ides with actual users, who should have a clear expectation from the OS. *"Most of them don't understand the idea ... It came 10 years before the app developers can recognize its benefit ... I have to change the idea into a more applicable product to get funding application approved by Innovation Norge ..."* (CEO of S12).

Interpretation: Challenges of early user involvement can be tracked to two problems, (1) to find appropriate early innovators and (2) whether there actually is a market for the product. On one hand, finding early lead users might be limited by the capacity of the startups, i.e. existing personal and professional networks, available human and financial resources. Hence, a lead user is often found as a suboptimal candidate for early stages. Many times, the first users are also startup team members. On the other hand, the startup products might have so small market that it is difficult to find relevant users.

4.2.6 Challenge 6: Evolving Throw-Away Prototypes

Description: Many prototypes are designed to eventually turn into a final software product. However, there are also many prototypes that accidentally become evolutionary ones. The modules that were not designed for a long-term usage was quickly fixed by some glue code and an ad-hoc reuse in the next prototype version. Along with learning and experimenting new technology, developers would emphasize the speed and ease of development over code robustness and maintainability. The increasing Technical debt caused by the lack of proper refactoring threatens the quality of product in later phases of software startups

Illustration: Startup S15 develops an in-class online quiz to check student understanding about lectures. Multiple prototypes developed by the CEO or as a student project, were experimented with different classes. The final prototype, which capture refined design and business ideas, were decided to become a launching version. However, the launch was delayed due to the low quality of the version. The reason was that the backend was not properly architected for scaling to a large number of users.

Interpretation: According to Dew et al. [13], startups, instead of avoiding the uncertainty as established organizations do, seek to leverage contingencies. Tolerating surprises during a series of prototypes might lead to utilize the business-fit prototype for long-term development. However, the prototype is not technical-fit for a long-term purpose, leading to the observed technical debts.

5   Discussion

5.1   Understanding Entrepreneurial Behavior of Startups

Entrepreneurship literature discusses the difference between causation and effectuation startups [13, 14, 23]. Startups adopting causation has a given goal and searches for means to reach his goal, while startups using effectuation will start with the means he has and from this point he looks at possible goals. By using an effectuation theory [13], we can explain different technical challenge startups facing with during their evolution journey. Effectuation-based entrepreneurial processes at the business level seem to mismatch with the agile, product-oriented approach at the technical level.

Collaboration, including efficient communication of visions and tasks among startup teams and interaction with external stakeholders, is important for shortening the idea-to-launch process. Besides, how customers are involved in the prototyping loops has an impact on the duration of the prototyping. From the product perspective, inappropriate customer feedback delays the learning and creates more prototyping loops, too many requests from customers delay the time-to-release and introduce complexity to product management. From the market perspective, startups might actually end up with so small market segment that is difficult to find early customers.

Paternoster et al. present that startups adopt fast releases to build a prototype in an evolutionary fashion and quickly learn from the users' feedback to address the uncertainty of the market [7]. In this study, we highlighted a new type of prototype, which is evolving throwaway prototypes. Intentionally or not, software startups do not throw away quick-and-dirty prototypes and evolve them (or part of them) into the final products. Giardino et al. point out two characteristics of the early stage development, which are neglect of software quality and evolutionary approach [6]. Our study complements to this work by add in an intention factor to explain for the evolving throw-away prototypes. While the evolving throw-away prototypes contain a lot of technical debts, the quality problem they face with sometimes so critical to be resolved by code refactoring.

5.2 Threats to Validity

One possible classification of validity concerns includes internal, external, construct and conclusion validity [16]. In our study, an internal threat to validity is the bias in the data collection, as the data might not represent the comprehensive case. In order to mitigate this threat, we selected CTO and CEO as interviewees, who have the best understanding about their startups. We also adopted different information source, i.e. observation, social media and press release to increase our understanding about the cases.

A construct validity threat is the possible inadequate descriptions of constructs. When analyzing data, the coding process of interview transcripts was assisted by the authors' prior knowledge about prototyping and validated learning. While codes and themes were mainly performed by the first author, the interpretation of the results was collectively discussed and refined with other co-authors. The viewpoint triangulation, especially with one of the co-authors as an entrepreneur makes us confident with the interpretation.

An external validity, which concerns about how can we generalize the results into a startup population, is more interesting to discuss. Our cases offer a good variety with regards to company size, application domain, financial model, and growth stage and organization structure. Startup cases are from Finland, Norway, Italy, UK, Netherland and Vietnam, however, the sample is dominant by Norwegian companies (70% total cases). The observed startups are mainly small size (three to seven people) and operate bootstrapping financial model. We do not consider other types of startups, for example, internal cooperate startups, venture capital invested startups, and American startups. The findings can be observable in other companies in countries in North Europe, because the contextual settings would be similar (e.g. culture, government regulations, innovative thinking and incentives surrounding start-up activities).

6 Conclusions

This paper portrayed a state-of-practice product development in twenty software startups. We systematically collected evidence about how long does it take a software startup to launch and what technical challenges do they face during the launch phase. Six engineering related challenges were identified and discussed from the viewpoint of behavior theory of entrepreneur firm. Our main finding provide evidence that there is a mismatch between the effectuation-based approach of business development and the iterative, evolutionary-oriented approach of product development in many early stage European software startups. Driven by the existing means and resource, startups search for local optimal solutions, emphasize on short-run feedback rather than long-run strategies. This results in technical challenges, such as vague prototype planning, paradox of demonstration and evolving throw-away prototypes.

There are several possibilities for future work on software startups. Our next step is to extend the map of startups challenge to include non-technical challenges that we identify from the cases, such as lock-in to external resources, changing team composition and market uncertainty. Furthermore, we found that entrepreneurial theories are helpful in understanding and explaining the context of technical challenges and decision-making. Future work would investigate more on how other theories can be adopted in software startup research.

References

1. Ries, E.: The Lean Startup: How Today's Entrepreneurs Use Continuous Innovation to Create Radically Successful Businesses, p. 103. Crown Publishing, New York (2013)
2. Maurya, A.: Running Lean. O'Reilly, Sebastopol (2012)
3. Nguyen-Duc, A., Wang, X., Abrahamsson, P.: What influences the speed of prototyping? an empirical investigation of twenty software startups. In: XP2017, Essen, Germany (2017)
4. Olsson, H.H., Alahyari, H., Bosch, J.: Climbing the stairway to heaven - a multiple-case study exploring barriers in the transition from agile development towards continuous deployment of software. In: 38th EuroMicro SEA, Izmir, Turkey (2012)
5. Fagerholm, F., Guinea, A.S., Mäenpää, H., Münch, J.: Building blocks for continuous experimentation. In: 1st International Workshop on Rapid Continuous Software Engineering (RCoSE 2014), Hyderabad, India (2014)
6. Giardino, C., Paternoster, N., Unterkalmsteiner, M., Gorschek, T., Abrahamsson, P.: Software development in startup companies: the greenfield startup model. IEEE Trans. Softw. Eng. **42**(6), 585–604 (2016)
7. Paternoster, N., Giardino, C., Unterkalmsteiner, M., Gorschek, T., Abrahamsson, P.: Software development in startup companies: a systematic mapping study. Inf. Softw. Technol. **56**(10), 1200–1218 (2014)
8. Teixeira, L., Saavedra, V., Ferreira, C., Simões, J., Sousa Santos, B.: Requirements engineering using mockups and prototyping tools: developing a healthcare web-application. In: Yamamoto, S. (ed.) HCI 2014. LNCS, vol. 8521, pp. 652–663. Springer, Cham (2014). doi:10.1007/978-3-319-07731-4_64
9. Nguyen-Duc, A., Ambrahamsson, P.: Minimum viable product or multiple facet product? the role of prototyping in early stage software startups. In: XP2016, Edinburg, Scotland (2016)
10. Kordon, F., Luqi.: An introduction to rapid system prototyping. IEEE Trans. Software Eng. **28**(9), 817–821 (2002)
11. Brandt, J., Guo, P.J., Lewenstein, J., Dontcheva, M., Klemmer, S.R.: Opportunistic programming: writing code to prototype, ideate, and discover. IEEE Softw. **26**(5), 18–24 (2009)
12. Grevet, C., Gilbert, E.: Piggyback prototyping: using existing, large-scale social computing systems to prototype new ones. In: CHI 2015, Seoul, Korea, pp. 4047–4056 (2015)
13. Dew, N., Read, S., Sarasvathy, S.D., Wiltbank, R.: Outlines of a behavioral theory of the entrepreneurial firm. J. Econ. Behav. Organ. **66**, 37–59 (2008)
14. Cyert, R.M., March, J.G.: A Behavioral Theory of the Firm. Prentice-Hall, Englewood Cliffs (1963)
15. Yin, R.K.: Case Study Research: Design and Methods (Applied Social Research Methods), 5th edn. SAGE Publications Inc, Thousand Oaks (2014)
16. Runeson, P., Höst, M.: Guidelines for conducting and reporting case study research in software engineering. Empir. Softw. Eng. **14**(2), 131–164 (2009)

17. Boyatzis, R.E.: Transforming Qualitative Information: Thematic Analysis and Code Development. Sage Publications, Thousand Oaks (1998)
18. Snowden, D.J., Boone, M.E.: A leader's framework for decision making. Harv. Bus. Rev. **85**(11), 69–76 (2007)
19. Tushman, M.L., Scanlan, T.J.: Boundary spanning individuals: their role in information transfer and their antecedents. Acad. Manag. J. **24**(2), 289–305 (1981)
20. Simon, H.A.: Strategy and organizational evolution. Strateg. Manag. J. **14**, 131–142 (1993)
21. Eisenhardt, K.M.: Building theories from case study research. Acad. Manag. Rev. **14**(4), 532–550 (1989)
22. Nguyen-Duc, A., Seppnen, P., Abrahamsson, P., Hunter-gatherer cycle: a conceptual model of the evolution of startup innovation and engineering. In: 1st Workshop on Open Innovation on Software Engineering, ICSSP (2015)
23. Sarasvathy, S.D.: Causation and effectuation: toward a theoretical shift from economic inevitability o entrepreneurial contingency. Acad. Manag. Rev. **26**(2), 243–263 (2001)
24. Startups & High-Growth Businesses: The U.S. Small Business Administration. SBA.gov
25. von Hippel, E.: Lead users: a source of novel product concepts. Manag. Sci. **32**(7), 791–805 (1986)

Little Big Team: Acquiring Human Capital in Software Startups

Pertti Seppänen[✉], Kari Liukkunen, and Markku Oivo

M3S/M Group, University of Oulu, FI 90015 Oulu, Finland
{pertti.seppanen,kari.liukkunen,markku.oivo}@oulu.fi

Abstract. *Background* – Resource-based-view and human capital theories have been used for decades when studying firms, their strategies, organizations, businesses, and successes. The value of the theories as general frameworks has commonly been recognized, especially because of their flexibility in adopting new perspectives, such as the dynamic character of the resources and human capital. Startup companies represent an interesting area on a map of firms because of their specific characteristics and tendency not to strictly follow the processes common in more established companies. Despite the differences, it is reasonable to assume that startups face similar phenomena as established companies do when building up their firms and operations. *Aim* – In this research, we studied software startups from the perspective of resource-based-view and human capital theories. We examined what human capital resources, capabilities, knowledge, and skills, were needed in the early stages of software startups and how the startups acquired such human capital. *Method* – We conducted a multiple-case study on a group of software startups in Norway and Finland. *Results* – We identified six high-level capability areas, nine means to acquire those capabilities, and nine drivers affecting the utilization of different means. We concluded that the capabilities in software startups are dynamic, evolving by growth and learning from the basis of the founders' prior capabilities, and the utilization of different acquiring means is a case-dependent thing with a varying set of drivers. We also found the uniqueness of the resources, as proposed by the resource-based-view theory, was not reached in our case startups, but replaced with a combination of commonly-available resources, innovation, and application-specific capabilities.

Keywords: Software startup · Initial team · Product development · Product development process · Capability needs · Resource-based-view theory · Human capital theory

1 Introduction

A software startup's ability to transform an innovation to a product and a business case is largely affected by the challenges it faces during its early stages, such as time pressure, a small and inexperienced team, dependency on a single product, and general lack of resources [1]. It is crucial that a startup should be able to gather the knowledge, skills, and capabilities needed to create a product based on the innovation.

© Springer International Publishing AG 2017
M. Felderer et al. (Eds.): PROFES 2017, LNCS 10611, pp. 280–296, 2017.
https://doi.org/10.1007/978-3-319-69926-4_20

Recent studies [1–3] revealed the software startups' characteristics that partly contradicted one another and these startups' contributions to the latest technical and economic developments. On one hand, typical software startups are immature [2, 3], characterized by small and inexperienced teams, limited resources, and third-party dependency [1]. On the other hand, they are innovative, rapidly evolving [1], and have created some of the most successful products of the past years.

We explored the software startups from the perspective of two interrelated business and economic theories defining the competitive potentials of firms—the resource-based-view (RBV) theory [4, 5] and the human capital (HC) theory [6, 7]. Research based on the RBV theory studies a firm's sustainable competitive advantage as a function of its resources, covering different categories. The HC theory focuses on knowledge-oriented human attributes as a basis of creating economic value. The focus of HC research varies from individuals to firms and further to nations, addressing a broad palette of human capabilities, knowledge, and skills, as well as ways to obtain them. The linkage of both theories by defining HC as one resource category of the RBV theory was already proposed by Barney [4], and a broader study on their convergence had been conducted [8].

In this research, we studied software startups' HC resources—capabilities, skills, and knowledge. We have chosen this research focus because several characteristics of software startups are tied to the availability of resources [1].

For our study, we asked the following research questions:

RQ1: What are the engineering-related capabilities in a software startup?
RQ2: What are the means to acquire those capabilities?
RQ3: What are the reasons for deploying different capability-acquiring means?

The research was conducted on two Norwegian and nine Finnish software companies. Nine companies were developing products of their own, while two were offering experienced resources to software startups on a subcontracting basis.

Comparing our empirical findings with the results of prior research on the theories, we identified both commonalities and differences. The importance of the availability of HC was recognized. Acquiring HC through experience and learning was also in line with the findings of prior literature. The uniqueness of the resources, as proposed by the RBV, was not identified in our study. Based on our results, we suggest that the software startups' business advantage does not depend on the uniqueness of their resources in general but on their ability to make a small team large by combining commonly available resources with unique innovation and application domain knowledge.

The rest of this paper is structured as follows. Section 2 focuses on the background of and the motivation for the study, reviewing prior research on software startups and the RBV and the HC theories. Section 3 presents the research design, including the case selection and research data analysis. Section 4 deals with the results, and Sect. 5 discusses the study's findings and relevance. Section 6 concludes the paper and offers suggestions for future research.

2 Prior Research

In this section, we review prior research on RBV and HC theories in the context of startups and entrepreneurship. We summarize the software startups' characteristics that were identified in previous studies.

2.1 Prior Research on Resource-Based View

The RBV is a business theory claiming that sustainable competitive advantage is gained when a company has access to valuable resources that the competitors lack and are rare, difficult to imitate, or difficult to substitute. The theory's development has led to various definitions and classifications of a company's resources.

Barney [4] divided the resources into three categories—physical capital, HC, and organizational capital. He further classified HC into such areas as training, experience, and personal characteristics of an individual. Several authors further developed the RBV by refining details and proposing various additional resources, such as strategic resources [9], managerial resources [10], or a division of resources into tangible and intangible ones [11].

In further developments of the RBV, a capability approach was defined, separating the so-called capabilities from the generic definition of resources. Research on the capability approach addressed companies very broadly, covering a multitude of definitions of capabilities [12–14]. Amit and Shoemaker [12] defined capabilities as firm specific and unavailable outside the company. A similar definition was presented by Makadok [15], claiming that the key characteristic of capabilities was that they must be built within the company and could not be bought.

To address the challenges caused by continuous changes in business and technology, the capability approach was further developed to address so-called dynamic capabilities [16–18]. Teece et al. defined in [16] the dynamic capabilities as "the firm's ability to integrate, build, and reconfigure internal and external competences to address rapidly changing environments". Dynamic capabilities had further been defined by different authors in the contexts of processes and routines [17, 18] and of product development-related competencies [19].

From our study's perspective, some definitions are of special interest, including capabilities as self-created [15], as company-internal processes and routines improving the usage of resources [14, 20, 21], as core competencies deployed in product development and gained through learning [11], and as dynamic phenomena [16–18, 21].

2.2 Prior Research on Human Capital Theory

The HC theory [6] is old and established in economics, focusing on human capacity, such as knowledge, intelligence, and talents, as a source of economic value creation. In the context of businesses and companies, the HC theory states that such human attributes as the personnel's education, experiences, and skills affect a firm's business performance [22].

In a broad study on Dutch startups, Bosma et al. reported that the founders' investments in human and social capital significantly affected the startups' performance, measured in three dimensions – survival, profits, and generated employment [23]. Thus, it is reasonable to assume that HC is a valuable resource for a startup, and investments in it further increase its value.

Based on the findings of an empirical study, Lazear [24] concluded that entrepreneurs were generalists with a broad variety of skills without necessarily being experts in any. Martin et al. in [25] found evidence that entrepreneurship-specific education positively contributed to entrepreneurship-specific HC, meaning that education was a valid source of such HC.

The effects of the technology entrepreneur's HC on innovation radicalness were studied by Marvel and Lumpkin [26], based on the understanding that breakthrough innovations were among the key competitive factors of a new enterprise. As general HC was proposed to build on the two main concepts of experience and education [6], Marvel and Lumpkin further divided experience into two different views on its depth and breadth. The study's results indicated that experience depth and education positively correlated to innovation radicalness, while experience breadth did not, differing from the results of Lazear [24].

Unger et al. [27] presented the results of a broad meta-analysis on HC research in entrepreneurship over the last three decades. The authors identified a significant relationship between HC and success. Interestingly, *a priori*-gained HC (existing capabilities, knowledge, and skills) showed a larger contribution to success than investments in HC in the form of education or learning. The HC that was specific for an actual task made the greatest positive contribution, and the positive contribution was stronger in the case of new businesses than in old established ones.

Shrader and Siegel in [28] found that a key determinant of the enterprises' long-term performance was the fit between the strategy and the team experience, and the most important determinant of a differentiation strategy's success was the team's technical experience. However, prior studies on software startups concluded that the initial team was often inexperienced [1, 29]. On the other hand, Hatch et al. [30] identified that utilizing external HC with prior industrial experience significantly reduced learning, while indicating that such compensation would not necessarily provide a startup with sustainable solutions to issues related to its team's missing experience.

2.3   Prior Research on Characteristics of Software Startups

Table 1 lists the characteristics of software startups that were identified in a broad literature review [1].

When reviewing the above-mentioned results from the HC and the RBV theories' perspectives, potential conflicts can be observed. The RBV theory points out valuable, rare, and inimitable resources as key determinants of sustainable business advantage [4]. Later studies proposed that a category of such inimitable resources was based on unique company developments, routines, and processes that tied together the capabilities of individuals [14, 20, 21]. Compared with the findings of other studies [1, 29], it may be concluded that software startups are missing several resource categories identified as building blocks of sustainable business advantage [4, 11, 17, 18].

Table 1. Identified characteristics of software startups [1].

ID	Characteristic	Explanation
C1	Lack of resources	Limited economic, physical, and human resources
C2	Highly reactive	Ability to quickly react to changes in market, technology, and products
C3	Innovation	Given a competitive ecosystem, startups need to focus on highly innovative segments of the market
C4	Uncertainty	Dealing with highly uncertain ecosystem from many perspectives: market, product, competition, people, and finance
C5	Rapidly evolving	Successful startups aim to grow and scale rapidly
C6	Time pressure	External pressure to release fast and to work under constant pressure
C7	Third-party dependency	Due to lack of resources, startups heavily rely on external solutions, such as open-source software and outsourcing
C8	Small team	Small number of members of the initial team
C9	One product	Activities gravitate toward one product or service only
C10	Low-experienced team	Many of the team members have less than 5 years of experience and are often recent graduates
C11	New company	The company has been recently created
C12	Flat organization	The company is usually founder centric, and all team members have major responsibilities with no need for high management
C13	Highly risky	The failure rate of startups is extremely high
C14	Not self-sustaining	Especially in the early stage, startups need external funding
C15	Little work history	The basis of an organizational culture is not present initially

Similarly, some characteristics identified in a study [1], such as a small and low-experienced team, third-party dependency, and little work history, seem to be in conflict with the established HC theory.

3   Research Design

To answer the research questions, we carried out a multiple-case study on a group of software startups, following the guidelines set out in an article [31].

3.1   Case and Subject Selection

Our research data was collected in three European locations, including two companies in Trondheim, Norway; two in Helsinki, Finland; and seven in Oulu, Finland. Nine companies were startups with their own products, while two were service providers offering highly experienced human resources. The startups were chosen to represent different products, business cases, evolution phases, and business statuses, using local startup incubators as the starting point of the selection. The service providers brought another viewpoint on the capability development in software startups, deepening our study. Out of the startup group, four case companies had embedded products, while five were developing pure software products. Table 2 summarizes the case companies and their application areas, customer cases, and current statuses.

Table 2. Descriptions of the case startups.

Case	Location	Product	Customers	Interviewee(s)	Status
A	Norway	Pure software	B2C, B2B	Founder, expert	Product on market
B	Norway	Pure software	B2C, B2B	Founder, expert	Product on market
C	Finland	Embedded	B2C	Founder	Dissolved
D	Finland	Embedded	B2C	Co-founder	Prototype series
E	Finland	Pure software	B2B	Founder	Established business
F	Finland	Pure software	B2B	Founder	Prototype series
G	Finland	Embedded	B2B	Co-founder	Established business
H	Finland	Pure software	B2C, B2B	Founder	Established business
I	Finland	Embedded	B2C	CEO	Prototype series
J	Finland	Service	B2B	Founder	Selling services
K	Finland	Service	B2B	Founder	Selling services

Legend: B2C business to customer, B2B business to business, CEO chief executive officer

The sizes of the startups in terms of the staff ranged from four to twelve employees. The operational age was between one and five years. One service provider was an established company with over ten years of operational history, while the other was a startup.

3.2   Data Collection

We collected the research data by conducting interviews and applying the key informant technique as defined by Marshall [32]. Most of the interviewees were founders or co-founders. One was a hired chief executive officer (CEO), who had a founder-level understanding of his company. We conducted semi-structured face-to-face interviews, using thematic interview guides [33]. All interviews were held in English, recorded, and transcribed.

3.3   Data Analysis

We analyzed the interview data by combining thematic synthesis and narrative synthesis [34]. Starting with thematic synthesis, the transcribed interview data were analyzed with the NVivo11 tool. The data that were related to the research questions were identified and coded. We continued the synthesis by combining the identified codes under themes in a hierarchical manner as described by Cruzes and Dybå [35]. The interview data and the qualitative codes are available as open data in [36].

To study the case companies' characteristics, we opted to use the narrative synthesis method [34]. A previous broad study [1] had identified fifteen characteristics typical of software startups (Table 1). In the narrative analysis, we figured out how those characteristics fitted each of our case startups. The results are presented in the next section.

4 Results

In this section, we discuss the findings identified from the research data in the context of the case companies.

4.1 Thematic Synthesis Results

In the thematic synthesis we found twenty four themes that we categorized into three categories according to the research questions: *identified capabilities*, *capability-acquiring means*, and *acquiring drivers* (Tables 3a, 3b, and 3c, respectively).

Table 3a. Found codes of top-level theme identified capabilities.

Capability	Knowledge about …
Application domain	The product's desired functionality and its value to the customers
Software development	How to conduct software development fitting the product
Hardware development	How to conduct hardware development fitting the product
Mechanics development	How to conduct mechanics development fitting the product
Systematic development work	How to conduct development according to systematic practices
Difficult technology domain	Especially difficult or rare technology needed in the product

Table 3b. Found codes of top-level theme capability-acquiring means.

Theme	Description
Founders' experience	Prior experience and knowledge of the founding team members
Other products	Learning from existing similar products
Prototyping and testing	Learning from developing prototypes and testing them
Customer cooperation	Learning from cooperating with the customer
Research	Learning from conducting empirical or literature research
Team growth: inexperienced	Acquiring new human capital by hiring inexperienced persons
Team growth: experienced	Acquiring new human capital by hiring experienced persons
Team growth: unconventional	Acquiring new human capital by offering unconventional remuneration or benefits instead of a conventional salary
Team growth: subcontracted	Acquiring new human capital by subcontracting

Table 3c. Found codes of top-level theme acquiring drivers.

Theme	Description
Founders' experience	The knowledge that founders bring to the startup
Customer cooperation	Customer cooperation possible
Skills	Knowledge and skills needed in the startup
Known persons	Seeking already known persons
Special interests	Seeking persons with special interests
Stable economy	Company has necessary economic resources
Challenging economy	Company has challenges in economic resources
Avoiding economic risks	Company wants to avoid additional economic risks
Ensuring innovativeness	Allocation of the key persons' work on innovation instead of routines

In the research data, we identified two capability domains where special knowledge was required – capabilities needed to solve difficult technical issues and capabilities needed to implement systematic routines and processes.

For the discussion section, we group the capability-acquiring means into three categories, as follows: (a) the original HC (founders' experience), (b) increasing the HC by growth (in-house hiring and subcontracting), and (c) increasing the HC by learning.

We identified nine drivers for utilizing different means of acquiring the needed capabilities. As shown in Table 3c, the drivers varied from the level of the individual up to the level of the whole company. At the individual level, personal attributes were dominating, while at the company level, the economic situation was a key factor.

4.2 Company Characteristics

The case companies A to I were software-intensive startups, each with a single product that had either just entered the markets or was in the prototype phase. Other characteristics listed in Table 1 were also common, such as highly reactive, rapidly evolving, time pressure, small team, new company, flat organization, and little work history. The resource situations varied, but only one case company, E, had a good situation in economic, physical, and human resources. All the other cases lacked resources in some areas. Uncertainty was another common characteristic. Companies E and G, having established businesses, were the only ones not facing greater uncertainty in the market, product, competition, people, or finance areas.

The team experience varied a lot among the companies and individual team members. Some of the founders were experienced professionals, while others were recent graduates with no prior industrial experience. A mixed team with both experienced and inexperienced members was a common setup. All case companies were somehow dependent on third parties. Most of the companies were subcontracting, and case company G utilized lots of open-source software.

Table 4. Themes' distribution among the case companies.

Case	Capability domains	Founders' experience	Acquiring means	Drivers
A	Application, software, systematic development	Just graduated	Other products, team growth – experienced and inexperienced	Stable economy
B	Application, software, systematic development	Just graduated	Other products, customer cooperation, team growth – experienced, inexperienced, unconventional and subcontracting	Customer cooperation, challenging economy
C	Application, software, hardware, mechanics, systematic development, difficult technology	Software, hardware, mechanics, systematic development	Founders' experience, team growth – experienced and subcontracting, research	Founders' experience, avoiding economic risks
D	Application, software, hardware, mechanics, difficult technology, systematic development	Application	Founders' experience, customer cooperation, team growth – experienced and subcontracting	Founders' experience, customer cooperation, avoiding economic risks
E	Application, software, systematic development, difficult technology	Application, software, systematic development, difficult technology	Founders' experience, team growth – experienced and inexperienced	Founders' experience, stable economy, special interest, ensuring innovativeness
F	Application, software, systematic development	Application, software, systematic development	Founders' experience, team growth – experienced and inexperienced	Founders' experience, known persons, avoiding economic risks
G	Application, software, hardware, mechanics, systematic development, difficult technology	Application, software, hardware, systematic development, difficult technology	Founders' experience, other products, team growth – experienced, inexperienced, unconventional and subcontracting, prototyping and testing, customer cooperation, research	Founders' experience, customer relationship, avoiding economic risks, ensuring innovativeness

(continued)

Table 4. (*continued*)

Case	Capability domains	Founders' experience	Acquiring means	Drivers
H	Application, software, systematic development	Only managerial experience in software development	Customer cooperation, team growth – experienced, unconventional	Customer relationship, avoiding economic risks
I	Application, software, hardware, mechanics, systematic development, difficult technology	Application, difficult technology	Founders' experience, growth – experienced, subcontracting	Founders' experience, stable economy, known persons, ensuring innovativeness

Three companies, E, G, and H, having established businesses, were self-sustaining. Other companies depended on external funding. However, the actual financial situation varied in all companies and affected their setup and operations.

The companies' innovativeness also varied. Most case companies were modifying existing product innovations to fit a new market, another price segment, or a new application domain. Three companies, C, E, and I, developed more innovative, totally new products. All companies utilized the latest technology, and companies C and G created new, technically challenging, multidisciplinary solutions.

Case companies J and K differed from the others; their business was to offer human resources to customer companies. Case company J was a software house that provided excellent software development knowledge, with over ten years of accumulated experience in different application domains. Case company K offered services to build up company structures and systematic work approaches. The company employed few but very experienced personnel. Company K had created the position of hired chief information officer (CIO) to support the customers in building up solid administration structures.

4.3   Prevalence of Capability-Related Themes

We combined the results of the thematic synthesis with the company narratives to find out the distribution of the themes among the case companies and to highlight the potential dependencies between the themes and the company characteristics. Table 4 shows the results. Note that the acquiring driver 'skills' is not listed in the table because it was common for all case companies and self-evident in any selection of a new hire or a subcontractor. All case companies performed prototyping and testing though this theme is mentioned only in company G, where it played an especially significant role in learning.

5   Discussion

In this section, the answers to the research questions are discussed. The findings are then explained in the context of the HC and the RBV theories. The discussion on the validity of the results and their relevance to the academia and to practitioners completes the section.

5.1   Answering the Research Questions

RQ1: What are the engineering-related capabilities in a software startup?
We identified six high-level capability domains (Table 3a). Application knowledge and software development domains were common in almost all the case companies; the service provider K focused on the systematic work domain. The research data further revealed that the application domain and software development capabilities must be available from the very beginning. Companies A and B failed in building their first software development teams, causing difficulties with the first versions of their respective products.

Hardware and mechanics development were present in all cases with embedded products. The companies differed the most in two capability areas—systematic development and difficult technology domains.

RQ2: What are the means to acquire those capabilities?
We identified nine means used in startups to acquire the capabilities (Table 3b). The most common one was the original HC—the prior knowledge and experience brought by the founder to the company. In three companies, A, B, and H, the founders' missing capabilities in software development were compensated by hiring experts.

Increasing the capabilities by learning was common. The sources included learning from existing similar products, customer cooperation, and prototype-oriented development. In the case of difficult technology domains, research in the form of searching results from the scientific literature and conducting empirical studies was used.

Additional capabilities were typically also acquired through growth, by hiring new employees or subcontracting. In companies B, G, and H, new employees were offered other benefits but normal salaries. For in-house growth, both experienced and inexperienced individuals were hired, while the subcontractors were selected based on their prior experiences and skills.

RQ3: What are the reasons for deploying different capability-acquiring means?
We identified nine drivers affecting the means deployed to acquire the needed capabilities (Table 3c). While the basis of the startups' HC was their founders' prior experience and knowledge, other means identified in our study could be perceived as compensation for the founders' missing capabilities.

Three companies, E, G, and I, had a special arrangement for administrative tasks, ensuring their respective founders' continuous focus on innovation and product development. In companies E and I, a CEO was hired at an early phase from outside of the company. Company K's special service, hired CIO, confirmed the value of ensuring continuous innovativeness instead of concentrating on administration.

The major division line between in-house hiring and subcontracting seemed to be the financial situation. In cases of a solid funding situation, new persons were hired, while in the opposite circumstances, subcontracting was preferred. Subcontracting was also common in cases of hardware and mechanics development and in some situations when difficult technology was deployed. Avoiding economic risks affected the selection of the hired persons; experts with well-known careers or former workmates were recruited for key positions, while the implementation work was many times performed by students.

In companies B, G, and H, the missing economic resources led to offering shared ownership instead of normal salaries when hiring new team members. The founder of company H pointed out that this option was used simply because the firm needed an experienced software developer but had no possibility to pay the costs of normal employment or subcontracting.

The individuals' skills had an effect on when a company sought new employees or subcontracting partners. The service provider companies, J and K, pointed out their specific capabilities as the key sales arguments presented to startup companies.

Table 4 summarizes that both the utilization of the means and the reasons were strongly depending on the context. Several means were used to acquire a specific capability, and several capabilities acquired by the same means. Similarly, the same reason led to utilization of different capability acquiring means, and the utilization of a means was driven by several reasons. Thus, in this study we were not able to create any proposal of a generic theory linking the capabilities, acquiring means, and reasons.

5.2   Findings in the Context of Prior Research

We discuss our study's results in the context of the prior knowledge presented in Sect. 2, covering the previous research on software startups, the HC theory, and the RBV theory.

Our study's findings are in line with those of the prior research on software startups [1, 29], though the companies, their products, and targeted customer segments varied. Eight out of the fifteen characteristics listed in Table 1 could be identified in all product-developing case companies. The rest of the characteristics were also identified in one or more cases. The research data from the service-providing companies, J and K, confirmed the findings; their business with startups was based on the customers' lack of specific HC and need to avoid financial risks.

From a larger perspective, our findings are consistent with those of the earlier research on the HC theory [6, 22–28, 30]. Becker's [6] definition of HC as composed of experience and education should preferably be broadened in the context of startups to cover learning, as proposed by Hatch and Dyer [30]. In all case companies, the initial capabilities were both broadened and deepened by learning from different sources, as shown in Table 4. The need for additional learning was also recognized in the case companies with founders possessing broader and deeper experiences because they tended to opt for more challenging technology.

A potential conflict exists between the results of Lazear's study [24], pointing out that the entrepreneurs are generalists, and those of Shrader and Siegel's work [28], noting the importance of technical experience for a startup. Our results are more in line with the latter. Five out of nine founders had strong technical experience, and even the rest (four) hired technical experts to compensate for their missing capabilities.

Companies C, E, G, and I confirmed the linkage between the depth of experience (especially in technology) and the radicalness of the innovation. The findings of Unger et al. [27], claiming that *a priori* experience had a more positive effect than education, were partly confirmed by the significant role of the founders.

Hatch and Dyer's [30] results, indicating that utilizing external HC with prior industrial experience significantly reduced learning, were not found in our study. External HC in the form of subcontracting was broadly used in the case companies in parallel with learning. In the resource-limited and risk-avoiding reality of a software startup, it can be regarded as a rational decision to reach the immediate product-related targets.

Generally, the resources to which the competitors lacked access, as defined in the RBV [4], were also unavailable in our case companies. The definition of capabilities as firm specific and unavailable outside the company, as proposed by Amit and Schoe-maker [12], was not supported. All companies were building capabilities through learning as proposed in prior research [11], but those capabilities could not be classified as rare and difficult to imitate [4]. In most cases, potential competitors would have been able to develop the same competencies or pay for them from outside. Companies C, E, G, and I owned technology-related capabilities that could be considered rare but not inimitable.

All but one capability acquiring means were related to growth or learning, creating dynamic capabilities and supporting the findings of prior research [1, 16]. Dynamic capabilities, defined as company-internal processes and routines improving the usage of resources [14, 20, 21], were identified especially in companies A, B, and F.

In summary, we conclude that our case companies' situations aligned well with the findings of the prior research on software startups. The HC theory and the RBV theory were partly applicable in the case companies. The partial applicability could be perceived as an expected result due to the theories' broad coverage of different types of companies. The important role of the availability of HC in the form of knowledge and capabilities was particularly identified in our study. Creating HC through education, experience, and learning, as proposed in the prior literature, was also consistent with our study's results.

The largest deviation from the HC and the RBV theories involved the uniqueness of the HC resources. Working with small and inexperienced teams under time pressure did not allow the startups to pursue uniqueness but forced them to acquire external knowledge and capabilities, which could not be considered exceptional.

Based on our study's results, we conclude that in the context of software startups, a company's ability to rapidly create difficult technology and complex products with a small team is the key component of its HC, especially in the form of its organizational capital as defined by Barney [4]. We also suggest that this ability represents uniqueness and sustainable advantage in the context of the RBV though a startup needs to deploy various external, publicly available resources to make use of its distinctive ability.

5.3 Validity Discussion

Our study focused on exploring phenomena related to the HC and the RBV theories in software startups. We conducted the study by interviewing a group of startups, analyzing the research data, and drawing conclusions from the analyzed research data. From the validity perspective, we now discuss construct validity, external validity, and reliability, as described by Runeson and Höst [31]. Our findings highlighted the context-dependent nature of the capabilities, acquiring means and reasons, and did not allow us to draw generic conclusions on the causal relationships them. Thus, we omit the internal validity discussion [31].

We addressed the construct validity by building our study out of well-established components, using a pre-prepared semi-structured interview as the means for collecting the research data, applying the key informant technique by interviewing persons in senior positions [32], and analyzing the data systematically with thematic and narrative analysis methods [34].

We collected the research data from nine Finnish and two Norwegian software companies, using interviews as the data gathering method. The sample's limited size, its geographical extent, and the single data gathering method restrict the external validity of our results though the case companies represent fairly large variations of business cases, technologies, and evolution phases. Further studies that will broaden the base of the research data are needed to improve the generalizability of the findings.

To address the reliability issues, we utilized peer work in the steps of our study. Our research team created the interview schema to enable a broad coverage of the phenomena in software startups. The research data were transcribed by an external professional. The results of the qualitative data analysis performed by the first author were reviewed by the co-authors.

5.4 Relevance to Academia and Practitioners

Our study focused on software startups from the perspective of two established theories about firms – HC and RBV. The results indicate that software startups represent a specific case under those theories. Because some key aspects of the theories, such as uniqueness of resources [4], seem unattainable in startups, it would be interesting to more closely examine what characteristics of a successful startup would compensate for those shortages on the resource side.

The theories referred to in this research can be perceived as focusing on a firm's success from the *how and by whom* perspective. Innovativeness, a characteristic of startups, addresses the *what* question. Because innovativeness is generally regarded as a key success factor of a startup, it would be important to conduct studies that compare the value of *what* with that of *how and by whom*.

From the practitioner's viewpoint, our study identifies the means utilized for acquiring HC-related resources in different software startups. It highlights the importance of knowledge and capabilities as key resources. Table 3b shows that all identified HC-acquiring means, besides the founders' own prior experiences and increasing the team size, are related to learning. This fact points out that a startup's early stages to a great extent constitute a learning story, and the founder has to utilize all relevant means for nurturing the necessary learning.

6   Conclusions and Future Research

We empirically explored what the elements of the HC in software startups were and how they were acquired. We identified six high-level capability areas, nine means to gather the required capabilities, and nine contextual drivers affecting the utilization of those means. We found that increasing the capabilities could be divided into three categories—the capabilities brought to the startup by the founders, the capabilities of the hired or subcontracted team members, and the capabilities developed by learning.

Our results indicate that the contextual features of a software startup drive the utilization of different capability-acquiring means, including both in-house and external types. The most important drivers are the founder's prior experience and the startup's economic situation.

Referring to the theories and prior research on a company's resources, we found that from an overall perspective, the startups follow the RBV and HC theories. The deviations in the uniqueness of the resources are due to specific characteristics of software startups, that is, small and inexperienced teams and limited economic resources.

In our study, learning was identified as a key means to increase the HC in a startup. Keeping in mind that software startups have managed to tackle the obstacles related to small and inexperienced teams, it would be interesting to investigate learning more closely. Is learning more effective in the small, flat, and new organization of a startup than in a larger and more established company?

Our study was based on a fairly small group of software startups located in two North European countries. Further studies that will increase the sample size and the geographical coverage would be needed to validate and generalize our results.

Acknowledgments. This study was partly funded by TEKES as part of the HILLA program. We thank the members of the Software Startups Global Research Network Anh Nguyen Duc, Pekka Abrahamsson, and Nirnaya Tripathi for their valuable help, as well as all the interviewees for their friendly contributions to the research data gathering.

References

1. Paternoster, N., Giardino, C., Unterkalmsteiner, M., Gorschek, T., Abrahamsson, P.: Software development in startup companies: a systematic mapping study. Inf. Softw. Technol. **56**, 1200–1218 (2014)
2. Blank, S.A.: The four steps to the epiphany: Successful Strategies for Products that Win (2005). CafePress.com
3. Crowne, M.: Why software product startups fail and what to do about it. Evolution of software product development in startup companies. In: 2002 IEEE International Engineering Management Conference, 2002, pp. 338–343. IEEE (2002)

4. Barney, J.B.: Firm resources and sustained competitive advantage. J. Manag. **17**, 99–120 (1991)
5. Barney, J., Wright, P.: On becoming a strategic partner: the role of human resources in gaining competitive advantage. Hum. Resour. Manag. **37**, 31–46 (1998)
6. Becker, G.S.: Human Capital: A Theoretical And Empirical Analysis, With Special Reference To Education (1993)
7. Becker, G.: Human capital revisted. J. Chem. Inf. Model. **53**, 1689–1699 (1994)
8. Wright, P.M., Dunford, B., Snell, S.: Human resources and the resource based view of the firm. J. Manag. **27**, 701–721 (2001)
9. Combs, J.G., Ketchen Jr., D.J.: Explaining interfirm cooperation and performance: toward a reconciliation of predictions from the resource-based view and organizational economics. Strateg. Manag. J. **20**, 867–888 (1999)
10. Peteraf, M.A., Bergen, M.E.: Scanning dynamic competitive landscapes: a market-based and resource-based framework. Strateg. Manag. J. **24**, 1027–1041 (2003)
11. Galende Del Canto, J., Súarez González, I.: A resource-based analysis of the factors determining a firm's R&D activities. Res. Policy **28**, 891–905 (1999)
12. Amit, R., Schoemaker, P.J.H.: Strategic assets and organizational rent. Strateg. Manag. J. **14**, 33–46 (2007)
13. Grant, R.M.: The Knowledge-Based View of the Firm, vol. 3, pp. 367–381 (2006)
14. Wagner, H.-T., Weitzel, T., Koenig, W.: Modeling the impact of alignment routines on IT performance: an approach to making the resource based view explicit. In: Proceedings of the 38th Hawaii International Conference on System Sciences (HICSS), pp. 1–10 (2005)
15. Makadok, R.: Toward a synthesis of the resource based and dynamic capability views of rent creation. Strateg. Manag. J. **22**, 387–401 (2001)
16. Teece, D.J., Pisano, G., Shuen, A.: Dynamic capabilities and strategic management. Strateg. Manag. J. **18**, 509–533 (1997)
17. Eisenhardt, K.M., Martin, J.A.: Dynamic capabilities: what are they? Strateg. Manag. J. **21**, 1105–1121 (2000)
18. Prieto, I.M., Easterby-Smith, M.: Dynamic capabilities and the role of organizational knowledge: an exploration. Eur. J. Inf. Syst. **15**, 500–510 (2006)
19. Mathiassen, L., Vainio, A.M.: Dynamic capabilities in small software firms: a sense-and-respond approach. IEEE Trans. Eng. Manag. **54**, 522–538 (2007)
20. Foss, K., Foss, N.J.: Learning in firms: knowledge-based and property rights perspectives. Working Paper, vol. 2, p. 34 (2000)
21. Winter, S.G.: Understanding dynamic capabilities. Strateg. Manag. J. **24**, 991–995 (2003)
22. Hitt, M.A., Bierman, L., Shimizu, K., Kochhar, R.: Direct and moderating effects of human capital on strategy and performance in professional service firms: a resource-based perspective. Acad. Manag. J. **44**, 13–28 (2001)
23. Bosma, N., Van Praag, M., Thurik, R., De Wit, G.: The value of human and social capital investments for the business performance of startups. Small Bus. Econ. **23**, 227–236 (2004)
24. Lazear, E.P.: Balanced skills and entrepreneurship. Am. Econ. Rev. **94**, 208–211 (2004)
25. Martin, B.C., McNally, J.J., Kay, M.J.: Examining the formation of human capital in entrepreneurship: a meta-analysis of entrepreneurship education outcomes. J. Bus. Ventur. **28**, 211–224 (2013)
26. Marvel, M.R., Lumpkin, G.T.: Technology entrepreneurs' human capital and its effects on innovation radicalness. Entrepreneurship Theory Pract. **31**, 807–828 (2007)
27. Unger, J.M., Rauch, A., Frese, M., Rosenbusch, N.: Human capital and entrepreneurial success: a meta-analytical review. J. Bus. Ventur. **26**, 341–358 (2011)

28. Shrader, R., Siegel, D.S.: Assessing the relationship between human capital and firm performance: evidence from technology-based new ventures. Entrepreneurship Theory Pract. **31**, 893–908 (2007)
29. Giardino, C., Unterkalmsteiner, M., Paternoster, N., Gorschek, T., Abrahamsson, P.: What do we know about software development in startups? IEEE Softw. **31**, 28–32 (2014)
30. Hatch, N.W., Dyer, J.H.: Human capital and learning as a source of sustainable competitive advantage. Strateg. Manag. J. **25**, 1155–1178 (2004)
31. Runeson, P., Höst, M.: Guidelines for conducting and reporting case study research in software engineering. Empir. Softw. Eng. **14**, 131–164 (2009)
32. Marshall, M.N.: The key informant technique. Fam. Pract. **13**, 92–97 (1996)
33. Lethbridge, T.C., Sim, S.E., Singer, J.: Studying software engineers: data collection techniques for software field studies. Empir. Softw. Eng. **10**, 311–341 (2005)
34. Cruzes, D.S., Dybå, T., Runeson, P., Höst, M.: Case studies synthesis: a thematic, cross-case, and narrative synthesis worked example. Empirical Software Engineering, pp. 1–32 (2014)
35. Cruzes, D.S., Dybå, T.: Recommended steps for thematic synthesis in software engineering. In: International Symposium on Empirical Software Engineering and Measurement, pp. 275–284. IEEE (2011)
36. Seppänen, P., Liukkunen, K., Oivo, M.: Supplementary data: raw interview data and NVivo11 analysis summary (2017). https://doi.org/10.5281/zenodo.809184

How Do Software Startups Approach Experimentation? Empirical Results from a Qualitative Interview Study

Matthias Gutbrod[1]([⊠]), Jürgen Münch[1], and Matthias Tichy[2]

[1] Faculty of Informatics, Reutlingen University, Alteburgstraße 150,
72762 Reutlingen, Germany
{matthias.gutbrod,
juergen.muench}@reutlingen-university.de
[2] Institute of Software Engineering and Programming Languages,
Ulm University, Ulm, Germany
matthias.tichy@uni-ulm.de

Abstract. Software startups often make assumptions about the problems and customers they are addressing as well as the market and the solutions they are developing. Testing the right assumptions early is a means to mitigate risks. Approaches such as Lean Startup foster this kind of testing by applying experimentation as part of a constant build-measure-learn feedback loop. The existing research on how software startups approach experimentation is very limited. In this study, we focus on understanding how software startups approach experimentation and identify challenges and advantages with respect to conducting experiments. To achieve this, we conducted a qualitative interview study. The initial results show that startups often spent a disproportionate amount of time focusing on creating solutions without testing critical assumptions. Main reasons are the lack of awareness, that these assumptions can be tested early and a lack of knowledge and support on how to identify, prioritize, and test these assumptions. However, startups understand the need for testing risky assumptions and are open to conducting experiments.

Keywords: Experimentation · Experiment · Software startups · Lean startup · Minimum viable product

1 Introduction

Drew Houston, the co-founder and CEO of Dropbox, got his idea for developing a file-sharing tool on a long bus ride to New York when he wanted to work but could not because he had forgotten his USB stick [9]. Developing a file sharing tool such as Dropbox requires significant resources such as time, effort, and money. The founders of Dropbox wanted to avoid waking up after years of development to see that nobody wants their product. Therefore, they decided to run a small experiment in order to test the most critical assumption, i.e., to test if most people have the problem of file synchronization and would give the product a try. They built a three-minute demo video and uploaded it to Hacker news together with a call to action to join the waiting

© Springer International Publishing AG 2017
M. Felderer et al. (Eds.): PROFES 2017, LNCS 10611, pp. 297–304, 2017.
https://doi.org/10.1007/978-3-319-69926-4_21

list for the private beta program. The video "drove hundreds of thousands of people to the website", Houston reported after the experiment and continued, "our beta waiting list went from 5,000 people to 75,000 people literally overnight. It totally blew us away." With this experiment, the founders validated the most critical assumption that there was real interest for their product [8]. The development of new products and services in startups typically faces many uncertainties. For all these uncertainties, startups need to make assumptions based on their current knowledge. Startups need to transform the riskiest assumptions into testable hypotheses and test them early, in order to avoid proceeding based on the wrong assumptions, which could have high-risk business impacts. Different techniques for testing assumptions can be used. These techniques are all fundamentally based on scientific experimentation principles. One approach that focuses on experimentation is the Lean Startup approach which has been popularized by Eric Ries [8]. It fosters hypothesis testing by applying experimentation as part of a constant build-measure-learn feedback loop. The build-measure-learn feedback loop can be seen as a motor that should always run and produce learning data about critical assumptions. There is only limited research about how startups approach experimentation. In this study, we focus on understanding how especially software startups approach experimentation and identify challenges and advantages with respect to conducting experiments.

The rest of this paper is organized as follows: Sect. 2 presents related work. Section 3 defines the research questions and describes how the study was executed. In Sect. 4 we present the findings followed by Sect. 5 with a discussion. Section 6 summarizes the paper and outline future research.

2 Related Work

The scientific literature offers several frameworks for experiment-driven product de-velopment based on empirical findings. Bosch, for instance, proposes a framework for building products as innovation experiment systems [1]. Fagerholm et al. present build-ing blocks for a continuous experimentation system and an infrastructure [2].

Several studies exist that focus on dealing with uncertainties. Nquyen-Duc et al. emphasize the role of prototyping for experimenting with business ideas. In a study, they identified factors influencing a prototype-centric learning loop. One important finding from their study is that it is necessary to align the prototyping approach with the learning goals [7]. Another study by Nguyen-Duc and Abrahamsson explored the role of minimum viable products (MVPs) in early stage startups. Among other findings, they found that MVPs play an important role in bridging knowledge gaps between the entrepreneur team and stakeholders [6]. These knowledge gaps could be seen as critical assumptions that need to be tested. Other studies focus on the challenges and benefits of organizing and conducting business-oriented experiments. Bosch et al. conducted a study that was aimed at typical challenges when finding a product idea worth scaling. They found that only very few companies "worked with continuously validating product concepts with customers to try to identify problems before building a full solution." Based on their findings they identified several key areas where support is needed. One of these key areas is the validation of product ideas [4].

Hassi and Tuulenmäki focused in a study on how to organize the innovation practices for experimentation. One result was that the design and organization of innovation activities has a major impact on the ability to unlock the full potential of experimentation [3]. In a study, Lindgren and Münch explored the state of the practice of experimentation in the software industry. The study found that experimentation is rarely done systematically and continuously in practice [5]. The study described in this paper focusses on understanding how software startups approach experimentation and identifies challenges and advantages with respect to conducting experiments in startups.

3   Research Approach

In practice, the actual situations in which startups use experiments are not clear. And if they are using experimentation, how do they conduct the experiments? To get a better understanding we defined the following Research Questions:

RQ1: *How do startups use experimentation in practice?*
RQ2: *What challenges do startups have with conducting experiments?*
RQ3: *What benefits do startups see with respect to experimentation?*

Given the exploratory nature of our study and the "how" research question, we decided to use a qualitative interview study in the context of a multiple case study approach [10]. All selected cases were software startups in their early phases before the product market fit with different products. With the term software startups, we refer to human institutions searching for scalable, repeatable, and profitable business models in order to create new software-based products or services, in the context of extreme uncertainty and unpredictable dynamic technology markets. The data collection method was semi-structured interviews with open-ended questions. The interview duration time was between 15–75 min. At the beginning and end of each interview, we included a "warm-up" and "cool down" question. Before every interview, the participants got a declaration of consent form to sign, which included ethical guidelines and the data privacy protection. All interview participants have the role of CIO or CTO in their company, of which they are also the co-founder. Each interview was recorded and transcribed for detailed analysis. The data analysis followed procedures suggested by Yin [10]. The interviews were conducted with German startups companies by the primary researcher from March to June 2017. Table 1 presents a short profile overview.

4   Results

Case 1: This startup provides a web-based toolbox for designing web applications that can be connected to the external and internal services of companies. The solution aims at helping companies to digitize their actual processes. It can be used without any programming skills and provides many reusable modules from a toolbox.

The startup conducts several kinds of experiments. It primarily conducts landing page tests. The main goal of these tests is to increase the conversaion rate and transform more visitors into prospective buyers. The CEO gave an example in the interview:

Table 1. Profiles of the software startups cases

Software startup	Business domain	Founded	Number of founders	Current product development phase
Case 1	Software as a service	2015	3	Functional product with a few large customers
Case 2	Online marketplace	2016	4	Functional product
Case 3	Job portal	2017	3	Prototype
Case 4	Software as a service	2016	2	Functional prototype

"On our landing page we use A/B testing for positioning call to action buttons in order to increase the conversion rates." He added that the duration of such experiments depends on how the team members vote, and is on average 2–3 weeks.

The startup also does implicit experimentation with some kinds of minimum viable products (MVPs) and calls customers regularly to test assumptions. The startup also exhibits at trade fairs and uses these opportunities to do small experiments.

One of the main challenges the startup faces is to drive enough visitors to its landing pages so that the results from the A/B tests are significant. The CEO mentioned: *"At the beginning we were happy if we had two visitors on our page"*. He also mentioned technical challenges with respect to A/B testing: "We change the content on the website with JavaScript and this can lead to conflicts with the actual JavaScript code on the page."

Case 2: This startup focuses on developing a web-based market place for vintage cars. The marketplace consists of an online platform for selling and buying. In addition to the online platform, the startup provides a hybrid mobile app. The founder and CEO of this startup explained that the startup is currently not conducting experiments in a systematic way. However, when developing new features or making changes to the current system, he feels a need to better understand customers: *"Sometimes you ask yourself after the 10th start of the application: are the customers happy? Do they have new ideas for improvements?"* Currently, new product ideas mainly stem from the startup itself: *"We develop the ideas in our heads. There are only a few which come from customers."* The startup visits fairs such as trade fairs, and uses these opportunities to test assumptions about products and features through interviews with potential visitors and investors. According to the CEO, the main challenge that hinders the conduction of experiments is the lack of resources. He mentioned: *"We are 2–8 people in the startup and there is no time to do experiments. However, in the future we will do more in this direction."*

The CEO of this startup had already founded another startup before, that focused on the creation of a speech recognition app. Based on the vision of this startup and ideas for features that were proposed by customers, the startup created MVPs and observed, how new features resonated with users. The startup acquired users for these MVP tests from their friends, through their networks and through Facebook groups. The CEO mentioned that some testers were very engaged: *"We had a super contact from Munich, which tested our software very deeply and wrote us 50–60 pages reports with weakness or strengths from our product. All for free."* The CEO also mentioned that he used some testers outside of the target customer segment and gained interesting insights from these testers. The startup also conducted customer interviews and A/B tests. The duration of experimentation was from 2 h to 2 weeks.

Another strategy that the CEO applied at his former startup was to partner with influencers: "We had some meetings with influencer with about 4–5 million followers in social media channels. These influencers started to use their audience to test our product assumptions. In this way we got important insights before the implementation".

The CEO summarized his thinking about testing product ideas as the following: "You should first find out how customers like your product before you go to market. We recognized several times that the customers understood our product ideas in another way than we expected. It happened that 9 from 10 people said: 'go that direction not the other'. In case that ideas from customers were tested successfully and got implemented, the customer identified themselves with the product and told others: 'Look, they did this because of me'. In this case, the customers are feeling that they are the co-creator and this is gold".

Case 3: This startup has the vision to create a web-based online platform to connect good job applicants to the right companies. With an intelligent psychological matching system, it aims at finding the perfect match between a job offer and an applicant. Additionally, the startup wants to help people to better understand different education and career choices in order to select those that fit their preferences and abilities. This aims at opening the spectrum of options with respect to education and career and to help people avoid choosing the wrong path.

The CTO of the startup explained that the first experiments were telephone interviews: *"It costs a lot of time and kilometers to drive to different companies and ask their hr manager questions. On the phone, we could find the responsible person faster"*. The questions were prepared in the following manner: *"We made a short brainstorming session and fixed 16 questions, from which some were around our idea. But in the first calls we found out that the interview partners did not have enough time. Therefore, we reduced the questions to eight."* The experiment duration was one week.

A challenge with conducting interviews was making cold calls. In addition, the CTO mentioned in the interview: "I have a little problem to motivate myself make calls for a whole week." A second challenge was to convince the companies to talk with the startup and answer the questions. The CTO already had experience with contacting customers from his last job as a support person. However, the other founders had no experience. In addition, he explained that *"you should know how to talk to a person on a phone and how to convince them to answer our questions."*

Actually, the first kind of customer-related study that the startup conducted was a market research study with data from statistica.com. Based on this study, the startup concluded that the assumed problem exists. In consequence, the startup started to develop a solution partly based on wrong assumptions. The CTO explained: *"I wish we could turn back time and do the interview study first and get its results. We lost 1,5 years."*

Case 4: This startup has the vision to support persons at a gym with a training software. The startup developed a combination of hardware and software as a solution. This startup started directly with the development of the product. The CEO explained: *"We built our product because the core was clear.* He mentioned how the startup comes up with ideas for new features and improvements: *"At first, we try to take the customer's perspective. This is always the fastest way. We also use our friends and they give us feedback."* He adds that friends are good testers, but they have a weakness: *"It is hard to get a honest feedback, if we do interviews with our friends. We use our own question catalogue."* We asked the CEO why he did not create a landing page for the product. He answered that he considers the product as an *innovation: "We want to keep the range of the people under control who are knowing our product."*

Table 2 gives a summary of the experiment types and the perceived challenges and benefits found in the studied software startups.

Table 2. Experimentation summary overview

Conducted experiment types	Perceived challenges with experimentation	Perceived benefits from experimentation
Interviews Trade show testing Landing page A/B testing MVP testing Testing with influencers	Getting enough subjects for experiments Fear of contacting customers Fear of making cold calls Technical challenges with setting up an infrastructure for experimentation Lack of skills for conducting customer interviews Lack of resources/staff for experimentation Lack of motivation to conduct experiments Fear that people steal the startup idea	Early feedback Better understanding of customer's needs, priorities, and behaviors Better prioritization of development activities Avoidance of unnecessary development efforts Early testing of market demand

5 Discussion

The studied software startups mainly address these uncertainties by getting feedback about product ideas from potential customers or friends. They basically use qualitative techniques such as unstructured or structured interviews to test ideas, or more light-weight approaches such as testing ideas at trade fairs.

Another approach that some of the studied startups are using is to create initial versions of products or features, expose them to existing or potential customers, and observe customer reactions in an unsystematic way. To some extent, this is similar to experimentation with an MVP, although a clear hypothesis or a learning goal is usually not explicitly stated.

Some of the studied startups use specific types of experiments for specific purposes, such as A/B testing in order to optimize a web site design, or landing pages for testing value propositions and generating leads. Our study shows significant challenges that startups are facing with respect to experimentation. Examples are problems with getting enough subjects, lack of motivation, and technical challenges. A major challenge identified in this study is the lack of knowledge about experimentation techniques and startup tactics, such as tactics for finding experimental subjects or showing potentially secret product ideas to others. Although software startups already apply techniques such as qualitative customer interviews that are well suited for problem exploration and solution testing, they do not have sufficient knowledge on how to use these techniques in a way that creates valuable insights.

The lack of knowledge about experimentation techniques and startup tactics might be a reason for the identified fears that hinder startups to conduct experiments. Another challenge that the study reveals is a lack of support for startups with respect to conducting experiments.

Such support might comprise training (e.g., how to conduct customer interviews), technical expertise (i.e., how to implement A/B tests), and infrastructure for experimentation (i.e., infrastructure for observing customer behavior). The studied startups lack the awareness that risk mitigation needs to be done early and is crucial for survival. In addition, it is not well known that risks can be mitigated early and systematically through experiments. Indicators for this lack of awareness are that (1) all studied software startups focused on testing ideas and none of them systematically validated the problem and the customer segments (usually, both should be done before validating solutions), (2) the statement by the CEO from case three that they have difficulties in motivating themselves and thus infects the other founders to conduct experiments negative. The lack of awareness that risks can be mitigated early and systematically through experiments is probably the most important challenge as it is an "unknown unknown" that significantly threatens the success of a startup. The integration of startups in accelerator programs, and a more wide-spread entrepreneurship education might help to overcome this challenge. It should be mentioned, that the studied software startups have shown a widely positive attitude towards experimentation. The startups understood some of the major benefits of experimentation, especially with respect to avoiding solution risks. In addition, customer centricity was seen as a valuable means towards developing successful products and services.

The study has several shortcomings with respect to validity. The first validity threat is related to generalization. Qualitative case studies are a suitable approach to understand how software startups use experimentation in the real world. To get more generalizable results, more case studies and quantitative studies should be conducted. The second validity threat is the construct validity which especially addresses misunderstandings between the researchers and participants. Before each interview, the participant got a short introduction about the goals of the study. Furthermore, the use of the interview guide enables asking clear questions. Another validity threat is related to the degree of knowledge about the history of the startup. To diminish this risk, we only interviewed founders or cofounders who generally have the best knowledge of their startup process.

6 Conclusions

The studied software startups apply some ad hoc validation of solution-related testing, the majority of the studied startups are not aware of the importance of risk mitigation and have a lack of knowledge on how to do this. Simply speaking, the studied startups do not systematically identify the riskiest assumptions, they do not have sufficient knowledge on how to describe such assumptions in a testable way, and they do not know how to test assumptions efficiently by means of experiments. Finally, they do not have sufficient support for conducting experiments in terms of training, technical competence, and infrastructure. Despite this, they are open to learn and improve their capabilities in order to increase the odds of their success.

We are planning to further investigate on how startups approach experimentation and on how to better support them in doing so. Further studies need to be conducted in order to increase the generalizability of the results.

Acknowledgements. We wish to thank all participants for their time and contributions.

References

1. Bosch, J.: Building products as innovation experiment systems. In: Cusumano, Michael A., Iyer, B., Venkatraman, N. (eds.) ICSOB 2012. LNBIP, vol. 114, pp. 27–39. Springer, Heidelberg (2012). doi:10.1007/978-3-642-30746-1_3
2. Fagerholm, F., Sanchez Guinea, A., Mäenpää, H., Münch, J.: The RIGHT model for continuous experimentation. J. Syst. Softw. **123**, 292–305 (2017). doi:10.1016/j.jss.2016.03.034
3. Hassi, L., Tuulenmäki, A. (eds.): Experimentation-driven approach to innovation: developing novel offerings through experiments. In: ISPIM Conference, Manchester (2012)
4. Bosch, J., Holmström Olsson, H., Björk, J., Ljungblad, J.: The early stage software startup development model: a framework for operationalizing lean principles in software startups. In: Fitzgerald, B., Conboy, K., Power, K., Valerdi, R., Morgan, L., Stol, K.-J. (eds.) LESS 2013. LNBIP, vol. 167, pp. 1–15. Springer, Heidelberg (2013). doi:10.1007/978-3-642-44930-7_1
5. Lindgren, E., Münch, J.: Raising the odds of success. the current state of experimentation in product development. Info. Softw. Technol. **77**, 80–91 (2016). doi:10.1016/j.infsof.2016.04.008
6. Nguyen-Duc, A., Abrahamsson, P. (eds.): Minimum Viable Product or Multiple Facet Product? The Role of MVP in Software Startups. In: XP2016 (2016)
7. Nguyen-Duc, A., Wang, X., Abrahamsson, P. (eds.): What influences the speed of prototyping? An empirical investigation of twenty software startups. In: XP2017 (2017)
8. Ries, E.: The Lean Startup. How Constant Innovation Creates Radically Successful Businesses/ Eric Ries. The Lean Series. Portfolio Penguin, London (2011)
9. Victoria Barret (2011). https://www.forbes.com/sites/victoriabarret/2011/10/18/dropbox-the-inside-story-of-techs-hottest-startup
10. Yin, R.K.: Case study research. Design and methods. SAGE, Los Angeles (2014). Robert K. Yin

Scrum

A Study of the Scrum Master's Role

John Noll[1]([✉]), Mohammad Abdur Razzak[2], Julian M. Bass[3],
and Sarah Beecham[2]

[1] University of East London, University Way, London E16 2RD, UK
j.noll@uel.ac.uk
[2] Lero, The Irish Software Research Centre, University of Limerick, Limerick, Ireland
{abdur.razzak,sarah.beecham}@lero.ie
[3] University of Salford, The Crescent, Salford M5 4WT, UK
j.bass@salford.ac.uk

Abstract. Scrum is an increasingly common approach to software development adopted by organizations around the world. However, as organizations transition from traditional plan-driven development to agile development with Scrum, the question arises as to which Scrum role (Product Owner, Scrum Master, or Scrum Team Member) corresponds to a Project Manager, or conversely which Scrum role should the Project Managers adopt?

In an attempt to answer this question, we adopted a mixed-method research approach comprising a systematic literature review and a case study of a commercial software development team. Our research has identified activities that comprise the Scrum Master role, and which additional roles are actually performed by Scrum Masters in practice.

We found ten activities that are performed by Scrum Masters. In addition, we found that Scrum Masters also perform other roles, most importantly as Project Managers. This latter situation results in tension and conflict of interest that could have a negative impact on the performance of the team as a whole.

These results point to the need to re-assess the role of Project Managers in organizations that adopt Scrum as a development approach. We hypothesize that it might be better for Project Managers to become Product Owners, as aspects of this latter role are more consistent with the traditional responsibilities of a Project Manager .

Keywords: Agile software development · Scrum · Scrum Master role · Empirical software engineering

1 Introduction

Scrum [1,2] is an increasingly common approach to software development adopted by organizations around the world. According to the annual State of Agile Survey [3], *94%* of organizations surveyed practice agile development.

However, while the vast majority of *organizations* are moving towards a form of agile development, for most of these organizations, more than half of their

© Springer International Publishing AG 2017
M. Felderer et al. (Eds.): PROFES 2017, LNCS 10611, pp. 307–323, 2017.
https://doi.org/10.1007/978-3-319-69926-4_22

teams are still following traditional, plan-driven methods [3]. Therefore, as organizations transition from traditional plan-driven development to agile development with Scrum, the question arises as to which Scrum role (Product Owner, Scrum Master, or Scrum Team Member) is the Project Manager, or conversely which Scrum role should Project Managers adopt?

In an attempt to answer this question, we used a mixed method research approach comprising a systematic literature review, and a case study of a commercial software development organization. Firstly, we reviewed the literature on agile software development in order to identify which activities are conventionally performed by Scrum Masters. Then, we conducted observations and practitioner interviews in order find out which activities are actually performed, and which additional roles Scrum Masters perform.

We found ten activities that are performed by Scrum Masters. Of these, only three are conventional Scrum Master activities. Others would traditionally be considered the responsibility of the Product Owner or Scrum Team. In addition, we found that Scrum Masters also double in other roles, most importantly as Project Managers. This latter situation results in tension and conflict of interest that could have a negative impact on the performance of the team as a whole.

These results point to the need to re-assess the role of Project Managers in organizations that adopt Scrum as a development approach. We suggest that it might be better for Project Managers to become Product Owners, as this latter role is more consistent with the traditional responsibilities of a Project Manager.

The rest of this paper is organized as follows: in the next section, we present the background related to Scrum and Scrum roles. Next, we describe our research method. Following that, in Sect. 4 we present our results, and a discussion of those results in Sect. 5. Section 6 ends with our conclusions.

2   Background

There are three key roles defined in the Scrum development approach: the self-organizing Scrum Team of developers, the Scrum Master, and the Product Owner [2]. The Product Owner represents the external stakeholder interests (customer, users, product management) and so is the primary interface between these stakeholders and the software development team [4]. The Scrum Team is responsible for the actual software development. A further role, Product Manager, who "defines initial content and timing of the release, then manages their evolution as the project progresses and variables change... [and] deals with backlog, risk, and release content" was also described in the original description of Scrum [1]; this role is mostly performed by the Product Owner in modern versions of Scrum [5].

The Scrum Master is responsible for facilitating the development process, ensuring that the team uses the full range of appropriate agile values, practices and rules. The Scrum Master conducts daily coordination meetings and removes any impediments that the team encounters [2]. Six Scrum Master activities have been identified in a large-scale distributed organisational context: process anchor, stand-up facilitator, impediment remover, sprint planner, scrum of scrums facilitator and integration anchor [6]. The process anchor nurtures adherence to agile methods. The stand-up facilitator ensures that team members share status and impediment information during each sprint. The impediment remover ensures developers can make progress with their work. The sprint planner supports the user story triage and workload planning that occurs prior to development work starting in each sprint. The scrum of scrums facilitator coordinates work with the other Scrum Masters in the development program. The integration anchor facilitates the merging of code bases developed by cooperating teams working in parallel.

According to Schwaber and Sutherland's Scrum guidelines, "the Scrum Master is a servant-leader for the Scrum Team. The Scrum Master helps those outside the Scrum Team understand which of their interactions with the Scrum Team are helpful and which aren't. The Scrum Master helps everyone change these interactions to maximize the value created by the Scrum Team" [7]; in summary, the Scrum Master serves the development team. This is in contrast to the Product Owner, who is responsible for maximizing the value of the product and the work of the Scrum Team. Schwaber and Sutherland [7] state that although there is great flexibility in how this is achieved, the Product Owner is the sole person responsible for managing the Product Backlog.

According to Schwaber and Sutherland [7], Product Backlog management tasks include: "1. ordering the items in the Product Backlog to best achieve goals and missions; 2. optimizing the value of the work the Development Team performs; 3. ensuring that the Product Backlog is visible, transparent, and clear to all, and shows what the Scrum Team will work on next; and, 4. ensuring the Development Team understands items in the Product Backlog to the level needed. [7]"

Evidence from practice shows that the Scrum Master role is evolving. For example, the role is sometimes shared, and activities performed by the Scrum Master are varied and somewhat different from the original vision. This was observed by Gupta et al. [8], who found that the challenges of adapting Scrum in a globally distributed team were helped by more than one person sharing the Scrum Master and Product Owner roles. Gupta et al. developed a new Scrum Master taxonomy in which three new roles were created to reflect the complexity involved in managing a global software development team, and transitioning from Waterfall to Scrum, the roles were: Scrum Master cum Part Product Owner (where development leads were also acting in part as product owners), Bi-Scrum Master (where a development leads worked remotely with the development team) and Chief Scrum Master (fulfilling the need to co-ordinate among scrum teams).

According to the ISO/IEC/IEEE standard on user documentation in agile [9] the Scrum Master and Product Manager have similar responsibilities when it comes to explaining, changing or new requirements. "The scrum master and information development lead or project manager should provide guidance to the technical writers and other members of the agile development teams on how to handle changing or new requirements." Perhaps this conflating of roles is largely due to organizations converting the traditional project manager role to a Scrum Master role, "As more and more of our Project Managers become

Scrum Masters and the Portfolio Managers becomes the Group Scrum Master, our Portfolio Management Office needed to become Agile itself [10]."

Adapting Scrum roles and creating new roles to manage large scale projects is observed in other studies, where an 'Area Product Owner' (APO) role was created; this APO role was shared by two people: a system architect and a product management representative. The system architect worked closely with the team, while the product management representative did not interact directly with the teams [11]. This combined role (shared between two people) worked well for this organisation and was reported as one of the successes of the project. However, in a later study, the same authors noted that line managers had a double role: that of Scrum Master, and that of traditional line management duties involving personnel issues such as performance evaluation. Over use of the Scrum Master role, who acted as a team representative at common meetings rather than rotate the role, was found problematic. The team felt that these meetings were a waste of time, and sent the Scrum Master instead of taking turns [12]. The frequent meetings in Scrum were also a problem in [13]. A Scrum Master's role is to facilitate daily coordination meetings where coordination meetings are used to communicate status of development work within the team and to product owners. However, the efficacy of daily coordination meetings was often compromised by too many stakeholders attending, or because the meetings were held too frequently to be beneficial for attendees [13].

Corrupting the careful balance between Scrum roles leads to other problems. For example Moe et al. [14] observed that the Scrum Master also did estimates and did not involve all the team in discussing a task. This lead to developers working alone, poor team cohesion, and problems emerging at the end of the sprint rather than at the beginning. A lack of thorough discussion was said to reduce the validity of the common backlog "making the developers focus more on their own plan. Since the planning had weaknesses and none of the developers felt they had the total overview, this probably was one of the reasons for design-problems discovered later."

Yet, in a recent survey that looked into whether project managers still exist in agile development teams, Shastri, et al. were surprised to learn that 67% of organisations surveyed reported that they still had the Project Manager role. These authors call for more research into why the Project Manager continues to be present on agile software development projects, and how their role may have changed [15]. Conventional wisdom suggests that Project Managers use a command and control style of management, whereas Scrum Masters focus on leading and coaching [16]. As such, Scrum masters are not line managers for their sprint team members. Further, Scrum Masters do not assign work items to the members of their team, since the teams are self-organising [6].

In summary, there is an emerging theme in the literature, namely that the original balance of Scrum Master, Product Owner and team roles are being adapted, conflated, and possibly corrupted, to suit the needs of organizations transitioning from Waterfall to Scrum, or scaling Scrum to large scale organisations. The extent to which the Scrum Master role has changed is unknown.

Therefore, in this study we now look to the wider literature, and specifically ask two questions:

RQ1: What activities do Scrum Masters perform according to the empirical literature?
RQ2: What other roles do Scrum Masters perform in practice?

We ask these questions in order to establish a broader understanding of a key Scrum role that has clearly evolved since its inception in 1995 [17] and later refinement [7], and consider whether adapting the theory proposed by Schwaber, Sutherland and Beedle is something to be embraced or resisted.

3   Method

In order to address our research questions, we adopted a mixed method approach comprising a systematic literature review and a case study of a commercial software development team [18]. We performed a systematic literature review [19] to identify the set of activities and additional roles performed by Scrum Masters. Then, using observations and transcripts of semi-structured interviews we undertook as part of an empirical study, we attempted to identify benefits or issues related to these activities and roles.

3.1   Systematic Literature Review

Two researchers were involved in the systematic literature review process (see Fig. 1), which comprised five steps.

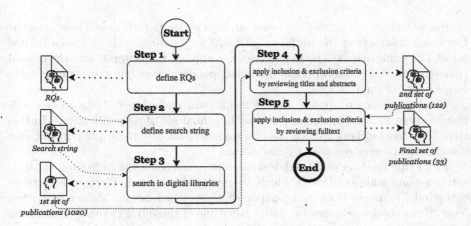

Fig. 1. Systematic literature review process

First, we defined two research questions:

1. What are the activities a Scrum Master performs?
2. What roles does the Scrum Master perform in addition to the Scrum Master role?

Next, we defined a search string. For expediency, we used one search string (or variants of the search string to fit the various databases) that combined both our research questions, as follows:

```
(activit* OR task* OR responsibilit* OR action* OR role* OR job*)
AND (''Scrum Master'')
```

We then used this search string to search five well-established digital libraries listed in Table 1 for potentially relevant publications. This search yielded 1,020 candidate publications.

Table 1. List of databases and number of publications.

Database	# of publications
IEEEXplore	13
ACM Digital library	378
Scopus	30
Elesevier Science Direct	282
SpringerLink	317
Total	**1020**

Subsequently, we applied inclusion and exclusion criteria (see Table 2) to the titles and abstracts of the initial set of 1,020 publications; this yielded a refined set of 122 publications. The first researcher applied the criteria, and the second researcher validated this application by independently applying the same criteria to a sample of publications.

Finally, we again applied the inclusion and exclusion criteria to the full-text of these 122 publications, resulting in a final set of 33 publications. In this step, both reasearchers applied the criteria independently to all 122 publications; disagreements were resolved by discussion.

From this final set of 33 publications, we extracted a list of Scrum Master's activities and additional roles, which are reported in Sect. 4. The first researcher extracted fragments from every paper that described Scrum Master activities. Next, the second researcher validated every one of these fragments by examining them in context to verify that each did indeed describe a Scrum Master activity. Then, working together, both researchers coalesced the validated set of fragments into ten higher level themes that represent Scrum Master activities. Finally, again working together, both researchers identified other roles performed by a Scrum Master.

Table 2. Inclusion and Exclusion criteria.

Inclusion criteria	Exclusion criteria
IC1: Publication year: 2006-2017	**EC1:** Is an experience report, book, presentation, or blog entry
IC2: Language: English	**EC2:** Is a duplicated study (where authors report similar results in two or more publications–e.g. a journal paper that is an extension of a conference paper); exclude the least detailed paper, or if unclear include the paper that is published in the more notable venue.
IC3: Full text available and accessible	
IC4: Focus on Scrum, in the field of software engineering	
IC5: Peer reviewed work	
IC6: Answers one or more of the research questions	

3.2   Case Study

The company we studied, which we will call PracMed, is a medium-sized Irish-based software company that develops practice and lab management software for the optical industry.

Research Site. PracMed employs approximately seventy staff members in its software development organization, including support and management staff. PracMed's annual sales approach €20 million, from customers across the British Isles, continental Europe, Scandinavia, North America and China.

Our study focused on TeamA, who are responsible for tailoring the company's product for a large customer in North America. The members of TeamA are distributed over four countries on two continents, with up to eight hours difference in timezones between locations. They are using Scrum to develop their software, with two weekly sprints. Table 3 shows the distribution of team members; of these, two team members share the Product Owner role, five are developers, one is the QA/Test lead, and one is Project Manager. In TeamA, the Project Manager also plays role of Scrum Master. Also, the Product Owners report to the Product Manager, who is based in Spain and is responsible for the strategic direction of the product.

Data Collection. We observed TeamA from January, 2016 through to March, 2017. Specifically, one of the authors observed approximately 200 of TeamA's Scrum ceremonies, including daily standups, sprint planning, backlog grooming, and sprint retrospectives. Due to team members being distributed across Europe and North America, the observations were made via video conference for each ceremony. The same author also conducted semi-structured interviews of each member of TeamA, which were recorded and transcribed. The interviews took approximately one hour, and resulted in 136 pages of transcribed verbatim data. The interview protocol is available from [20].

Table 3. Team Distribution.

Country	Agile Roles	No of Team Members
Ireland	Product Owner	1
	Software Developer	3
	Quality Assurance	1
Canada	Scrum Master (Project Manager)	1
	Product Owner	1
	Software Developer	1
USA	Technical Lead (Software Developer)	1
Spain	Product Manager	1

The observer also made contemporaneous hand-written notes during both the ceremony observations and interviews. Finally, the interviewer summarized the interviews using a mind-map, and presented the result to five interviewees in an online workshop to validate the insights gained from the interviews.

Data Analysis. Interview recordings and transcripts were carefully reviewed. An open coding approach was used to identify topics in interview transcripts and contemporaneous notes of ceremonies. An approach informed by thematic analysis was used to group codes into concepts [21].

4   Findings

In this section we summarise our results and in response to our research questions, describe each of the Scrum Master's activities identified in our data analysis. As noted in our method, for consistency, where possible we adopt the activity name given in the literature.

4.1   Systematic Literature Review

Our paper selection process identified a total of 33 publications that fit our search and inclusion criteria (Table 4).

Table 4. Publication by year.

Year	2006	2008	2009	2010	2011	2012	2013	2014	2015	2016	2017	Total
Publications	1	1	1	3	4	4	1	8	2	6	2	**33**

Table 5. Scrum Master activities.

Activities	Ideal Scrum role	Source
Process facilitation	Scrum Master	[6, 22–24]
Ceremony facilitation (incl. Scrum of Scrums)	Scrum Master	[6, 23, 25–27]
Impediment removal	Scrum Master	[6, 23, 28]
Prioritization	Product Owner	[29, 30]
Sprint planning	Scrum Team	[6, 31–33]
Sprint reviewing	Scrum Team	[34, 35]
Estimation	Scrum Team Member	[36]
Integration	Scrum Team Member	[6, 37]
Travelling	None	[26, 28]
Project management	None	[24, 29, 38–40]

Activities. From these papers, we identified ten activities performed by Scrum Masters; these are shown in Table 5. These activities are defined as follows:

Process facilitation involves guiding the Scrum Team on how to use Scrum to achieve their objectives.

Ceremony facilitation involves moderation of the daily standup, backlog grooming, sprint planning, and sprint retrospective meetings that occur during each sprint.

Impediment removal is part of the Scrum Master as "servant manager" role: the Scrum Master serves as a buffer between the Scrum Team and external pressures, and also attempts to secure resources or remove blockers to progress that come from outside the team.

Prioritization involves ordering stories on the product and sprint backlogs by order of importance.

Sprint planning identifies those stories on the product backlog that will fit into a single sprint, taking into account team velocity and capacity, and story estimates.

Sprint reviewing is part of the Sprint Retrospective ceremony where the team identifies what went well, what could be improved, and might be added or removed from their process to be more effective.

Estimation assigns a value in "story points" or ideal engineering time representing the effort required to complete a story.

Integration facilitates amalgamation of software elements.

Travelling is an activity associated with distributed teams that involves visiting different sites where teams are located, to facilitate communications [41].

Project management is a traditional management activity found in Waterfall-style development projects.

Roles. Fifteen papers mentioned other roles that Scrum Masters hold in addition to that of Scrum Master. These are summarized in Table 6.

Table 6. Scrum Master additional roles.

Role	Company-size	Source
Project Manager	Large-scale	[42–46]
Product Owner	Unclear	[29,44]
Architect/Software Designer	Large-scale	[47,48]
Project Lead	Large-scale	[49]
Developer/Senior Engineer	Large-scale	[30,43,49–51]
Team Leader	Large-scale	[42,49,52]
Test Lead	Unclear	[43]
Head of Department/Dir. of Eng/Dev. Mgr	Large-scale	[30,43,53,54]

Of these eight roles, four (Architect/Software Designer, Developer/Senior Engineer, Team Leader, and Test Lead) would be considered technical roles, and three (Project Manager, Project Lead, Head of Department) are management roles. In total, nine of fifteen papers reported the Scrum Master also taking on some kind of management role, with six explicitly mentioning "Project Manager" or "Project Lead."

4.2   Case Study

We observed this tension and conflict of interest in our case study organization. On the one hand, the Scrum Master performs project management duties:

> *So, we do all the traditional project management roles as in doing the scope statement, the planning, change control process, communication management plan and all that stuff. And, then internally [we act as] Scrum Master.*

The planning part of this role has a Waterfall characteristic:

> *When I got to start working on this project when there was a contract – there is a very specific set of requirements. . . . there is a very specific budget for example, and the timeline is normally set as well [at] a high level.*

In PracMed, project management for projects involving customization for large accounts, also involves interfacing with the customer. The Scrum Master admits balancing these two roles creates tension:

... Madness! It's hard. ... if you know about one role not the other, I think it's easier because you do the best you can in your Scrum Master role or you do the best in your Project Manager role ignoring the other. Now, the dilemma is as a Project Manager I still know what the Scrum Master role is, I know the Agile team – I know I am not supposed to break their rules and let them be self-organizing and do all of that. At the end you have the client to answer [to], you have management to answer to. So, you can't just say oh well it's in the sprint or they plan for it or I don't know when its gonna get done because team is self-organizing.

In particular, there is tension between the Project Manager as customer interface, and the Scrum Master role:

... Yah, pressure will always be there ... An example would be, the client would want to know ... exactly when all [features] are going to get done. Now, in an Agile world there is no way that I could tell them when they are going to get done until the estimates are there. ... with a client it's hard because I cannot just tell them we are doing Agile.

5 Discussion

Scrum defines only three roles: Product Owner, Scrum Team Member, and Scrum Master [2]. This results in a balance between the customer, user, and other stakeholder interests, which are represented by the Product Owner, and the technical realities of software development, which are represented by the Scrum Team. The Scrum Master facilitates the interaction between these two interests, and also serves to insulate the team as a whole from external distractions (hence the description "servant-leader" that is often used to describe Scrum Masters [5]).

Three Scrum Master activities (Process facilitation, Ceremony facilitation, and Impediment removal) that formed part of our ten activities observed from the literature would be considered "traditional" Scrum Master activities, as defined by Schwaber and Beedle [2]. Prioritizing, on the other hand, is supposed to be the responsibility of the Product Owner, and Estimation is supposed to be performed by the Scrum Team members [2]. While the Scrum Master may *facilitate* these activities, he or she is not supposed to perform them; this is because Scrum relies on a balance of power between "business" and "technical" interests in order to set realistic sprint goals [2,55]. Given the Scrum Master's role as facilitator, and mediator between the Product Owner and the Scrum Team, overloading the Scrum Master role with project management introduces a conflict of interest that can compromise the Scrum Master's ability to ensure a balance between the interests of external stakeholders and the Scrum Team: the Scrum Master is supposed to insulate the team and remove impediments, but as Project Manager, he or she would also have responsibilities to achieve objectives set by higher levels of the organization. Stray and colleagues observed that when the Scrum Master is viewed as a manager rather than facilitator, the daily standup becomes a management reporting exercise rather than a team communication meeting [13].

5.1 The Way Ahead

If tensions are created when the Scrum Master activities are combined with Project Manager activities, which Scrum role is the right role to perform Project Manager activities?

To answer this question, it's useful to consider what project management involves in Scrum, especially considering Scrum teams are supposed to be "self organizing." Schwaber defines five project management activities that must be carried out when undertaking development using the Scrum approach:

1. Vision management – establishing, nurturing, and communicating the product vision.
2. ROI management – monitoring the project's progress against Return on Investment goals, including updating and prioritizing the product backlog to reflect these goals.
3. Development iteration management – expanding items on the Product Backlog into items for the Sprint Backlog, then implementing those items in order of priority.
4. Process management – facilitating ceremonies, removing impediments, and shielding the team from outside interference.
5. Release management – deciding when to create an official release, in response to market pressures and other investment realities.

Of these, only *Process management* is the responsibility of the Scrum Master; *Development iteration management* is the responsibility of the development team, and the remaining activities (Vision management, ROI management, and Release management) are the *Product Owner's* responsibility.

This suggests that, when organizations decide to adopt Scrum, their existing Project Manager's should be assigned to the Product Owner role. The advantages are twofold: first, as Product Owners, Project Managers could advocate for business requirements without feeling tension with their Product Owner responsibilities, since such advocacy is consistent with the Product Owner role.

Second, the Scrum Master would be free to support the Scrum Team when business requirements conflict with technical reality, and to support the Product Owner when business priorities differ from Scrum Team Member preferences (for example, when certain mundane functionality must be developed to keep the product roadmap progressing, at the expense of more technically interesting features), and to support both when upper management pressure threatens to override or compromise the team's own decisions.

Limitations. Practitioner roles, such as that of Scrum Master, are rapidly evolving and hence, while literature is important, it cannot be solely relied upon for an up-to-date perspective. On the other hand, an empirical case study, while providing more up-to-date insights, necessarily derives those insights from at most a handful of settings.

This research adopts a mixed method approach to compensate for the weaknesses of each research approach used in isolation, by combining a systematic literature review with an empirical case study in a mixed method approach to provide a broad perspective based on the literature that is supported by observations from a case study.

Our insights into the tensions and conflicts created by combining the Scrum Master and Project Manager roles are based on observations of a single development team and interviews of one Scrum Master/Project Manager. As such, we must be extremely cautious about generalizing our results. However, our observations do suggest two propositions that can serve as the basis for further research:

P1: When adopting Scrum, teams will be more successful if the former Project Manager adopts the Product Owner role rather than the Scrum Master role.

Conversely,

P2: When adopting Scrum, teams that combine the Scrum Master and Project Manager roles will experience tension resulting from the conflict of interests between these two roles.

6   Conclusions

In this study, we adopted a mixed method research approach to try to answer two research questions:

1. What activities do Scrum Masters perform according to the empirical literature?
2. What other roles do Scrum Masters perform in practice?

We first performed a systematic literature review related to the Scrum Master role and then a case study to uncover empirical evidence of what activities Scrum Master's actually perform, and what additional roles they take on. This review revealed ten activities that are performed by Scrum Masters, and eight additional roles that Scrum Masters also play.

Combining the findings from the literature with observations from a case study of a medium-sized development organization, we identified tensions and conflicts between the Scrum Master role and the Project Manager role that are often combined in practice. As such, we propose that, when adopting Scrum, organizations appoint existing Project Managers to the role of Product Owner, rather than that of Scrum Master.

Acknowledgments. We thank the members of TeamA and members of the Project Management Team for their generous and thoughtful collaboration on this study, and PracMed, for allowing us to study their software development efforts. This work was supported, in part, by Science Foundation Ireland grants 10/CE/I1855 and 13/RC/2094 to Lero - the Irish Software Research Centre (www.lero.ie).

References

1. Schwaber, K.: SCRUM development process. In: Sutherland, J., Casanave, C., Miller, J., Patel, P., Hollowell, G. (eds.) Business Object Design and Implementation, OOPSLA 1995 Workshop Proceedings, pp. 117–134. Springer, London (1995)
2. Schwaber, K., Beedle, M.: Agile software Development with Scrum, vol. 1. Prentice Hall Upper Saddle River, NJ (2002)
3. VERSIONONE.COM: 11th annual state of agile™ survey. Technical report, VersionOne, Inc. (2017)
4. Schwaber, K.: Agile Project Management with Scrum. Microsoft press, WA (2004)
5. Cohn, M., Schwaber, K.: The need for agile project management. Agile Times, vol. 1, January 2003
6. Bass, J.M.: Scrum master activities: process tailoring in large enterprise projects. In: 2014 IEEE 9th International Conference on Global Software Engineering (ICGSE), pp. 6–15. IEEE (2014)
7. Schwaber, K., Sutherland, J.: The Scrum guide-the definitive guide to Scrum: The rules of the game (2016). http://www.scrum.org/storage/scrumguides/Scrum%20Guide
8. Gupta, R.K., Reddy, P.M.: Adapting agile in a globally distributed software development. In: 2016 49th Hawaii International Conference on System Sciences (HICSS), pp. 5360–5367, January 2016
9. ISO/IEC/IEEE: Systems and software engineering - developing user documentation in an agile environment. Technical report, International Standards Organization, March 2012
10. Tengshe, A., Noble, S.: Establishing the agile PMO: managing variability across projects and portfolios. In: Agile 2007 (AGILE 2007), pp. 188–193, August 2007
11. Paasivaara, M., Lassenius, C.: Scaling Scrum in a large distributed project. In: 2011 International Symposium on Empirical Software Engineering and Measurement, pp. 363–367, September 2011
12. Paasivaara, M., Lassenius, C.: Scaling Scrum in a large globally distributed organization: a case study. In: 2016 IEEE 11th International Conference on Global Software Engineering (ICGSE), pp. 74–83, August 2016
13. Stray, V.G., Lindsjorn, Y., Sjoberg, D.I.: Obstacles to efficient daily meetings in agile development projects: a case study. In: 2013 ACM/IEEE International Symposium on Empirical Software Engineering and Measurement, pp. 95–102. IEEE (2013)
14. Moe, N.B., Dingsyr, T., Dyb, T.: Understanding self-organizing teams in agile software development. In: 19th Australian Conference on Software Engineering (ASWEC 2008), pp. 76–85, March 2008
15. Shastri, Y., Hoda, R., Amor, R.: Does the project manager still exist in agile software development projects? In: 2016 23rd Asia-Pacific Software Engineering Conference (APSEC), pp. 57–64, December 2016
16. Berczuk, S., Lv, Y.: We're all in this together. IEEE Softw. **27**(6), 12–15 (2010)
17. Sutherland, J.V., Schwaber, K.: Business object design and implementation: OOPSLA 1995 workshop proceedings. The University of Michigan. Technical report (1995). ISBN 3-540-76096-2
18. Creswell, J.W.: Research Design: Qualitative, Quantitative, and Mixed Methods Approaches, 4th edn. SAGE Publications Inc., Thousand Oaks, California (2013)

19. Kitchenham, B., Charters, S.: Guidelines for performing systematic literature reviews in software engineering, v. 2.3. Technical report EBSE-2007-01, Software Engineering Group, School of Computer Science and Mathematics, Keele University (2007)
20. Beecham, S., Noll, J., Razzak, M.A.: Lean global project interview protocol (2017). http://www.lero.ie/sites/default/files/Lero_TR_2017_02_Beecham_Noll_Razzak-Lean%20Global%20Project%20Interview%20Protocol.pdf
21. Braun, V., Clarke, V.: Using thematic analysis in psychology. Qual. Res. Psychol. **3**(2), 77–101 (2006)
22. Andriyani, Y., Hoda, R., Amor, R.: Reflection in agile retrospectives. In: Baumeister, H., Lichter, H., Riebisch, M. (eds.) XP 2017. LNBIP, vol. 283, pp. 3–19. Springer, Cham (2017). doi:10.1007/978-3-319-57633-6_1
23. Baumgart, R., Hummel, M., Holten, R.: Personality traits of Scrum roles in agile software development teams-a qualitative analysis. In: ECIS (2015)
24. Costa, N., Santos, N., Ferreira, N., Machado, R.J.: Delivering user stories for implementing logical software architectures by multiple Scrum teams. In: Murgante, B., et al. (eds.) ICCSA 2014. LNCS, vol. 8581, pp. 747–762. Springer, Cham (2014). doi:10.1007/978-3-319-09150-1_55
25. Dorairaj, S., Noble, J., Malik, P.: Understanding team dynamics in distributed agile software development. In: Wohlin, C. (ed.) XP 2012. LNBIP, vol. 111, pp. 47–61. Springer, Heidelberg (2012). doi:10.1007/978-3-642-30350-0_4
26. Alzoubi, Y.I., Gill, A.Q., Al-Ani, A.: Empirical studies of geographically distributed agile development communication challenges: a systematic review. Inf. Manag. **53**(1), 22–37 (2016)
27. Maranzato, R.P., Neubert, M., Herculano, P.: Moving back to Scrum and scaling to Scrum of Scrums in less than one year. In: Proceedings of the ACM International Conference Companion on Object Oriented Programming Systems Languages and Applications Companion, pp. 125–130. ACM (2011)
28. Bless, M.: Distributed meetings in distributed teams. In: Sillitti, A., Martin, A., Wang, X., Whitworth, E. (eds.) XP 2010. LNBIP, vol. 48, pp. 251–260. Springer, Heidelberg (2010). doi:10.1007/978-3-642-13054-0_27
29. Cajander, Å., Larusdottir, M., Gulliksen, J.: Existing but not explicit - the user perspective in Scrum projects in practice. In: Kotzé, P., Marsden, G., Lindgaard, G., Wesson, J., Winckler, M. (eds.) INTERACT 2013. LNCS, vol. 8119, pp. 762–779. Springer, Heidelberg (2013). doi:10.1007/978-3-642-40477-1_52
30. Gulliksen Stray, V., Moe, N.B., Dingsøyr, T.: Challenges to teamwork: a multiple case study of two agile teams. In: Sillitti, A., Hazzan, O., Bache, E., Albaladejo, X. (eds.) XP 2011. LNBIP, vol. 77, pp. 146–161. Springer, Heidelberg (2011). doi:10.1007/978-3-642-20677-1_11
31. Drury, M., Conboy, K., Power, K.: Obstacles to decision making in agile software development teams. J. Syst. Softw. **85**(6), 1239–1254 (2012)
32. Heikkilä, V.T., Paasivaara, M., Rautiainen, K., Lassenius, C., Toivola, T., Järvinen, J.: Operational release planning in large-scale Scrum with multiple stakeholders-a longitudinal case study at f-secure corporation. Inf. Softw. Technol. **57**, 116–140 (2015)
33. Vlietland, J., van Vliet, H.: Towards a governance framework for chains of Scrum teams. Inf. Softw. Technol. **57**, 52–65 (2015)
34. Chamberlain, S., Sharp, H., Maiden, N.: Towards a framework for integrating agile development and user-centred design. In: Abrahamsson, P., Marchesi, M., Succi, G. (eds.) XP 2006. LNCS, vol. 4044, pp. 143–153. Springer, Heidelberg (2006). doi:10.1007/11774129_15

35. Stray, V., Fægri, T.E., Moe, N.B.: Exploring norms in agile software teams. In: Abrahamsson, P., Jedlitschka, A., Nguyen Duc, A., Felderer, M., Amasaki, S., Mikkonen, T. (eds.) PROFES 2016. LNCS, vol. 10027, pp. 458–467. Springer, Cham (2016). doi:10.1007/978-3-319-49094-6_31
36. Daneva, M., Van Der Veen, E., Amrit, C., Ghaisas, S., Sikkel, K., Kumar, R., Ajmeri, N., Ramteerthkar, U., Wieringa, R.: Agile requirements prioritization in large-scale outsourced system projects: an empirical study. J. Syst, Softw. **86**(5), 1333–1353 (2013)
37. Alaa, G., Samir, Z.: A multi-faceted roadmap of requirements traceability types adoption in Scrum: an empirical study. In: 2014 9th International Conference on Informatics and Systems (INFOS), p. SW-1. IEEE (2014)
38. Baskerville, R., Pries-Heje, J., Madsen, S.: Post-agility: what follows a decade of agility? Inf. Softw. Technol. **53**(5), 543–555 (2011)
39. Caballero, E., Calvo-Manzano, J.A., San Feliu, T.: Introducing scrum in a very small enterprise: a productivity and quality analysis. In: O'Connor, R.V., Pries-Heje, J., Messnarz, R. (eds.) EuroSPI 2011. CCIS, vol. 172, pp. 215–224. Springer, Heidelberg (2011). doi:10.1007/978-3-642-22206-1_19
40. Santos, R., Flentge, F., Begin, M.-E., Navarro, V.: Agile technical management of industrial contracts: scrum development of ground segment software at the european space agency. In: Sillitti, A., Hazzan, O., Bache, E., Albaladejo, X. (eds.) XP 2011. LNBIP, vol. 77, pp. 290–305. Springer, Heidelberg (2011). doi:10.1007/978-3-642-20677-1_21
41. Bass, J.M.: How product owner teams scale agile methods to large distributed enterprises. Empirical Softw. Eng. **20**(6), 1525–1557 (2015)
42. Gren, L., Torkar, R., Feldt, R.: Group development and group maturity when building agile teams: a qualitative and quantitative investigation at eight large companies. J. Syst. Softw. **124**, 104–119 (2017)
43. Hoda, R., Murugesan, L.K.: Multi-level agile project management challenges: a self-organizing team perspective. J. Syst. Softw. **117**, 245–257 (2016)
44. Tuomikoski, J., Tervonen, I.: Absorbing software testing into the Scrum method. In: Bomarius, F., Oivo, M., Jaring, P., Abrahamsson, P. (eds.) PROFES 2009. LNBIP, vol. 32, pp. 199–215. Springer, Heidelberg (2009). doi:10.1007/978-3-642-02152-7_16
45. Stray, V., Sjøberg, D.I., Dybå, T.: The daily stand-up meeting: a grounded theory study. J. Syst. Softw. **114**, 101–124 (2016)
46. Moe, N.B., Dingsøyr, T.: Scrum and team effectiveness: theory and practice. In: Abrahamsson, P., Baskerville, R., Conboy, K., Fitzgerald, B., Morgan, L., Wang, X. (eds.) XP 2008. LNBIP, vol. 9, pp. 11–20. Springer, Heidelberg (2008). doi:10.1007/978-3-540-68255-4_2
47. Díaz, J., Pérez, J., Garbajosa, J.: Agile product-line architecting in practice: a case study in smart grids. Inf. Softw. Technol. **56**(7), 727–748 (2014)
48. Sekitoleko, N., Evbota, F., Knauss, E., Sandberg, A., Chaudron, M., Olsson, H.H.: Technical dependency challenges in large-scale agile software development. In: Cantone, G., Marchesi, M. (eds.) XP 2014. LNBIP, vol. 179, pp. 46–61. Springer, Cham (2014). doi:10.1007/978-3-319-06862-6_4
49. Diebold, P., Ostberg, J.-P., Wagner, S., Zendler, U.: What do practitioners vary in using Scrum? In: Lassenius, C., Dingsøyr, T., Paasivaara, M. (eds.) XP 2015. LNBIP, vol. 212, pp. 40–51. Springer, Cham (2015). doi:10.1007/978-3-319-18612-2_4

50. Garbajosa, J., Yagüe, A., Gonzalez, E.: Communication in agile global software development: an exploratory study. In: Meersman, R., Panetto, H., Mishra, A., Valencia-García, R., Soares, A.L., Ciuciu, I., Ferri, F., Weichhart, G., Moser, T., Bezzi, M., Chan, H. (eds.) OTM 2014. LNCS, vol. 8842, pp. 408–417. Springer, Heidelberg (2014). doi:10.1007/978-3-662-45550-0_41

51. Li, J., Moe, N.B., Dybå, T.: Transition from a plan-driven process to Scrum: a longitudinal case study on software quality. In: Proceedings of the 2010 ACM-IEEE international symposium on empirical software engineering and measurement, p. 13. ACM (2010)

52. Galster, M., Angelov, S., Meesters, M., Diebold, P.: A multiple case study on the architect's role in Scrum. In: Abrahamsson, P., Jedlitschka, A., Nguyen Duc, A., Felderer, M., Amasaki, S., Mikkonen, T. (eds.) PROFES 2016. LNCS, vol. 10027, pp. 432–447. Springer, Cham (2016). doi:10.1007/978-3-319-49094-6_29

53. Alahyari, H., Svensson, R.B., Gorschek, T.: A study of value in agile software development organizations. J. Syst. Softw. **125**, 271–288 (2017)

54. Vlaanderen, K., van Stijn, P., Brinkkemper, S., van de Weerd, I.: Growing into agility: process implementation paths for Scrum. In: Dieste, O., Jedlitschka, A., Juristo, N. (eds.) PROFES 2012. LNCS, vol. 7343, pp. 116–130. Springer, Heidelberg (2012). doi:10.1007/978-3-642-31063-8_10

55. Leffingwell, D.: Scaling software agility: Best practices for large enterprises. Addison Wesley, Boston (2007)

An Exploratory Study on Applying a Scrum Development Process for Safety-Critical Systems

Yang Wang[✉], Jasmin Ramadani[✉], and Stefan Wagner[✉]

University of Stuttgart, Stuttgart, Germany
{yang.wang,jasmin.ramadani,stefan.wagner}@informatik.uni-stuttgart.de

Abstract. *Background:* Agile techniques recently have received attention from the developers of safety-critical systems. However, a lack of empirical knowledge of performing safety assurance techniques, especially safety analysis in a real agile project hampers further steps. *Aims:* In this article, we aim at (1) understanding and optimizing the S-Scrum development process, a Scrum extension with the integration of a systems theory based safety analysis technique, STPA (System-Theoretic Process Analysis), for safety-critical systems; (2) validating the Optimized S-Scrum development process further. *Method:* We conducted a two-stage exploratory case study in a student project at the University of Stuttgart, Germany. *Results:* The results in stage 1 showed that S-Scrum helps to ensure safety of each release but is less agile than the normal Scrum. We explored six challenges on: priority management; communication; time pressure on determining safety requirements; safety planning; time to perform upfront planning; and safety requirements' acceptance criteria. During stage 2, the safety and agility have been improved after the optimizations, including an internal and an external safety expert; pre-planning meeting; regular safety meeting; an agile safety plan; and improved safety epics and safety stories. We have also gained valuable suggestions from industry, but the generalization problem due to the specific context is still unsolved.

Keywords: Agile software development · Safety-critical systems · Case study

1 Introduction

To reduce the risks and costs for reworking and rescheduling, agile techniques have aroused attention for the development of safety-critical systems. Traditionally standardised safety assurance, such as IEC 61508 [1], is based on the V-model. Even though there is no prohibition to adapt standards for lightweight development processes with iterations, some limitations cannot be avoided during the adaptation [2]. Existing research in agile techniques for safety-critical systems is striving for consistency to standards. Safe Scrum [3] is a considerable success due to a comprehensive combination between Scrum and IEC 61508.

© Springer International Publishing AG 2017
M. Felderer et al. (Eds.): PROFES 2017, LNCS 10611, pp. 324–340, 2017.
https://doi.org/10.1007/978-3-319-69926-4_23

However, an integrated safety analysis to face the changing architectures inside each sprint still needs to be enhanced. Therefore, in 2016, we proposed S-Scrum to integrate a systems theory based safety analysis technique, STPA (System-Theoretic Process Analysis) [7], which was proposed by Leveson in 2012, inside each sprint to guide a safe design [16].

Problem statement. We proposed to integrate STPA in a Scrum development process to enhance the safety in agile development. However, it has not been validated in practice. As far as we know, there exists no empirical data on applying Scrum for a safety-critical project with the integration of STPA.

Research objective and research questions. In this article, we aim to explore the agility and safety of S-Scrum as well as challenges and their relevant optimizations for developing a safety-critical system called "Smart Home". The research questions are as follows:

RQ 1 *How does S-Scrum handle agility and safety in safety-critical systems?*
RQ 2 *What are the challenges of S-Scrum in such a context?*
RQ 3 *How could S-Scrum be optimized to overcome the challenges?*
RQ 4 *What are the effects of the optimized S-Scrum on safety and agility?*

Contribution. This paper provides the first case study on applying a Scrum development process for safety-critical systems. We investigated the effects and challenges of S-Scrum in the 1st stage of the case study. We proposed an optimized S-Scrum and validated it in the 2nd stage of the case study. To this end, we preliminarily discussed the optimized S-Scrum in industry.

Outline. The paper is organized as follows. First, we present the related work on using Scrum for safety-critical systems and normal Scrum development process improvement (Sect. 2). Then, we present the background about STPA and our previous work about S-Scrum (Sect. 3). After that, we describe the approach and results of the 1st stage of the case study (Sect. 4.1), and the 2nd stage of the case study (Sect. 4.2). Finally, we discuss the threats to validity (Sect. 5), and draw the conclusions (Sect. 6).

2   Related Work

To the best of our knowledge, few empirical studies of applying Scrum or other agile processes for safety-critical systems exist. Most of the research is still in the stage of theoretical illustration and validation [8,9].

Safe Scrum is a Scrum development process for safety-critical systems, which was developed to adhere to the general functional safety standard IEC 61508 [3,6]. Previous research of Safe Scrum has been synergized with other safety standards in different domains [4] [5]. However, purely theoretical validation is unable to cover the details of the process. More practical experiences are becoming crucial.

Despite the limited practical experiences in applying Scrum for safety-critical systems, there are a lot of Scrum development process experiences that could be taken as a reference for the agile software process improvement of our project [25, 26]. Diebold et al. [10] investigated the industrial usage of Scrum with various sprint length, events, team size, requirements engineering, roles, effort estimations and quality assurance. Cho [11] conducted an in-depth case study in two organizations. The data was analyzed along 4 dimensions, including human resource management; structured development process; environment; information systems and technology. These factors were covered in our assessment of agility considering our criteria to improve the S-Scrum.

3   STPA and S-Scrum

STPA is a new hazard analysis technique by Leveson in 2012. It has been successfully used in various domains, such as aviation, automobiles and healthcare. Compared with the traditional safety analysis techniques, such as FMEA (Failure Mode and Effects Analysis) and FTA (Fault tree analysis), STPA bases on the systems theory rather than the traditional reliability theory. Due to an increasing complexity of systems, the accidents are not caused by single function failures or chains of failure events, but resulted from inadequate control actions. To ensure the safety of today's complex systems, the use of STPA is becoming necessary. Besides, we proposed using STPA in a Scrum development process [16], as current safety analysis techniques start from a complete design, which is not consistent to agile methodologies, which advocate a lightweight up-front planning and design. STPA, on the contrary, provides the necessary information to start from a high-level architecture and to guide the incremental design process. In S-Scrum, we integrate STPA mainly in three aspects: (1) During each sprint, we integrate STPA as safety-guided design. (2) At the end of each sprint, we use STPA on the product instead of a Reliability, Availibility, Maintainability and Safety (RAMS) validation. (3) We replace the final RAMS validation with STPA. The other parts are kept consistent to Safe Scrum: (1) The environment description and the SSRS phases 1–4 (concept, overall scope definitions, hazard and risk analysis and overall safety requirements). (2) Test Driven Development. (3) Safety product backlog. (4) A safety expert [30]. We aim to fill the gap of a lack of safety analysis in agile development and enhance the safety on the basis of a standard-based Scrum development process for safety-critical systems.

4   Case Study

To explore S-Scrum further, we conduct this study following the guideline by Runeson [17] and Yin [18]. We design this case study with a multi-staged procedure. Each stage has different objectives and research questions. We explored the challenges and optimizations in **S-Scrum** in stage 1, while we validated the **optimized S-Scrum** in stage 2.

4.1   Research Context

The case study (including stage 1 and stage 2) was performed in the project developing safety-critical systems, Smart Home, between March, 2016 and March, 2017 at the Institute of Software Technology, University of Stuttgart. The project had 400 planned working hours per head with a headcount of 14 students. The students have taken part in a training program for agile development and STPA before joining the project and a course on automation systems during the project. The Scrum Master was one research assistant with experienced project management background, while the Product Owner and Safety Expert was another research assistant majoring in using agile for safety-critical systems. All the students were supervised by three research assistants. The project was to work on an IoT based smart home with a smart coffee machine, smart light alarm system, autonomous parking system, door-open system, and smoke detector alarm system through the IoT server - KAA[1]. The project "Smart Home" is openly available in GitHub[2].

4.2   Case Study - Stage 1

The objective of stage 1 is to validate the safety and agility of S-Scrum and optimize it. In stage 1, we focus on answering RQ 1, RQ 2, and RQ 3. The general research strategy in stage 1 is shown in Table 1.

Data Collection in Stage 1. Stage 1 spans from sprint 1 to sprint 9. Each sprint lasts three weeks. The agility-related quantitative data, M1 to M15, were collected through 13 questionnaires[3]. Our participant observation as the Product Owner (the first author), the Scrum Master, and the customer imposed also an evaluation and review of the results. The safety-related data, M16.1 to M16.3 and M17.1 to M17.3, were quantitatively collected during sprint 6 and sprint 7. From sprint 1 to sprint 5, we executed normal Scrum without safety analysis for the adaptation and preparation for the project. The STPA was performed by the safety expert and recorded privately by using the STPA tool, XSTAMPP[4], while the hazards and safety requirements were recorded in the safety product backlog in Jira.

Based on the quantitative data for agility and safety, we then designed semi-structured interviews with 6 voluntary participants from the development team, including the Scrum Master and five developers. The interviews lasted 270 min overall. The questions began with a specific set of questions regarding the observations. Further, we asked about the causalities. Finally, the optimizations were collected in an open-ended mode. The interview guideline[5] was provided before

---

[1] https://www.kaaproject.org/overview/.

[2] https://github.com/ywISTE/student-project---Smart-Home.

[3] The questionnaire is available: https://zenodo.org/record/439696#.WODCovl96Uk.

[4] http://www.xstampp.de/.

[5] The interview guideline is available: https://zenodo.org/record/439696#. WODCovl96Uk.

Table 1. Research strategy in stage 1 ("DL"-Developer, "SH"-Stakeholder, "SM"-Scrum Master)

Time	Sprint 1 to sprint 5	Sprint 6 to sprint 7	Sprint 8	Sprint 9
Process	Scrum	S-Scrum	S-Scrum	S-Scrum
Data collection	Participant observation	Participant observation	Questionnaires	Semi-structured interviews
	Scrum artifacts	Scrum artifacts		
	Documentation review	Documentation review		
Participants	DLs	DLs	13 voluntary DLs	5 voluntary DLs
	SHs	SHs		1 SM
Data types	Quantitative	Quantitative	Quantitative	Qualitative
Analysis	Sum of the numbers	Sum of the numbers	Median MAD	Coding
Output	No safety data	Safety data: M16.1-M16.3 M17.1-M17.3	Agility data: M1-M15	Challenges and optimizations of S-Scrum

each interview. We recorded interview data in field notes and we used the audio recordings for text transcription.

Data Analysis in Stage 1. We analyzed the data using the combination of GSN [14] and GQM [15] referring partially to the VMF framework [13], as shown in Fig. 1. The data are from two aspects: agility (S1) and safety (S2). To evaluate and optimize agility (S1), we set 15 goals (G1 to G15) considering Comparative Agility Survey [12]. They are: G1 (Team work composition); G2 (Team work management); G3 (Communication); G4 (Requirement emergency); G5 (Technical design); G6 (Planning levels); G7 (Critical variables); G8 (Progress tracking); G9 (Sources of dates and estimates); G10 (When do we plan); G11 (Customer acceptance test); G12 (Timing); G13 (Quality focus); G14 (Reflection); G15 (Outcome measure). To reach G1 to G15, we analyzed M1 to M15 indirectly by setting sub-metrics. For example, M1 (Team work composition) was analyzed by M1.1 (Team members are kept as long as possible), M1.2 (Specialists are willing to work outside their specialty to achieve team goals), M1.3 (Everyone required to go from requirements to finished system is on the team), and M1.4 (People are no more than two teams). Each sub-metric was analyzed on an ordinal scale of 5 (e.g., from 1 to 5 means "Negative", "More negative than positive", "Neither negative nor positive", "More positive than negative", and "Positive"). To investigate the in-depth challenges, we found out either the negative values of the results or the significant differences between the normal Scrum and S-Scrum to formulate further interview questions. To analyze the

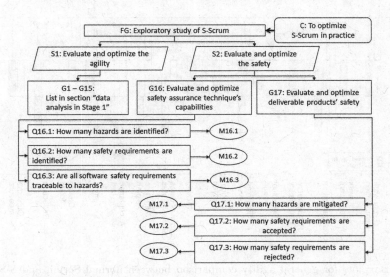

Fig. 1. General data analysis strategy ("FG"-Final Goal, "S"-Strategy, "G"-Goal, "C"-Context, "Q"-Question, "M"-Metric)

interview results, we used NVivo11 for text encoding [19]. Concerning safety, G16 is extended with 3 questions together with 3 metrics including: number of software hazards (M16.1), number of software safety requirements (M16.2), and number of safety requirements traceable to hazards (M16.3). G17 is extended to be evaluated by the number of mitigated hazards (M17.1), number of accepted safety requirements (M17.2) in the present sprint, and number of rejected safety requirements (M17.3) in the project.

Results in stage 1 - RQ 1: How does S-Scrum handle agility and safety in safety-critical systems? We investigate the effect on agility by comparing the normal Scrum and the S-Scrum according to the 15 metrics in Fig. 2. From the general overview, we can conclude that most of the values regarding agility in S-Scrum are slightly worse than those in the normal Scrum, while one metric shows strongly negative values ("when do we plan"). We discussed the results with the technical support from the Comparative Agility Survey and got the feedback: *when most of the values are more positive than negative (more than "3"), we could say that the process is agile enough.* Moreover, most values show relatively small differences between normal Scrum and S-Scrum. Thus, we consider the agility of S-Scrum to be acceptable. Yet, optimizations are needed. Regarding the safety of S-Scrum, we performed STPA two rounds in sprint 6. We found 6 software hazards (M16.1) and 15 safety requirements (M16.2), which can all be traced back to software hazards (M16.3). Three hazards were mitigated (M17.1), while 14 safety requirements were accepted (M17.2). In sprint 7, we performed two rounds of STPA analysis. We found 10 software hazards (M16.1)

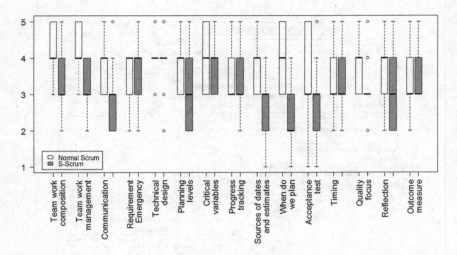

Fig. 2. Boxplots for general agility comparison between normal Scrum and S-Scrum (From "1"to "5" means less agile ("negative") to very agile ("positive"))

and 24 safety requirements (M16.2), which can also all be traced back to software hazards (M16.3). Six hazards were mitigated (M17.1), while 23 safety requirements were accepted (M17.2). Each sprint has 1 rejected safety requirement due to hardware limitation (M17.3).

Results in stage 1 - RQ 2 and RQ 3: What are the challenges of S-Scrum in such context? and How could S-Scrum be optimized to overcome the challenges? To optimize S-Scrum, we derived six challenges from the six abnormal values (see data analysis in stage 1) from the sub-metrics inside these 15 metrics.

Challenge 1: The priority management of safety requirements and functional requirements has conflict. In the normal Scrum, the management and development team determine the sprint backlog with functional requirements in the sprint planning meeting. All the team members have a clear overview of and commitment to the sprint plan with relatively high-level features. The developers accomplish each item with their own detailed tasks. The requirements from the management and the concrete realizations from the developer reach a consensus during each sprint. In S-Scrum, the integrated STPA and the safety requirements break the balance. The functional requirements are correlated with the safety requirements. However, some developers preferred: *functional requirements are more important than the safety requirements.* It was found that the need for long-term quality was given a lower priority than the need for short-term progress [27]. Moreover, the safety expert spent a relatively short time working with the team members which influences also the decision making. As one developer mentioned: *The safety expert is not working in the same room with the development team and has an inconsistent working time.* Thus, a lack of an in-time decision maker on the safety requirements together with the ignorance of safety requirements in the development team cause the conflict.

To face this challenge, a **safety culture** should be integrated into a lightweight development process. We suggest to include an **internal safety expert** in the development team to (1) spread the safety culture; (2) increase the safety expert's working time with the team members; (3) clarify the bewilded safety requirements. An **external safety expert** is necessary to keep the communication with other stakeholders. To fill the gap between the external safety expert and the development team, the development team suggests that the external safety expert should join at least once the weekly Scrum meeting. The discussion between the management, the external safety expert and the internal safety expert could strive a fresh balance on the priorities.

Challenge 2: The communication between team members and safety expert is disturbed. To start with, the unclear safety-related documentation influences an effective communication. The team members mentioned: *it is difficult to comprehend the purpose of the safety expert and integrate into our daily work from the existing documents.* Moreover, a lack of safety-related knowledge of the development team influences the discussion concerning safety issues. Finally, the insufficient time spent between safety expert and development team causes also a poor communication. Without a non-obstacle work place to communicate within the team about the work progress, the safety assurance could either be a superficial decoration or even worse, a roadblock during fast product delivery.

To face this challenge, in addition to the separated **internal safety expert** and **external safety expert**, a **weekly safety meeting** is suggested by an interviewee: *The internal safety expert and external safety expert should meet each other at least once a week to exchange the status of the development team. Because the discussion should be deep in the safety area, it is not supposed to be established during the normal weekly Scrum meeting.* Last but not least, we improve our **safety epics** and **safety stories** to support an effective communication [31], as shown in Sect. 4.3 (Optimized S-Scrum).

Challenge 3: The safety requirements are not determined early enough to appropriately influence design and testing. In sprint 6 and sprint 7, the safety requirements were determined by the development team and the safety expert together in the sprint planning meeting. However, as one interviewee mentioned: *the determination of safety requirements from the safety product backlog is too late to avoid a conflict between the functional requirements and their suitability for the coming sprint.* Thus, sometimes the functional design and testing have to start without the in-time safety requirements.

To face this challenge, we propose **a pre-planning meeting** for solving the time pressure problem. First, the internal, external safety experts and product owner discuss the safety product backlog and the functional product backlog in the pre-planning meeting. Then they brainstorm the results with the whole development team in the sprint planning meeting to gather more ideas and make each safety requirement clear.

Challenge 4: The planning at the start of each iteration is insufficient. In the normal Scrum, the development team and the product owner plan the upcoming sprint in the sprint planning meeting by formulating the sprint backlog with estimated items, which makes the development team sufficiently confident about their plan. However, the estimation and planning for the safety product backlog seem not ideal, as well as the interconnection with the functional product backlog, which make an in-time identification of the sprint backlog difficult. An interviewee said: *It is difficult to determine the safety requirements when the development team has not planned the functional requirements for the coming sprint.*

To face this challenge, we suggest and adapt an **agile safety plan** [21] in connection with the **pre-planning meeting** to increase the understanding of safety issues and enhance confidence. In our project, the results of STPA are part of the agile safety plan.

Challenge 5: The time to perform upfront planning is late. A team member said: *'the pre-planning meeting for safety issues should start before the sprint planning meeting. But the concrete time should be decided between the external safety expert, the internal safety expert and the product owner.* Based on the experience of the previous sprints, it is better to start upfront planning one week before the sprint planning meeting (3 weeks/sprint). The time could be changed depending on the sprint length. More explanations are in challenge 4.

Challenge 6: The safety requirements lack well-defined completion criteria. In the normal Scrum, we have various testing methods to determine the completion of each feature such as unit testing, system testing, regression testing, and acceptance testing, which are promoted to be automated in an agile context. However, few agile testing methods are suitable for validating safety requirements, as the safety requirements are either from standard requirements or the safety analysis, which differentiates safety testing and functional testing. In S-Scrum, we use UAT (User Acceptance Testing) for validating safety requirements. Thus, a suitable safety criterion becomes important.

To face this challenge, we use a "Given-When-Then" format [23] as **safety requirements' criteria**. The development team suggest that the external safety expert could decide the **safety stories' criteria** and the internal safety expert could decide the **safety tasks' criteria**. The whole development team could **brainstorm** both criteria. To this end, the product owner and safety expert perform the acceptance testing.

4.3   Case Study - Stage 2

After the optimizations described above, the objective of stage 2 is to validate the safety and agility of the optimized S-Scrum and discuss it in industry. We focus on answering the RQ 4 together with some discussion from industry. The general research strategy in stage 2 is shown in Table 2.

Table 2. Research strategy in stage 2 ("DL"-Developer, "SH"-Stakeholder, "SM"-Scrum Master, "PO"-Product Owner)

Time	Sprint 10 to sprint 11	Sprint 12	Sprint 13
Process	optimized S-Scrum	Optimized S-Scrum	Optimized S-Scrum
Data collection	Participant observation	Questionnaires	Semi-structured interviews
	Scrum artifacts		
	Documentation review		
Participants	DLs	8 voluntary DLs	1 PO (from EPLAN)
	SHS		1 SM (from EPLAN)
Data types	Quantitative	Quantitative	Qualitative
Analysis	Sum of the numbers (compare with the data from stage 1)	Median and MAD (compare with the data from stage 1)	Coding
Output	Safety data: M16.1-M16.3 M17.1-M17.3	Agility data: M1-M15	Preliminary discussion in industry

Optimized S-Scrum. To have a clear overview, we compare the optimized S-Scrum to the normal Scrum and the S-Scrum in our project respectively in Table 3. In the optimized S-Scrum, we differentiate between an internal safety expert and an external safety expert. A pre-planning meeting and weekly safety meetings are established between safety experts. We include the safety epics, to satisfy <the overall safety needs>, the system must <always be able to reach a safe state> [22], in the story map. The safety product backlog is improved with optimized safety story: To keep <control action> safe, the system must <achieve or avoid something>. An agile safety plan based on STPA technology is suggested for a clear overview. The safety culture is expected to be enhanced by the additional activities.

Data Collection in Stage 2. Stage 2 is from sprint 10 to sprint 13. The safety-related data, M16.1 to M16.3 and M17.1 to M17.3, were collected in the same way as in stage 1. The safety results were collected by both internal and external safety experts. The agility-related data, M1 to M15, were collected by the second round questionnaires[6]. We further discussed the optimized S-Scrum by conducting 2 semi-structured interviews with one Scrum Master and one Product Owner from EPLAN GmbH, Germany. The interview lasted 2 h. We formulated questions about the status of the Scrum development process in the company projects; the feasibility of the optimized S-Scrum in industry; and further suggestions from the industrial perspective. A project background illustration was

---

[6] The questionnaire is available: https://zenodo.org/record/439696#.WODCovl96Uk.

Table 3. Normal Scrum, S-Scrum and optimized S-Scrum in Smart Home ("DL"-Developer, "SM"-Scrum Master, "PO"-Product Owner, "SE"-Safety Expert)

Normal Scrum	14 DLs	Sprint planning meeting	Story map
	1 SM	Weekly Scrum meeting (2 times/week)	Product backlog
	1 PO	Sprint review meeting	Sprint backlog
		Sprint retrospective meeting	
S-Scrum	14 DLs	Sprint planning meeting (with safety planning)	Story map
	1 SM	Weekly Scrum meeting (2 times/week) (with safety discussion)	Functional product backlog
	1 PO	Sprint review meeting (with safety review)	Safety product backlog
	1 SE	Sprint retrospective meeting	Sprint backlog
Optimized S-Scrum	13 DLs	Pre-planning meeting	Story map (with safety epics)
	1 SM	Sprint planning meeting (brainstorming requirements and criteria)	Functional product backlog
	1 PO	Weekly Scrum meeting (2 times/week)	Safety product backlog (with safety stories)
	1 internal SE	Weekly safety meeting (1 time/week)	Sprint backlog
	1 external SE	Sprint review meeting (with safety review)	Safety plan
		Sprint retrospective meeting	

provided before the interviews, together with the interview guidelines[7]. The field notes, interview transcripts, and voice recordings were all preserved for backup.

Data Analysis in Stage 2. The quantitative data were compared with the numbers in stage 1. The interview results from the industry were text encoded with: status, challenges, possible solutions, and the feasibility of S-Scrum.

---

[7] The interview guideline is available: https://zenodo.org/record/439696#.WODCovl9 6Uk.

Results in Stage 2 - RQ 4: What Are the Effects of the Optimized S-Scrum on Safety and Agility? As shown in Fig. 3, most of the evaluated agility aspects sustained a good level of satisfaction with little variance. However, the "technical design" is slightly reduced. Due to the new role, the collaborative part of design between safety work and development work fell on the internal safety expert. The personal capability is becoming important. To improve the technical design, cooperation shall increase between the external safety expert and the development team.

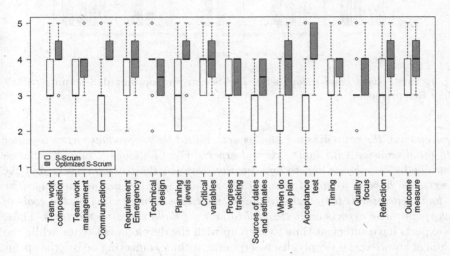

Fig. 3. Boxplots for agility comparison between S-Scrum and optimized S-Scrum (From "1" to "5" means less agile ("negative") to very agile ("positive"))

Regarding the safety of optimized S-Scrum, as we can see in Fig. 4, safety aspects improved (M16.1, M16.2, M16.3, M17.1, M17.2). We also rejected few safety requirements (M17.3): 1 (sprint 6), 1 (sprint 7), 0 (sprint 10), 2 (sprint 11). We can conclude that, in general, the optimized S-Scrum has better safety assurance capabilities. However, there are still some abnormal values in sprint 7. The number of safety requirements, the number of safety requirements traceable to hazards and the number of accepted safety requirements in sprint 7 are more than in sprint 10. This may be traced back to the fitting-in phase of the optimized S-Scrum. Since the training of STPA for the internal safety expert, we finished STPA in sprint 10 only once. In sprint 6, sprint 7, and sprint 11, we finished STPA twice. After the adaption of the new role, the safety data rose in sprint 11.

Results in Stage 2 - Discussion. To strength the study further, we discussed our results preliminarily in industry. For *Challenge 1*, the conflict between functional requirements and non-functional requirements seems not obvious. As one interviewee mentioned: *Since we have a relative small amount of non-functional*

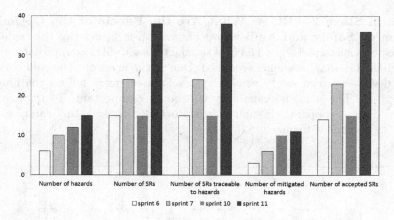

Fig. 4. Safety data comparison between S-Scrum and optimized S-Scrum ("SRs"-Safety Requirements)

requirements, the priorities are always determined by the product owner together with the discussion with some external experts. For *Challenge 2*, one interviewee mentioned: *To enhance the communication between the team members and the experts, we have a technical meeting before each sprint planning meeting. The product owner sends the emails to the relevant experts depending on the goals of each sprint. The experts are welcomed to join the daily stand-up meetings.* Thus, the experts have sufficient time to keep up with the development team, while the technical knowledge is deeply discussed in the technical meeting before the sprint planning meeting. The project has also a good knowledge sharing mechanism to support the communication during each sprint. One interviewee mentioned: *We use pair programming, formal guidelines to teach new colleagues, chat clients, and screen sharing. When the team includes experts, the product owner will contact 2–3 colleagues to discuss technical stuff, who will inform other colleagues.* A hierarchical communication mode is preferred for a multi-expert team. For *Challenge 3*, the industrial projects have also mentioned this problem: *Internal user stories are used to record the non-functional requirements. The execution of internal user stories is up to the team.* For *Challenge 4*, the two teams execute a sufficient planning. An interviewee mentioned: *We have a refinement time slot to get all product backlog items approved (each team member has understood) and not so much discussion in the sprint planning meeting.* The team members are beginning the refinement in the present sprint for the user stories in the next sprint. In Scrum, not all requirements have to be at the same level of detail at the same time [24]. The progressive refinement could be further extended for the safety planning and assessment to: (1) avoid a premature development decision from the high-level safety requirements; (2) reserve sufficient time for managing priorities between safety requirements and functional requirements; (3) increase the rework possibilities; (4) enhance the likelihood of using conversation to clarify safety requirements. That could also illustrate the *Challenge 5.*

For *Challenge 6*, the refinement phase helps building a pre-understanding of each requirement and reaching a common criterion in the sprint planning meeting. The *external expert* is a regular member in industry. An interviewee mentioned: *We prefer some experts with deep knowledge in the team, but the arrangement of an internal expert has to take more issues into account, such as training, responsibility, and even personal development.* An external safety consultant to test the products and delivered trainings and an internal safety initiative [20] to promote safety practices across groups in industry could be align with our internal and external safety expert. *Safety culture* in industry is enhanced either by setting the regulations or by the established organization structure and activities. An *agile safety plan* is also required from some standards. They draw the safety plan either in the technical meeting or in parallel with the refinement. The technical meeting suggested in industry could also be considered as an *extra (weekly) safety meeting*. The *pre-planning meeting* seems to be a suitable form for realizing progressive refinement in industry. This alignment motivates more combinations between our optimizations and existing industrial practices. All the requirements and *acceptance criteria* are retrieved by *brainstorming*. An effective communication plays a vital role in executing acceptance testing.

5   Threats to Validity

Construct validity: The first threat to construct validity is the general data analysis framework. To apply Scrum for safety-critical systems, we focus primarily on safety aspect and agility aspect in our exploratory study. In terms of agility, we referred to an official agility comparative survey [12] for ensuring the coverage of measurement. In terms of safety, S-Scrum was extended from Safe Scrum, which was originally developed in accordance with the general functional safety standard IEC 61508. Thus, the validation regarding to the consistency with IEC 61508 has not been included in the framework. Furthermore, in S-Scrum we mainly integrate STPA. We aim to validate the enhanced safety concerning the integrated safety analysis technique. Thus, the safety assurance technique's capability and the deliverable products' safety are set as two relevant goals. Yet, the goals and metrics seem not enough and the validation framework is possible to be extended. The second threat to construct validity is the validation periods for S-Scrum and optimized S-Scrum are shorter than our expectations. We executed the normal Scrum in the first five sprints to strengthen students' background knowledge of agile techniques and prepare the detailed organization structure, which took us a lot of time.

Internal validity: The first threat to internal validity is the arrangement of team roles. One of the authors acted as the product owner and the safety expert concurrently in sprint 6 and sprint 7. To avoid this threat in alignment with the optimizations in sprint 10 and sprint 11, the product owner acted further as an external safety expert. An internal safety expert has been arranged in the development team. The second threat to internal validity exists in the qualitative data from the semi-structured interviews. The interviews have been performed by one of the authors together with the audio record. The language we used has also partial German. To avoid subjective and language bias, the audio recording has been transcribed independently by two researchers (one is a native German speaker) and compared to formulate a final result.

External validity: A student project is different from an industrial project. However, Höst et al. [28], Tichy, Kitchenham et al. [29] proposed that students could be acceptable. To consider this debatable issue, we mainly referred to an empirical study conducted by Falessi in 2017 [33]. 16 statements are provided by 65 empirical researchers. They mentioned: *Conducting experiments with professionals as a first step should not be encouraged unless high sample sizes are guaranteed or performing replicas is cheap.* In our research, there exists few industrial projects for developing safety-critical systems fully adopted a Scrum development process according to the preliminary research [32]. S-Scrum was also proposed in 2016 as a high-level process model. In addition, the long learning cycles and a new technology are two hesitations for using professionals. STPA was developed in 2012. In industry, there is still a lack of experts. Thus, we believe that in our research area, a student project is a relative suitable way to aggregate contributions. Even though, the generalizability is considered critical.

Reliability: The student project is a suitable way for a first validation. Yet, the results from the students are limited by their personal experience. Besides, the "grading power" of the researchers may influence the results. We separated our research work from the final examination of the product to mitigate this threat.

6   Conclusion

The main benefit of our research is that it provides a first empirical and practical insight into applying Scrum for safety-critical systems with the integration of STPA. Moreover, the presented challenges existing in priority management, communication, time pressure on determining safety requirements, safety planning, safety requirements' acceptance criteria and solutions including the split of the safety expert, pre-planning meeting, regular safety meeting, improved safety epics, STPA-based safety stories and an agile safety plan could arouse interest in practitioners and show future research directions. The effects on safety and agility aspects indicate the feasibility to align STPA with a Scrum development process. The discussion in industry motivates the further step of transmitting the optimized S-Scrum from the academic environment towards industry environment. However, the execution of S-Scrum and optimized S-Scrum was in a specific context. We can rely our improvements on an academical project only. The generalization in industry of the optimizations remains subject to future work. Finally, regarding safety and security in agile development in today's cyberphysical systems, even though special attention has to be paid to the respective norms and standards, problems' exploration in practice seems also necessary.

Acknowledgements. We want to thank Dr. A. Nguyen-Duc for proof reading and his valuable suggestions. We are grateful to all participants involved during the case study. Finally, we want to thank all the feedback on previous versions. The first author is supported by the LGFG (Stipendien nach dem Landesgraduiertenfördergesetz).

References

1. IEC61508: Functional safety of electrical/electronic/programmable electronic safety-related systems. International Electrotechnical Commission (2010)
2. Turk, D., France, R., Rumpe, B.: Limitations of agile software processes. arXiv preprint arxiv:1409.6600 (2014)
3. Stålhane, T., Myklebust, T., Hanssen, G.K.: The application of safe Scrum to IEC 61508 certifiable software. In: 11th International Probabilistic Safety Assessment and Management Conference and the Annual European Safety and Reliability Conference (2012)
4. Stålhane, T., Vikash, K., Myklebust, T.: Scrum and IEC 60880. Enlarged Halden Reactor Project meeting, Storefjell, Norway (2013)
5. Stålhane, T.: Safety standards and Scrum A synopsis of three standards
6. Hanssen, G.K., Haugset, B., Stålhane, T., Myklebust, T., Kulbrandstad, I.: Quality assurance in Scrum applied to safety critical software. In: Sharp, H., Hall, T. (eds.) XP 2016. LNBIP, vol. 251, pp. 92–103. Springer, Cham (2016). doi:10.1007/978-3-319-33515-5_8
7. Leveson, N.: Engineering a Safer World: Systems Thinking Applied to Safety. MIT press, Cambridge (2011)
8. Ge, X., Richard, F.P., John, A.M.: An iterative approach for development of safety-critical software and safety arguments. In: AGILE Conference, IEEE (2010)
9. Vuori, M.: Agile development of safety-critical software. Tampere University of Technology 14 (2011)
10. Diebold, P., Ostberg, J.-P., Wagner, S., Zendler, U.: What do practitioners vary in using scrum? In: Lassenius, C., Dingsøyr, T., Paasivaara, M. (eds.) XP 2015. LNBIP, vol. 212, pp. 40–51. Springer, Cham (2015). doi:10.1007/978-3-319-18612-2_4
11. Cho, J.J.: An exploratory study on issues and challenges of agile software development with Scrum. All Graduate theses and dissertations (2010). 599
12. Williams, L., Kenny, R., Mike, C.: Driving process improvement via comparative agility assessment. In: AGILE Conference, IEEE (2010)
13. Cruickshank, K.J., James, B.M., Man-Tak, S.: A validation metrics framework for safety-critical software-intensive Systems. IEEE International Conference System of Systems Engineering, SoSE 2009, IEEE (2009)
14. Kelly, T., Rob, W.: The goal structuring notation a safety argument notation. In: Proceedings of the Dependable Systems and Networks 2004 Workshop on Assurance Cases, Citeseer (2004)
15. Basili, V.R.: Software modeling and measurement: the goal/question/metric paradigm (1992)
16. Wang, Y., Wagner, S.: Toward integrating a system theoretic safety analysis in an agile development process. In: Software Engineering (2016)
17. Runeson, P., Höst, M.: Guidelines for conducting and reporting case study research in software engineering. Empirical Softw. Eng. **14**(2), 131 (2009)
18. Yin, R.K.: Case Study Research: Design and Methods. Sage publications, CA (2013)

19. Strauss, A., Corbin, J.M.: Grounded Theory in Practice. Sage, CA (1997)
20. Poller, A., Kocksch, L., Türpe, S., Epp, F.A., Kinder-Kurlanda, K.: Can security become a routine?: a study of organizational change in an agile software development group. In: Proceedings of the 2017 ACM Conference on Computer Supported Cooperative Work and Social Computing, ACM (2017)
21. Myklebust, T., Stålhane, T., Lyngby, N.: The Agile Safety Plan. In: PSAM13 (2016)
22. Myklebust, T., Stålhane, T.: Safety stories a new concept in agile development. In: Fast Abstracts at International Conference on Computer Safety, Reliability, and Security (SAFECOMP 2016) (2016)
23. Garg, S.: Cucumber Cookbook. Packt Publishing Ltd, UK (2015)
24. Rubin, K.S.: EssentiaL Scrum: A Practical Guide to the Most Popular Agile Process. Addison-Wesley, Boston (2012)
25. Moe, N.B., Torgeir, D., Tore, D.: A teamwork model for understanding an agile team: a case study of a Scrum project. Inf. Softw. Technol. **52**(5), 480–491 (2010)
26. Begel, A., Nachiappan N.: Usage and perceptions of agile software development in an industrial context: an exploratory study. In: First International Symposium on Empirical Software Engineering and Measurement, ESEM 2007, p. 2007. IEEE (2007)
27. Moe, N.B., Aybüke, A., Dybå, T.: Challenges of shared decision-making: a multiple case study of agile software development. Inf. Softw. Technol. **54**(8), 853–865 (2012)
28. Höst, M., Björn, R., Wohlin, C.: Using students as subjects a comparative study of students and professionals in lead-time impact assessment. Empirical Softw. Eng. **5**(3), 201–214 (2000)
29. Tichy, W.F.: Hints for reviewing empirical work in software engineering. Empirical Softw. Eng. **5**(4), 309–312 (2000)
30. Wang, Y., Wagner, S.: Towards applying a safety analysis and verification method based on STPA to agile software development. In: IEEE/ACM International Workshop on Continuous Software Evolution and Delivery (CSED), IEEE (2016)
31. Wang, Y., Bogicevic, I., Wagner, S.: A study of safety documentation in a Scrum development process. In: Proceedings of the XP2017 Scientific Workshops, ACM (2017)
32. Theocharis, G., Kuhrmann, M., Münch, J., Diebold, P.: Is *Water-Scrum-Fall* reality? on the use of agile and traditional development practices. In: Abrahamsson, P., Corral, L., Oivo, M., Russo, B. (eds.) PROFES 2015. LNCS, vol. 9459, pp. 149–166. Springer, Cham (2015). doi:10.1007/978-3-319-26844-6_11
33. Falessi, D., Juristo, N., Wohlin, C., Turhan, B., Münch, J., Jedlitschka, A., Oivo, M.: Empirical software engineering experts on the use of students and professionals in experiments. J. Empirical Softw. Eng. 1–38 (2017). Springer

Exploring the Individual Project Progress
of Scrum Software Developers

Ezequiel Scott[✉] and Dietmar Pfahl

University of Tartu, Tartu, Estonia
{ezequiel.scott,dietmar.pfahl}@ut.ee

Abstract. Scrum based software development has become increasingly popular in recent years. Scrum requires teams following agile practices and their principles. One of them includes having room for the reflection of the team on how to become more effective. In this context, measuring and enhancing the performance of teams is still an area of interest for the Scrum community. Traditional Scrum metrics have often been used to measure the performance and productivity; however, individual contributions of team members to the project are often shaded by the team overall performance. In this paper, we propose a metric for measuring individual differences in project progress based on the traditional Burndown chart. We also show preliminary results of applying it in a particular training context, highlighting how learning-styles based instruction can improve the individual project progress of students.

Keywords: Agile software development · Scrum · Agile metrics

1 Introduction

Scrum based software development has become increasingly popular in recent years [3]. In fact, the latest State of Agile Survey reports that Scrum and its variants are used by more than the 75% of respondents [14]. This acceptance stems from the fact that many Scrum teams have reported relevant results regarding the quality of the software, the working synergy, the user satisfaction, and the enjoyable working environment [12].

To put Scrum into practice, teams not only have to follow the Scrum practices but also adhere to the agile manifesto and their principles. One of them includes having room for the reflection of the team on how to become more effective, in order to tailor their behavior accordingly [1]. In this context, measuring and enhancing the performance of teams is still an area of interest for Scrum practitioners. As a result, many metrics for measuring performance in Scrum have been proposed such as the *Velocity* of the team and their *Burndown chart*, among many others [4].

These metrics have been successfully used for monitoring how certain data points affect the progress of teams. However, individual contributions are often

© Springer International Publishing AG 2017
M. Felderer et al. (Eds.): PROFES 2017, LNCS 10611, pp. 341–348, 2017.
https://doi.org/10.1007/978-3-319-69926-4_24

shaded by the team overall performance since Scrum stresses teamwork and collective responsibility for the final outcome of a project [6]. Knowing the individual project progress could help teams in different ways. For example, teams can get a better understanding of the progress of the project and use this knowledge as a first indicator of possible problems. In addition, training contexts can take advantage of individual metrics since they can serve as an indicator of students' performance. Thus, studies on metrics for assessing individual project progress are beneficial for the Scrum community.

In this study, we aim to make a two-fold contribution. First, we propose a metric for measuring individual project progress based on Scrum. Second, we show the preliminary results of applying the metric in a particular training context. Our results highlight how learning-styles based instruction can improve the individual project progress of students.

2   Related Work

There are many metrics often used to deal with project monitoring and control activities in Scrum. All of them usually rely on the use of agile artifacts such as *Backlogs* and *User Stories*. Although these metrics are popular, the agile community agrees with the idea of improving the measurement in Scrum. Dawney and Sutherland [4] have defined a set of Scrums metrics which aim at improving the traditional ones. The goal of these metrics, like many of the traditional ones, is to measure the team productivity.

The team productivity and the factors which correlate with it have been studied by many authors. For example, performance has been studied in their relationship with the stakeholder-driven process [9], and the stress and empowerment of the teams [8]. In addition, researchers and practitioners seem to agree about the importance of both technical and non-technical skills of developers regarding productivity [13]. So far, however, there has been little discussion about individualized metrics in Scrum.

In particular, studies focused on individuals have been connected with the educational field. For example, Gamble and Hale [6] have defined four individualized metrics: Contribution, Influence, Impact, and Impression. These metrics are based on the interaction of the students with a collaborative tool. In contrast, this study is more focused on the individuals' amount of work done during the software development than in the level of social engagement. Other studies have proposed metrics that rely on self-reporting activity, project evaluation rubrics, and grades based on individual submissions related to the project [2,7]. Surprisingly, the analysis of metrics derived from traditional agile artifacts like the Burndown chart have not been closely examined.

Exploring the individual characteristics of team members allows for studying their achievements in Scrum from a training point of view. In this line, Scott et al. [11] have explored how to improve the students' understanding of Scrum topics when learning preferences are used. Measuring the individual project progress in these contexts could be useful for determining the effectiveness of training approaches.

3 Method

The method used to explore the individual project progress mainly comprises three steps. The first step involves an initial training in Scrum. In the second step, the trainees put the Scrum framework into practice by developing a small software product. Finally, their individual project progress is analyzed. We describe these steps in the following sections.

3.1 Initial Training in Scrum

The initial Scrum training is based on previous experiences using the Felder-Silverman learning style model [5] in capstone projects. This model has been widely used in Computer Science and proposes classifying students into different learning styles which have their corresponding teaching style. Previous studies have shown that students can improve their understanding of Scrum concepts when they are exposed to instructional methods tailored according to their learning style [11].

To analyze the individual project progress when students receive the instructional method according to their learning styles, we rely on the recommendations of Pashler et al. [10]. The authors propose several guidelines to design a controlled experiment and obtain thoroughly evidence from it when learning styles are involved. According to these guidelines, we organize the initial training as follows.

First, students are assigned to two different groups according to their learning style. The students' learning styles are collected through an online questionnaire that allows for classifying the students into *active* or *reflective* students. Briefly speaking, *active* students prefer doing tasks or talking about concepts whereas *reflective* students are likely to manipulate and examine the information introspectively [5].

Once students are grouped by learning style, we randomly assign the students to two different instructional-method groups related to the *active* and *passive* teaching styles. These groups determine the instructional methods received by the students and the random assignment guarantees that both instructional-method groups have the same numbers of *active* and *reflective* students.

Finally, students receive the training in Scrum on the basis of their assigned instructional method. One group of students receive the instructional method according to one learning style (i.e. the *active* method) whereas the second group is trained using the remaining instructional method (i.e. the *passive* method). Thus, both groups receive the same topics, yet in different ways. The topics and the instructional methods used are described in more detail in previous research [11].

After receiving the training in Scrum, the students are expected to put the Scrum concepts into practice through the development of a small software project. We organize the software development as follows.

3.2   Software Development

To put the Scrum concepts into practice, the students are allocated to different teams. Each team is asked for developing the same software product: a small software application that allows teachers to manage courses and their topics. They are also asked for following the Scrum practices they learned before and track the project monitoring and control information into an online spreadsheet. Figure 1 shows an example of a user story in the spreadsheet.

#User Story	User Story Description	Story Points (SP)	#Task	Task Description	Resp.	Task SP
1	As a teacher, I want to manage the topics of my course to easily define the syllabus online.	5	1	Allow for adding new topics to the course	X	1
			2	Allow for removing topics from the course	Y	1
			3	Develop the printing module	Z	1
			4	Support linking topics	X	1
			5	Allow for listing all the topics of the syllabus	Y	1

Fig. 1. Example of the spreadsheet used to monitor and control the projects.

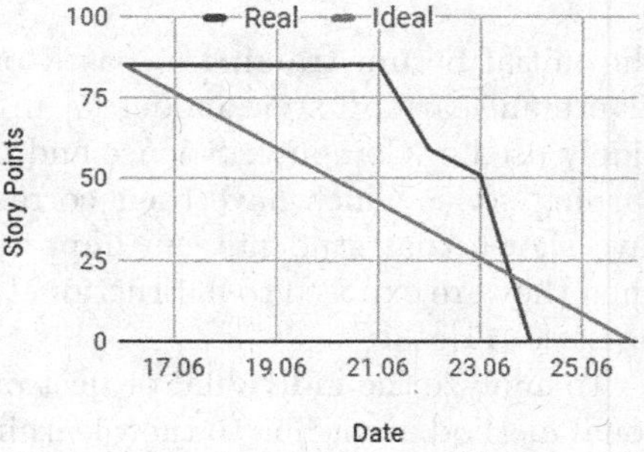

Fig. 2. Example of Burndown chart.

In this context, the students have to create User Stories from the requirements given by the Product Owner (the teacher) to build the Product Backlog. Then, they have to define the Sprint Backlog and estimate the User Stories to be done during the Sprint by using Planning Poker. The students also have to split User Stories into Tasks and allocate them into a Release Plan. Following these practices, the User Stories belong to the team whereas Tasks are self-assigned to team members.

During the development, the students record all the data about User Stories, Story Points, Tasks, and their statuses in the spreadsheet. At the end of the Sprint, the students are expected to generate a product increment and integrate it into the working product. Then, they present the product and receive feedback from the Product Owner during the Sprint Review. Finally, the students are encouraged to carry out the Scrum ceremonies within the team such as the Sprint Retrospective.

At the end of the Sprint, it is also possible to calculate several traditional Scrum metrics such as Velocity, Technical debt, and the Burndown chart, if the students use the spreadsheet properly. In particular, we focus on studying the individual project progress of the students through the data recorded on the spreadsheet.

3.3   Project Progress Measurement

To analyze the project progress of a team, we can analyze the number of Story Points they have done during the Sprint. The spreadsheet used by the teams allow us to identify the completed User Stories on each day of the Sprint. This way, we can build a Burndown chart for each team. This chart is a commonly used measurement tool for planning and monitoring the progress in agile methods [4].

The Burndown chart represents the amount of work remaining that needs to be accomplished till the end of the Sprint. The horizontal axis shows the days of a Sprint whereas the vertical axis shows the number of remaining Story Points. The trend line of remaining Story Points, also known as *ideal*, indicates whether the Team will accomplish the tasks committed by the end of the Sprint. Figure 2 shows an example of Burndown chart.

However, this chart is not suitable for studying the individual contribution of the team members to the overall project progress. This is because the chart shows the remaining Story Points of the User Stories, and User Stories belong to all the members of the team. To deal with it, we apply a straightforward strategy that is focused on the Tasks done by the team members and not in the User Stories.

The strategy consists in dividing the number of Story Points of each User Story among their Tasks. For example, if a User Story has been estimated with 5 Story Points and it has 5 linked Tasks, we consider that the amount of work of each linked Task is 1 Story Point. Figure 1 shows this example. This way, it is possible to measure the size of a Task in Story Points based on its User Story. In consequence, we can calculate the number of spent Story Points and build an individual Burndown chart representing the contribution of the team member to the project progress.

Using the individual Burndown chart, we study how far the individual project progress is from the average expected rate determined by the *ideal* line. To address this question, we calculate the area of the region between the *real* and the *ideal* progress lines of the Burndown chart. This area is calculated following the Trapezoidal Rule (Eq. 1) since its result is exact when the integrand is a linear function.

$$A = \int_a^b f(x)dx \approx \Delta x(\frac{y_0}{2} + y_1 + \cdots + \frac{y_n}{2}) \tag{1}$$

In our case, a represents the first day of the Sprint and b the last one, $f(x)$ is the function of interest (i.e. the difference between the *ideal* and the *real* progress lines of the Burndown chart), y_n represents the value of $f(x)$ at day n and we determine the value of Δx according to the intersection of both lines. Thus, the area of the region between the real and the ideal lines A can be considered as a measure of the individual progress of a team member. Values closer to zero indicate better performance whereas further values indicate worst performance.

4   Results

We explored the data from a pilot study which involved 35 students. The students received the initial training in Scrum according to their learning styles by following the aforementioned procedure. Among the total number of students, 18 were assigned to the active instructional method (12 of them were *active* students and 6 *reflective* students). The remaining 17 students were assigned to the passive instructional method (12 of them were *active* and 5 *reflective*).

After receiving the tailored instruction, the students were allocated to 8 teams for developing the same software product. At the end of the first Sprint, we processed all the data from the spreadsheets. We removed the data of those students who were not able to record the spent Story Points. We also removed data outliers of those who spent an excessive number of Story Points (more than 100) since these values are unrealistic. As a result, we analyzed the data about 27 students in total, 13 who received the active instructional method (10 of them were *active* and 3 *reflective*) and 14 who received the passive one (10 of them were *active* and 4 *reflective*).

We computed 27 Burndown charts in total, one chart per student. We also calculated the value of the area A for each one. We analyzed the arithmetic mean of these differences with regard to the different learning and teaching style groups. According to Pashler et al. [10], the evidence about using learning styles is reliable if the experiment reveals what is commonly known as a cross-over interaction between the learning style and the instructional method. In this case, the cross-over interaction occurs when the value of A of students being taught with a suitable instructional method is lower than students being taught with an unsuitable method. Table 1 shows these results in terms of arithmetic mean ($\bar{x}$) and standard deviation (s^2) and Fig. 3 depicts the crossover interaction.

Table 1. Mean and standard deviation of the area between real and ideal.

	Active students ($\bar{x} \pm s^2$)	Reflective students ($\bar{x} \pm s^2$)
Active method	34.89 $\pm$ 28.11	54.80 $\pm$ 35.43
Passive method	38.24 $\pm$ 41.11	57.02 $\pm$ 49.58

We also studied the statistical significance of the difference in the mean areas of both groups: students who were taught with suitable instructional methods (Group A) and students who were taught in a way that did not correspond to their learning style (Group B). Therefore, we conducted a *t-test* for independent samples. Although the mean of Group A ($\bar{x}_A = 27.041$) is lower than the mean of Group B ($\bar{x}_B = 37.216$), the results of the *t-test* show that there is no statistically significant difference between both means ($T = -0.623$, $p = 0.537$). A possible explanation for this results could be the small samples used.

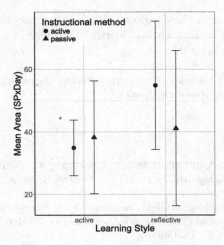

Fig. 3. Distribution of individual project progress according to the instructional methods and the students' learning style.

5   Discussion, Limitations, and Conclusion

In this paper, we explored a metric for measuring the individual project progress of Scrum developers. The metric is mainly based on adapting the traditional Burndown chart to the individual and then studying the area of the region between the real progress and the ideal one. We also showed the utility of applying this metric in a training context, pointing out how learning-styles based instruction can improve the students' individual project progress.

Using the proposed metric, we have found interesting differences in the individual project progress of students who were exposed to different instructional methods. Although these results are not statistically significant yet, they suggest that these differences can be measured in a traditional Scrum environment and how the individual project progress can be interpreted as a learning outcome.

There are threats to validity that should be carefully evaluated in future research. As for construct validity, more indicators have to be considered to determine the individual project progress. We suggest to use this metric as a first indicator of possible problems and analyze the context to find the root causes of the problems. Regarding external validity, there are factors that jeopardize the generalization of the results. In educational contexts, we suggest to use the metric carefully, bearing in mind that it is only one learning outcome among many others. Moreover, different groups of individuals are affected by their history, cultural background, and previous experience differently, and it can conduct to different conclusions.

In terms of directions for future research, further work could explore the previous knowledge on Scrum as well as different metrics that allow for measuring different aspects of the software development process. These aspects are not only performance indicators such as the number of incomplete tasks but also psychological constructs of the developer. In addition, including communication metrics of the team is a research line worth to explore in order to understand the problems that can arise in a project.

Acknowledgements. This research was supported by the institutional research grant IUT20-55 of the Estonian Research Council.

References

1. Beck, K., Beedle, M., Van Bennekum, A., Cockburn, A., Cunningham, W., Fowler, M., Grenning, J., Highsmith, J., Hunt, A., Jeffries, R., et al.: The agile manifesto (2001)
2. Cooley, W.L.: Individual student assessment in team-based capstone design projects. In: 34th Annual Frontiers in Education, FIE 2004, p. F1G-1. IEEE (2004)
3. Dingsøyr, T., Nerur, S., Balijepally, V.G., Moe, N.B.: A decade of agile methodologies: towards explaining agile software development (2012)
4. Downey, S., Sutherland, J.: Scrum metrics for hyperproductive teams: how they fly like fighter aircraft. In: 2013 46th Hawaii International Conference on System Sciences (HICSS), pp. 4870–4878. IEEE (2013)
5. Felder, R.M., Silverman, L.K.: Learning and teaching styles in engineering education. Eng. Educ. **78**(7), 674–681 (1988)
6. Gamble, R.F., Hale, M.L.: Assessing individual performance in agile undergraduate software engineering teams. In: 2013 IEEE Frontiers in Education Conference, pp. 1678–1684. IEEE (2013)
7. Hayes, J.H., Lethbridge, T.C., Port, D.: Evaluating individual contribution toward group software engineering projects. In: Proceedings of the 25th International Conference on Software Engineering, pp. 622–627. IEEE Computer Society (2003)
8. Laanti, M.: Agile and wellbeing-stress, empowerment, and performance in Scrum and Kanban teams. In: 2013 46th Hawaii International Conference on System Sciences (HICSS), pp. 4761–4770. IEEE (2013)
9. Mahnic, V., Vrana, I.: Using stakeholder driven process performance measurement for monitoring the performance of a scrum based software development process. Electrotech. Rev. **74**(5), 241–247 (2007)
10. Pashler, H., McDaniel, M., Rohrer, D., Bjork, R.: Learning styles concepts and evidence. Psychol. Sci. Public Interest **9**(3), 105–119 (2008)
11. Scott, E., Rodríguez, G., Soria, Á., Campo, M.: Towards better scrum learning using learning styles. J. Syst. Softw. **111**, 242–253 (2016)
12. Stellman, A., Greene, J.: Learning Agile: Understanding Scrum, XP, Lean, and Kanban. O'Reilly Media Inc., Sebastopol (2014)
13. Trendowicz, A., Münch, J.: Factors influencing software development productivity - state-of-the-art and industrial experiences. In: Advances in Computers, vol. 77, pp. 185–241 (2009)
14. VersionOne: 11th annual state of agile survey (2017). https://explore.versionone.com/state-of-agile

Software Testing

Is 100% Test Coverage a Reasonable Requirement? Lessons Learned from a Space Software Project

Christian R. Prause[1]([✉]), Jürgen Werner[2], Kay Hornig[2], Sascha Bosecker[2], and Marco Kuhrmann[3]

[1] German Aerospace Center, Bonn, Germany
christian.prause@dlr.de
[2] Test Spacecom GmbH, Backnang, Germany
{Juergen.Werner,Kay.Hornig,Sascha.Bosecker}@tesat.de
[3] Institute for Applied Software Systems Engineering,
Clausthal University of Technology, Goslar, Germany
kuhrmann@acm.org

Abstract. To ensure the dependability and safety of spaceflight devices, rigorous standards are defined. Among others, one requirement from the European Cooperation for Space Standardization (ECSS) standards is 100% test coverage at software unit level. Different stakeholders need to have a good knowledge of the implications of such a requirement to avoid risks for the project that this requirement might entail. In this paper, we study if such a 100% test coverage requirement is a reasonable one. For this, we interviewed the industrial developers who ran a project that had the sole goal of achieving 100% unit test coverage in a spaceflight software. We discuss costs, benefits, risks, effects on quality, interplay with surrounding conditions, and project management implications. We distill lessons learned with which we hope to support other developers and decision makers when considering a 100% unit test coverage requirement.

Keywords: Validation and verification · Software quality · Unit testing · Test coverage · Expert interviews · Spaceflight · Software criticality · Process requirements

1 Introduction

Software has become key to spacecrafts. It is the devices' brain that, among other things, maintains altitude and orbit, reads and analyzes sensor data, and controls the hardware. In particular, software is key to detect, isolate, and recover from unexpected situations and failures and, eventually, software ensures communication with ground stations. Due to the special environment, once deployed, a spacecraft has to 'survive' autonomously. Maintenance of its hardware is—if at all possible—impractical.

More fatal than crashing software is software that performs in the wrong way, as it may give commands that destroy a device or the whole spacecraft.

© Springer International Publishing AG 2017
M. Felderer et al. (Eds.): PROFES 2017, LNCS 10611, pp. 351–367, 2017.
https://doi.org/10.1007/978-3-319-69926-4_25

For instance, recently, the *Hitomi* telescope was erroneously commanded by its software to start spinning faster and faster until it disintegrated [22]. A software problem caused the recent crash of the *Schiaparelli* lander, which prematurely released its parachute several hundred kilometers above ground: Contradicting calculations of sensor data made the navigation software erroneously assume the lander had already touched Mars' surface [20]. Another software problem hit the Mars rover *Spirit* 18 Sols[1] after landing. The rover was caught in the rebooting cycle as it could not read a full fixed-memory block. The rover successfully passed a 10-Sol test concerning exactly this kind of problem prior to landing, yet, the memory bank was full at Sol 18, and the rover could only be put back into operation by using some 'backdoors' in the system [1]. Hence, software failures in space devices can be costly. Malfunctioning spacecrafts, moreover, may seriously threaten human life or the environment, e.g., remnants of space probes orbiting Earth endanger other satellites[2], uncontrolled reentry might endanger whole regions, e.g., ROSAT's uncontrolled reentry [18], and so forth. Software of a space device has to be dependable (i.e., reliable, available, and maintainable) and safe. To ensure high dependability and safety, space software and systems are developed under a strict quality and product assurance regime according to an extensive system of standards [19].

Context. The standards of the *European Cooperation for Space Standardization* (ECSS) are a coherent and comprehensive collection of standards addressing all areas of spaceflight. At the highest level, the ECSS standards are divided into management, engineering, and product assurance (quality) branches, and further subdivided into so-called areas. Each standard comprises a large number of requirements prescribing what is to be achieved. The standards ECSS-E-ST-40C (Software Engineering; [6]) and ECSS-Q-ST-80C (Software Product Assurance; [8]) address the development and product assurance of software for space applications. One of the standards' requirements for highly-critical software is that "100% code branch coverage at unit testing level" must be achieved. However, ECSS prescribes 100% for classes[3] A and B only [6], but leaves coverage for classes C and D open to negotiation. Achieving a high—or even a full—coverage

---

[1] A Sol is a day on Mars, which is 24 h 37 min, while a day on Earth is 23 h 56 min. The time unit Sol is used to run Mars operations and to not have the demand of continuously converting time.

[2] Estimates mention more than 500,000 pieces of junk, so-called 'space debris', orbiting Earth at high speeds of dozens of km/s [17]. Due to their extreme speeds, the kinetic energy of even small particles of only a few millimeters can cause impact craters of several dozen centimeters on the spacecraft, and lead to fatal and catastrophic effects like disintegration of the target.

[3] The ECSS standards define four levels for criticality from A to D (ECSS-Q-ST-30C [7]). For instance, criticality class A comprises catastrophic events, e.g., loss of life, launch site facilities, or the entire spacecraft. Class B is for the risk of losing the ability to perform the mission (loss of mission), and Class C for a major mission degradation. The LCT system, which is the subject of this paper (see Sect. 2) is classified as B (system), and its software as C.

is demanding, though. Adopting Tom Cargill's 90/90 rule [4] to unit testing, one could state: *The first 90% of the unit test code accounts for the first 90% of the development time. The remaining 10% of the unit test code accounts for the other 90% of the development time.* So, what happens, if contracting bodies ask for a 100% unit test coverage?

Contribution. In this paper, we report lessons learned from a space software project that had the goal of reaching a test coverage of 100% using unit tests for the flight software of a laser communication device (LCT). While the project very closely reached the goal of 100% test coverage (>99.5%), the effort turned out to be tremendous. Two developers spent two years developing the unit tests for a software of about 25,000 lines of code. Using semi-structured expert interviews, we studied how the project incrementally increased the test coverage to achieve the 100%-goal. We present lessons learned to stimulate a critical discussion about cost, benefits, and reasonableness of the 100% test coverage requirement.

Outline. The remainder of the paper is organized as follows: Sect. 2 provides the background of the project reviewed. Section 3 presents the research design, before we present our findings in Sect. 4. Section 5 discusses related work. Finally, Sect. 6 concludes the paper.

2   Background

The 'information society' relies on data and data exchange; and the amount is increasing year-by-year. More than 100 communication satellites in service build the communication backbone providing communication, bringing internet to remote locations, and broadcasting tens of thousands of television and radio programs worldwide.

The *Copernicus* program of the European Commission aims to establish a European capacity for earth observation by providing atmosphere, maritime, land, climate, emergency and security services. Several *Sentinel* satellites are the program's heart and produce large amounts of data. For instance, *Sentinel-2A* orbits Earth at an altitude of 786 km, delivering optical images on 13 spectral channels at a depth of 12 Bit per channel at resolutions of up to 10 m. A typical image is a tile of 100 km^2, or approx. 500 MB. A setup of two *Sentinel* satellites generates up to 1.6 TB of compressed raw image data per day, or 160 MBit/s continuously. Having access to imagery as quickly as possible is crucial for a number of *Copernicus* applications. However, earth's curvature prevents continuous radio communication with ground stations in Europe (broken line-of-sight) [9].

Laser Communication. To overcome this limitation, *Sentinel* satellites use the *European Data Relay System* (EDRS). EDRS features geostationary satellites at 36,000 km altitude that have a permanent link to European ground stations (Fig. 1). EDRS and *Sentinel* satellites carry novel *Laser Communication Terminal* (LCT) devices to establish laser links among one another to overcome

Fig. 1. Sentinel and AlphaSat satellite link, and relay to Earth (source: Tesat Spacecom GmbH).

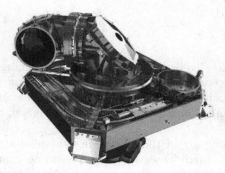

Fig. 2. The Laser Communication Terminal (source: Tesat Spacecom GmbH).

bandwidth limitations and to reduce off-line windows (Fig. 2). LCT devices allow for data transfer rates of up to 1.8 GBit/s. For this, the LCT laser has to hit a target of 200 m in diameter from a distance of 45,000 km, which corresponds to a moving 2-Euro coin from a 6.8 Km distance. Besides 'housekeeping' activities, the LCT software is primarily responsible for laser-targeting and controlling the hardware, e.g., power management or controlling the coolant system for the laser. Using software allows for precise targeting of the laser and, moreover, the software allows for compensating degrading hardware, and failure detection, isolation and recovery (FDIR).

The LCT Device. LCT plays a key role for the *Sentinel* and EDRS satellites, and for the *Copernicus* program as a whole. Due to the criticality, software quality is crucial and, therefore, quality assurance is a vital part of the system's development. Development of the LCT device itself stretched over several projects and lasted longer than a decade, resulting in several changes of key personnel. Furthermore, the LCT project involves several stakeholders: The LCT devices are developed by Tesat Spacecom GmbH, which was contracted by the national space agency, the German Aerospace Center (DLR) that also defined the quality requirements. Those requirements are, basically, grounded in ECSS standards, yet differ in some aspects, and, in particular, are tailored to project characteristics according to different technical, programmatic and risk criteria [19]. The *Sentinel 2* and *EDRS-A* satellites that host the LCTs are manufactured by Airbus DS on behalf of the European Space Agency (ESA), which applies mostly unmodified ECSS.

Within the conglomerate of partners involved and standards to implement, the ECSS standards received a major revision (*Issue B* to *Issue C*) while the LCT devices were produced. The new revision makes test coverage a first-class-citizen. Even though LCT was rigorously quality assured[4], the manufacturer did not yet collect test coverage data. This led to a situation in which test coverage was unknown while contracting agencies insisted on the new 100% test coverage requirement and proving its fulfillment. To overcome this situation, an agreement among the involved parties was made to initiate a separate project, which had the goal of increasing test coverage to 100% before the launch of the satellite.

3 Research Design

This section describes our research design, starting with describing the research objective and the research questions in Sect. 3.1. Section 3.2 describes the data collection procedures, including the interview instrument and the subjects selection. The analysis procedures are described in Sect. 3.3, and we discuss threats to validity in Sect. 3.4.

3.1 Research Objective and Questions

The overall objective of this study is to shed light on what a 100% coverage-requirement entails. We aim to study whether 100% test coverage is a reasonable requirement, what experienced practitioners "normally" consider good/high quality, and what benefits practitioners see in going beyond "normal" coverage

---

[4] The product assurance process performed so far includes several parties and procedures. The device manufacturer's product assurance reports to and is supervised by the customer's product assurance (cf. [19]). Further involved on satellite-level are the customer's and the prime contractor's product assurance. At the technical level V&V activities include, inter alia, static analyses, verification controls' and reviews. At device level, separate test teams carry out software tests in isolation and as part of the integrated device prior to shipment for full integration and system testing.

and towards 100%. We collect information about the practitioners' perception of the requirement's effects on costs, benefits, risks, its interplay with surrounding conditions, and project management implications. Hence, the overall research question investigates:

RQ: *Is 100% test coverage a reasonable requirement?*

3.2 Implementation

The study was conducted as semi-structured interview with experts in a 2-day workshop. We talked to all interviewees separately.

Interview Instrument. Table 1 shows the guideline of the semi-structured interview. The table shows the eight top-level 'entry' questions and (selected) detailed questions. In total, the guideline comprises a maximum of 66 questions in eight categories to ensure all relevant topics are addressed in every interview. In the interview, the participants were asked the entry question of the respective category to start the conversation. The interviewers traced the guideline and only asked follow-up questions from the question pools if information was not provided or if responses required clarification.

Interview Subjects. This paper reports on the interviews with the project's core personnel, i.e., the two developers and the project manager. For the developers, it was their first space project. The project manager already had a few years of experience in the space domain. All interviewees previously worked in other embedded software domains, mostly automotive software. They all look back on an industrial development experience of 10–25 years, working primarily with the languages C and C++ (C is the predominant language in space projects).

Interview Procedure. Before the interviews, we informed interviewees about the interview and its purpose, and asked them to prepare themselves. Participation was voluntary; no test development team member opted out. The interviews were conducted individually and face-to-face at the company's site and took between 60–90 min. One researcher preceded the interview using the guideline. The second one made short notes and only asked clarifying or follow-up questions. Each interview was audio recorded. Finally, all participants were summoned for a wrap-up session to clarify possibly remaining open points, ask things we might have missed, and to provide room for further discussion.

Project Performance Data. Complementing the qualitative data collected in the interview, we had access to project performance data, notably, the test coverage statistics. These data sets were included in our analysis to complement and to help interpret the qualitative data.

Table 1. Summary of the interview guideline, including (selected) detailed questions used to drive the interview.

No.	Top-level Question/Question Category	#Q
1.	Demographics	5
	Questions: Role in the organization? Role in the project? Years of experience in Space projects? Years of experience in using the development environment? Did you do something like this before?	
2.	Is achieving 100% test coverage a reasonable goal?	13
	Selected Detailed Questions: What level of test coverage do you consider 'normal'? What level of test coverage do you consider efficient from an economical perspective? Which minimum level of test coverage do your clients usually expect you to deliver? For what kind of critical software do you consider a 100% test coverage always necessary? Which methods and techniques do you apply to maximize test coverage? Related to your personal experience, do you expect positive impact on the overall system quality?	
3.	Have you achieved the project goals?	10
	Selected Detailed Questions: Have you reached the 100% test coverage? What were the biggest organizational challenges? What were the biggest technical challenges? Are there further factors that positively/negatively affect the reachability of the 100% goal? Did the quality of the system improve (due to the 100% goal)?	
4.	Development tools and methods	20
	Selected Detailed Questions: Which positive/negative impact did the programming language(s) have on the 100% goal? Did you have to adhere to an external standard (multiple standards)? If yes, were these standards supportive for the management, developers, or quality assurance? If yes, how did these standards influence your selected approach? If yes, does your software fulfill all requirements set by the standards completely? Which tool to measure test coverage was used? Would you rate your chosen approach more 'agile' or more 'traditional'?	
5.	Extra (general) questions	4
	Questions: How many errors were found through unit testing? When were the most errors found? (time, at coverage rate of x%, distribution function) How big is the overall software system? How big is the test system?	
6.	Static Verification	5
	Questions: Which tools and methods were used in the project to support the static verification? Was there a considerable flow of information to and from static verification? If yes, how was the information flow implemented, and what did the information exchange comprise? Were synergy effects between both approaches observed? Did the testing make the static verification dispensable (or vice versa)?	
7.	Software Metrics	4
	Questions: Why did you collect KPIs in your project? Was collecting KPIs beneficial to the project (KPIs, e.g., coverage, test lines, etc.)? Would you have liked to collect even more or more sophisticated KPIs? What other KPIs would you have liked to collect?	
8.	Lessons Learned	5
	Questions: What should others know, who face the same situation? What should be the learning for the space agency as client? What is a general take-away for clients concerning the 100% goal? What are your own lessons learned from this project? From your experience, what are the biggest risks in this kind of project?	

#Q: Number of questions per top-level question/question category

3.3 Analysis Procedures

To qualitatively analyze the interview data, both researchers performed an initial review to plan the transcription and to revise the data analysis plan. A secretary was appointed to transcribe the interviews, which was performed interactively with regular consultations and quality assurance on (tentative) results. Based on the transcripts, we qualitatively analyzed the data to extract the required information and to answer the research questions. Project performance data amended the analysis[5].

3.4 Validity Considerations

The lessons learned are based on the experts' opinions expressed during the interviews. Although the experts are experienced industrial developers, we still convey opinions related to one particular project only. The interviews were conducted during the final week of the project. One of the interviewers was also the customer's appointed software quality manager during the project. While this situation possibly affected interviewees' responses (see also disadvantages of interviews as stated in [23]), it has to be noted that the project was conducted primarily on demand from the prime/satellite customer. To improve the objectivity of the interview, an external researcher, who was not involved in the project, was called in. Due to this interview setup, the participants could speak rather freely. The interviews were conducted in the participants' mother tongue (German), and quotes presented in this paper were translated to English from the German interview transcripts afterward. We tried to preserve as many intricacies of the responses as possible, yet, there is the risk that a few subtleties have been lost during translation. The interviewees were given the opportunity to review the completed paper, and encouraged to provide clarifications and comments.

4 Results

In this section, we analyze quantitative project performance data (Sect. 4.1) and condense lessons learned based on qualitative findings from interviews in Sect. 4.2.

4.1 Quantitative Data

The project tracked test-coverage progress on a daily basis. This resulted in approx. 400 data points covering approx. 700 days. The actual project duration was longer than two years because of the necessary management activities (ramp-up times, creation of documents, reviews, delivery and acceptance, etc.). Figure 3 plots the percentage of code covered. The curve is quite linear for the most part of the project. However, it bends when it reaches approximately 90% of coverage. This indicates that the last few percent of coverage require significantly more effort.

---

[5] Due to the sensitivity of the data, we only present excerpts and anonymized results.

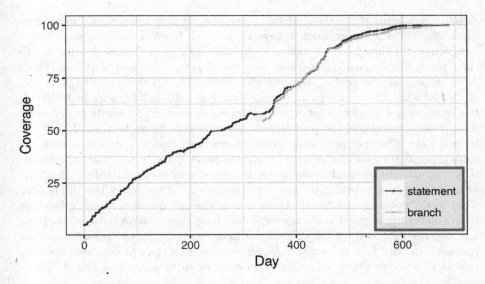

Fig. 3. Statement and branch coverage over time.

Figure 3 also compares statement coverage to branch coverage. Branch coverage was not monitored in the first place. The data shows that—by its nature—it tends to be a bit lower than statement coverage if not monitored. At the same time, however, it is not far out. Once monitored, branch coverage can be improved in conjunction with statement coverage without much additional effort. This changed upon reaching approx. 90% of coverage, when branch coverage started to fall behind, until it again catches up when getting closer to 100%. As stated in the interviews: *"In the beginning, coverage increased quite linearly. Of course, there were some disturbances* [e.g., Christmas]. *But the last few percent were really difficult."* The unit test development project found between 20 to 30 issues that could have been interpreted as actual errors. Less than three of these errors detected were considered having a potentially serious impact on the device's functionality. The project caused a development effort of four person years plus support staff for about 25,000 lines of code (LoC).

4.2 Lessons Learned

This study aimed at collecting experience from a project in which a test coverage of 100% should have been achieved in order to meet requirements defined by an external standard. From the qualitative analysis of the interviews conducted, we extract the following lessons learned.

100% Coverage Is Unusual but Achievable. To start the interviews, we asked participants if they ever faced a similar requirement before. Prior to this project, all participants worked for different companies. Yet, all of them faced *"such a requirement for the first time, and for the first time it was stated that explicitly."* Furthermore, neither have they faced *"such a high coverage ratio"* before nor did they have to realize it *"in this way, as a follow-up project."* In their previous experience, coverage *"was not directly being looked at"*, and *"was an issue only in the area of [complex electronics, i.e.,] ASIC and FPGA"*.

Asked what they consider a 'normal' coverage, the participants had difficulties in naming a precise number, as *"it depends on what one wants to achieve"*. As a general reference, the participants mentioned it *"may be around 80% [... because] the effort per percentage point of coverage, typically increases dramatically towards the end of a project."* Yet, one participant stated that, in general, referring to all static and dynamic verification techniques available, *"when you have reached more than 90%, you are doing well."* This raises the discussion, what 'good' coverage is after all; because over the last decades, the threshold for what constitutes a 'good' coverage ratio may have risen: *"With reasonable effort, I would say 90% is a lot. In this project here, everything went smooth until we reached 95% and then it became difficult, because you start to deal with the code that is difficult to reach. [...] My experience in early years was that 85% was excellent."*

Nevertheless, participants basically agreed that a 100% coverage can be achieved. Nitpicking, the project reached "only" a coverage of 99.9% and one participant stated: *"100%—you can say good-bye to that—but 100 minus epsilon is probably possible."*, but another one disagreed: *"100%, and I really mean 100 dot zero percent, is definitely achievable."* In fact, true 100% or 100%-epsilon, is probably an academic question, as from a practical perspective other problems are more relevant.

100% Coverage Is Sometimes Necessary. One participant considers 100% as *"a necessary, but not a sufficient condition for quality"*. He explained that coverage *"should be 100%"* because otherwise there is the *"risk of fair-weather tests [..., i.e.,] that potentially the most complex, hardest to understand, or most difficult to reach functionality is left untested."* If less was the target, developers might *"pick the 80% most beautiful tests that they can wangle most easily, [... and think that as they] satisfied the metric, now everything is fine."* The remaining 20%, *"what harm can it do?"*. But if *"the remaining 20% are full of bugs"*, then the other 80% are useless.

However, all participants were in agreement that *"for criticality class A, i.e., loss of human live or catastrophic consequences, I would demand 100%"*. Also *"a high financial loss"* was seen as justification. But for criticality class B— *"i.e., loss of mission, that is an economic loss"* or for *"a smaller satellite that just orbits some place where nobody cares"*, participants agreed that *"less may be potentially fine."* One participant, however, mentioned that *"one should always target 100%. The reason is: if I aim at less than 100%, what do I leave out? How do I justify not testing something?"*

100% Coverage Brings in New Risks. All participants agree that the 100% coverage requirement introduces risks to a project. In particular, the participants saw a risk to the schedule, i.e., that they might *"lock jaws in some problem and let the project slip out of control already at its beginning."* A development team needs to be aware of and have a strategy to cope with this risk. Moreover, they all agreed that a fixed and high coverage ratio imposes a financial risk as it is difficult to say in advance what and how many *"hard nuts"* are in the project. If developers *"postponed the difficult things"*, the real difficulties will start at some point. This point may be somewhere between 80% and 95% (so-called Pareto Principle[6]) and the 100% coverage requirement is likely beyond this point. In the studied project, two developers required two years to achieve 100% coverage for about 25,000 lines of code. A customer demanding this should know that *"it will cost a lot. It is going to be expensive"*.

Don't Optimize for the 100%-Metric. On the one hand, a clear point was made: *"100%: it sounds really good. But I think those who demand it, do not know what they are asking for."* On the other hand, participants mentioned several risks of setting a 100%-requirement. Therefore, it is necessary that all stakeholders understand the implications of such a requirement. As mentioned before, the higher the coverage, the more expensive. The question is, however, whether this relationship is linear. The project curve in Fig. 3, which is extracted from the project performance data, is fairly linear and just bends at about 90%. The remaining 10%, however, do not account for about 80% of project effort. Consequently, the *Pareto principle* only applies very roughly here. This is in contrast to a quick analysis we did in preparation of the test coverage project. On the basis of test coverage data from a randomly chosen open source project, we found that to 'organically grown' unit tests (i.e., without using coverage metrics) the Pareto principle seems to fit better. While more rigorous verification of this observation is needed, it seems that the use of metrics effected the relationship between effort for developing tests and coverage. The use of metrics seems to be responsible for the linear relationship for most of the project duration. While using coverage measurements during the project made good (linear) progress possible, optimizing for a metric might have hidden downsides (see Sect. 5).

In the same vain as 'standard' discussions on metrics, 100% coverage is also just a metric, and focusing too much on it could mean that one *"loses track of the actual goal; which is to increase the quality."* Instead, testers might know best where to find bugs and how to use their *"available resources so that he will find all errors."* A misunderstood metric can create a sense of false security: *"I just want to say that I think it is bad to say: Now we have 80% unit tests, now it's fine."* A high coverage is not a guarantee of good quality.

---

[6] This is also called the "Pareto principle"; according to Joseph M. Juran who proposed the 80/20-rule, which roughly says that the first 80% are easy to achieve while the remaining 20% are not.

Develop a Proper Strategy to Maximize Coverage. Monitoring using metrics is important and a prerequisite to achieve a high coverage. However, aiming at high coverage also requires an appropriate development approach. When production code is developed, testing must already be planned to avoid problems that the participants faced in the project: *"Testability is a goal that one actually has to code into the code. It does not come automatically, along the way, or for free. It is a goal that one must prescribe."* Furthermore, when setting a test coverage requirement, customers should be careful that a plain 100% coverage may be too undifferentiated: *"What can be tested very well with unit tests is business logic* [e.g., a PI controller[7]] *because it abstracts from the hardware and the operating system, and because it can be reused. Here unit tests make a lot of sense"* and are *"economically reasonable"*. *"The hardware* [...] *and the operating system, and all the things at those lower layers are hard to test, and require a lot of effort, and they are not really what unit tests are intended for. You leave these things out, and the resulting percentage is what is economically reasonable."* So, if there is *"10% hardware-specific stuff,* [...] *90% are good tests."*

This includes that a test strategy has to pay attention to the different system parts. Hence, the participants also argued for considering a combination of different V&V techniques: unit tests are not an end in itself, but should be considered in the scope of the whole V&V ecosystem, where they complement each other. For example, *"reading from or writing to a register,* [...] *these are things* [...] *on a different level. They will certainly be caught by integration tests,"* and *"there were integration tests that covered large areas"*, so unit tests do not find many errors (see Sect. 4.1). Instead, *"unit tests were done to ensure certification of the software."* One may also consider the metric results of other static and dynamic *"verification techniques that have a notion of coverage"*. In this regard, the role of unit tests was also critically discussed by the participants: test-driven development leads to a high coverage (*"we certainly would have had 90%"*) but does not lead to 100%. It is *"not relevant whether or not you really reached 100%, but that interfaces were covered"*.

Eventually, even though a strategy needs to be in place to achieve a high coverage, our participants ended up with a fairly pragmatic approach: *Do easy things first.* One participant noted that *"it is normal: first one does the things that can be easily done."* It allows the team *"to get into a decent flow,* [...] *to carve out some lead initially, to be able to crack the hard nuts at the end."* If, at some later point, the project should *"slip out of control"*, it could be easier for negotiations if good progress has been made so far. Nonetheless—also regarding the 'special' setup of the studied project—the findings from the interview, again, confirm the saying: *You can't test quality into a product.* It has to be built in right from the start. The participants noted that unit testing cannot *"be done after the code freeze* [... when] *not a single bit is allowed to be changed."* Testing

---

[7] A proportional-integral (PI) controller is a control loop feedback mechanism that continuously computes the difference between an expected and an actual value for a variable (e.g., temperature, electrical current flow, angles,...) and applies a correction based on proportional, integral, and derivative terms.

"has to happen in parallel, or [... *as*] *test after coding.* [...] *It all depends on when one starts with the tests."* An extreme target value of 100% must be set early on and reflected in the quality assurance approach, or, otherwise, it may cause serious trouble.

100% Coverage Is Not a Sufficient Condition for Good Quality. The participants concluded that *"100% coverage is not a sufficient condition for good quality."* In fact, it might *"have a slight impact on quality"* because in the *"extreme case, one can achieve 100% coverage by just'running all code' but without doing a single test."* One just *"claims that one tested something"* but only shows that *"the functions did not crash".* It does not necessarily mean that *"the software/the functions really do what they are supposed to."* Hence, coverage is *"a start,* [...but] *one may not forget, there is also test depth. Test depth is difficult to measure."*

5   Related Work

According to Bennet and Wennberg [3], bug-fixing cost increases by magnitudes in later system lifecycle stages. In particular for space systems, however, bug-fixing cost could mean the system's cost in total, as a software failure might cause a complete system loss, e.g., as recently happened to ESA's *Schiaparelli* lander [20].

Therefore, rigorous software quality assurance as part of the overall product assurance is crucial. Hence, and as also found in our interviews, a 100%-coverage can be a reasonable requirement. However, the implications need to be considered as well, especially concerning the efficiency and effectiveness of the instrument (i.e., unit test) on the project's operation. For instance, Gokhale and Mullen empirically investigated the marginal value of increased testing [12]. In their tests, they observed an asymptotic convergence of test coverage towards 100%. The marginal coverage as a function of the number of tests decreases logarithmically, reaching almost zero at about 1,000 tests. Approximately linear growth of coverage ends between 50% and 80% of coverage. However, Arthur Lowell stated ironically that *"20% of the code has 80% of the errors. Find them, fix them!"* [2]. If he is right, then just a few percent of uncovered code might still contain many (critical) errors (see also [5]). And, eventually, Mockus et al. [16] found that, on the one hand, cost increases dramatically if achieving higher coverage rates, but on the other hand, reduction of field issues increases linearly. They conclude that, for most projects, (economically) optimal coverage rates are below 100%. However, it has to be mentioned that, to the best of our knowledge, test coverage and its economic implications to the space domain has not yet been investigated in detail as most of the papers listed above are concerned with 'normal' software-intensive systems. For instance, although Mockus et al. [16] might be right, in the space domain, even one 'field issue' might lead to a complete system loss. Referring to the *Schiaparelli* lander [20], there is no bug-fixing strategy; the probe is just gone.

Practitioners also have to be careful to not be trapped in 'chasing the rabbit'. In particular, Marick [14] describes the misuse of coverage metrics, e.g., in the problematic different perception of developers, managers, and product testers, and their respective constraints and requirements. He makes a clear statement that coverage (tools) should enhance thought, not replace it. On the other hand, Martin [15] demands a high coverage to be a goal of any professional development team. Yet, he is often criticized for this opinion, since people argue that a high coverage does not necessarily lead to meaningful tests. In this regard, the *2016 Software Testing Technology Report* by Vector Software [21] makes a strong statement that one of the most misunderstood issues with code coverage is its relevance to software quality. Authors conclude that a 100% code coverage should not be the goal of software testing, rather than the result of complete testing—a statement that we also found in our interviews.

Regarding the strategy to achieve a high coverage, our study revealed a fairly pragmatic approach. This comes as no surprise, as recent research illustrated a significantly different perspective on software testing [11]. That is, even though using the same terminology, industry and academia quite often put emphasis on different 'things'. On the other hand, empirical evidence on particular methods/approaches is rare. For example, Fucci et al. [10] found no difference in applying test-first or test-last approaches. Only thing that counts is the granularity (and quality) of the work packages and requirements specifications. Furthermore, even though driven by standards, quite often, safety-related requirements are implemented and assured in a mixed approach. For instance, Ingibergsson et al. [13] found a discrepancy between method- and development-level implementation of standards to adhere to quality requirements in the field of autonomous robotics—providing further support for [11]. Also, our interview participants emphasized the importance of combining different testing techniques, and that an improved combination of different verification and validation approaches (including e.g., static analyses), would be wiser than a fairly 'academic' (not to say 'bureaucratic') 100% coverage requirement; maybe even more efficient.

The paper at hand thus adds to the body of knowledge by studying high test coverage ratios in the domain of software and system development for space systems. This paper adds an experience report and lessons learned from a space project and shows a still present need to study (economic) reasonableness of a 100% coverage goal.

6   Conclusion

Space systems are critical systems that require substantial quality assurance during development. If errors occur, such systems might be completely lost. However, what is substantial quality assurance? According to the ECSS standards, software for space systems shall have 100% test coverage (for criticality classes A and B). Is this a reasonable goal? In order to answer this question, we studied a project performed in which a software system's test suite was to be improved towards meeting a 100% unit test coverage goal. Eventually, the team managed to achieve >99.5% test coverage (statement and branch coverage), yet, it became obvious that the effort required to implement such a comprehensive test suite was tremendous. Therefore, we wanted to reflect on the project and we wanted to study if the 100%-goal is a reasonable one.

This paper presents the findings of an interview study performed at *Tesat Spacecom* in the final phase of the *LCT* project (Sect. 2). Our leading question, *"Is 100% test coverage a reasonable requirement?"* was studied from different perspectives, e.g., need for 100% coverage, break-even points, and strategies to achieve this goal. The interviews provided numerous of valuable insights from which we condensed a set of lessons learned. There is some justification for setting 100% coverage as a requirement. However, a plain 100% requirement may be too undifferentiated, and one should really understand the effects and possible alternatives (which might find possible errors more cost-efficiently). In a nutshell, our interviews resulted in the following key lessons:

- 100% coverage is unusual but achievable
- 100% coverage is sometimes necessary
- 100% coverage brings in new risks
- Don't optimize for the 100%-metric
- Develop a proper strategy to maximize coverage
- 100% coverage is not a sufficient condition for good quality

Our findings include that there seems to be a break-even point between 80% and 95%, and everything beyond this points is increasingly costly and could introduce new project risks—which confirms findings reported so far in literature (Sect. 5). However, the interview revealed that, still, 100% coverage can be a reasonable quality requirement; even though a 100% requirement is not a good indicator for the software quality as such. Especially for dependable systems, the decision to test less also includes a decision of what *not* to test, i.e., which parts of the system to exclude from the tests. Feedback from an author of the test coverage requirements in ECSS standard was: Only the idea that some statements may never have been exercised at all by any test should be a source of anxiety. Yet, such a rule should not be taken and applied too literally, and be discussed carefully.

Furthermore, we found the participants arguing that 100% should not become a 'formal' goal only, which leads to a situation in which just a metric is optimized. 100% coverage should always be the result of good testing but it makes few sense as a goal in itself. So how should the issue be treated on the contractual and standards level? As a customer, one wants to have 100% unit test coverage but achieving it by a formal demand (requirement) does not guarantee quality.

Moreover, the test depth and applying different V&V techniques should be considered. Nonetheless, all participants agreed that lifting the unit test coverage to 100% ex-post has to be criticized (time, effort, no options to change the software due to already performed certification). If a high coverage must be achieved in a project, the respective approach needs to be defined upfront and implemented continuously.

Finally, regarding the question whether or not the ECSS goal of 100% test coverage is reasonable: if there is only a small chance to avoid an extreme risk from materializing, it should be seized. However, when resources are limited, one has to make the decision whether effort should be spent on increasing the unit test coverage ratio, or to better put emphasis on other V&V activities. Hence, the answer to the question whether 100% is a reasonable requirement still is: "It depends".

Limitations. As stated in Sect. 3.4, our interview only covers one particular project, which was in the special situation that the high degree of test coverage had to be achieved ex-post. Furthermore, we only interviewed one project team. Hence, our findings are grounded in a few developers' opinions and, therefore, are hard to generalize. Also, in the project studied, 100% coverage was not required from the beginning. That is, it remains unclear if the lessons learned would be the same if a project starts with such a requirement right from the beginning. Finally, further implications on the system as such were not in the scope of this study.

Future Work. As part of the future work, we plan to include the remaining interviews conducted with project support personnel into the evaluation. Furthermore, since the interviews revealed numerous interesting findings not directly aligned with the major research question, future work will put more emphasis on the other parts of the interviews. We also want to investigate links between techniques like "defensive programming" and their effect on coverage, and as a justification for not achieving 100% coverage. Finally, even though we already collected and presented some qualitative data (Sect. 4.1), we also plan to include more quantitative data into the study to gather further insights. We might still be able to obtain and to take into consideration some data that has high correlation with hard-to-test modules, like complexity, nesting depth, fan-in, fan-out, etc.

Acknowledgements. We thank our colleagues Karin Schmitz for transcribing the several hours of recorded interviews, and Björn Gütlich and Sabine Philipp-May for supporting our undertaking.

References

1. Adler, M.: Spirit Sol 18 Anomaly, September 2006. http://web.archive.org/web/20110605095126/www.planetary.org/blog/article/00000702
2. Arthur, L.J.: Quantum improvements in software system quality. Commun. ACM **40**(6), 46–52 (1997)
3. Bennett, T., Wennberg, P.: Eliminating embedded software defects prior to integration test. Qual. Assur. Inst. J. (2006)
4. Bentley, J.: Programming pearls. Commun. ACM **28**(9), 896–901 (1985)
5. Boehm, B., Basili, V.R.: Software defect reduction top 10 list. Computer **34**(1), 135–137 (2001)

6. ECSS-E-ST-40 Working Group: ECSS-E-ST-40C: Space engineering - Software. Standard, ECSS Secretariat, March 2009

7. ECSS-Q-ST-30 Working Group: ECSS-Q-ST-30C: Space product assurance - Dependability. Standard, ECSS Secretariat, March 2009

8. ECSS-Q-ST-80C Working Group: ECSS-Q-ST-80C: Space product assurance - Software product assurance. Standard, ECSS Secretariat, March 2009

9. ESA: Sentinel online (2017). https://sentinel.esa.int

10. Fucci, D., Erdogmus, H., Turhan, B., Oivo, M., Juristo, N.: A dissection of test-driven development: does it really matter to test-first or to test-last? IEEE Trans. Softw. Eng. (2017, in Press)

11. Garousi, V., Felderer, M.: Worlds apart: a comparison of industry and academic focus areas in software testing. IEEE Softw. (2017, in press)

12. Gokhale, S.S., Mullen, R.E.: The marginal value of increased testing: an empirical analysis using four code coverage measures. J. Braz. Comput. Soc. **12**(3), 13–30 (2006)

13. Ingibergsson, J.T.M., Schultz, U.P., Kuhrmann, M.: On the use of safety certi-fication practices in autonomous field robot software development: a systematic mapping study. In: Abrahamsson, P., Corral, L., Oivo, M., Russo, B. (eds.) PRO-FES 2015. LNCS, vol. 9459, pp. 335–352. Springer, Cham (2015). doi:10.1007/978-3-319-26844-6_25

14. Marick, B.: How to misuse code coverage. In: Proceedings of the 16th International Conference on Testing Computer Software, pp. 16–18 (1999)

15. Martin, R.C.: The Clean Coder: A Code of Conduct for Professional Programmers. Pearson Education, Upper Saddle River (2011)

16. Mockus, A., Nagappan, N., Dinh-Trong, T.T.: Test coverage and post-verification defects: a multiple case study. In: 2009 3rd International Symposium on Empirical Software Engineering and Measurement, pp. 291–301, October 2009

17. NASA: NASA Missions: Space Station, September 2013. https://www.nasa.gov/mission_pages/station/news/orbital_debris.html

18. NBC News: German satellite crashed over Asia's Bay of Bengal, October 2011. http://www.nbcnews.com/id/45032034/ns/technology_and_science-space

19. Prause, C.R., Bibus, M., Dietrich, C., Jobi, W.: Managing software process evo-lution for spacecraft from a customer's perspective. In: Kuhrmann, M., Münch, J., Richardson, I., Rausch, A., Zhang, H. (eds.) Managing Software Process Evolu-tion: Traditional, Agile and Beyond – How to Handle Process Change, pp. 137–163. Springer, Cham (2016). doi:10.1007/978-3-319-31545-4_8

20. Tolker-Nielsen, T.: EXOMARS 2016 - Schiaparelli anomaly inquiry. Report DG-I/2017/546/TTN, European Space Agency (ESA), May 2017

21. Vector Software, Inc.: Software testing technology report, p. 2016. Technical report, Vector Software, September 2016

22. Witze, A.: Software error doomed Japanese Hitomi spacecraft. Nature **533**, 18–19 (2016)

23. Wohlin, C., Runeson, P., Höst, M., Ohlsson, M.C., Regnell, B., Wesslén, A.: Exper-imentation in Software Engineering. Springer, Heidelberg (2012). doi:10.1007/978-3-642-29044-2

Exploratory Testing of Large-Scale Systems – Testing in the Continuous Integration and Delivery Pipeline

Torvald Mårtensson[1]([⊠]) [iD], Daniel Ståhl[2] [iD], and Jan Bosch[3] [iD]

[1] Saab AB, Linköping, Sweden
torvald.martensson@saabgroup.com
[2] Ericsson AB, Linköping, Sweden
daniel.stahl@ericsson.com
[3] Chalmers University of Technology, Gothenburg, Sweden
jan@janbosch.com

Abstract. In this paper, we show how exploratory testing plays a role as part of a continuous integration and delivery pipeline for large-scale and complex software products. We propose a test method that incorporates exploratory testing as an activity in the continuous integration and delivery pipeline, and is based on elements from other testing techniques such as scenario-based testing, testing in teams and testing in time-boxed sessions. The test method has been validated during ten months by 28 individuals (21 engineers and 7 flight test pilots) in a case study where the system under test is a fighter aircraft. Quantitative data from the case study company shows that the exploratory test teams produced more problem reports than other test teams. The interview results show that both engineers and test pilots were generally positive or very positive when they described their experiences from the case study, and consider the test method to be an efficient way of testing the system in the case study.

Keywords: Continuous delivery · Continuous integration · Exploratory testing · Large-scale systems · Software testing

1 Introduction

Exploratory testing was coined as a term by Cem Kaner in the book "Testing Computer Software" [1] 1988, and was then expanded upon as a teachable discipline by Kaner, Bach and Pettichord in their book "Lessons Learned in Software Testing" [2] in 2001. The test technique combines test design with test execution, and focuses on learning about the system under test.

Different setups exist for planning, execution and reporting exploratory testing. Testing can be organized as charters [3, 4] or tours [3, 5] which are conducted as sessions [3, 4] or threads [3]. Janet Gregory and Lisa Crispin [3] describe the test technique with the following words: "Exploratory testers do not enter into a test session with predefined, expected results. Instead, they compare the behavior of the system against what they might expect, based on experience, heuristics, and perhaps oracles. The difference is subtle, but meaningful." The core of the test technique is the focus on

© Springer International Publishing AG 2017
M. Felderer et al. (Eds.): PROFES 2017, LNCS 10611, pp. 368–384, 2017.
https://doi.org/10.1007/978-3-319-69926-4_26

learning, shown in for example Elisabeth Hendricksson's [4] definition of exploratory testing: "Simultaneously designing and executing tests to learn about the system, using your insights from the last experiment to inform the next".

Coevally with the evolution of exploratory testing, continuous integration and other continuous practices emerged during the 1990s and early 2000s. The exact moment for the birth of each practice is up for debate. Continuous integration is often referred to as a term coming from either Kent Beck's book "Extreme Programming" [6] in 1999 or Martin Fowler's popular article [7] in 2006, and the term continuous delivery seems to have been established by Jez Humble and David Farley in the book "Continuous Delivery" [8] in 2011. Automated testing is described as a corner stone of continuous practices, and automated tests tend to be the focus when test activities are assembled to a continuous integration and delivery pipeline (shown in Fig. 1). This pipeline splits the test process into multiple stages, and is described with different terminology by Duvall as "stage builds" [9], by Larman and Vodde as "multi-stage CI system" [10] or by Humble and Farley as the "deployment pipeline" or "integration pipeline" [8]. Humble and Farley [8] include exploratory testing in the final stage before release to the customer. We believe that exploratory testing also can play an important role early in the integration flow, especially when developing large-scale systems with many dependencies between the subsystems.

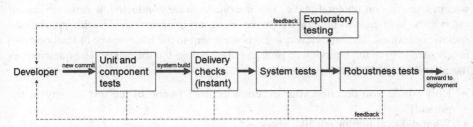

Fig. 1. An example of a continuous integration and delivery pipeline (including exploratory testing), showing the flow of test activities that follows a commit of new software

Based on this, the topic of this paper is to answer the following research question: *How can exploratory testing be used in the continuous integration and delivery pipeline during development of large-scale and complex software products?*

The contribution of this paper is three-fold. First, it presents a test method for large-scale and complex software products. Second, the paper shows how exploratory testing plays a role as part of a continuous integration and delivery pipeline for large-scale and complex software products. Third, it provides quantitative data and interview results from a large-scale industry project. The remainder of this paper is organized as follows. In the next section, we present the research method. This is followed in Sect. 3 by a study of related literature. In Sect. 4 we present the test method, followed by validation in Sect. 5. Threats to validity are discussed in Sect. 6. The paper is then concluded in Sect. 7.

2 Research Method

The first step to answer the research question stated in Sect. 1 was to conduct a systematic literature review (according to Kitchenham [11]), which is presented in Sect. 3. The question driving the review was "Which test methods related to exploratory testing and testing of large-scale and complex systems have been proposed in literature?"

The test method for exploratory testing of large-scale systems was developed based on related published literature and experiences in the case study company. The test method was validated using the following methods to achieve method and data triangulation [12]:

- *Systematic literature review*: Comparison of the test method and related work found in literature.
- *Validation interviews*: Interviews with 18 engineers and 7 flight test pilots who used the test method during ten months.
- *Analysis of quantitative data*: Exploratory analysis of quantitative data (problem reports and time used in the test rig) retrieved from the case study.

Interviews were held with 25 of the 28 individuals who were participating in the test activity in the case study. The remaining three had in two cases changed jobs, and was in one case on parental leave. The interviews were conducted as semi-structured interviews, held face-to-face or by phone using an interview guide with pre-defined specific questions. The interview questions were sent to the interviewee at least one day in advance to give the interviewee time to reflect before the interview. The questions in the interview guide were:

- How would you describe your experiences from [name of the test activity in the project]?
- What did you like or not like about...
  - The planning meetings?
  - The briefings before testing?
  - The test sessions in the rig?
  - The debriefings after testing?
- What do you like or not like about [name of the test activity in the project] compared to other types of test activities?
- Are you interested in participating in this type of activity again?

The interview results were analyzed based on thematic coding analysis as described by Robson [13, pp. 467–481], resulting in three main themes corresponding to the characteristics of the test method (each supported by statements or comments by between 15 and 20 of the interviewees). The process was conducted iteratively to increase the quality of the analysis. Special attention was paid to outliers (interviewee comments that do not fit into the overall pattern) according to the guidelines from Robson [13], in order to strengthen the explanations and isolate the mechanisms involved.

Detailed data on e.g. types of scenarios selected by the test teams, types of issues found during the test sessions or detailed interview results are not included in this research paper due to non-disclosure agreements with the case study company.

3 Reviewing Literature

3.1 Criteria for the Literature Review

To investigate whether solutions related to the research question have been presented in published literature, a systematic literature review [11] was conducted. A review protocol was created, containing the question driving the review ("Which test methods related to exploratory testing and testing of large-scale and complex systems have been proposed in literature?") and the inclusion and exclusion criteria. The inclusion criterion and the exclusion criterion for the review are shown in Table 1.

Table 1. Inclusion and exclusion criteria for the literature review

Inclusion criterion	Yield
Publications matching the Scopus search string TITLE-ABS-KEY ("exploratory testing" AND software) on March 27, 2017	52
Exclusion criterion	Remaining
Excluding duplicates, conference proceedings summaries and publications with no available full-text	39

To identify published literature, a Scopus search was conducted. The search was updated before writing this research paper, in order to include the state-of-the-art. The decision to use only one indexing service was based on the fact that we in previous work have found Scopus to cover a large majority of published literature in the field, with other search engines only providing very small result sets not already covered by Scopus.

3.2 Results from the Literature Review

An overview of the publications found in the systematic literature review is presented in Table 2. The review of the 39 publications retrieved from the search revealed that five of the publications were not directly related to exploratory testing. These papers use the term "exploratory testing" as a keyword without a single mention in the article itself or only mentioning it in passing. In addition to that, one of the papers was a poster which contained the same information as another paper found in the search.

Ten of the papers were related to methods and tools, typically combining two test techniques such as model-based testing and exploratory testing [14–18]. Two papers proposed different approaches to combine script-based testing and exploratory testing [19, 20] and one paper described how to extract unit tests and from exploratory testing [21]. One paper discussed "guidance for exploratory testing through problem frames" [22] and finally one paper investigated the feasibility of using a multilayer perceptron neural network as an exploratory test oracle [23].

Table 2. An overview of the publications found in the systematic literature review

Topic of the publications	Number of papers
Not relevant	5
Poster	1
Methods/tools	10
Effectiveness and efficiency of test methods	14
How exploratory testing is used	5
Reporting experiences	4
Summary	39

Fourteen of the publications discussed the effectiveness and efficiency of different test methods. Two of those were systematic literature reviews [24, 25] and one combined a systematic literature review and a survey [26]. Eight papers [27–34] compared exploratory testing and scripted testing (also referred to as test case based testing or confirmatory testing). The comparisons were based on either true experiments or experiences from industry projects. Sviridova et al. [35] discuss effectiveness of exploratory testing and proposes to use scenarios. Micallef et al. [36] discuss how exploratory testing strategies are utilized by trained and not trained testers, and how this affect the type of defects the testers find. Raappana et al. [37] report the effectiveness of a test method called "team exploratory testing", which is defined as a way to perform session-based exploratory testing in teams.

Five papers describe in different ways how exploratory testing is used by the testers, based on either a true experiment [38], a survey [39], video recordings [40] or interviews [41, 42]. Itkonen and Rautiainen [42], Shoaib et al. [38] and Itkonen et al. [40] describe how the tester's knowledge, experiences and personality are important while performing exploratory software testing in industrial settings. Itkonen et al. [41] present the results of a qualitative observation study on the manual testing practices, and presents a number of exploratory strategies: "User interface exploring", "Exploring weak areas", "Aspect oriented testing", "Top-down functional exploring", "Simulating a real usage scenario", and "Smoke testing by intuition and experience".

Finally, four papers [43–46] report experiences from exploratory testing in industry, but without presenting any quantitative or qualitative data as validation. Suranto [44] describes experiences from using exploratory testing in an agile project. Pichler and Ramler [46] describes experiences from developing and testing a visual graphical user interface editor, and touches upon the use of exploratory testing as part of an iterative development process. Gouveia [43] reports experiences from using exploratory testing of web applications in parallel with automated test activities in the continuous integration and delivery pipeline.

In summary, we found no publications that discussed exploratory testing in the context of large-scale and complex software system. Some publications touched on topics related to the subject, such as iterative development and continuous integration (which are commonly used during development of large-scale and complex software systems).

4 Exploratory Testing of Large-Scale Systems

4.1 Characteristics of the Test Method

The *test method for exploratory testing of large-scale systems* is based on related published literature and experiences from the case study company. In this case, exploratory testing is used to test a large-scale and complex system, which may consist of a range of subsystems that are tightly coupled with a lot of dependencies.

The motivation behind developing the test method was an interest in the case study company to increase test efficiency, and to find problems related to the integration of subsystems earlier in the development process. The transformation to continuous development practices implies a transformation from manual to automated testing. This requires large investments, both a large initial investment in implementing automated test cases and later costs for maintaining the test cases to keep up with changes in the system under test. For test activities that is likely to not remain static (the same specification is run over and over again) it is an alternative to utilize the flexibility of experienced engineers in manual test activities. ·

The test method is designed to complement automated testing in the continuous integration and delivery pipeline, and to provide different feedback and insights than the results from an automated test case. The characteristics of the test method are:

- *Exploratory testing as an activity in the continuous integration and delivery pipeline*: Testing is conducted with an exploratory approach where the testers simultaneously learn about the system's characteristics and behavior. Testing is done regularly on the latest system build, which has passed the test activity in the preceding step in the continuous integration and delivery pipeline.
- *Session-based testing in teams with experienced engineers representing different subsystems:* Testing is conducted in time-boxed sessions by teams of hand-picked experienced engineers, representing the different subsystems of the product. If the size or complexity of the system under test cannot be covered by a single team, the test scope can be split between several teams.
- *Scenario-based testing with an end-user representative as part of the test team*: Testing is conducted in scenarios, which represent how the product will be used by the end-user. An end-user representative is participating in both planning and test execution, securing that the scenarios are reflecting appropriate conditions.

The characteristics of the test method are in different ways described or touched upon in published literature. Exploratory testing has been described (at least briefly) in the context of agile or iterative development [3, 44, 46] and one report describes how exploratory testing is used in the "continuous integration pipeline" [43]. Exploratory testing is often combined with the use of sessions [3, 4, 28, 37, 40] and the concept of testing in teams has been described [37] or at least touched upon [3]. There are also publications that enhance the importance of experience and knowledge [38, 40, 42]. The use of scenarios is also described in different ways [3, 5, 35, 41], but not specifically with an end-user representative as part of the test team.

4.2   Using the Test Method

The test team work together in planning workshops, test sessions and debriefing meetings (shown in Fig. 2).

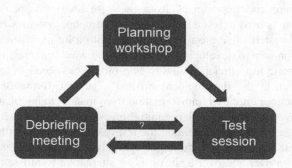

Fig. 2. The flow between planning meetings, test sessions and debriefing meetings

At the *planning meeting*, the test team discusses ideas for testing that could result in finding uncovered problem areas. The team members prioritize and group the test ideas into scenarios, which could be executed during a test session. A scenario is a chain of events that could be introduced by either the product's end-user, derive from a problem in the product's software or hardware systems, or be coming from other systems or the environment where the product is operated (e.g. change of weather if the product is a car). The test team is monitoring the reports from other test activities in the continuous integration and delivery pipeline, in order to follow new or updated functions or new problems that have been found which could affect the testing.

During the *test session*, the scenarios are tested in a test environment which is as production-like as possible. The test environment must also be equipped so that the test team is able to test fault injection and collect data using recording tools. Before the test session the team must also decide on test approaches for the planned test sessions: Should the team observe as many deviations as possible or stop and try to find root causes? Should the team focus on the intended scope or change the scope if other issues come up?

The *debriefing meeting* is used by the team to summarize the test session. The responsibility to write problem reports or follow up open issues found in the test session is distributed among the team members. The team should consider if a problem should have been caught at a test activity earlier in the pipeline, and report this in an appropriate way. Decisions are made if the tested scenarios should be revisited at the next session or not. The team should also discuss how team collaboration and other aspects of test efficiency could be improved.

5 Validation

5.1 The Case Study

The case study company is developing airborne systems and their support systems. The main product is the Gripen fighter aircraft, which has been developed in several variants. Gripen was taken into operational service in 1996. An updated version of the aircraft (Gripen C/D) is currently operated by the air forces in Czech Republic, Hungary, South Africa, Sweden and Thailand. The next major upgrade (Gripen E/F) will include both major changes in hardware systems (sensors, fuel system, landing gear etc.) and a completely new software architecture.

The test method described in Sect. 4 was applied to a project within the case study company for ten months. The system under test was the aircraft system with functionality for the first Gripen E test aircraft, which was tested in a test rig. The test pilot was maneuvering the aircraft in a cockpit replica, which included real displays, panels, throttle and maneuvering stick. In the rig the software was executing on the same type of computers as in the real aircraft. The aircraft computers were connected to an advanced simulation computer, which simulated the hardware systems in the aircraft (e.g. engine, fuel system, landing gear) as well as a tactical environment. A visual environment was presented on an arc-shaped screen. The test team communicated with the pilot from a test leader station in a separate room. From the test leader station the tester could observe the pilot's displays and the presentation of the aircraft's visual environment. The test team could also observe the behavior of the software in the aircraft computers and inject faults in the simulator during flight (e.g. malfunction of a subsystem in the aircraft).

Continuous integration practices such as automated testing, private builds and integration build servers were applied in the development of software for the Gripen computer systems. When a developer committed new software to the mainline, the new system baseline was tested in multiple stages in a pipeline similar to the example shown in Fig. 1. All test activities on unit, component and system level which were effectuated up to weekly frequency were automated tests, followed by exploratory testing and other manually executed test activities.

Testing was conducted in sessions, starting with four hours per session which after two months was changed to three hours. The testing started with two teams, followed by a third team after a month. The teams tested at a frequency of one test session per week for two weeks out of three, meaning that generally two of the three teams tested every week. The testers were handpicked from the development teams, all being senior engineers representing different subsystems in the aircraft. A test pilot (from the flight test organization) was maneuvering the aircraft in the simulator. The engineers (in total 21 individuals) were allocated to the three test teams, each of which focused on one cluster of subsystems in the aircraft. The last two months the teams were merged to one test team, due to that no new functions were introduced and not so many new problems where found during the test sessions.

5.2   Validation Interviews

The interviewed 18 engineers who participated in the test activity were generally very experienced, all with many years of experience from industry software development. The interviewed 7 pilots were all employed as flight test pilots, with training from military pilot schools and experience from many years of service in both the air force and as test pilots in the industry. Both engineers and test pilots were generally positive or very positive when they described their experiences. "Relevant and good testing", to quote one of the test pilots. One of the engineers described it with the following words: "It was fantastic! We identified a lot of problems. And we learned how the system worked."

The three test teams used the way of working described in Sect. 4 with planning meetings, test sessions and debriefing meetings. The interviewees described that they "built a backlog" of things to test at the planning meetings, which was then used during the upcoming test sessions. The planning meetings were described with words as "creative" or "at least as interesting as the testing itself". Interviewees from one of the test teams described that they at first did very little preparations before the testing, resulting in some unprepared and inefficient test sessions. This changed when the team focused more on the planning meetings.

All teams held a short briefing (10–15 min) right before the test session, in order to go through the program for the test session. This was appreciated by both engineers and test pilots, as it gave everyone a picture of what would happen. During the briefing roles and responsibilities were also clearly distributed (communicating with the pilot, taking notes etc.). The testing itself was generally described as efficient, where engineers and the test pilot were working together as a team. One voice asked for better tools for some of the fault injection procedures, and someone else asked for better recording capabilities. After the test session the team had a short debriefing, with the purpose to summarize the findings and decide who was to write problem reports or further examine open issues. The teams often also had a follow-up meeting the day after the test, focusing on improving test efficiency and ways of working.

Both the engineers and the test pilots were generally very generous with comments and thoughts regarding their experiences from the test activities. Many engineers described their experiences with a lot of enthusiasm, and in some cases even referring to the testing as "great fun". The experiences shared by the interviewees are summarized in themes corresponding to the characteristics of the test method:

- Exploratory testing as an activity in the continuous integration and delivery pipeline
- Session-based testing in teams with experienced engineers representing different subsystems
- Scenario-based testing with an end-user representative as part of the test team

Exploratory testing as an activity in the continuous integration and delivery pipeline: Both engineers and test pilots described the benefits with exploratory testing, where the test teams not plainly follow the instructions in a test case step by step. As one interviewee described it: "We could test according to the ideas we had. We wanted to understand the system that we were building and to find the weaknesses in the system". A few interviewees also described that they during this test activity were looking for the root cause of the problems that were found, whereas they in other test activities just wrote down a brief description of the problem. Besides talking about the benefits from the higher level of freedom, many engineers also described the need for structure and discipline. A field of improvement seemed to be communication of the results from other test activities in the continuous integration and delivery pipeline. Several interviewees described situations where the team was not sure if a problem was already known, or even if a function was complete or still under development. However, according to the interviewees the synchronization with other test activities improved over time.

Session-based testing in teams with experienced engineers representing different subsystems: Almost all engineers described benefits from testing in teams. According to the interviewees, many of the questions that came up at a test session could be solved directly during the test session. Another engineer described that "the quality of the problem reports improves if there are people from different subsystems participating at the test". The engineers described that they were "learning about the system" and "learning about other subsystems". A few voices talked about the importance of having the right people onboard, referring to personality as well as knowledge and experience from the different subsystems of the product. To have a team of six or up to eight people participating during the same test session could also be challenging. Several interviewees described that it sometimes was difficult to see what was going on at the displays, and it was important that the test leader was good at involving all team members in the test process.

Scenario-based testing with an end-user representative as part of the test team: Almost all interviewees described or touched upon that scenarios was a good way to test the complete system. Both engineers and test pilots described that most of the other test activities focused on a subsystem in the aircraft, whereas this test activity focused on the complete aircraft. The interviewees seemed to like to use scenarios as a description of the tests, seeing it as a description that everyone could understand and more flexible than a traditional test case. Several engineer commented on the value to use a real test pilot, who could describe how the product would be used by the end user. The test pilots also described that they could "learn a lot from the engineers". To quote one of the test pilots: "During this test activity the engineers who design the product came in direct contact with the pilots who use it". A few voices (especially from the test pilots) asked for more clear objectives with each scenario test.

One of the questions in the interview guide asked the interviewee to compare the exploratory test activity and other types of test activities. None of the interviewees wanted to describe one way of testing as better than the other, but did instead in different ways describe that exploratory testing and specification-based testing are different types of testing with different purposes. To quote one of the engineers: "Testing according to [a test specification] verifies that the function is implemented according to the specification. This type of testing checks that it is good enough, that we can use the product."

Two of the engineers were a bit less positive than the others. One of them described it like "it never worked quite well", but explained this with that the subsystem he was representing had very little coupling to other subsystems. The other engineer described his situation in the following way: "I was never fully in, I do not know why. I had no clear vision of the whole system. I wished I had known more about my own subsystem, to be able to answer questions from the others."

The last question in the interview guide was if the interviewee was interested in participating in this type of activity again. Twenty-three of the 25 interviewees answered the question with "yes". Some of the engineers and some of the test pilots added that their participation were depending on priority decisions from management. Two of the participants answered the question with "maybe". One of them just added "we'll see when the question comes up". The other described himself as "not completely negative, but not completely positive either" but did not expand this further.

5.3   Problem Reports and Testing Time

Each test session in the case study resulted in a number of found defects in the system or open issues. The open issues were discussed with other developers or system managers, which sometimes clarified that the behavior was according to design, and sometimes confirmed that this was a defect in the system. All defects were documented as problem reports in the organization's issue management tool. All test sessions were conducted in one of the test rigs. The test rig was a scarce and valued test resource, as it was constructed with the same bespoke hardware as a real aircraft and a complex system for the visual environment (as described in Sect. 5.1).

Figure 3 shows for every month during the test period how many percent of all problem reports that month that came from the exploratory test teams. The figure also shows how many percent of all time in the rig that month (rig maintenance not included) that were booked by the exploratory test teams. The figure shows that except for May (and July when almost no testing was done due to vacation period) the exploratory test teams produced a larger share of the problem reports than the exploratory test teams' share of the rig time. As problem reports from other test activities were also written based on testing in other rigs and test environments, the share of time in all related rigs and test environments is actually even lower.

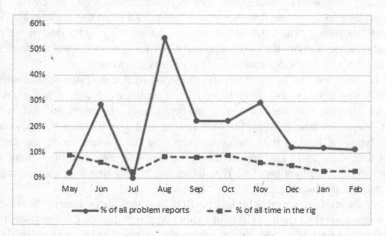

Fig. 3. The exploratory test teams' share of problem reports (in percent) and share (in percent) of all time in the rig

Figure 4 shows how the problem reports from the exploratory test teams are distributed over the ten months when the test activity was conducted. The figure also shows how all testing time in the rig used by the exploratory test teams is distributed over the same period of time. Figures 3 and 4 together show that the three test teams started a bit slow, and did not generate so many problem reports the first month. This changed during June, and peaked during August. Then the trends seem to stabilize for three months, followed by a period of time when the activity was run less intensively due to that no new functions were introduced.

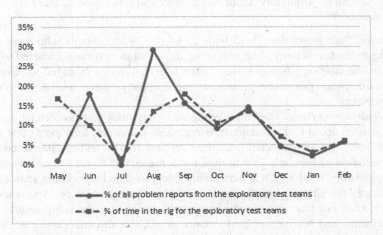

Fig. 4. Distribution of problem reports and testing time for the exploratory test teams

6   Threats to Validity

6.1   Threats to Construct Validity

One must always consider that a different set of questions and a different context for the interviews can lead to a different focus in the interviewees' responses. In order to handle threats against construct validity, the interview guide was designed with open questions (presented in Sect. 2). In this paper, we present both the interview guide and the background for both the interviewees and the case study in order to provide as much information as possible about the context.

The test rig was considered to be a scarce and valued resource. Therefore, we measure the number of problem reports (defects found) per unit of rig time in order to discuss the efficiency of the test method. We do not claim to discuss efficiency on more general terms, such as comparing the importance of the problem reports from different types of test activities (which we consider much harder to measure or quantify).

The observed effectiveness of exploratory testing in terms of number of problem reports may have been influenced by a focus on new functionality. It is conceivable that using the test method with a more clear focus on regression testing would provide a different result.

It is conceivable that the effectiveness of the studied test method is affected by the knowhow and experience of the participants in the study. As the studied test method was new for the participants, the study represents an early usage phase or basically the introduction of the test method. Results and feedback from participants may be different once the test method has turned into an established practice.

6.2   Threats to Internal Validity

Of the 12 threats to internal validity listed by Cook, Campbell and Day [47], we consider Selection, Ambiguity about causal direction and Compensatory rivalry relevant to this work:

- *Selection*: Interviews were held with 25 of the 28 individuals who were participating in the test activity. The remaining three had in two cases changed jobs, and was in one case on parental leave. As the interview series managed to cover all of the participants that were present at the company, there was no selection of interviewees.
- *Ambiguity about causal direction*: While we in this study discuss correlation, we are very careful about making statements regarding causation. Statements that include cause and effect are collected from the interview results, and not introduced in the interpretation of the data. Due to this, we consider this threat to be mitigated.
- *Compensatory rivalry*: When performing interviews and comparing scores or performance, the threat of compensatory rivalry must always be considered. The questions in our interviews were deliberately designed to be value neutral for the participants, and not judging performance or skills of the interviewee or the interviewee's organization. Generally, the questions were also designed to be opened-ended to avoid any type of bias and ensure answers that were open and accurate. However, our experiences from previous work is that we found the interviewees more prone to self-criticism than to self-praise.

6.3   Threats to External Validity

The validation of the test method is based on interviews and quantitative data from a single company. It is conceivable that the findings from this study are only valid for this company, for companies that operate in the same industry segment (military aircraft), or for similar products in different types of industry segments (e.g. other types of vehicles). The characteristics of the test method are in different ways described in related work (as described in Sect. 4), which we argue supports the generalizability of the results of this study (external validity). We have also presented detailed information about both the case study company and the project in the case study, in order to support attempts to replicate our results in other studies.

7 Conclusion

In this paper, we have discussed how exploratory testing can be used in the continuous integration and delivery pipeline during development of large-scale and complex software products. We have proposed a new test method with the following characteristics:

- Exploratory testing as an activity in the continuous integration and delivery pipeline
- Session-based testing in teams with experienced engineers representing different subsystems
- Scenario-based testing with an end-user representative as part of the test team

The characteristics of the test method are in different ways described or touched upon in published literature, which we argue strengthens the validation of the test method. However, none of the found publications presents a test method focusing on large-scale and complex systems, which we argue strengthens this paper's position as a valid contribution. The test method has been validated in a case study, where the system under test was a fighter aircraft. The test method was used during ten months by 28 individuals (21 engineers and 7 flight test pilots). Validation is based on quantitative data and interviews with 25 of the 28 participants.

Quantitative data from the case study company (presented in Sect. 5.3) shows that the exploratory test teams produced more problem reports than other test teams. The three test teams started a bit slow, and did not generate so many problem reports the first month. This changed the following months, and the number of problem reports peaked during the fourth month.

The interview results (summarized in Sect. 5.2) show that the characteristics of the test method are considered valuable by the interviewed 18 engineers and 7 flight test pilots, and that they consider the test method to be an efficient way of testing the system in the case study. Both engineers and test pilots embraced exploratory testing, and appreciated more freedom. Coordination with other test activities in the continuous integration and delivery pipeline was described as a problem at the beginning of the case study, but this improved later on. Many of the engineers described that they were able to test that the subsystems worked together, and that they learned about other subsystems due to that the team consisted of engineers from different subsystems. Engineers and test pilots thought that testing with scenarios was a good way to test the complete system, and described it as valuable to have the test pilot as an end-user representative participating in the test activity. The interviewees were generally positive or very positive when they described their experiences from the case study, using phrases like "relevant and good testing" or "we learned a lot".

Consequently, we find that the test method presented in this paper succeeds in incorporating exploratory testing in the continuous integration and delivery pipeline and is an efficient test method for large-scale and complex software products. This is a significant result, as we see great value in how automated testing and exploratory testing could be complementing one another, each mitigating the weaknesses of the other by addressing unique concerns. Whereas automated test activities in the pipeline are able to rapidly provide feedback to developers and to verify requirements, exploratory testing can provide more in-depth insights about the system under test. Based on this research study, we believe that exploratory testing should be used in a continuous integration and delivery pipeline, preferably to test new functions and systems in a large-scale system.

7.1   Further Work

As the validation in this paper is based on a single case study, this calls for validation from other case studies using the same test method. As a suggestion, the system under test could be another type of vehicle, such as a car or a truck. This type of study could also be combined with the use of other methods to compare the efficiency of the test method (preferably using quantitative data).

References

1. Kaner, C.: Testing Computer Software. TAB Books, Blue Ridge Summit (1988)
2. Kaner, C., Bach, J., Pettichord, B.: Lessons Learned in Software Testing. Wiley, New York (2001)
3. Gregory, J., Crispin, L.: More Agile Testing. Addison Wesley, Boston (2015)
4. Hendrickson, E.: Explore It! The Pragmatic Bookshelf, Dallas (2013)
5. Whittaker, J.: Exploratory Software Testing. Addison Wesley, Boston (2010)
6. Beck, K.: Extreme Programming Explained: Embrace Change, 1st edn. Addison-Wesley Professional, Boston (1999)
7. Fowler, M.: Continuous integration (2006). http://www.martinfowler.com/articles/continuousIntegration.html
8. Humble, J., Farley, D.: Continuous Delivery. Addison Wesley, Boston (2011)
9. Duvall, P.: Continuous Integration. Addison Wesley, Boston (2007)
10. Larman, C., Vodde, B.: Practices for Scaling Lean & Agile Development – Large, Multisite, and Offshore Product Development with Large-Scale Scrum. Addison Wesley, Boston (2010)
11. Kitchenham, B.: Procedures for performing systematic reviews. Keele UK Keele University, vol. 33, pp. 1–26 (2004)
12. Runeson, P., Höst, M.: Guidelines for conducting and reporting case study research in software engineering. Empirical Softw. Eng. 14(2), 131–164 (2009). doi:10.1007/s10664-008-9102-8
13. Robson, C., McCartan, K.: Real World Research, 4th edn. Wiley, London (2016)
14. Frajtak, K., Bures, M., Jelinek, I.: Exploratory testing supported by automated reengineering of model of the system under test. Cluster Comput. 20(1), 855–865 (2017). doi:10.1007/s10586-017-0773-z
15. Frajtak, K., Bures, M., Jelinek, I.: Model-based testing and exploratory testing: is synergy possible? In: 6th International Conference on IT Convergence and Security, ICITCS 2016 (2016). 7740354
16. Gebizli, C.Ş., Sözer, H.: Automated refinement of models for model-based testing using exploratory testing. Softw. Qual. J., 1–27 (2016). doi:10.1007/s11219-016-9338-2
17. Schaefer, C.J., Do, H.: Model-based exploratory testing: a controlled experiment. In: Proceedings of IEEE 7th International Conference on Software Testing, Verification and Validation Workshops, ICSTW 2014, pp. 284–293 (2014). 6825674

18. Schaefer, C., Do, H., Slator, B.M.: Crushinator: a framework towards game-independent testing. In: Proceedings of 2013 28th IEEE/ACM International Conference on Automated Software Engineering, ASE 2013, pp. 726–729 (2013). 6693143

19. Shah, S.M.A., Gencel, C., Alvi, U.S., Petersen, K.: Towards a hybrid testing process unifying exploratory testing and scripted testing. J. Softw. Evol. Process. **26**(2), 220–250 (2014). doi:10.1002/smr.1621

20. Rashmi, N., Suma, V.: Defect detection efficiency of the combined approach. In: Satapathy, S., Avadhani, P., Udgata, S., Lakshminarayana, S. (eds.) ICT and Critical Infrastructure. AISC, vol. 249, pp. 485–490. Springer, Cham (2014). doi:10.1007/978-3-319-03095-1_51

21. Kuhn, A.: On extracting unit tests from interactive live programming sessions. In: Proceedings of International Conference on Software Engineering, pp. 1241–1244 (2013). 6606688

22. Kumar, S., Wallace, C.: Guidance for exploratory testing through problem frames. In: Proceedings of Software Engineering Education Conference, pp. 284–288 (2013). 6595262

23. Makondo, W., et al.: Exploratory test oracle using multi-layer perceptron neural network. In: 2016 International Conference on Advances in Computing, Communications and Informatics, ICACCI 2016, pp. 1166–1171 (2016). 7732202

24. Thangiah, M., Basri, S.: A preliminary analysis of various testing techniques in Agile development - a systematic literature review. In: Proceedings of 3rd International Conference on Computer and Information Sciences, ICCOINS 2016, pp. 600–605 (2016). 7783283

25. Garousi, V., Mäntylä, M.V.: A systematic literature review of literature reviews in software testing. Inf. Softw. Technol. **80**, 1339–1351 (2016)

26. Ghazi, A.N., Petersen, K., Börstler, J.: Heterogeneous systems testing techniques: an exploratory survey. In: Winkler, D., Biffl, S., Bergsmann, J. (eds.) SWQD 2015. LNBIP, vol. 200, pp. 67–85. Springer, Cham (2015). doi:10.1007/978-3-319-13251-8_5

27. Itkonen, J., Mantyla, M.V., Lassenius, C.: Test better by exploring: harnessing human skills and knowledge. IEEE Softw. **33**(4), 90–96 (2016). 7155417

28. Afzal, W., et al.: An experiment on the effectiveness and efficiency of exploratory testing. Empirical Softw. Eng. **20**(3), 844–878 (2015). doi:10.1007/s10664-014-9301-4

29. Itkonen, J., Mäntylä, M.V.: Are test cases needed? Replicated comparison between exploratory and test-case-based software testing. Empirical Softw. Eng. **19**(2), 303–342 (2014). doi:10.1007/s10664-013-9266-8

30. Shah, S.M.A., et al.: Exploratory testing as a source of technical debt. IT Prof. **16**(3), 44–51 (2014). 6475929

31. Shah, S.M.A., Alvi, U.S., Gencel, C., Petersen, K.: Comparing a hybrid testing process with scripted and exploratory testing: an experimental study with practitioners. In: Cantone, G., Marchesi, M. (eds.) XP 2014. LNBIP, vol. 179, pp. 187–202. Springer, Cham (2014). doi:10.1007/978-3-319-06862-6_13

32. Prakash, V., Gopalakrishnan, S.: Testing efficiency exploited: scripted versus exploratory testing. In: 2011 3rd International Conference on Electronics Computer Technology, ICECT 2011, vol. 3, pp. 168–172 (2011). 5941824

33. Itkonen, J., Mäntylä, M.V., Lassenius, C.: Defect detection efficiency: test case based vs. exploratory testing. In: Proceedings of 1st International Symposium on Empirical Software Engineering and Measurement, ESEM 2007, pp. 61–70 (2007). 4343733

34. Do Nascimento, L.H.O., Machado, P.D.L.: An experimental evaluation of approaches to feature testing in the mobile phone applications domain. In: Workshop on Domain-Specific Approaches to Software Test Automation - In Conjunction with the 6th ESEC/FSE Joint Meeting, DoSTA 2007, pp. 27–33 (2007)

35. Sviridova, T., Stakhova, D., Marikutsa, U.: Exploratory testing: management solution. In: 2013 12th International Conference on the Experience of Designing and Application of CAD Systems in Microelectronics, CADSM 2013, p. 361 (2013). 6543293
36. Micallef, M., Porter, C., Borg, A.: Do exploratory testers need formal training? An investigation using HCI techniques. In: Proceedings of 2016 IEEE International Conference on Software Testing, Verification and Validation Workshops, ICSTW 2016, pp. 305–314 (2016). 7528977
37. Raappana, P., et al.: The effect of team exploratory testing - experience report from F-Secure. In: Proceedings of 2016 on IEEE International Conference on Software Testing, Verification and Validation Workshops, ICSTW 2016, pp. 295–304 (2016). 7528976
38. Shoaib, L., Nadeem, A., Akbar, A.: An empirical evaluation of the influence of human personality on exploratory software testing. In: 2009 IEEE 13th International Multitopic Conference, INMIC 2009 (2009). 5383088
39. Pfahl, D., et al.: How is exploratory testing used? A state-of-the-practice survey. In: International Symposium on Empirical Software Engineering and Measurement (2014)
40. Itkonen, J., Mäntylä, M.V., Lassenius, C.: The role of the tester's knowledge in exploratory software testing. IEEE Trans. Softw. Eng. 39(5), 707–724 (2013). 6298893
41. Itkonen, J., Mäntylä, M.V., Lassenius, C.: How do testers do it? An exploratory study on manual testing practices. In: 2009 3rd International Symposium on Empirical Software Engineering and Measurement, ESEM 2009, pp. 494–497 (2009). 5314240
42. Itkonen, J., Rautiainen, K., Exploratory testing: a multiple case study. In: 2005 International Symposium on Empirical Software Engineering, ISESE 2005, pp. 84–93 (2005). 1541817
43. Gouveia, N.: Agile testing on an online betting application. In: Sharp, H., Hall, T. (eds.) XP 2016. LNBIP, vol. 251, pp. 193–200. Springer, Cham (2016). doi:10.1007/978-3-319-33515-5_16
44. Suranto, B.: Exploratory software testing in agile project. In: 2015 2nd International Conference on Computer, Communications, and Control Technology, Art Proceeding, I4CT 2015, pp. 280–283 (2015). 7219581
45. Moss, C.: Big visible testing. In: Proceedings of AGILE 2013, pp. 94–100 (2013). 6612884
46. Pichler, J., Ramler, R.: How to test the intangible properties of graphical user interfaces? In: Proceedings of the 1st International Conference on Software Testing, Verification and Validation, ICST 2008, pp. 494–497 (2008). 4539578
47. Cook, T.D., Campbell, D.T., Day, A.: Quasi-Experimentation: Design & Analysis Issues for Field Settings, vol. 351. Houghton Mifflin, Boston (1979)

Process and Tool Support for Internationalization and Localization Testing in Software Product Development

Rudolf Ramler[1](✉) and Robert Hoschek[2]

[1] Software Analytics and Evolution, Software Competence Center Hagenberg GmbH, Softwarepark 21, 4232 Hagenberg, Austria
rudolf.ramler@scch.at
[2] OMICRON Electronics GmbH, Oberes Ried 1, 6833 Klaus, Austria
robert.hoschek@omicronenergy.com

Abstract. Software globalization is an inevitable step for many companies. Developing for a global market requires the internationalization of software products and their localization to different countries, regions, and cultures. Internationalization and localization testing verifies that localized variants of the software product work, look and feel as expected. The highly repetitive task of testing of multiple language variants makes localization testing a perfect candidate for automation with a high potential to reduce the involved human effort and to speed-up release cycles. However, there is surprisingly little support for localization testing by existing test automation tools. Furthermore, there are only few empirical results or practical insights available as the topic is rarely addressed in the scientific literature. In this paper we describe the process and tools applied for automated testing of the different localized variants of a large commercial software product, we report on the issues detected with automated localization tests, and we discuss our experiences and lessons learned.

Keywords: Internationalization · Localization · I18N · L10N · Multilingual software · Internationalization testing · Localization testing · GUI testing

1 Introduction

Developing successful software products for a global market requires meeting the demands of users all over the world and supporting their local languages and customizations. Problems in localized product variants can be devastating for the reputation of a software product since they are commonly visible to end users. They can manifest in the form of inappropriate or misleading translations, misaligned and irritating screen layouts, or corrupted data and crashes. Thus, even relatively "simple" translation bugs can quickly create an exceptionally negative impression [1].

To support a global audience software products have to be designed and built with internationalization (i18n) in mind. World-ready software products [2] are adjustable to different countries, regions, and cultures. Localization (l10n) is the step of adapting the internationalized software product by configuration, translation or creation of region-specific variants. Consequently, *internationalization testing* extends functional testing

© Springer International Publishing AG 2017
M. Felderer et al. (Eds.): PROFES 2017, LNCS 10611, pp. 385–393, 2017.
https://doi.org/10.1007/978-3-319-69926-4_27

of the software system to its ability to be adjusted by switching to a different language, format, measurement system etc. *Localization testing* makes sure that the localized variants of the software system work – and look and feel – as expected.

A major focus of localization testing is usually on checking the graphical user interface (GUI) for missing translations, grammar and spelling issues, and layout problems. These properties are often verified manually. Thus, localization testing becomes a resource-intensive and time-consuming task. The effort multiplies for software products supporting many different localized variants. Furthermore, localization testing is often performed towards the end of software development, when the functionality has reached a stable state and all translations are available. Hence, internationalization and localization bugs are usually found very late, which is in conflict with fast feedback encouraged by continuous delivery and agile development principles [3].

There is surprising little support for localization testing by existing tools for test automation. In this paper we describe the approach we applied for automating testing of localized variants of a large software product developed by *OMICRON electronics*. We report on the various bugs found and discuss our experiences and lessons learned.

2   Industry Context

OMICRON electronics[1] is an international company in the domain of electrical engineering and energy systems. The company is a world leader in electrical power system diagnostics and monitoring solutions. It serves customers in over 150 countries all around the world and offers localized versions of its products and services.

2.1   System Under Test

One of these products – the system under test (SUT) investigated in this paper – is a large software suite for analyzing of protection and measurement devices in power systems. Technically, the system is a Windows application designed to run on a PC or laptop. It offers more than 30 different modules for monitoring, measurement, diagnostics and reporting. The entire application consists of about 2.700 screens (e.g., dialog windows, message boxes and menus) containing over 85.000 GUI elements with textual representations (e.g., buttons, labels, text fields, lists, menu entries).

The application supports 16 different languages including, for example, English, German, French, Indonesian, Russian, Chinese, Japanese and Korean. All languages are installed with the software system and switching to a different language is possible at any time without restarting. Especially in international projects, commissioning engineers from different countries are working together and exchanging data. Moreover, customers often wish (or have the legal obligation) to generate a measurement report in a specific language other than the engineer's preferred working language.

---

[1] https://www.omicronenergy.com.

2.2   Internationalization and Localization Process

The default language of the application is English. The first step is the internationalization of the application as part of GUI design and software development. English text
strings to be localized are stored in separate resource files from which the application
loads them at runtime. The current version of the software system contains 141 resource
files containing 25.430 localizable text strings in English. In addition, designing the
application requires considering that translated text strings are usually longer than in
English. Growth rates of strings can be from 10 to 100% [2]. GUI design needs to provide
extra space to display strings in all languages without clipping or unwanted wrapping
to subsequent lines.

In every release and throughout development new text strings are added, changed or
removed. To keep track of new or changed text strings that need to be translated, a
software tool developed in-house scans all source code folders for resource files, extracts
the localizable text resources, and stores them in a central terminology database. The
database contains the terms (i.e., words, phrases or sentences) in the default language
English and the available translations in the supported local languages. Identical text
resources that appear in several resource files are consolidated to one entry. The database
is compared to the source code in every nightly build and changed or new terms with
missing translations are reported. For the current software version the terminology database contains 11.170 unique entries.

The actual translation is done by specialized translation agencies. Terms needing
translation are exported and sent to agencies together with optional annotations and hints
for the translator. This is necessary because terms in the database are missing context
information, which makes them ambiguous and hard to translate. Translated terms are
reviewed, e.g., by engineers from offices in different countries.

Finally the translation tool is used to generate the localized resource files containing
the translated text strings from the terminology database. More than 10 different resource
file types are supported. The generation process runs as part of the nightly build, which
makes the latest translation results available on a frequent basis and allows exploring
the system in all supported languages already in the development phase. About 2.300
resource files are generated in every build.

3   Automation Support for Localization Testing

Internationalization and localization testing are performed as part of regression testing
for every release. However, localization testing is a highly time consuming and resource
intensive task when performed manually via the GUI. Testers have to verify the correct
localization by opening every single screen to check its visual appearance, to inspect all
localized text strings (including "hidden" elements such as collapsed tree and list
elements, context menus and tooltips), to assert that no elements overlap and none of
the text strings has been truncated, etc. All these test steps have to be repeated in the
same manner for each of the 16 supported languages. The repetitive character of localization testing makes it a natural candidate for automation, which helps to save time and
resources and, furthermore, allows running the localization tests more frequently. In the

past, due to the high manual effort, the tests were executed infrequently, usually only once at the end of the release cycle.

Figure 1 shows the steps and artifacts involved in automated localization testing. Testing is based on *automated GUI test scripts* that exercise the application in each of the 16 languages. The outcome is a *localization test report* that contains an annotated comparison of the localized version of all screens with the English default version.

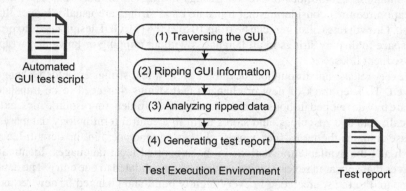

Fig. 1. Process and automation approach for localization testing.

(1) Traversing the GUI: First, for each module, a GUI test script has been developed using a commercial GUI test automation tool. These test scripts perform a round trip over all screens. The scripts differ from conventional functional tests as they are not related to specific usage scenarios. They only open each of the different screens. Input is provided by the scripts to proceed to the next screen or to trigger error message dialogs. The scripts contain checks verifying that a certain screen has been actually been opened, but they do not verify the correctness of the output on the screens.

The scripts are based on an in-house library and GUI interaction is defined as a sequence in tables that can be easily maintained. They were created by testers with detailed knowledge about where to locate all screens in the navigation structure and how to access them. The testers also decided what constitutes a "screen" relevant for testing. Typically a screen corresponds to a dialog window. However, complex dialogs contain frames or tabs that represent distinct screens, i.e., one per frame or tab.

For localization testing, the test scripts had to be executable on each localized versions of the SUT. Therefore, the scripts themselves had to be internationalized, which means that language-specific references to GUI elements (e.g., button label "Next") had to be replaced by neutral references (e.g., index or position in the GUI hierarchy).

(2) Ripping GUI information: For each module, the corresponding test script is executed in the default language English as well as in each localized variant. The scripts take a screenshot of each visited screen. Furthermore the scripts traverse the hierarchy of GUI elements of each screen to extract various properties of the GUI elements such as their element type, displayed text, visibility status, position and size. Only data from GUI elements relevant for testing was extracted, e.g., buttons, text fields, lists containing text strings; structural elements were ignored. The programming interface of the applied

GUI test automation tool has been used to access the properties of the GUI elements. This approach allowed to process visible as well as hidden GUI elements. Actually a large number of relevant GUI elements were "hidden". They were either outside the visible part of a scrollable area, a collapsed list or tree, they were set invisible in a particular system state, or they become visible on certain events such as tooltips that are activated by hoovering over an element.

(3) **Analyzing extracted data:** In a post-processing step, the data extracted during test execution is analyzed by comparing the different localized variants with the reference version in English. The comparison is based on an extensible set of checks. They check for missing translations, e.g., the same text string appears in the reference language and a localized variant, whereby a list of exceptions is maintained for terms that should not be translated. Similarly, a list of illegal and obsolete terms is used in a related check. Further checks search for missing or inconsistent keyboard shortcuts. Violations of basic style guidelines [4] are identified, for example, capitalization and punctuation issues in labels. The size, location and alignment of the GUI elements are checked to reveal corrupted screen layouts. These checks perform the actual verification step in localization testing. Currently we have implemented more than 20 checks for various properties that can be easily extended or adapted.

(4) **Generating test report:** Finally, reports are generated that show the analyzed screens in the reference language English and the localized variants side-by-side (Fig. 2). For every screen the corresponding screenshot is shown and details about the analyzed GUI elements are listed, including annotations about potential localization issues detected by the implemented checks. The reports are used to investigate the detected issues and for further manual analysis. The report generator is also able to output summary information and statistics over all reports to determine the overall test status and to compute trends when included in the build process.

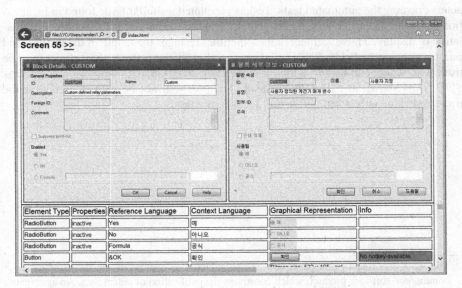

Fig. 2. Localization test report showing reference language and localized variant side-by-side.

4 Results and Discussion

Automated localization testing was introduced when the Korean language version was added [5]. Test reports were generated as support for the review of Korean translations. They show the translated terms in context of the dialogs where they are used, which makes it easier to verify that the translations are appropriate and consistent. The tests were also used to find regression bugs introduced during the internationalization/localization process when running the SUT in the Korean localization with corresponding fonts and character sets installed. Subsequently, localization testing was also established for all other languages. Therefore the localization tests are run for all supported languages as part of the build pipeline on a central test execution server that is also used for performing other automated testing. The summary test results are monitored and when a deviation occurs in the overall trend, e.g., when several checks fail after an update, the detailed results are investigated further.

4.1 Detected Defects

Automated localization testing was applied for 30 modules of the SUT in the Korean language. They include 2.663 screens containing a total of 84.165 GUI elements. The automated tests revealed 59 additional issues, despite running them after manual testing conducted by the test team and a Korean native speaker. Table 1 provides an overview of the different types of detected bugs[2].

Despite being real bugs, many of the found problems are characterized as cosmetic issues with low severity. Two issues, however, were found to be critical. The first is related to an incorrectly initialized GUI element that contained arbitrary values in localized versions. When interpreted as text, these values formed illegal, non-Unicode characters crashing the automated tests. Testers recounted a similar issue found in localization testing of an earlier version that actually crashed the entire SUT. Second, the translation of displayed measurement units sometimes changes the length of data values and numbers shown in fields. Since numbers are aligned right, the highest digits may be truncated, which can lead to a highly misleading situation, e.g., when a value such as "110 V" is shown as "10 volts" instead. The user will not be able to recognize the truncated value unless setting the edit focus to the field.

---

[2] The work reported in this paper has been conducted in context of the development of a commercial software product, which constrains the publication of defect data. An aggregated overview of detected issues is provided in Table 1.

Table 1. Detected issues in automated localization testing of the Korean language version.

Issue category	Description	Share
Missing translations	Text strings that have not been translated can be detected automatically by comparing the text extracted from the localized and the reference variant. We found several issues including false positives as this often occurs during development, when translations are still missing.	24%
Incorrect translations	The automated tests detected syntactical defects related to typos and punctuation issues. Correctness of translations can only be determined by human reviewers knowing in the target language.	36%
Corrupted text and illegal characters	Translated text strings may contain control characters (e.g., tabs or line breaks) as well as placeholders for parameters. Their incorrect use results in corrupted labels or the display of illegal characters. In one case an uninitialized GUI element contained random characters that led to a crash of the tests.	3%
Truncation and overlap	Translations vary in length which may lead to labels being truncated if the layout is static or overlapping with other GUI elements if dynamic layout is used. Related issues were detected by checking the size and position of the bounding box of the GUI elements.	14%
Misalignment	The tests check basic layout properties such as alignment or spacing between elements. The detected layout issues were not caused by localization bugs but they were already present in the reference version.	14%
Incorrectly formatted data	Due to translation of text data and measurement units the length of displayed data values changes. When truncated, it requires the user to set the focus to the field to see the entire value. For numbers aligned to the right, the highest digits may be truncated, which can cause misleading situations that are hard to recognize for the user.	2%
Disrupted sort order	Related to translations of data values such as "none" or "n/a" we also found an impact on the sort order in lists and drop down menus.	2%
Missing or inconsistent shortcuts	While the SUT does not support keyboard shortcuts in the Korean language version, the tests detected labels that contained misleading hints for the use of shortcuts.	5%
Other	Miscellaneous issues not directly related to localization.	2%

4.2 Observations and Lessons Learned

There are several observations and lessons learned from developing an automation approach for localization testing that scales to a large, real-world software product.

- *Automation inherits testability issues from GUI testing:* Since our localization testing approach is based on the SUT's GUI, we encountered the same testability issues as in conventional GUI testing (e.g., timing issues, missing unique IDs to identify GUI elements, and a zoo of different GUI technologies and frameworks not supported by the test automation tool). What makes it even more challenging is the need to develop language-independent, "internationalized" test scripts that run on all localized versions of the software product.

- *Finding localization issues requires executing the SUT:* Can localization testing be performed by analyzing the text strings in the terminology database, avoiding the struggles of accessing the GUI? No, because most localization issues (more than 80%) were only detectable in context of the screen on which the translated text appears when executing the SUT. For example, truncated labels can only be spotted when the GUI elements are rendered, inconsistencies between correct translations become apparent when they are displayed in context of a particular screen, and elements missed in internationalization are not stored in the database at all.

- *Testing visual representations is not enough:* Localization issues often affect the visual appearance of screens (e.g., overlapping elements, illegal characters, corrupted layouts). However, a visual inspection of the screenshots is not sufficient to detect all issues as a large share of information relevant for localization testing is only shown on user interaction (e.g., tooltips, entries menus, content of lists and scrollable areas). Less than half of the available information (46%) was found to be visible on screenshots. Thus, we extracted the "hidden" information from screens at runtime using GUI ripping and also extended our test reports accordingly.

- *Detailed knowledge of the SUT is inevitable for localization testing*: Although most automated tasks in localization tests appear to be generic (e.g., traversing screens, extracting data from GUI elements, comparing localized variants), they involve questions that can only be answered with detailed knowledge about the SUT. Where to find a particular screen in the navigation structure? What constitutes a unique "screen" (e.g., a dialog, tab or frame) relevant for testing? Furthermore, involvement of human experts is also required for developing the checks that detect localization issues when questions arise such as how to interpret the style guide or which screens have to be treated differently as they are based on system dialogs.

4.3 Related Work

Localization testing contains many simple, highly repetitive tasks (e.g., traversing each language version of the SUT, extracting and comparing text from each screen) that encourage automation. Moreover, many localization problems are caused by "simple" bugs that are easily detectable by automated checks. There is, however, surprising little support for localization testing by existing tools for test automation. Key tasks such as making automated GUI tests language independent in order to run on different localizations requires considerable effort but are not well supported.

With a few exceptions, localization testing is also rarely addressed in the scientific literature. Archana et al. [6] show examples of localization issues that can be detected automatically by using a testing approach similar to our work. Martinez et al. [7] applied random testing to search the GUI for mistranslations based on a predefined list of incorrect terms. Zaraket et al. [8] developed GUICop, a tool that searches for violations of properties defined with their GUI specification language. Furthermore, in the area of Web and mobile application development, automation approaches have been proposed for detecting presentation failures caused by localization bugs [9, 10].

5   Summary and Future Work

In this paper we described the internationalization/localization process and the approach we applied for automated testing of the different localized variants of a large software product. Our work contributes empirical results on the various bugs we found (including critical ones that caused crashes or resulted in highly misleading situations for the user) and practical insights on how to develop a scalable, industry-strength automation approach. The results show that test automation allows continuous regression testing of localized versions. It supports finding localization bugs early and it helps to speed-up release cycles and to save human effort in testing.

The implemented testing approach generates a wealth of data about the software systems' GUI that can also be used to gain new insights and to support other quality assurance tasks. For example, we plan to extend our testing approach to detect presentation and layout issues when scaling the GUI to high resolution displays.

Acknowledgments. This research has been supported by the Austrian Research Promotion Agency, the Austrian Ministry for Transport, Innovation and Technology, the Federal Ministry of Science, Research and Economy, and the Province of Upper Austria in the frame of the COMET center SCCH (FFG 844597).

References

1. Alameer, A., Halfond, W.G.J.: An empirical study of internationalization failures in the web. In: International Conference on Software Maintenance and Evolution (ICSME). IEEE (2016)
2. Kano, N.: Developing International Software, 2nd edn. Microsoft Press, Amsterdam (2002)
3. Ressin, M., Abdelnour-Nocera, J., Smith, A.: Defects and agility: localization issues in agile development projects. In: Sillitti, A., Hazzan, O., Bache, E., Albaladejo, X. (eds.) XP 2011. LNBIP, vol. 77, pp. 316–317. Springer, Heidelberg (2011). doi:10.1007/978-3-642-20677-1_23
4. Microsoft Corp.: Microsoft Manual of Style, 4th edn. Microsoft Press, Amsterdam (2012)
5. Ramler, R., Hoschek, R.: How to test in sixteen languages? Automation support for localization testing. In: 10th International Conference on Software Testing, Verification and Validation (ICST). IEEE Computer Society (2017)
6. Archana, J., Chermapandan, S.R., Palanivel, S.: Automation framework for localizability testing of internationalized software. In: International Conference on Human Computer Interactions (ICHCI). IEEE Computer Society (2013)
7. Martinez, M., Esparcia, Anna I., Rueda, U., Vos, Tanja E.J., Ortega, C.: Automated localisation testing in industry with test*. In: Wotawa, F., Nica, M., Kushik, N. (eds.) ICTSS 2016. LNCS, vol. 9976, pp. 241–248. Springer, Cham (2016). doi: 10.1007/978-3-319-47443-4_17
8. Zaraket, F., Masri, W., Adam, M., Hammoud, D., Hamzeh, R.: GUICOP: specification-based GUI testing. In: 5th International Conference on Software Testing, Verification and Validation (ICST). IEEE Computer Society (2012)
9. Alameer, A., Mahajan, S., Halfond, W.G.J.: Detecting and localizing internationalization presentation failures in web applications. In: International Conference on Software Testing, Verification and Validation (ICST), pp. 202–212. IEEE Computer Society (2016)
10. Awwad, A.A., Slany, W.: Automated bi-directional languages localization testing for android apps with rich GUI. Mob. Inf. Syst. **2016**(27), 1–13 (2016)

Workshop: HELENA 2017

2nd Workshop on Hybrid Development Approaches in Software Systems Development

Marco Kuhrmann[1(✉)], Philipp Diebold[2], Stephen MacDonell[3], and Jürgen Münch[4]

[1] Department of Computer Science, Institute for Applied Software Systems Engineering, Clausthal University of Technology, Goslar, Germany
marco.kuhrmann@tu-clausthal.de
[2] Fraunhofer IESE, Kaiserslautern, Germany
Philipp.Diebold@iese.fraunhofer.de
[3] Auckland University of Technology, Auckland, New Zealand
stephen.macdonell@aut.ac.nz
[4] Reutlingen University, Bögblingen, Germany
Juergen.Muench@Reutlingen-University.de

Abstract. Software and system development is complex and diverse, and a multitude of development approaches is used and combined with each other to address the manifold challenges companies face today. To study the current state of the practice and to build a sound understanding about the utility of different development approaches and their application to modern software system development, in 2016, we launched the HELENA initiative. This paper introduces the 2nd HELENA workshop and provides an overview of the current project state. In the workshop, six teams present initial findings from their regions, impulse talk are given, and further steps of the HELENA roadmap are discussed.

Keywords: Software process · Process description · Process improvement · Agile methods · Hybrid development approaches

1 Introduction

Practitioners face numerous challenges in selecting the appropriate development approach for an organization, a team or a project. Since there is no "Silver Bullet" [2] in software system development, software engineers are on the quest for suitable development approaches, yet facing a huge variety of dynamic contextual factors influencing the definition of appropriate processes [3,10]. Hence, a variety of development approaches compete for the users' favor: standard approaches as well as home-grown approaches, more traditional and/or more agile ways of work, and projects influenced by the need to adhere to standards, norms, or regulations.

In 2015, West claimed that "Water-Scrum-Fall" had become reality [9]. A systematic review to investigate the current state-of-practice in software process use [8] revealed a considerable imbalance in the research concerning traditional

© Springer International Publishing AG 2017
M. Felderer et al. (Eds.): PROFES 2017, LNCS 10611, pp. 397–403, 2017.
https://doi.org/10.1007/978-3-319-69926-4_28

and agile software system development. As a consequence, we initiated HELENA that aims to study the use of "Hybrid dEveLopmENt Approaches in software systems development". This initiative grew to a real project involving about 80 researchers[1] from (currently) 26 countries. Each of these 26 sites has a local head supporting the general organization team, and we owe special thanks to all our colleagues, who helped us quality assuring the survey instrument, translating the instrument, and spreading the word among their local peers. Initial results—in particular from the HELENA trials and the first stage of the study—have been presented at the annual meeting of the *Software Process* special interest group of the German Computer Society [6], at the *International Conference on Software System Process* (ICSSP) 2017 [4], and in [5].

The remainder of the paper is organized as follows: In Sect. 2, we provide a brief overview of the current state of the study. Section 3 introduces the workshop as such, and Sect. 4 provides a summary of future work.

2   The HELENA Study: Overview and Current State

In this section, we provide a quick overview of the current state of the HELENA study from a global perspective. Information provided concerns the current dissemination of the survey (Sect. 2.1) and few selected results (Sect. 2.2) grounded in a data dump from mid August 2017. Furthermore, detailed results can be obtained from the region-specific reports, which are introduced in Sect. 3.

2.1   Current State

The second HELENA workshop aims at discussing preliminary results from HELENA's stage 2. For this, the participating teams were invited to provide an initial analysis of a dataset, which was dumped from the survey tool on August 15, 2017. This dataset comprised 501 complete[2] data points, i.e., completely answered questionnaires. Figure 1 illustrates the countries from which we received answers. In total, we received data points from 31 countries. Among these data points, more than 20 data points each come from 10 countries and 14 countries provided fewer than 5 data points. The stage 2 questionnaire of HELENA was made available to the public on May 2, 2017 and accepts answers until September 30, 2017.

2.2   Selected Results

As already found in [4], the HELENA dataset is rich with information. Thus, in this section, we only provide a quick overview of selected results. The questionnaire was made available in English (35% of all answers), German (26%),

---

[1] The full list of all HELENA contributors can be depicted from: https://helenastudy. wordpress.com/helena-team.

[2] It has to be mentioned that we have more that 1,100 data points in the database. Nevertheless, for the preliminary analyses, we only include those data points from completed questionnaires.

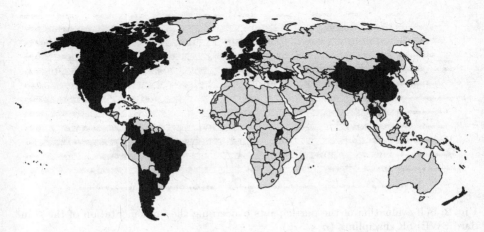

Fig. 1. Overview of the countries from which we received answers to the questionnaire (status: August 15, 2017).

Spanish (25%), and Portuguese (14%). Included in this analysis are the "complete" answers only, which results in an $n = 501$. Yet, since the questionnaire has a number of optional and multiple-selection questions, we have a varying n, which is reported in the respective answers. In the following, we provide some basic parameters:

Company Size ($n = 501$): We provided five categories for the company size from which the participants could choose: micro-sized (11.58% of the participants), small (14.97%), medium (27.54%), large (23.95%), and very large (21.76%). Only 0.2% of the participants did not provide information regarding the company size.

Distributed work ($n = 501$): The participants were asked to state their distributed work pattern. In total 38.12% of the participants stated that they do not work in a distributed manner, 25.75% use distributed work within the same country, 11.98% in the same region, i.e., the same continent. Finally, 23.95% use globally distributed work. Again, 0.2% of the participants did not provide information.

Product/Project Size ($n = 501$): A considerable share of the participants classifies the projects they refer to in their answers as very large, i.e., more than one person year in effort (60.88%). For the remaining categories, we received the following answers: large: 17.76%, medium: 15.37%, small (less than one person month): 4.19%, and very small (less than two person weeks): 1.8%.

Experience ($n = 501$): In total, 63.07% of the participants stated that they have more than 10 years of experience. Another 15.97% have 6–10 years, 13.97% have 3–5 years, and 4.59% of the participants has 1–2 years of experiences. Only 2.40% mentions to have less than one year of experience.

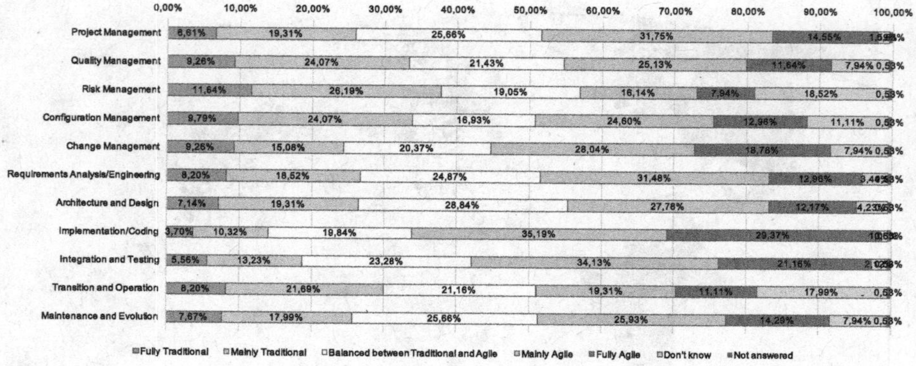

Fig. 2. Self-evaluation of the participants concerning the implementation of the standard SWEBoK disciplines ($n = 378$).

In the survey, we asked the participants if they (intentionally) combine different development approaches, and 74.85% positively answered this question. In the regard, we are interested—similar to [4]—in the self-perception of the participants' way of work. To this end, we asked the participants to rate their way of implementing the standard SWEBoK disciplines [1]. Figure 2 shows that the participants aim at implementing a balanced process ecosystem, yet with a strong tendency toward agile.

Concerning the development approaches as such, we provided the participants with two lists: one comprising 24 (large, integrated) development methods and frameworks, and a second list comprising 35 techniques and practices. We did not provide an explicit categorization, whether a method or a practice is "traditional" or "agile", but provided the alphabetically sorted lists only. In total, we received 30,060 selections on the 7-point Likert scale answers that will help us to identify particular combination patterns. Just these few pieces of information show the richness of the HELENA dataset; further exciting insights are reported by the presenters of this workshop.

3   The Workshop

This 2nd HELENA workshop aims at continuing the community work initiated at ICSSP 2016 (Austin, Texas); in particular, the HELENA survey. It continues the 1st workshop held in conjunction with ICSSP 2017 (Paris; [7]).

3.1   Overview

In this workshop, we aim at bringing together all academic and industry contributors and further interested people to:

1. Report the current state and (preliminary) outcomes of the HELENA survey
2. Develop a work program and define next steps within the whole community

3. Build working groups to work on selected (sub-)topics of interest
4. Create a research agenda for hybrid software and system development

This second workshop comprises reports from the regions presenting the current state of the data collection and analysis, posters that report status and/or present research questions, and (external) "lightning" talks given by researchers and practitioners not involved on the HELENA core activities to challenge the HELENA community. For the regions' reports, we asked the regions to submit short position papers, which were thoroughly reviewed by the HELENA core coordination group. Six regional and cross-regional papers have been invited for presentation. Hence, this second workshop also aims at informing the research community as well as practitioners about the current state of practice.

3.2 Workshop Organization

The 2nd HELENA workshop is a 1-day workshop aiming at bringing together all the contributors of the HELENA project. Table 1 shows the general workshop schedule. Besides the reports on the current state of the work in the different regions all across the globe, a key activity in the workshop is working in *Breakout Sessions*. These sessions aim at identifying and further developing topics

Table 1. Overview of the workshop topics and schedule.

No.	Topic
1	*Introduction (Organizers)*
2	Report of the current state from a global perspective (Organizers)
3	Reports from the regions (*followed by a discussion of the global and regional status in the whole group*):

1. Initial Results of the HELENA Survey Conducted in Estonia with Comparison to Results from Sweden and Worldwide; *Ezequiel et al.* for Estonia and Sweden
2. Hybrid Software and Systems Development in Practice: Perspectives from Sweden and Uganda; *Nakatumba-Nabende et al.* for Uganda and Sweden
3. HELENA Stage 2—Danish Overview; *Tell et al.* for Denmark
4. HELENA Study: Reasons for Combining Agile and Traditional Software Development Approaches in German Companies; *Klünder et al.* for Germany
5. Hybrid Software and System Development in Practice: Initial Results from Austria; *Felderer et al.* for Austria
6. HELENA Study: Initial observations of Software Development Practices in Argentina; *Paez et al.* for Argentina

No.	Topic
4	Wrap up of results and work that happened since the first workshop
5	Lightning talks and poster presentations
6	Setup of working groups and continuing work in breakout session
7	Presentation of the working groups and their plans
8	Development of the HELENA Agenda and next steps
9	*Closing (Organizers)*

of interest that allow for (i) continuing the survey research, and (ii) to form working groups within the HELENA team. Different to the first workshop, we also provide room for *Lightning Talks* in which HELENA team members and interested "externals" discuss different topics of interest and/or challenge the team and the research findings obtained so far. Finally, this workshop will also continue developing a research agenda to steer further work on the use of hybrid development approaches.

4   Conclusion and Future Work

Research conducted in the HELENA community so far strongly indicates the high relevance of the topic. Specifically, the combination of different software and system development approaches has become reality (see Fig. 2) and, moreover, as we could show in [5], it happens to all companies—independent of their size or the respective industry sectors. With this second workshop, we can also add the "region" as a further parameter (Table 1) and, thus, conclude that combination of different development approaches also happens independently from the actual region. That is, hybrid software and system development is a worldwide phenomenon, which requires further attention.

This second workshop is the last one performed during the HELENA stage 2 data collection. The third HELENA workshop will be held in conjunction with the *Evaluation and Assessment in Software Engineering Conference* (EASE) 2018, June 28–29, 2018 in Christchurch, New Zealand.

Acknowledgements. We want to thank the Profes 2017 Chairs and organization board for providing us with the opportunity to held the second workshop in conjunction with Profes 2017. We look forward to a fruitful and long-term collaboration with the Profes community.

References

1. Bourque, P., Fairley, R.E. (eds.): Guide to the Software Engineering Body of Knowledge, Version 3.0. IEEE Computer Society, Washington, DC (2014)
2. Brooks, F.P.: No silver bullet essence and accidents of software engineering. IEEE Comput. **20**(4), 10–19 (1987)
3. Clarke, P., O'Connor, R.V.: The situational factors that affect the software development process: towards a comprehensive reference framework. Inf. Softw. Technol. **54**(5), 433–447 (2012)
4. Kuhrmann, M., Diebold, P., Münch, J., Tell, P., Garousi, V., Felderer, M., Trektere, K., McCaffery, F., Prause, C.R., Hanser, E., Linssen, O.: Hybrid software and system development in practice: waterfall, scrum, and beyond. In: Proceedings of the International Conference on Software System Process, ICSSP, pp. 30–39. ACM, New York, July 2017
5. Kuhrmann, M., Diebold, P., Münch, J., Tell, P., Trektere, K., McCaffery, F., Garousi, V., Felderer, M., Linssen, O., Hanser, E., Prause, C.R.: Hybrid software development approaches in practice: a European perspective. IEEE Softw. (2017, in press)

6. Kuhrmann, M., Münch, J., Diebold, P., Linssen, O., Prause, C.R.: On the use of hybrid development approaches in software and systems development: construction and test of the HELENA survey. In: Proceedings of the Annual Special Interest Group Meeting Projektmanagement und Vorgehensmodelle (PVM). Lecture Notes in Informatics (LNI), vol. P-263, pp. 59–68. Gesellschaft für Informatik (GI), Bonn (2016)
7. Kuhrmann, M., Münch, J., Tell, P., Diebold, P.: Summary of the 1st international workshop on hybrid development approaches in software systems development. ACM SIGSOFT Softw. Eng. Notes (2017, submitted)
8. Theocharis, G., Kuhrmann, M., Münch, J., Diebold, P.: Is *Water-Scrum-Fall* reality? On the use of agile and traditional development practices. In: Abrahamsson, P., Corral, L., Oivo, M., Russo, B. (eds.) PROFES 2015. LNCS, vol. 9459, pp. 149–166. Springer, Cham (2015). doi:10.1007/978-3-319-26844-6_11
9. West, D.: Water-Scrum-Fall is the reality of agile for most organizations today. Technical report, Forrester (2011)
10. Xu, P., Ramesh, B.: Using process tailoring to manage software development challenges. IT Prof. **10**(4), 39–45 (2008)

Initial Results of the HELENA Survey Conducted in Estonia with Comparison to Results from Sweden and Worldwide

Ezequiel Scott[1]([⊠]), Dietmar Pfahl[1], Regina Hebig[2], Rogardt Heldal[2], and Eric Knauss[2]

[1] University of Tartu, Tartu, Estonia
{ezequiel.scott,dietmar.pfahl}@ut.ee
[2] Chalmers University of Gothenburg, Gothenburg, Sweden
{hebig,heldal,knauss}@chalmers.se

Abstract. The way how software is developed in industry has considerably changed with the advent of the agile development paradigm about 20 years ago. The HELENA initiative tries to investigate the current state of practice in software and system development. This paper reports about initial results of an online survey that was conducted in 26 countries simultaneously, focusing on results from Estonia and comparing these results with results from Sweden as well as with the joint results from all participating countries worldwide.

Keywords: Agile software development · HELENA · Survey

1 Introduction

The acronym HELENA stands for Hybrid Software and System Development Approaches. The associated project aims to investigate the use of hybrid development approaches in software system development - from emerging and innovative sectors to regulated domains. For this purpose an online survey form was created[1]. The overall goal of this survey is to investigate the current state of the practice in software and systems development. In particular, researchers involved in the HELENA project are interested to collect data about the types of development approaches (traditional, agile, main-stream, or home-grown) used in practice and how those approaches are combined, how such combinations were developed over time, and if and how standards (e.g., safety standards) affect the used development processes. This information will help push forward systematic process design and improvement activities resulting in more effective and efficient software development.

---

[1] HELENA Survey - https://www.soscisurvey.de/HELENA/.

© Springer International Publishing AG 2017
M. Felderer et al. (Eds.): PROFES 2017, LNCS 10611, pp. 404–412, 2017.
https://doi.org/10.1007/978-3-319-69926-4_29

HELENA has been designed as a 3-staged international research endeavor. The first stage, which has been completed (cf. [1]), aimed at preparing the data collection and to test the survey instrument. The project is now in the second stage, i.e., international "mass data" collection using a revised survey instrument. The second stage is conducted in a large international consortium that comprises more than 60 partners from more than 30 countries. More details can be found in the official web site[2]. The results of the second stage will fuel the third project stage by focusing follow-up in-depth research on particularly interesting outcomes of the second stage.

In this paper we present first results from the second stage of the survey for Estonia and compare it to the joint results from all countries as well as to the results from Sweden. We picked Sweden as a point of comparison since Sweden is similar to Estonia in terms of being a Nordic country with a highly digitalized society but at the same time very different from Estonia in terms of the type of software industry.

2 Initial Results

Table 1 shows the communication channels used in Estonia and Sweden. In both countries, most effort was invested in direct emailing, with comparable response rates. Data collection in Estonia was mostly done through emailing contact persons in software development companies in the time period May 20 to June 20 (one reminder was sent). In addition, we posted the survey in a blog of a community of software testers as well as in a mailing list. In total, we received 12 responses by June 20, 2017, all responses coming from the direct mailing initiative (30.8% response rate). Similarly, data collection in Sweden was mainly

Table 1. Communications channels used.

Channel	Estonia			Sweden		
	Requests	Answers	Response rate	Request	Answers	Response rate
Personal contact	39	12	30.8%	35	13	37%
Mailinglist	1	0	0%	0	-	-
Twitter	0	-	-	1	0	0%
Blog post	1	0	0%	0	-	-
Other	0	-	-	2	0	0%
Total	41	12	-	38	13	-

---

[2] HELENA Web Site - https://helenastudy.wordpress.com.

based on direct emails to existing contacts, complemented by posting the survey in social media such as Twitter. All 13 responses received in Sweden are accounted for through direct mailing, leading to a response rate of 37%. Overall, i.e. across all 26 participating countries, 513 responses were collected until August 23, 2017, when we conducted our analyses.

The differences of company sizes reported by Estonian respondents as compared to Swedish respondents was roughly as we expected, i.e., many of the Estonian respondents (41.7%) work in small companies (11–50 employees) while most of the Swedish respondents work in large companies (251–2499 employees), compared to only 7.7% who work in small companies. The difference of company size becomes even more explicit when merging the numbers for respondents working in small and medium size companies (11–250 employees) and those for respondents working in large and very large companies (above 250 employees). While the number of respondents is equally distributed over both classes, i.e., 50% in each class, only about 15% of the Swedish respondents work in small and medium size companies while about 85% work in large or very large companies.

When comparing the company size distributions of the Estonian and Swedish respondents one can observe that the two countries are either balanced with regards to company size (Estonia) or strongly leaning towards larger companies (Sweden). The distribution of company sizes among the responses from all participating countries can be placed somewhere between the Estonian and Swedish distributions. In addition, worldwide, 11.6% of the respondents work in micro companies (<10 employees). None of the respondents from Estonia and Sweden works in such small companies (Fig. 1).

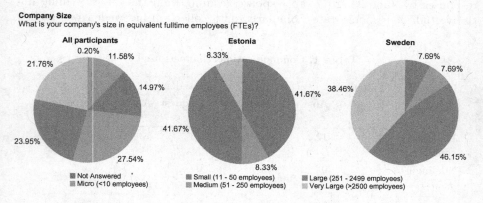

Fig. 1. Distribution of company sizes among the responses from all the participants, Estonia, and Sweden.

Frameworks/Methods
Which of the following frameworks and methods do you use?

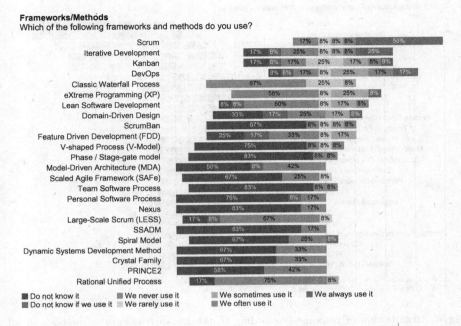

Fig. 2. Distribution of responses according to the use of frameworks/methods in Estonia.

Frameworks/Methods
Which of the following frameworks and methods do you use?

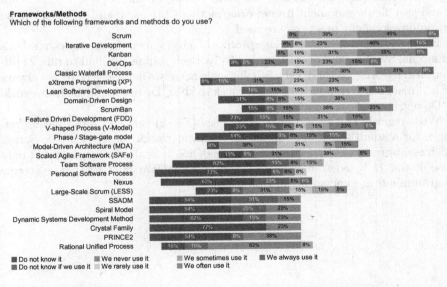

Fig. 3. Distribution of responses according to the use of frameworks/methods in Sweden.

Frameworks/Methods
Which of the following frameworks and methods do you use?

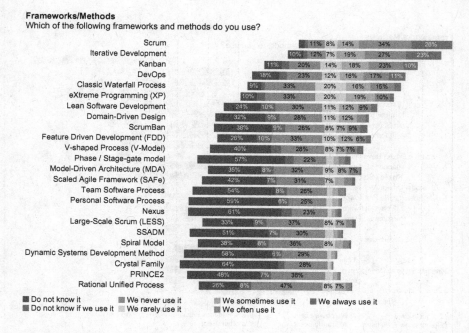

Fig. 4. Distribution of responses according to the use of frameworks/methods in all the countries.

In the following, we discuss two main results of the survey, i.e., to what extend specific development frameworks/methods are used, and to what extend certain development practices are used.

Figures 2, 3 and 4 show the usage profiles of development frameworks/methods in Estonia, Sweden, and overall, respectively. Each respondent had to rate 24 different frameworks/methods on a 5-point scale from 'we never use it' to 'we always use it'. In addition, respondents could check the box 'Do not know the framework' or 'Do not know if we use it'.

With regards to the Estonian responses (Fig. 2) one can see a clear preference for a small set of agile development frameworks, clearly lead by Scrum which is 'always used' by 58% of the respondents. It is also interesting that only three of the 24 listed frameworks (Scrum, Classic Waterfall Process, eXtreme Programming) are known by all respondents.

When looking at the responses from Sweden (Fig. 3) one can again see a frequent use of Scrum but only 8% of the respondents use it always. Similarly often used as Scrum are Iterative Development, Kanban - and the Classic Waterfall Process. Only 46% of the respondents said that they use eXtreme Programming 'rarely' or 'sometimes', nobody said they use it 'often' or 'always'.

When comparing the results from Estonia and Sweden with the overall results from all participating countries (Fig. 4), one can see that the three most frequently used frameworks (Scrum, Iterative Development, and Kanban) are the same as in Sweden. However, one can observe that the usage frequency of Scrum is between those of Estonia and Sweden.

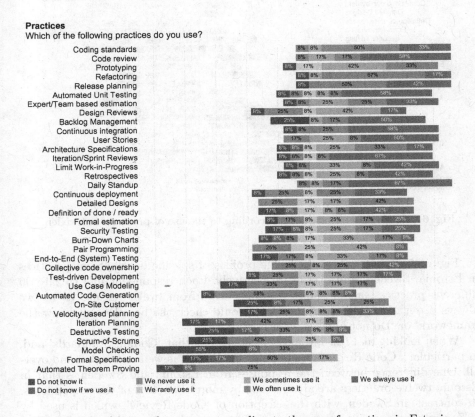

Fig. 5. Distribution of responses according to the use of practices in Estonia.

Practices
Which of the following practices do you use?

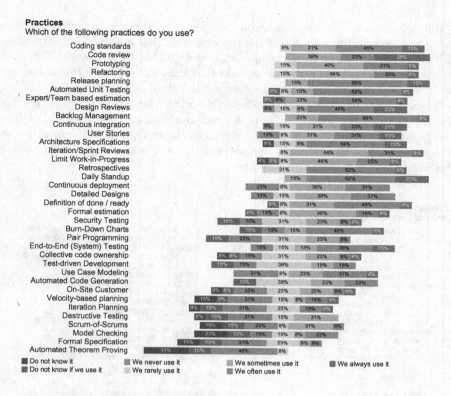

Fig. 6. Distribution of responses according to the use of practices in Sweden.

Figures 5, 6 and 7 show the usage profiles of specific development practices in Estonia, Sweden, and overall, respectively. Each respondent had to rate 36 different practices, again using a 5-point scale from 'we never use it' to 'we always use it'. In addition, respondents could check the box 'Do not know the framework' or 'Do not know if we use it'.

When looking at Figs. 5, 6 and 7 it sticks out that 'Coding Standards' and, in particular, 'Code Review' are popular in Estonia as well as Sweden and overall. One difference between the responses from Estonia and Sweden is that in Estonia twelve practices are always used by more than 40% of the respondents. In contrast, in Sweden, with the exception of 'Code Review', which is used by 38% of the respondents always, none of the practices is used more than 23% always. As could be expected, the project usage profile of development practices aggregated over all survey participants lies in-between Estonia and Sweden.

Practices
Which of the following practices do you use?

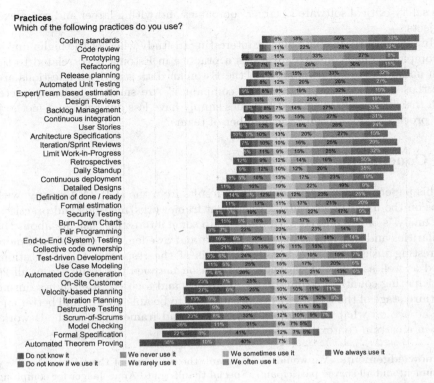

Fig. 7. Distribution of responses according to the use of practices in all the countries.

3   Discussion

Initial results of the second stage of the HELENA project show interesting similarities and differences between the usages of development frameworks/methods and practices when comparing responses from Estonia and Sweden.

One clear similarity is, for example, that Scrum is the most used development framework/method in both Estonia and Sweden, as well as overall. A similar statement could me made regarding the use of the practices 'Coding standards' and 'Code review'. An explanation for the high popularity of agile approaches and techniques could be that both countries have very competitive software industries that are constantly striving to improve their processes and adopt effective techniques.

One of the main differences between Estonian and Swedish responses is related to the popularity of non-agile framework/methods - they seem to be used more often in Sweden than in Estonia. One possible explanation for this could be that Sweden has not only young, small and medium-sized software houses that mainly build web-applications and business software but, in addition, a well-established software industry producing a large amount embedded and safety-critical software in larger companies and within larger and complexer projects.

In future work, it would also be interesting to study whether the high number of companies that claim to always us a practice in Estonia is correlated to the high number of small companies in the Estonian data set. Open questions are: Are these numbers due to the small companies? Are small companies stricter with their process? Do small companies simply have less diverse use of methods and processes, due to the lower number of teams?

4   Conclusions

In this paper, we only presented partial results from the HELENA survey, with focus on the usage of software development frameworks/methods and practices. The analysis of the related data brought up some interesting insights about the similarities and differences between Estonia and Sweden. We expect even more interesting insights from a broader analysis of the responses to all questions asked as well as a more systematic comparison between the results from all 26 participating countries. From follow-up surveys and focused case studies during the third stage of the HELENA project we hope to be able understand better and give advice on what combination of practices and frameworks/methods works best in a certain context.

Acknowledgements. We would like to thank the designers of the HELENA survey instrument and all survey participants. Special thanks go to Anne Jääger for compiling the list of contacts in Estonian companies and sending out emails to them, as well as to Nauman bin Ali, Rashidah Kasauli, Grischa Liebel, and Kai Petersen for their help in survey design and data collection as part of the Swedish group. Ezequiel Scott and Dietmar Pfahl were financially supported by the institutional research grant IUT20-55 of the Estonian Research Council as well as the Estonian IT Center of Excellence (EXCITE).

Reference

1. Kuhrmann, M., Diebold, P., Münch, J., Tell, P., Garousi, V., Felderer, M., Trektere, K., McCaffery, F., Linssen, O., Hanser, E., et al.: Hybrid software and system development in practice: waterfall, scrum, and beyond. In: Proceedings of the 2017 International Conference on Software and System Process, pp. 30–39. ACM (2017)

Hybrid Software and Systems Development in Practice: Perspectives from Sweden and Uganda

Joyce Nakatumba-Nabende[1]([✉]), Benjamin Kanagwa[1], Regina Hebig[2], Rogardt Heldal[2], and Eric Knauss[2]

[1] Makerere University, Kampala, Uganda
{jnakatumba,bkanagwa}@cis.mak.ac.ug
[2] Chalmers University of Technology, Gothenburg, Sweden
{regina.hebig,heldal,eric.knauss}@cse.gu.se

Abstract. Many organizations are adapting the use of hybrid software development approaches by combining traditional methods with flexible agile practices. This paper presents the initial results from the survey on the use of hybrid software and systems approaches. The results are from twenty one respondents from Sweden and Uganda. Our results show that the iterative model is the most widely used process model in both Sweden and Uganda. However, the traditional process models are also used in combination with the more agile models like Scrum. From the results, we also show that the large sized companies face the biggest problems during implementation of agility since they have to adhere to standards and control measures.

Keywords: Software process · Hybrid development approaches · HELENA survey

1 Introduction

Software development methodologies cover a range of techniques that are useful for planning, executing and monitoring the process of developing software systems. These methodologies are diverse and organizations are quickly adopting to new technologies [4]. This paper analyzes initial results from a survey carried out with an overall goal of investigating the current state of practice in software and systems development. The aim of the HELENA[1] survey was to collect data from software developers and practitioners to help determine the main software development approaches used in practice and how these approaches are combined in project development [3]. This paper presents preliminary results of the data collected as part of the second phase of HELENA. The results discussed here are from Sweden and Uganda. As part of the second phase of HELENA, Uganda is the only country from Africa that is participating in the survey and

---

[1] Hybrid dEveLopmENt Approaches in software systems development.

© Springer International Publishing AG 2017
M. Felderer et al. (Eds.): PROFES 2017, LNCS 10611, pp. 413–419, 2017.
https://doi.org/10.1007/978-3-319-69926-4_30

therefore we decided to compare results from a developing country to those from a Nordic country like Sweden. The first reason is that we were interested in establishing any differences and similarities between these two countries in terms of the type of software industry. The second reason is that Uganda and Sweden share a program to educate PhD students, which gives us the unique possibility to have young researchers visiting both sites for future studies in phase three of HELENA.

The survey was sent out to several practitioners in industry and based on their responses, Sweden received 13 data points while Uganda received 8 data points. The data collection was mainly done through personal contacts, via email, mailing lists and telephone contacts. In Uganda, the link to the survey was sent out to 15 companies and was filled out by eight of those resulting in a response rate of 53%. In Sweden the survey was mainly distributed through direct emails to existing contacts, complemented by posting the survey in social media such as Twitter. All 13 responses received in Sweden are accounted for through direct mailing, leading to a response rate of 37%.

The remainder of the paper is organized as follows: Sect. 2 provides an overview of the initial results from Sweden and Uganda. Section 3 provides a discussion of the results. Finally, we conclude the paper in Sect. 4.

2 Initial Results

In this section we present results from the HELENA survey [3]. The survey consists of five categories of questions belonging to: Metadata, Process Use, Process Use and Standards, Process use in the lifecycle and Experience. The results presented in this section were selected from three of the five sections in the survey, i.e., Metadata, Process Use (PU) and Process Use and Standards (PS). As indicated in the previous section, we received a total of 21 data points from both Sweden and Uganda; the analysis in this section is based on these data points.

2.1 Demographics

In this section, we cover the responses from the Metadata section of the survey. We analyzed responses on the company sizes and the roles that the respondents have in the projects they are part of. Table 1 provides an overview of the comparison of the company sizes and the roles from Sweden and Uganda.

The result set provided answers from all categories, i.e., micro-sized organizations to the very large organizations. As seen from the results, five of the organizations were micro-sized organizations and they all belonged to respondents from Uganda while five of the organizations were very large companies and these were only observed in Sweden. All the Uganda respondents had defined roles that they performed on the projects while from the Sweden respondents, there was the "other" category with two respondents. The respondents also highlighted the roles that they were frequently assigned to. From the results, it is

Table 1. Overview of the comparison of the number of participants from Sweden (SW) and Uganda (UG) under different company sizes and the roles of the participants ($n = 21$).

	Micro	Small		Medium	Large		Very large	Sum
	UG	SW	UG	SW	SW	UG	SW	
C-level Manager	-	-	1	-	-	-	-	1
Product Manager	-	1	-	-	-	1	1	3
Project/Team Manager	1	-	-	-	2	-	2	5
Analyst/Req. Engineer	1	-	-	-	-	-	-	1
Architect	1	-	-	1	2	-	1	5
Developer	2	-	1	-	1	-	-	4
Other	-	-	-	-	1	-	1	2
$\sum$	5	1	2	1	6	1	5	**21**

seen that the architect and project/team managers were the most frequently stated roles in Sweden while in Uganda the developers were the most frequently stated roles.

2.2 Process Use

Under process use, we were interested in determining the patterns in software development, as there is move towards agile software development process [3]. We aimed to establish the least used/unknown process models and the always/often used process models. Figure 1 provides an overview of these results from the Sweden and Ugandan respondents.

We picked the top five software development models based on the results from the survey. All processes that tied for the fifth position were included. From the results in the Fig. 1, Crystal Family and Nexus are the either not known or never used in most software companies for both Uganda and Sweden. It is also interesting to note that whereas the Dynamic Systems Development Method (DSDM) is unknown in Sweden, it is one of the most commonly used models in Uganda. We find the opposite result for Kanban, for which is known by most of the Swedish companies, but never used for five of the Ugandan companies.

2.3 Process Use and Standards

The authors in [2,3] argue that external standards, norms and regulations are major initiators brought about by the increasing complexity of software-intensive systems. In this subsection, we investigate if external standards facilitate the creation of hybrid development approaches. From the survey results, it was

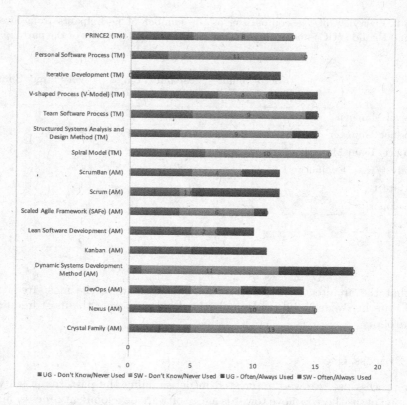

Fig. 1. Overview of the comparison of the least used/unknown development approaches verses the often/always used development approaches in Sweden (SW) and Uganda (UG) (TM: Traditional Method; AM: Agile Method).

established that 61.5% of the Swedish companies implemented external standards in comparison to the 37.5% of Uganda companies. For both countries, more than 50% of the participants indicated that they implemented the standards due to the requirements of the company/project businesses. Table 2 shows whether using standards, norms and regulations challenge companies in the implementation of agility. However, we note that the responses received for this questions were quite few $(n = 11)$ in comparison to the responses from the previous questions. Therefore, we did not carry out a comparison of Sweden and Uganda but rather we considered an aggregated view of the responses from both countries. From the results, it is evident that the large companies face the biggest problems during implementation of agility.

Table 2. Results of the number of respondents that identified whether standards, norms and regulations challenge the implementation of agility in their organizations (n = 11).

Company size	Challenged by agility?	
	Yes	No
Micro	1	1
Medium	1	-
Large	2	1
Very large	3	1

3   Discussion

In this section, we discuss the results presented in the previous section. We highlight any commonalities and differences between the respondents from Sweden and Uganda. As shown in Table 1, the role distributions are reflective of the company sizes. For example, we observe that larger companies from Sweden had more roles compared to the small sized companies which is also consistent with the results presented in [3]. In Uganda, the greater number of the respondents were software developers since there is a growth in software development industry as compared to the architects and project managers from the Sweden results.

From the results shown in Fig. 1, the iterative method of software development is the most commonly used model in Uganda and Sweden. This is possibly due to fact that it is one of oldest development processes. Furthermore, from the results we observe that there is a widespread use of V-shaped traditional model in Sweden while it is one of the least used development methods in Uganda. The wide spread use of the model could be attributed to the model being an extension of one of the oldest process models and also this is in line the with large size of companies as established in Sect. 2. More companies in Sweden indicated consistent use of agile software related approaches as opposed to Uganda, e.g., the use of Scrum, Kanban and DevOps. From these initial results, it is evident that organizations tend towards using hybrid approaches for software development.

The results shown in Table 2 are consistent with the initial survey results as reported in [3], that large companies face the biggest problems during the implementation of agility. From the results, there were no significant differences between the responses from Sweden and Uganda. Many of the respondents gave justification as to why implementation of agility was a problem. Some of the views received from the individual respondents were that:

"There is a perceived level of control; deviations identified can lead to deadlocks and schedule conflicts with other projects; increased need for speed is slowed down by safety regulations, e.g. traceability, documentation levels, formal reviews; ISO26262 assumed process is pure waterfall and cause problems to run in an agile setup; conforming to standards from different domains, sometimes standards are not easily changed or flexible even when the business environment points to the need for change."

Many of these problems highlighted here are consistent with findings from previous studies on the challenges of agile implementation [1].

Based on these observations, we raise some questions for future research. We observe that agile methods are less known by Ugandan companies, while they use iterative development. Similarly DSDM is largely unknown by Swedish companies. By taking more data in future, we hope to understand questions that relate to any correlations between the used processes and the contextual environment of the companies including education, maturity of software industry and nature of projects carried. Other questions relate to re-occurring combinations of approaches and effect of the observed differences on internationalization and outsourcing.

4   Conclusion

In this paper, we have provided an overview of the results from the HELENA survey based on responses from Sweden and Uganda. Particularly, we have focused on the questions relating to demographics, process use, and processes and standards. Based on the results received from respondents in Uganda and Sweden, we carried out a comparative review of the main software development approaches used in industry. We categorized the company sizes from Uganda and Sweden while highlighting the roles that the respondents play in these organizations. We also analyzed the main process models that are used in both countries and found out that companies do not adhere to one development method but rather employ hybrid approaches in practice.

The main limitation of this study is the number of data points that were received from Sweden and Uganda were small and the results presented here may not provide a generalization of the software development approaches in Sweden and Uganda. For future work, we aim to get more data points before the close of the survey period and also survey other research questions and areas as discussed in the previous section. Furthermore, we also hope to compare our results with results from other regions.

Acknowledgments. We would like to thank Nauman bin Ali, Rashidah Kasauli, Grischa Liebel, Kai Petersen for their help in survey design and data collection as well as all participants in the survey.

References

1. Dikert, K., Paasivaara, M., Lassenius, C.: Challenges and success factors for large-scale agile transformations: a systematic literature review. J. Syst. Soft. **119**, 87–108 (2016)

2. Kuhrmann, M., Münch, J., Diebold, P., Linssen, O., Prause, C.R.: On the use of hybrid development approaches in software and systems development: construction and test of the HELENA survey. In: Proceedings of the Annual Special Interest Group Meeting Projektmanagement und Vorgehensmodelle (PVM). Lecture Notes in Informatics, vol. 263, pp. 59–68 (2015)
3. Kuhrmann, M., Diebold, P., Münch, J., Tell, P., Garousi, V., Felderer, M., Prause, C.R.: Hybrid software and system development in practice: waterfall, scrum, and beyond. In: Proceedings of the 2017 International Conference on Software and System Process, pp. 30–39. ACM (2017)
4. Vijayasarathy, L.R., Butler, C.W.: Choice of software development methodologies: do organizational, project, and team characteristics matter? IEEE Soft. **33**(5), 86–94 (2016)

HELENA Stage 2—Danish Overview

Paolo Tell[1(✉)], Rolf-Helge Pfeiffer[2], and Ulrik Pagh Schultz[3]

[1] IT University of Copenhagen, Copenhagen, Denmark
`pate@itu.dk`
[2] Copenhagen Business Academy, Copenhagen, Denmark
`rhp@cphbusiness.dk`
[3] University of Southern Denmark, Odense, Denmark
`ups@mmmi.sdu.dk`

Abstract. Since the early days of software engineering, a number of methods, processes, and practices to design and develop software systems have been proposed and applied in industry, e.g., the Rational Unified Process, Agile Software Development, etc. However, since no silver bullet exists, organizations use rich combinations of agile and/or traditional methods and practices, rather than following a single process by the book. To investigate this reality, an international exploratory multistage research project named HELENA (Hybrid DEveLopmENt Approaches in software systems development) was initiated. Currently, the HELENA survey is conducted globally (second stage of HELENA project). This short paper presents and discusses the results of the survey in Danmark compared to the global results based on the data from August 15, 2017.

Keywords: Hybrid development approaches · HELENA

1 Introduction to the HELENA Project

HELENA is an international exploratory multistage survey-based study on the use of "**H**ybrid d**E**ve**L**opm**EN**t **A**pproaches in software systems development". The project aims at: *(a)* researching the practical application of methods, processes, and practices in software engineering, and *(b)* development and deployment of new systematic processes to enable more efficient and effective software development. To achieve these goals the project is designed to collect data through a survey[1], which has been refined over several iterations. After being successfully tested within Europe in project stage one [2], the HELENA project is currently in stage two, in which the survey is conducted globally in more than 25 countries. A third and final stage will conclude the project. In stage three, focus groups will perform in depth research on community-defined topics of interest, based on the results of stage two.

With this paper, we aim (i) to identify potentially interesting similarities and differences of the current Danish results compared to the overall global ones;

---

[1] HELENA survey accessible from www.soscisurvey.de/HELENA/.

© Springer International Publishing AG 2017
M. Felderer et al. (Eds.): PROFES 2017, LNCS 10611, pp. 420–427, 2017.
https://doi.org/10.1007/978-3-319-69926-4_31

(ii) to assess whether results from stage one can be confirmed focusing on the Danish population; and (iii) to establish a base for more in-depth research at the end of the survey, at the end of Sept. 2017.

In particular, Sect. 2 presents and discusses an overview of the results of the survey in Danmark compared to the global results (including the Danish ones) based on the data from August 15, 2017. Furthermore, focusing only on the Danish data set, in Sect. 3 we replicate the analysis performed on the data set from project stage one [3], and we assess whether the main results of stage one are in line with the ones collected from Denmark in stage two. Finally, Sect. 4 wraps up the main finding and briefly suggests future directions that the Danish team will consider.

1.1 The Danish Participation

The Danish HELENA research team consists of 4 members (see Table 1 for contacts and affiliations). Since the beginning of project stage two, the team invited 132 individuals via personal email (127) or mailing lists and physical meetings (5) to answer the survey. Of these, 22 fully completed the survey, i.e., response rate of ca. 16.6%. Finally, at least 13 (ca. 9.8%) individuals started the survey but did not complete it.

Table 1. Danish team—contacts.

Paolo Tell	pate@itu.dk	IT University of Copenhagen, Copenhagen
Rolf-Helge Pfeiffer	rhp@cphbusiness.dk	Copenhagen Business Academy, Copenhagen
Brad Beach	brbe@mmmi.sdu.dk	University of Southern Denmark, Odense
Ulrik Pagh Schultz	ups@mmmi.sdu.dk	University of Southern Denmark, Odense

2 Demographics

Except of two, all respondents have at least three years of working experience and the majority (13 out of 32) are senior with more than ten years of experience, see Fig. 1. This distribution is similar to the world-wide demographics, see orange line in Fig. 1.

The Danish respondents are mostly product managers/owners, developers, and architects, see Fig. 2. That is interesting, as it is firstly, different from the world-wide population, see orange bars in Fig. 2, and secondly, it suggests a more agile development environment in those companies as fewer project/team managers participated and no participant selected positions like analyst/requirement engineer, quality manager, tester, and trainer. Of course, these Danish results

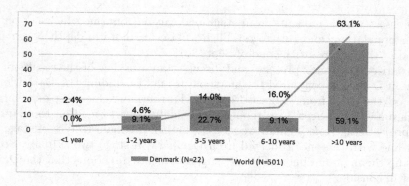

Fig. 1. Overview of the experience level as stated by the participants.

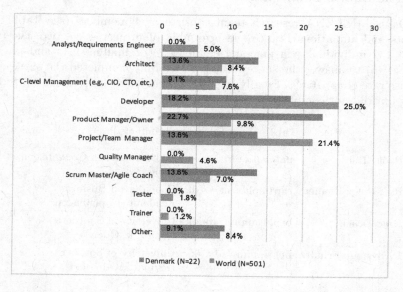

Fig. 2. Overview of the roles as stated by the participants.

may be heavily biased by the selection of survey participants (in essence we activated every practitioner we know) and may be not representative of the entire
Danish software industry.

Nonetheless, Fig. 3 illustrates, that not only small and medium-sized
enterprises are represented—which might favor a more agile development
environment—but that approx. a third of the respondents works in large companies.

The application domain of the companies is very diverse. Most respondents
work in the areas of cloud-, web-applications and services, see Fig. 4. However,
also robotics, home automation, and automotive software is represented, which

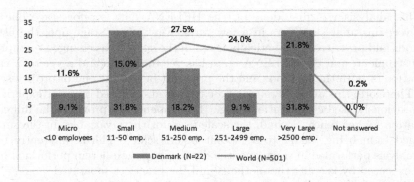

Fig. 3. Overview of the size of the companies as stated by the participants.

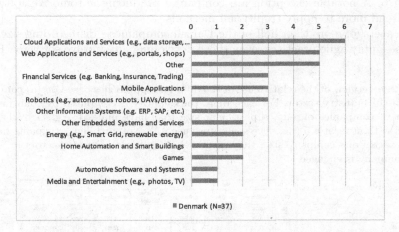

Fig. 4. Overview of the application domain of the companies as stated by the participants. Note: multiple selection was enabled.

is interesting for a country without car manufacturing. Even though existent in Danmark, there are no responses from the healthcare domain. This particular domain has been discussed within the 'safety' focus point identified during the first HELENA workshop[2] [4].

3   Applied Methods and Practices in Danmark

Currently, our hypothesis is that the Danish software industry is more inclined to apply agile software development. To investigate this, we focused on the data set generated by Danish respondents, and we analyzed the list of methods and practices selected. This section presents the breakdown of the methods and practices based on the company size and the industry sectors (see Fig. 2).

---

[2] The first international HELENA workshop was held co-located with the 2017 International Conference on Software and Systems Process (ICSSP).

This analysis was first done on the HELENA data set for stage one [3]. However, this analysis differs in a few ways. First, since stage one, the list of methods and practices alphabetically listed in the survey has changed to improve the instrument, and the HELENA team has yet to discuss and agree on a categorization of both the methods and the practices before the end of project stage two. Therefore, this analysis relies on a categorization based on prior experience and previously used classifications (e.g., [1]). Appendix A provides the full categorization for reference. Second, the scale used for these variables in the survey changed from being binary to a 7-point Likert scale[3]. Third, differently from the analysis performed in stage one, the data aggregation herein performed have been executed by keeping the methods and the practices separated.

Table 2, shows clearly that the majority of Danish software producers apply agile methods—on average $\geq 63.0\%$—independent of company size and sector, see Fig. 5. A notable exception are companies producing automotive software, which tend more to apply traditional methods.

On average, more than half of the Danish companies—disregarding size and sectors—apply agile practices, even those developing automotive software. How-

Table 2. Overview of the relative use of the different approaches based on (a) company size and (b) industry sector. For each item, the quantity is computed by counting the number of companies of, e.g., a particular size that have marked, e.g., a traditional method with at least a 5 (i.e., "we sometimes use it"). Note: while participants had to select exactly one company size, they could select multiple industry sectors in which their company is engaged.

	QTY	Method			Approaches Selected	Practice			Approaches Selected
		Traditional	Agile	Both		Traditional	Agile	Both	
Micro (<10)	2	0.0%	60.0%	40.0%	5	10.5%	36.8%	52.6%	19
Small (11-50)	7	0.0%	79.4%	20.6%	34	8.3%	56.5%	35.2%	108
Medium (51-250)	4	21.1%	57.9%	21.1%	19	12.9%	55.7%	31.4%	70
Large (>250)	2	21.1%	63.2%	15.8%	19	12.1%	53.4%	34.5%	58
Very Large (>2500)	7	24.4%	58.5%	17.1%	41	15.4%	52.3%	32.2%	149
Average		13.3%	63.8%	22.9%		11.8%	51.0%	37.2%	
Deviation		10.6%	6.2%	6.8%		1.9%	5.6%	6.2%	
Cloud Applications and Services (e.g., data storage, SaaS)	6	0.0%	75.0%	25.0%	32	9.0%	54.1%	36.9%	111
Web Applications and Services (e.g., portals, shops)	5	0.0%	70.8%	29.2%	24	10.9%	51.1%	38.0%	92
Other	5	26.7%	60.0%	13.3%	30	16.3%	52.0%	31.6%	98
Financial Services (e.g. Banking, Insurance, Trading)	3	13.3%	80.0%	6.7%	15	8.0%	60.0%	32.0%	50
Mobile Applications	3	0.0%	75.0%	25.0%	12	7.8%	52.9%	39.2%	51
Robotics (e.g., autonomous robots, UAVs/drones)	3	20.0%	55.0%	25.0%	20	16.1%	46.4%	37.5%	56
Other Information Systems (e.g. ERP, SAP, etc.)	2	30.0%	50.0%	20.0%	10	13.0%	50.0%	37.0%	46
Other Embedded Systems and Services	2	0.0%	66.7%	33.3%	3	19.0%	47.6%	33.3%	21
Energy (e.g., Smart Grid, renewable energy)	2	23.8%	61.9%	14.3%	21	12.7%	52.7%	34.5%	55
Home Automation and Smart Buildings	2	42.9%	50.0%	7.1%	14	19.5%	51.2%	29.3%	41
Games	2	11.1%	66.7%	22.2%	9	6.9%	58.6%	34.5%	29
Automotive Software and Systems	1	50.0%	25.0%	25.0%	4	12.5%	50.0%	37.5%	16
Media and Entertainment (e.g., photos, TV)	1	0.0%	83.3%	16.7%	6	5.3%	57.9%	36.8%	19
Average		16.8%	63.0%	20.2%		12.1%	52.7%	35.3%	
Deviation		14.3%	11.7%	6.6%		3.8%	3.1%	2.5%	

---

[3] The survey variables PU09 and PU10 changed scale from project stage one to two. Earlier they were binary, now they are on a 7-point Likert scale: **1**: 'Do not know the framework'; **2**: 'Do not know if we use it'; **3**: 'We never use it'; **4**: 'We rarely use it'; **5**: 'We sometimes use it'; **6**: 'We often use it'; **7**: 'We always use the framework'.

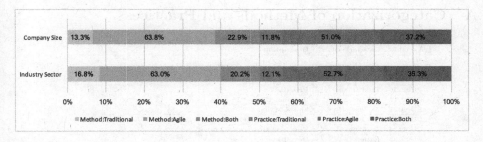

Fig. 5. Overview of the breakdown provided in Table 2 generated based on the averages.

ever, companies with less than ten employees appear to be less agile in practice, likely due to the lack of 'teams' as such.

Furthermore, the analysis in Table 2 supports one of the main results of project stage one [3], namely, that hybrid approaches emerge regardless of company size and industry sector ($\geq 20.2\%$).

Notably, and differently from earlier results [3], it seems that companies with less than 50 employees in Denmark do not use 'traditional' methods and only some 'traditional' practices. Similarly, it seems that 'younger' sectors, such as *media and entertainment, games,* and *mobile applications* are least 'traditional' in their practices. Interestingly, *financial services* report similar low application of 'traditional' practices, all below 10%.

We are aware that this analysis is premature and potentially misleading as only 22 respondents from Danmark are registered so far. To strengthen our analysis and to confirm the tendencies we encourage more participants from the Danish software industry to take the survey.

4   Conclusion and Final Remarks

In this short paper, we have presented and analyzed the current results of the Danish HELENA stage two survey, based on the data from August 15, 2017.

The trends seem to be in line with the entire data set as well as the results identified during the first stage of the project: traditional and agile methods and practices are combined with each other regardless of company size and industry sector. Nevertheless, some interesting differences are present in both the population and the data, which seem to indicate that Danish enterprises might favor a more agile development environment. The grounds for these differences and the extend to which methods and practices are combined will be further investigated once the survey will be closed. To this end, the Danish team will certainly attempt to promote and advertise more the HELENA survey, as attracting additional participation will be crucial to reach deeper and statistically sound insights.

Acknowledgements. We would like to thank—also on behalf of the entire HELENA team—all those who took part in the survey and that helped us collecting data.

A   Categorization of Methods and Practices

Variable	Categorization[a]	Description
Methods		
PU09_01	Traditional	Classic Waterfall Process
PU09_15	Traditional	Phase/Stage-gate model
PU09_16	Traditional	PRINCE2
PU09_17	Traditional	Rational Unified Process
PU09_21	*Traditional**	Spiral Model
PU09_22	Traditional	Structured Systems Analysis and Design Method (SSADM)
PU09_24	Traditional	V-shaped Process (V-Model)
PU09_03	Agile	DevOps
PU09_05	Agile	Dynamic Systems Development Method (DSDM)
PU09_06	Agile	eXtreme Programming (XP)
PU09_07	Agile	Feature Driven Development (FDD)
PU09_09	Agile	Kanban
PU09_10	Agile	Large-Scale Scrum (LESS)
PU09_11	Agile	Lean Software Development
PU09_13	Agile	Nexus
PU09_18	Agile	Scaled Agile Framework (SAFe)
PU09_19	Agile	Scrum
PU09_20	Agile	ScrumBan
PU09_02	Both	Crystal Family
PU09_04	Both	Domain-Driven Design
PU09_08	Both	Iterative Development
PU09_12	Both	Model-Driven Architecture (MDA)
PU09_14	Both	Personal Software Process
PU09_23	Both	Team Software Process
Practices		
PU10_01	Traditional	Architecture Specifications
PU10_03	Traditional	Automated Theorem Proving
PU10_16	Traditional	Detailed Designs/Design Specifications
PU10_19	Traditional	Expert/Team based estimation (e.g. Planning Poker)
PU10_20	*Traditional**	Formal estimation (e.g. COCOMO, FP)
PU10_21	Traditional	Formal Specification
PU10_24	Traditional	Model Checking
PU10_36	Traditional	Use Case Modeling (as Requirements Engineering Practice)
PU10_05	Agile	Backlog Management
PU10_06	Agile	Burn-Down Charts (as Progress Monitoring Practice)
PU10_09	Agile	Collective code ownership
PU10_10	Agile	Continuous deployment
PU10_11	Agile	Continuous integration
PU10_12	Agile	Daily Standup
PU10_13	Agile	Definition of done/ready
PU10_15	*Agile**	Destructive Testing
PU10_23	Agile	Iteration/Sprint Reviews
PU10_17	Agile	Limit Work-in-Progress (e.g., using Kanban board)
PU10_25	Agile	On-Site Customer
PU10_28	*Agile**	Refactoring
PU10_29	Agile	Release planning
PU10_30	Agile	Retrospectives
PU10_31	Agile	Scrum-of-Scrums
PU10_34	Agile	User Stories (as Requirements Engineering Practice)
PU10_35	Agile	Velocity-based planning
PU10_02	Both	Automated Code Generation
PU10_04	Both	Automated Unit Testing
PU10_07	Both	Code review
PU10_08	Both	Coding standards
PU10_14	Both	Design Reviews
PU10_18	Both	End-to-End (System) Testing
PU10_22	Both	Iteration Planning
PU10_26	Both	Pair Programming
PU10_27	Both	Prototyping
PU10_32	Both	Security Testing
PU10_33	Both	Test-driven Development (TDD)

[a]Note that the items which categorization is marked in *italic with a * symbol* are considered particularly debatable.

References

1. Diebold, P., Zehler, T.: The right degree of agility in rich processes. In: Kuhrmann, M., Münch, J., Richardson, I., Rausch, A., Zhang, H. (eds.) Managing Software Process Evolution, pp. 15–37. Springer, Cham (2016). doi:10.1007/978-3-319-31545-4_2
2. Kuhrmann, M., Diebold, P., Münch, J., Tell, P., Garousi, V., Felderer, M., Trektere, K., McCaffery, F., Linssen, O., Hanser, E., Prause, C.R.: Hybrid software and system development in practice: waterfall, scrum, and beyond. In: Proceedings of the 2017 International Conference on Software and System Process, ICSSP 2017, pp. 30–39. ACM, New York (2017)
3. Kuhrmann, M., Diebold, P., Münch, J., Tell, P., Trektere, K., McCaffery, F., Garousi, V., Felderer, M., Linssen, O., Hanser, E., Prause, C.R.: Hybrid software development approaches in practice: a European perspective. IEEE Softw. (2017, in press)
4. Kuhrmann, M., Münch, J., Tell, P., Diebold, P.: Summary of the 1st international workshop on hybrid development approaches in software systems development. ACM (2017)

HELENA Study: Reasons for Combining Agile and Traditional Software Development Approaches in German Companies

Jil Klünder[1]([✉]), Philipp Hohl[2], Masud Fazal-Baqaie[3], Stephan Krusche[4], Steffen Küpper[5], Oliver Linssen[6], and Christian R. Prause[7]

[1] Leibniz Universität Hannover, Software Engineering Group, Hannover, Germany
jil.kluender@inf.uni-hannover.de
[2] Daimler AG, Research and Development, Ulm, Germany
philipp.hohl@daimler.com
[3] S&N CQM GmbH, Paderborn, Germany
masud.fazal-baqaie@sn-cqm.de
[4] Technische Universität München, Munich, Germany
krusche@in.tum.de
[5] Technische Universität Clausthal, Clausthal-Zellerfeld, Germany
steffen.kuepper@tu-clausthal.de
[6] FOM University of Applied Sciences for Economics and Management,
Essen, Germany
oliver.linssen@fom.de
[7] German Aerospace Center, Bonn, Germany
christian.prause@dlr.de

Abstract. Many software development teams face the problem of selecting a suitable development approach fitting to their specific context. According to them, the combination of agile and traditional approaches seems to be the solution to handle this problem. However, the current state of practice with respect to hybrid approaches is not sufficiently examined. Most studies focus either on traditional or on agile methods, but the combination of both is not well investigated yet. The "Hybrid dEveLopmENt Approaches in software systems development" (HELENA) study performs a large-scale international survey in order to gain insights into the distribution of hybrid approaches. So far, the study indicates several reasons why companies combine agile and traditional approaches. The hybrid approaches aim at improving the frequency of delivery to customers, the adaptability and the flexibility of the process to react to change. Furthermore, it is the aim to increase the productivity. In this publication, we present the current state of the German results and outline the next steps.

Keywords: HELENA study · Hybrid software development · Empirical study in Germany

© Springer International Publishing AG 2017
M. Felderer et al. (Eds.): PROFES 2017, LNCS 10611, pp. 428–434, 2017.
https://doi.org/10.1007/978-3-319-69926-4_32

1   Introduction

Nowadays, there exist various methods and practices to develop software. The methods consist of agile and plan-driven processes [6]. However, it seems to be a best practice to combine both approaches. While the plan-driven process provides clear process models with an overall project structure, the agile approach enables more flexibility and individuality by focusing on shorter time-to-market and customer satisfaction [1]. In order to obtain the advantages of both approaches, hybrid software development seems to increasingly spread into industry. To investigate this topic in detail, the HELENA study was brought to life. The study investigates the combinations of agile, traditional, and other kinds of software development approaches in use. Furthermore, the study examines how agile methods and practices are integrated into traditional development approaches and why they are selected.

Currently, 85 researchers from 26 countries contribute to the study of hybrid development approaches. This paper presents the current state of the data collection in Germany, shows an overview of preliminary results and outlines the next steps with respect to data analysis.

2   Related Work

There are only a few publications focusing on the prevalence of hybrid approaches: Boehm and Turner [3] motivate the combination of agile and plan-driven approaches. They mention that a changing world needs agile and disciplined development methods. They characterize "home grounds" where the approaches are most likely to succeed and identify five critical dimensions. With a classification within the critical dimensions, it is possible to set up a balanced strategy for a successful combination of agile and plan-driven approaches. The presented risk-based method takes advantage of the strengths and mitigates the weaknesses of both approaches.

Diebold and Zehler [4] examine the process of combining agile and traditional development methods. They distinguish between the revolutionary and the evolutionary approach, which differ in the order of occurrence of the methods. The authors describe the coexistence of both development methods, but they do not investigate their distribution.

Kuhrmann and Linssen [5] examine the use of process models in Germany. They compare the data from 2006 with the data of 2013 and observe the emergence of many different models and approaches. They point out that the combination of traditional process models and agile development approaches is pervasive. However, agile approaches are not as dominating as promoted by the agile community. Theocharis et al. [7] report of a high popularity of hybrid approaches. They experience the lack of quantitative data representing the use of development methods. The HELENA study aims at examining this research gap in detail.

3   Data Collection in Germany

Since May 2, 2017, the questionnaire of the HELENA survey is available online in German, English, Spanish and Portuguese. The German team of HELENA consists of 14 researchers from 11 different institutions. The researchers encouraged practitioners from different German organisations including SMEs and companies to participate in the study. Therefore, they sent personalized emails to contacts within organisations and used mailing lists of software engineering communities. Like teams from other countries, they also distributed the questionnaire using social media via Twitter, XING and ResearchGate.

The data points collected until this intermediate report seem to indicate selection and response biases resulting from the invitation method (personal emails). To mitigate these biases, the researchers started a Google AdWords campaign in order to find additional participants without a personal relationship to the researchers. (Note that the data collected during this campaign is not included in this report.) After 10 days, advertisements to "participate in the scientific survey" were displayed 40K times and 300 people clicked through the survey. Until now, five people completed the questionnaire over this campaign (one of them from Peru as advertisements were initially not restricted to Germany).

4   Overview of Preliminary Results

Based on the data collection until August 15, 2017, the German team collected 95 complete data records from German software developers. Most of the participants (33%) are employed in very large organizations with more than 2500 employees. 31% work in large organisations with more than 250 employees (cf. Table 1). There have been 45 more responses from larger organisations than from smaller ones. Among the selection bias, a possible reason might be that hybrid approaches are more interesting for large companies because they are more likely to use traditional development processes and aim to speed up development. Hybrid approaches promise them an improved development process. Small software companies tend to apply agile methods and practices right from the beginning. Hence, they often do not think about implementing hybrid approaches so far.

Table 1. Number of companies using hybrid approaches

Company size	# Participants	# Companies using hybrid approaches
<10	10	7 (70%)
10–50	5	5 (100%)
51–250	20	14 (70%)
251–2500	29	22 (76%)
>2500	31	25 (71%)

The HELENA study also asks about the size of the developed software products and the project length. In three of four cases, the product size is more than one person year (76%). Only 2% of the projects do not last longer than two person months. One third of the teams is not distributed (35%). Half of the teams is distributed either globally (26%) or nationally (same country) (24%). 15% of the projects are regionally distributed, i.e. distributed on the same continent.

One third of the participants either works in the automotive domain (16%) or in the financial sector (15%). The automotive sector is strong in Germany. Hence, it is plausible that there is a high participation from automotive software developers. 12% of the participants work in the space domain. However, these 12% do not represent the real-world industry distribution of the space domain in Germany and hence may indicate skewed representation.

26 project or team managers (27%) and 16 developers (17%) from German companies participated in the survey. Eleven participants are quality managers (12%). Most participants have more than ten years of working experience (62%). The findings in Table 1 show that the combination of agile and traditional development methods do not depend from the size of the company. In each company size category, more than 70% of the interviewed participants use hybrid approaches.

39 participants in our study (41%) stated that each project within their company can individually decide which process should be used. 20 participants (21%) report that decisions are made on business unit level. 38% of the projects are operated according to a in-house standard process. Projects either decide about specific practices and methods on demand during the project (37%) or a project manager tailors the process in the beginning (19%). In 15% of the cases, the customer is taken into account when selecting the practices and methods.

Figure 1 gives an overview of some goals, companies want to reach by selecting individual development approaches, such as time-to-market, employee satisfaction and improved delivery pace.

Most very large (>2500 employees) companies combine agile and traditional approaches to improve the frequency of delivery to customers (64%), to improve the adaptability and flexibility of the process to react to change (64%) and to improve the productivity (64%). Large companies (251–2500) also aim at improving the productivity (81%), the planning and estimation (67%) and the adaptability and flexibility of the process to react to change (62%). Micro companies (<10 employees) also want to increase the productivity (57%) and the external product quality (57%). The small companies mostly want to satisfy the employees (80%), which seems to be less important for companies which are either smaller (29%) or larger (33% resp. 19%). The very large companies also want to increase employee satisfaction (50%).

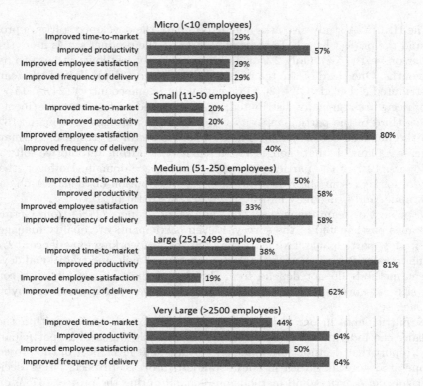

Fig. 1. Reasons for companies to implement hybrid approaches (extract)

5   Future Work

This paper presents ongoing research. So neither the data collection nor the analysis are complete yet. Next, we present a set of initial research questions for exploring the distribution of hybrid approaches in Germany and worldwide.

In order to examine the distribution of hybrid development approaches within different company sizes, we are interested in analysing domain-specific contexts. In the future, we want to examine, if there is a correlation between organization size, the implemented new roles and the way of working in order to gain insights into advantages and disadvantages, difficulties and experiences with more or less suitable combinations. Therefore, we aim at answering the following research questions:

RQ1:   Are there any domains working with a purely agile approach?

RQ1.1: Are there context factors that enable the implementation of agile?
RQ1.2: Which agile approaches are in use when implementing agile?

RQ2: Are there any domains working with a purely plan-driven approach?

RQ2.1: Are there context factors that inhibit the integration of agile and lead to the implementation of plan-driven approaches?

RQ3: Which domains primarily use hybrid approaches?

RQ3.1: Which domain-specific context factors support the implementation of hybrid approaches?
RQ3.2: Which combinations are widely distributed and which ones are less suitable?
RQ3.3: Are there best practices when implementing hybrid approaches?
RQ3.4: Do common practice and best practice differ from each other?

According to Boehm [2], agile and plan-driven software development approaches have different home grounds, i.e., agile development is favourable for fast-paced markets, while domains with high failure costs tend to favour traditional development models.

RQ4: What is the effect of software criticality on the choice of development approach?

RQ4.1: Is there a clear relationship between the choice of the development approach and the criticality of developed software?
RQ4.2: Do domains with expected higher failure costs (e.g., aerospace, automotive, medicine) favour more traditional development approaches?

6   Conclusion

The results of our study indicate a high popularity of hybrid development approaches in Germany. Independent of the size of the organization, many project teams combine individually selected development approaches. Most of the organisations aim at improving the productivity, the customer's perceived product quality, planning and estimation as well as the frequency of delivery to the customer. We plan to extend our data collection and analysis in future work.

References

1. Beck, K., Beedle, M., Van Bennekum, A., Cockburn, A., Cunningham, W., Fowler, M., Grenning, J., Highsmith, J., Hunt, A., Jeffries, R., et al.: Manifesto for Agile Software Development (2001)
2. Boehm, B.: Get ready for agile methods, with care. Computer **35**(1), 64–69 (2002)
3. Boehm, B., Turner, R.: Balancing Agility and Discipline: A Guide for the Perplexed, Portable Documents. Addison-Wesley Professional, Boston (2003)
4. Diebold, P., Zehler, T.: The right degree of agility in rich processes. In: Kuhrmann, M., Münch, J., Richardson, I., Rausch, A., Zhang, H. (eds.) Managing Software Process Evolution, pp. 15–37. Springer, Cham (2016). doi:10.1007/978-3-319-31545-4_2

5. Kuhrmann, M., Linssen, O.: Welche Vorgehensmodelle nutzt Deutschland? Projektmanagement und Vorgehensmodelle **2014**, 17–32 (2014)
6. Kuhrmann, M., Münch, J., Diebold, P., Linssen, O., Prause, C.R.: On the use of hybrid development approaches in software and systems development: construction and test of the HELENA survey. Projektmanagement und Vorgehensmodelle **2016**, 59–68 (2016)
7. Theocharis, G., Kuhrmann, M., Münch, J., Diebold, P.: Is *Water-Scrum-Fall* reality? On the use of agile and traditional development practices. In: Abrahamsson, P., Corral, L., Oivo, M., Russo, B. (eds.) PROFES 2015. LNCS, vol. 9459, pp. 149–166. Springer, Cham (2015). doi:10.1007/978-3-319-26844-6_11

Hybrid Software and System Development in Practice: Initial Results from Austria

Michael Felderer[1(✉)], Dietmar Winkler[2], and Stefan Biffl[2]

[1] University of Innsbruck, Innsbruck, Austria
michael.felderer@uibk.ac.at
[2] Vienna University of Technology, Vienna, Austria
{dietmar.winkler,stefan.biffl}@tuwien.ac.at

Abstract. The application of software process models in industry includes traditional processes, agile processes, and process variants that aim at balancing traditional and agile with focus on specific industry needs. To investigate the characteristics of such hybrid software and system development approaches that combine agile and traditional approaches the HELENA project was initiated. HELENA is based on a large international survey. Based on the first HELENA survey, conducted in 2016, in 2017 a second round of surveys has been launched. This paper focuses on initial results and discussions of the data from Austria where 22 persons participated. Results showed a good balance of small and medium enterprises and large organizations. Iterative development processes and Scrum are widely spread in these organizations where traditional approaches are often combined with some agile practices.

Keywords: Agile software development · Hybrid development approaches · Software process · Survey

1 Introduction

The adoption of suitable software and system development methods and practices has become essential for business success in the age of digitalization. There are many agile, e.g., Scrum, or traditional approaches, e.g., Waterfall, with a high number of different methods and practices available, which are often combined ad-hoc in industry. However, systematic investigations for their combination in a specific context to a so-called hybrid software development approach are missing. A hybrid software development approach (short: hybrid approach) is any combination of agile and traditional (plan-driven or rich) approaches that an organizational unit adopts and customizes to its own context needs [1].

To investigate characteristics of hybrid approaches, the research project HELENA[1] (Hybrid DEveLopmENt Approaches in software systems development) was initiated. The first round of surveys has been scheduled in 2016 in a large-scale international context [1]. The main outcome was that organizations typically use some combinations

---

[1] Helena Survey: https://helenastudy.wordpress.com/.

© Springer International Publishing AG 2017
M. Felderer et al. (Eds.): PROFES 2017, LNCS 10611, pp. 435–442, 2017.
https://doi.org/10.1007/978-3-319-69926-4_33

where traditional processes serve as a framework for agile practices. These combinations are independent of the size of an organization. The authors concluded that such hybrid approaches are the results of a natural process evolution, driven by experience and pragmatism [1, 3]. Based on lessons learned and feedback in 2017 a second round of improved surveys have been launched. By August 15, 2017 more than 500 participants from around 20 participating countries all over the world have contributed to this replicated survey.

In this paper we provide initial results and discussion of the data received from Austria, where 22 persons participated in the survey. This paper provides a contribution to in-depth discussions on HELENA at the 2nd Workshop on Hybrid Software and System Development Approaches collocated with PROFES 2017.

The remainder of this paper is structured as follows. Section 2 presents initial survey results collected in organizations, located in Austria with focus on organization demographics, personal roles of respondents, and applied software engineering frameworks and methods. In Sect. 3 we discuss the results and provide candidate next steps.

2   Initial Results

In this section we provide an overview of the demographics and initial results from Austria. Initially, we invited 55 selected individuals covering 40 different organization in Austria. Organizations include small and medium enterprises as well as large organizations. Overall, we received 22 responses, which corresponds to a response rate of 40%.

2.1   Company Size, Business Sector, and Industrial Sector

Figure 1 shows demographical data on the size of organizations based on collected data from Austria.

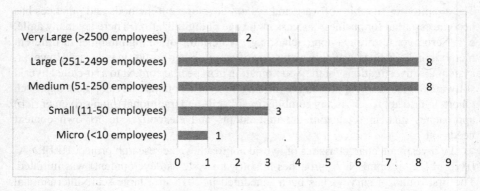

Fig. 1. Company data: distribution of the company size [number of organizations].

Results include 1 micro organization (5%), 11 small and medium enterprises (50%), and 10 large and very large organizations (45%). Thus, there is a good balance of very large/large and small/medium enterprises.

Figure 2 illustrates the share of business areas of the related organizations. The respondents reported 49 different business domains in their organizations. Please note that multiple business areas are covered especially by large and very large organizations. The top-three rated business areas are: (a) Customer-specific Software Development (15 responses), (b) Standard Software Development (10 responses), and (c) System Development (8 responses). Furthermore, some organizations focus on supporting and consulting business areas, such as Project Management Support (5 responses), IT Consulting, Training, and Services (5 responses), and Software Process Management (3 responses). One organization declares Research & Development as a core business area and 2 responses did not provide any details on their businesses.

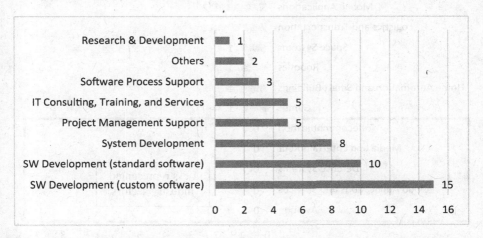

Fig. 2. Company data – distribution of business areas [number of business areas, multiple answers accepted].

Figure 3 presents the distribution of the industrial sector. Similar to business areas, multiple answers were possible. The Austrian result set includes 50 industrial sector nominations. The six most reported industry sectors include (a) financial services (8 nominations), (b) Public Sector, (c) Medical Devices, (d) Energy (6 nomination each), (e) Web applications, and (f) Automotive Software and Systems (4 nominations each). In the Austrian results, none of the respondents work in organizations who see Telecommunication, Media and Entertainment, Defense Systems, Cloud Applications and Services, and Aviation as targeted industry sectors.

These analysis results are typically biased by the selection of the survey participants and responses. However, in context of the application of software processes and practices the industry sector this limiting factors have to be considered in the analysis.

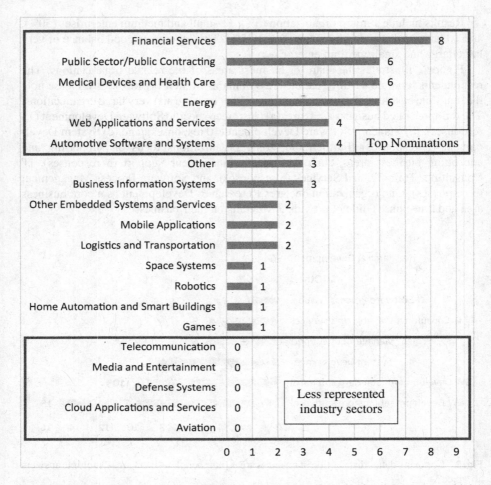

Fig. 3. Company data – distribution of industrial sectors [number of industrial sectors, multiple answers accepted].

2.2 Roles and Experiences

To complete the demographic analysis, this section summarizes individual roles and experiences of respondents. Figure 4 illustrates the distribution of the main role of the respondents based on 22 responses. Note that participants had to declare their main role in typical projects. Thus, multiple answers were not possible.

The main roles of the respondents are (a) Project/Team Manager (5 nomination = 23%), (b) Quality Manager, (c) C-Level Manager, (d) Product Manager/Owner, and (e) Developers (3 nominations = 14% each). Note that the respondent group does not include Analysts/Requirements Engineers and Testers. Again, these results are biased by the selection of the survey participants and responses.

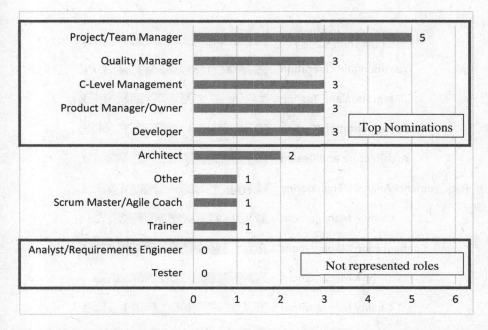

Fig. 4. Respondents data: distribution of project roles [number of main roles of respondents].

In addition, we captured the experience level of the respondents. The results showed highly experienced survey participants in Austria, i.e., 4 participants (i.e., 18%) with 6–10 years of professional experience and 18 participants (i.e., 82%) with more than 10 years of experiences.

These experience levels corresponds to the main roles of the respondents as typically more experienced participants take management tasks and roles.

2.3 Application of Traditional/Agile Software Engineering Best-Practices

Based on standard project activities according to the SWEBOK [2], Fig. 5 presents the distribution of best-practice nominations of respondents of industry practice data in Austria. Note that we received an overall number of 17 survey responses (some participants did not provide any data for this evaluation).

The results show a balance of traditional and agile software engineering best-practices. Traditional approaches are mainly used for architecture and design, configuration management, and risk management. Agile approaches are focused on integration and testing, change management, quality management, and project management. It is also observable that for architecture and design, requirements analysis/engineering, quality management, and project management hybrid approaches are used to overcome limitations of traditional and agile approaches. For transition and operation, change management, and risk management, we received responses, that these best-practices seem to be

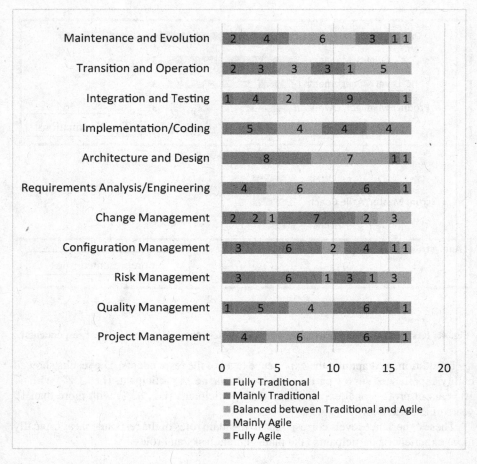

Fig. 5. Software engineering phases – traditional vs. agile approaches [number of the application of agile practices]

unknown or it is unknown to the respondents how these approaches are applied. Detailed analysis of these results require further investigations.

2.4 Software Engineering Frameworks/Methods

Figure 6 shows the industrial relevance of different software engineering frameworks and methods. In the survey response sample from Austria iterative development approaches and Scrum are widespread and frequently used. Kanban, the waterfall process approach and the V-shaped process model are also used to some extent. Other process models (both agile and traditional approaches) are either unknown or less frequently used.

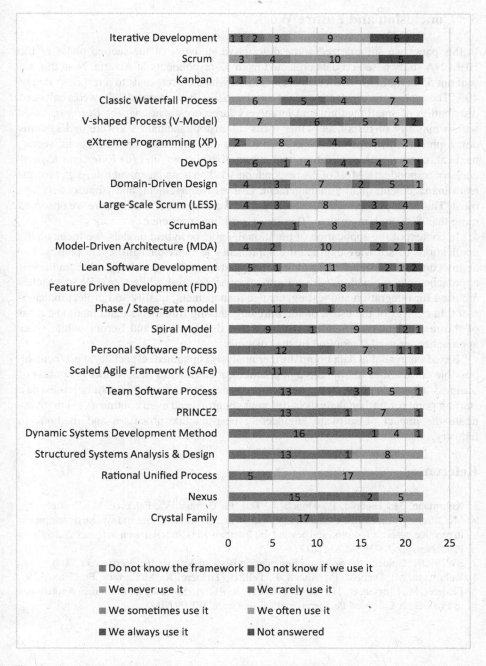

Fig. 6. Used software engineering frameworks and methods [number of applied frameworks/ methods].

3   Conclusion and Future Work

In this paper we summarized some descriptive statistics of the second phase of the HELENA study based on data collected from 22 respondents in Austria. Note that we sent out 55 invitations in selected organization which corresponds to a response rate of 40%. The analysis results focus on (a) *Company Size* where the results showed a balanced distribution of small/medium and large/very large organizations; (b) *Business Areas* with a majority of respondents that focus on custom/standard software and systems development; (c) *Industry Sectors* with a focus on financial services, public sector, medical, energy, web application, and automotive sectors; and (d) *Roles and Experiences* of respondents. Most of the respondents work in a management role, e.g., project/team management, quality management, C-level management, and (senior) development. This is also supported by the analysis of working experience, where we observed more than 80% with more than 10 years of working experience.

In context of the application of traditional, agile, or hybrid models, we focus on the applications of software engineering approaches in individual life cycle phases. For architecture and design, configuration management, and risk management traditional approaches or combinations with agile practices are favored, while core agile approaches are used for integration and testing, change management, quality and project management. In context of the usage of software engineering frameworks and methods, most of the respondents are familiar with iterative development and Scrum, while other approaches are used if required by the customer.

Based on available data points further analysis is planned, especially with focus on possible correlations on the usage of practices, methods and frameworks in context of business area, industry sectors, and company size. In addition, the results represent a starting point for further analysis in different countries and even continents [3] to investigate the impact of software engineering best-practice processes and methods in industry.

References

1. Kuhrmann, M., Diebold, P., Münch, J., Tell, P., Garousi, V., Felderer, M., Trektere, K., McCaffery, F., Linssen, O., Hanser, E., Prause, C.R.: Hybrid software and system development in practice: waterfall, scrum, and beyond. In: International Conference on Software and System Processes, pp. 30–39. ACM (2017)
2. SWEBOK: Guide to the Software Engineering Body of Knowledge, Version 3 (2004)
3. Kuhrmann, M., Diebold, P., Münch, J., Tell, P., Trektere, K., McCaffery, F., Garousi, V., Felderer, M., Linssen, O., Hanser, E., Prause, C.R.: Hybrid Software Development Approaches in Practice: A European Perspective. IEEE Software. IEEE (2017)

HELENA Study: Initial Observations of Software Development Practices in Argentina

Nicolás Paez, Diego Fontdevila[✉], and Alejandro Oliveros

Universidad Nacional de Tres de Febrero, Caseros, Argentina
nicopaez@computer.org, {dfontdevila,aoliveros}@untref.edu.ar

Abstract. HELENA Survey is a worldwide initiative that aims to investigate the use of hybrid software development approaches ranging from agile to traditional and how they combine. This article presents the initial results and observations on software development practice in Argentina, and briefly discusses two patterns of interest related to software development practice usage.

Keywords: HELENA · Software development practices · Practices usage

1 Introduction

HELENA Survey is a multi-national initiative that aims at investigating the current state of practice in software and systems development. More specifically the goal of this initiative is to study how different development approaches are used in practice and how practitioners combine them. It uses a hybrid development perspective integrating agile and traditional approaches, and ranges from emerging and innovative sectors to regulated domains [1]. There are currently more than 40 institutions worldwide involved in the initiative. The study was designed in 3 stages. This article was written during the second stage that focuses on massive data collection.

In this paper we present initial results and observations of software development practices in Argentina. We also briefly discuss two patterns of interest related to the usage of organizational and technical practices, and the relevance of agile practices usage.

2 Results

At this point, the Argentinian sample contains 53 data points while the global sample contains 501 data points. Figure 1 shows the results in terms of company size for the global and Argentinian samples. It is interesting to note that in the Argentinian sample the highest percentage of respondents corresponds to medium sized companies (51–250 employees).

© Springer International Publishing AG 2017
M. Felderer et al. (Eds.): PROFES 2017, LNCS 10611, pp. 443–449, 2017.
https://doi.org/10.1007/978-3-319-69926-4_34

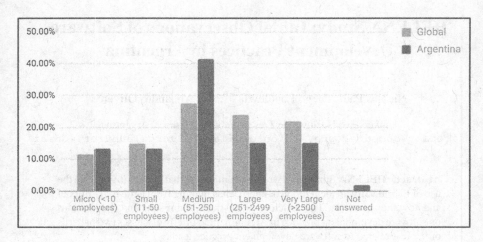

Fig. 1. Company size distribution.

Figure 2 shows the results in terms of Product size. In this case the Argentinian and global distributions follow the same pattern.

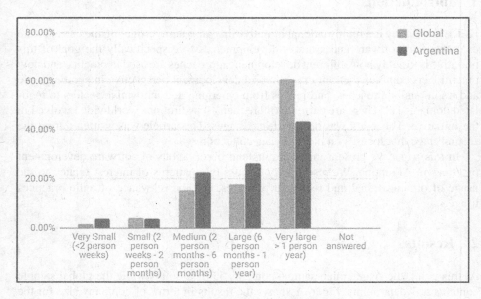

Fig. 2. Product size distribution.

Figure 3 shows the results in terms of business area. In both samples the main area is *Custom Software Development*. At the same time there is a big difference in favor of the global sample in the *Hardware/Embedded Software development* area.

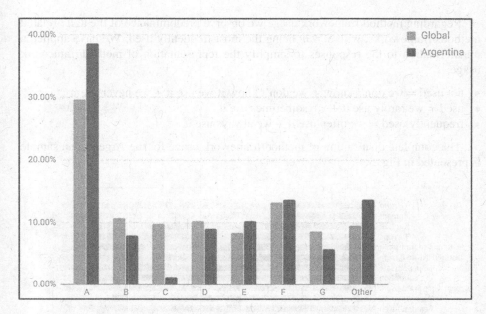

Fig. 3. Business area distribution: (A) Custom Software Development, (B) Standard Software Development, (C) Hardware and Software/Embedded Software, (D) Consulting/Project Management Support, (E) Consulting/Software Process Support, (F) IT Consulting, Training, and Services.

When looking at roles in the Argentinian sample we see that the two biggest groups are *Developers* and *Project/Team Managers*, the distribution of roles is shown in Fig. 4.

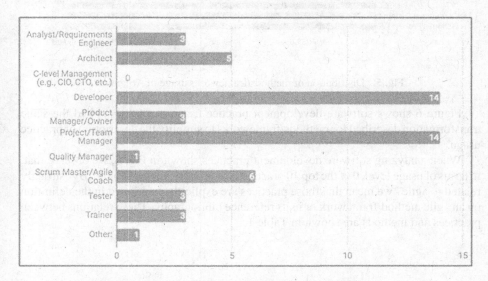

Fig. 4. Respondent's role distribution in Argentina

Regarding method/framework usage we observe predominance of the agile-related methods/frameworks, with *Scrum* being the most frequently used. We have applied a transformation to the responses to simplify the representation of method/framework usage:

- not used = we don't know + we don't know if we use it + we never use it
- used = we rarely use it + we sometimes use it
- frequently used = we often use it + we always use it

The complete distribution of method/framework usage for the Argentinian sample is presented in Fig. 5.

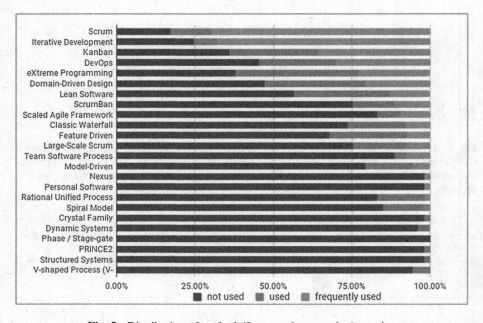

Fig. 5. Distribution of methods/frameworks usage in Argentina

Figure 6 shows software development practice usage, we have applied the same transformation described for methods/frameworks to simplify the description of practice usage.

When analyzing software development practices shown in Fig. 6, we observe that, in terms of usage level, 9 of the top 10 practices are strongly related to agile. By "strongly related to agile" we mean that those practices are explicitly mentioned in the definition on an agile method/framework or in its reference bibliography. These relations between practices and methods are shown in Table 1.

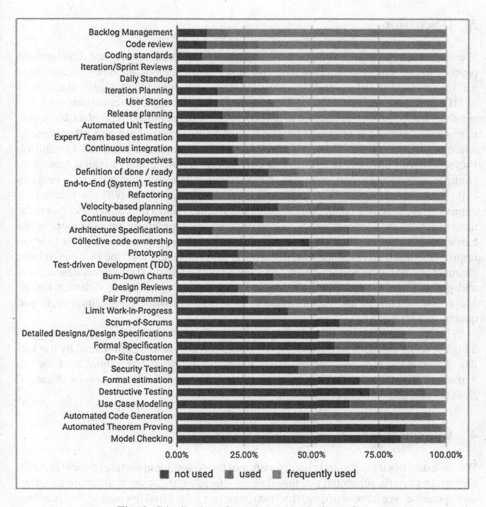

Fig. 6. Distribution of practices usage in Argentina

Table 1. Relation between practices and agile methods

Practice	Method	Reference bibliography
Backlog management	Scrum	Scrum guide [2]
Coding standards	XP	Extreme programming explained [3]
Iteration/Sprint reviews	Scrum	Scrum guide
Daily standup	Scrum	Scrum guide
Iteration planning	Scrum	Scrum guide
User stories	XP	Extreme programming explained
Release planning	Crystal	Crystal clear [4]
Automated unit testing	Crystal	Crystal clear
Expert/Team based estimation	XP	Extreme programming explained

3 Discussion

We center our discussion on two particular patterns related to software development practice usage. The first pattern is based on the categorization of practices into technical and organizational. When looking at the top 10 practices used in the Argentinian results of HELENA, we see that most of them are organizational. This is consistent with our previous study [5]. A right balance between technical and organizational practices seems reasonable, given that technical practices support product quality and effectiveness, while organizational practices in general affect cost, schedule and team sustainability. Projects lacking severely in any of these two aspects are more likely to fail (Chow et al. identify engineering practices as one of the three main success factors in agile projects [6]). Furthermore, cost-effectiveness might probably depend heavily on a balanced approach taking into account costs, quality and productivity. This could mean that technical practices are harder to adopt, or that organizational practices are used more in the earlier stages improvement processes (and that there is a predominance of early stage improvement initiatives in the sample). This is also consistent with the fact that Scrum, the most popular method/framework, does not have any technical practices. Researchers and practitioners have applied this categorization, although it takes different forms: Meyer uses technical and organizational/managerial [7] while Pantiuchina et al. use quality and speed [8].

The second pattern we want to focus on is the fact that agile-related practices have a high level of usage. We consider that this situation may also be influenced by the fact that *Scrum* is the most used development method/framework. Even more, 4 of the top 5 methods/frameworks (in terms of usage) are also agile-related: *Scrum*, *Kanban*, *DevOps* and *Extreme Programming*.

4 Conclusions

We have described the general characteristics of the Argentinian sample of the HELENA Survey and briefly presented our initial observations on the state of software development practice. We have also described two patterns that we find interesting, the predominance of organizational over technical practices, and the relevance of agile practices usage.

In the short term we plan to continue with data collection in Argentina and compare the observed trends in Argentina with the global sample. Once the data collection is completed, further studies may be conducted to identify potential causes and implications of the two patterns of interest described in the previous section.

References

1. Kuhrmann, M., et al.: On the use of hybrid development approaches in software and systems development: construction and test of the HELENA survey. In: Proceedings of the Annual Special Interest Group Meeting Projektmanagement und Vorgehensmodelle (PVM). Lecture Notes in Informatics (LNI), vol. 263 (2016)

2. Kchwaber, K., Sutherland, J.: Scrum Guide. http://www.scrumguides.org/scrum-guide.html. Accessed 10 Aug 2017
3. Beck, K., Andres, C.: Extreme Programming Explained: Embrace Change, 2nd edn. Addison-Wesley, Boston (2004)
4. Cockburn, A.: Crystal Clear: A Human-Powered Methodology for Small Teams. Addison-Wesley Professional, Boston (2004)
5. Paez, N., Fontdevila, D., Oliveros, A.: Characterizing technical and organizational practices in the agile community. In: Proceedings of the CONAIISI, Salta, Argentina (2016)
6. Chow, T., Cao, D.B.: A survey study of critical success factors in agile software projects. J. Syst. Soft. **81**(6), 961–971 (2008). http://doi.org/10.1016/j.jss.2007.08.020
7. Meyer, B.: Agile!: The Good, the Hype and the Ugly, 2014th edn. Springer, New York (2014)
8. Pantiuchina, J., Mondini, M., Khanna, D., Wang, X., Abrahamsson, P.: Are software startups applying agile practices? The state of the practice from a large survey. In: Baumeister, H., Lichter, H., Riebisch, M. (eds.) Agile Processes in Software Engineering and Extreme Programming, pp. 167–183. Springer, Cham (2017). doi:10.1007/978-3-319-57633-6_11

Workshop: HuFo 2017

3rd International Workshop on Human Factors in Software Development Processes (HuFo): Measuring System Quality

Silvia Abrahao[1(✉)], Maria Teresa Baldassarre[2], Danilo Caivano[2], Yvonne Dittrich[3], Rosa Lanzilotti[2], and Antonio Piccinno[2]

[1] Universitat Politecnica de Valencia (UPV), Valencia, Spain
sabrahao@dsic.upv.es
[2] Università degli Studi di Bari "Aldo Moro", Bari, Italy
{mariateresa.baldassarre,danilo.caivano,rosa.lanzilotti,
antonio.piccinno}@uniba.it
[3] IT University of Copenhagen, Copenhagen, Denmark
ydi@itu.dk

Abstract. The two communities of Software Engineering and Human-Computer Interaction tackle issues related to the software development process differently although with the same final goal: that of developing high quality software most effectively. This workshop has reached its third edition and is continuing to pursue the positive results achieved in previous years. The research question discussed is: how can we assure high quality software from a HCI and SE perspective?

Keywords: Human factors · System quality · Measurement · Metrics

1 Workshop Theme and Rationale

HuFo workshop is at its third edition. In fact, the success of the first two editions allowed us to organize this edition in conjunction with PROFES 2017 in Innsbruck, Austria. The first edition of the HuFo was held in Bozen-Bolzano, Italy, during the 16th International Conference on Product-Focused Software Process Improvement (PROFES 2015), while the second HuFo edition was held in Trondheim, Norway, during the PROFES 2017 (for more information see the HuFo workshop website at: http://hufo2015.serandp.com and http://hufo2016.serandp.com).

The main theme of this edition of the workshop is "measuring system quality" in order to address aspects both from users' side (Human-Computer Interaction (HCI) aspects) and software system (Software Engineering (SE) side). The SE and HCI communities are collaborating to create better software products, but the two communities are still far from being synergic while they could both gain from a better integration. Recent efforts have contributed to increase the synergy between SE and HCI. Nevertheless, this has not led to expected results and impacts with respect to the software development process. Indeed, recent literature has pointed out how in most empirical

© Springer International Publishing AG 2017

M. Felderer et al. (Eds.): PROFES 2017, LNCS 10611, pp. 453–456, 2017.
https://doi.org/10.1007/978-3-319-69926-4_35

evaluations only a small number of works include human participants. Moreover, there is still little experience in conducting empirical studies with human participants.

The overall goal of this interdisciplinary workshop is to raise the level of engagement and discussion about human factors in software product engineering and development processes. A further goal of the workshop is to identify opportunities to improve the quality of scientific discourse and progress on human aspects of software development, as well as to identify opportunities able to educate researchers about how to conduct sound human-centered evaluations in the context of software engineering.

To achieve these goals, it is important to bring together researchers and practitioners who face the problem of integrating human factors in software development processes and have tried effective methods to resolve it. The workshop will provide a forum to discuss the following research questions:

- What are the key methods that allow the integration of human factors in software development processes?
- What methods do current software development teams use to engage users in development processes?
- How can the level of human factor involvement be objectively verified during and after software development?
- How to educate researchers on performing human-centered evaluations in the software engineering processes?

2   Workshop Contributions

Four papers were accepted to be presented for the third edition of the HuFo workshop. The first paper, titled "Don't Underestimate the Human Factors! Exploring Team Communication Effects" and written by Fabian Kortum, Jil Klünder, and Kurt Schneider of the Leibniz Universität (Hannover, Germany), explores one of the main critical issue in software development process, i.e. the team communication. The goal of the research was to increase the awareness for often insufficiently interpreted human factors. Thus, the authors investigate several team communication effects with data records from an empirical study with 34 academic software projects. An approach to compare between conventional linear dependency analyses and a novel technique for automatized characterization onto team communication effects is described. In other words, the authors wanted to provide a substantive case study about interpreting communication effects more accurately through exploratory techniques compared with conventional linear methods. The results of the study showed that applying the MINE technique revealed to achieve a higher overall interpretation capability due to its multivariate statistical and functional property analyses. Visualizing of effects will help project managers and stakeholders to understand previous team behavior through extensive cognitive perception, thus to improve the building conciseness of diagnoses models together with external analysts.

The second paper, titled "A Systematic Literature Review of Social Network Systems for Older Adults" and written by Bilal Ahmad, Ita Richardson, and Sarah Beecham of the University of Limerick (Ireland), investigates what older adults think about social network systems in order to identify whether their needs are met. A snowballing approach was performed and 51 primary studies on social network systems for older adults were analyzed. The results showed that since 2005 there is an evident increase in social network systems designed for older adults. In addition, the study revealed that simplicity, ease of use, privacy and access to useful information are the most important quality aspects of the social network systems for older adults. The authors conclude their paper highlighting that social network systems remain a potential way to reduce the social isolation of older adults, and that it is also important to investigate important aspects largely unexplored, such as the extent to which social network systems replace real human contact and whether they can trigger the creation of new supportive communities.

The third paper, titled "Applying Extreme Engineering and Personality Factors to Improve Software Development under a Heayyweight Methodology" and written by Mercedes Ruiz, Germán Fuentes of the University of Cádiz (Puerto Real, Cádiz, Spain), describes a process improvement proposal for the V-model based on team creation and task allocation strategies that take into account the personality of workers and its impact on productivity and quality. The study has been performed in a real company of the defense sector, where the use of the V-model is mandatory. The results showed that a possible real application of the improvement designed for the current process model is possible. The improvement introduces the novel concept of extreme engineering, that extends the concept of pair-programming to all the phases of the software life cycle, applies the concept of cross-functional teams to software engineering and pioneers in the use of the Cattel's model of 16PF to improve productivity in processes under the V-model.

The fourth paper, titled "Different Views on Project Success When Communication Is Not The Same" and written by Jil Klünder, Oliver Karras, Fabian Kortum, Mathias Casselt, and Kurt Schneider of the Leibniz Universität (Hannover, Germany), describes the results of a study aiming at examining which factors are perceived to be important for a successful project execution. A total of 97 student participants and 8 customers were involved. The results showed that communication is most important for both the team and the customer for project success, even if the term "communication" has different meanings. For the customer, a regular information exchange with the development team is mandatory and the most important factor for project success. For the developers, the collaboration and communication with the customer are less important than the team-internal communication and collaboration as well as the distribution of tasks in the team, which are most important to enable project success. Based on these results, the authors suggest to increase the awareness on both sides, in particular for newcomers, on the importance of communication between customers and development team, since "communication" can facilitate collaboration and smooth the way to a successful project execution.

3   Audience and Expected Outcomes

The overall goal of this interdisciplinary workshop has been to raise the level of engagement and discussion about human factors in software engineering. A further goal of the workshop has been to promote the synergic encounter between the two communities of HCI and SE with respect to topics related to human aspects of software evaluation from both a researcher and practitioner perspective.

Once again, in this year's edition, the workshop has received a positive response from both HCI and SE communities with several interesting and valuable contributions. The submissions were peer-reviewed by international committee members for their quality, topic relevance, innovation, and potentials to foster discussion.

Acknowledgment.   We would like to thank the organizers of PROFES 2017 for giving us the opportunity to organize this workshop. We are also grateful to our international program committee of experts in the field for their reviews and collaboration.

Don't Underestimate the Human Factors! Exploring Team Communication Effects

Fabian Kortum[✉], Jil Klünder, and Kurt Schneider

Software Engineering Group, Leibniz Universität Hannover,
Welfengarten 1, 30167 Hannover, Germany
{fabian.kortum,jil.kluender,kurt.schneider}@inf.uni-hannover.de

Abstract. Team communication addresses a critical issue for software developments. Understanding human behavior and communication take an important role for cost optimized scheduling and adjustment of dysfunctional manner. But team phenomena are often not trivial to interpret. Empirical studies can disclose practical information. Many kinds of research with the focus on human factors justify findings solely through linear statistics. This leads to an estimation problem of formally interpreted effects, in particular for diagnosis models. In this paper, we investigate several team communication effects with data records from an empirical study with 34 academic software projects. In general, we want to increase the awareness for often insufficiently interpreted human factors. We apply conventional linear correlation statistics in comparison with the novel exploratory analysis MINE on three sample cases concerning team meetings and communication behavior. Both analyzing techniques approved to be capable in identifying the relevant team communication effects within the case studies, even though with different estimation of relevances. The study demonstrates how quickly e.g. group behavior and communication effects can be insufficiently interpreted with dangerous gaps for factor estimation in modeling approaches.

Keywords: Team communication · Human factors · Data visualization · Exploratory analysis · Interpretation problem

1 Introduction

Software engineering is a discipline that involves human activities and performances during the development process. These human factors sometimes cause dynamic phenomena that are not always trivial to interpret. Especially the way how teams communicate, collaborate, hold meetings or prioritize next tasks address critical conditions for the success of innovative software projects [8,15]. Well performing teamwork can smooth the way for innovative software projects [6]. Vice versa, insufficient communication can negatively influence the final product, and therefore the customer's satisfaction. A better understanding of central communication behavior in teams can help project associates, team leader, and even single team members to recognize the inadequate structures earlier [9,12].

© Springer International Publishing AG 2017
M. Felderer et al. (Eds.): PROFES 2017, LNCS 10611, pp. 457–469, 2017.
https://doi.org/10.1007/978-3-319-69926-4_36

Thus, a faster recognition of suboptimal team condition enables adjustments before destructive habits endanger the project. Empirical studies are suitable to disclose knowledge about software developers' practices and project condition changes over time. The gathered information often provide valuable insides e.g. for conceptualizing and formalizing of experience based diagnosis or tendency models. Many of these studies with the focus on human factors thoroughly interpret their findings through linear correlation statistics. However, it often requires more extensive analyses with more detailed dependency characterizations [7]. But this is often associated as time-consuming without knowing or considering for modern techniques that could cover additionally required effort while achieving equivalent or even better interpretations.

This paper describes an approach to compare between conventional linear dependency analyses and a novel technique for automatized characterization onto team communication effects. We want to investigate, whether exploratory analyzing techniques like MINE [17] can keep the analyst's manual effort low when interpreting also non-linear effects. Furthermore, we want to qualify if the exploratory interpretation provides differences compared to solely linearity results. In particular, we apply both analyzing methods in three case studies about team communication effects in student software projects. The data originates from a previously conducted empirical study observing communication behavior of teams from 34 software projects at university environment. The collected information consists of weekly reports about communication structures, meeting practices and each member's mood, elicited from 165 student participants [18]. Previous studies and related work about early team diagnose [10, 11] revealed the importance of understanding the teams' behavior in more detail, and therefore human-centered communication effects [15].

1.1   Motivation

Estimation Problems Through Interpretation Gaps. Empirical studies are often applied to confirm or understand, e.g. active practices and experiences [14]. Gathered information about team communication behavior or collaboration structures can be systematically used to characterize occurring group manners. Some phenomena appear from social aspects and can be sophisticated for conventional dependency methods. Therefore, they cannot always be solely expressed through linear correlation methods [17]. Consequently, the strength and significances of interpretations may remain lower than their possible maximum.

For instance, the productivity interpretation for the LOC data variable in Fig. 1 can be described as a strong linear outcome when using standard Pearson correlation. The linear interpretation fits strong dependency criteria with $r = 0.74$ and a significance of $p < 0.01$. However, not every dependency interpretations seem to be adequate solved in this way. For this particular example, an exploratory analysis could achieve a better interpretation due to additional e.g. polynomial property consideration as in Fig. 1. However, the statistical outcome for the shown exploratory dependency analyses measures a significance $p < 0.01$ but with a stronger relevance factor $r = 0.88$.

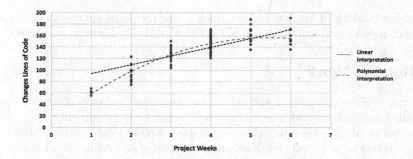

Fig. 1. Example for interpretation gaps of data dependencies

This result should set alarm bells ringing since it presents a 14% interpretation difference for the same data dependency. Such differences can influence the accuracy of a system-based diagnosis, especially if several estimators consists of inaccuracies. For the conceptualization of these models, the identification of relevant key factors can be endangered due underestimated or insufficient interpretations. Findings of team communication effects become subsequently visualized as force-based network diagrams to provide an enhanced overall understanding of the characterized effects. All study results become in the later on sections validated, interpreted and summarized.

Case Studies for Analyzing Statistical Interpretation Gaps. We limited the study scope to the interpretation of team communication effects that cover the use of digital communication [4], the belief, and the morale of teams in projects.

> (1) *Face-to-face communication perceives a higher collaboration intensity compared to communication sessions through digital channels.*
> (2) *The use of digital communication channels decreases a developer's belief in the own team and its integrity.*
> (3) *The positive belief of a developer in his team supports an overall positive team thinking, and also increases his team's motivation.*

Case 1 covers developer's perceived communication intensity through face-to-face interaction compared with more decentralized, e.g. digital communication. Such decentralization indeed tends to have a lower recognized intensity based on member's reduced attention or participation through virtual closeness [4].

Case 2 describes the use of digital communication channel that also leads to a downward slope of team's atmosphere. Thus, the impressions of members tend to consist of a more decentralized team belief, which is reasonable due to the loss of personal contact, compared with face-to-face communication [1,6].

Case 3 concerns on developer's belief and goals in his or her team and if it can be positively associated with the team's satisfaction. This has relevances for the understanding of human factors since a positive atmosphere in teams also indicates a good performing group behavior [5] and development condition [18].

2   Related Work

This study relies on concepts and achievements in the field of exploratory analysis, data visualization and human factors in software development.

Reshef et al. [17] established an extensive empirical evaluation of the equitability, power against independence, and runtime of several leading measures of dependence. They could validate that their MINE technique, and in particular, the use of Maximal Information Coefficient (MIC) presents an efficient strategy to identify and classify even complex types of relationships in data sets. The authors' algorithm additionally covers conventional linearity statistics. Thus it provides the maximum information needed to express a particular dependency.

McGuffin [16] presents strategies for data visualization of communities and system structures. He describes mechanics for basic graph representation, as well as advanced techniques for visualizing network data for a wide variety of situations, such as relationships structures as force-based or mutual information diagrams. Many data sets can be most naturally interpreted and depicted as networks [16]. Considering his work helps us to improve the cognitive understanding and visual representation for statistic measures.

Hoegl et al. [6] established a concept about teamwork quality with relevances for the success of software projects. The authors clarified a definition of teamwork and investigated on success factors, like team performance and satisfaction. They identified six aspects with impact on teamwork: communication, coordination, a balance of contribution, mutual support, effort, and cohesion. Their results rely on an empirical study, providing data from 575 developers and project leader in 145 German software development laboratories [6].

In previous studies, Kortum et al. [10,12] started exploring team behavior in academic software projects and how they differ to practitioners. Schneider et al. [18] primarily examined factors for the mood and communication in groups. On behalf of the authors' findings, we investigated the feasibility of early diagnoses on team manner during software projects. First models have been established [10,11] through a set of machine learning classifier and enabled forecasts for key communication metrics with linearity estimation, likewise to Hoegl et al.'s [6] research on teamwork. The estimator interpretations for the diagnosis model led us to the question whether solely linearity expressions are a sufficient method for modeling approaches, especially when human behavior is involved.

3   Empirical Study

The Software Engineering Group at Leibniz Universität Hannover frequently collects empirical data from teams in yearly offered student software projects [18]. We collected team conditions with typical group sizes of five members developing a software product for real customers. Towards, the students have to perform through all phases of a waterfall oriented development process. This includes the requirements elicitation, design, implementation, and testing. The products' fulfillment according to the requirement specification will be verified with customer acceptance tests. Every customer was limited in time and availability. Thus, teams had to arrange interviews and feedback meetings with their client individually. Teams were responsible to self-manage themselves which was one of the casual experience goals. At the end of each project, customers were held to grade the success and progressing of a team, as well as to verify the compliance of implemented features. In a subsequent retrospective, students' reflected their experiences and impressions made during the project.

3.1 Framework Condition of Academic Software Projects

The team communication records used for this approach rely on a data collection of 165 student participants in 34 teams. The software projects were comparable due to framework conditions, complexity and had a lifespan of 15 weeks [10, 18]. All teams passed quality gates at the end of each phase. This was necessary for an adequate process assurances of achieved tasks versus the planned. Teams scheduled and managed e.g. the essential tasks themselves during the project. The students reported weekly about their team communications and meetings in categorical rating that have been mainly realized through Likert scales. These cover 5-stages of agree- or disagreement for a particular condition question. All weekly reports provide status information about each team's communication ambitions, atmosphere conditions, and project progress. The reporting categories related to human behavior rely on established studies from organizational and social psychology [6, 8]. An overview of all reported categories is shown in Fig. 2.

Member Atmosphere	Members' Belief in Team	Member Communication
• Mood (+) • Mood (-) • Motivation	• Produced Quality • Keeping Deadlines • Fulfill Cuts. Expectation • Finish Project in Time • Continuous Dev. Proc.	• Who to Whom • Type (local face-to-face, video, telephone, chat, email) • perceived intensity
Team Meetings	**Project Condition**	**Customer Grading**
• Duration • Number of Meetings • Team Completeness • Number of Attendance • Duration of Attendance	• Lifespan • Current Week • Development Phase • Events (Quality Gate) • Team Size	• Acceptance Test

Fig. 2. Report information in academic software projects

4 Methodology

Team communication is a prerequisite for the success of projects and, due to human involvement, often difficult to estimate. Some researchers recommend plotting experience-based information about behavior changes over time for recognizing effects [3, 14]. Others connote interpretations through statistical correlation analyses [2, 7]. The former often rely upon linear dependencies that barely consider more extensive analyses. Since we want to identify potential interpretation gaps e.g. about team communication effects, MINE is applied to detect complex factors with relevance for the three team communication cases of this study, also to express their characteristics and dependency strengths extensively.

4.1 Exploratory Analyses Using MINE

Empirical data in software engineering sometimes require analyzing on hundreds, thousands or millions of possible dependency combinations. Based on this, information often becomes solely studied with linearity measures, such as significance and correlation between two data variables. Modern solutions with advantages for dependency interpretations are rarely taken into account. Reshef et al.'s [17] MINE application supports such a systematic exploration. It uses a maximal information coefficient (MIC) which is a novel measure for relationships capturing linearity and complex associations between pairs of data variables. The algorithm interprets mutual information of data pairs, thus each dependencies functional properties. The resulting MIC score represents statistical measures that are comparable to the coefficient of determination r^2.

Relationship Type	MIC	Pearson	Spearman	Mutual Information (KDE)	(Kraskov)	CorGC (Principal Curve-Based)	Maximal Correlation
Random	0.18	-0.02	-0.02	0.01	0.03	0.19	0.01
Linear	1.00	1.00	1.00	5.03	3.89	1.00	1.00
Cubic	1.00	0.61	0.69	3.09	3.12	0.98	1.00
Exponential	1.00	0.70	1.00	2.09	3.62	0.94	1.00
Sinusoidal (Fourier frequency)	1.00	-0.09	-0.09	0.01	-0.11	0.36	0.64
Categorical	1.00	0.53	0.49	2.22	1.65	1.00	1.00
Periodic/Linear	1.00	0.33	0.31	0.69	0.45	0.49	0.91
Parabolic	1.00	-0.01	-0.01	3.33	3.15	1.00	1.00
Sinusoidal (non-Fourier frequency)	1.00	0.00	0.00	0.01	0.20	0.40	0.80
Sinusoidal (varying frequency)	1.00	-0.11	-0.11	0.02	0.06	0.38	0.76

Fig. 3. Dependency interpretation: power of MIC algorithm [17]

Figure 3 shows some functional dependency types that are interpretable in MINE. The MIC algorithm considers several relationship interpretations e.g. by the Pearson's linear correlation, mutual information estimation [13], maximal correlation estimation and curve-based analyses [3]. The systematic processing of MINE allows an almost automatic analysis of up to 27 different dependency characteristics and explore even complex associations.

4.2   Pre-investigation on Team Communication Records

Linearity Analysis. We first analyzed our empirical data set with the Pearson's correlation and Fisher's exact test for measuring the significance of each dependency. The data consist of 29 record variables, each with 2475 rows of each team's consequently reporting over 15 weeks. We derived with R-statistics $406 = \frac{n \cdot (n-1)}{2}$ linearity analyses (Gaussian Sum Formula) covering all possible combinations of variable pairs.

Exploratory Analysis. We applied the same data information also to MINE. The exploratory analysis results in a ranked list of variable dependencies sorted top down by the strongest interpreted MIC due to the identified mutual information and functional properties. The MIC scoring is defined as an equivalent to the coefficient of determination r^2 [17]. Thus, considering the square root of MIC $\sqrt{(MIC)}$ allows a direct comparison with the Pearson correlation coefficient r.

Table 1. Interpretation differences for MIC and Pearson: Observed means

Observations: 406 Pairs of Variables		
	∅ r coef.	∅ p-value
SQRT(MIC)	0.34196	0.01754
Pearson r	0.09200	0.10926
Δ	0.24996	0.09172

Comparing both the overall mean results of linear correlations and the MIC scores obtains whether the team behavior records can be adequately interpreted through solely linear expression or might achieve a better interpretability by extensive analyses. Table 1 shows the resulted mean differences for both interpretation strategies. However, whether the mean measures also indicate relevant gaps for our three case studies about decentralized communication behavior requires a more channelized analyzing scope.

Visualization. We developed a Java application that adapts the MINE algorithm and visualizes results as force-based network graphs through an embedded R-server. The graph relies on an R-library called *igraph*. Our application gives the user a simplified understanding about the different communication dependencies through additional cognitive perception. Furthermore, it provides a function to channelize investigation scopes to only those variables of interest. An entire system visualization of all 29 empirical data variables would result in a system graph covering 29 nodes and 406 edges. Thus it grows extremely complex. This scoping feature allows us to primarily limit the system variables, e.g. as a sub-system that only provides the top 19 identified team report variables as in Fig. 4. Our application allows to chose particular variables to identify all affecting or effected variables within the data records. The node sizes in Fig. 4 depend on the resulted MIC scoring, and so do the edges which vary in the width, expressing the relevance of interpreted relationship. A force describes the positive and negative orientation of effect, likewise the course of interpreted function.

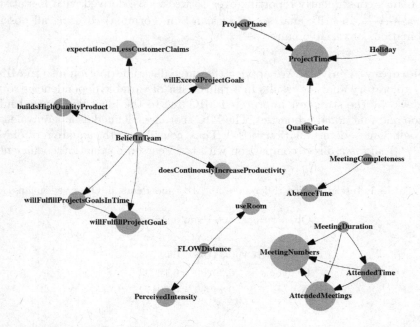

Fig. 4. Force-based sub-network derived from top down ranked MINE findings

4.3   Analyzing Interpretation Gaps of Case Studies

Our case studies consider the use of decentralizing communication and its effects on the team atmosphere, belief in the team, also the perceived intensity due to the chosen communication type. The channelize function of our application helps us to limit the system scope to only those variables with related to the cases.

Case 1 states that face-to-face communications between team member have a positive effect for perceived communication intensities. We first selected the variable *PerceivedIntensity* from our ranked MINE list. Subsequently, we wanted to identify all potential incoming effects for this variable. Running the embedded exploratory analyses once again results in a new ranked list of all identified influencing factors relating to the *PerceivedIntensity*. However, this findings require an additional selection for the variables *face-to-face communication (useRoom)*, *useVideo, useChat, useTelephone and useEmail*. The subsequent derive as force-based sub-network is shown in Fig. 5.

The interpreted *PerceivedIntensity* dependencies through MINE confirm the *Case 1* statement. All five ingoing edges show positive effects towards the

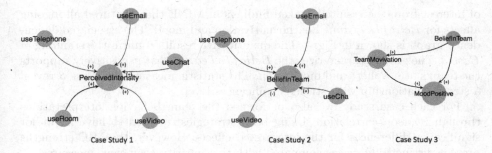

Fig. 5. Case study findings from MINE generated as force-based sub-networks

perceived communication intensity in teams. The force between the local face-to-face communication and the *PerceivedIntensity* has a stronger width compared to the four digital communications. This means that a more frequent use of face-to-face interaction also positively affects the *PerceivedIntensity* due to the given information exchange. The MINE results for *Case 1* are listed in Table 2.

We repeated the variable selecting procedure as in the previous case, this time with concern for relevant variables from *Case 2*. The case describes the use of digital communication channel, which has an adverse effect on the belief in teams. The associated force-based network due to the sub-selected variable scope and MINE analyzing results is shown in Fig. 5. The overall graphical outcome reveals a weak positive effect on the belief in teams when using digital communication channel. In particular, the use of emails, chats, and telephone calls have a positive effect on the belief in the own team. In contrast, the use of video chats has an adverse influence on the team belief. The statistically measured significances and dependency strengths are listed in Table 2.

Case 3 states that the belief in teams supports a positive thinking and motivates team members. Once more, we selected only the relevant variable labeled *BeliefInTeams* in our Java application. Subsequently, we chose the variables

Table 2. Statistical interpretation differences of Case Studies

	X Variable	Y Variable	MIC	SQRT(MIC)	p-value	Pearson r	p-value
Case 1	useRoom	PerceivedIntensity	0.39783	0.63074	0.02380	0.67620	0.00000
	useEmail	PerceivedIntensity	0.11664	0.34153	0.01441	0.30727	0.00000
	useChat	PerceivedIntensity	0.09730	0.31193	0.01277	0.22925	0.00000
	useTelephone	PerceivedIntensity	0.03433	0.18528	0.01255	0.18129	0.00000
	useVideo	PerceivedIntensity	0.00703	0.08385	0.01137	0.04852	0.01578
Case 1	useEmail	BeliefInTeam	0.04228	0.20562	0.00714	0.19477	0.00000
	useChat	BeliefInTeam	0.04206	0.20509	0.00605	0.14116	0.00000
	useTelephone	BeliefInTeam	0.02186	0.14785	0.00498	0.00460	0.81908
	useVideo	BeliefInTeam	0.01745	0.13210	0.00533	-0.00116	0.95386
Case 3	Motivation	MoodPositive	0.39446	0.62806	0.02015	0.70180	0.00000
	BeliefInTeam	Motivation	0.30437	0.55170	0.00615	0.37754	0.00000
	BeliefInTeam	MoodPositive	0.30221	0.54974	0.01262	0.61967	0.00000

of interest from the resulted ranked findings in MINE that captured all ingoing affects for $BeliefInTeams$, i.e. the motivation and mood. The associated dependency graph is shown in Fig. 5. The quantitative results confirm the standing of $Case\ 3$. The graph characterizes the $BeliefInTeams$, that it positively supports the team's atmosphere and motivation. The statistic measures for $Case\ 3$ reveal a strong relationship with strong significances level.

For each case study, we also performed the team behavior interpretations through Pearson correlation. Using both strategies revealed to have no major significance differences for the interpreted effects. However, the MIC strengths present distinct differences compared with the linearity coefficient measures.

5   Validity and Discussion of Results

Applying correlation measures for interpreting team behavior in empirical studies requires an maximal adequate interpretation of investigated effects [5,6].

5.1   Study Results and Interpretation

We compared conventional linear measures in R-statistics and exploratory analyses in MINE. The analyzing subjects were weekly team communication reports from 34 educational software projects. We derived coefficients of determinations with both techniques, to identify the interpretation gaps for communication factors. Each result was applied to Fisher's exact test for capturing its significance level. Table 2 lists all results from both strategies, with and particular scope on communication effects with relevance for the case studies. The Pearson correlation only detected linearities, whereas the exploratory analyses also characterized more complex effects. Thus, MINE could identify the strengths for 9 of 12 relationships more accurately. The gray-colored fields in Table 2 indicate the analyzing method with better interpretation outcome for a particular cases relationship. However, both variants provided strong significances with moderate to strong findings according to the case studies.

For the qualitative overall validation, we statistically compared both techniques for the entire empirical team records. As shown in Table 1, the MINE technique achieved an overall stronger mean correlation coefficient $r = 0.25$ and a significance improve of $p = 0.09$. The distribution of all identified data dependencies is shown in Fig. 6. The box-plot characterizes that the Pearson correlation detects relationship strengths within a weak range, differently to the MIC. Both findings determined strong significance measures, whereas the p-value of MIC has a more consistent range with less extreme outliers and $p < 0.01$.

5.2   Threats to Validity

Construct validity: We interpreted team communication solely through linear and exploratory statistics; other techniques became not considered. Findings with strong significances but only weak correlation measures were tolerated.

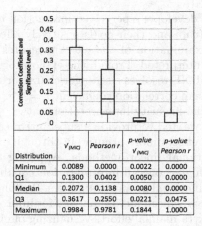

Distribution	V_(MIC)	Pearson r	p-value V_(MIC)	p-value Pearson r
Minimum	0.0089	0.0000	0.0022	0.0000
Q1	0.1300	0.0402	0.0050	0.0000
Median	0.2072	0.1138	0.0080	0.0000
Q3	0.3617	0.2550	0.0221	0.0475
Maximum	0.9984	0.9781	0.1844	1.0000

Fig. 6. Distribution of interpretation differences: Linear vs. MIC

Internal validity: All interpretations are based on previously elicited empirical data [18]. The reporting was a volunteer activity. We assume that people freely replied the truth when submitting information. There were no parallel courses or gradings for the software projects that would bias the reported data.

External validity: The results might not be overgeneralized since we interpreted student teams in educational projects. Data from practitioners, industry or other university software projects may lead to alternative team communication effects. Due to human factors and unknown other influences, the investigated interpretation of behavior can never completely ensure all real world factors.

Conclusion validity: All interpretations are reliable and statistically verified with normalized data. Since we focus on human factors, there might be different reports when repeating the empirical study. Changing framework conditions may also lead to different results. The exploratory data analyses can be generalized for plenty other kinds of investigation that provide empirical data [6,17].

6 Conclusion

An early recognition of communication phenomena and dysfunctional habits is important in software projects [12]. Empirical studies can help gathering data about team behavior. When building diagnoses models, effect interpretations throughout linearity correlations often result as an insufficient strategy [17].

We approached the statistical interpretation differences for Pearson linear correlation and exploratory analyses using MINE. We qualified both strategies and their capabilities on dependency characterization for three case studies about team communication effects. We show that both strategies were capable of identifying all case studies relevant communication effects with statistical significance $p < 0.05$. For instance, we show that the use of digital communication channel has an adverse effect on developer's perceived interaction intensity, also that the member's belief in the team and their goals positively affects the team's overall atmosphere. A closer examination of the effect measures reveals, that 9 of 12 effects could be better interpreted through the exploratory analyses. An overall analysis discloses that MINE resolves a stronger characterization for dependency strengths with better mean correlation coefficient $r = 0.34$ and significance level $p < 0.02$, compared to the linearity interpretations.

With this study, we wanted to provide a substantive case study about interpreting communication effects more accurately through exploratory techniques compared with conventional linear methods. Applying the MINE technique revealed to achieve an higher overall interpretation capability due to its multivariate statistical and functional property analyses. We follow up with the aim to enrich the awareness for advanced factor analyses for improved dependency characterizations without extra manual effort. Visualizing of effects will help project managers and stakeholders to understand previous team behavior through extensive cognitive perception, thus to improve the building conciseness of diagnoses models together with external analysts.

Acknowledgment. This work was funded by the German Research Foundation (DFG) under grant number *263807701* (Project TeamFLOW, 2015–2017).

References

1. Ambler, S.W., et al.: Agile modeling (2002)
2. Breiman, L., Friedman, J.H.: Estimating optimal transformations for multiple regression and correlation. J. Am. Stat. Assoc. **80**, 614–619 (1985)
3. Delicado, P.: Another look at principal curves and surfaces. J. Multivar. Anal. **77**, 84–116 (2001)
4. Dennis, A.R., Valacich, J.S.: Rethinking media richness: towards a theory of media synchronicity. In: 1999 Proceedings of the 32nd Annual Hawaii International Conference on Systems Sciences, HICSS-32. IEEE (1999)
5. Hinsz, V., Park, E., Sjomeling, M.: Group interaction sustains positive moods and diminishes negative moods. In: Annual Meeting of the Midwestern Psychological Association, Chicago (2004)
6. Hoegl, M., Gemuenden, H.G.: Teamwork quality and the success of innovative projects: a theoretical concept and empirical evidence. Organ. Sci. **12**, 435–449 (2001)
7. Houghton, J., Siegel, M., Goldsmith, D., Moulton, A., Madnick, S., Wirsch, A.: A survey of methods for data inclusion in system dynamics models: methods, tools and applications (2013)
8. Kauffeld, S., Lehmann-Willenbrock, N.: Meetings matter: effects of team meetings on team and organizational success. Small Group Res. **43**, 130–158 (2012)
9. Klünder, J., Schneider, K., Kortum, F., Straube, J., Handke, L., Kauffeld, S.: Communication in teams - an expression of social conflicts. In: Bogdan, C., et al. (eds.) HCSE/HESSD -2016. LNCS, vol. 9856, pp. 111–129. Springer, Cham (2016). doi:10.1007/978-3-319-44902-9_8

10. Kortum, F., Klünder, J.: Early diagnostics on team communication: experience-based forecasts on student software projects. In: 10th International Conference on the Quality of Information and Communications Technology. IEEE (2016)

11. Kortum, F., Klünder, J., Schneider, K.: Miscommunication in software projects: early recognition through tendency forecasts. In: Abrahamsson, P., Jedlitschka, A., Nguyen Duc, A., Felderer, M., Amasaki, S., Mikkonen, T. (eds.) PRO-FES 2016. LNCS, vol. 10027, pp. 731–738. Springer, Cham (2016). doi:10.1007/978-3-319-49094-6_62

12. Kortum, F., Klünder, J., Schneider, K.: Characterizing relationships for system dynamics models supported by exploratory data analysis. In: 29th International Conference on Software Engineering and Knowledge Engineering. KSI Research Inc. (2017)

13. Kraskov, A., Stögbauer, H., Grassberger, P.: Estimating mutual information. Phys. Rev. E **69**, 066138 (2004)

14. Madachy, R.J.: Software Process Dynamics. Wiley, Hoboken (2007)

15. McChesney, I.R., Gallagher, S.: Communication and co-ordination practices in software engineering projects. Inf. Soft. Technol. **46**, 473–489 (2004)

16. McGuffin, M.J.: Simple algorithms for network visualization: a tutorial. Tsinghua Sci. Technol. **17**, 383–398 (2012)

17. Reshef, D.N., Reshef, Y.A., Finucane, H.K., Grossman, S.R., McVean, G., Turnbaugh, P.J., Lander, E.S., Mitzenmacher, M., Sabeti, P.C.: Detecting novel associations in large data sets. Science **334**, 1518–1524 (2011)

18. Schneider, K., Liskin, O., Paulsen, H., Kauffeld, S.: Media, mood, and meetings: related to project success? ACM Trans. Comput. Educ. **15**, 1–33 (2015)

Applying Extreme Engineering and Personality Factors to Improve Software Development Under a Heavyweight Methodology

Mercedes Ruiz[1(✉)] and Germán Fuentes[2]

[1] University of Cádiz, Avda. de la Universidad de Cádiz, 10, 11519 Puerto Real, Cádiz, Spain
mercedes.ruiz@uca.es
[2] Navantia, Carretera de la Carrraca s/n, 11100 San Fernando, Cádiz, Spain
gfuentesl@navantia.es

Abstract. Companies of the defense sector use heavyweight methodologies such as the V-model to develop large systems in which reliability is a crucial factor. This model has well-known disadvantages but the necessity to maintain all the phases under control and its mandatory use by the public institutions prevent the companies from altering the methodology. This paper describes a process improvement proposal for the V-model based on the concepts of Extreme-Engineering, team creation and task allocation strategies that take into account the personality of workers and its impact on productivity and quality. The study has been performed in a real company of the defense sector. The proposal has been tested and validated using a multiparadigm simulation model that makes use of the company historical data.

Keywords: V-model · Extreme-Engineering · Team creation · Personality factors · Process improvement · Simulation

1 Introduction

In an increasingly competitive global market, companies struggle to find their place and gain business success. There are several factors for this success, but quality and price are the two factors that mostly determine the success or failure of a product or service.

Since the articulation of the agile manifesto in 2001[1], agile methods such as XP or Scrum have transformed the way we build software. However, they do not seem to penetrate adequately in large projects, where a heavyweight methodology such as the V-model [1] is usually preferred [2]. This is mainly because the customers of such projects, usually governments, demand rigid control, with strict plans and abundant documentation.

Nevertheless, disregarding the use of light or heavyweight methodologies, a common objective and a widely accepted assumption are shared by all types of projects: (a) to deliver working software that meets the requirements and quality goals, within a

---

[1] http://www.agilemanifesto.org.

© Springer International Publishing AG 2017
M. Felderer et al. (Eds.): PROFES 2017, LNCS 10611, pp. 470–481, 2017.
https://doi.org/10.1007/978-3-319-69926-4_37

reasonable time and budget, and (b) the crucial role that teamwork plays to meet this objective.

Teamwork is considered to have a positive effect on people's productivity due to the increase of the synergies among the members of the same team, their sense of fulfillment and the personal satisfaction, factors that lead to an improvement in work efficiency [3].

However, there are situations in which this general law may not always lead to more productive teams. Grouping people with opposing or conflicting personalities can lead to negative synergy, with teamwork producing just the opposite effect to the intended one. The right thing to do would be to carefully select the right *and* compatible human resources before starting a project, but since this is not always possible, we need techniques to organize people in a project so that we get the most out of them.

In this work, we present the initial results of a process improvement experience developed in a real company of the defense sector, in which the use of a heavyweight methodology such as the V-model was compulsory. The solution acts on the strategies used for team creation and task allocation management, leading to an improvement of the team productivity and the product quality, without altering the nature of the V-model. The strategy developed grounds on concepts such as cross-functional teams, personality factors, team synergy and Extreme-Engineering. The proposal has been validated using a multiparadigm simulation model that has been created and validated with company's historical data. The model allows to compare the results of the existing process and the improved one without the risks of testing the proposal in the real world.

This paper is structured as follows: Sect. 2 describes the current situation and the problems found. Section 3 summarizes the published works in the scope of the V-model improvement. Sections 4 and 5 describe our proposal and its results obtained by simulation, respectively. Finally, Sect. 6 summarizes the paper, draws our conclusions and describes our future work.

2 Problem Description

This work describes the experience carried out in a real Spanish company that is a worldwide reference in the design and construction of military systems solutions. The company also is specialized in providing technical assistance for the development of control and combat systems. For confidential reasons, we will refer this company as SeaVessels. The projects developed by SeaVessels follow the V-model and are very large and complex, being some of them R&D ones. The projects usually last approximately three to six years. The customers of these projects are mostly governments from different countries. SeaVessels has a team of 30 people working in these projects. The team is divided into two groups: one for systems engineering, responsible for the analysis and testing phases of the project, and another group for software engineering, responsible for the phases of software design, development and unit testing. Each work group has an area manager who is responsible for the planning of each area, work coordination and resources balance.

The following subsections describe briefly the V-model followed in SeaVessels projects and the problems the company encountered in its application.

2.1 The V-Model

The V-model is usually used on very large projects, generally developed for public organizations or for systems engineering typical of the defense environment [4, 5]. The V- model for software development can be considered as an extension of the waterfall model that gives more emphasis to testing. Figure 1 shows the general structure of the V-model for software development.

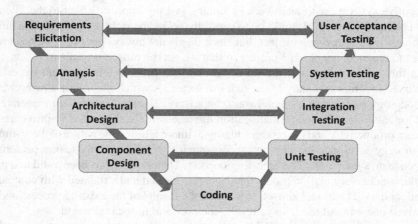

Fig. 1. The V-model for software development.

The V-model is mostly characterized by the following features:

- There is a direct relationship between each phase of the project lifecycle with a testing phase. As a result, each phase is tested at its level of abstraction.
- Each testing phase is a milestone, normally set and controlled by the customer.
- It requires test procedures to be written as soon as possible.
- It gives the same importance to the development and testing phases.
- It provides a simple and easy way to follow the software process.
- It is suitable for projects involving hardware and software development.

2.2 The V-Model Problems in Real-Life Projects

In the application of the V-model to real-life projects, SeaVessels has found several general problems:

- The V-model lacks flexibility, which is contrary to the nature of software development. The simple fact of not being able to begin the next phase without having finished the previous one is unreal. It is very common that:
    - The customer is not clear about the high-level requirements, normally because the projects can have a great difficulty.
    - The requirements of the customers may not be fully, clearly and unambiguously described in the software specifications in the first attempt, preventing the designers/developers from making software that meets the customer expectations.

The level of difficulty of the projects, or the fact that they maybe R&D ones are the frequent reasons for this lack of quality in the software specifications.

- Inside the company, there is a general belief that the success of the projects that use this methodology is thanks to the flexibility that the program managers and technical leaders introduce and allow during the process.
- Due to the crucial importance for both the customer and the program managers of the start-up and last testing phases of a project, there is a danger of losing control in the lower phases of the V. This lack of control adds pressure to the managers of those phases to have the product ready to meet a milestone, giving the false appearance of control to the customer. This pressure forces sometimes to apply inefficient testing methods.
- The V-model produces a false belief that everything is under control by running a testing phase for each process.
- Usually the project team is organized in several groups of people working unrelated, that is, some analysts generate the highest-level specification that are passed to lower-level specification by other analysts and developers. The communication between them occurs mainly through documentation and not through conversations and discussions.

2.3   Current Process Model

The current process model implemented in SeaVessels strictly follows the V-model and is the following:

- When a new analysis task arrives, it is assigned to a free analyst. The analyst studies the available documentation, performs the analysis, and writes the Software Requirements Specification document (SRS).
- Once the SRS is completed, a free designer/programmer performs the Software Design Document (SDD).
- When the SDD is completed, a free designer/programmer (it can be the same person who wrote the SDD, depending on the available resources) is assigned to the development and unit testing of the software.
- Once a software version with unit tests is released, it is passed to an available analyst/tester (it may or may not be the same person who wrote the SRS) that executes the Engineering Testing and Evaluation (ET&E) procedure.
- After executing the tests, changes in the specification (DCN, Documentary Change Note) or changes in the code (SCP, Software Change Proposal) may occur, which makes the task return to its initial phase or to the implementation phase, respectively.

The main problems observed when using this process model are:

- Dead times of some people due to deadlocks between people and phases.
- There is little review of results, as each person is responsible for their work. The work could be reviewed by the area manager in charge of the phase, but it does not seem feasible for a single person to review everything.

- There is no team feeling and workers often perceive their task as a whole and not as an element of a higher set, which negatively affects the subsequent integration of these elements.
- Having a person per task at each phase can help detect errors more easily. However, every time a new person is assigned to a new task, some learning time is needed which, if reduced or eliminated, has an impact on quality.
- During the analysis tasks of complex elements, it can take a lot of time (order of months) to understand the problem and be able to specify an appropriate solution to the problem. The single analyst assigned to the task is responsible for expressing with the maximum quality possible, the results of their analysis. Sometimes, the designers or/and programmers do not fully understand the problem and the solution posed by the analyst. Due to time constraints, the necessary re-analysis of the problem cannot be done and the solution lacks quality or is developed with a significant delay. The problem is also increased because the analysts and programmers are in two different groups, leading to some frictions and lack of communication between both groups. Incidentally, this impacts negatively on the final quality of the product, the fulfillment of deadlines and the motivation of the people involved.
- The assignment of tasks to people is done according mostly to their availability and the experience of the person in charge of the assignment. However, no formal model is used to perform this important activity [6].

3   Improvements to the V-Model

Once the problems that the use of the V-model have been identified, the next step should be to find what improvements have been proposed to the V-model without altering its nature.

Not many formal improvements of the V-model can be found in the literature. For example, Mathur and Malik [7] propose the Advanced V-model. This model improves the V one by adding a maintenance phase, which it is considered to improve the efficiency, stability and reliability of the process. Another improvement is presented in [8]. This work proposes the W model for component-based software development. The improvement consists in a different procedure to validate and verify components and systems. Finally, Liu et al. [9] introduce inv-V, a development process for automotive industry that improves the conventional V-model and variants by introducing and institutionalizing early and continuous integrated verification. None of these improved models addresses most of the problems found in SeaVessels.

As already mentioned, the use of the V-model as a heavyweight development methodology is an obligation in the defense sector. However, in the literature there are some attempts to apply certain concepts of agile methodologies to these projects without altering its rigorous use. For example, Fruhling et al. [10] performed an experiment in a military project where some XP concepts such as incremental developments and short iterations were successfully applied, whereas other concepts such as pair programming or test-oriented development did not achieve their purpose. In any case, the authors conclude that the application of XP had a positive effect on the project in a general way. This positive effect is, in part, due to emphasizing teamwork in the scope of the V-model.

As mentioned before, in order to get the benefits of teamwork, teams have to be carefully designed. When designing a team, several aspects need to be taken into consideration. For example, [11] makes use of the Cattell model [12] to measure the personality of each worker and thus be able to determine which role within a project to assign to each one. Gómez, in her dissertation [13], studies the influence of personality and work climate on software development. It makes use of the Big Five personality model as a simpler model that integrates other models, including Cattell's one.

4   Our Proposal

4.1   Assumptions

In order to design a proposal to improve the current results of the process model of SeaVessels without modifying the development methodology, we considered to act on the strategies for team creation and task allocation management. Specifically, our proposal is based on the following assumptions:

- Workers will be more productive if they belong to a well-defined team, so as to maintain homogeneity, shared leadership, fruitful brainstorming, etc. [14].
- The application of the Extreme Programming (XP) and agile concepts to the analysis, design and testing phases will lead to an improvement in quality, task completion times and worker motivation. This concept is called Extreme Engineering (XE). It improves the communication between different teams as well as the product quality, since the same people are allocated to the same tasks during the whole task life-cycle [15].
- Pairing people for a task according to their personality will provoke positive synergy. The use of Cattell's 16PF model is suitable for this purpose as it measures the normal dimensions (non-pathological viewpoint) of the personality with an ambitious scope as it encompasses ability, temperament, dynamics, moods and the situations [16].
- All workers, regardless of the team they belong, will feel part of a whole, that is, not two teams fighting but cooperating for the sake of quality and the proper completion of tasks [17].

4.2   Using Cattell's 16 Personality Factors Model

For Cattell, personality is the determinant of behavior in a given situation. The basic component of personality is its traits. Cattel developed a taxonomy of 16 personality primary traits, based on the assumption that each person contains all of these 16 traits to a certain degree. In addition to the 16 primary factors, the taxonomy covers another group of broader second order factors that are obtained from the decatype scores obtained on the first-order factors. Cattel's model the result of psychological research, with empirical basis of more than 10 years of factorial experimentation on thousands of elements [12].

For the purpose of this work, we have used 11 decatypes, we considered to be the most influential decatypes in professional software development. These decatypes were measured for each worker in the team using Cattel's 16 PF Personality Questionnaire. In addition, a cross-matrix representing whether there is a positive, negative or zero synergy in the union of two workers with all the possible combinations of decatypes has been developed. The full matrix cannot be included here due to space reasons. As an example, Table 1 shows the synergy of four decatypes, where a positive/negative sign stands for positive/negative synergy and a blank cell means neutral synergy.

Table 1. Cross-matrix of synergy per decatype.

	Reserve	Forthright	Unconcerned	Submissive
Reserve	−	+	−	−
Forthright	+	−	+	+
Unconcerned	−	+	−	
Submissive	−	+		−

4.3   Improved Process Model

The proposed process model can be broadly defined according to the following characteristics:

- Workers are grouped by phase, as in the current model, but also by functionality, i.e., they belong to a team of people (analysis/test or design/programming), but, at the same time, to a functional group (data processing, graphical interface or signal processing). As a consequence, cross-functional teams are formed [18]. Tasks are assigned to two people, one from each team. Depending on the phase, one worker will have more workload in the task than the other.
- Workers are allocated to the tasks according to their personality and technical skills.
- When a phase is completed, the task moves to the next phase of the life cycle, but the same people will continue allocated. It goes without saying that in the Test phase, the person of the design/programming team should only be there to give support and not to test. The task performs the cycle of analysis/design/programming/test until it is proven the task is done. In each iteration, the task is assigned to the same pair of people at each phase. As a result, at each moment a worker has two tasks allocated, each one with a different workload depending on the phase and the worker's technical skills.

The following algorithm shows how each new task is allocated to a pair of workers:

1. Pre-select workers, from both teams analysts/testers and designers/programmers, that are available or partially available.
2. Rank and order each pre-selected worker according to their area experience skills in the functional area the task belongs to.
3. Make pairs of workers, starting from the ones who have more experience.
4. Calculate, for each pair of workers, the synergy of their union according to their personality. When the union of the two factors of personality of the two workers in

the pair has a positive sign (see Table 1), a value in the range (0,1] will be added to the synergy factor. Oppositely, if the union of their personalities has a negative sign, a value will be added to the synergy factor in the range [−1.0). The value that is added in each case is obtained from the concrete value of the decatypes of each worker. Table 2 shows the adjustment that is made to the union of each pair of decatypes according to the individual value of each worker.

Table 2. Adjustment of sinergy.

	Very high	High	Slightly high	Normal	Slightly low	Low	Very low
Very high	100%	90%	70%	60%	50%	30%	10%
High	90%	80%	60%	50%	40%	20%	5%
Slightly high	70%	60%	50	40%	30%	10%	0%
Normal	60%	50%	40%	30%	20%	5%	0%
Slightly low	50%	40%	30%	20%	10%	0%	0%
Low	30%	20%	10%	5%	0%	0%	0%
Very low	10%	5%	0%	0%	0%	0%	0%

5. Allocate to the new task the pair of workers who, having the greatest possible experience, have the greatest positive synergy points.

If there are no staff available that meets the above criteria, allocate equally according to the lowest negative synergy possible.

5   Evaluation of the Proposal Through Simulation

5.1   Multimethod Simulation Model

We first built the AS-IS simulation model that represents the current process model used by the company. This initial model consists of a pure discrete event network of tasks and resources in which the time needed to perform a task is a function of the experience of the worker allocated. In this model, as in real life, workers are allocated to tasks based on who is free at the required moment. The time it takes to perform a task is determined by the experience of the worker in that type of task. In the AS-IS model the tasks enter the system as a stream of arrivals defined by the historical data of the company. When a new task enters, it is directed to the queue representing the Analysis phase and waits for an available resource in the Analyst_Testers resource pool. Once a resource is available, it is allocated to the task for the time needed by that resource to perform that type of task. Once finished, the task moves to the next phase and so on until either it comes back for rework or it is done.

The TO-BE simulation model represents the improved process. In this model, the AS-IS model is extended with an agent-based simulation model. The agent-based model represents each worker as an individual agent, with their own personality and technical skills that affect how the workers interact with each other and develop their tasks, resulting in a more realistic simulation. The agent-based model is represented as a state transition diagram that describes the workers event- and time-driven behavior. In the TO-BE model, the algorithm that allocates workers to each new task implements the steps described in Sect. 4.3.

5.2   Simulation Runs

The base scenario for the simulation is defined with an initial population of 30 agents, representing each one a member of the real team. Their personality factors, skills profile and average time needed to develop each type of task are read from a csv file containing real data from the last three projects developed under the V-model. The scenario simulates the development of a project with a job creation rate of one a week, starting on July 3, 2009 and finishing on July 31, 2017 (420 weeks duration).

Figures 2 and 3 represent the mean time spent on software analysis tasks in the last year of the simulated project using the AS-IS and the TO-BE model, respectively. The tasks have been classified into areas, namely HMI, for Human-Machine interaction software, SIGNAL, for signal processing software, and Data_Process, for data processing software.

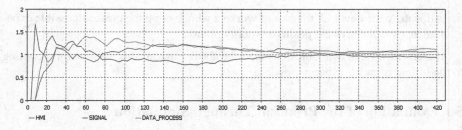

Fig. 2. Analysis mean time: AS-IS model.

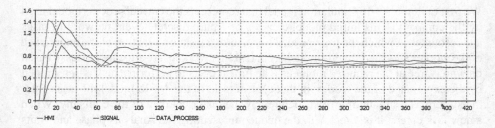

Fig. 3. Analysis mean time: TO-BE model.

In this case, whereas in the AS-IS process the mean time needed for the analysis tasks was 0.97 weeks, in the improved process was 0.77 weeks, leading to 20% reduction of the time needed to perform the analysis tasks.

Figures 4 and 5 represent the mean time spent on software development tasks using the AS-IS model and the TO-BE model, respectively.

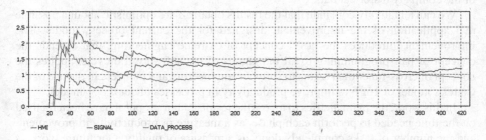

Fig. 4. Programming mean time: AS-IS model.

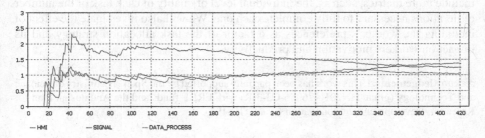

Fig. 5. Programming mean time: TO-BE model.

In this case, the mean time of the development tasks in the current process model was 1.45 weeks and in the improved process model 1.20 weeks, leading to a reduction of 17.24% of the time needed to programming tasks.

If we shift our focus to quality, the number of tasks completed with the maximum quality at the time of finishing the project was the following:

- AS-IS model: 135 finished tasks, with an average of 30.81 weeks duration.
- TO-BE model: 162 completed tasks, with an average of 31.73 weeks duration.

This implies an improvement in the number of tasks of 20%. However, the average duration of the completed tasks was worsened by 2.98%.

Finally, if we compare the workers' busy time, in the AS-IS model, 21 out of the 30 workers had 100% occupancy through the project's lifecycle. In the TO-BE model the number of workers with full occupancy rose to 24, representing an improvement of 12.5%

6   Conclusions and Future Work

This work describes a process improvement proposal for the V-model based on team creation and task allocation strategies that take into account the personality of workers and its impact on productivity and quality. The study has been performed in a real company of the defense sector, where the use of the V-model is mandatory. The proposal has been tested and validated using a multiparadigm simulation model that makes use of the company historical data.

We can tentatively conclude that the results obtained are optimistic about a possible real application of the improvement designed for the current process model. The improvement introduces the novel concept of extreme engineering, that extends the concept of pair-programming to all the phases of the software life cycle, applies the concept of cross-functional teams to software engineering and pioneers in the use of the Cattel's model of 16PF to improve productivity in processes under the V-model.

In this work, the main metrics to assess the results of our proposal have been focused on the time needed to perform each phase, as a measure of productivity improvement, and the number of tasks completely done, as a measure of quality. Our future work, is planned to extend the analysis to the different phases of software development and include more metrics, such as, the individual level of quality of each task or the number of iterations necessary to fully complete each one. We will also investigate the effect of including the worker's preferences as a factor of the task allocation strategy and its impact on workers motivation and productivity.

Acknowledgements. This work has been partially supported by the Spanish Ministry of Science and Technology (grant TIN2016-76956-C3-3-R) with ERDF funds and the Andalusian Plan for Research, Development and Innovation (grant TIC-195).

References

1. Haskins, C.: Systems Engineering Handbook: A Guide for System Life Cycle Processes and Activities (ver. 3). International Council on Systems Engineering (2006)
2. Aitken, A., Ilango, V.A.: Comparative analysis of traditional software engineering and agile software development. In: 46th HICSS, pp. 4751–4760. IEEE Computer Society (2013)
3. Hertel, G.: Synergetic effects in working teams. J. Manag. Psychol. **26**(3), 176–184 (2011)
4. Department of Defense of USA: MIL-STD-498 (1994)
5. Department of Defense of USA: Defense Systems Software Development (DOD-STD-2167A) (1985)
6. André, M., Baldoquín, M.G., Acuña, S.T.: Formal model for assigning human resources to teams in software projects. Inf. Soft. Technol. **53**(3), 259–275 (2011)
7. Mathur, S., Malik, S.: Advancements in the V-model. Int. J. Comput. Appl. **1**(12), 30–35 (2010)
8. Lau, K.K., Taweel, F.M., Tran, C.M.: The W model for component-based software development. In: 37th EUROMICRO Conference on Software Engineering and Advanced Applications, pp. 47–50 (2011)
9. Liu, B., Zhang, H., Zhu, S.: An incremental V-model process for automotive development. In: 23rd Asia-Pacific Software Engineering Conference, pp. 225–232 (2016)
10. Fruhling, A., McDonald, P., Dunbar, C.: A case study: introducing eXtreme programming in a US government system development project. In: 41st HICSS, pp. 464–464 (2008)
11. Acuña, S.T., Juristo, N.: Assigning people to roles in software projects. Soft. Pract. Experience **34**(7), 675–696 (2004)

12. Cattell, R.B., Eber, H.W., Tatsuoka, M.M.: Handbook for the Sixteen Personality Factor Questionnaire (16 PF). Institute for Personality and Ability Testing (1988)
13. Nieves, M.: Estudios experimentales sobre la influencia de la personalidad y el clima en el desarrollo de software. Guías para gestión de equipos en proyectos de ingeniería del software, Ph.D. Dissertation (in Spanish). Universidad Autónoma de Madrid (2010)
14. Maslow, A.: Motivation and Personality. Harper & Brothers, New York (1954)
15. Begel, A., Nagappan, N.: Usage and perceptions of agile software development in an industrial context: an exploratory study. In: First International Symposium on Empirical Software Engineering and Measurement, ESEM 2007, pp. 255–264 (2007)
16. Harrington, H.J., Harrington, J.S.: Total Improvement Management: The Next Generation in Performance Improvement. McGraw-Hill Professional, New York (1995)
17. Shaw, R.B.: Extreme Teams. AMACOM (2017)
18. Parker, G.M.: Cross-Functional Teams: Working with Allies, Enemies, and other Strangers. Jossey-Bass, San Francisco (2003)

A Systematic Literature Review of Social Network Systems for Older Adults

Bilal Ahmad[✉], Ita Richardson, and Sarah Beecham

Lero, The Irish Software Research Centre, University of Limerick, Limerick, Ireland
{bilal.ahmad,ita.richardson,sarah.beecham}@lero.ie

Abstract. Background. The proportion of older adults (OAs) is increasing throughout the developed world. Social isolation is a recognised problem for this sector. Technology is regarded as a possible way to create a more inclusive society, where for example social network systems (SNSs) can keep OAs in contact with local communities, create new communities, reduce adverse impact of geographic separation, reduced mobility and lifestyle changes. **Objective.** As end-users of SNSs, this paper looks at the current state of practice of SNSs for OAs. We explore what OAs think about SNSs, what they want from SNSs and whether these needs are met. **Method.** Taking a snowballing approach, we examined 51 primary studies on SNSs for OAs. **Results.** There is a discernible increase in SNSs designed for OAs since 2005, which claim to meet needs such as simplicity, ease of use, privacy and access to useful information. Yet, sustained use over time is unknown. **Conclusion.** SNSs remain a potential way to reduce the social isolation of OAs, however the extent to which SNSs can replace real human contact is largely unexplored, as is whether SNSs can trigger the creation of new supportive communities.

Keywords: Older adult · User needs · Snowballing · Social isolation · Social network systems · Systematic literature review

1 Introduction

The proportion of older adults is increasing throughout the developed world. For example, in Ireland the proportion of younger OAs - aged over 65, is predicted to triple between 2006 and 2041 and the proportion of older OAs - aged over 80, will quadruple in next couple of decades [40]. This projected increase requires long-term planning to ensure that we have systems, structures and supports for this segment of population. Social isolation and loneliness are pronounced challenges for the OAs [5,9,16,31,36,37], and can lead to a low quality of life [8], which in turn can lead to physical ill-health [6], and depression [12]. OAs can suffer from a lack of communication and declining interaction [23] which can lead to social isolation - "the state of having minimal contact and integration with others and a generally low level of involvement in community life" [33]. This problem is not limited to OAs, but it is exacerbated with ageing. In general, SNSs

© Springer International Publishing AG 2017
M. Felderer et al. (Eds.): PROFES 2017, LNCS 10611, pp. 482–496, 2017.
https://doi.org/10.1007/978-3-319-69926-4_38

such as Facebook, Twitter and Skype are shown to connect people and create virtual communities [22]. According to Boyd, SNSs are on-line environments in which people create a self-descriptive profile and then make links to other people they know on the site, creating a network of personal connections [2]. These are considered as a potential solution to solve the problem of loneliness and social isolation [6,12,42]. However, differences in media preferences between the younger generation and OAs are preventing the older adult from engaging with the wider community [20]. It appears that OAs are unable to take full advantage of the stimulus and interaction these SNSs provide [13]. This paper presents a systematic literature review (SLR) that identifies the SNSs from the lens of the OA over the last two decades. The main contributions are:

- In-depth sensitivity analysis;
- Elicitation of the requirements for the development of SNSs for OAs as described in the literature;
- Categorization and characteristics of SNSs used by OAs;
- Comparison between take up of general and special SNSs used by OAs.

The remainder of this paper is organized as follows. Section 2 describes the systematic literature review protocol. Section 3 presents results of the review. Section 4 discusses the lessons learned and Sect. 5 presents limitations of this work, while Sect. 6 concludes this study and gives directions for future work.

2   Literature Review Protocol

Conducting an in depth literature review is a way to gain a broad understanding of the domain because it provides a balanced and objective summary of research for a particular topic [3]. We decided to use a snowballing approach to identify the relevant studies in the literature. Claes Wohlin conducted a comparative study of systematic literature review (SLR) methods [45] and concluded that snowballing is an efficient and effective way to identify the studies with less noise and lower chance of missing a relevant paper than using string-based searches in electronic databases. These two points motivated us to choose snowballing over electronic database searches. Also our topic falls in an inter-disciplinary category, hence there were chances of missing an important study by just looking at computer science and software engineering venues. Due to space limitations our full protocol is reported in a technical report [1]. In our case, a quick review of the related literature revealed that SNS development spanned from 1990's to date. We therefore opted to take a forward and backward snowballing approach, adopting guidelines from Wohlin [45] that calls for several iterations. In our case, two iterations of snowballing were sufficient as this resulted in a considerable number of relevant studies and saturation.

2.1   Goals and Research Questions

The goal of this SLR is to identify and document all the SNSs used by OAs, mentioned in the literature since 1990. We wanted to synthesize the findings to create a summary of the typical expectations of OAs from SNSs and whether these are met or not. Our research questions and associated rationales are:

RQ1. What does the Older Adult look for in SNSs?
Rationale: Elicitation of needs of OA to be met by a social networking system.
RQ2. What are the characteristics of SNSs used by the Older Adult?
Rationale: To understand characteristics of SNSs used by OA, and by implication, what works for the OA.
RQ3. How are OA using SNSs?
Rationale: To give a level of rigor to the findings, we need to understand the level to which the SNSs have been used by OA.
RQ4. Is there a difference between the take-up of general SNSs and SNSs developed specially for the OA?
Rationale: Highlight whether there is a need for more SNSs for OAs.

2.2   Study Selection Process

Search Strings. Search strings validated by a senior researcher and details of the databases on which they were applied are described in Sect. 2 of the technical report [1]. An example of a search string applied in ScienceDirect is:
("social networking service" OR social media* OR SNS*) AND (older adult* OR OA* OR OAP* OR elder* OR senior*).

Snowballing. A literature review on SNSs for the OAs conducted in 2016 [10] led to a starter set of papers [6,8,15,16,31,41,43]. However, the 7 review papers, though a good start, did not address our research questions fully. Being published between 1993 to 2013 suggested the need for both forward and backward snowballing. Also, the sources searched were very narrow. Additionally, this survey did not use standard SLR guidelines. The need for further studies to be included was confirmed since we found a further 18 papers post-2013 that published research on SNSs used by OAs.

Study Refinement and Data Extraction Process. Inspecting references (217) and citations (370) of the start set, left 594 studies to be investigated. We followed a five-step refinement process (detailed in Sect. 4 of technical report [1]) to select the final set of 51 primary studies as shown in Fig. 1.

3   Results

Section 3.1 identifies the types of studies reporting on SNSs for OAs to uncover any bias. Sensitivity analyses [38] provides an important context for answering our research questions by providing information on where the data used to answer the research questions might be biased. It helps with generalisation, scoping, sampling, limitations, for example, over representation of one country, domination by group, or elimination of one gender. After this, Sects. 3.2, 3.3, 3.4 and 3.5 aim to answer the four research questions presented in Sect. 2.1.

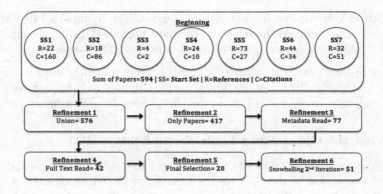

Fig. 1. Steps for selection of papers

3.1 Sensitivity Analysis

SNSs Used by OAs. There is a growing body of research in SNSs for the OAs on which we can build. More attention is given to designing technically-oriented solutions for the so-called baby boomers during the last decade in comparison with previous years. Figure 2 shows that both general and special SNSs for OAs have captured the interest of researchers with a slight emphasis on SNSs designed specially for OAs rather than adopting existing SNSs.

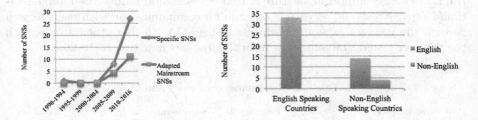

Fig. 2. SNSs used by older adults   **Fig. 3.** Language spoken v/s used in SNSs

Countries Involved. The published literature indicates that the USA and UK are taking the lead in terms of exploring, understanding and exploiting the potential of SNSs for OAs. However, this is likely to be in part due to our inclusion criteria that stipulates that we only include studies written in the English language.

Types of Research. 31 studies use qualitative research methods i.e. 61%, with 16 % using quantitative methods. Mixed methods were observed in the other studies.

Inclusion of Older Adults. Shannon [40] defines three categories of OAs i.e. younger (aged > 65), older (aged > 75 and < 85) and oldest OA (aged > 85).

The oldest OA are at the highest risk of independent living [12,14]. Paradoxically, it has been observed that they are the most neglected during the elicitation, analysis, design, development and evaluation of the SNSs for OAs.

Language Spoken v/s Used in SNSs. English is predominantly used in the SNSs for OAs. Obviously, the countries whose native language is English have used it, but interestingly, as shown in Fig. 3 other languages are represented.

3.2   What the Older Adult Looks for in SNSs – RQ1

The primary purpose of many of the studies was to describe the design, development and evaluation of the SNS for the OA. A list of OA needs extracted from the studies is shown in Table 1 that presents the most prevalent requirements, associated references and frequencies. The requirements are classified into functional and non-functional, where functional is considered as "a statement of a piece of a required functionality or a behaviour that a system will exhibit under specific conditions" [44] and non-functional as "a property, or quality, that the product must have, such as appearance, or a speed or accuracy property" [35].

Access to useful information is the top feature that OAs expect from a SNS. Therefore, SNSs were focused on providing information according to the demands of OAs e.g. health, horoscope, entertainment [16,20]. Asynchronous communication allows OAs to reciprocate at their convenience and is the second most important feature in these SNSs. It was especially useful for OAs suffering from chronic disease, as there are times when they do not feel well enough to respond [14,17]. Another important feature is that SNSs should reduce the intergenerational gap. SNS should serve as a medium for communication with peers as well as with the younger generation which will help OAs to share their stories with the younger generation and learn from them about new things [18,26].

Table 1. Requirements of older adults

ID	Requirements	Frequency	ID	Requirements	Frequency
	Functional			**Non-Functional**	
Req1	Provides access to useful information	26	Req6	Privacy management	39
Req2	Asynchronous communication	24	Req7	Requires less memory/cognitive load	38
Req3	Reduce intergenerational gap	7	Req8	Liberty	29
	Non-Functional		Req9	Stable	19
Req4	Ease of use	49	Req10	Device should be nearby	15
Req5	Simplicity	47			

The top non-functional requirement for OAs is ease of use. This means that the systems should be designed to ensure that they achieve the goals of OAs effectively and efficiently, leading to satisfactory use, whereas simplicity means that the SNS should have only those features, which are essential. For example Norval et al. [34] developed a simplified version of Facebook by removing advertisements and apps and by using very easy terminology. Privacy is a major concern and should be managed in any system developed for OAs [41,43].

They are very sceptical about what they share or write on a system, and are concerned that it may be accessed by someone other than the intended person. Cognitive load indicates that the SNSs specially for the OA should require less mental effort to understand and use. SNSs must not be over-emphasised in the life of OAs. Rather, they should be designed with liberty or independence of the OA in mind. This means that OA should be able to operate the SNS without seeking help and at their own preferred time. Stability of the system is another important feature that needs to be incorporated in the SNSs for OAs, because if a system breaks down the motivation level of the OA will reduce significantly. In addition, the device (e.g. tablet, LED, mobile) should be deployed near the room of the OA, in order to make it physically accessible.

3.3   Characteristics of SNSs Used by OAs – RQ2

There are two kinds of SNSs for the OAs i.e. general and special SNSs. The term general is used for those solutions that are exploiting the features of conventional SNSs such as Facebook and adapting it according to the needs of OAs. On the other hand, special SNSs are those social networking systems that are novel and built specially for the OAs. The list of both general and special SNSs selected as primary studies is presented in Sect. 6 of the technical report [1]. These are developed in different parts of the world and are targeted towards OA problems and requirements, which are either taken directly via interviews/focus groups or based on literature. One important feature that could be generalized from these SNSs is that all of these have tried to propose an easy and innovative way for communication. Some researchers have opted for typical computer machines while others focused on the use of tablets or the daily living objects such as tables, lamps, books etc. for making technology accessible and familiar to the older segment of population. There are two types of characteristics of SNSs used by OAs i.e. functional and non-functional. If we look at the functional aspects, then text based, audio and video based interaction is provided by these SNSs. The non-functional characteristics of these applications include multimodality, ambience, ease of use, source of enjoyment and liberty. Table 2 presents the full list of characteristics with their frequency and references. Some of the most important of these include simplicity, usability and privacy. (FoCh is short for functional and NoFoCh for non-functional characteristics. Their definitions are same as discussed in the answer of RQ1). It is inferred from here that some of the expectations of the OAs are met by the current offerings. Although OAs have used these solutions during the evaluation period of these studies, the motivation towards using these SNSs keeps on diminishing with the passage of time. This could be due to a number of factors e.g. lack of interest of the researcher to further investigate or the evolution of expectations of OAs from the SNSs. Therefore, in order to incorporate these new ways of communication and engagement with the society as a part of their daily routine, new ways of thinking and more novel and holistic approaches are needed that cater for enhancements in the system as well. We also tested the quality of SNS research via evaluation methods, duration of evaluation, sample, and data collections methods. Briefly, 21 out of 51 studies have used home-deployment for evaluation. 70% of SNSs were evaluated for less than 3 months and 74% of the sample were female. The top most data collection method used was interviews. More results along with figures are made available in the Sect. 7 of the technical report [1].

Table 2. Characteristics of SNSs used by older adults

ID	SNSs Characteristics	Frequency	ID	SNSs Characteristics	Frequency
	Functional			**Non-Functional**	
FoCh1	Text-based communication	47	NoFoCh10 Tangible		19
FoCh2	Photo-based communication	35	NoFoCh11 Asynchronous		19
FoCh3	Video-based communication	18	NoFoCh12 Ease of Use		17
FoCh4	Audio-based communication	17	NoFoCh13 Privacy Management		16
FoCh5	Hand-written communication	3	NoFoCh14 Involves New people		15
	Non-Functional		NoFoCh15 Valuable		14
NoFoCh1	Internet Dependency	51	NoFoCh16 Natural Form of Communication		13
NoFoCh2	Simplicity	32	NoFoCh17 Synchronous		13
NoFoCh3	Involves Friends	31	NoFoCh18 Source of Enjoyment		12
NoFoCh4	Involves Family	25	NoFoCh19 Adaptive		12
NoFoCh5	Involves Caregivers	23	NoFoCh20 Richer		10
NoFoCh6	Ubiquitous	22	NoFoCh21 Liberty		8
NoFoCh7	Useful	21	NoFoCh22 Ambient		6
NoFoCh8	Multimodality	20	NoFoCh23 Unique		6
NoFoCh9	Interesting	19	NoFoCh24 Gender oriented		5

3.4   Older Adult Experiences with SNSs – RQ3

In order to understand how OAs are using SNSs, we first consider the level of rigor associated with the findings. The codes that are extracted from the reading of the literature related to the usage of these SNSs by OAs include the location, training, classification of participants, integration with existing systems, core functionality (e.g. communication) and finally the response received. The following 6 subsections elaborate these themes.

Location. In most of the cases OAs were given the opportunity to choose a location according to their preference [20] e.g. living room and kitchen. They showed less inclination for SNSs to be in their bedrooms.

Training. OAs were provided training to understand the concept and functionality of the SNSs. The methods for guidance used were face-to-face introduction and recorded training videos [16].

Classification of Participants. The participants involved in the evaluation of the SNSs are classified into two categories: heterogeneous and homogeneous.

Heterogeneous. If family members, caregivers, friends or younger generation are involved during the different phases, then these have heterogeneous participants. The studies that lie in this category include [14,20,26,31,32].

Homogeneous. If only OAs are involved in the evaluation then these studies have homogeneous participants. One of the examples is the evaluation of

Fridgenet [28], which involved 15 OAs using the system and communicating with each other for the enhancement of their social wellbeing.

Integration with Existing Systems. The researchers had chosen a pragmatic approach whilst designing and developing SNSs for OAs. They created a simplified interface for OA, but on the other hand relatives, friends and caregivers can use their preferred social media technologies to reciprocate e.g. Facebook, Skype.

Core Functionality. The ultimate objective of almost all of these SNSs is to provide a mechanism for communication that can lead to increased social contact and overcoming isolation of OAs. Different researchers have opted for different features according to the needs posed by OAs. Some of the functionalities include emailing, access to information, sharing of information (e.g. pictures), broadcasting content, posting comments (audio, textual), instant messaging, phone calls, searching information, private messaging, video conferencing, discussion forum.

Feedback. Almost every study claimed that their solution served the purpose well for which it was made e.g. social isolation. Some of the assertions made by the authors with respect to the feedback received by OAs, include electronic family newspaper [36], which is portrayed as a partial solution to alleviate social isolation. Building bridges [20] device helped in creating connections outside the system as well. Tlatoque [14] is known for enhancing asymmetric relations and face-to-face communication. Sharetouch [42] encouraged users to make more friends. Pinteresce and Social connector [4,32] facilitated social interaction consequently alleviating the communications breakdown.

3.5 Difference Between General and Special SNSs Used by OAs – RQ4

In order to understand and analyse the differences between the take up of general and special SNSs for OAs several parameters were selected. In general, if something is used for a longer period of time than the study, this is an indication that it has a level of longevity. Secondly, the number of people interested in that SNS also indicates potential interest in the system - hence we selected the number of OAs using the SNSs for comparison. Thirdly, we selected the age group under study, as it gives insight as to the popularity of SNSs within a sample of the population. Lastly, we also wanted to look at whether gender might have an influence on take-up and interest in SNSs. Table 3 shows the minimum, average and maximum values for these parameters. It is important to note that the data presented in this table is extracted from the primary studies only. Although, in some cases the differences in the level of adoption are very subtle they reveal that researchers were inclined towards developing special SNSs instead of tweaking the general ones. A larger number of parameters could prove useful for validation in our future work.

Difference in Duration of Evaluation. OAs used the general SNSs for a maximum of 4 weeks in comparison with special SNSs, some of which were used for 6 months. The average time for usage of general SNSs is 5.6 days while for

Table 3. Difference in the level of adoption of general and special SNSs

Sr. No.	Parameters	Variation		General SNSs	Special SNSs
		Minimum		45 minutes	2 months
1	Duration of Evaluation	Average		5.6 days	3.3 months
		Maximum		4 weeks	6 months
		Minimum		8	4
2	Number of OAs	Average		18.6	16.2
		Maximum		31	36
		Minimum		58	55
3	Age of OAs involved	Average		72.8	75.2
		Maximum		92	95
			Minimum	4	0
		Male	Average	6.4	3.4
4	Gender Division w.r.t. Number		Maximum	11	7
			Minimum	4	1
		Female	Average	12.2	12.8
			Maximum	20	36

special SNSs it is nearly 3.3 months. The usage time here indicates the evaluation duration mentioned in the studies, which implies that more attention was paid by the researchers to evaluate the special SNSs as shown in Table 3.

Difference in Number of OAs. The figures about the number of OAs involved in the different phases of the SNSs are interesting. The minimum number of OAs evaluating special SNSs is less than for general SNSs i.e. four compared to eight. Also, on average, 18.6 OAs contributed in the studies that are presenting general SNSs while 16.2 OAs evaluated special purpose SNSs. Once again, a threat to validity could be the correlation between the circumstances under which these solutions were developed and the number of OAs involved.

Difference in Age Range of OAs. The age range of the OAs who participated during the course of the general SNSs is between 58 and 92. Special SNSs were advantaged because, during their progression, the OAs involved were of a broader age range i.e. from 55 to 95. The average age for the included seniors was 72.8 and 75.8 for general and special SNSs respectively.

Difference in Gender Distribution of OAs. More females were involved for both general and special purpose SNSs. This could be due to their availability, paying attention to new advancements in technology or desire to be in touch with their relatives more than their male counterparts. The number of males involved in the studies presenting general SNSs ranged from 4 to a maximum of 11. On the other hand, for special SNSs, the inclusion of males was even less, as indicated in Table 3. In one study, there was no male involved and the maximum number in any study was seven. The average number of males involved for general and special SNSs was 6.4 and 3.4 respectively. Conversely, the average number of female participation is almost double for both types of SNSs. Therefore, we can conclude that these studies are gender biased.

It can be concluded from this section that OAs cannot use conventional SNSs on an as-is basis and they have their special needs due to a number of factors such as manual dexterity, lack of purpose and fear of technology. Several studies have tried to modify conventional SNSs and to introduce them to OAs, but the results did not demonstrate success. Therefore research has been undertaken in recent years where researchers have gone directly to OAs and ask them about their needs and create special SNSs for them. Some of the needs of OAs were met by both general and special SNSs, but they never became part of the daily lives of OA. One of the reasons was the evaluation period, which was from a few minutes to a maximum of 6 months. One possible thing that could be done in the future is to increase that duration. This might serve as a better source of integration of SNSs in the lives of OAs over the long-term. Another important point that is highlighted from Table 3 is that special purpose SNSs are now on the horizon, so this is also an evidence that there exists a need for more inclusion and special SNSs for OAs.

4   Discussion and Lessons Learned

This study has analysed the collective impact of the growing number of SNSs on the life of OAs. Most of SNSs are domestic ones developed in native languages. None have a global influence. This is partly due to a finite social range of the elderly and partly due to different cultures of different countries [9]. This will be further investigated during interviews with OAs where we will ask about awareness, familiarity and experience with technology, especially SNSs. The implications of the existing SNSs include increased social integration and intergenerational communication leading to health benefits. So these factors suggest that there is a need to develop further tools with new ideas e.g. volunteer hub by ensuring that things like ease of use, cognitive impairment, visual acuity etc. are adhered to, which is the ultimate purpose of our research. Following paragraph presents the lessons learnt through a synthesis of the studies in this review.

SNSs are changing continuously, so a wide variety of barriers to their adoption might arise in the future [34]. By default, the privacy level of SNSs should be high and easy to access for the OAs, because this is the most prevalent issue raised by them [7,21,25,29,46]. An effective SNS for OAs can be designed by knowing their history, because they are very heterogeneous [39] e.g. how they acquired education. The included studies were gender biased which means that the requirements stated earlier may be more relevant for female OAs. If OAs are provided with right circumstances to use new SNSs, it will be very effective because OAs are becoming interested in adopting new technologies [27]. SNSs alone are not the complete solution to overcome social isolation [24]. They must be augmented with community involvement. Culture is also an important factor in increasing or decreasing the motivation towards the use of SNSs by OAs [30]. SNSs could be fully adopted by OAs if they are incorporated into objects which are already used by them e.g. TV, book [11].

Researchers and practitioners can use the results of this study as evidence to indicate the need of more special and inclusive SNSs for OAs. They can also benefit by adopting the top requirements that are presented in this review for developing SNSs. During evaluation phase, they can use this study's recommendations by deploying the SNSs in the homes of OAs for a longer duration. This will provide more accurate results about adoption and diffusion of the system in their lives. To avoid gender bias, which is observed in existing studies, it is highly recommended to select subjects in equal numbers from both genders.

5   Threats to Validity

This research also has certain limitations like any other study in the field of science. The main limitation is that our analysis was based on two iterations of snowballing, so further assessment is needed. However, the results have provided some valuable insights and we believe our review met its goal.

External Validity. Forward and backward snowballing was conducted on seven specific studies. Although these cover a broad range of years, the results might not be generalizable if a different review protocol is used for conducting further studies. Also, we cannot be sure that even if we did capture all published work in the area, that this is a fair reflection of all the SNSs in the market, since it is likely that some developers of SNSs do not publish their results.

Internal Validity. Snowballing guidelines [45] were applied to a selection of studies. Snowballing is not an alternative to database searches and ideally a mixed approach to identifying relevant literature should be used to ensure the best possible coverage of the literature. Here, the notion was avoidance of noise. Also key authors were not contacted at the time of writing this paper which could be a valuable way to check if any study is missed or not.

Reliability. The technique for the extraction and analysis of data was applied in such a way that others can replicate it. Also, every choice or paper selection made by the first researcher was validated by a second researcher.

6   Conclusion and Future Work

The 51 studies in the review helped identify what OAs would like from SNSs, and to what extent current SNSs meet their needs. Desired characteristics of SNSs such as privacy, simplicity and ease of use were the most frequently mentioned features. Many studies claim they are providing these, but they were unable to prove the uptake of their proposed solutions over time [12, 20, 36]. Indications are that motivation to use the SNSs drop with the passage of time. It is unclear as to why this is the case or whether SNSs have in any way solved the problem of social isolation. We propose therefore that there is a need for more inclusive SNSs that have the capability to make a positive difference to the lives of OAs, and for more in-depth and longitudinal studies to be conducted to observe the impact SNSs have on the lifestyle of the OA. An example of how SNSs could make a positive impact was presented in a study by Fang et al. [19], who proposed a SNS that suggested volunteer opportunities for OAs. Through this engagement, OAs were connected with the local community, and the problem of social isolation for OAs was solved indirectly. This, in turn, improve their physical and mental health [19]. This kind of intervention might be useful to propose in future work. The next step in our research will be to identify a sample of the OA population and study their current needs regarding SNSs. We plan to develop an SNS to reflect a local community, and tap into a real need, with the aim that SNSs can integrate OAs with the wider community. Thus, we propose to prevent a growing proportion of our population becoming socially isolated due to lifestyle changes.

Acknowledgments. This work was supported, in part, by Science Foundation Ireland grant 13/RC/2094 & co-funded under the European Regional Development Fund through the Southern & Eastern Regional Operational Programme to Lero - the Irish Software Research Centre (www.lero.ie).

References

1. Ahmad, B., Richardson, I., Beecham, S.: Protocol for a systematic literature review of social network systems for older adults. Technical report 3, Lero, The Irish Software Research Centre, University of Limerick, Ireland (2017). https://goo.gl/fo4Thx

2. Boyd, D.M., Ellison, N.B.: Social network sites: definition, history, and scholarship. J. Comput. Mediat. Commun. **13**(1), 210–230 (2007)

3. Brereton, P., Kitchenham, B.A., Budgen, D., Turner, M., Khalil, M.: Lessons from applying the systematic literature review process within the software engineering domain. J. Syst. Softw. **80**(4), 571–583 (2007)

4. Brewer, R.N., Jones, J.: Pinteresce: exploring reminiscence as an incentive to digital reciprocity for older adults. In: Proceedings of the 18th ACM Conference Companion on Computer Supported Cooperative Work, CSCW 2015 Companion, pp. 243–246. ACM, New York (2015)

5. Brunette, K., Eisenstadt, M., Pukinskis, E., Ryan, W.: Meeteetse: social well-being through place attachment. In: CHI 2005 Extended Abstracts on Human Factors in Computing Systems, pp. 2065–2069. ACM, New York (2005)

6. Burmeister, O.K.: What seniors value about online community. J. Commun. Inform. **8**(1) (2012)

7. Campos, W., Martinez, A., Sanchez, W., Estrada, H., Castro-Sánchez, N.A., Mujica, D.: A systematic review of proposals for the social integration of elderly people using ambient intelligence and social networking sites. Cogn. Comput. **8**(3), 529–542 (2016)

8. Chen, Y.: Usability analysis on online social networks for the elderly. Helsinki University of Thechnology (2009)

9. Coelho, J., Duarte, C.: Socially networked or isolated? Differentiating older adults and the role of tablets and television. In: Abascal, J., Barbosa, S., Fetter, M., Gross, T., Palanque, P., Winckler, M. (eds.) INTERACT 2015. LNCS, vol. 9296, pp. 129–146. Springer, Cham (2015). doi:10.1007/978-3-319-22701-6_10

10. Coelho, J., Duarte, C.: A literature survey on older adults' use of social network services and social applications. Comput. Hum. Behav. **58**, 187–205 (2016)

11. Coelho, J., Rito, F., Luz, N., Duarte, C.: Prototyping TV and tablet Facebook interfaces for older adults. In: Abascal, J., Barbosa, S., Fetter, M., Gross, T., Palanque, P., Winckler, M. (eds.) INTERACT 2015. LNCS, vol. 9296, pp. 110–128. Springer, Cham (2015). doi:10.1007/978-3-319-22701-6_9

12. Cornejo, R., Hernández, D., Favela, J., Tentori, M., Ochoa, S.: Persuading older adults to socialize and exercise through ambient games. In: 2012 6th International Conference on Pervasive Computing Technologies for Healthcare (PervasiveHealth) and Workshops, pp. 215–218, May 2012

13. Cornejo, R., Favela, J., Tentori, M.: Ambient displays for integrating older adults into social networking sites. In: Kolfschoten, G., Herrmann, T., Lukosch, S. (eds.) CRIWG 2010. LNCS, vol. 6257, pp. 321–336. Springer, Heidelberg (2010). doi:10.1007/978-3-642-15714-1_24

14. Cornejo, R., Tentori, M., Favela, J.: Ambient awareness to strengthen the family social network of older adults. Comput. Support. Coop. Work (CSCW) **22**(2), 309–344 (2013)

15. Cornejo, R., Tentori, M., Favela, J.: Enriching in-person encounters through social media: A study on family connectedness for the elderly. Int. J. Hum. Comput. Stud. **71**(9), 889–899 (2013)

16. Czaja, S., Guerrier, J., Nair, S., Landauer, T.: Computer communication as an aid to independence for older adults. Behav. Inf. Technol. **12**(4), 197–207 (1993)

17. David, J.M., Benjamin, A., Baecker, R.M., Gromala, D., Birnholtz, J.: Living with pain, staying in touch: exploring the communication needs of older adults with chronic pain. In: CHI 2011 Extended Abstracts on Human Factors in Computing Systems, CHI EA 2011, pp. 1219–1224. ACM, New York (2011)

18. Davis, H., Pedell, S.: Older adults' use of a novel communication system: client goals versus participant experiences. In: Proceedings of the Annual Meeting of the Australian Special Interest Group for Computer Human Interaction, OzCHI 2015, pp. 269–273. ACM, New York (2015)

19. Fang, W.C., Hsieh, M.C., Yang, P.C., Li, W.G., Chiu, C.J., Chiang, J.H.: iDianNao: an orange technology that recommends volunteer opportunities to older adults. In: 2015 International Conference on Orange Technologies, pp. 38–41, December 2015

20. Garattini, C., Wherton, J., Prendergast, D.: Linking the lonely: an exploration of a communication technology designed to support social interaction among older adults. Univ. Access Inf. Soc. **11**(2), 211–222 (2012)

21. Gibson, L., Moncur, W., Forbes, P., Arnott, J., Martin, C., Bhachu, A.S.: Designing social networking sites for older adults. In: Proceedings of the 24th BCS Interaction Specialist Group Conference, pp. 186–194. British Computer Society, Swinton (2010)

22. Grosinger, J., Vetere, F., Fitzpatrick, G.: Agile life: addressing knowledge and social motivations for active aging. In: Proceedings of the 24th Australian Computer-Human Interaction Conference, pp. 162–165. ACM, New York (2012)

23. Haris, N., Majid, R.A., Abdullah, N., Osman, R.: The role of social media in supporting elderly quality daily life. In: 2014 3rd International Conference on User Science and Engineering (i-USEr), pp. 253–257, September 2014

24. Harley, D., Howland, K., Harris, E., Redlich, C.: Online communities for older users: what can we learn from local community interactions to create social sites that work for older people. In: Proceedings of the 28th International BCS Human Computer Interaction Conference on HCI 2014, pp. 42–51. BCS, Swinton (2014)

25. Hope, A., Schwaba, T., Piper, A.M.: Understanding digital and material social communications for older adults. In: Proceedings of the SIGCHI Conference on Human Factors in Computing Systems, pp. 3903–3912. ACM, New York (2014)

26. Hsu, C.-L., Tseng, K.C., Tseng, C.-L., Liu, B.-C.: Design and development a social networks platform for older people. In: Stephanidis, C. (ed.) UAHCI 2011. LNCS, vol. 6766, pp. 186–195. Springer, Heidelberg (2011). doi:10.1007/978-3-642-21663-3_20

27. Karahasanović, A., Brandtzæg, P.B., Heim, J., Lüders, M., Vermeir, L., Pierson, J., Lievens, B., Vanattenhoven, J., Jans, G.: Co-creation and user-generated content-elderly people's user requirements. Comput. Hum. Behav. 25(3), 655–678 (2009)

28. Lee, Y., Huang, M.C., Zhang, X., Xu, W.: FridgeNet: a nutrition and social activity promotion platform for aging populations. IEEE Intell. Syst. 30(4), 23–30 (2015)

29. Lehtinen, V., Näsänen, J., Sarvas, R.: "A little silly and empty-headed": older adults' understandings of social networking sites. In: Proceedings of the 23rd British HCI Group Annual Conference on People and Computers: Celebrating People and Technology, pp. 45–54. British Computer Society, Swinton (2009)

30. Michailidou, E., Parmaxi, A., Zaphiris, P.: Culture effects in online social support for older people: perceptions and experience. Univ. Access Inf. Soc. 14(2), 281–293 (2015)

31. Morris, M.E.: Social networks as health feedback displays. IEEE Internet Comput. 9(5), 29–37 (2005)

32. Muñoz, D., Cornejo, R., Gutierrez, F.J., Favela, J., Ochoa, S.F., Tentori, M.: A social cloud-based tool to deal with time and media mismatch of intergenerational family communication. Future Gener. Comput. Syst. 53, 140–151 (2015)

33. Naufal, R.: Addressing social isolation amongst older victorians: an evidence based approach (2008)

34. Norval, C., Arnott, J.L., Hanson, V.L.: What's on your mind?: Investigating recommendations for inclusive social networking and older adults. In: Proceedings of the SIGCHI Conference on Human Factors in Computing Systems, CHI 2014, pp. 3923–3932. ACM, New York (2014)

35. Robertson, S., Robertson, J.: Mastering the Requirements Process: Getting Requirements Right, 3rd edn. Addison-Wesley Professional, Upper Saddle River (2012)

36. Rodríguez, M.D., Gonzalez, V.M., Favela, J., Santana, P.C.: Home-based communication system for older adults and their remote family. Comput. Hum. Behav. 25(3), 609–618 (2009)

37. Romero, N., Markopoulos, P., Baren, J., Ruyter, B., Ijsselsteijn, W., Farshchian, B.: Connecting the family with awareness systems. Pers. Ubiquit. Comput. 11(4), 299–312 (2007)

38. Saltelli, A., Chan, K., Scott, E.M., et al.: Sensitivity Analysis, vol. 1. Wiley, New York (2000)

39. Sayago, S., Santos, P., Gonzalez, M., Arenas, M., López, L.: Meeting educational needs of the elderly in ICT: two exploratory case studies. Crossroads 14(2) (2007)

40. Shannon, S.: The New Agenda on Ageing - To Make Ireland the Best Country to Grow Old In. College Green, Dublin (2012)

41. Sillanpää, N., Älli, S., Övermark, T.: Easy-to-use social network service for people with cognitive or speech and language impairments (2009)

42. Tsai, T.H., Chang, H.T., Chang, Y.M., Huang, G.S.: Sharetouch: a system to enrich social network experiences for the elderly. J. Syst. Softw. 85(6), 1363–1369 (2012)

43. Waycott, J., Vetere, F., Pedell, S., Kulik, L., Ozanne, E., Gruner, A., Downs, J.: Older adults as digital content producers. In: Proceedings of the SIGCHI Conference on Human Factors in Computing Systems, pp. 39–48. ACM, New York (2013)

44. Wiegers, K.E.: Software Requirements, 2nd edn. Microsoft Press, Redmond (2003)
45. Wohlin, C.: Guidelines for snowballing in systematic literature studies and a replication in software engineering. In: Proceedings of the 18th International Conference on Evaluation and Assessment in Software Engineering, EASE 2014, pp. 38:1–38:10. ACM, New York (2014)
46. Xie, B., Watkins, I., Golbeck, J., Huang, M.: Understanding and changing older adults' perceptions and learning of social media. Educ. Gerontol. **38**(4), 282–296 (2012)

Different Views on Project Success
When Communication Is Not the Same

Jil Klünder[(✉)], Oliver Karras, Fabian Kortum, Mathias Casselt,
and Kurt Schneider

Software Engineering Group, Leibniz Universität Hannover,
Welfengarten 1, 30167 Hannover, Germany
{jil.kluender,oliver.karras,fabian.kortum,
kurt.schneider}@inf.uni-hannover.de, m.casselt@stud.uni-hannover.de

Abstract. Software project success has various facets and definitions
ranging from customer satisfaction over software quality to the degree of
implemented vs. not implemented requirements. Customers, developers
and project leaders strive for project success. During the development
process, they try to pay attention to aspects which are perceived to be
important for a satisfying project execution from their individual point
of view. These aspects may vary according to the underlying definition
and understanding of project success. Different views on the importance
of aspects like communication can cause problems and complicate the
collaboration due to different expectations and misunderstandings.

In a study with 97 student participants and eight customers, we examine which factors are perceived to be important for a successful project
execution. In order to unfold discrepancies, we analyze whether the views
of customers and developers on the relevance of aspects like communication and fulfilling the requirements specification differ from each other.
According to our results, communication is most important for both the
team and the customer. But they have different ideas of the term: The
correct exchange of information between the team and the customer as
well as the team-internal communication.

In particular rather inexperienced developers and customers should
be aware of different ideas of terms like communication for a successful project execution. It is not sufficient to know that communication is
important. Being aware of different ideas can facilitate the collaboration
and avoid problems due to misunderstandings.

Keywords: Human factors · Communication · Collaboration · Project
success · Student software projects

1 Introduction

The overall goal in software development is a successful project execution. There
are many different approaches to define project success [10]. A software project
may be successful, if the resulting software contains the desired features [5] or

© Springer International Publishing AG 2017
M. Felderer et al. (Eds.): PROFES 2017, LNCS 10611, pp. 497–507, 2017.
https://doi.org/10.1007/978-3-319-69926-4_39

if the software is of high quality [1]. Some approaches also deal with internal or external influences during the process. Verner et al. [12] identify good requirements and their effective management as best criteria of project success. According to Hofmann and Lehner [4], requirements engineering practices also have a strong influence on the result. Taking the stakeholders into account increases customer satisfaction due to requirements fulfillment [4].

The underlying definition of success influences the project. Agile teams who want to satisfy the customer may reveal a higher importance on the collaboration with the customer than teams who primary want to fulfill the requirements specification. Hence, different definitions of project success may lead to different expectations from the team's and the customer's point of view. This can complicate the collaboration between the team and the customer. Hoda et al. [3] examine the so-called "Lack of Customer Involvement" as one of the biggest difficulties in agile teams. An inadequate information exchange between the team and the customer and this "Lack of Customer Involvement" may endanger project success due to misinterpreted and badly communicated information [3]. In contrast, being aware of possible different understandings between the team and the customer may smooth the way towards a successful project execution [3].

To reduce this problem of possibly mistaken issues related to project success, we want to gain an overview of the different ideas from both the customers' and the developers' point of view. We want to find answers for the following research question:

RQ: *Which factors are perceived to be most important for project completion from the developers' and the customers' point of view?*

To clarify and answer our research question from the developers' point of view, we conducted a study with 97 participants in twelve student software projects at a university environment. The student participants resemble potential newcomers in companies. Their opinion represents the views of new developers in industry. The customers' perspective is covered by the expectations from eight customers from industry of the student projects. Both students and customers filled in questionnaires at project's end.

The main contribution of this paper is the insight that developers and customers have different views on aspects like communication and fulfilling the requirements specification as prerequisites for project success. Our results reflect the importance of increasing the students', i.e. newcomers', awareness of different understandings of an adequate information exchange during the process. Communicating in software development teams is more than just team-internal communication. Increasing the awareness may help to satisfy the customer. This is very important for project success [4].

This paper is structured as follows: In Sect. 2, we consider related work. Section 3 presents our study design with the methodology and the results related to our research question. We interpret our results and present implications for education and industry in Sect. 4 and conclude our work in Sect. 5.

2   Related Work

Different factors influencing and defining project success, in particular the collaboration between the customer and the team, have already been addressed by some researchers.

Philippo et al. [8] analyze the relevance of requirement ambiguity as a factor for project success. Based on empirical data, they investigate the relation between these two aspects. According to their results, there does not exist a correlation between requirements ambiguity and project success. The ambiguity does not increase the number of defects during the test phase. They validated their results by conducting an interview study with experts. These interviews resulted in a framework outlining factors which have an influence on requirement-ambiguity risk by increasing or mitigating it [8].

Surian et al. [11] analyze socio-technical aspects of successful and failed projects to predict the outcome using machine learning techniques. They focus on the interactions and the collaboration between the involved team members by considering a so-called "collaboration graph" [11]. For instance, they consider the number of already finished successful software projects of a team member and the time the person is part of the team. Using machine learning, they find patterns apparently appearing in successful projects. In contrast to our approach, Surian et al. [11] focus on rather technical measures which can be quantified.

Keil and Carmel [6] emphasize the relevance of customers or end users for new products or improvements. In their contribution, they present several possibilities to link the customer and the developers. The "customer-developer links" describe various ways of information exchange between customers and the development team. Resulting from the experiences from 17 companies with 31 projects, they determine three lessons for the collaboration between team and customer. First, the number of used links increases the value of each link only up to a specific point [6]. Second, the authors propose to "reduce the reliance on indirect links" [6, p. 39]. Third, they recommend also to consider new links, i.e. links which are not traditionally used in the company [6].

Hofmann and Lehner [4] focus on requirements engineering as one determining factor for project success in software projects. The authors state deficient requirements as the biggest cause of project failure. Hofmann and Lehner [4] analyze the importance of different practices in requirements engineering for project success. They perform a study with 15 requirements engineering teams focusing on team-internal aspects, but they do not analyze particularly the relevance of the collaboration between the team and the customer for project success. Nonetheless, they state that the teams often struggle with "adequately involving customers to identify high-priority requirements" [4, p. 63].

Hoda et al. [3] analyze customer collaboration in agile teams. They increase the awareness of the importance of an adequate customer collaboration by outlining the impact of an inadequate amount of customer involvement. According to Hoda et al. [3], the "Lack of Customer Involvement" is one of the biggest difficulties in agile teams. They outline consequences of this lack such as problems in gathering and clarifying requirements and loss of productivity. In our contribution, we focus on the problem of missing mutual understanding between the customer and the team which is not addressed by Hoda et al. [3].

Agarwal and Rathod [1] present developers', project managers' and customer account managers' views on project success based on an exploratory study. For the participants, it is most important to fulfill the scope of software projects including functionality and quality. For external stakeholders, target cost and time are important. In the end, the criteria for project success of both groups do not match [1]. Meanwhile Agarwal and Rathod [1] mostly consider "hard" factors and concrete criteria, we focus on the way to achieve them.

3   Study

This paper is based on an empirical study which was conducted at Leibniz Universität Hannover using student software projects.

3.1   Student Software Projects

The Software Engineering Group at Leibniz Universität Hannover yearly offers a course called *Software-Project (SWP)*. The students have to attend in this course before finishing their bachelor studies. Most of them are in the third year of their computer science studies.

In the winter term 2016/2017, 97 students participated in the SWP. They formed 12 teams with seven to ten team members. Within the duration of 15 weeks, each team developed a software for one of the eight customers. Most of the customers have been externals for example from the Police Department for Cyber Criminal Affairs in Hannover, a sports club, the medical school in Hannover, and industrial environments. They had a real interest in the project being successful, particularly because the final products should be applied in existing real life projects or applications and used for a long time. To avoid problems and to facilitate teamwork, each team was supported by a tutor who helped in the case of organizational questions. But the tutor was not allowed to help the team with task-related conflicts.

The software projects followed the waterfall model but also contained some agile artifacts [7]. The projects had a rather strict timetable with an obligatory weekly meeting. Based on the concept of the on-site customer, the students and the customers met once a week to discuss project process and the current development state. Each of these meetings contained a weekly Scrum: Each member reported about the progress since the last meeting, the plans until the next meeting and problems.

The development was divided into four main phases visualized in Fig. 1: requirements analysis, two iteration phases, and polishing. The first phase was about clarifying the customer's requirements and ended in writing a requirements specification, which was adjusted and granted by the customer. The two following phases were the main development iterations for implementing the basic

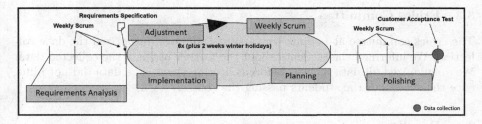

Fig. 1. Process of the observed student software projects (Color figure online)

functionalities. During the polishing phase, the participants had the opportunity to implement last change requests of the customer as well as to improve the product's quality or using the time for fixing bugs. The project ended with an acceptance test carried out by the customers.

3.2 Study Design

The survey took place right after project completion (see also Fig. 1; the dark blue dot represents the time slot of the data collection). The survey has been answered during the weekly meeting of developers and customers and was conducted with a paper-pencil-questionnaire. Due to absence, 94 of 97 students (97%) and 7 out of 8 customers (87,5%) participated in the survey.

The structure of the survey was adjusted for developers and customers. The survey consisted of simple checkbox questions and tasks to prioritize prescribed answers to guarantee a certain amount of easily set up data. Some questions were also designed to encourage the interviewed person to provide preferably individually formulated answers for instance with open questions. This allows receiving new opinions and views. Hence, these kinds of questions were valuable, but the results required some sort of processing. In this case, manual clustering [2] was used to extract recurring and hence important factors from the large gained data set of raw answers.

The objective of the survey was to determine the opinions and views regarding the perceived relevance of different factors for a successful completion of software projects. Hence, it contained questions about factors leading to or affecting project success. In this paper, we investigate the most important factors of project success from both points of view in order to compare them.

The survey was conducted anonymously. The aim was to receive better results in terms of more reliable answers, particularly with critical statements. A transparent answering might have led to biased answers. But due to an individual identifier, it was possible to provide both anonymity and the ability to analyze the course of answers.

3.3   Ethics Committee

The ethics committee at Leibniz Universität Hannover authorized the data collection. We informed the students about the further usage of the collected data. We anonymized all data records before collecting them. The data did not influence the success of the students passing the course.

3.4   Results

The following results focus on the most important requisites for software project success.

Both the developers and the customers state that the student projects are ordinary completed according to the customer requirements. Only one of the projects was not successful from the customer's perspective and 7.9% of the developers have not been fully satisfied with the results. The information exchange between developers and customers was considered as good (80.6% developers, 91.7% customers).

More than half of the developers (52.3%) stated that the fulfillment of previously agreed requirements (in this case in a requirements specification) is sufficient for a successful project completion. Other students stated that the following aspects are more important: customer satisfaction (20.4%), flexibility and motivation of the developers (17.2%) as well as teamwork (5.4%) and usability of the software (3.2%).

40% of the customers did not consider the fulfillment of requirements as the most important and sufficient aspect. For these customers, it was more important that the developers accept change requests and react on those. Some customers clarified that a product which simply fulfills the requirements is not valuable if the customer's views and ideas changed during the process but have not been included.

Table 1. Most important aspects for project success from the customers' point of view.

Aspect	Mentioned by
1. Communication	5 out of 7
2. Time management	5 out of 7
3. Preparation for customer meetings	3 out of 7
4. Programming skills of developers	3 out of 7
5. Suitable prioritization of requirements	3 out of 7

The participants were also asked to state the most important factors for project success according to their perception. The five factors that are perceived to be most important for both customers and developers are shown in Tables 1 and 2. It should be highlighted that from the developers' point of view the four

Table 2. Most important aspects for project success from the developers' point of view.

Aspect	Mentioned by
1. Team-internal communication and collaboration	50 out of 94
2. Distribution of tasks in the team	26 out of 94
3. Motivation and mood	22 out of 94
4. Expertise	18 out of 94
5. Communication and collaboration with the customer	18 out of 94

most important aspects were team-internal ones. Unlike from the view of the customers, where the most frequent aspect besides time management (71%) was the communication between customers and developers (71%). In contrast, the latter was only the fifth most important aspect of the developers with 19.15% valuing the communication with the customer as important for project success. But nonetheless, both the developers and the customers revealed communication as the factor perceived to be most important for project success. They only consider different kinds of communication: the team-internal information exchange and the information exchange between the team and the customer.

3.5 Study Limitations and Threats to Validity

Due to the limitations of our academical environment with respect to the real world, there are some aspects which may threaten the validity of our results. In accordance with the classifications of threats to validity by Wohlin et al. [13], we consider *construct, internal, conclusion* and *external validity*.

Construct validity. The results of this contribution are based on a wider survey. Although we do not expect any reciprocal effects with the other questions and items, we are not able to eliminate this problem. Nonetheless, the questions are formulated in a very general manner and arranged in groups to reduce this threat.

Internal validity. Any results and newly obtained knowledge are based on the opinions of the interviewed persons. Hence, the results are subjective and make no claim for completeness.

Conclusion validity. Using a survey as empirical strategy leads to the problem of limited possibilities for the validation of the survey results. For instance, it is not possible to verify the honesty in an answer. Our students had neither advantages nor disadvantages by participating in the study. The students were free to deny the participation in our study without any consequences. But nonetheless, there may be incorrectly given answers due to mistaken issues or items which can lead to wrong results.

External validity. Due to the student subjects, we do not have a representative sample of developers. But we have a set of subjects representing potential newcomers in industry. Furthermore, we only considered student software projects with comparable project scopes. Hence, we are not able to generalize our results for projects in real world environment. Real-world customers and experienced developers may answer our questions differently.

4   Interpretation

Our study with 97 students, i.e. developers, and eight customers supported our impressions of differences in the idea of which aspects are important for project success from both points of view.

From the customers' point of view, a continuous exchange of information between the customer and the team during the project is the most important aspect to guarantee project success. This includes a close cooperation with a regular exchange about the current development state. Therefore, according to the customers' point of view, it is essential that the developers are flexible and yield a high amount of motivation, which also means to develop own ideas and suggestions. Software should not only be developed for the customer but rather together with the customer. Mostly at the start of software projects, the majority of all involved parties is not completely sure about aspects like structure, look, and behavior of the final product. Hence, it is important to take customer wishes and altered requirements into account, especially outside the predefined specification. The customers clarified that software cannot be used when the implemented requirements do not fit the customer expectations, which may have changed during the project process.

According to our results, more than half of the student developers and the customers think that fulfilling the requirements specification suffices for project success. The others state that it helps to satisfy the customer, but it is not a sufficient criterion. Only a few interviewed customers stated that a successful project can be defined by only having a high degree of fulfilled pre-agreed requirements. In fact, an inflexible focus of the developers on unique discussed requirements counteracts a successful project closure and may be harmful to the success of the project in general. The students attach a greater importance to the requirements specification than the customers. From the developers' point of view, the specification contains all customer requirements. They consider the specification rather as a document of unlimited validity than as a document in time. For the developers, it is much easier to fulfill the written requirements than to react on more or less spontaneous change requests like in agile software development.

Our examination of factors with a large perceived relevance for project success revealed a wide difference between the customers' and rather inexperienced developers' point of view. On first sight, communication is the most important factor from both points of view. But on the second sight, there are differences in the meaning of "communication". For the customers, information exchange between customer and team is the most important aspect. But for the team, the team-internal communication exchange is most important.

This gap can complicate the collaboration between team and customer – in particular for inexperienced development teams mostly consisting of newcomers who are not aware of the problem. Not knowing about the other side may lead to misunderstandings and misinterpretation which in turn lead to dissatisfaction on both sides. The customer has to know about the relevance of team-internal issues. Otherwise, he might be dissatisfied with the collaboration. And the team needs to know about the relevance of a continuous information exchange between the team and the customer.

Summarizing, we can answer our research question as follows:

Research Answer:

- *For the customers, communication, time management, the preparation of customer meetings, programming skills and a suitable prioritization for requirements are the five most important factors. For developers, team-internal communication and collaboration, the distribution of tasks, motivation, mood, expertise and communication and collaboration with the customer are the five most important factors.*
- *For both, communication is very important for project success – but different kinds of communication. For the customers, communicating with the team is the most important factor for project success. But for the team, it is the team-internal communication which is most important.*
- *Fulfilling the requirements specification is less important for the customers than implementing changed or new requirements. For the developers, fulfilling the previously agreed requirements is very important and may be considered as a mandatory criterion.*

4.1 Implications for Education

Our study revealed different views on aspects like communication or the requirements specification from the customers and the rather inexperienced student developers. This is a difficulty, the university teaching should deal with.

In particular, the value of the requirements specification should be transported to the students in order to avoid the students strictly following the specification without reacting on the customer's change requests. This big issue should be faced in academical lectures. Students and newcomers need to be aware of the importance of also fulfilling change requests which are not covered by the specification in order to satisfy the customer.

Within the context of the student software projects, developers perceived major changes in the requirements along the project process as disruptive – what led to complications. Otherwise, this freedom in terms of describing wishes and requirements was very appreciated by the customers. It is recommended to find a good balance to which extent additional requirements are compatible. Nonetheless, the students need to know that they have to fulfill change requests if desired by the customer – independently from the effort needed to implement them.

According to our experience, a weekly meeting with the customer in student software projects is a good approach to ensure an adequate exchange of information. In addition, it increases the students' awareness of the importance of change requests and their relevance for a successful project closure.

4.2   Implications for Industry

Irrespective of whether academical lectures deal with the aforementioned problems, the responsible persons in industry should also be aware of them in order to facilitate a newcomer's start in real software projects and to avoid difficulties.

To increase the awareness of the importance of customer collaboration, a newcomer may be integrated into the whole exchange with the customer. It is important that the newcomer does not only know about the in-house development process but also to look at the process beyond their own noses. Getting to know the extent of customer involvement also increases the newcomer's respect of the customer. A wrong assessment of change requests can endanger the project.

Polanyi [9] classifies knowledge as tacit, i.e. implicit, and explicit. According to the definition, most people are not able to verbalize their tacit knowledge. But most of a person's knowledge is tacit. It cannot be directly transported to other persons because it is hardly or even impossibly tangible. Observing people can help to gain parts of the tacit knowledge. Hence, working with experienced persons is very important and helpful for newcomers. It helps to gain (tacit) knowledge about the "right" amount of interaction with the customer, the team work and the importance of aspects during the whole process. It is highly recommended to enable team members to learn from the experiences from other team members. Therefore, having teams with mixed experiences and knowledge is better than having a team only consisting of newcomers.

5   Conclusion

There are mainly two involved parties in small software projects: the development team and the customer: the team having the ability to influence project success, and the customer deciding in the end whether he is satisfied with the remaining product or not.

In a study with 97 student developers and eight customers, we examined the factors which are perceived to be most important for project success from their points of view. Our results show that there are differences in the prioritization of these aspects.

For both the teams and the customers, communication is very important for project success. But the term "communication" has different meanings. For the customer, a regular information exchange with the team is mandatory and the most important factor for project success. But for the developers, factors such as team-internal communication and collaboration as well as the distribution of tasks in the team are most important to enable project success. The collaboration and communication with the customer are less important.

While the requirements specification is only a document in time and has not unlimited validity from the customers' point of view, the students state that fulfilling the requirements in the specification ensures project success.

These differences in the prioritization can complicate the collaboration between both parties due to a missing mutual understanding. Increasing the awareness on both sides, in particular for newcomers, is very important. A mutual understanding of the term "communication" from both sides can facilitate collaboration and smooth the way to a successful project execution.

Acknowledgment. This work was funded by the German Research Foundation (DFG) under grant number *263807701* (Project TeamFLOW, 2015–2017).

References

1. Agarwal, N., Rathod, U.: Defining "Success" for software projects: an exploratory revelation. Int. J. Proj. Manag. **24**(4), 358–370 (2006)
2. Forza, C.: Survey research in operations management: a process-based perspective. Int. J. Oper. Prod. Manag. **22**(2), 152–194 (2002)
3. Hoda, R., Noble, J., Marshall, S.: The impact of inadequate customer collaboration on self-organizing agile teams. Inf. Softw. Technol. **53**(5), 521–534 (2011)
4. Hofmann, H.F., Lehner, F.: Requirements engineering as a success factor in software projects. IEEE Softw. **18**(4), 58 (2001)
5. Karras, O., Klünder, J., Schneider, K.: Indicating potential risks for project success based on requirements fulfillment - analyzing requirements compliance in student software projects. In: Gesellschaft fr Informatik, Fachgruppentreffen Requirements Engineering, Stuttgart (2016)
6. Keil, M., Carmel, E.: Customer-developer links in software development. Commun. ACM **38**(5), 33–44 (1995)
7. Klünder, J., Unger-Windeler, C., Kortum, F., Schneider, K.: Team meetings and their relevance for the software development process over time. In: Proceedings of 43th Euromicro Conference on Software Engineering and Advanced Applications (SEAA) (2017)
8. Philippo, E.J., Heijstek, W., Kruiswijk, B., Chaudron, M.R.V., Berry, D.M.: Requirement ambiguity not as important as expected—results of an empirical evaluation. In: Doerr, J., Opdahl, A.L. (eds.) REFSQ 2013. LNCS, vol. 7830, pp. 65–79. Springer, Heidelberg (2013). doi:10.1007/978-3-642-37422-7_5
9. Polanyi, M.: The Tacit Dimension. University of Chicago Press, Chicago (2009)
10. Savolainen, P., Ahonen, J.J., Richardson, I.: Software development project success and failure from the supplier's perspective: a systematic literature review. Int. J. Proj. Manag. **30**(4), 458–469 (2012)
11. Surian, D., Tian, Y., Lo, D., Cheng, H., Lim, E.P.: Predicting project outcome leveraging socio-technical network patterns. In: Proceedings of the 17th European Conference on Software Maintenance and Reengineering (CSMR). pp. 47–56. IEEE (2013)
12. Verner, J., Cox, K., Bleistein, S., Cerpa, N.: Requirements engineering and software project success: an industrial survey In Australia and the US. Australas. J. Inf. Syst. **13**(1), 225–238 (2005)
13. Wohlin, C., Runeson, P., Höst, M., Ohlsson, M.C., Regnell, B., Wesslén, A.: Experimentation in Software Engineering. Springer, Heidelberg (2012). doi:10.1007/978-3-642-29044-2

Workshop: QuASD 2017

1st QuASD Workshop: Managing Quality in Agile and Rapid Software Development Processes

Claudia Ayala[1] , Silverio Martínez-Fernández[2(✉)] ,
and Pilar Rodríguez[3]

[1] GESSI Group, Universitat Politècnica de Catalunya (UPC) - BarcelonaTech,
Barcelona, Spain
cayala@essi.upc.edu
[2] Fraunhofer Institute for Experimental Software Engineering (IESE),
Kaiserslautern, Germany
Silverio.Martinez@iese.fraunhofer.de
[3] M3S Group, University of Oulu, Oulu, Finland
pilar.rodriguez@oulu.fi

Abstract. Optimal management of software quality calls for appropriate integration of quality management activities into the whole software (engineering) life-cycle. However, despite the competitive advantage of ensuring and maintaining high quality levels, software development methodologies still offer little support for the integration and management of quality. This is especially true for, and essential in, agile software development processes and the recent trends towards rapid and continuous software development. The premise is that faster and more frequent release cycles should not compromise quality. This workshop aims to exchange challenges, experiences, and solutions among researchers and practitioners to bring agile and rapid software processes a step further towards seamless integration of quality management activities into their practices.

Keywords: Quality · Agile software development · Rapid and continuous software development

1 Introduction

Welcome to the First International Workshop on Managing Quality in Agile and Rapid Software Development Processes (QuASD).

The QuASD workshop aims at investigating the current challenges that companies using agile software development and rapid release cycles face when integrating quality management activities into their practices. The objective of the workshop is to exchange experiences and solutions to bring agile and rapid software development processes a step further towards seamless integration of quality management activities into their practices. To strengthen this objective, QuASD 2017 has been held in the context of one of the top-recognized software development and process improvement

C. Ayala, S. Martínez-Fernández and P. Rodríguez—**Program Committee Chairs.**

© Springer International Publishing AG 2017
M. Felderer et al. (Eds.): PROFES 2017, LNCS 10611, pp. 511–514, 2017.
https://doi.org/10.1007/978-3-319-69926-4_40

conferences: the International Conference on Product-Focused Software Process Improvement (PROFES 2017) on November 29, 2017, in Innsbruck, Austria.

2 Keynote: Agile and Rapid Software Development at Nokia Base Station R&D

The keynote focuses on the changes and adaptations of agile software development processes to deal with quality requirements at Nokia. Nokia is a global leader in technologies that connect people and things. It combines global leadership in mobile and fixed network infrastructure with software, services, and advanced technologies to transform how smart devices and sensors tap the power of connectivity. With state-of-the-art software, hardware, and services for any type of network, Nokia is uniquely positioned to help communication service providers, governments, and large enterprises deliver on the promise of 5G, the Cloud, and the Internet of Things.

In this context, Merja Jokiniva (5G R&D Release Manager) shares her experience on leading content and schedule planning as well as progress follow-up of Base Station SW deliveries.

Merja Jokiniva has worked almost 20 years at Nokia Base Station R&D in various roles in Finland and in the USA. Her most recent role is 5G R&D Release Manager where she started at the end of 2016. As R&D Release Manager she leads content and schedule planning as well as progress follow up of Base Station SW deliveries. Before the current role, she worked seven years as a line manager of 4G R&D Program Management team and as a 4G R&D Release Manager. Earlier she has worked in Program, Product and Quality Management. Before joining Nokia, she worked for the University of Oulu several years. There her last tasks were in area of program management by teaching the graduate students and by consulting local companies in program management practices.

3 Accepted Papers

We received a total of eleven contributions in different categories (technical papers, experience reports, emergent research, vision papers, and practitioner messages). These contributions were peer reviewed by three members of the Program Committee, composed of prominent researchers from the community and practitioners. After a tough revision process, eight high-quality works addressing issues on quality in agile software development from different perspectives were accepted. The effort and dedication of the Program Committee and the additional reviewers who collaborated in the revision process were outstanding and deserve recognition (see Sect. 4).

The accepted papers composing the QuASD workshop program are:

- **3 technical papers** (12 pages long) describing beyond-state-of-the-art methods, tools, or techniques in support of the management of quality in agile and rapid software development and continuous software development contexts:
  - Marcus Ciolkowski, Liliana Guzmán, Adam Trendowicz and Felix Salfner: *"Lessons Learned from a research project on the strategical planning of Technical Debt"*.

- Michael Mohan and Des Greer: "*MultiRefactor: Automated Refactoring To Improve Software Quality*".
- Mohammad Abdur Razzak, Sarah Beecham, John Noll and Ita Richardson: "*Transition from Plan Driven to SAFe: Periodic Team Self-Assessment*".
- **4 emergent research papers** (8 pages long) describing research endeavors that have just started. These works present preliminary findings without full-fledged validation:
  - Woubshet Behutiye, Pertti Karhapää, Dolors Costal, Markku Oivo and Xavier Franch: "*Non-functional Requirements Documentation in Agile Software Development: Challenges and Solution Proposal*".
  - Frank Elberzhager, Konstantin Holl, Britta Karn and Thomas Immich: "*Rapid Lean UX Development through User Feedback Revelation*".
  - Lidia Lopez Cuesta, Woubshet Behutiye, Pertti Karhapää, Jolita Ralyté, Xavier Franch and Markku Oivo: "*Agile Quality Requirements Management Best Practices Portfolio: A Situational Method Engineering Approach*".
  - Sven Theobald and Philipp Diebold: "*Beneficial and Harmful Agile Practices for Product Quality*".
- **1 practitioner message** (4 pages long) that reports on the practitioners' perspective of managing quality in agile and rapid software development:
  - Michael Klaes and Frank Elberzhager: "*Managing Development Using Active Data Collection*".

4 Program Committee

The program committee was composed of prominent researchers from several universities and the industrial sector.

Sanja Aaramaa	Nokia, Finland
Jan Bosch	Chalmers University of Technology, Sweden
Javier Criado	University of Almeria, Spain
Xavier Franch	Technical University of Catalunya, Spain
Matthias Galster	University of Canterbury, New Zealand
Juan Garbajosa	Technical University of Madrid, Spain
Lidia López	Technical University of Catalunya, Spain
Michael Mlynarski	QualityMinds GmbH, Germany
Elisa Nakagawa	University of Sao Paulo, Brazil
Anh Nguyen Duc	Norwegian University of Science and Technology, Norway
Markku Oivo	University of Oulu, Finland
Marc Oriol Hilari	Technical University of Catalunya, Spain
Paulo Sérgio Santos	Federal University of Rio de Janeiro, Brazil
Dan Tofan	UberResearch (Digital Science), Romania
Guilherme Travassos	Federal University sof Rio de Janeiro, Brazil
Anna Maria Vollmer	Fraunhofer IESE, Germany
Agustin Yague	Technical University of Madrid, Spain

5 Activities

The workshop has been structured to promote discussions and interchange of ideas among participants from both industry and academia sectors.

The keynote will open the workshop activities and is expected to shake the audience. It will be followed by presentations of the accepted papers in various sessions. In the last session, we will organize an open brainstorming space through a wall of ideas, where the participants will post their key messages on particular topics, followed by a plenary discussion on the hottest emerging topics.

All these activities are aimed to:

- Scope the current state of quality management in agile and rapid software development in both research and practice.
- Compile success and failure experiences.
- Produce a research agenda.
- Establish a community to foster long-term collaboration on this emerging topic.

We hope that the workshop participants will enjoy the topics presented here and perhaps find the inspiration to push the field a step further, or open the door for new collaborations.

Finally, we would like to acknowledge all the people who have enabled the organization of QuASD 2017: the authors, who submitted their papers; the Program Committee members, who made possible the conference program; Nokia for being willing to give the keynote and share their experiences on managing quality and quality requirements in the context of agile and rapid software development; and the organizing committee members, who handled all the complexity of arranging an event such as PROFES 2017 and the associated workshops.

Non-functional Requirements Documentation in Agile Software Development: Challenges and Solution Proposal

Woubshet Behutiye[1]([✉]) [iD], Pertti Karhapää[1] [iD], Dolors Costal[2] [iD], Markku Oivo[1] [iD], and Xavier Franch[2] [iD]

[1] University of Oulu, Pentti Kaiteran Katu 1, 90014 Oulu, Finland
{woubshet.behutiye,Pertti.karhapaa,markku.oivo}@oulu.fi
[2] Universitat Politècnica de Catalunya, Campus Nord, Jordi Girona, 1-3, 08034 Barcelona, Spain
{dolors,franch}@essi.upc.edu

Abstract. Non-functional requirements (NFRs) are determinant for the success of software projects. However, they are characterized as hard to define, and in agile software development (ASD), are often given less priority and usually not documented. In this paper, we present the findings of the documentation practices and challenges of NFRs in companies utilizing ASD and propose guidelines for enhancing NFRs documentation in ASD. We interviewed practitioners from four companies and identified that epics, features, user stories, acceptance criteria, Definition of Done (DoD), product and sprint backlogs are used for documenting NFRs. Wikis, word documents, mockups and spreadsheets are also used for documenting NFRs. In smaller companies, NFRs are communicated through white board and flip chart discussions and developers' tacit knowledge is prioritized over documentation. However, loss of traceability of NFRs, the difficulty in comprehending NFRs by new developers joining the team and limitations of documentation practices for NFRs are challenges in ASD. In this regard, we propose guidelines for documenting NFRs in ASD. The proposed guidelines consider the diversity of the NFRs to document and suggest different representation artefacts depending on the NFRs scope and level of detail. The representation artefacts suggested are among those currently used in ASD in order not to introduce new specific ones that might hamper actual adoption by practitioners.

Keywords: Non-functional requirements · Quality requirements · NFR · Agile software development · Non-functional requirements documentation

1 Introduction

Non-functional requirements (NFRs) also referred to as quality requirements [21], represent software requirements that describe how software should perform [5]. These, for instance include software requirements about performance, usability, maintainability, reliability, and security. NFRs are characterized as vague and hard to define [17] and quite often result in being under/un-specified and undocumented. In particular, this is reflected in agile software development (ASD) where working software is prioritized over comprehensive documentation [2].

© Springer International Publishing AG 2017
M. Felderer et al. (Eds.): PROFES 2017, LNCS 10611, pp. 515–522, 2017.
https://doi.org/10.1007/978-3-319-69926-4_41

ASD's focus on "individuals and interaction over processes and tools" encourages minimal documentation [2]. ASD relies on tacit knowledge of the team and leans towards reducing the focus on requirements specification and documentation. Additionally, ASD is characterized with short iterations and it focuses on the quick delivery of working software. In such cases, developers face time pressure, mainly focus on delivery of functionalities and often do not give consideration to NFRs [6]. However, in such scenarios, neglecting NFRs may result in documentation debt with further consequences of increase in maintenance cost and effort [16].

NFRs play important role in the success of software systems [5, 9]. In ASD, existing requirements engineering practices fail short regarding the documentation of NFRs. For instance, user stories of ASD have limitations in specifying and documenting NFRs [15]. When NFRs are not documented, traceability becomes difficult, the likelihood of forgetting NFRs increases and consequences such as weak user acceptance may also result [7].

The findings from the scientific literature acknowledge the significance of handling NFRs in ASD [3, 8, 15]. The challenges of NFRs documentation in ASD, the limitations of ASD for handling NFRs, solution proposals for handling NFRs in ASD and the need for further investigation of the topic are reported frequently.

In this paper, we present the challenges of NFRs documentation in ASD and NFRs documentation practices identified from scientific literature and an ongoing empirical study in the Q-Rapids project[1] [10], about managing NFRs in ASD. We also present guidelines for addressing challenges of NFRs documentation in ASD.

The rest of the paper is structured as follows. Section 2 describes the related work on challenges of documentation of NFRs and current ASD practices for documenting NFRs. Section 3 presents analysis of NFRs documentation practices and challenges identified from the ongoing empirical study about management of NFRs in ASD. Section 4 presents guidelines proposal for addressing documentation of NFRs in ASD. Finally, Sect. 5 presents the conclusion.

2   Related Work

2.1   Non-functional Requirements Documentation Challenges and Practices in Agile Software Development

Research in the documentation and optimal integration of NFRs in ASD has paramount importance considering the vague nature of NFRs [17] and limitations in documentation practices of ASD [15]. Consequently there have been many studies investigating the topic area [8, 14, 15, 20]. In what follows, we present some challenges of NFRs management and current practices for documenting NFRs in ASD.

ASD puts less emphasis on the documentation of NFRs. Instead, its reliance on the continuous interaction with customers is thought to minimize the need for specifying NFRs [20]. In ASD, NFRs are ill defined and rarely documented, and there are no formal acceptance tests for NFRs. As a result, problems arise at later stages of development [14].

---

[1] http://q-rapids.eu/.

The negligence of NFRs appears to be a major concern of many agile projects and is reported frequently [4, 14, 17]. For instance, Cao and Ramesh [4] identified the neglect of NFRs and minimal documentation as major challenges of agile requirements engineering in an empirical investigation of 16 software development organizations. According to their findings, NFRs are given less priority in the early stage of ASD as customers instead prioritize core functionality. Consequently, minimal documentation and negligence of NFRs in ASD result in challenges of scalability of the software, and introduce difficulty for new members joining the development team.

Failure to consider NFRs in the early stages of software development may result in poor quality software, increased maintenance costs and time [5]. Indeed, when NFRs are omitted in the early stages of development, they result in major issues at later stages. ASD methods face challenges in addressing specific NFRs such as security [1]. For instance, Scrum's lack of consideration for integrating security (NFRs) in the development process opens vulnerability to the software [1]. Absence of documentation for security, limited amount of time for testing security in sprints, and difficulty for integrating security related activities are major security issues in Scrum.

ASD mainly utilizes index cards, paper prototypes and storyboards to document features and requirements [14]. Practices such as user stories are used for documenting high level requirements [4]. However, they have limitations for specifying and documenting NFRs [11, 12, 15]. Martakis et al. [15], found that agile developers face challenges while using user stories for documenting NFRs such as security and internationalization.

Consequently, there have been proposals for integrating, planning and managing NFRs in ASD (e.g. AFFINE framework, NORMAP, NORPLAN, security backlog for Scrum etc.) [3, 8, 15]. Lightweight practices and systematic solutions that integrate NFRs in ASD without compromising quality of software and agility of the development process are of high importance.

3   Non-functional Requirements Documentation Practices and Challenges in ASD Projects

We conducted case studies following [19], in four case companies that are part of the Q-Rapids project, in order to synthesize knowledge regarding management of NFRs in ASD. We collected data through semi-structured interviews and applied qualitative analysis on the transcriptions of the interviews. The four case companies providing the use cases (UCs) for the project are of varying size and domain. The first company has over 900 employees while the second has over 600 employees. The third is large scale global company with over 100,000 employees while the fourth has less than 100 employees. We conducted 12 interviews, with roles that include product owners, project managers, developers and quality assurance engineers, DevOps Specialist, and Scrum masters.

Agile practices and iterative development are applied in all the UCs, of which three are close to Scrum. In UC1, the company follows in-house tailored agile and iterative development. However, they do not have any fixed sprint cycles. In comparison, the development applied in UC2 and UC4 is the closest to Scrum with daily sprints and weekly, or biweekly sprints. In UC3, which is the large-scale company, Scrum, or variations of it, is applied in some of the development teams at lower levels of the organization. In UC3, a team can apply any development model they see fit. Continuous integration is applied in all the UCs.

The interview findings reveal that the companies employ varying practices for documenting both functional requirements (FRs) and NFRs. UC1 prefers to focus effort on development and documents requirements in detail only when implementing features that the developers are unfamiliar with. NFRs are communicated through whiteboards during meetings. On the other hand, UC2 and UC3 document both FRs and NFRs. Partly this is enforced through standards that the companies must comply with. In UC2 requirements are documented in epics, features, and user stories, and NFRs are also in the acceptance criteria and Definition of Done (DoD). Additionally, word documents, PowerPoints and wikis are used for documentation during the development. Along the process, the documentation in the wikis becomes more of a technical description of the software and the connection to the original high level requirements is lost. The interviewees suggested including more design documentation in the user stories to preserve this link. Using Word and PowerPoint for documentation is perceived challenging, as these documents become easily detached from the actual software. This is due to the fact that it is easy to forget updating a certain document with every change to the code.

In the case of UC3, which is a large and distributed organization, documentation is important as there are teams in different locations that may be working on the same feature. There is complex backlog structure and all the requirements are also documented in features that are broken down into sub features and further into tasks that can be coded. Additionally, NFRs are documented in DoD and acceptance criteria. At the lower task level, however, there are no NFRs in the backlog as such, but the tasks need to meet the DoD including quality criteria. In UC3, documentation of NFRs is identified as problematic. Our interviewees find the requirements management tool under use and complexity of backlogs difficult and stated that they are not able to identify dependent NFRs. Additionally, internally inherited NFRs such as operability are rarely documented and prioritized. UC4 documents all the requirements (FRs and NFRs) in the epics and user stories. DoD and acceptance criteria (at user story, task and ticket levels) are used for documenting NFRs. Additionally, excel spread sheets, mock-ups, product backlogs and sprint backlogs are used for documenting NFRs.

In summary, we observe that three of the UCs follow up procedures for documenting NFRs in ASD. The UCs followed a formal approach to specify and document NFRs. However, in one UC, NFRs were not documented and were rather communicated in face-to-face meetings facilitated by whiteboards and flip charts. In such cases, companies relied on the tacit knowledge of the developers. These developers discuss NFRs in meetings (e.g. daily stand-ups, sprint planning meetings) and avoid detailed documentations. Table 1 summarizes NFRs documentation practices and challenges identified from the UCs.

Our findings reveal that companies may face challenges when they fail to document NFRs properly. For instance, in UC1 when relying on tacit knowledge of developers', the traceability of NFRs becomes difficult in later stages of development. The interviewees pointed out that this introduces challenge to new developers joining the team

Table 1. Summary of NFRs documentation practices and challenges in ASD UC companies

Use case	NFRs documentation practice	NFRs documentation challenge
UC1	NFRs are not formally documented, however communicated through white board and when necessary documented in word documents	NFRs not documented properly and resulted in the lack of traceability of NFRs, difficulty for new developers joining team
UC2	NFRs documented in epics, features, and user stories, acceptance criteria and DoDs, wiki pages, word docs with FRS	Lower-level details are lost in documentation, word and power point documents disconnected from actual software
UC3	NFRs documented in features, acceptance criteria and DoDs in complex backlogs	Complexity of backlogs makes it hard to identify dependent NFRs, internally generated NFRs are not documented
UC4	NFRs documented in epics, user stories, in DoD and acceptance criteria (at user story, task and ticket levels), in product and sprint backlogs. Mockups, wireframes, word, spreadsheet are also used for documenting NFRs while Whiteboards and flip charts facilitate communication of NFRs.	Not reported by interviewees

as they will have limited visibility of the NFRs. Scientific literature depicts similar findings [11]. On the other hand, difficulty in identifying interdependent NFRs in complex backlogs is another challenge identified in UC3.

The significance of NFRs for the success of software projects and specific challenge of ASD in documenting NFRs that is also reflected in the UCs, prompt us to propose lightweight and systematic guidelines for documenting NFRs in ASD.

4   Guidelines Proposal for Documenting NFRs in ASD

In order to cope with the diversity of approaches to represent requirements in agile methods, we take the following assumptions that do not compromise the general applicability of our approach: (1) FRs are specified using both epics and user stories, (2) user stories may include one or more acceptance criteria and (3) user stories will be derived from epics and this link will be recorded.

The system NFRs to document may be quite diverse. Remarkably the scope of NFRs may vary significantly. A NFR may refer to quality properties of the entire system to be developed but it also may define quality properties for a particular service, function or system component [18]. We distinguish three different types of scope for NFRs: system-wide for those that apply to the entire system, group-wide for those that apply to a set of user stories (or a group of functionalities) and local for those that apply to a single user story (or functionality). Additionally, the level of detail in which a NFR is specified may vary. Accordingly, we distinguish among generic NFRs, i.e., specified at a high level of abstraction (near to the notion of goal) [13], and detailed NFRs, i.e., specified as a concrete feature or tied to a concrete solution. Quite often, a generic NFR may be specified in an earlier development stage and, later on, it may be refined into a set of detailed NFRs that operationalize it (e.g. the generic NFR "The system must be usable" may be refined into "The system must allow reaching any functionality in no more than 3 clicks" among other detailed NFRs). All combinations of scope and detail are possible when specifying a NFR. For instance, "The critical functions of the system must take less than 0.25 s, 90% of the times" is group-wide and detailed while "The functionality for checking the account balance must have a good response time" is local and generic.

The variability of NFRs both in scope and detail suggests that there is not a single representation artefact that is adequate to cope with all of them. Therefore, a proposal for documenting NFRs in ASD should provide different artefacts for representing them and a set of guidelines to select the most adequate representation depending on the features of each specific requirement. In our opinion, the artefacts should preferably be those currently used in ASD in order not to introduce new specific artefacts that might damage the agility of the process and hamper actual adoption by practitioners. Therefore, our guidelines proposal, summarized in Table 2, consists of using either acceptance criteria, user stories or epics to represent NFRs.

Table 2. Guidelines for documenting NFRs according to their scope and detail

Scope	Detail	Representation artefact	Observation
Local	Generic	User story (NFR user story)	With a link to the functional user story to which it applies
	Detailed	Acceptance criteria	Appearing in the functional user story to which it applies
Group wide	Generic	Epic	The description of the epic must clarify to which group of functionalities it applies (e.g. "critical functions of the system")
	Detailed	(1) User story or	(1) The description of the user story must clarify to which group of functionalities it applies or include links to the user stories it applies
		(2) Acceptance criteria	(2) Appearing in the functional user stories to which it applies
System wide	Generic	Epic	The description of the epic must clarify it is system-wide (e.g. by referring to "the system")
	Detailed	User story	The description of the epic must clarify to which group of functionalities it applies (e.g. "critical functions of the system")

In the following, we describe the rationale used in our proposal (see Table 2) to select the adequate representation artefact for a NFR based on the scope and detail of the NFR.

The simplest case is that of local and detailed NFRs. They can be locally represented, in the affected user story, as acceptance criteria, because these NFRs neither affect the other user stories nor need further refinements. Conversely, local and generic NFRs cannot be documented as acceptance criteria because they are not concrete enough. Therefore we propose to document them as user stories that should be linked to the functional user story to which they apply. Then, the acceptance criteria of this latter user story may refine the generic NFR.

For system-wide NFRs, we propose to use epics if they are generic and user stories if they are detailed. System-wide and generic NFRs are documented by epics because they are high level qualities of the whole system and thus they are relevant requirements that will probably need to be further detailed by means of user stories (derived from that epic). These latter user stories will then be representing system-wide and detailed NFRs.

For group-wide NFRs, our proposal is similar to that of system-wide NFRs. However, if they are detailed and the group of functionalities affected by the NFRs is small, we propose, as an additional option to document them as acceptance criteria of the user stories to which they apply (like local and detailed NFRs).

5   Conclusion

In this paper, we presented the findings of NFRs documentation practices in ASD projects. We identified that NFRs are documented together with FRs. The UCs applied epics, features, user stories, acceptance criteria and DoD of user stories, and backlogs to document NFRs. Whiteboard and flip charts are used to facilitate the communication of NFRs in cases where they are not documented. The difficulty in the traceability of NFRs, problems in identifying interdependent NFRs and detached documentation from actual software, were among the challenges of NFRs identified in the UCs. Moreover, we propose guidelines for documenting NFRs in ASD. The proposed guidelines acknowledge diversity of NFRs and utilize existing ASD artefacts such as epics, user stories and acceptance criteria for documenting NFRs. In addition, the guidelines consider different levels for the scope and details of abstraction of NFRs.

Acknowledgments.   This work is a result of the Q-Rapids project, which has received funding from the European Union's Horizon 2020 research and innovation program under grant agreement N° 732253.

References

1. Azham, Z. et al.: Security backlog in scrum security practices. In: 2011 5th Malaysian Conference in Software Engineering, MySEC 2011, pp. 414–417 (2011)
2. Beck, K. et al.: Agile Manifesto. http://agilemanifesto.org/
3. Bourimi, M., et al.: AFFINE for enforcing earlier consideration of NFRs and human factors when building socio-technical systems following agile methodologies. In: Bernhaupt, R., Forbrig, P., Gulliksen, J., Lárusdóttir, M. (eds.) HCSE 2010. LNCS, vol. 6409. Springer, Heidelberg (2010). doi:10.1007/978-3-642-16488-0_15
4. Cao, L., Ramesh, B.: Agile requirements engineering practices: an empirical study. Softw. IEEE **25**(1), 60–67 (2008)
5. Chung, L., et al.: Non-Functional Requirements in Software Engineering. Springer, New York (2000). doi:10.1007/978-1-4615-5269-7

6. Cysneiros, L.M., Yu, E.: Non-functional requirements elicitation. In: do Prado Leite, J.Ć.S., Doorn, J.H. (eds.) Perspectives on Software Requirements, pp. 115–138. Springer, Boston (2004)

7. Eckhardt, J., Vogelsang, A., Méndez Fernández, D.: On the distinction of functional and quality requirements in practice. In: Abrahamsson, P., Jedlitschka, A., Nguyen Duc, A., Felderer, M., Amasaki, S., Mikkonen, T. (eds.) PROFES 2016. LNCS, vol. 10027, pp. 31–47. Springer, Cham (2016). doi:10.1007/978-3-319-49094-6_3

8. Farid, W.M., Mitropoulos, F.J.: NORPLAN: non-functional requirements planning for agile processes. In: 2013 Proceedings of IEEE, Southeastcon, pp. 1–8 (2013)

9. Glinz, M.: On non-functional requirements. In: 15th IEEE International Requirements Engineering Conference, RE 2007, 21–26 (2007)

10. Guzmán, L., Oriol, M., Rodríguez, P., Franch, X., Jedlitschka, A., Oivo, M.: How can quality awareness support rapid software development? – A research preview. In: Grünbacher, P., Perini, A. (eds.) REFSQ 2017. LNCS, vol. 10153, pp. 167–173. Springer, Cham (2017). doi: 10.1007/978-3-319-54045-0_12

11. Heikkilä, V.T. et al.: A mapping study on requirements engineering in agile software development. In: 2015 41st Euromicro Conference on Software Engineering and Advanced Applications, pp. 199–207 (2015)

12. Inayat, I. et al.: A systematic literature review on agile requirements engineering practices and challenges. Comput. Hum. Behav. **51**, 915–929 (2015). doi:10.1016/j.chb.2014.10.046

13. Van Lamsweerde, A. et al.: Goal-oriented requirements engineering: a guided tour. In: Proceedings of Fifth IEEE International Symposium on Requirements Engineering, pp. 249–262 (2001)

14. De Lucia, A., Qusef, A.: Requirements engineering in agile software development. J. Emerg. Technol. Web Intell. **2**(3), 212–220 (2010)

15. Martakis, A., Daneva, M.: Handling requirements dependencies in agile projects: a focus group with agile software development practitioners. In: Proceedings - International Conference on Research Challenges in Information Science (2013)

16. Mendes, T.S., et al.: Impacts of agile requirements documentation debt on software projects. In: Proceedings of the 31st Annual ACM Symposium on Applied Computing - SAC 2016, pp. 1290–1295 (2016)

17. Paech, B., Kerlow, D.: non-functional requirements engineering - quality is essential. In: Proceedings of 10th Anniversary of International Workshop on Requirements Engineering, Foundational Software Quality, pp. 237–250 (2004)

18. Pohl, K.: Requirements Engineering: Fundamentals, Principles, and Techniques. Springer, Heidelberg (2010)

19. Runeson, P. et al.: Case Study Research in Software Engineering, Wiley (2012). doi: 10.1002/9781118181034

20. Sillitti, A., Succi, G.: Requirements engineering for agile methods. In: Engineering and Managing Software Requirements, pp. 309–326 (2005)

21. Wagner, S.: Software Product Quality Control. Springer, Heidelberg (2013). doi: 10.1007/978-3-642-38571-1

Lessons Learned from the ProDebt Research Project on Planning Technical Debt Strategically

Marcus Ciolkowski[1]([✉]), Liliana Guzmán[2], Adam Trendowicz[2], and Felix Salfner[3]

[1] QAware GmbH, Aschauer Str. 32, 81549 Munich, Germany
marcus.ciolkowski@qaware.de
[2] Fraunhofer IESE, Fraunhofer-Platz 1, 67663 Kaiserslautern, Germany
{liliana.guzman,adam.trendowicz}@iese.fraunhofer.de
[3] Seerene GmbH, August-Bebel-Str. 26-53, 14482 Potsdam, Germany
felix.salfner@seerene.com

Abstract. Due to cost and time constraints, software quality is often neglected in the evolution and adaptation of software. Thus, maintainability suffers, maintenance costs rise, and the development takes longer. These effects are referred to as "technical debt". The challenge for project managers is to find a balance when using the given budget and schedule, either by reducing technical debt or by adding technical features. This balance is needed to keep time to market for current product releases short and future maintenance costs at an acceptable level.

Method: The project ProDebt aimed at developing an innovative methodology and a software tool to support the strategic planning of technical debt in the context of agile software development. In this project, we created quality models and collected corresponding measurement data for two case studies in two different companies. Altogether, the two case studies contributed 5–6 years of data, from the end of 2011, resp. mid-2012, until today. Using measurement and effort data, we trained a machine-learning model to predict productivity based on measurement data—representing the technical debt of a file at a given point in time.

Result: We developed a prototype and a prediction model for forecasting potential savings based on proposed refactorings of key drivers of technical debt identified by the model. In this paper, we present the approach and the experiences made during model development.

Keywords: Technical debt · Agile software development · Quality management

1 Introduction

Agile software development (ASD) represents a complex decision-making situation, which is characterized by short development cycles and a focus on the delivery of customer-specific software features. Frequent changes of software artifacts (primarily source code) without corresponding quality assurance measures, however, quickly lead to a decrease in software quality, with a concurrent increase in the costs for further development and evolution due to the increase in technical debt (TD). As these features

© Springer International Publishing AG 2017
M. Felderer et al. (Eds.): PROFES 2017, LNCS 10611, pp. 523–534, 2017.
https://doi.org/10.1007/978-3-319-69926-4_42

are of major importance for the product's end user, however, sufficient quality assurance is often forgone. This gradually leads to a strong increase in the amount of TD.

Countermeasures are only taken if TD hinders the development of new features. In this reactive process, as much TD as possible is reduced with as little effort as possible—for example, through refactoring—so that enough budget (time) can be assigned to the development of new features. If, however, the quality assurance measures employed in the development iterations are too stringent, they require a substantial proportion of the available development budget. This leads to the situation that there is always less budget available for the actual development of new product features and that the market is not satisfied. Thus, good balancing between quality assurance measures and the evolution respectively development of new product features is necessary.

To achieve this, TD must be planned proactively and prospectively. That is, managers in ASD need tool-supported approaches for identifying TD, precisely estimating it, and assessing its impact on future development costs. However, current approaches focus only on the evaluation of the quality of a software product [4] by measuring violations of predefined quality requirements [3] on software artifacts. Thus, there is a lack of approaches for properly analyzing and managing TD.

In this paper, we contribute to a comprehensive analysis of TD. First, we will summarize the state of the art and practice regarding TD. Then we will describe our approach for analyzing TD, namely the ProDebt approach, and sketch its evaluation. The ProDebt approach was developed and evaluated in collaboration with three German companies. It includes a tailorable quality model, which allows differentiated estimation of the quality and prediction of TD, as well as a cockpit that visualizes both the quality model and the prediction of TD. The prediction model forecasts potential savings based on proposed refactoring of key TD drivers. Finally, we will summarize the lessons learned during the development of the ProDebt approach.

2   Related Work

In 1992, Ward Cunningham introduced the term 'technical debt' (TD) to signify immature or 'not really proper' software source code [1]. TD refers to both unintentional quality deficits of a software product and intentional quality compromises that are made; for example, to bring a product to market faster. In practice, TD as a result of conscious compromises is predominant [5]. The crucial question, particularly in ASD, is: *How much TD can I accept and which compromises should I make now so that I can get my software to the market on time and can still repay the associated TD in future releases?*

From the perspective of a software company, TD is unavoidable—yet the strategic planning of TD in software projects has not been addressed to date. In recent years, numerous approaches have been presented for determining the actual degree of immaturity of a software product, but not for the characterization of the resulting TD. Most approaches focus on the evaluation of the quality of a software product [4] by measuring violations of predefined internal and external quality requirements [3] on software artifacts such as architecture or code. These requirements are normally defined for static features of software artifacts such as complexity, coupling, code duplicates, or commenting. Although quality deficits are associated with incomplete work (either intentionally or unintentionally), current approaches rarely deal with this association when it comes to cost estimates for immature products.

Effective planning of TD requires a custom-tailored approach in which project data and human expertise from a given context are elicited and analyzed to identify TD, to understand its nature as well as the impact factors, and to predict its development over time. To reliably assess quality deficits, stakeholder-specific preferences regarding product quality must be considered; that is, all relevant quality aspects must be quantified, measured, and interpreted along a transparent quality model. The impact of context-specific cost drivers must also be taken into account for the estimation, respectively prediction, of the costs associated with TD (i.e., principal, interest). Moreover, a continuous chain of automated tools is needed for collecting relevant information, analyzing links between the uncompleted work and the resulting immature software products, and predicting the evolution of the associated debt over time.

3   The ProDebt Approach

3.1   The ProDebt Project

The ProDebt approach was developed as part of the ProDebt research project funded by the German Federal Ministry for Education and Research. The research project aims at developing a tool-supported methodology for assessing and proactively managing software quality and technical debt in the context of ASD.

Whereas the ProDebt approach for analyzing TD was developed by Fraunhofer IESE, the German company Seerene was responsible for implementing the ProDebt tool. Members from two German small and medium enterprises—QAware and Insiders Technologies—also took part in the ProDebt project. QAware develops information systems for customers in several application domains. Insiders Technologies develops and sells its own range of products, mainly document management solutions for the public, insurance, and commercial sectors.

3.2   Case Studies

We aimed at analyzing TD in one project of each case study partner, one of QAware and one of Insiders Technologies:

Case study A (QAware project): The project has been running since mid-2012 using a Scrum-like process. It focuses on the development of an enterprise search web application using Java, .Net, and Objective-C for the automotive and after-sales domains. The current development team includes 22 developers working in sprints that last between three and nine weeks. The software quality is managed using SonarQube. The project uses JIRA as a ticket system to manage user stories, and spreadsheets for recording effort. The current software release has approximately 160,000 lines of code without third-party libraries in 32 components.

Case Study B (Insiders Technologies project): The project has been running since 2000. It focuses on the development of a software for processing, extracting, and classifying information from any kind of business correspondence for the insurance domain using C++. The releases have been developed using Scrum since 2009. The current Scrum team includes nine developers working in sprints of two weeks. Software quality is managed ad-hoc without any specific tool support. Effort and user stories are managed with a custom ticket tool. The current software release has approximately one million lines of code and 50 components.

3.3   Vision and General Approach

Figure 1 illustrates the vision of the ProDebt approach. Its central element is the assessment of the software quality of relevant quality aspects with a quality profile. Based on the current and target quality values, the quality gap (quality deficit) is identified. Ideally, the quality deficit is the source for quantifying TD. The basis for quality assessment is a so-called quality model, which specifies which aspects of quality are a relevant source of TD, how to measure them, and how to interpret the respective measurement data. The cost of quality deficits (i.e., TD) consists of the cost of removing the deficit (principal) and the additional cost of software development imposed by remaining quality deficits (interest). The objective is to estimate these costs and thus support software managers in deciding which quality deficits should be removed and when not to exceed software development costs and schedule objectives.

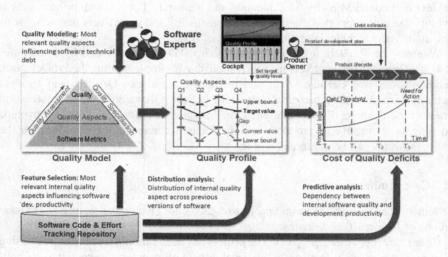

Fig. 1. Vision and core elements of the ProDebt approach.

The ProDebt approach implemented within the project runtime focuses on specifying and measuring a quality model derived from expert input and data analysis. The quality profile is derived from an analysis of baseline measurement data (approx. 5 years of project history) corresponding to the quality model. The cost of TD is approximated by predicting productivity improvement or deterioration based on the measured quality model—if productivity decreases, the cost for developing new features rises. This will be explained in the next sections.

3.4 Creating the Quality Model

Managers with different experiences often perform TD assessments multiple times during a development project and over multiple projects. Thus, one of the critical business requirements on managing TD during the project ProDebt was to reduce the involvement of human experts and thus the subjectivity and total cost of TD assessments.

We applied a hybrid approach for developing one company-specific quality and TD prediction model for QAware and one for Insiders Technologies by combining expert judgment with the analysis of quantitative software project data. For each company, we proceeded as follows (see Fig. 2):

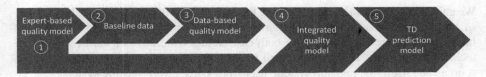

Fig. 2. Creating the quality and prediction model

First, we developed an **expert-based quality model** using experts' knowledge acquired in on-site workshops and an offline survey with software developers and managers. We prepared and designed the workshops and survey taking into account the outcomes of the survey on quality management practices at the project partners. We compared, related, and integrated the results of the workshops and survey into a quality model. This step created company-specific quality models.

Second, we collected **baseline data** by implementing the quality model in the companies' case studies. To do so, each case study partner measured historical data and implemented a continuous measurement process for their case study projects. The resulting baseline data were used for creating the data-based model as well as for training a prediction model.

Third, we developed a **data-based quality model** using the baseline project data available in the context of case studies A and B. After preparing the data, we analyzed the available measurement data on software code quality and development cost (measured in terms of personal effort) in order to identify which software quality aspects have the greatest impact on development and maintenance cost; that is, the key TD drivers. On the one hand, we analyzed measurement data on software quality to find a minimal set of relevant indicators of software quality (unsupervised analysis using, among others, attribute, distance-based, and correlation-based clustering). On the other hand, we analyzed software quality data in relation to software development data in order to identify those quality aspects that have the greatest impact on development productivity (supervised learning using random forests).

Fourth, the **integrated quality model** was derived by combining the outcomes of expert- and data-based quality modeling and selecting, in particular, those measurable quality aspects that have the greatest impact on software TD. We integrated the expert- and data-based quality models using a combination of top-down and bottom-up approaches. Top-down meant excluding expert-based quality aspects for which no measurement data were available. Bottom-up meant adding quality aspects represented by the metrics having a relevant impact on TD.

Finally, we developed a **prediction model for TD** using the same supervised analysis methods as for building the data-based quality model; that is, we applied the random forest modeling method. We developed the prediction model in several iterations, developing a model on part of the data (training set) and evaluating its predictive performance on the remaining data (testing set). The resulting prediction model forecasts potential savings based on proposed refactorings of the identified key drivers of TD.

3.5 Measuring Baseline Data

We gained baseline data by implementing the quality models in each case study. In doing so, we extracted measurements of historical data. In addition, we installed a continuous integrated measurement process for both case studies from 2016 onwards, which also included effort data. This measurement process used the following data sources: the source code itself, the revision system, user stories, and effort tracking systems.

For case study A (the QAware project), the baseline includes historical data from mid-2012 to the time of this writing (July 2017) with at least one measurement per week since 2016. In total, we measured the quality model for 145 points in time. Code measurement is based on SonarQube and on the Seerene measurement tool. Effort data are contained in spreadsheets and are aligned with user stories managed in JIRA. Effort data are recorded per day and per feature.

For case study B (the Insiders Technologies case study), the baseline includes historical data from the end of 2011, measured at the end of each sprint (i.e., every two weeks). In total, we measured the quality model for 167 points in time. Code measurement is based on the Understand tool. Effort data are integrated within a custom ticket system (storyteller) and refer to the total effort for a user story.

3.6 Creating the Prediction Model

The software's source code is organized in files. We applied static software analysis tools to measure the quality model's metrics in each file of the software. These metrics also included size-related metrics such as lines of code. Metrics were captured multiple times at intervals of one sprint (case study B) or one week (case study A) for more than five years into the past. In Fig. 3, these metrics are indicated by M_0, which is the set of metrics for the present time, M_{-1} for the metrics obtained at the previous measurement point, etc.

We also used data about how the software was modified (revision information) and how much effort had to be invested by the developers for each of their development tasks (extracted from ticket information). Revision data were obtained from the source code version control system (e.g., GIT or SVN) and data on the cost of development were extracted from the ticketing systems (e.g., JIRA). The relationship between files,

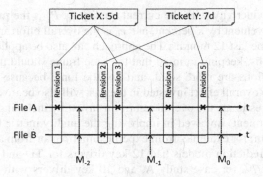

Fig. 3. Data sources used to train the prediction model.

revisions, and tickets is depicted in Fig. 3: Commit messages allow alignment of changed files within revisions to tickets and thus to effort spent on a feature in total or (in case study A) per week. Simultaneously, changes to the source code can be derived by comparing, for example, lines of code (LoC) at two different measurement points.

Based on coding effort and changes to the source code, we measured productivity by

$$P = \frac{\text{Coding output}}{\text{Effort invested}} = \frac{\Delta LoC}{\text{reported effort}} \tag{1}$$

The basic assumption of our approach is that productivity depends (amongst other factors) on the quality of the source code. That is, we have a function $f : \bar{q} \rightarrow P$, where $\bar{q}$ is the vector of metrics in the quality model. Given that the function f is generally unknown, we applied machine learning (more precisely, a random forest algorithm) to approximate f from the collected baseline data. Using the productivity approximator f, we computed productivity for a hypothetical quality level $\bar{q}_x$, obtained by modifying one quality metric by x percent and keeping all other quality metrics at the same level. This approach is depicted in Fig. 4.

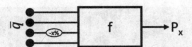

Fig. 4. Computing a hypothetical productivity P_x by varying one quality metric by x percent

The saved effort (and thus, the approximated TD) for a hypothetical improvement of x percent can be computed by reformulation of Eq. (1) as follows:

$$e_x = e_0 \left(1 - \frac{P_0}{P_x} \right), \tag{2}$$

where P_0 is the productivity with the current quality $\bar{q}_0$, P_x is the productivity for the hypothetical improvement by x percent, and e_0 is the overall effort invested into modifying the code for the last 12 months. The approach can also be applied for time frames other than 12 months, keeping in mind that the time frame should not be too short, to ensure that estimations are more solid, and not too long, because of the underlying assumption that the overall effort invested in the past will also be invested in the future.

It is possible to estimate the overall return-on-invest by including an estimation for the cost (i.e., investment) involved in improving the quality metric by x percent. This estimation may stem, for example, from expert estimations or from an effort database.

The resulting prediction models had 12 key drivers for TD and a median relative prediction error of 7% for case study A, and 10 key drivers with a median relative prediction error of 31% for case study B. That is, given the training and test sets of data from the baselines, the prediction model had high to medium precision.

3.7   Applying the Prediction Model

The ProDebt prototype implements the prediction model as follows. First, the user selects one of the key drivers for productivity variation. Then the prototype uses a tree map visualization to display the current state of TD regarding this key driver in the project (see Fig. 5). Each box represents a resource (e.g., module or file); the area of a box is proportional to the effort invested into the related resource within the last 12 months; and color represents the metric values for the selected key driver of this resource. The prototype uses a color scale from green to red to identify the minimum and maximum values of the key driver for the resources displayed in the tree map, respectively. This map uses a configurable aggregation to compute metric values for each resource based on metric data per file (e.g., sum or average). In, the key driver "unexplained McCabe points" has been selected in case study A. This metric computes the number of McCabe points that are not explained or documented by a method name or inline comment. The idea of this metric is that unexplained complexity decreases maintainability and thus increases TD. The range of unexplained complexity for case study A is between 0 and 27, on average, for each file (Fig. 5).

Fig. 5. Tree map visualization of current TD regarding prediction model (Color figure online)

Using this tree map, the user can identify potential investments by investigating, for example, large red areas: Metric values are below average, and a lot of effort has been invested within the past year—meaning that most likely, much effort will be invested again, and thus reducing the TD will most likely pay off. In addition, the user can drill down into the resources by clicking on the related box, making it possible to focus on specific resources.

In the next step, the user can compute potential savings for the selected module and key driver. As outlined in the previous section, the prototype will compute savings in terms of person-days. Figure 6 shows an example output of the prediction model. In this case, the model predicts that modifying the key driver "unexplained McCabe points" by 2% (i.e., write comments for code blocks that represent roughly 70 McCabe points in total) will save two person-days of effort during the next year.

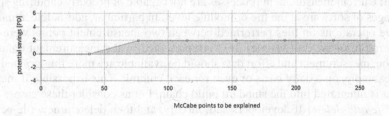

Fig. 6. Potential savings computed with the prediction model

4 Evaluation

We evaluated the ProDebt approach iteratively using the empirical design reported in [2], i.e., a mixed-method study design. Whereas the first evaluation focused on managing quality deficits, the second focused on managing TD.

In the first evaluation, eleven subjects used the ProDebt prototype to analyze quality deficits—six developers and two managers from QAware and two developers and one manager from Insiders Technologies. The participants rated the information provided by this prototype—i.e., quality metrics and associated analysis—as understandable and relevant for analyzing quality deficits and the impact of refactoring tasks. Though the prototype was considered as easy to use, the participants identified improvement potentials, in particular with regard to its system quality. For example, they claimed the need for visualizing quality deficits together with the corresponding source code and other information sources. A detailed report of the first evaluation design and results can be found in [2].

In the second evaluation, again eleven participants used the ProDebt prototype to analyze technical debts—six developers and one manager from QAware, and three developers and one manager from Insiders Technologies. Analyzing TD in this evaluation meant identifying possible savings based on proposed refactorings of key drivers of TD. The participants claimed the information provided by this prototype—i.e., key drivers of TD and the associated analysis—is understandable and useful for analyzing potential savings associated with future refactoring tasks. They also confirmed that the prediction models for managing technical debt are valuable and relevant. They emphasized that the prediction models for managing TD will gain acceptance only if they are accurate and their findings are easy to interpret. That is, potential savings are easily traceable to concrete development tasks.

5   Lessons Learned and Conclusions

Although the two project partners were quite different with respect to their organizational characteristics and the type of software products and services, both were shown to face very similar challenges with respect to managing TD:

1. **Under- and overrepresentation of actual software changes in the measurement data:** Current measurement processes are not capable of properly capturing specific changes of software at the file or module level. In particular, add-delete, rename, or move operations on files performed between two measurement points were either underrepresented (not visible) or overrepresented in the measurement data. As a lesson, measurement and effort data should be available at a more fine-grained level; for example, on a daily basis or even for each commit. This is possible if measurement is integrated into the standard build chain. Let us consider these cases:
    - *File add-delete:* If developers add, modify, and then delete a new file between two measurement points, this change will not appear in the outcome measurement data. In such cases, the effort consumed for adding/modifying/deleting the file will not be traceable to any change in the software code.
    - *File rename or move*: If developers rename or move an existing file to another location, code measurement tools interpret this change as deletion of the original file and addition of a new file. In such cases, although the factual change and the associated effort were small, the change reflected in the measurement data will be large. In extreme cases, renaming or moving a complete project folder will be interpreted as deletion and addition of multiple files.
2. **Missing traceability between software changes and associated development effort:** The organizations collected software quality data and development effort (cost) data independent of each other using separate data collection processes and tools. Software quality was measured for software code across subsequent versions, whereas development effort was reported for user stories. Yet, because software changes and user stories were in an n:m relation with each other, it was hardly possible to associate the exact effort with the observed software changes. On the one hand, implementing one user story may require performing multiple changes of multiple files over time; on the other hand, one measured change of a file may actually result from implementing multiple user stories.
3. **Insufficient data quality:** The quantitative data suffered from significant quality deficits, which influenced the applicability of quantitative analyses and the reliability of the analysis outcomes. Two of the most critical quality deficits were:
    - *Correctness of data*: The data on several attributes did not comply with predefined business rules or were inconsistent with other attributes. For example, the effort

reported as being actually required for implementing a user story was equal to zero, whereas the expected value should be greater than zero.

– *Completeness of data*: Data entries for a number of attributes were missing; for many of them the rate of missing values ranged from 50% to 100%. Causes for this are manifold and range from measurement errors to tools storing zero values ("0") as missing data for some metrics.

4. **Inability to distinguish between new feature development and quality improvement in the data:** Not all organizations distinguish between user stories dedicated to developing new software features and user stories for improving software quality (so-called refactoring or bug fixes). According to the "Boy Scout" (or "feature-driven refactoring") principle of ASD, quality improvements occur only in association with the development of new features; i.e., code quality is improved only when the code has to be touched due to development tasks. Consequently, the effort for quality improvement was included in the total effort for developing a new feature.

5. **Diverse challenges in data quality:** Every company had specific data quality problems. This made it impossible to use the same analysis chain (procedure, algorithms, parameters, tools). Consequently, context-specific approaches would be needed.

Moreover, we elicited further lessons learned regarding predicting TD:

6. **Identification of key drivers of TD:** Developers and managers from QAware and Insiders technologies perceived the identified key drivers of TD as useful for analyzing possible savings related to refactoring tasks. However, further and continuous analyses are needed to identify a set of sufficient and reliable key drivers and keep them up-to-date over time. The identification of key drivers of TD is a complex task that should (1) consider and analyze several types of files (e.g., code, generated code, and test cases) differently; (2) take into account the use of different coding practices (e.g., clean code) over time; and (3) consider and analyze factors besides static code metrics (e.g., developers' task load and experience).

7. **Credibility of prediction model for TD:** On the one hand, developers from QAware and Insiders Technologies considered the prediction models for forecasting savings by refactoring key drivers of TD as very important and useful. On the other hand, managers from both companies claimed they needed support at a higher level of abstraction, commenting, e.g., that they required further support to allocate plausible and significant savings to concrete user stories. Developers and managers emphasized that the prediction model for TD is relevant, but will gain acceptance if and only if it shows very high accuracy and is easy to interpret. Random forests have the disadvantage of being discontinuous. It may be helpful for the credibility of the model to investigate whether other types of prediction models may be beneficial.

Overall, the participants from both companies perceived the ProDebt prototype and approach to have high potential for managing TD. However, in its current state, they also perceived it to be too immature to use. Yet they stated that it would complement TD management in both companies. Moreover, we learned through the evaluations which features are needed in a cockpit for managing technical debt to increase user acceptance.

Acknowledgments. Parts of this work were funded by the German Ministry of Education and Research (BMBF) under research grant no. 01IS15008A-D (ProDebt - A Method and Tool for the Strategic Planning of TD in Agile Software Projects).

References

1. Cunningham, W.: The WyCash portfolio management system. ACM SIGPLAN OOPS Messenger **4**(2), 29–30 (1992)
2. Guzmán, L., Vollmer, A.M., Ciolkowski, M., Gillmann, M.: Formative evaluation of a tool for managing software quality. In: Proceedings of the International Symposium on Empirical Software Engineering and Measurement, November 2017. (Accepted Full Paper)
3. ISO/IEC 25010:2011, Systems and software engineering – Systems and Software Quality Requirements and Evaluation (SQuaRE) – System and software quality models. International Standardization Organization (2011)
4. Kläs, M., Heidrich, J., Münch, J., Trendowicz, A.: CQML scheme: a classification scheme for comprehensive quality model landscapes. In: Proceedings of the 35th EUROMICRO Conference (SEAA 2009), Patras, Greece, 27–29 August 2009
5. Lim, E., Taksande, N., Seaman, C.: A balancing act: what software practitioners have to say about TD. IEEE Softw. **29**(6), 22–27 (2012)

Rapid Lean UX Development Through User Feedback Revelation

Frank Elberzhager[1(✉)], Konstantin Holl[1], Britta Karn[2], and Thomas Immich[2]

[1] Fraunhofer IESE, Fraunhofer Platz 1, 67663 Kaiserslautern, Germany
{frank.elberzhager,konstantin.holl}@iese.fraunhofer.de
[2] Centigrade GmbH, Science Park 2, 66123 Saarbrücken, Germany
{britta.karn,thomas.immich}@centigrade.de

Abstract. The development of software within short timeframes calls for concepts like minimum viable products with lean development. An agile development setting allows software products to be put on the market in time. Nevertheless, quality, especially in terms of user requirements, suffers when the focus is on the speed of the development. Therefore, we have developed the approach Opti4Apps, which considers user feedback automatically. This automation enables rapid user feedback to be revealed, which is needed for lean development in order to achieve high software quality in accordance with the users' needs. This paper shows how the approach can be applied smoothly in agile development settings by analyzing common agile practices with regard to our user-centric feedback approach Opti4Apps. It turned out that with most practices, the additional effort is low, and the positive influence can be highly beneficial.

Keywords: Quality assurance · User experience · Lean development · User-centered · Feedback · Agile practices

1 Introduction

With the rise of applications that have a short time to market, quality has often become subordinated to features. Since it is both relevant for companies to be the first on the market and to increase the quality of mobile applications, ensuring high quality is moving into the focus of development to help companies remain competitive. To achieve this quality, companies need to invest in quality assurance strategies and define new priorities [1]. This requires the investigation of product and process quality in the context of agile and rapid software development.

To improve current practices for quality assurance in agile settings, we focus on early feedback from users in this publication. According to our observations from practical environments, but also in line with other researchers, users are often not given the priority they deserve, and companies struggle when it comes to gathering and analyzing user feedback efficiently [6]. However, on the other hand, feedbacks are a rich source for improving the software products. In order to make this efficient, automation should play a role. A reasonable instrument for realizing such a procedure is a semi-automated feedback elicitation, analysis, and processing framework, so the effectiveness and

© Springer International Publishing AG 2017
M. Felderer et al. (Eds.): PROFES 2017, LNCS 10611, pp. 535–542, 2017.
https://doi.org/10.1007/978-3-319-69926-4_43

efficiency of early user feedback consideration during further development can be examined with the goal of assuring the quality and acceptance of a mobile application developed in a minimalistic way [2].

While MVP development enables early feedback and very fast time to market, the quality of the resulting product suffers in comparison to traditional development. In contrast, with traditional development, there is no early feedback and time to market is longer.

Our approach Opti4Apps for automated consideration of user feedback could realize and extend the benefits of MVP development through the development and use of a framework based on the automatable elicitation and analysis of feedback as well as through the use of an effective and efficient quality assurance methodology. This rapidly focuses the lean development on the user's requirements. Furthermore, the feedback and the insights from one development could be reused in parallel or subsequent developments.

Nevertheless, in order to reap the benefits of automated consideration of user feedback, compatibility with existing agile processes is required. Therefore, we show the compatibility of a selected set of common agile practices with our Opti4Apps approach.

This article is structured as follows: Sect. 2 describes the related work, in particular basic concepts, prior work, and an agile references process. Section 3 presents top-down the feedback-based lean UX development process followed by the assessment of selected agile practices. Section 4 wraps up the results and experiences followed by ideas for future work.

2   Related Work

2.1   Lean UX

The development of mobile apps calls for concepts like minimum viable products produced in lean development due to short timeframes. The Lean UX approach is a concept that combines three development methodologies: design thinking, agile development, and Lean Start-up [5].

1. The principles of design thinking show that design methods can be used in every phase of a project from any discipline. Non-designers should be encouraged to use design methods based on this approach, as it supports teams in collaborative design across roles. Furthermore, it is a customer-centered approach as it takes not only the user needs into account but also the technological possibilities and the business view.
2. The second methodology in Lean UX is agile development. It has been an important approach for software developers for a long time, especially the Scrum process. The important elements of Lean UX are the iterative and incremental approach, which enables the team to respond to change immediately (compared to the waterfall model), collaboration in teams and with the customer to ensure continuous feedback, and a strong communication culture.
3. The third methodology is Lean Start-up. The basis of this approach is the "build-measure-learn" loop, which helps teams to minimize project risks and supports quick

feedback and faster completion of projects. This faster completion results from the Minimum Viable Products (MVPs) that the teams are building to get user feedback as soon as possible with the help of rapid prototyping. According to Lean UX [5], an MVP is, on the one hand, the smallest thing that helps to test assumptions with the help of a prototype or other product developed by the team. In this case, the MVP is built to learn something and the team benefits from it, but there is no immediate benefit for the user. On the other hand, an MVP in Lean UX is defined as the smallest version of the end product that is delivered to the users and addresses a problem or need the user has. In this case, the focus of the MVP is on the benefit for the user. In the Opti4Apps context, we define MVP in the latter way: a product that is usable and valuable for the user who benefits from it.

The Lean UX approach of continuous learning and testing leads to the following principle, which also defines the start of a Lean UX project: Assumptions before requirements! The first step in the Lean UX process is to declare assumptions that should be validated along the process.

2.2 Prior Work

Figure 1 provides a conceptual overview of the previously defined user feedback approach [2]. There is a mobile application as an MVP on a mobile device and users who use the application. The users can give feedback. This feedback comprises the application's usage data (e.g., usage frequency, duration, or misentries), state (e.g., installation and online state), and explicit user feedback (reviews, bug reports). Such feedback can be provided by the user automatically (e.g., via a specific agent running on the mobile device), semi-automatically (e.g., some data is tracked by the mobile device and has to be sent manually to a backend), or manually (e.g., users provide some written feedback in the app store). In other words, feedback can be provided explicitly by the user or implicitly through measurement by technical means.

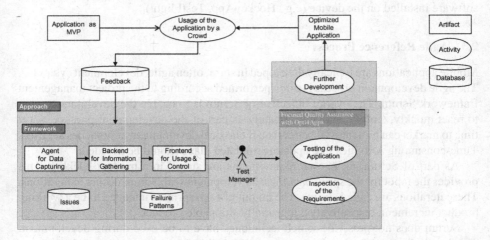

Fig. 1. Automated user feedback consideration in the Opti4Apps approach.

The feedback then has to be edited, analyzed, and provided in a suitable way so that the company developing the application gets information it can use to improve the application. A framework is used for this purpose. It uses, for example, the data provided by the agent integrated into the mobile application, direct feedback, or feedback gathered by performing data mining analyses to detect existing deficiencies or reveal improvement ideas. All such data is consolidated by a backend and classified to generate a more suitable overview.

The analysis of the collected information in the backend via data mining is intended to enable a fast learning effect with respect to existing deficiencies. Thus, it can provide a baseline for effective further development as well as for focused quality assurance. Identified failure patterns (based on mobile-specific failure classes [3]) can increase the effectiveness of the quality assurance of the current development. Because of the reusability of failure patterns, these can also be used for parallel and subsequent developments.

One of the main aspects of the framework could be the recognition of usage patterns that may be considered as failures as part of the mentioned failure patterns, which constitute a collection of typical failure causes and impacts in the area of mobile applications.

The control of the framework and the utilization of the produced information result in several role-specific tools, which form the frontend. A dashboard with different views depending on the data analysis is used by a test manager. This role is responsible for taking further actions based on the results of the feedback analysis. The main tasks include controlling quality assurance (i.e., deriving new test cases based on the identified problems) or sharing the results with a requirements engineer in case new feature wishes are identified.

By using the failure patterns during the inspection of the requirements specification as well as during testing of the mobile application, focused quality assurance is established, thus optimizing the mobile application. Based on the user feedback, the optimized mobile application is again distributed to the users. This is realized by a distribution software installed on the device (e.g., HockeyApp, TestFlight).

2.3   Agile Reference Process

Mobile applications are typically developed in short, often agile, development cycles [4]. The agile development process is often performed according to the project management framework Scrum. The overall objective of Scrum is to enable the development team to react quickly, simply, and appropriately as part of the development process. Short time to market can be achieved better than if classical development approaches are used. Time-consuming activities like updating outdated plans should be avoided.

As part of Scrum, all known requirements are stored in a product backlog. This provides the input for the sprint backlogs. Development with Scrum occurs in iterations. These iterations are called sprints. The output of each sprint is intended to be a working product increment, respectively a potentially shippable product.

Scrum does not prescribe which techniques have to be used during development. This is mostly up to the development team [7]. Neither does Scrum dictate the types of tests that have to be performed [4]. Independent of the specific technique selected as part of Scrum (e.g., Extreme Programming, Test First), testing in agile development can be assigned to the fundamental test process, just like testing in classical software engineering.

3   Process Integration

3.1   Conceptual Picture of Feedback-Based Lean UX Development

The Lean UX framework is our starting point. The UX team starts an MVP project with a pre-process. Elements of the pre-process are, e.g., Scoping, User Research, Conceptual Design, and Design Engineering Workshops. The exact content of this pre-process is not determined by this model; rather, the objective is to derive user stories from user needs, which will be the working basis in the following sprint process. Hence, it is necessary to clarify user needs that are evaluated based on real user feedback. Those user stories that are most relevant for the current scope are taken into the following sprints and form the basis for the resulting MVP. It is possible to run parallel processes for multiple MVPs with different teams as well as to operate sequentially. In addition, it is possible to develop the same user story in different ways on different tracks, e.g., to do A/B-testing later on. Of course, it is important to continuously consider the "big picture", i.e., the project as a whole, to ensure that it will be possible to consolidate the results of different MVPs in one overall product or system.

The objective of the lean process for Opti4Apps is to gain user feedback at any time of the process, which is shown in the area below the model, despite the short timeframe. The classical feedback approaches make heavy use of concept testing (which serves the designer) and mostly will not work in this timeframe, as there are too many iterations. With Opti4Apps, the user feedback is gathered during product testing by a tracking agent that automatically obtains relevant usage data from users.

Nevertheless, this model is initially an idealization and does not consider all "real-world circumstances" of projects. The process must be adapted depending on diverse influencing factors, for example team size and constellation, project domain, "type" of customer (internal, external), and the take-off point of the project (an all-new development vs. a refinement of an existing product). Many other influencing factors are conceivable. All these factors determine what a more detailed view of the model would look like. In order to understand how different instances of agile processes behave when such a user-centric approach is considered, we analyzed common agile practices with respect to invasiveness and benefit. The results are presented in the next section.

3.2   Assessment of Selected Agile Practices

In order to make the lean UX process more concrete, we analyzed how common agile practices cooperate with Opti4Apps and what the potential benefit is when Opti4Apps is applied in an agile process (i.e., if agile practices are followed). Two experienced researchers (more than 10 years of experience) performed an evaluation of the most common agile practices. We addressed 11 top-level topics from Diebold and Dahlem

[7] (some of the 18 originally mentioned ones have no connection to user feedback, such as refactoring), and considered a total of 21 concrete agile practices. We evaluated invasiveness and benefit on a four-point scale (see legend in Table 1):

- Invasiveness: When Opti4Apps is applied, how much is the agile practice influenced (under the assumption that the agile practice is applied) and how much adaptation may be necessary (which might result in higher effort to apply the agile practice)?
- Benefit: How strong does the agile practice (and indirectly the overall agile development process) benefit when Opti4Apps is applied?

Table 1. Invasiveness and benefit rating of using agile practices with Opti4Apps

Top-Level Topic	Agile Practice	Invasiveness	Benefit	Remarks
Quality Check	Pair Programming	↝	↝	Feedback from pair
	Code Review	↝	↝	Suggestions from Opti4Apps framework
	Usability Expert Review	↝	⇒	Defect patterns from Opti4Apps framework for review
Customer Involvement	Product Owner	⇧	⇧	User researcher role, controlling Opti4Apps framework
Validation	Test-driven Development	⇒	⇒	Defect patterns from Opti4Apps framework for test
	Explorative Testing	↝	⇧	Suggestions from Opti4Apps framework
	Crowd Testing	⇧	⇧	Systematic crowd test and automatic clustering/interpretation
Learning Loop	Retrospective	↝	⇒	Dashboard shows quality details / feature requests
Planning Meeting	Planning Poker	↝	⇩	Maybe more user stories lead to more complex planning poker
	Feature Freeze	⇩	⇩	-
	Jour Fixe	↝	⇒	Dashboard shows quality details / feature requests
Progress Monitoring	Burn Chart	⇩	⇩	-
	Definition of Done	⇩	⇩	-
Product Vision	Product Backlog	↝	⇧	More features, more bug reports
Specification	Sprint Backlog	↝	⇧	More features, more bug reports
	Personas	↝	⇧	New information about stakeholders / customers
	Design Thinking	⇒	⇒	Automated feedback regarding early prototypes
	User Stories	↝	⇒	More user stories with requested features / bug corrections
Continuous Delivery	Continuous Integration	⇩	↝	Supports prioritization
Frequent Releases	Code Generation	⇩	⇩	-
Daily Discussions	Standup Meeting	↝	⇒	Dashboard shows quality details / feature requests

Legend: high ⇧, medium ⇒, low ↝, none ⇩

Let's consider the topic "Quality check" as a first example to understand the rating: During pair programming, a second person watches what is being programmed, and can give direct feedback. When the feedback cannot be implemented directly, it can be documented in the Opti4Apps framework. This requires little effort (=low invasiveness), but the benefit from such feedback is also rather limited as the amount of such additional feedback is expected to be low. For a code review, experiences regarding typical issues stored in the Opti4Apps framework can be used and checked. However, their number is again expected to be low. During a usability review, defect patterns might be used to control the review, which makes it more effective. The level of invasiveness is again low, as just some information is consumed, but the benefit is, on average, medium.

Besides crowd testing, customer involvement is the only agile practice that has a high level of invasiveness. The reason is that either a new role is needed (a user researcher who controls the Opti4Apps tasks) or that a role such as the product owner has to perform it, which also results in some effort. However, the benefit of such a dedicated role, respectively the product owner who owns the relevant tasks, is highly beneficial, and to a certain extent forms the core of Opti4Apps, as this role controls, for example, how to handle all the feedback and determines consequences resulting from the analyzed feedback.

There are also agile practices that have no influence (and usually no benefit), for instance burn charts. It is simply a mechanism for visualizing the current status, but new feedback has no direct influence on this practice.

Certain practices support the same benefits. For example, a retrospective, a jour fixe, and a standup meeting are all influenced in a minimal way by Opti4Apps (mainly due to some more feedback which needs little extra time to mention), but have at least a medium positive influence due to new feature ideas or bug indications that may be revealed. There also exist further agile practices that we did not consider in our analysis; however, we picked a set of the most common practices [7] to start our analysis. Table 1 shows the complete evaluation results together with a short explanation of every agile practice.

Of course, the individual ratings can be further discussed and might lead to adaptations depending on the concrete context. On purpose, we did not use a number schema, but tendency arrows, which indicate the general evaluation direction for every agile practice. The agile practices should also be assessed by other researchers and practitioners in order to get a more stable evaluation. Moreover, Opti4Apps should be applied in concrete agile development settings in order to get higher confidence in the initial rating. The current evaluation is mainly based on arguments and on our own experience from several development environments, and serves as a starting point for initial discussions and further evaluations. However, though slight adaptations are reasonable, the trends will probably mainly remain.

The evaluation results show that Opti4Apps is compatible with many agile practices, and that the additional effort or need for changes (expressed as invasiveness here) is rather low. Of course, any new methodology requires some investment effort, but considering the benefit that customer feedback provides in terms of new features and features that are really expected by customers, as well as in terms of indications about quality issues, it is worthwhile the effort.

Practitioners might use the evaluation of these agile practices to check how much Opti4Apps influences their concrete agile development process, and to get further ideas regarding which practices to use in order to gain an even higher benefit and get concrete feedback from customers for further development. Researchers can further analyze agile practices and check whether our rating fits in other settings.

4   Conclusion and Future Work

In this article, we again took up the challenge of how software-developing companies can consider user feedback more strongly. To this end, we provided an overview of our Opti4Apps approach, which gathers user feedback from several sources automatically. Modern software development tends to become ever faster, with trends such as continuous delivery and DevOps. At the same time, it still has to ensure high quality and develop those features that users really demand. To deal with this situation, we introduced our Opti4Apps approach and showed its compatibility with several agile practices. The approach does, of course, require some investment; however, it turned out that the challenge of really considering the user during development can be highly supported by our approach without large investments or changes in the agile processes.

In the future, we will substantiate our initial classification and rating of agile practices by discussing them with more experts, but also by observing real applications of the Opti4Apps framework in agile developments. We are convinced that this will contribute to stronger consideration of the user during development, as intended by the Agile Manifesto, and that our approach will provide specific guidance for practitioners.

Acknowledgments. The research described in this paper was performed in the project *Opti4Apps* (grant no. 02K14A182) of the German Federal Ministry of Education and Research (BMBF). We also thank Sonnhild Namingha for proofreading.

References

1. Buenen, M., Teje, M., Carrel, I.: Testing and SMAC Technologies: Ensuring a Seamless and Secure Customer Experience. World Quality report 2014–2015, Sixth edn., Capgemini, HP, Sogeti (2014)
2. Holl, K., Elberzhager, F., Tamanini, C.: Optimization of mobile applications through a feedback-based quality assurance approach. In: 15th International Conference on Mobile and Ubiquitous Multimedia, Finland, pp. 1–3 (2016)
3. Holl, K., Elberzhager, F.: A Mobile-specific failure classification and its usage to focus quality assurance. In: 40th Euromicro Conference on Software Engineering and Advanced Applications (SEAA 2014), Italy, pp. 385–388 (2014)
4. Linz, T.: Testing in Scrum: A Guide for Software Quality Assurance in the Agile World, 1st edn. dpunkt.verlag, Heidelberg (2014)
5. Gothelf, J., Seiden, J.: Lean UX: Applying Lean Principles to Improve User Experience. O'Reilly, Sebastopol (2013)
6. Fabijan, A., Olsson, H.H., Bosch, J.: Customer feedback and data collection techniques in software R&D: a literature review. In: Fernandes, J.M., Machado, R.J., Wnuk, K. (eds.) Software Business ICSOB 2015. LNBIP, vol. 210, pp. 139–153. Springer, Cham (2015). doi: 10.1007/978-3-319-19593-3_12
7. Diebold, P., Dahlem, M.: Agile practices in practice: a mapping study. In: 18th International Conference on Evaluation and Assessment in Software Engineering (2014)

Managing Development Using Active Data Collection

Michael Kläs[✉] and Frank Elberzhager

Fraunhofer IESE, Kaiserslautern, Germany
{michael.klaes,frank.elberzhager}@iese.fraunhofer.de

Abstract. Problems commonly observed in Big Data and Predictive Analytics projects that try to provide data-driven innovations motivate the need for a general paradigm shift from passive to active data collection. A possible active data collection framework based on Big Data technology is outlined and possible implications for research are identified.

Keywords: Software development · Big Data · Experimentation · Measurement

1 Motivation for Active Data Collection

Current trends subsumed under Big Data and Predictive Analytics promise interesting new opportunities for software-developing companies, especially in the context of the ongoing digitization of products and services. This is not only true for companies developing the required technology stack, but also for companies using the new technologies to enhance their existing products and services or provide new ones.

However, Heudecker argued that most Big Data projects will not be successful [1]. Based on many informal discussions with practitioners from different companies and first-hand experience with Big Data and Predictive Analytics projects, there are many reasons for such projects to fail, but most of these fit into one of the following three categories: (1) *unclear analysis goals*, (2) *serious data quality issues*, or (3) *lack of user acceptance*.

1. The analysis problem to be solved is not understood or was defined too generically. ('Here are our data. Please find some new and useful insights.')
2. The underlying data suffer from unexpected quality problems jeopardizing or even negating the applicability of available analysis approaches.
3. The developed solution is not accepted by the intended users (such as the notorious Microsoft Office assistant Clippit, which most users considered annoying rather than intelligent or helpful [2]).

This work is being partially funded by the German Federal Ministry for Economic Affairs and Energy in the context of the technology program "Smart Data - Innovations in Data", grant no. 01MD15004E and by the Ministry of Education Research in the context of the Abakus project, grand no. 01IS1550.

© Springer International Publishing AG 2017
M. Felderer et al. (Eds.): PROFES 2017, LNCS 10611, pp. 543–547, 2017.
https://doi.org/10.1007/978-3-319-69926-4_44

There are approaches that can support practitioners in identifying these kinds of problems at an early stage, such as Design Thinking [3], doing a potential analysis in advance [4], or testing their assumptions with a minimal viable product [5].

Nevertheless, a common issue that occurs in most data-driven innovation projects is a mismatch between the data collected to date and the data that would actually be needed to solve the analysis problem. The reason for this mismatch is simple; the existing data was usually collected for other purposes. For example, sensor data collected in the automotive industry to optimize the motor control unit are not necessarily the same data that would be useful for building a predictive maintenance model. Another example are resellers who collected data to enable smooth sales processes and now want to make use of these data to provide customer-specific product recommendations. In consequence, it is rarely possible to solve an innovative analysis problem relying only on existing data collections. These observations are also in line with Gartner's prediction that 90% of deployed data lakes will turn out to be useless [6].

Based on experience from former projects – especially from industry environments – our *first assertion* is that companies should focus less on collecting and storing all kinds of data or making big investments analyzing previously collected data in the hope of finding some useful new insights, but instead should make efforts to build up an infrastructure to efficiently define, collect, and analyze data that are relevant for their current analysis problems. Because the scope of data collection as well as the relevant analysis problems at a given time may change over time, the infrastructure not only needs to be scalable but also easy to adjust to emerging information needs.

Our *second assertion* is that an infrastructure for data collection should not be designed as a passive monitoring component but as a component that can also actively influence the data collection situation in order to leverage the full potential of the collected data. This requirement is motivated by the observation that analysis problems of the highest relevance commonly address similar types of questions:

- Which is the better option with respect to X, a1 or a2?
- Does the value of A influence X and to what extent?
- How does X change if the values of A, B, and C are changed?

The commonality among all these questions is that they ask about causalities. However, data analysis approaches, including machine learning, performed on data collected without any active influence on the data collection situation cannot be applied to determine such causal relationships. The best thing these analyses can achieve is to detect and quantify correlations among different variables. The difference between correlation and causality becomes clearer if we consider an example: The number of storks was shown to correlate very well with the number of newborns in certain cities. However, contrary to existing myths, it might not be a good idea to rely on a repopulation program for storks to increase low fertility rates in industrialized countries.

In contrast to passive data collection, active influence on the collection situation allows conducting experiments to validate assumptions and quantify causal effects with a given error probability. Experiments can investigate the variable of interest by systematically varying this variable and measuring changes in the target variable. Further variables that might influence the target variable are kept constant during such experiments or controlled through the experimental design using randomization.

In software companies, experimentation is currently mainly used by large Internet companies or in online marketing in the form of split-run tests [7], where websites are presented to the user with different layouts or content and the impact on the conversation rate or other KPIs is measured and tested for statistically relevant differences.

However, considering the ongoing trend to shorten release cycles using continuous deployment [8] and software as a service (SaaS), the potential of active data generation goes beyond simple statistical tests. It allows providing statistically validated answers to key questions of developers, product and quality managers:

- What are the true needs and requirements of our customers?
- What are missing features and which are used only rarely?
- How can user experience and interaction with the product be improved?
- What is the impact of a specific code change on product quality?
- Are performance and stability of the new release sufficient?

Section 2 illustrates the idea for an open framework supporting active data collection and experiments in an efficient way. Section 3 concludes the paper with implications and possible directions we see for future research.

2 Towards a Framework for Active Data Collection

This section provides an overview of a framework for active data collection (see Fig. 1).

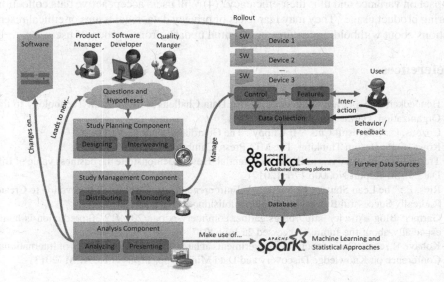

Fig. 1. Illustration of an active data collection framework using a Big Data stack.

546 M. Kläs and F. Elberzhager

An active data collection study is designed based on analysis questions or hypotheses of the stakeholders and is then interwoven with other concurrent studies. As soon as a software version with required changes (e.g., new features) is rolled out on the devices, the study management component can distribute the respective control information to the selected devices and monitor further progress of the study.

Data collection and interaction of the device with the user are influenced by the study control component, i.e., different devices may behave differently depending on the investigated treatment. Kafka as a highly scalable messaging system writes the collected study data in a distributed database. The data can then be analyzed using Spark as a scalable data processing framework and visualized to allow decision-making on the further development of the software and to derive new questions and hypotheses.

3 Possible Implications for Research

From our point of view, an open framework for active data collection can offer significant advantages for companies in managing their product development. This is in line with a current study on experimentation in product development, which can be seen as a specific application of active data collection. The study found rising interest in industry and identified technical tools as the success factor mentioned most often [9].

However, several questions arise that require a more detailed investigation: (1) Are the effect sizes that will be investigated in practice high enough to get reliable feedback also for companies that are not Google or Microsoft? (2) What designs are most efficient to quantify effects, and can we use data mining to optimize these designs in advance or even during runtime based on prior knowledge? (3) How can we interweave a high number of concurrent studies without invalidating their results and minimizing the impact on variance and thus their efficiency? (4) Will users accept active data collection during product usage? They may fear leaks of privacy data, legal issues or ethical reservations about withholding features or essential updates from a group of users.

References

1. Heudecker, N.N., et al.: Predicts 2015: Big Data Challenges Move from Technology to the Organization. Gartner report, November 2014
2. Cozens, C.: Microsoft Cuts 'Mr Clippy'. The Guardian, London (2001)
3. Rowe, G.P.: Design Thinking. The MIT Press, Cambridge (1987)
4. Trendowicz, A.: Analysis of Big Data Potential: How to demonstrate the business value of Big Data. IESE-Report No. 006.17/E (2017)
5. Ries, E.: The Lean Startup: How Today's Entrepreneurs use Continuous Innovation to Create Radically Successful Businesses. Crown Publishing, New York (2011)
6. Gartner Blog Article. http://blogs.gartner.com/merv-adrian/2014/12/30/prediction-is-hard-especially-about-the-future/. Accessed 25 July 2017
7. Kohavi, R., et al.: Online controlled experiments at large scale. In: Proceedings of International Conference on Knowledge Discovery and Data Mining, pp. 1168–1176. ACM (2013)

8. Rodríguez, P.P., Haghighatkhah, A., Lwakatare, L.E., Teppola, S.: Continuous deployment of software intensive products and services: a systematic mapping study. JSS **123**, 263–291 (2017)
9. Lindgren, E., Münch, J.: Raising the odds of success: the current state of experimentation in product development. Inform. Softw. Technol. **77**, 80–91 (2016)

Agile Quality Requirements Management Best Practices Portfolio: A Situational Method Engineering Approach

Lidia López[1(✉)], Woubshet Behutiye[2], Pertti Karhapää[2], Jolita Ralyté[3], Xavier Franch[1], and Markku Oivo[2]

[1] Universitat Politècnica de Catalunya (UPC), Barcelona, Spain
{llopez,franch}@essi.upc.edu
[2] University of Oulu, Oulu, Finland
{woubshet.behutiye,pertti.karhapaa,markku.oivo}@oulu.fi
[3] University of Geneva, Geneva, Switzerland
jolita.ralyte@unige.ch

Abstract. Management of Quality Requirements (QRs) is determinant for the success of software projects. However, this management is currently under-considered in software projects and in particular, in agile methods. Although agile processes are focused on the functional aspects of the software, some agile practices can be beneficial for the management of QRs. For example, the collaboration and interaction of people can help in the QR elicitation by reducing vagueness of requirements through communication. In this paper, we present the initial findings of our research investigating what industrial practices, from the agile methods, can be used for better management of QRs in agile software development. We use Situational Method Engineering to identify, complement and classify a portfolio of best practices for QR management in agile environments. In this regard, we present the methodological approach that we are applying for the definition of these guidelines and the requirements that will lead us to compile a portfolio of agile QR management best practices. The proposed requirements correspond to the whole software life cycle starting in the elicitation and finalizing in the deployment phases.

Keywords: Quality requirement · Non-functional requirement · Agile development · Situational Method Engineering

1 Introduction

Agile methods are becoming increasingly popular in the software industry [1–3]. Customer satisfaction through early and continuous delivery of valuable software, adaptability to late requirements changes, short and iterative development cycles are some principles of agile software development (ASD) methods [4]. Another important aspect of software development that has attracted a lot of attention is software quality, mainly represented by the quality requirements (QRs; also referred to as non-functional requirements –NFRs) of the product [5]. However, it has been documented that the management of QRs in software development in general [5] and in ASD in particular [6] is problematic, e.g. important QRs might be neglected in ASD [7].

© Springer International Publishing AG 2017
M. Felderer et al. (Eds.): PROFES 2017, LNCS 10611, pp. 548–555, 2017.
https://doi.org/10.1007/978-3-319-69926-4_45

One aspect of ASD is that agile principles put emphasis on communication and linking of people [4]. The closer collaboration between people within a development team, e.g. requirements engineers and testers, helps in generating an understanding of the requirements so that development can progress and testing can be conducted properly despite lower quality of the requirements and lack of documentation [8]. Agile practices can also help the QR elicitation by reducing vagueness of requirements through communication [9], QRs in particular, since defining good, verifiable, and complete QRs is quite difficult.

Improving the management of QRs in agile projects is the ultimate goal of the Q-Rapids (Quality-aware Rapid Software Development) project[1]. In order to achieve this goal, we aim at defining a set of guidelines for integrating QR management into the ASD life cycle. There are several methods, techniques and models that can be applied for managing QRs, making difficult the definition of a unique method to be applied in any organization. In the context of ASD, Qumer and Henderson-Sellers applied Situational Method Engineering (SME) to create a software development method combining agile and formal practices in a large software development organization [10]. Following the same approach, in this paper we propose using SME to identify, complement, and classify a portfolio of best industrial practices in order to define a method for QR management in agile environments.

The rest of the paper is organized as follows. Section 2 introduces the research approach followed, including the background necessary to apply SME. The construction of the method is based in the software development process detailed in Sect. 3. Section 4 includes the definition of the method requirements, and Sect. 5 includes an example of the guidelines associated to the QRs prioritization. Finally, Sect. 6 concludes the presentation of the work included in this paper and discusses our future work.

2   Situational Method Engineering

2.1   Background

In this work we apply the assembly-based Situational Method Engineering (SME) approach [11] as underpinning theory for capitalizing best practices in the domain of QR management in ASD, and for reusing them in the construction of situation-specific methods. Following this approach, the knowledge of such methods has to be formalized in terms of reusable method chunks. A method chunk describes the method process (i.e., the guidelines) and its related products (i.e., the concepts and artefacts used/transformed/created by applying the guidelines). It also specifies the situation in which it can be applied (i.e., the required input artefacts) and the intention (i.e., the engineering goal) to be reached. The method chunks are used as building blocks for constructing a situation-specific method, which can be a project-specific method or even a configurable method family including several method chunk variants for each method step. In both cases, the approach consists of defining method requirements and then selecting and assembling method chunks satisfying these requirements. Method requirements (also

---

[1] http://q-rapids.eu/.

called requirements map) are specified as a desired process model by using the Map process modeling formalism [12], which allows to express methods in terms of intentions and strategies to reach the intentions. The variability and flexibility of a method is reached by defining several strategies for achieving an intention.

The sources for engineering method chunks can be various: existing methods, standards, templates, and best practices. Depending on their formalization and level of detail, the creation of method chunks consist in reengineering the existing method knowledge or defining it from scratch.

2.2   Application

The assembly-based SME approach has been applied in various software and information systems engineering domains. For instance, Ralyté et al. reengineered the RESCUE Requirements Process into a modular method (a collection of method chunks organized into a multi-level process map) allowing to assess the quality of the method, to identify omissions and weaknesses, and to reason about its improvements [13]. This case also demonstrated the effectiveness of the SME approach for modelling large-scale engineering processes. In a different domain, López et al. presented the OSSAP method [14], applying assembly-based SME approach to construct a method for OSS adoption business processes. The OSSAP chunks correspond to the different ways of adopting OSS and the pieces of processes to be adopted by the organization, depending on the way they want to be involved with the OSS community producing the OSS.

3   Software Development Process in Agile Projects

In this section, we present the analysis of the software development process employed in four use cases (UCs) of the Q-Rapids project. The results are based on preliminary findings of case studies conducted to understand the software development processes and QR management practices adopted in selected projects of the Q-Rapids industrial partners. The Q-Rapids industrial partners are representatives of small, medium, and large sized companies from three different countries (Finland, France and Poland), all produce software in different domains (telecommunications, secure solutions, modeling and ad-hoc solutions). Qualitative analysis was done on the 12 semi-structured interviews conducted in the UCs to get an understanding of the development processes.

Our findings reveal that all of the UCs adopt variants of Scrum tailored to their specific context of development. The UCs operate in predefined release cycles that range from two weeks to six months. The sprint cycle varied from one to four weeks. Medium and large companies are characterized by complex backlog structure and multiple teams. The smaller companies utilized a single backlog and consist of a small sized team. Additionally, the ASD maturity level applied in the UCs also varied. We observed both similarities and differences in the practices, roles and tools utilized in the UCs.

During initial stages of the development process, the UCs elicit requirements (both functional requirements and QRs) mainly based on customer needs. At this stage, high level features are elicited together with the customer. Features that bring more value to the customer are prioritized. However, the level of customer involvement, as well as the practices and roles involved in the process, varies among the UCs. For instance, two UCs from small and medium sized companies mainly utilize the customer for eliciting requirements. The other two UCs from medium and large sized companies consider additional factors such as product roadmaps, the status of the market and problems of potential customer segments. Roles involved in higher level requirements elicitation included product owners, product and technical managers, sales team, and usability experts. Product and technical managers made requirements prioritization decision in UCs of medium and large companies. On the other hand, smaller companies relied on the product owners' decisions for requirements elicitation and prioritization. Elicitation of the higher-level features considered both functional requirements and QRs.

The higher level features are refined and specified into lower level features or user stories and tasks. In medium and large organizations, higher level features were refined in several steps due to the product size. On the other hand, in smaller companies, the number of refinement steps were fewer.

Communication happens throughout the development process in all of the UCs. Face-to-face communication serves as the main source of communication in small sized companies. In such cases, face-to-face communication facilitates the development process, as the developers are close to each other and usually in the same room. Additionally, there was less emphasis on the documentation practices. However, in medium and large sized companies, documentation and shared tools serve as sources of communication. Face-to-face communication was adopted only at lower (local) level.

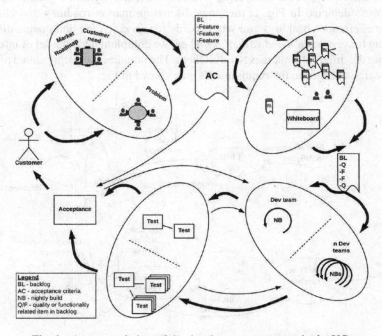

Fig. 1. Aggregated view of the development processes in the UCs

All UCs employ continuous integration in their development process. Nightly builds, integration tests, and acceptance tests are applied in the verification and validation process. The testing practices also varied with the size of the companies. Figure 1 depicts the generic view of the development process adopted in the UCs.

4   QR Management Method Requirements

The analysis of the software development process of the UCs, described in the previous section, uncovered that they do not use a predefined existing method for QR management. The organizations use and combine different methods and techniques in different ways for setting their own agile oriented development process. The aim of this work is setting up a portfolio of best practices organizing and complementing these techniques to improve QR management in the context of ASD processes.

Due to this diversity of methods and techniques, we are developing this portfolio applying SME, concretely creating a new method constructed from scratch [15]. In order to identify the needed guidelines, we applied a process-driven strategy to elicit the method requirements, which is more relevant in the case of a new method construction [16]. In order to specify the requirements for the method, we need to (1) identify the set of intentions related to the QR management in the current processes, and (2) identify the possible strategies for fulfilling these intentions.

During the UCs analysis, we collected the initial set of intentions to be fulfilled by the new method: *Elicit, Specify, Communicate,* and *Verify and Validate* QRs. These intentions correspond to the underlying goals for each activity of the generic development process depicted in Fig. 1: meetings discussing market roadmap and customer needs for *elicitation*, backlogs and whiteboards for *specification* and *communication*, and testing for *verification and validation*. Then, we complemented the set of intentions identifying the different strategies to fulfill them. The intentions are represented as nodes and strategies as edges in the requirements map shown in Fig. 2.

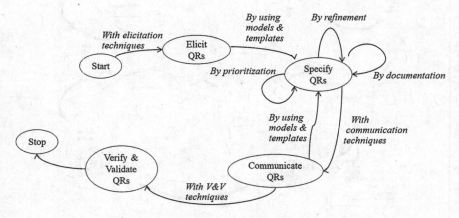

Fig. 2. QR management method requirements map

Most of the strategies included in the requirements map are still generic, except for the strategies to fulfill the *Specify QR* intention. The Q-Rapids UC providers (see Sect. 3), pointed out that we can find different levels of requirements in ASD processes, from high-level requirements (coming from the elicitation activity) to lower-level requirements (defined in later stages), which are the refined requirements that can be translated to user stories, features or tasks to be communicated to the development team. Therefore, refinement is the strategy to specify new lower-level requirements. Prioritization is really important in agile environments, requirements need to be arranged by priority to be fully specified before they are communicated to the development teams.

5   Example: Chunks for QR Prioritization

In this section, we describe the possible strategies for fulfilling the *Prioritize QRs* intention. From the analysis of the UC processes, we identified the following two situations: the prioritization by urgency (issue-driven) and prioritization based on value (value-driven). The prioritization by urgency occurs when some blocking situation arises during the software development process that affects the expected workflow. For example, if there is a specific problem/issue in the development of a critical feature, the development team should reprioritize the work focusing on fixing this situation. On the other hand, when no critical situations should be handled, the organization can prioritize their requirements with no specific problem to solve.

For the value-driven strategy, we identified an existing method chunk included in [17] for cost-value requirements prioritization. This value-driven prioritization chunk proposes having two criteria for evaluating requirements: relative value and relative cost, which are used for ranking the requirements. Figure 3 reproduces the process map for this chunk.

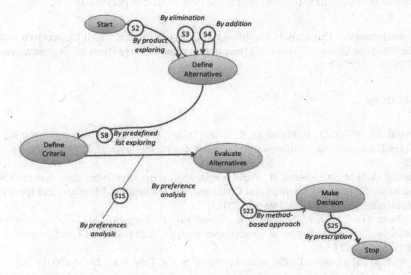

Fig. 3. Cost-value requirements prioritization approach chunk [17]

We did not find any existing method for the Issue-driven prioritization, so we envisage that we are going to create one. It could be based on the idea of identifying the features related to the issue, and then the dependencies for this feature, the features would be ranked depending on the dependency to the critical issue to solve.

According to SME process, we refined the strategy named "by prioritization" into two: Value-driven prioritization and Issue-driven prioritization.

6   Conclusions and Future Work

Organizations do not use a predefined existing method for QR management. In this paper we present the initial findings of our research investigating what industrial practices, from the agile methods, can be used for better management of QRs in agile software development.

In this paper, we present how we are using Situational Method Engineering (SME) to identify, complement and classify a portfolio of best practices for agile QR management. SME is used to construct methods that can be customized to fulfill the organization needs. The first results reported in this paper correspond to the initial set of intentions that are leading our method requirements elicitation. The guidelines should include best practices to fulfill four different intentions: *QR elicitation*, *specification*, *communication*, and *verification and validation*, and the three strategies for fulfilling the specification intention: *by refinement, documentation* and *prioritization*. So far, we identified two concrete strategies for the prioritization: the prioritization by urgency (issue-driven) and prioritization based on value (value-driven), and the paper includes the method chunk corresponding to the value-driven strategy.

We are in the initial stages of identification of different strategies to achieve identified intentions. Our future work is to select current strategies and create new ones to produce a complete set of chunks that will shape our best practices portfolio.

Acknowledgments.   This work is a result of the Q-Rapids project, which has received funding from the European Union's Horizon 2020 research and innovation program under grant agreement N° 732253.

References

1. Cristal, M., Wildt, D., Prikladnicki, R.: Usage of Scrum practices within a global company. In: IEEE International Conference on Global Software Engineering, ICGSE 2008, pp. 222–226
2. Hamed, A.M.M., Abushama, H.: Popular agile approaches in software development: review and analysis. In: 2013 International Conference on Computing, Electrical and Electronics Engineering (ICCEEE), pp. 160–166 (2013)
3. Matharu, G.S., Mishra, A., Singh, H., Upadhyay, P.: Empirical study of agile software development methodologies: a comparative analysis. ACM SIGSOFT Softw. Eng. Notes **40**(1), 1–6 (2015)
4. Fowler, M., Highsmith, J.: The agile manifesto. Softw. Dev. **9**(8), 28–35 (2001)

5. Nuseibeh, B., Easterbrook, S.: Requirements engineering: a roadmap. In: Proceedings of the Conference on the Future of Software Engineering, pp. 35–46 (2000)
6. Schön, E.M., Thomaschewski, J., Escalona, M.J.: Agile requirements engineering: a systematic literature review. Comput. Stand. Interfaces **49**, 79–91 (2017)
7. Ramesh, B., Cao, L., Baskerville, R.: Agile requirements engineering practices and challenges: an empirical study. Inform. Syst. J. **20**(5), 449–480 (2010)
8. Uusitalo, E.J., Komssi, M., Kauppinen, M., Davis, A.M.: Linking requirements and testing in practice. In: 16th IEEE International Requirements Engineering, RE 2008, pp. 265–270 (2008)
9. Inayat, I., Salim, S.S., Marczak, S., Daneva, M., Shamshirband, S.: A systematic literature review on agile requirements engineering practices and challenges. Comput. Hum. Behav. **51**, 915–929 (2015)
10. Qumer, A., Henderson-Sellers, B.: Construction of an agile software product-enhancement process by using an Agile Software Solution Framework (ASSF) and situational method engineering. In: Annual International Computer Software and Applications Conference (COMPSAC), pp. 539–542 (2007)
11. Ralyté, J., Rolland, C.: An assembly process model for method engineering. In: Dittrich, K.R., Geppert, A., Norrie, M.C. (eds.) CAiSE 2001. LNCS, vol. 2068, pp. 267–283. Springer, Heidelberg (2001). doi:10.1007/3-540-45341-5_18
12. Rolland, C., Prakash, N., Benjamen, A.: A multi-model view of process modelling. Requir. Eng. J. **4**(4), 169–187 (1999)
13. Ralyté, J., Maiden, N., Rolland, C., Deneckère, R.: Applying modular method engineering to validate and extend the RESCUE requirements process. In: Delcambre, L., Kop, C., Mayr, H.C., Mylopoulos, J., Pastor, O. (eds.) ER 2005. LNCS, vol. 3716, pp. 209–224. Springer, Heidelberg (2005). doi:10.1007/11568322_14
14. López, L., Costal, D., Ralyté, J., Franch, X., Méndez, L., Annosi, M.C.: OSSAP – a situational method for defining open source software adoption processes. In: Nurcan, S., Soffer, P., Bajec, M., Eder, J. (eds.) CAiSE 2016. LNCS, vol. 9694, pp. 524–539. Springer, Cham (2016). doi:10.1007/978-3-319-39696-5_32
15. Henderson-Sellers, B., Ralyté, J.: Situational method engineering: state-of-the-art review. J. Univ. Comput. Sci. **16**(3), 424–478 (2010)
16. Ralyté, J., Deneckère, R., Rolland, C.: Towards a generic model for situational method engineering. In: Eder, J., Missikoff, M. (eds.) CAiSE 2003. LNCS, vol. 2681, pp. 95–110. Springer, Heidelberg (2003). doi:10.1007/3-540-45017-3_9
17. Kornyshova, E., Deneckère, R., Rolland, C.: Method families concept: application to decision-making methods. In: Halpin, T., Nurcan, S., Krogstie, J., Soffer, P., Proper, E., Schmidt, R., Bider, I. (eds.) BPMDS/EMMSAD -2011. LNBIP, vol. 81, pp. 413–427. Springer, Heidelberg (2011). doi:10.1007/978-3-642-21759-3_30

MultiRefactor: Automated Refactoring to Improve Software Quality

Michael Mohan[✉] [iD] and Des Greer

Queen's University Belfast, Belfast, Northern Ireland, UK
{mmohan03,des.greer}@qub.ab.uk

Abstract. In this paper, a new approach is proposed for automated software maintenance. The tool is able to perform 26 different refactorings. It also contains a large selection of metrics to measure the impact of the refactorings on the software and six different search based optimization algorithms to improve the software. This tool contains both mono-objective and multi-objective search techniques for software improvement and is fully automated. The paper describes the various capabilities of the tool, the unique aspects of it, and also presents some research results from experimentation. The individual metrics are tested across five different codebases to deduce the most effective metrics for general quality improvement. It is found that the metrics that relate to more specific elements of the code are more useful for driving change in the search. The mono-objective genetic algorithm is also tested against the multi-objective algorithm to see how comparable the results gained are with three separate objectives. When comparing the best solutions of each individual objective the multi-objective approach generates suitable improvements in quality in less time, allowing for rapid maintenance cycles.

Keywords: Search Based Software Engineering · Automated maintenance · Refactoring tools · Multi-Objective optimization · Software metrics

1 Introduction

Search based optimization has been used extensively in various areas of engineering and in recent years has also been applied to software engineering. Search Based Software Engineering (SBSE) is an area of research that attempts to apply search heuristics to solve complex problems in software development [1]. Software maintenance is one of the more expensive parts of the software development cycle [2]. SBSE applied to maintenance, known as Search Based Software Maintenance (SBSM), is used to assist the manual aspects of maintaining a software project and minimize the time necessary to do so. To aid with this research various tools [3–11] have been used to assist with the refactoring of a software project. An increasing amount of SBSM research is looking at multi-objective techniques [12–20]. Many multi-objective search algorithms are built with genetic algorithms, as their ability to generate multiple possible solutions is suitable for a multi-objective approach. Instead of focusing on only one property, the multi-objective algorithm will be concerned with a number of different objectives.

© Springer International Publishing AG 2017
M. Felderer et al. (Eds.): PROFES 2017, LNCS 10611, pp. 556–572, 2017.
https://doi.org/10.1007/978-3-319-69926-4_46

The MultiRefactor tool uses refactorings to improve Java projects using metric functions to guide the search. Many of the other tools available have a limited selection of refactorings or metrics available to use. The effort has been made to equip the Multi-Refactor tool with a large range of available refactorings and metrics to choose from, in order to promote maximum configurability within the tool. MultiRefactor combines the ability to use a multi-objective approach with the more practical ability to improve the source code itself, while checking the semantics of the refactorings being applied so that the changes in the code are valid with respect to the application domain.

In order to assess the capabilities of the MultiRefactor approach, a set of experiments have been set up to compare different procedures available within the tool. Experiments have previously been conducted comparing the other metaheuristic searches [21], so the experimentation here focuses on the use of the genetic algorithms in the tool and aims to find out two things. The first aim is to test the available software metrics within the tool and discover which are more successful. Some metrics may be more useful than others in measuring the changes made by the available refactorings. These will be more helpful when trying to analyze the changes made to a solution and as such, a metric function made from these metrics may assist in creating a more prosperous solution. The second aim is to compare the mono-objective approach with the multi-objective search available and see whether using a multi-objective algorithm to automate maintenance of a software solution is as practical as using a mono-objective algorithm. We wish to test whether, in a fully automated solution, a multi-objective algorithm using similar settings can yield comparable results across all the objectives, and whether it is worth the time taken to do so. The following research questions have been formed to address these concerns, along with a corresponding set of hypotheses and null hypotheses for each factor investigated in **RQ2**:

RQ1: Which set of software metrics have the most variability when used with a mono-objective genetic algorithm to refactor software?

RQ2: Does a multi-objective refactoring approach give comparable results on all objectives to corresponding mono-objective refactoring runs?

H1: The overall objective improvements in the multi-objective searches are not significantly worse than the overall objective improvements in the mono-objective search.

H1$_0$: The overall objective improvements in the multi-objective search are significantly worse than the overall objective improvements in the mono-objective searches.

H2: The overall time taken to run the multi-objective search is no higher than the time taken to run any of the three mono-objective searches.

H2$_0$: The overall time taken to run the multi-objective searches is higher than time taken to run one of more of the three mono-objective searches.

The remaining sections go into more detail about the capabilities of the MultiRefactor approach and showcase its abilities with the set of experimental studies. Section 2 discusses the design of the tool as well as the refactorings, metrics and search techniques available. Section 3 explains the details of the experiments conducted. The results are presented in Sect. 4 and discussed in Sect. 5. Section 6 presents related literature within SBSE and with multi-objective techniques in SBSM. Finally, Sect. 7 gives the conclusion.

2 MultiRefactor

The MultiRefactor approach[1] is in common with those of Moghadam and O' Cinnéide [10] and Trifu et al. [7] in using the RECODER framework[2] to modify source code in Java programs. RECODER extracts a model of the code that can be used to analyze and modify the code before the changes are applied and written to file. The tool takes Java source code as input and will output the modified source code to a specified folder. The input must be fully compilable and must be accompanied by any necessary library files as compressed jar files. The numerous searches available in the tool have various input configurations that can affect the execution of the search. The refactorings and metrics used can also be specified. As such, the tool can be configured in a number of different ways to specify the particular task that you want to run. If desired, multiple tasks can be set to run one after the other.

A previous study [22] used the A-CMA [9] tool to experiment with different metric functions but needed to be modified to produce an output. The tool could only produce bytecode (likewise, the TrueRefactor [3] tool only modifies UML and Ouni et al.'s [17] approach only generates proposed lists of refactorings) so the MultiRefactor tool was developed in order to be a fully automated search-based refactoring tool that produces compilable, usable code as an output. The tool can therefore be used for research purposes or for maintaining actual projects, as demonstrated in Sect. 3 where open source projects are used for experimentation. Along with the Java code artifacts, the tool will produce an output file that gives information on the execution of the task. The output gives information about the parameters of the search executed, the metric values at the beginning and end of the search, and details about each refactoring applied. The metric configurations can be modified to include different weights and the direction of improvement of the metrics can be changed depending on the desired outcome. These configurations can be read in a number of ways including as text files or xml files. There are a few ways the metrics functions can be calculated. An overall metric value can be found using a weighted metric sum or Pareto dominance can be used to compare individual metrics within the functions. Figure 1 gives a brief overview of the process used in the MultiRefactor tool to generate refactored Java code.

---

[1] https://github.com/mmohan01/MultiRefactor.
[2] http://sourceforge.net/projects/recoder.

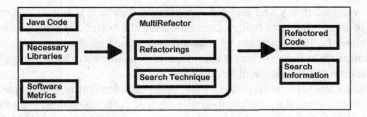

Fig. 1. Overview of the MultiRefactor process

2.1 Searches

MultiRefactor contains six different search options for automated maintenance, with three distinct metaheuristic search techniques available. For each search type there is a selection of configurable properties to signify how the search will run. For the searches used in this paper (the genetic algorithm and the multi-objective genetic algorithm) the details of how they are implemented and the configurable properties available are given below.

The *Genetic Algorithm* is based on the process of genetic replication. The representation used in MultiRefactor is based on the implementation used by Seng et al. [23] and further adapted by O' Keeffe and O' Cinnéide [24]. The search algorithm stores model information to represent multiple different genomes in a population, avoiding the expensive memory costs needed to store multiple different models. The initial population is constructed by applying a selection of random refactorings to the initial model to create a single genome, and repeating for the required amount. The crossover process uses the cut and splice technique, generating two offspring from two different parent genomes. A single, separate point is chosen for each parent in order to facilitate the technique. The point is chosen at random along the refactoring sequence in each of the parent solutions, with at least one refactoring present on each side. For each child, the two sets of refactorings are then mixed together. The first set of refactorings in one parent will be applied first and then the second set of refactorings from the other parent will be applied. Any inapplicable refactorings during this process will be left out although the child genome will still be able to be generated using the remaining refactorings. Mutation will choose from the new offspring and apply a single random refactoring to the end of the refactoring sequence for that genome. Crossover will be applied at least once during each generation and may happen more depending on the input parameters specified. Likewise, mutation will be applied a certain amount of times each generation depending on the parameters specified, or may not happen at all.

In order to choose parent genomes for crossover, a rank selection operator is used. Once the mutation process is complete for a generation, the new offspring is combined with the current population and the solutions are ordered according to fitness. The genetic algorithm can either store the entire final population of solutions resulting from the process, or only the fittest solution. The amount of generations specified will determine when the search terminates and the population size will determine how many genomes are generated during initialization and how many will survive each generation.

The crossover probability and mutation probability (between 0 and 1) determine the likeliness of these processes being executed during the search. The refactoring range will determine the initial amount of refactorings applied to the genomes during the initialization process. For each initial solution, a random amount of refactorings between one and the refactoring range will be chosen.

The *Multi-Objective Genetic Algorithm* is largely identical to the simple genetic algorithm, and contains the same configuration options (although it must store the whole population when finished). The algorithm is an adaptation of the NSGA-II [25] algorithm and as such, differs mostly in how the fitness is calculated. The selection operator used is the binary tournament operator, in order to avoid the need to rely on ranks during selection. The multi-objective algorithm allows the user to choose multiple metric functions as separate objectives to guide the search. The genomes in the population will then be sorted using a non-dominated approach, allowing each objective to be considered separately. Unlike the approach used by Ouni et al. [17], the refactorings used will be checked for semantic coherence as part of the search, and will be applied automatically, eliminating the need to check and apply the refactorings manually and ensuring the process is fully automated. There is also a many-objective search available in the tool to handle problems with more than three objectives.

2.2 Refactorings

The refactorings used in the tool are mostly based on Fowler's list of refactorings [26], and consist of 26 field-level, method-level and class-level refactorings, as listed in Table 1. Each refactoring will initially deduce whether a program element can be refactored. It will make all the relevant semantic checks and return true or false to reflect whether it is applicable as a refactoring and whether the code will be able to compile after it is applied. The checks applied will depend on the refactoring, and are important in order to exclude elements that are not applicable for that refactoring. These checks, as well as the refactoring process itself, ensure that the refactorings chosen are behavior preserving, and that the program will still be compilable after the refactorings are applied to the solution. The RECODER framework allows the tool to apply the changes to the element in the model. This may consist of a single change or, as in the case of the more complex refactorings, may include a number of individual changes to the model. Specific changes applied with the RECODER framework consist of either adding an element to a parent element, removing an element from a parent element, or replacing one element with another in the model. The refactoring itself will be constructed using these specific model changes.

In some cases new elements will be created for use in the refactoring (for instance, new imports may need to be created when moving an element to a new class), and where possible, these will be constructed from existing elements to minimize the potential for issues. The refactorings can be reversed to undo the changes made in the last instance of the refactoring. This allows the hill climbing and simulated annealing searches to check neighboring refactorings from the current state and measure their impact on the program, before deciding which one to use. For some refactorings, choices have to be made in relation to how specifically the refactoring is applied. The Move Field Down and Move Method Down refactorings involve moving program elements down to a sub class. Here, the subclass to be used needs to be chosen before the refactoring is applied. Likewise, the Extract Subclass refactoring involves picking a subset of the elements of a class to extract into a new sub class. Here the elements to be moved will need to be chosen beforehand.

Table 1. Available refactorings in MultiRefactor tool

Field level	Method level	Class level
Increase Field Visibility	Increase Method Visibility	Make Class Final
Decrease Field Visibility	Decrease Method Visibility	Make Class Non Final
Make Field Final	Make Method Final	Make Class Abstract
Make Field Non Final	Make Method Non Final	Make Class Concrete
Make Field Static	Make Method Static	Extract Subclass
Make Field Non Static	Make Method Non Static	Collapse Hierarchy
Move Field Down	Move Method Down	Remove Class
Move Field Up	Move Method Up	Remove Interface
Remove Field	Remove Method	

The *Increase/Decrease Visibility* refactorings change a field or method declaration up or down one level between public, protected, package and private visibility (where an increase moves towards private and a decrease moves towards public). The *Make Final/Non Final* refactorings will either apply or remove the final keyword from a field, method or class declaration. Likewise, the *Make Static/Non Static* refactorings are concerned with added or removing the static keyword from a global field or method declaration. Also, *Make Class Abstract/Concrete* will add or remove the abstract keyword from a class declaration. The *Move Down/Up* refactorings will either move the global field or method declaration to its immediate super class or to one of its available sub classes. *Extract Subclass* will choose a selection of local field and/or method declarations from a class that relate to each other as a distinct unit, and will move them to a newly created sub class. *Collapse Hierarchy* is applied by taking all the elements of a class (except any existing constructors for the class) and moving them up into the super class. It will then remove the class from the hierarchy. The *Remove* refactorings will remove the element related to that type of refactoring.

2.3 Metrics

The metrics in the tool are used to measure the current state of a program and deduce whether an applied refactoring has had a positive or negative impact. Due to the multi-objective capabilities of MultiRefactor, the metrics can be measured as separate objectives to be more precise in measuring their effect on a program. A number of the metrics available in the tool are adapted from the list of metrics in the QMOOD [27] and CK/MOOSE [28] metrics suites. Table 2 lists the 23 metrics currently available in the tool and the metrics not adapted from elsewhere are described below.

Table 2. Available metrics in MultiRefactor tool

QMOOD based metrics	CK based metrics	Others
Class Design Size	Weighted Methods Per Class	Abstractness
Number Of Hierarchies	Number Of Children	Abstract Ratio
Average Number Of Ancestors		Static Ratio
Data Access Metric		Final Ratio
Direct Class Coupling		Constant Ratio
Cohesion Among Methods		Inner Class Ratio
Aggregation		Referenced Methods Ratio
Functional Abstraction		Visibility Ratio
Number Of Polymorphic Methods		Lines Of Code
Class Interface Size		Number Of Files
Number Of Methods		

Abstractness measures the ratio of interfaces in a project over the overall amount of classes. *Abstract Ratio* gives the average ratio of abstract methods (as well as the class itself if it is abstract) per class. *Static Ratio* and *Final Ratio* give the average ratios of static and final elements per class (static amount looks at classes and methods, whereas final amount also looks at fields), and *Constant Ratio* calculates the average ratio of elements (classes, methods and global fields) that are both static and final pre class. *Inner Class Ratio* calculates the ratio of the amount of inner classes over the amount of classes in a project. *Referenced Methods Ratio* finds the average ratio of inherited methods referenced per class. In each class, the metric measures the amount of distinct external methods (methods defined outside the current class) referenced amongst the methods of the class. For each class, the ratio of the amount of these methods that are inherited by the class over the amount referenced is calculated. *Visibility Ratio* calculates an average visibility ratio per class. In a class, each method and global field declaration (as well as the class itself) is given a visibility value, where a private member has a value of 0 and a public member has a value of 1. The visibility ratio for that class will calculate the accumulated visibility values over the amount of elements. The smaller this is, the more inaccessible the elements of the project are. Finally, *Lines Of Code* gets the overall amount of lines of code in a project and *Number Of Files* counts the amount of Java files in a project.

3   Experimentation

Five open source programs are used in the experimentation to ensure a variety of different domains are tested. The programs range in size from relatively small to medium sized, as shown in Table 3. These programs were chosen as they have all been used in previous SBSM studies and so there is an increased ability to compare the results and also because they promote different software structures and sizes. The source code and necessary libraries for all of the programs are available to download in the GitHub repository for the MultiRefactor tool. The experiments are run on a PC using an Intel Core i7 CPU and with 8 GB of RAM. The experimentation is split into two parts. The first experiment measures the effect of each individual metric available on a range of inputs using the mono-objective genetic algorithm. The second experiment compares the more effective metrics in a mono-objective set up against a multi-objective approach. In order to choose configuration parameters for the genetic algorithms used, trial and error is used to find the most effective settings. First, the crossover and mutation probabilities are compared using a baseline metric and input. The largest input, JHotDraw, is used with a metric assumed to be volatile due to it being directly related to the increase/ decrease visibility refactorings, visibility ratio. Nine different tasks are used to compare crossover and mutation probabilities of 0.3, 0.5 and 0.8. Each task is run five times to get an average value. As shown in Fig. 2, the most improved configuration has a mutation value of 0.8 and a crossover value of 0.2.

Table 3. Java programs used in experimentation

Name	LOC	Classes
JSON 1.1	2,196	12
Mango	3,470	78
Beaver 0.9.11	6,493	70
Apache XML-RPC 2.0	11.616	79
JHotDraw 5.3	27,824	241

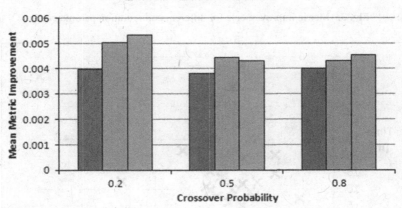

Fig. 2. Mean metric improvement values with different crossover and mutation probabilities

Next, the other configuration parameters are compared using these mutation and crossover values to find the best tradeoff between software improvement and time taken. 27 different tasks are set up to compare different combinations of generation amounts, population sizes and refactoring ranges. The generation amounts tested are 50, 100 and 200. The refactoring ranges used are likewise and the population sizes used are 10, 50 and 100. Figure 3 shows the metric improvement values for each permutation of the generation, population size and refactoring range genetic algorithm settings. Figure 4 compares them against the time taken to run them. As shown in Fig. 4, one configuration stands out as having a larger increase in quality without having a similar increase in necessary time. This configuration with 100 generations, a refactoring range of 50 and a population size of 50 is used for the experimentation. The final settings are shown in Table 4.

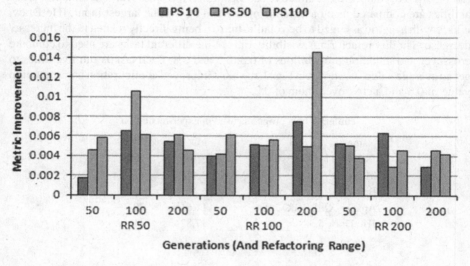

Fig. 3. Metric improvements for different configuration parameters

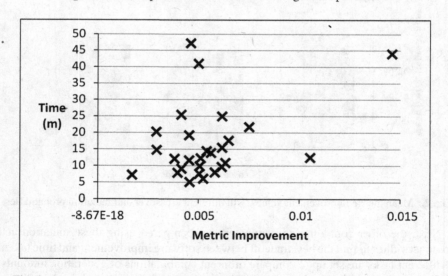

Fig. 4. Improvements mapped against time taken for different configuration parameters

Table 4. Genetic algorithm configuration settings

Configuration parameter	Value
Crossover Probability	0.2
Mutation Probability	0.8
Generations	100
Refactoring Range	50
Population Size	50

In the first experiment, each metric is run as an individual fitness function with a genetic algorithm using the configuration parameters outlined in Table 4. The metrics are run with each of the input programs five times, giving an overall average improvement value. The average values are then compared for each metric to find the most volatile metrics with the available refactorings in the tool. In the second experiment, a set of metric functions are constructed using the results from the first, by excluding the metrics that have the least effect. The relevant metrics are split into three functions in order to be used as separate objectives in a multi-objective genetic algorithm. To compare the multi-objective approach with a mono-objective analogue, the three objectives are used as separate metric functions in different runs of the mono-objective algorithm. Each objective with the mono-objective search is run six times for each of the five inputs, giving 30 runs of the search. Likewise, the multi-objective genetic algorithm with the three objectives is run six times for each input. Therefore, across all four different search approaches, there are 120 tasks run.

For each objective, the mono-objective genetic algorithm is run using the configuration parameters from Table 4 for each input, and the average metric improvement is calculated for the top solution across the different inputs. For the purposes of this study, we are not interested in whether the multi-objective approach can generate a single solution with comparable results across all three objectives, but in whether each separate objective can be comparable. Therefore, the best solutions in the final population for each individual objective are found and the average improvements are calculated across the different inputs. In order to aid in finding the top scores for each objective in the final population of the multi-objective tasks, the search has been modified in this experiment to update the relevant results files to state that they contain the highest score for the corresponding objective, circumventing the need to manually check the scores in each solution.

The metric changes are calculated using a normalization function. The function finds the amount that a particular metric has changed in relation to its initial value at the beginning of the task. These values can then be accumulated depending on the direction of improvement of the metric and the weights given to provide an overall value for the metric function or objective. A negative change in the metric will be reflected by a decrease in the overall function/objective value. In the case that an increase in the metric denotes a negative change, the overall value will still decrease, ensuring that a larger value represents a better metric value regardless of the direction of improvement. For the experiments used in this paper, no weighting is applied to any of the metrics used. The directions of improvement used for each metric is defined in Table 5, where a plus indicates a metric that will improve with an increase and a minus indicates a metric that will improve with a decrease. Equation 1 defines the normalization function used, where C_m is the current metric value and I_m is the initial metric value. W_m is the applied weighting for the metric and D is a binary constant that represents the direction of improvement of the metric. n represents the number of metrics used in the function.

$$\sum_{m=o}^{n} D.W_m \left(\frac{C_m}{I_m} - 1 \right)$$

(1)

Table 5. Average metric gains

Metrics	Direction	Average metric gain
Class Design Size	+	0
Number Of Hierarchies	+	0
Number Of Files	+	0
Average Number Of Ancestors	+	0.0009662
Number Of Children	+	0.0009662
Aggregation	+	0.0028846
Functional Abstraction	+	0.00878788
Number Of Polymorphic Methods	+	0.00640564
Abstractness	+	0.0034176
Inner Class Ratio	+	0.0028846
Lines Of Code	−	0.0034388
Data Access Metric	+	0.07267708
Direct Class Coupling	−	0.011253
Cohesion Among Methods	+	0.0335982
Number Of Methods	−	0.047224824
Weighted Methods Per Class	−	0.07551
Abstract Ratio	+	0.06006748
Referenced Methods Ratio	+	0.02487444
Visibility Ratio	−	0.02984252
Class Interface Size	+	0.10246376
Static Ratio	−	0.17167356
Final Ratio	+	0.60217196
Constant Ratio	+	0.24485396

4   Results

Table 5 gives the average quality gains conceived by each individual metric across all of the inputs. They are grouped into metrics that have a similar level of volatility. Three of the metrics, Class Design Size, Number Of Hierarchies and Number Of Files, showed no improvement at all. These metrics are more abstract, relating to the project design and class measurements as opposed to other metrics measuring more low level attributes like methods and fields. The most volatile metrics captured in the bottom group all relate to more low level aspects of the code. The metric functions used in experiment two were taken from the metric groups derived in Table 5. The least volatile metrics from the top two groups were left out and the remaining metrics were split into three individual objectives to be used in a multi-objective setup by using the three remaining groupings of metrics to each represent an objective. These particular groupings are informed by the average quality gains, with similarly volatile metrics being grouped together, although these groupings are used more as example objectives for the current experiment. These three groups of metrics may be combined to represent an overall improvement function for a generalized measure of software quality, with the average quality gain values across numerous different input programs informing its composition. Table 6 gives the list of metrics associated with each objective.

Table 6. Individual objectives derived from metric experimentation

Objective 1	Objective 2	Objective 3
Class Interface Size	Data Access Metric	Aggregation
Static Ratio	Direct Class Coupling	Functional Abstraction
Final Ratio	Cohesion Among Methods	Number Of Polymorphic Methods
Constant Ratio	Number Of Methods	Abstractness
	Weighted Methods Per Class	Inner Class Ratio
	Abstract Ratio	Lines Of Code
	Referenced Methods Ratio	
	Visibility Ratio	

Figure 5 and Table 7 compare the average objective values with the separate mono-objective runs against the values generated with the multi-objective approach. The values for objective one were the most disparate with the largest ranges of results. The mono-objective approach for objective 1 and objective 2 yielded improvements 1.2 and 1.3 times greater than the multi-objective approach, respectively. The other objective was slightly better with the multi-objective approach, though both improvement values where relatively small. The objective values for the two search approaches with the first and second objective were compared using a two-tailed Wilcoxon rank-sum test (for unpaired data sets) with a 95% confidence level ($\alpha = 5\%$). The multi-objective values were found to not be significantly lower than the mono-objective values in either case.

The execution times for the two approaches were also compared to analyze how much more time is needed in the multi-objective approach to handle the three objectives simultaneously. Figures 6 and 7 compare the overall times taken for the mono-objective and multi-objective approaches. In Fig. 6, the overall times taken for each individual objective of the mono-objective search are compared with the overall time taken to run the three objectives in the multi-objective approach. Figure 7 compares the overall time taken to run all three objectives in the mono-objective approach against the multi-objective counterpart. It stacks the times for each separate objective in the mono-objective search to show the influence of each one on the time. The average time taken for the mono-objective algorithm to run for each objective was 3 h, 46 min and 17 s. For the

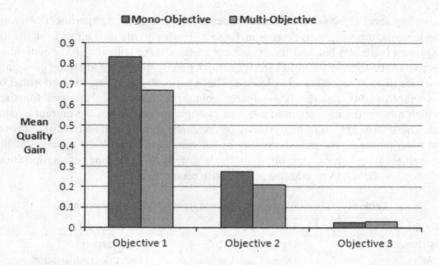

Fig. 5. Mean metric gains for each objective in a mono-objective and multi-objective setup

Table 7. Individual objective metric gains for mono-objective and multi-objective optimization

	Objective 1	Objective 2	Objective 3
Mono-Objective	0.8335831	0.2732774	0.028064733
Multi-Objective	0.672707033	0.210753367	0.028501433

multi-objective approach to run for all the inputs it took 3 h, 14 min and 49 s, a reduction against the mono-objective average of 31 min and 28 s. For the mono-objective approach to run the inputs for all three objectives would have taken over 11 h, meaning 71.3% of time is saved running one multi-objective search against running three separate mono-objective searches.

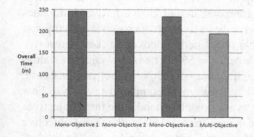

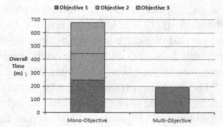

Fig. 6. Overall time taken to run each objective of the mono-objective approach and the multi-objective approach

Fig. 7. Overall time taken for each approach, with each objective of the mono-objective approach stacked on top of each other

5 Discussion

Of the metrics tested, three of the more abstract metrics showed no improvement. Although class level refactorings do exist in the MultiRefactor tool, they will be less likely to be applied due to the conditions necessary to apply them without modifying the program functionality. Likewise, the most volatile metrics all relate to more low level aspects of the code. It seems that these types of software metric may be more useful for driving change in an automated refactoring system due to the increased likelihood that structure level refactorings will be able to affect them.

To address **RQ2** and the answer the hypotheses constructed, statistical tests were used to decide whether the data sets were significantly different. While the other objective was better with the multi-objective approach, the statistical test was run for the first and second objectives where the multi-objective approach was worse. The values in the multi-objective approach were not significantly worse than in the mono-objective approach for either objective, thus rejecting the null hypothesis $H1_0$. In none of the three cases did the multi-objective approach take longer to run than the mono-objective approach, thus rejecting the null hypothesis $H2_0$. The experiments conducted suggest that this fully automated approach may be feasible and can allow for multiple separate objectives to be considered in a single run within an acceptable amount of time, although the improvement of a subset of these objectives may take a hit.

6 Related Work

The term SBSE was first coined by Harman and Jones in 2001 [1]. Further research in the area was identified, as well as open problems in 2007 [29]. Clarke et al. [30] discussed ways to apply metaheuristic search techniques to software engineering problems and proposed other aspects of software engineering to apply them to in 2003. There are literature reviews on the subject [31, 32]. Numerous tools have been proposed that can automate the maintenance process of software refactoring to some extent, although many are limited, and not all are fully automated. Many of the proposed tools isolate design smells in the code using detection rules [3–8]. Most of the tools using this approach have focused on a limited amount of detection rules to isolate certain types of design smell, due to the uncertainty involved in constructing these metric based detection rules. Other tools use metrics to determine ideal refactorings to make to the code that will improve the quality and remove design smells as a by-product of the process [9–11].

More recent research has explored the use of multi-objective techniques. White et al. [12] used a multi-objective approach to attempt to find a tradeoff between the functionality of a pseudorandom number generator and the power consumption necessary to use it. De Souza et al. [13] investigated the human competitiveness of SBSE techniques in four areas of software engineering, and used mono-objective and multi-objective genetic algorithms in the study. Ouni et al. [14] created an approach to measure semantics preservation in a software program when searching for refactoring options to improve the structure, by using the NSGA-II search. Ouni et al. [15] then explored the potential of using development refactoring history to aid in refactoring a software project by using

NSGA-II. Ouni et al. [17] also expanded upon the code smells correction approach of Kessentini et al. [16] by replacing the genetic algorithm used with NSGA-II. Mkaouer et al. [18] experimented with combining quality measurement with robustness using NSGA-II to create solutions that could withstand volatile software environments. Mkaouer et al. [19, 20] also used the successor algorithm to NSGA-II, NSGA-III, to experiment with automated maintenance. These studies only suggest refactoring sequences to be applied, and do not check the applicability of the refactorings.

7   Conclusion

In this paper we have presented the MultiRefactor approach and associated automated refactoring tool containing both mono-objective and multi-objective search techniques. Six separate search techniques are available as well as 23 different metrics and 26 refactorings. The tool works with Java source code (as well as accompanying library files) as input and is a fully automated tool that can generate refactored, compilable Java code as an output, along with information about the refactoring process. The tool is highly configurable, allowing the user to set up different tasks with different sets of metrics to use and different refactorings to activate. The available search techniques have numerous configurable properties to be set, influencing how the search process will work. No other known refactoring tool currently allows the user to use multi-objective techniques to improve the software without having to manually apply the refactorings.

Two experiments were run to test various aspects of the approach. The configuration parameters of the genetic algorithm were tested to analyze the effect that they can have on the refactoring process and to deduce what settings can have a better tradeoff between metric improvement and time taken. Each of the available metrics were then tested with the genetic algorithm across a number of real world, open source Java programs to find the least volatile metrics interacting with the available refactorings. It was found that the more low level metrics produced greater average improvements compared to the more abstract, class level metrics. The results of this experiment were then used to construct metric functions to compare a mono-objective refactoring approach against a multi-objective approach. The more volatile metrics were split into three separate objectives to see if the multi-objective approach could generate comparable results to the mono-objective counterparts. The individual mono-objective approaches gave better results for two out of the three objectives but the multi-objective approach managed to generate suitable improvements for all of the objectives and took less time than each mono-objective approach, with the single multi-objective run taking 71% less time than the three combined mono-objective runs.

Acknowledgments. The research for this paper contributes to a PhD project funded by the EPSRC grant EP/M506400/1.

References

1. Harman, M., Jones, B.F.: Search-based software engineering. Inf. Softw. Technol. **43**, 833–839 (2001). doi:10.1016/S0950-5849(01)00189-6
2. Bell, D.: Software Engineering: A Programming Approach. Addison Wesley, Boston (2000)
3. Griffith, I., Wahl, S., Izurieta, C.: TrueRefactor: an automated refactoring tool to improve legacy system and application comprehensibility. In: 24th International Conference on Computer Application in Industry and Engineering, ISCA 2011 (2011)
4. Li, H., Thompson, S.: Refactoring support for modularity maintenance in Erlang. In: Proceedings of the 2010 10th IEEE Working Conference on Source Code Analysis and Manipulation, SCAM 2010, pp. 157–166. IEEE (2010)
5. Di Penta, M.: Evolution doctor: a framework to control software system evolution. In: 9th European Conference on Software Maintenance and Reengineering, CSMR 2005, pp. 280–283. IEEE (2005)
6. Tsantalis, N., Chaikalis, T., Chatzigeorgiou, A.: JDeodorant: identification and removal of type-checking bad smells. In: 12th European Conference on Software Maintenance and Reengineering, CSMR 2008, pp. 329–331 (2008)
7. Trifu, A., Seng, O., Genssler, T.: Automated design flaw correction in object-oriented systems. In: 8th European Conference on Software Maintenance and Reengineering, CSMR 2004, pp. 174–183. IEEE (2004)
8. Dudziak, T., Wloka, J.: Tool-Supported Discovery And Refactoring Of Structural Weaknesses In Code (2002)
9. Koc, E., Ersoy, N., Andac, A., Camlidere, Z.S., Cereci, I., Kilic, H.: An empirical study about search-based refactoring using alternative multiple and population-based search techniques. In: Gelenbe, E., Lent, R., Sakellari, G. (eds.) Computer and Information Sciences II, pp. 59–66. Springer, London (2011). doi:10.1007/978-1-4471-2155-8_7
10. Moghadam, I.H., Cinnéide, M.Ó.: Code-Imp: a tool for automated search-based refactoring. In: 4th Workshop on Refactoring Tools, WRT 2011, pp. 41–44 (2011)
11. Fatiregun, D., Harman, M., Hierons, R.M.: Evolving transformation sequences using genetic algorithms. In: IEEE International Workshop on Source Code Analysis and Manipulation, SCAM 2004, pp. 65–74. IEEE Computer Society (2004)
12. White, D.R., Clark, J., Jacob, J., Poulding, S.: Searching for resource-efficient programs: low-power pseudorandom number generators. In: Proceedings of the 10th Annual Conference on Genetic and Evolutionary Computation, GECCO 2008, pp. 1775–1782 (2008)
13. De Souza, J.T., Maia, C.L., De Freitas, F.G., Coutinho, D.P.: The human competitiveness of search based software engineering. In: 2nd International Symposium on Search Based Software Engineering, SSBSE 2010, pp. 143–152. IEEE (2010)
14. Ouni, A., Kessentini, M., Sahraoui, H., Hamdi, M.S.: Search-based refactoring: towards semantics preservation. In: 28th IEEE International Conference on Software Maintenance, ICSM 2012, pp. 347–356 (2012)
15. Ouni, A., Kessentini, M., Sahraoui, H.: Search-based refactoring using recorded code changes. In: Proceedings of the 2013 17th European Conference on Software Maintenance and Reengineering, CSMR 2013, pp. 221–230 (2013)
16. Kessentini, M., Kessentini, W., Erradi, A.: Example-based design defects detection and correction. In: 2011 IEEE 19th International Conference on Program Comprehension, ICPC 2011, pp. 1–32 (2011)
17. Ouni, A., Kessentini, M., Sahraoui, H., Boukadoum, M.: Maintainability defects detection and correction: a multi-objective approach. Autom. Softw. Eng. **20**, 47–79 (2013). doi: 10.1007/s10515-011-0098-8

18. Mkaouer, W., Kessentini, M., Bechikh, S., et al.: Software refactoring under uncertainty: a robust multi-objective approach. In: Proceedings of the Companion Publication of the 2014 Annual Conference on Genetic and Evolutionary Computation, GECCO 2014 (2014)
19. Mkaouer, W., Kessentini, M., Bechikh S, et al.: High dimensional search-based software engineering: finding tradeoffs among 15 objectives for automating software refactoring using NSGA-III. In: Proceedings of the 2014 Annual Conference on Genetic and Evolutionary Computation, GECCO 2014 (2014)
20. Mkaouer, W., Kessentini, M., Kontchou, P., et al.: Many-objective software remodularization using NSGA-III. ACM Trans. Softw. Eng. Methodol. 24(3) (2015). Article No. 17
21. O'Keeffe, M., Cinnéide, M.Ó.: Search-based software maintenance. In: Proceedings of the 10th European Conference on Software Maintenance and Reengineering, CSMR 2006, pp. 251–260 (2006)
22. Mohan, M., Greer, D., McMullan, P.: Technical debt reduction using search based automated refactoring. J. Syst. Softw. 120, 183–194 (2016). doi:10.1016/j.jss.2016.05.019
23. Seng, O., Stammel, J., Burkhart, D.: Search-based determination of refactorings for improving the class structure of object-oriented systems. In: Proceedings of the 8th Annual Conference on Genetic and Evolutionary Computation, GECCO 2006, pp. 1909–1916 (2006)
24. O'Keeffe, M., Cinnéide, M.Ó.: Getting the most from search-based refactoring. In: Proceedings of the 9th Annual Conference on Genetic and Evolutionary Computation, GECCO 2007, pp. 1114–1120 (2007)
25. Deb, K., Pratap, A., Agarwal, S., Meyarivan, T.: A fast and elitist multiobjective genetic algorithm: NSGA-II. IEEE Trans. Evol. Comput. 6, 182–197 (2002). doi: 10.1109/4235.996017
26. Fowler, M.: Refactoring: Improving The Design Of Existing Code. Pearson Education, Fort Collins (1999)
27. Bansiya, J., Davis, C.G.: A hierarchical model for object-oriented design quality assessment. IEEE Trans. Softw. Eng. 28, 4–17 (2002). doi:10.1109/32.979986
28. Chidamber, S.R., Kemerer, C.F.: A metrics suite for object oriented design. IEEE Trans. Softw. Eng. 20, 476–493 (1994)
29. Harman, M.: The current state and future of search based software engineering. In: Future of Software Engineering, FOSE 2007, pp 342–357 (2007)
30. Clarke, J., Dolado, J.J., Harman, M., et al.: Reformulating software engineering as a search problem. IEE Proc. Softw. 150, 1–25 (2003)
31. Harman, M., Mansouri, S.A., Zhang, Y.: Search based software engineering: trends, techniques and applications. ACM Comput. Surv. 45, 1–64 (2012). doi: 10.1145/0000000.0000000
32. Harman, M., McMinn, P., de Souza, J.T., Yoo, S.: Search Based Software Engineering: Techniques, Taxonomy, Tutorial. In: Meyer, B., Nordio, M. (eds.) LASER 2008-2010. LNCS, vol. 7007, pp. 1–59. Springer, Heidelberg (2012). doi:10.1007/978-3-642-25231-0_1

Transition from Plan Driven to SAFe®: Periodic Team Self-Assessment

Mohammad Abdur Razzak[1(✉)], John Noll[2], Ita Richardson[1],
Clodagh Nic Canna[3], and Sarah Beecham[1]

[1] Lero, The Irish Software Research Centre, University of Limerick, Limerick, Ireland
{abdur.razzak,ita.richardson,sarah.beecham}@lero.ie
[2] University of East London, University Way, London E16 2RD, UK
j.noll@uel.ac.uk
[3] Ocuco Ltd., Blanchardstown Corporate Park, Dublin D15 N5DX, Ireland
clodagh.niccanna@ocuco.com

Abstract. Context: How to adopt, scale and tailor agile methods depends on several factors such as the size of the organization, business goals, operative model, and needs. The Scaled Agile Framework (SAFe®) was developed to support organizations to scale agile practices across the enterprise.

Problem: Early adopters of SAFe® tend to be large multi-national enterprises who report that the adoption of SAFe® has led to significant productivity and quality gains. However, little is known about whether these benefits translate to small to medium sized enterprises (SMEs).

Method: As part of a longitudinal study of an SME transitioning to SAFe we ask, *to what extent are SAFe® practices adopted at the team level?* We targeted all team members and administrated a mixed method survey in February, 2017 and in July, 2017 to identify and evaluate the adoption rate of SAFe® practices.

Results: Initially in Quarter 1, teams were struggling with PI/Release health and Technical health throughout the organization as most of the teams were transitioning from plan-driven to SAFe®. But, during the transition period in Quarter 3, we observed discernible improvements in different areas of SAFe practice adoption.

Conclusion: The observed improvement might be due to teams merely becoming more familiar with the practices over-time. However, management had also made some structural changes to the teams that may account for the change.

Keywords: SAFe · Scrum · Inter-team coordination · Global software engineering · metrics · Process assessment · Software process improvement

1 Introduction

Software development is still driven by *Infinite Diversity in Infinite Combinations* [1]. As a consequence, practitioners ask themselves *why they need to adopt* a

© Springer International Publishing AG 2017
M. Felderer et al. (Eds.): PROFES 2017, LNCS 10611, pp. 573–585, 2017.
https://doi.org/10.1007/978-3-319-69926-4_47

practice, and *how to scale* a practice. This leads to two challenges: first, recognising *the purpose of a practice* and second, *scaling practices*. Scaling agile continues to be a challenge in software development where the associated growth calls for strong coordination among teams as well as within the project [2–4]. Scaling agile in globally distributed projects adds to the complexity [5] since *"Distance"* creates new challenges for successful scaling of agile practices.

A number of frameworks have been proposed for scaling agile across the enterprise and the Scaled Agile Framework (SAFe®) is one of the most adopted of these models according to the Annual State of Agile Report [6]. SAFe® has gained rapid attention amongst practitioners and is an important choice for organisations scaling agile development. Yet, the literature indicates that SAFe® is aimed at large-scale organizations. However, small-medium-enterprises (SMEs) are also interested in SAFe® as it provides an enterprise roadmap for adopting agile. As the adoption of SAFe® increases, little research exists to identify how SAFe® is adopted in SMEs. We conducted a study to measure the adoption of SAFe® recommended practices at the team level over time, in order to address the question *How can the Scaled Agile Framework be implemented in an SME?*

This paper is organised as follows: Sect. 2 provides a background to scaling agile frameworks, Sect. 3 presents the method we used in our empirical study, while Sect. 4 summarises our key findings and Sect. 5 discusses the implications of these results. Section 6 gives some conclusions to the study.

2   Background

Agile Scaling Frameworks. Scaling agile covers the movement from a few agile teams to multiple agile development teams, where the number of teams can be in the hundreds [7]. Scott Ambler [7] pointed out several factors that need to be considered when scaling agile such as team size, geographical distribution, entrenched culture, system complexity, legacy systems, regulatory compliance, organizational distribution, governance and enterprise focus. In general, productivity and quality are the two main concerns of any organization when adopting a scaling agile paradigm.

The choice of scaling agile framework which a company adopts or how the framework is tailored will depend on the organization's size or on "what works" based on their own business goals, operative model, and needs. The Agile Scaling Knowledgebase (ASK)[1] developed a matrix of different Agile frameworks namely *Scrum-of-Scrum (SoS)*[2], *Large Scale Scrum (LeSS)*[3], *Scaled Agile Framework (SAFe)*[4], *Disciplined Agile Delivery (DAD)*[5], *Spotify Model*[6], *Nexus*[7], and *Scrum*

---

[1] http://www.agilescaling.org/home.html.

[2] https://www.agilealliance.org/glossary/scrum-of-scrums/.

[3] https://less.works.

[4] http://www.scaledagileframework.com.

[5] http://www.disciplinedagiledelivery.com.

[6] http://blog.crisp.se/2012/11/14/henrikkniberg/scaling-agile-at-spotify.

[7] https://www.scrum.org/resources/nexus-guide.

at Scale[8]. This matrix shows that SAFe®, launched in 2012 by Dean Leffing-well [8] focuses on large enterprises and takes a scaled approach to agile adoption.

In comparison to (SAFe®), the other scaling agile frameworks (e.g.; SoS, LeSS, Nexus, Spotify) provide few artefacts, roles, and events in addition to Scrum. SAFe® provides more roles, events, artefacts and practices compared to other frameworks that enables SAFe® to scale on an organization level. The 11th Annual State of Agile report [6] reported that, SAFe® is the most used scaling method used by 28% respondents. In contrast, LeSS, DAD, and Nexus are reported to have a significantly lower take-up rate.

Scaled Agile Framework (SAFe®). SAFe® is essentially a container for several existing agile approaches that is scalable and modular, and is primarily developed for organizing and managing agile practices in large enterprises. These qualities allow an organization to apply SAFe® in a way that suits their needs. Early adopters of SAFe® report that the application of the practices contained in this framework led to significant productivity and quality improvements [9]. The literature also claims that SAFe® adoption is widespread including sectors such as manufacturing, software, and financial services [5,9–11]. SAFe® 4.0 is organized into four layers: (1) *Portfolio* – Funding and coordinating programs, (2) *Value Stream* – Used when a single Agile Release Train (ART) cannot deliver the full solution, (3) *Program* – Contains 5–12 teams working towards a common goal, and (4) *Team* – Teams, which practice Scrum and/or eXtreme Programming and/or Kanban.

In SAFe®, all teams are part of the Agile Release Train (ART) and ARTs are the central construct of the program level. Teams are collectively responsible for defining, building and testing software in fixed-length iterations and releases. The team events (Backlog Refinement, Sprint Planning, Sprint Review) are an integral part of SAFe® and help to reduce coordination overhead between teams. These teams typically consist of 7–9 members and teams operate on identical cadence and iteration lengths in order to provide better integration among teams [11]. But, adoption of only Scrum at the team level could lead to additional problems in task synchronization. To resolve this issue, SAFe® introduces the *Release Planning* meeting to synchronize team tasks after every five iterations [8]. All teams on an ART are synchronized and integrated via common iterations that provide a valuable increment of new functionality. At the end of each iteration, the team perform a system demo for ART integration.

3   Methods

The Case Organization. The company we studied, Ocuco, is a medium-sized Irish-based software company that develops practice and lab management software for the optical industry. Ocuco employs approximately seventy staff members in its software development organization, including support and management staff. Ocuco's annual sales approach € 20 million from customers across the British Isles, continental Europe, Scandinavia, North America, and China.

---

[8] https://www.scruminc.com/scrum-scale-case-modularity/.

Data Collection. As part of a company-wide longitudinal study, we administered a SAFe self-assessment survey[9] to 70 team members in February, 2017 and in July, 2017. However, before the actual survey, two of the authors took a participant-observer role by sitting in on each team's Scrum "ceremonies." One of us observed TeamA, daily, from January, 2016 to March, 2017, and TeamB, from May, 2017 to June, 2017; another of us observed TeamC, daily, from November, 2015 to July, 2016. We observed daily standups, sprint planning meetings, backlog grooming sessions, and sprint retrospectives. Due to the fact that the team members are distributed across Europe and North America, the observations were made by joining the video conference session for each ceremony. The observers also conducted semi-structured interviews with each member of the team he was observing, following an interview protocol [12].

Table 1. List of participants.

Role	Quarter 1 (n = 26)	Quarter 3 (n = 19)
Project manager (Scrum master)	9	7
Developer	9	6
Quality assurance	2	3
Development manager	1	–
Product manager	2	–
Director of eng.	1	–
Product owner	1	3
Unclear	1	–

The SAFe Self-Assessment survey comprises 25 questions that were sent to participants in an Excel Spreadsheet format. Each question has both a quantitative element (Likert scale), and an optional qualitative element (comment) that allowed participants to explain their ranking if needed. The Likert scale has six possible response options (ranging from 'never' to 'always' as shown in Table 2) to measure the frequency of practice use according to each area (Product Ownership Health, PI/Release Health, Sprint Health, Team Health, and Technical Health).

In Quarter 1, we received 28 responses out of 70. Two responses were excluded as they were incomplete, resulting in a final set of 26, and in Quarter 3 we received 19 responses. The results represent a range of responses from seven roles. Table 1 shows a breakdown of the roles of all 26 and 19 respondents (with one role unclear).

Data Analysis. To analyze the collected survey data, firstly, we extracted all qualitative and quantitative data. Secondly, we aggregated the 26 and then the

---

[9] http://www.scaledagileframework.com/metrics/#T4.

Table 2. SAFe Team Self-Assessment scale.

Value	0	1	2	3	4	5
Meaning	Never	Rarely	Occasionally	Often	Very Often	Always

19 data points from Quarter 1 and Quarter 3 to get an overall view of all team members and to measure the frequency of practices used by teams according to each area (Product Ownership Health, PI/Release Health, Sprint Health, Team Health, and Technical Health) within the organization. Finally, we compared and contrasted across the two data sets to identify any changes over time.

4 Findings

In this section, we present results of the qualitative and quantitative SAFe Team Self-Assessment. Figure 1 shows the median score across all participants. Of these, PI/Release health and Technical health were the most weak areas in Quarter 1 but responses to the repeated exercise undertaken in Quarter 3 indicates that there were marked improvements.

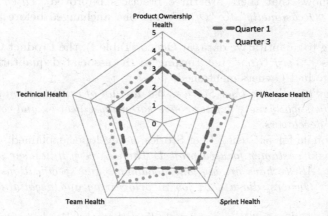

Fig. 1. SAFe Team Self-Assessment (values: 0 - Never, 1 - Rarely, 2 - Occasionally, 3 - Often, 4 - Very Often, 5 - Always).

Product Ownership Health. Product Ownership means ensuring the success of the product, providing support, making a difficult decision when necessary, and considering the consequences of that decision [13]. In Scrum, the on-site customer role is fulfilled by a Product Owner, who represents the interests of the customer and end-users on a development team. Product Owners are responsible for communication between the customer and development teams [14]. Product Owners also maintain the *product backlog*, a list of user "stories" that define

Table 3. Product Ownership Health.

Question	Stage	Median[a]	Mode[a]
Q1. Product Owner facilitates user story development, prioritization and negotiation	Quarter 1	3	3
	Quarter 3	4	4
Q2. Product Owner collaborates proactively with Product Management and other stakeholders	Quarter 1	4	4
	Quarter 3	4	4
Q3. User Stories are small, estimated, functional and vertical	Quarter 1	2, 5	2, 3
	Quarter 3	3	4
Q4. Product owner facilitates development of acceptance criteria which are used in planning, review and story acceptance	Quarter 1	3	4
	Quarter 3	4	4
Q5. Teams refine the backlog every sprint	Quarter 1	3	3
	Quarter 3	4	5

[a]Values: 0 - Never, 1 - Rarely, 2 - Occasionally, 3 - Often, 4 - Very Often, 5 - Always

requirements for the project. Table 3 shows the aggregated two stages result of Product ownership health at Ocuco.

Table 3 shows that there are three practices improved *"Often"* to *"Very Often"*, one *"Occasionally"* to *"Often"*, and one unchanged before and during operation.

According to quantitative data, at Ocuco (Table 3), the Product Owners use "User Stories" *"Very Often"* but turning to the associated qualitative results, one of the Product Owners mentioned,

... *We don't really use User Stories. We do a lot of prioritization and negotiation. We do a slightly more defined conversation/specification and communicate directly with developers.*

As a rationale for not using User Stories, a developer explained,

... *This is a customer focused project. There is very little user story development in it. All we have are big long documents and specifications. However, they [Product Owners] did a good job in prioritizing and negotiating with the customer.*

This statement results in our concluding that the Product Owner *"Very Often"* facilitates prioritization, and negotiation (in Table 3, Q1), and not user story development.

But, on the other hand, a Project Manager who also acts as a Scrum Master said,

... *There is not a lot of negotiation going on for our team as the estimates are done in advance. Due to nature of contract we don't work with User Stories. We have deliverables that have been defined as part of the contract.*

PI/Release Health. In SAFe®, the Program Increment (PI) is the largest plan-do-check-adjust learning cycle that comprises PI planning, PI execution, the system demo, and the Inspect & Adapt workshop respectively. Table 4 shows the aggregated result of PI/Release health at Ocuco.

Table 4. PI/Release Health.

Question	Stage	Median[a]	Mode[a]
Q1. Team participates fully in Release Planning and Inspect and Adapt	Quarter 1	3	3
	Quarter 3	4	4
Q2. Product backlog for the PI is itemized and prioritized	Quarter 1	3	3
	Quarter 3	4	4
Q3. Teams proactively interact with other teams on the train as necessary to resolve impediments	Quarter 1	3	3
	Quarter 3	3	3
Q4. Team participates in system demo every two weeks, illustrating real progress towards objectives	Quarter 1	3	3
	Quarter 3	4	5
Q5. Team reliably meet 80–100% of non-stretch PI Objectives	Quarter 1	3	3
	Quarter 3	3	3

[a]Values: 0 - Never, 1 - Rarely, 2 - Occasionally, 3 - Often, 4 - Very Often, 5 - Always

In Table 4, three practices improved from *"Often"* to *"Very Often"*, and two practices were unchanged. In response to release planning, we received contradictory statements from two teams. The Project Manager said,

... *We do not have a formal release planning, instead we plan continuously*

But, a Product Owner said,

... *All releases are planned. The whole team participates and know what is required for the version, and what can wait for the next in some cases.*

Sprint Health. In Scrum, a *sprint* is a set period of time during which specific work has to be done and made ready for review. During the planning meeting, the Product Owner and Agile team agree upon set of tasks needs to accomplish within a sprint based on the team bandwidth. Finally, the Product Owner defines the acceptance criteria for each assigned task to be completed at the end of a sprint. Table 5 shows the aggregated result of Sprint Health at Ocuco.

Table 5 shows, teams *"Often"* calculate velocity to plan for the upcoming sprint. Additionally, teams *"Very Often"* plans the sprint collaboratively, effectively and efficiently, but one of the team members said,

... *Sprints are not planned as such as we are at the tail end of the dev cycle. Almost all open tickets are go into the sprint.*

Though teams *"Often"* calculate velocity to plan for the upcoming sprint, but due to lack of proper estimation, team cannot meet the sprint goals.

... *We are often behind on doing the estimates, not taking the needed time or missing information enough to do a proper estimate*

A Project Manager identified, *"Over commitment"* and QA *"Speed"* are hindering the team in meeting the sprint goals. But, a Developer said,

Table 5. Sprint Health.

Question	Stage	Median[a]	Mode[a]
Q1. Team plans the sprint collaboratively, effectively and efficiently	Quarter 1	4	4
	Quarter 3	4	3,5
Q2. Team always has clear sprint goals, in support of PI objectives, and commits to meeting them	Quarter 1	3	3
	Quarter 3	4	3
Q3. Teams apply acceptance criteria and definition of done to story acceptance	Quarter 1	3	3
	Quarter 3	3	4
Q4. Team has a predictable, normalized velocity which is used for estimating and planning	Quarter 1	2.5	2
	Quarter 3	3	2,3,4
Q5. Team regularly delivers on their sprint goals	Quarter 1	3	3
	Quarter 3	3	3

[a]Values: 0 - Never, 1 - Rarely, 2 - Occasionally, 3 - Often, 4 - Very Often, 5 - Always

...It's a bit up and down, sometimes we succeed. It is like it is become common to always introduce new 'critical' issues into current sprint, instead of letting them wait for the next sprint planning.

Team Health. There are three key roles defined in the Scrum development approach: the self-organizing development Scrum Team, the Scrum Master, and the Product Owner [15]. The Scrum Master is responsible for facilitating the development process, ensuring that the team uses the full range of appropriate agile values, practices and rules [15]. The Scrum Master conducts daily coordination meetings and removes any impediments that the team encounters [15]. Table 6 shows the aggregated result of Team health at Ocuco.

According to Table 6, in Ocuco teams *"Always"* hold collaborative, effective and efficient planning meeting. Daily meetings are in place where all members participate, status is given clearly, issues are raised, obstacles are removed, and information exchanged among team members. Team members are self-organized, respect each other, *"Always"* help each other to complete sprint goals, manage interdependencies, and stay in-sync with each other.

Furthermore, team members are self-organized, respect each other, and help each other to complete sprint goals. A Product Owner states,

...Teams work well together and everyone is providing their part to making the best product. We just don't always agree on, which is good!

The Teams *"Always"* hold collaborative, effective and efficient planning and daily meetings where all members, including remote team members, participate, status is given clearly, issues are raised, obstacles are removed and information exchanged with other team members. But, the teams rarely hold retrospectives after each sprint:

Table 6. Team Health.

Question	Stage	Median[a]	Mode[a]
Q1. Team members are self-organized, respect each other, help each other complete sprint goals, manage interdependencies and stay in-sync with each other	Quarter 1	4	4
	Quarter 3	5	5
Q2. Scrum Master attends Scrum of Scrums and interacts with RTE as appropriate	Quarter 1	3	4
	Quarter 3	3	5
Q3. Stories are iterated through the sprint with multiple define-build-test cycles (e.g. the sprint is not a waterfalled)	Quarter 1	3	4
	Quarter 3	3	4
Q4. Team holds collaborative, effective and efficient planning and daily meetings where all members participate, status is given clearly, issues are raised, obstacles are removed and information exchanged	Quarter 1	4	4
	Quarter 3	5	5
Q5. Team holds a retrospective after each sprint and makes incremental changes to continually improve its performance	Quarter 1	3	4
	Quarter 3	4	5

[a]Values: 0 - Never, 1 - Rarely, 2 - Occasionally, 3 - Often, 4 - Very Often, 5 - Always

...I can only recall one retrospective during the last 2 years, it was done after a release and not after each sprint.

Technical Health. The Technical Health part of the survey helps a technology transformation team assess the current state of the technical maturity of a program/product line or organization. It can also be used later to have Agile teams assess their technical health and see if improvements have happened. The dimensions of the Technical Health part of the survey are: Continuous Delivery, Architecture, Technical Excellence, and Metrics. Table 7 shows the aggregated result of Technical health at Ocuco.

Interestingly, as Table 7 shows, teams *"Rarely"* adopt automated acceptance testing and unit testing as part of the story *definition of done (DoD)*[10] [15].

Most of the teams at Ocuco struggle with technical health, especially *"test automation"* and *"refactoring"*. Throughout the organization none of the teams perform automated testing, but some teams are planning to adopt automatic test strategies. On the other hand, a Developer mentioned, there is no refactoring at all, because,

...the customer keeps raising new requirements that contradicts with their previous requirements. Therefore, we kept adding new stuff while keeping the old one there because they might be worked on by a different developer, and we don't really know if they should just be removed/refactored. As a result, I can see quite

---

[10] A list of criteria which must be met before a product increment "often a user story" is considered "done".

Table 7. Technical Health.

Question	Stage	Median[a]	Mode[a]
Q1. Teams actively reduce technical debt in each sprint	Quarter 1	3	2
	Quarter 3	4	5
Q2. Team has clear guidance and understanding of intentional architecture guidance, but is free and flexible enough to allow emergent design to support optimal implementation	Quarter 1	3	3,4
	Quarter 3	4	4
Q3. Automated acceptance tests and unit tests are part of story DoD	Quarter 1	0	0
	Quarter 3	1	0
Q4. Refactoring is always underway	Quarter 1	2.5	3
	Quarter 3	3	5
Q5. CI, build and test automation infrastructure is improving	Quarter 1	2	0
	Quarter 3	3	0

[a]Values: 0 - Never, 1 - Rarely, 2 - Occasionally, 3 - Often, 4 - Very Often, 5 - Always

a lot of functionality in the system that previously does the job but now it doesn't do anything and nobody is going to take them out as time goes by.

5 Discussion

In software development, teams tailor their practices based on the metrics used to measure their system and evaluate their performance [8]. Agile teams continuously assess and improve their processes via a structured or periodic self-assessment as the first value of Agile Manifesto is to prefer *"Individuals and interactions over processes and tools"*. By applying self-assessment, a software development team can understand its current process maturity, identify practices to improve, and practices that are missing.

Improving towards expectation? The comparison shown in Table 8 (based on the Likert-scale results presented in Fig. 1) incorporating team improvement over time (5 months). In general, we observed a convincing improvement in four areas: Product Ownership Health, PI/Release Health, Team Health, and Technical Health but there was no discernible improvement in Sprint Health over the time.

There appear to be several reasons for these observed improvements. As part of the company-wide longitudinal study three new dedicated Product Owners have been appointed as Management recognised that this is a full time job. One new Product Owner has prior knowledge about SAFe®. According to Ocuco's Director of Development, "we realized our Product Owners were being pulled in different directions by their multiple responsibilities, and as a result their teams were drifting away from the product roadmap. So we decided to hire additional

Table 8. Comparison.

Area	Quarter 1 (n = 26) February, 2017	Quarter 3 (n = 19) July, 2017	Improvement 5 months
Product Ownership Health	3	4	+1
PI/Release Health	3	4	+1
Sprint Health	3	3	0
Team Health	3	4	+1
Technical Health	2.5	3	+0.5

staff so the Product Owners could focus solely on Product Ownership and keep the long-term product vision in-focus." This could a reason for the improvement Product ownership health as well as PI/Release health (Product backlog for the PI is *"Very Often"* itemized and prioritized).

There is some improvement in technical health moving from between *"Occasionally"/"Often"* to *"Often"*. According to Ocuco's Director of Development, "One of our new teams is adopting pure SAFe, to include *automated test strategy* and *continuous improvement* technique." That could be an another reason we are observing better results in Quarter 2 compared to Quarter 1. Ocuco's Director of Development also mentioned, some teams are building their experience and learning over time.

A major goal for Ocuco is to standardise their processes across all teams through transitioning to the SAFe® framework. They are starting to achieve this by tailoring SAFe® practices through modeling their "as-is" processes and identifying which practices need to be modified or added to achieve their target set of comprehensive "to-be" processes. Though SAFe® is primarily developed for organizing and managing agile practices in large enterprises it is clear that SME's are also interested in adopting SAFe®. However, SAFe® requires more roles, events, artefacts and practices compared to other frameworks to enable SAFe® to scale on an enterprise level. But, in SMEs it would be challenging if not impossible to adopt all the different ceremonies as well as fill all dedicated role such as Release Train Engineer (RTE). So, SME's need to consider which of the many ceremonies they want to adopt, and which roles they need to fill when adopting SAFe®. They may also need to look at the various levels of Team Health and consider what level they want to reach that they feel is acceptable, when assessing how well they are doing against the SAFe® self assessment survey results.

6   Conclusions

In this study, we employed a mixed method approach to identifying and evaluating the adoption rate of agile practices as well as health levels of different process areas within a medium-sized Irish-based software company. Initially, we found that teams were struggling with PI/Release and Technical health throughout the organization as most of the teams were transitioning from plan-driven to SAFe®. But, during the transition over time, we observed a convincing improvement.

SAFe® provides more roles, events, artefacts and practices compared to other frameworks that aim to support organizations to scale on an enterprise level. But, in smaller organizations, adopting the many different ceremonies as well as dedicated roles may not be possible or necessary to meet their business goals. The results gained from the self-assessment at the Team level, may be satisfactory (there are only two practices in Quarter 3 that were reported as being used *"Always"*, most reached a level of being used *"Often"*). Therefore, as a result of our longitudinal study, we suggests that successful SAFe® implementation teams need to tailor the many SAFe® practices to understand the:

Purpose of adopting a practice – *"Why"* – the Team needs to understand *"why"* they need adopt agile practices.

Implementation of a practice – *"How"* – the Team needs to learn *"how"* to implement a practice to get the best out of it by tailoring SAFe® practices.

Acknowledgments. We thank the members of TeamA, TeamB, and TeamC for their generous and thoughtful collaboration on this study, and for allowing us to study their software development efforts. This work was supported, in part, by Science Foundation Ireland grant 13/RC/2094 to Lero - the Irish Software Research Centre (www.lero.ie).

References

1. Kuhrmann, M., Fernández, D.M.: Systematic software development: a state of the practice report from Germany. In: 2015 IEEE 10th International Conference on Global Software Engineering (ICGSE), pp. 51–60. IEEE (2015)
2. Abrahamsson, P., Conboy, K., Wang, X.: "Lots done, more to do": the current state of agile systems development research (2009)
3. Maples, C.: Enterprise agile transformation: the two-year wall. In: Agile Conference, AGILE 2009, pp. 90–95. IEEE (2009)
4. Turk, D., France, R., Rumpe, B.: Limitations of agile software processes. In: Third International Conference on Extreme Programming and Flexible (2014)
5. Paasivaara, M.: Adopting safe to scale agile in a globally distributed organization. In: Proceedings of the 12th International Conference on Global Software Engineering, pp. 36–40. IEEE Press (2017)
6. VersionOne: 11th annual state of agile report. https://explore.versionone.com/state-of-agile/versionone-11th-annual-state-of-agile-report-2. Accessed 07 July 2017
7. Ambler, S.W.: Agile software development at scale. In: Meyer, B., Nawrocki, J.R., Walter, B. (eds.) CEE-SET 2007. LNCS, vol. 5082, pp. 1–12. Springer, Heidelberg (2008). doi:10.1007/978-3-540-85279-7_1
8. Leffingwell, D.: Scaled agile framework®4.0 (2015). http://scaledagileframework.com/. Accessed 15 Apr 2016
9. Laanti, M.: Characteristics and principles of scaled agile. In: Dingsøyr, T., Moe, N.B., Tonelli, R., Counsell, S., Gencel, C., Petersen, K. (eds.) XP 2014. LNBIP, vol. 199. Springer, Cham (2014)

10. Pries-Heje, J., Krohn, M.M.: The safe way to the agile organization. In: Proceedings of the XP2017 Scientific Workshops, XP 2017, pp. 18:1–18:3. ACM, New York (2017)
11. Turetken, O., Stojanov, I., Trienekens, J.J.: Assessing the adoption level of scaled agile development: a maturity model for scaled agile framework. J. Softw. Evol. Process **29**(6) (2017)
12. Beecham, S., Noll, J., Razzak, M.A.: Lean global project interview protocol (2017). http://bit.ly/2nPxaXH
13. Raithatha, D.: Making the whole product agile – a product owners perspective. In: Concas, G., Damiani, E., Scotto, M., Succi, G. (eds.) XP 2007. LNCS, vol. 4536, pp. 184–187. Springer, Heidelberg (2007). doi:10.1007/978-3-540-73101-6_33
14. Hoda, R., Noble, J., Marshall, S.: The impact of inadequate customer involvement on self-organizing agile teams. Inf. Softw. Technol. **53**(5), 521–534 (2011)
15. Schwaber, K., Beedle, M.: Agile Software Development with Scrum, vol. 1. Prentice Hall, Upper Saddle River (2002)

Beneficial and Harmful Agile Practices
for Product Quality

Sven Theobald[✉] and Philipp Diebold

Fraunhofer Institute for Experimental Software Engineering,
Fraunhofer-Platz 1, 67663 Kaiserslautern, Germany
{sven.theobald, philipp.diebold}@iese.fraunhofer.de

Abstract. There is the widespread belief that Agile neglects the product quality. This lack of understanding how Agile processes assure the quality of the product prevents especially companies from regulated domains from an adoption of Agile. This work aims to identify which Agile Practices contribute towards product quality. Hence, data from a survey study is analyzed to identify Agile Practices which are beneficial or harmful for the quality of the product. From 49 practices that were used in the survey so far, 36 were perceived to have a positive impact on product quality, while four practices were rated as being harmful. The results enrich understanding of how product quality can be achieved in Agile, and support selection of practices to improve quality.

Keywords: Agile · Agile practices · Product quality · Impacts

1 Introduction and Motivation

Agile already is a well-established software development approach, at least in non-regulated domains [1]. Its benefits such as more flexibility and a faster time to market are known. That is why companies from regulated domains such as the automotive or aerospace domains also want to benefit from these advantages. One adoption barrier is the fear of loosing compliance with regulations or certifications, caused by the widespread belief that Agile neglects the quality of the product. Boehm et al. [2] used a dichotomy between agility and discipline, which shows that Agile is not always seen as a disciplined approach. The Agile Manifesto demands: "Individuals and interactions over processes and tools" [3]. This can be misinterpreted as having no defined process. Hence, the quality of the product is often expected to be unpredictable.

This perception is one of many reasons why such companies stick to their traditional approaches with defined and rigorous verification and validation phases. While more flexibility and a faster reaction time to changes are one of the main drivers for Agile adoption [1], dealing with emerging requirements and architectures makes it difficult to plan quality assurance activities upfront and to achieve certifications.

On the other side, Agile processes are reported to produce higher quality [1, 4], e.g., based on focusing on a restricted number of most important requirements which are implemented with highest quality. Both different views could be explained by the insight that only the way of assuring quality is different: classical approaches rely on

© Springer International Publishing AG 2017
M. Felderer et al. (Eds.): PROFES 2017, LNCS 10611, pp. 586–593, 2017.
https://doi.org/10.1007/978-3-319-69926-4_48

heavy verification and validation activities, while Agile approaches incorporate the realization of quality into the process.

Instead of doing some specific practices (formal reviews, acceptance at certain stage gates, etc.), the contribution towards quality is spread over several practices throughout the whole development process. Therefore it is more difficult to identify which practices are contributing towards quality and to evaluate if a set of practices is sufficient to provide the same trust in the quality as is achieved in traditional approaches. For this reason, it is necessary to understand the contribution of Agile Practices on quality.

Commonly experienced in practice is the phenomenon that people adopt and adapt the method Scrum as their new development process during their Agile transition [1, 5]. Scrum is only supposed to be the minimal frame which has to be filled with further development practices. It therefore lacks a description of technical practices which are necessary for a disciplined software engineering. Knowing the effects of those single practices allows to evaluate and improve such a development method. In many cases, a combination of methods and practices is needed, e.g., the use of Scrum [6] enhanced by technical practices from XP [7].

The aim of this work is therefore to identify which elements of Agile, namely which Agile Practices, affect product quality. We use the preliminary results from a survey to analyze which of the practices were perceived by the survey participants as having an impact on product quality.

In Sect. 2, we shortly present the survey which is used as data source, as well as the research questions and analysis approach of this work. The results are presented and discussed in Sect. 3, and we finally conclude the paper together with some suggestions for future work (Sect. 4).

2   Research Method

In this work, data from a survey study was analyzed. We first present the background information about this survey study to clarify the origin of the data. Afterwards, the research goal is defined and research questions are derived. Finally, the data analysis approach is discussed.

2.1   Background

The data used for analysis in this work originate from an ongoing survey study [8]. In this study, the experiences of study participants concerning the impacts of Agile Practices on certain process improvement goals are collected. This is done using A0 posters with a printed matrix of Agile Practices and improvement goals. Participants can place sticky dots in the fields of the matrix, describing that there is an impact of the practice (row) on the improvement goal (column). This impact is rated with the help of color-coding on a scale from strongly positive (green) to strongly negative (red). More information about the research method is provided in [8].

In mid of July, the database contained 1846 data points collected at 17 venues with both academia and industry participants (see Table 1). The aggregated results are available on our website [9]. The subset of this data included and discussed in this paper will be those Agile Practices with a (positive or negative) impact on product quality, which is only one of several improvement goals considered in this study.

Table 1. Events, number of collected impacts and participants' information.

Events (ordered by date)	Impacts (on Quality/Overall)		Participants (Background/No. of)	
Agile in automotive 2016	15	118	Practitioners	170
Profes 2016	0	143	Mixed	150
OOP 2017	24	76	Practitioners	1500
Lean IT management 2017	7	78	Practitioners	100
AgileXChange 1-2017	31	112	Practitioners	80
AgileLab copenhagen 2017	19	123	Practitioners	50
Q-Rapids meeting 2017	23	83	Mixed	20
Agile in automotive USA 2017	20	99	Practitioners	90
CESI 2017 (@ICSE 2017)	4	22	Practitioners	10
XP 2017	99	513	Mixed	280
ScrumDay 2017	9	68	Practitioners	250
EASE 2017	9	101	Academics	90
AgileXChange 2-2017	13	79	Practitioners	80
SPA 2017	4	26	Practitioners	50
Agile Austria 2017	33	156	Practitioners	250
Agile on the beach 2017	6	37	Practitioners	400
ICSSP 2017	1	12	Academics	35

2.2   Research Goal

To overcome the lack of understanding how Agile assures quality, this study aims to identify Agile Practices that have an effect on product quality. The goal of this study was formulated using the GQM template [10]:

> *Identify* Agile Practices *with respect to* their effect on product quality *in the context of* an analysis of preliminary data from a survey study *from the perspective of* Agile practitioners and researchers.

Based on this goal, three research questions (RQs) are defined:

RQ1: Which Agile Practices have a positive effect on product quality?
RQ2: Which Agile Practices have a negative effect on product quality?
RQ3: Which Agile Practices have been rated without a common agreement?

These three research questions help to identify the beneficial and harmful practices, as well as those practices where the impact is varying depending on the context or the implementation of the practice.

2.3   Analysis

The existing data (1846 impacts) [9] was filtered to only include the 317 impacts on product quality, which is the improvement goal in the focus of this analysis. The impacts were collected at 16 different events. The reason why one event was missing is that for the first two events, product quality was not included on the poster. At one of those events, the Agile in Automotive (2016), a participant added product quality to the poster in order to report his experiences and we integrated product quality as a standard answer on future posters afterwards. To facilitate analysis, the scale (strongly positive, positive, negative, strongly negative) was transformed into a scale of +2, +1, −1, −2. This enables analysis based on descriptive measures such as the average value.

3   Results and Discussion

In this chapter, the results of the analysis are presented and discussed along the research questions, followed by a general discussion of results and threats to validity.

From the list of all 49 Agile Practices included in this study, eight practices were not set in relation with product quality at all. The other 41 practices were rated as having an impact on product quality: There were four practices with a negative impact (average <= 0.5), and 36 with a positive impact (average > = 0.5), while one practice, Backlog, received mixed ratings and ended up with a neutral average.

3.1   RQ 1 – Beneficial Practices

Overall, 36 of the 49 Agile Practices were perceived to have a positive impact on product quality. Since some of them only received a low number of ratings so far, the trust in the average value is not given for certain practices. Therefore, we provide only those Agile Practices with a more reliable average value in Table 2.

Table 2. Most beneficial Agile Practices with at least 10 ratings

Beneficial agile practice	Average	Count	+2	+1	−1	−2
Test driven development	1.93	15	14	1		
Pair programming	1.83	12	10	2		
Continuous Integration	1.77	13	10	3		
Cross-functional team	1.75	28	21	7		
Definition of done	1.75	24	18	6		
Definition of ready	1.75	12	9	3		
Unit testing	1.64	14	9	5		
Refactoring	1.58	19	14	4		1
Backlog grooming	1.57	14	10	3	1	
Iteration reviews	1.47	19	9	10		
Product owner	1.40	15	8	6	1	
Retrospective	1.36	14	9	5		
Scrum master	1.23	13	7	4	2	

For this selection, only practices which received at least 10 ratings were considered in order to increase the reliability of the data. All practices from this list origin from Scrum or XP, most likely because these are the Agile Methods which are most frequently used and known. Sorted by the average rating starting with the practice with the highest average, the list of all other beneficial practices is provided in the following, including the average rating and the number of ratings the practice received:

Collective Ownership (2/6), Continuous Delivery (2/3), Product Canvas (2/1), Product Vision board (2/2), Work-in-Progress Limit (2/2), Iterative development (1.75/4), Peer Reviews (1.67/3), Self-organizing team (1.67/3), Story Mapping (1.67/3), Personas (1.6/5), Architecture Sprint (1.5/2), Automated Builds (1.5/6), Minimum Viable Product (1.5/6), Shippable Increment (1.5/8), User stories (1.43/7), Coding Styleguides (1.4/5), Sign Up (1.4/5), Communities of Practice (1.33/6), Daily Meeting (1.33/6), Prototyping (1.25/4), Sprint Zero (1/1), Team-Based Estimation (1/1), Relative Estimation (0.5/2).

Name (Average/Count)

3.2   RQ 2 – Harmful Practices

Four practices ended up with a negative average, most of them based on a limited amount of ratings (see Table 3). It can be seen that velocity is perceived to have a negative contribution towards product quality. Participants rated this impact four times as strongly negative, and three times as negative. In addition, burn charts received a strongly negative rating (three times). The strongly negative ratings for those two practices came all from the XP 2017 conference.

Table 3. Practices with negative impact on product quality

Harmful agile practice	Average	Count	+2	+1	−1	−2
Taskboard	−1	1			1	
Velocity	−1.57	7			3	4
Burn chart	−2	3				3
Release planning	−2	1				1

A possible reason for the negative rating of velocity and burn charts could be a misuse of the increased transparency of those practices: If the burn chart shows that the end of the iteration comes closer, or when the current velocity is not as high as in previous iterations, quality is neglected in order to be able to show a better performance. This happens especially when Management uses burn charts or velocity to track the efficiency of the team or even individuals, sometimes also to decide on incentives. This aspect was also mentioned by one of the study participants, when we asked him why he reports a negative impact.

For the other two practices, we cannot tell whether they really have a negative impact or whether these are opinions by individuals. For further analysis, we have to wait for more data.

3.3   RQ 3 - Ambiguous Practices

While most practices were rated with a clear trend, there are some practices whose ratings are ambiguous. A clear trend means that the practice received either only positive values or only negative ones. In Fig. 1, we list all practices that received ambiguous ratings (some positive and some negative ratings).

For all practices with a clear trend, we can assume that, given enough data points, this practice is always beneficial or always harmful for a certain improvement goal, in our case product quality. We expect the participants of our survey to have various context, so we assume that these practices are applicable in different contexts with similar results. Additionally, practices are often adapted to be useable in a certain context or because of lack of knowledge, e.g., most Scrum practices are used with adaptations [5]. It seems, given enough data points, that a practice with a clear trend is always showing certain benefits or drawbacks, independent of the individual implementation and context.

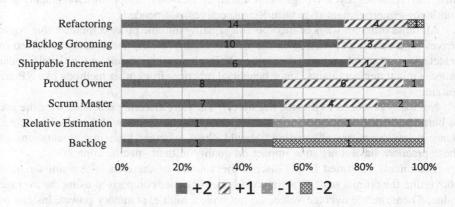

Fig. 1. Practices with ambiguous impact on product quality: Distribution of the amount of ratings over the scale (+2, +1,−1,−2).

But if experiences or perceptions of the practices' impacts vary, these practices could be dangerous to adapt or use in certain contexts. Therefore, it is necessary to be aware of those practices during introduction. It is necessary to identify whether those ambiguous ratings are outliers or whether the impact of the practice is really unsteady and context-dependent.

From the data in Fig. 1, the negative ratings of the first four practices (Refactoring, Backlog Grooming, Shippable Increment, Product Owner) can be considered as being individual outliers. For the last two practices (Relative Estimation and Backlog), not enough data is available to make any assumption. The Scrum Master received two negative ratings, which tells us that more than one person perceived this Agile role to have a negative contribution towards product quality. Without knowing the reason why those participants reported this harmful impact, we cannot tell whether the role was implemented wrongly, or whether there are certain aspects to this role which really affect quality negatively.

3.4 Discussion

The fact that most practices (36 out of 49) were reported as beneficial shows that quality is an important aspect in Agile development. Beside the practices that assure quality directly, such as Unit Testing, Test-Driven Development, Pair Programming and (Code) Reviews, there were other practices contributing towards a higher quality in different ways:

The responsibility for the quality of the product is shared with the help of Agile Practices, such as Collective Ownership, Sign Up/Pull principle, or Cross-functional Team. There is a shared understanding of the quality demands, supported by practices such as Coding Styleguides, Definition of Ready and Definition of Done. Another important aspect how Agile development achieves better quality is to prioritize requirements and focus to only build what the user really needs with a higher quality, using Minimum Viable Product, Product Owner, User Stories, and Personas. To do this, fast feedback cycles (e.g., with Iteration Reviews, Shippable Increment) and continuous improvement (e.g. with Retrospectives) are needed.

All those different ways of incorporating quality into the process indicate that Agile strives for a culture of focusing on the product quality. Discipline is demanded, also to select the right development practices. Only implementing Scrum as the development process might neglect quality, since beneficial practices from other methods like XP are missing.

Not many practices were rated negatively. The only alarming practices were the use of burn charts and velocity, which are frequently used together with Scrum. Therefore, many practitioners are affected and should check whether their implementations of these practices have a negative impact on quality in their specific context.

The threats identified in [8] discuss the validity of the data. The main threat is converting the ordinal scale to an interval scale for easier comparison using the average value. Therefore the average values do not have a high explanatory power. Instead of considering the detailed ranking, only the tendency towards positive or negative impact should be considered. The proposed practices are by no means complete, since not all available Agile Practices were covered by the survey. Only a limited amount of ratings were given so far, so the validity of results needs to be improved by increasing the size of the data set, which is continuously done with the ongoing survey.

4 Conclusion and Future Work

An analysis of the preliminary results [8] a survey study [8] showed that there exist many Agile Practices which contribute towards product quality. Out of the 49 practices used in the survey, 36 practices were reported as beneficial (RQ1). On the other hand, only four practices were reported with only a few ratings as being harmful for product quality (RQ2). Practitioners should especially be careful with the practice Velocity. There is very little disagreement on which practices contribute positively or negatively (RQ3). Thus, both academics and practitioners seem to have a common perception of the impacts of Agile Practices. Despite the assumed individual context variations and adaptations of practices, most practices show a stable impact.

The identified practices help to better understand how Agile addresses product quality. This knowledge can be used to select dedicated Agile Practices for adoption. Knowing which practices contribute to product quality facilitates a mapping of Agile Practices and certain regulations in order to identify how Agile approaches fulfill the requirements of such standards concerning the achievement of high quality products.

Since this is a continuous survey study, we rely on support by event organizers or event visitors who want to place our poster to collect experiences from the participants. This is your chance to contribute to the Agile community to increase our understanding of the impacts of Agile Practices. With a growing number of reported impacts, the validity of our analysis can be increased.

Additionally, qualitative statements have to be collected to provide some potential reasons for the reported impacts, e.g. in case studies or interviews. Further, the high-level improvement goals can be further refined to provide insights. In the case of product quality, future work could investigate which products or product parts and which refined quality aspects are addressed.

Acknowledgements. This work was partly funded by the German Federal Ministry of Education and Research in a Software Campus project (BMBF 01IS12053) and as part of the research project ProKoB (www.prokob.info) (BMBF 01IS15038).

References

1. VersionOne: 10th Annual State of Agile Development Survey (2016)
2. Boehm, B., Turner, R.: Balancing Agility and Discipline: A Guide for the Perplexed, Portable Documents. Addison-Wesley Professional, Boston (2003)
3. Beck, K., et al.: Manifesto for Agile Software Development (2001)
4. Komus, A., et al.: Status quo agile 2014 (2014)
5. Diebold, P., Ostberg, J.-P., Wagner, S., Zendler, U.: What do practitioners vary in using Scrum? In: Lassenius, C., Dingsøyr, T., Paasivaara, M. (eds.) XP 2015. LNBIP, vol. 212, pp. 40–51. Springer, Cham (2015). doi:10.1007/978-3-319-18612-2_4
6. Schwaber, K., Sutherland, J.: The Scrum Guide (2013)
7. Beck, K.: Extreme Programming Explained: Embrace Change. Addison-Wesley Professional, Boston (2000)
8. Diebold, P., Galster, M., Rainer, A., Licorish, S.A.: Interactive posters: an alternative to collect practitioners' experience. In: Proceedings of the 21st International Conference on Evaluation and Assessment in Software Engineering, pp. 230–235. ACM (2017)
9. Diebold, P., Theobald, S.: Collected Impacts of Agile Practices (2017). http://impact.iese.fhg.de/data.php. Accessed 11 July 2017
10. Basili, V., Caldiera, G., Rombach, D.: The goal question metric approach. Encycl. Softw. Eng. **2**(1994), 528–532 (1994)

Posters and Tool Demonstration Papers

Visual Programming Language for Model Checkers Based on Google Blockly

Seiji Yamashita[1], Masateru Tsunoda[1(✉)], and Tomoyuki Yokogawa[2]

[1] Department of Informatics, Kindai University, 3-4-1 Kowakae,
Higashiosaka City, Osaka 577-8502, Japan
tsunoda@info.kindai.ac.jp
[2] Faculty of Computer Science and Systems Engineering, Okayama Prefectural University,
111 Kuboki, Soja City, Okayama, 719-1197, Japan
t-yokoga@cse.oka-pu.ac.jp

Abstract. Recently, model checkers, such as SPIN, have played an important role in the enhancement of software reliability. To promote the use of model checkers, we propose a visual programming language for SPIN model checkers for educational use. Our prototype is based on Google Blockly.

Keywords: Model checking · Visual programming · Promela

1 Introduction

Recently, formal verification methods, such as model checking, have gained attention for their role in the enhancement of software reliability. Model checking can verify the correctness of a software system by checking whether the software system satisfies the given properties. SPIN [2] is one of the most successful implementations of the model checking algorithm. To promote the use of model checking, it is necessary to teach students how to express the system as a modeling language by using model-checking tools. To help introduce programming languages to students, visual programming languages, such as Scratch [4], are often used in education. In this paper, we propose a visual programming language for SPIN model checkers. The proposed language is developed based on Google Blockly. By using our language, students can express the model without typing any code. The proposed language has the following advantages:

- Students' difficulty in understanding a peculiar syntax of the modeling language for a model checker is reduced.
- The education cost (time and human resources) to correct syntax errors in the models written by students is reduced.

These advantages ease the teaching of model checking in a software engineering course. Note that we assumed a visual programming language for model checkers in this study for educational use and not for professional use.

© Springer International Publishing AG 2017
M. Felderer et al. (Eds.): PROFES 2017, LNCS 10611, pp. 597–601, 2017.
https://doi.org/10.1007/978-3-319-69926-4_49

2   Google Blockly

Google Blockly is a library for building visual programming editors. Demos that work on a Web browser are provided on the website [1]. We selected a Code Editor of the demos to convert a visualized program into a textual program such as JavaScript. Figure 1 shows a screenshot of the Code Editor. A user can create a program by placing statement blocks. By switching the language tab (such as JavaScript), the editor generates a source code described using the selected language. We can define new custom blocks and associate a source code with those blocks.

Fig. 1. Screenshot of Code Editor created using Google Blockly

The utilization of Google Blockly on model checking education gives us the following advantages:

- We can easily create visual programming editors for various model checkers.
- By partially concealing specifications of the programming language, students can easily understand the language.
- Students can create a visualized program on a Web browser. By preparing a model checker on a Web server, students need not install additional software.

Although there exist some visualized tools for model checkers [3], these advantages can only be acquired by adopting Google Blockly.

3   Prototype of Visualized Promela

By using Google Blockly, we implemented basic statements of Promela, which is a specification language for SPIN. We provided a prototype of visualized Promela, including its fundamental syntax, as we assumed that a teacher may introduce the SPIN model checker to students for few hours.

When a variable is added to the visual programming editor, its declaration is automatically added. In our prototype, the variable type is fixed to integer. When a statement is added, the declaration of the process is automatically added. Figure 2 illustrates a visualized code and the generated Promela code.

```
int x;

active proctype P() {
  x = 1;
}
```

Fig. 2. Example of the declaration of a variable and process

Figure 3 illustrates a loop statement. In this example, the variable x is iteratively incremented. In our prototype, a given condition is restricted to true because the condition is not an exit condition but an execution condition. That is, the condition is almost the same as an if statement, and can be written by using the statement. The break statement is used to finish the loop.

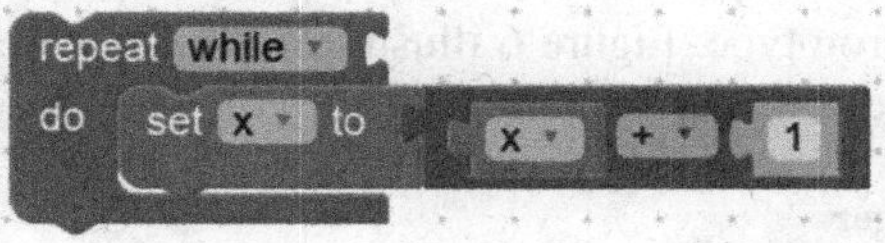

```
do
:: true-> x = x + 1;
od;
```

Fig. 3. Example of loop statement 3

Figure 4 illustrates an if statement. In the example, when the value of variable x is 0, it is set to 1. When the value is 2, it is set to 2. When the value does not satisfy the conditions, the value is set to 0. As shown, the reading and writing conditions are easier to implement by using the visual programming language than by using Promela for beginners.

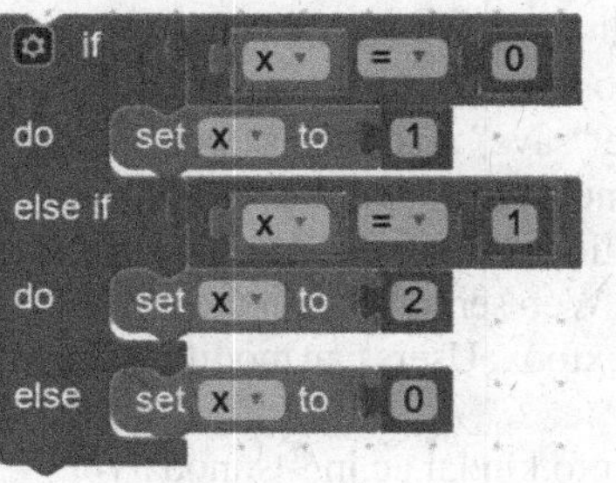

```
if
:: (x == 0) ->   x = 1;
:: (x == 1) ->   x = 2;
:: else ->   x = 0;
fi;
```

Fig. 4. Example of if statement

The easiest way to check the correctness of the program is by using an assertion. Figure 5 illustrates an assertion in a loop statement. A Boolean expression in the assertion represents a specification, which should be satisfied when the assertion is called. In the example, when $x = 0$ (or >0) before the loop, the assertion x > 0 is always satisfied in the loop. If the assertion is evaluated to false, SPIN returns an assertion error.

```
repeat while
do    set x to
                  x  +  1
      Assert
                  x  >  0
```

```
do
:: true->
   x = x + 1;
   assert{x > 0};
od;
```

Fig. 5. Example of assertion statement

A linear temporal logic (LTL) expression can also be used for checking the correctness of the program. An LTL formula can express temporal specifications such as "x is always larger than 0." LTL has temporal and Boolean operators. We implemented the following temporal operators: *globally*, *finally*, *next*, and *until*. We implemented the following Boolean operators: *not*, *and*, *or*, *implication*, and *equivalence*. We provided these LTL operators as blocks in our prototype. Figure 6 illustrates the block notation of the LTL formula expressing "x will eventually become 5."

```
ltl p0 {<>(x == 5)};
```

Fig. 6. Example of an LTL statement

Preliminary evaluation: Two subjects used the prototype, and we measured the time taken for developing a very simple code with and without the prototype. The time taken to develop the code by using the tools was not very different. This is because the searching blocks consumed more time. Therefore, we should improve the grouping blocks (In Fig. 1, left-most texts indicate block groups). In contrast, a code developed by a subject included syntax errors. The result suggests that our prototype suppresses such errors and reduces time to correct the errors of a lecture.

Other functions: Our prototype comprises the "save" and "SPIN" buttons. The "save" button can be used to save the visualized Promela code, and the "SPIN" button can be used to execute the code and obtain a verification result by SPIN. These functions are implemented by sending generated codes to a Web server. When the "SPIN" button is clicked, the generated code is also copied to a textbox. Users can modify this code before execution.

Our prototype is available on http://www.info.kindai.ac.jp/~tsunoda/vpl.

Acknowledgments. This research was partially supported by Japan Society for the Promotion of Science (JSPS) [Grants-in-Aid for Scientific Research (C) and (A) (No. 16K00113 and No. 17H00731)].

References

1. Google Blockly demos. https://blockly-demo.appspot.com/static/demos/index.html
2. Holzmann, G.: The model checker SPIN. IEEE Trans. Softw. Eng. **23**(5), 279–295 (1997)

3. Leue, S., et al.: v-Promela: a visual, object-oriented language for SPIN. In: Proceedings of International Symposium on Object-Oriented Real-Time Distributed Computing (ISORC), pp. 14–23 (1999)
4. Resnick, M., et al.: Scratch: programming for all. Commun. ACM **52**(11), 60–67 (2009)

Improving Communication in Scrum Teams

Marvin Wyrich[1(✉)], Ivan Bogicevic[2(✉)] [iD], and Stefan Wagner[2] [iD]

[1] AEB GmbH, Stuttgart, Germany
marvin.wyrich@aeb.com
[2] Institute of Software Technology, University of Stuttgart, Stuttgart, Germany
{ivan.bogicevic,stefan.wagner}@informatik.uni-stuttgart.de

Abstract. Communication in teams is an important but difficult issue.
In a Scrum development process, we use meetings like the Daily Scrum to
inform others about important problems, news and events in the project.
When persons are absent due to holiday, illness or travel, they miss
relevant information because there is no guarantee that the content of
these meetings is documented. We present a concept and a Twitter-like
tool to improve communication in a Scrum development process. We take
advantage out of the observation that many people do not like to create
documentation, but they do like to share what they did. We used the tool
in industrial practice and observed an improvement in communication.

Keywords: Scrum · Agile communication · Activity tracking

1 Introduction

Communication is an essential part of the work in any Scrum team. Many of
the everyday events and activities are communicated orally in the Daily Scrum.
Ratanotayanon et al. [2] even show in a case study that knowledge transfer over
a longer period of time can be managed with extensive communication alone.
However, the larger a team gets, the more difficult is the communication. One
of the most important challenges in large Scrum teams is inter-team coordination [1]. Coordination requires communication both between teams and within
a team. Important events that occur during development could be relevant to
others and are often not sufficiently documented or communicated [3]. Software
developers do not update relevant documents, do not see their benefits and wish
more automatic generation of documented content [4,5].

1.1 Problem Statement

Every day, a lot of activities and events happen in agile teams and some of them
are really important for other team members to know. Especially when decisions
are taken, new tasks emerge or unexpected incidents happen and team members
are not adequately informed, it can become problematic. The Daily Scrum allows
members of a Scrum team to keep up with the latest activities of their colleagues.

© Springer International Publishing AG 2017
M. Felderer et al. (Eds.): PROFES 2017, LNCS 10611, pp. 602–605, 2017.
https://doi.org/10.1007/978-3-319-69926-4_50

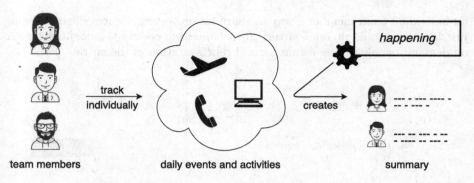

track individually

creates

happening

team members   daily events and activities   summary

Fig. 1. *happening* allows individual members of a Scrum team to efficiently track their activities. The tool then provides a summary of the whole team's activities.

The problem is that not every team member takes part in all meetings. We have also observed that not every important activity or event is communicated in the Daily Scrum. So even a documentation of the Daily Scrum would not cover the whole team's activities. The consequence when a team member is absent is that he or she has to seek for this information in different places and has to ask his or her colleagues. This costs time of several team members, and it is not guaranteed that the information seeker gets informed about every important event.

Simple communication tools used by developers like Slack[1], FlowDoc[2] or Gitter[3] provide basic chatting features, but do not support structuring, prioritizing, and summarizing adequately important events (and only these). An example of a tool with at least an automatic summarizer for daily scrum meetings has been proposed by Park [6].

1.2   Research Objectives and Contributions

The objective of our research is to lower the effort of getting a complete overview of what recently happened within a Scrum team. In particular we want to develop a tool for generating a summary based on activities and events tracked by individual team members. This summary should contain all relevant information for an individual team member to eliminate the need for most additional information sources. The tool aims to ensure better communication in large Scrum teams even when developers are absent for a while.

2   Concept and Solution

People usually do not like to create documentation, but they do like to share what they did. As a consequence *happening* serves as a documentation tool that gives

---

[1] https://slack.com/.
[2] https://www.flowdock.com/.
[3] https://gitter.im/.

an individual team member a way to share his or her experiences in short form, just like they would do on Twitter. Then *happening* creates the documentation on demand by generating a summarized representation of the entries (Fig. 1).

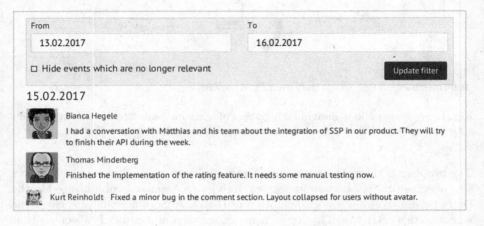

Fig. 2. Sample screenshot of the tool *happening*

The solution consists of two parts: a simple form for inserting individual events and a page for viewing the summary for a selected time period. The latter is shown in Fig. 2. It is an example page which summarizes activities and events of a Scrum team for a selected period of time. In the example, the entry of Kurt Reinholdt was given a lower priority and thus has a smaller avatar. Any event entry consists of a description, a manually selected priority and the date on which the event took place. The priority indicates for what period of time the event will be relevant to others. Thus the priority of an individual event has significant influence on what is shown in the summary if the user wants to hide events that are no longer relevant. Currently the solution is a stand-alone tool with a web interface and thus can be accessed by its users via any web browser. We also offer an online demo installation where the tool can be tried out without installation.[4]

3   Evaluation

We evaluated the tool in a productive environment of a Scrum team, which used the previously described tool in its day-to-day work. The team was made up of eight persons, from which one worked from home, one was located in Sweden and the others were at the same office in Germany during the evaluation period. The team members were told to track their activities and events on a daily basis and to use the summary of the tool as a reminder in their Daily Scrum. At the end of

---

[4] https://github.com/MarvinWyrich/happening.

the evaluation period the team members gave their feedback on the usefulness of the tool. We found that the summarizing presentation of the team's activities is not that useful in the Daily Scrum. The selected Scrum team was already used to have the JIRA task list opened during the Daily Scrum. So the developers wished to integrate *happening* as a plugin in JIRA to not have two tools open at the same time. However, seven out of eight participants said that *happening* was useful outside of the Daily Scrum and they think it would be a great help after a longer period of absence.

4   Conclusion

The concept and tool worked well in practice and helped improving the communication in agile teams. At first glance the tool contradicts the agile principles where direct communication is more important than tools and documentation. But when developers are absent, writing down otherwise missed information is the only way of replacing direct communication. The costs for using the tool are low as sharing the important information goes fast. A weakness of the tool is that it has only been used in a small environment so far, long-term evaluations are still missing. Further weaknesses of the tool are that there is no possibility to hierarchically structure the events. Future work on the concept and tool will try to eliminate these weaknesses.

Acknowledgements. We want to thank AEB GmbH who made this work possible and who provided the persons for the tool evaluation. We also thank Fujitsu Next who supported this work with a 5.000 Euro grant and the first prize of its *Agile IT*-Award 2016.

References

1. Dingsøyr, T., Moe, N.B.: Research challenges in large-scale agile software development. SIGSOFT Softw. Eng. Notes **38**(5), 38–39 (2013)
2. Ratanotayanon, S., Kotak, J., Sim, S.E.: After the Scrum: twenty years of working without documentation. In: Eighteenth International Conference on Software Engineering and Knowledge Engineering (SEKE), 5–7 July 2006, San Francisco, CA, USA (2006) 200–205
3. Visconti, M., Cook, C.R.: An overview of industrial software documentation practice. In: Proceedings of the XII International Conference of the Chilean Computer Science Society, SCCC 2002, pp. 179–186 (2002)
4. Forward, A., Lethbridge, T.C.: A survey. In: Proceedings of the 2002 ACM Symposium on Document Engineering, DocEng 2002, NY, USA, pp. 26–33
5. Lethbridge, T.C., Singer, J., Forward, A.: The state of the practice. IEEE Softw. **20**(6), 35–39 (2003)
6. Park, S.: A daily Scrum meeting summarizer for agile software development teams. Master thesis. University of Calgary, Canada, August 2007

Tool Support for Consistency Verification of UML Diagrams

Salilthip Phuklang[1], Tomoyuki Yokogawa[2]([⊠]), Pattara Leelaprute[1], and Kazutami Arimoto[2]

[1] Kasetsart University, 50 Thanon Ngam Wong Wan, Khwaeng Lat Yao, Khet Chatuchak, Bangkok 10900, Thailand
salilthip.p@ku.th, pattara.l@ku.ac.th
[2] Okayama Prefectural University, 111 Kuboki, Soja, Okayama 719-1197, Japan
{t-yokoga,arimoto}@cse.oka-pu.ac.jp

Abstract. Manual verification of the consistency between UML state machine diagrams and sequence diagrams is labor-intensive and prone to make mistakes. We provide an automatic tool written in Java that performs the verification by translating UML diagrams into a process description of CSP_M language. The tool takes in a PlantUML file and verifies the consistency with a model-checker FDR.

Keywords: Formal verification · UML · CSP · FDR

1 Introduction

UML is one of the most familiar specification languages and is the de-facto standard modeling language for object-oriented software. While it is less used in software development projects [5], it is well used in the model-driven software development [6]. Software systems are often documented with UML, and its mechanisms are reviewed on the documents. Such documents comprise multiple models and views related to each other, and their inconsistencies must be managed in software development [2]. An automatic consistency checking is expected because developers spend not a little effort to keep the consistency [3].

State machine diagrams and sequence diagrams of UML are widely used for software development. The automatic consistency checking methods between them have been proposed [1,8]. However, they adopted different semantics for modeling the diagrams and missed a formal definition of consistency property. Thus, we developed a method for inter-model consistency verification of sequence diagrams and state machine diagrams using model checking [4,7].

This paper describes a tool that implements our method in Java. It translates UML diagrams written in PlantUML language into a process representation described by CSP_M. Consistencies are checked by feeding it to a model checker FDR that supports the latest version of Failures-Divergence Refinement (FDR).

A state machine diagram is composed of *states*, *transitions*, *messages*, and an *initial state*. For each message m, m! and m? are *labels* which correspond to

© Springer International Publishing AG 2017
M. Felderer et al. (Eds.): PROFES 2017, LNCS 10611, pp. 606–609, 2017.
https://doi.org/10.1007/978-3-319-69926-4_51

sending and receiving of m, respectively. A transition connects source and target states and labeled by e? and a! as *trigger* and *action* (these labels are described "e/a" in a diagram). A transition $t = \langle x, e?, a!, y \rangle$ is executed if x is activated and e is received, and then the state machine sends a and y is activated. A sequence diagram is composed of *lifelines*, *occurrences*, messages, a partial order relation between occurrences, and a labeling function from an occurrence to a label. Figure 1 shows examples of UML diagrams.

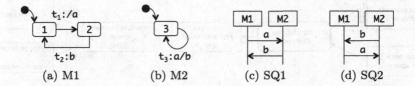

(a) M1   (b) M2   (c) SQ1   (d) SQ2

Fig. 1. Examples of UML diagrams

The semantics of the diagrams is defined with a set of *computations*, which is a sequence of labels. The state machine M1 has two states and alternately repeats two transitions $t_1 = \langle 1, -, a!, 2 \rangle$ and $t_2 = \langle 2, b?, -, 1 \rangle$. M2 repeats one transition $t_3 = \langle 3, a?, b!, 3 \rangle$. Since a? and b? can be respectively executed following a! and b!, the diagrams have only one computation a!a?b!b?a!a?b!b? . . .. The sequence diagram SQ1 and SQ2 describe two interactions between M1 and M2. SQ1 and SQ2 has one computation a!a?b!b? and b!b?a!a?, respectively.

The consistency of state machine diagrams and a sequence diagram is defined as an inclusive relation between the sets of computations [7]. Since a state machine diagram generally has infinite computations, we compare finite prefixes of the computation with computations of the sequence diagram. For example, the state machine diagrams M1 and M2 has a prefix of computation a!a?b!b?, and it corresponds to the computation of the sequence diagram SQ1. Thus M1 and M2 are consistent with SQ1, but not consistent with SQ2.

FDR can check a trace inclusion of processes by checking traces refinement relation. By representing state machine diagrams and a sequence diagram as processes whose traces correspond to their computations, a consistency verification can be done by checking traces refinement of the processes using FDR.

2   Tool Overview

Figure 2 shows the framework of consistency verification using FDR. Our tool reads state machine diagrams and a sequence diagram described in PlantUML language and then generates a process representation described by CSP_M. A model checker FDR takes in the representation and checks a trace refinement relation between the processes of the state machine diagrams and the sequence diagram. Passing the trace refinement check means that the computation of the sequence diagram is included by those of the state machine diagrams. Therefore, it can be said that the consistency of the diagrams is confirmed. In contrast, failing the check means that the diagrams are inconsistent.

In the case of failure, some computations of the sequence diagram are not included by those of the state machine diagrams, and FDR generates a counter example that shows the computation which is not included. The counter example can help to fix the inconsistency of diagrams.

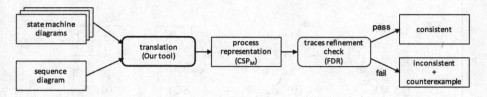

Fig. 2. The framework of consistency verification using FDR

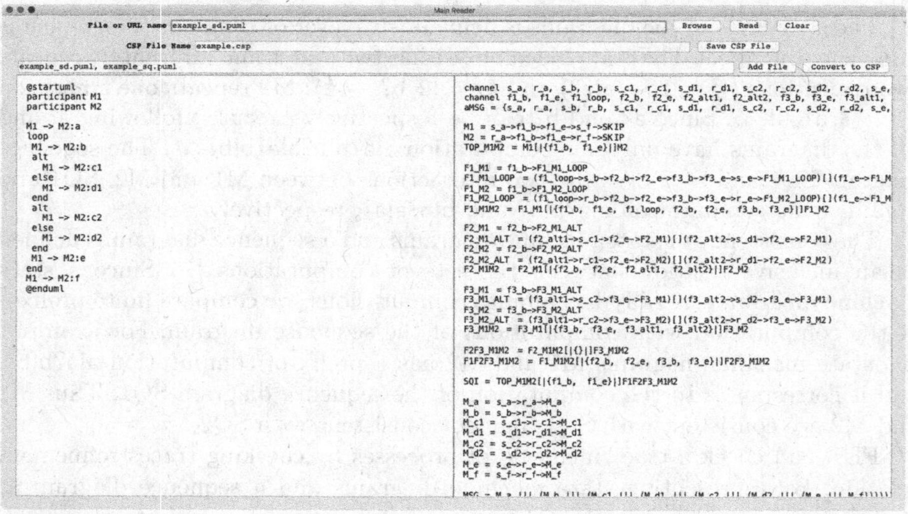

Fig. 3. Interface of our tool

Figure 3 shows a GUI interface of our tool. The left-side of window shows state machine diagrams and a sequence diagram. Users can translate the diagrams into process description by pushing the "`Convert to CSP`" button. The right-side of the window shows an obtained process description. The users can check the consistency of the diagrams by feeding it to FDR.

This tool supports the popular format and hides the tool-chain comprising formal verification tools. It helps a developer to verify consistency without detailed knowledge of formal methods.

3   Future Remarks

We provided a tool supporting consistency verification of state machine diagrams and sequence diagrams. Our tool can translate the diagrams into process description and the consistency is verified by checking traces refinement using FDR. Supporting inconsistency fixing using a counterexample is in our future plan.

References

1. Egyed, A.: Automatically detecting and tracking inconsistencies in software design models. IEEE Trans. Softw. Eng. **37**, 188–204 (2011)
2. Huzar, Z., Kuzniarz, L., Reggio, G., Sourrouille, J.L.: Consistency problems in UML-based software development. In: Jardim Nunes, N., Selic, B., da Silva, A.R., Rodrigues, A., Toval Alvarez, A. (eds.) UML 2004. LNCS, vol. 3297, pp. 1–12. Springer, Heidelberg (2005). doi:10.1007/978-3-540-31797-5_1
3. Lucas, F.J., Molina, F., Toval, A.: A systematic review of UML model consistency management. Inf. Softw. Technol. **51**(12), 1631–1645 (2009). http://dx.doi.org/10.1016/j.infsof.2009.04.009
4. Miyazaki, H., Yokogawa, T., Amasaki, S., Asada, K., Sato, Y.: Synthesis and refinement check of sequence diagrams. IEICE Trans. Inf. Syst. E **E95–D**(9), 2193–2201 (2012)
5. Petre, M.: UML in practice. In: Proceedings on International Conference on Software Engineering (ICSE 2013), pp. 722–731 (2013)
6. Torre, D., Labiche, Y., Genero, M.: UML consistency rules: a systematic mapping study. In: Proceedings of the 18th on International Conference on Evaluation and Assessment in Software Engineering (EASE 2014), pp. 1–10 (2014)
7. Yokogawa, T., Amasaki, S., Okazaki, K., Sato, Y., Arimoto, K., Miyazaki, H.: Consistency verification of UML diagrams based on process bisimulation (fast abstract). In: Proceedings of the 19th IEEE Pacific Rim International Symposium on Dependable Computing (PRDC 2013), pp. 126–127 (2013)
8. Zhao, Xiangpeng, Long, Quan, Qiu, Zongyan: Model checking dynamic UML consistency. In: Liu, Zhiming, He, Jifeng (eds.) ICFEM 2006. LNCS, vol. 4260, pp. 440–459. Springer, Heidelberg (2006). doi:10.1007/11901433_24

Tutorials

Analyzing the Potential of Big Data

A Tutorial for Business and IT Experts

Andreas Jedlitschka[✉]

Fraunhofer Insitute for Experimental Software Engineering (IESE), Kaiserslautern, Germany
andreas.jedlitschka@iese.fraunhofer.de

Abstract. Recent studies report that many Big Data projects fail due to insufficient alignment with the organization's strategic objectives and no consideration of its operational capabilities. Our method for the analysis of the potentials of Big Data supports companies in making a rational decision to use Big Data as well as in systematically conceptualizing and realizing a specific Big Data strategy. The Potential Analysis helps to find a Big Data solution for a specific business innovation idea that promises to deliver the best trade-off between the potential business benefits and the investments required for deploying it. The development of a suitable solution happens in several iterations during which both the anticipated data-driven business solution and the required Big Data solution concept are revised. This tutorial addresses experts from business and IT. The participants will learn a systematic approach for developing a company-specific Big Data strategy.

Keywords: Big Data · Potential Analysis · Tutorial

1 Introduction

Independent of any domain, all roadmaps and future scenarios clearly show: A service layer will be established in the future between products and customers. It will be oriented more towards the business processes of the market participants and will create benefit especially through the combination of systems and data – for manufacturers, suppliers, service providers, salespeople, workshops, and end customers [1]. "Data-driven business models" and "Big Data" are the big buzzwords in this context.

However, recent surveys report that 60% of Big Data projects fail to go beyond piloting and experimentation [2]. Furthermore, less than 50% of the organizations that have not started yet with Big Data, have sufficiently adjusted their culture or business model to allow them to benefit from Big Data [3].

One major reason for such failures is that the initiatives were neither aligned with the strategic objectives nor matched to the operational capabilities of a particular organization. Driven by the belief that more data will bring more benefit, organizations focus on creating data lakes without prior consideration of what they want to achieve with the data and how; 90% of deployed data lakes end up being useless as they are overwhelmed with information assets captured for uncertain use cases [3]. As the authors concluded

© Springer International Publishing AG 2017
M. Felderer et al. (Eds.): PROFES 2017, LNCS 10611, pp. 613–616, 2017.
https://doi.org/10.1007/978-3-319-69926-4_52

in their study [3], data and ecosystems are key drivers of future trends in software engineering and "the challenge isn't the big data but the organization's ability to make smart, timely decisions based on the data". It is the ability to collect relevant data, analyze it, and implement data-driven decision making that strongly affect the way a company functions, its architecture, and its workflows.

The effective use of data from and pertaining to today's products and services as well as the goal-oriented combination and analysis of existing and possibly the exploitation of new data sources do not only open up optimization potential but also new business opportunities. However, this also entails uncertainties that are difficult to assess, due to new technologies and analysis processes, frequently ambiguous data quality, and unverified or implicit assumptions [1].

Thus, the key question today is no longer "whether", but rather how Big Data can help an organization to achieve their business objectives. Further questions include:

- How can an organization benefit from Big Data?
- Which data "treasures" are already available in the organization?
- Are there any hidden business potentials in the available data?
- Are the required competencies available?
- Is the quality of the data sufficient to realize the anticipated business benefits?
- What investments are necessary to deploy a Big Data initiative?
- How does Big Data affect existing business models?

The answers should not be given by any specific part of the organization, e.g., solely by the IT or business unit, but should, in the best case, be developed by a group staffed from different units with heterogeneous skills. The analysis of the Big Data business potential offers answers to these questions, ideally, before any investments are made.

2   Analysis of Big Data Potential

The Fraunhofer IESE approach for analyzing the business potential of Big Data (cf. "Potential Analysis") [4] covers the ideation, derivation, evaluation, and maturation of business innovations based on Big Data and minimizing the risk and potential loss due to investments in Big Data solutions that do not create the expected business value.

The core element of the Potential Analysis is a concrete Big Data business case (see Fig. 1). It specifies particular Big-Data-driven business innovation, including its context with the underlying business need, the business solution with its expected benefits (value), and the Big Data solution including the organizational readiness to implement it. The Potential Analysis answers key questions that should precede any Big-Data-driven change: In what context should it happen? What business benefit (value) should be gained from the use of Big Data? Are the capabilities for implementing the Big Data solution available? How much will it cost?

The Potential Analysis starts by specifying the organizational scope and current situation. The purpose is to understand an organization's internal and external factors that (1) are the source of potential business challenges and opportunities and (2) influence the feasibility of potential Big Data solutions.

Fig. 1. Analysis of Big Data business potentials

The motivation for developing a business solution first is that evaluation and failing at this stage are cheap, whereas prototyping and testing already require considerable investments into infrastructure and staff. Developing a Big Data solution includes deciding about Big Data methods, infrastructure, and skills required for realizing the business solution. Similar to a business solution, a Big Data solution evolves through test-feedback-improve evaluation cycles. In each evaluation cycle, the readiness of the organization to implement and deploy a specific Big Data solution is assessed and the gap between the required and available organizational capabilities is determined. A capability gap can be addressed by either adjusting the business solution and/or the associated Big Data solution (i.e., necessary data, analysis methods, and infrastructure). As Porter says: "Success requires both the right strategy and operational effectiveness" [5].

To minimize the risk of failing with Big Data and to reduce potential business losses, the Big Data solution concept is evaluated and matured in several lab and piloting stages before being deployed in a productive environment. Each step is followed by an evaluation of the results according to pre-defined criteria (technical and business aspects). For instance, the accuracy of a prediction algorithm may directly influence the reliability of forecasts and thus affect customer acceptance of the realized business solution.

At each stage, the Big Data solution concept, the associated business case, and the organization's readiness are revised based upon the evaluation outcomes. In the very first stage, a blueprint of the Big Data solution is evaluated without any practical implementation. In the following stages, specific "in-use" aspects of the Big Data solution concept are implemented in test environments and then evaluated. For example, the performance and scalability of the selected data analysis approach are evaluated in a lab environment using simulated (or real) data. Evaluating integration with existing infrastructure and processes as well as user acceptance, on the other hand, requires piloting of the Big Data approach in the target environment. Based on the evaluation results, the solution concept and the corresponding business solution are revised and re-assessed. Only if the Big Data solution has successfully run through all intermediate stages will it be rolled out into a productive environment. Yet this is not the end; as the organizational context changes continuously, the effectiveness of the realized data-driven business model should be revised on a regular basis.

3 Details About the Tutorial

The goal of this tutorial is to raise the participants' awareness regarding the necessity to plan Big Data projects strategically and to align them with business goals.

The tutorial is targeted at experts from companies who are interested in Big Data and in how to approach their use. In particular, we aim at people who (1) are asking themselves whether Big Data provides a benefit for their company, (2) just started their first Big Data project, and (3) have first experience, either from successful or failed Big Data projects. We connect business (C-Level, Marketing, Portfolio/Product Management, …) with technical experts (IT, BI, …); therefore, no IT background is required.

To start with, the participants will get an overview of current trends in digitization and Big Data. From there, we will go through a hands-on example to explain the theoretical concepts behind a goal-oriented Big Data strategy. The participants will learn how to sketch a Big Data business model, estimate its benefits, and derive required capabilities, as well as how to check the model in terms of its benefits, associated risks, and technical feasibility. They will be actively involved through exercises and experience different moderation methods supporting the development of the strategy.

The Potential Analysis represents the first step of an incremental development and implementation process. It consists of three parts: scoping, benefit analysis, and readiness analysis. During the tutorial, the participants will get an introduction to all three parts. During the exercise, we will develop a common example.

During Scoping, we have a look at the target environment and make the constraints and success criteria for possible initiatives more concrete. During the subsequent Benefit Analysis, we identify business opportunities based on existing challenges and data sources and make them more concrete in terms of their information needs with the help of scenarios. An assessment of the contribution with regard to superordinate business goals supports prioritization. During the Readiness Analysis, we develop an initial solution concept for selected business opportunities and derive necessary skills. This provides the basis on which we assess the organization's readiness to implement this specific Big Data solution.

References

1. Heidrich, J., Trendowicz, A., Ebert, C.: Exploiting Big Data's benefits. IEEE Softw. **33**(1), 111–116 (2016). doi:10.1109/MS.2016.99
2. Heudecker, N., et al.: Predicts 2015: Big Data challenges move from technology to the organization, Gartner Report, November 2014
3. Bosch, J.: Speed, data, and ecosystems. The future of software engineering. IEEE Softw. **33**(1), 82–88 (2016). doi:10.1109/MS.2016.14
4. Trendowicz, A.: Big Data – Mountains of Gold or Garbage Dumps (Whitepaper). Fraunhofer IESE, Kaiserslautern (2017). https://bigdata.iese.fraunhofer.de
5. Porter, M.E.: What is strategy? Harv. Bus. Rev. **74**(6), 61–78 (1996)

Automatic Requirements Reviews - Potentials, Limitations and Practical Tool Support

Henning Femmer[✉]

Qualicen GmbH, Garching bei München, Germany
henning.femmer@qualicen.de

Abstract. Requirements are usually documented, and natural language is still the primary choice of syntax. However, in particular with natural language, the quality of the documentation is a key success factor for projects. To keep this risk in check, projects apply manual quality assurance in the form of reviews. Due to the shortcomings of manual reviews, more and more companies look into lightweight automatic support mechanisms to improve the quality of requirements documents.

1 Description

To document requirements, natural language is still the primary means. Requirements in natural language can be created and understood by all stakeholders without additional effort and specific requirements engineering background. However, natural language poses the risk of being imprecise or ambiguous. Badly written requirements have an expensive impact on the whole project. Incomplete or ambiguous requirements generate additional effort due to unnecessary feedback loops. In the end, bad requirements lead to misinterpretations and finally to the wrong product.

Manual reviews are an effective tool to create high quality requirements documents. Although effective, this method comes with considerable effort. The manual inspection of the requirements by multiple reviewers and the integration of review results are time consuming. As one review cycle often takes days or weeks to complete, the author of the requirements has to wait a long time before receiving feedback. The result of these problems is that reviews are often only performed sporadically or only superficially.

2 Potentials

The potential for automatic reviews detection lays in the aforementioned deficiencies of manual reviews; A claim that is also supported by practitioners and evaluated in practice (see, e.g. [5]).

Automatic reviews are cheap. As we discuss in [3], one of the key challenges to establishing manual reviews in practice are the high costs that come with a thorough analysis. Therefore, to have a mechanism that provides feedback free of charge is a promising advantage. (For the sake of the argument, we deliberately ignore the costs of setting up and maintaining such an analysis.)

© Springer International Publishing AG 2017
M. Felderer et al. (Eds.): PROFES 2017, LNCS 10611, pp. 617–620, 2017.
https://doi.org/10.1007/978-3-319-69926-4_53

Automatic reviews are fast. For many quality aspects, feedback can be given more or less instantaneously. For example, in the current configuration, our requirements scout receives, processes, and renders feedback for a paragraph in around 500 ms. This enables us to give feedback on-the-fly.

Automatic reviews are consistent. If you hand a requirements artifact to one reviewer on two different days, you might receive two very different results. The review process depends on various personal factors, such as the state of mind or the recent input of the reviewer. While this can be an advantage, for quality factors such as *Does the artifact follow a guideline?*, this subjectivity throws the doors wide open for inconsistencies. An automatic method works in a deterministic way, every day.

In an analysis of an industrial RE artifact guideline in [6], we estimate that 52% of the guideline rules can be automatically checked perfectly or with a good heuristic. Surprisingly, for detection of quality violations, most rules require just simple heuristics.

Accordingly, many researchers work on providing automatic support for REs [1,4,5,7–10].

3   Limitations

Various reasons imply that a quality factor cannot be automatically detected. This is analyzed in-depth, i.a. in [2] or [6]. The main reasons, why certain quality factor cannot be automatically detected are:

- Automatic reviews require an explicit quality definition.
- Automatic reviews struggle with noise in industrial data.
- Automatic reviews have no deep semantic understanding of text.
- Automatic reviews have no knowledge of domain and common sense.
- Automatic reviews do not know the goal of the system and the current project status.

4   Tooling: The Requirements Scout

Tooling for automatic requirements reviews can be seen from three roles: The central role is, of course, the requirements author, who produces the requirements. But there is also the reviewer, who proof-reads and validates the requirements. And finally, there is the QA-Engineer, responsible for the overall quality of all artifacts created during the engineering process. Each of these roles needs a different view on requirements and different tools in order to do their work efficiently and achieve a high requirements quality.

The author is interested in direct feedback. In a previous analysis [3], we found that receiving feedback directly within the tool increases the willingness of authors to use such a tool. Therefore, the requirements scout comes with various plugins, e.g. for the widespread RE tool PTC Integrity (see Fig. 1) or Microsoft Word.

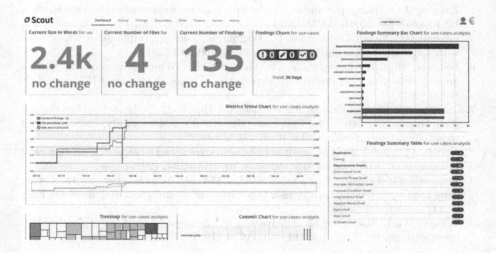

ID	Section	Text	QRC_Findings	QRC_Findings_Text
178	2.4.2	Because of base waterproof protection. Watch face be made out of glass.	☐ Passive Voice Smell	Because of base waterproof protection. Watch face be made out of glass.
188	2.5	**Time Zone Requirements**		**Time Zone Requirements**
190	2.5.1	All time zones must run of the same internal quartz crystal. To distinguish between the time zones, the embedded microprocessor must calculate the offset of each time zone and keep track of the time zones chosen by the user. yes		All time zones must run of the same internal quartz crystal. To distinguish between the time zones, the embedded microprocessor must calculate the offset of each time zone and keep track of the time zones chosen by the user. yes
192	2.5.1.1	As soon as one time zone time is changed, all others must adjust automatically. The only exception to this is a daylight savings time change. By knowing the offset of each time zone, the MPU can determine the new times for the other times zones using the appropriate offsets	☐ Passive Voice Smell ☐ Imprecise Phrase Smell	As soon as one time zone time is changed, all others must adjust automatically. The only exception to this is a daylight savings time change. By knowing the offset of each time zone, the MPU can determine the new times for the other times zones using the appropriate offsets
194	2.6	**Timer Requirements**		**Timer Requirements**
196	2.6.1	tbd.		tbd.
198	2.6.1.1	For the timer feature, the counter on the digital display must be counted down to 00:00:00.	☐ Passive Voice Smell	For the timer feature, the counter on the digital display must be counted down to 00:00:00.
200	2.7	**Chronometer Requirements**		**Chronometer Requirements**
202	2.7.1	The chronometer must have an easy-to-understand user interface which allows the user to quickly clear and restart the chronometer or restart timing from their previous stopped time.	☐ Long Sentence Smell	The chronometer must have an easy-to-understand user interface which allows the user to quickly clear and restart the chronometer or restart timing from their previous stopped time.

Fig. 1. PTC integrity integration of qualicen scout

The reviewer is interested in focussing on the most relevant quality factors. For example, he or she wants to analyze whether the specification validly meets the stakeholders' goals. Therefore, the scout offers the option to list all findings that the scout detects, so that the reviewer quickly picks the interesting ones from the list and then continues focussing on the content.

Lastly, the QA-Engineer (and also management) is interested in the development of quality over time. Therefore, the scout enables to set baselines, compare two versions, and analyze trends and tendencies in order to understand in which direction the quality is going (see Fig. 2).

Fig. 2. Qualicen scout quality dashboard

5   Summary

Automatic review techniques have matured over the last years: A substantial set of widespread quality defects in requirements documents can now be found automatically. Examples of such defects are ambiguous wording or overly complex sentences. Also more complex defects, such as cloning, inadequate levels of abstraction, or wrong references in documents can be detected automatically.

However, there are also strong limitations to automatic review techniques. In a recent study [6] we quantified this, estimating that 52% of the guideline rules can be automatically checked perfectly or with a good heuristic. As a conclusion, automatic reviews do not replace, but complement manual reviews. It is assumed, however still remains to be shown, that automatic reviews reduce the time needed for manual reviews and provide faster and less expensive feedback for requirements authors.

References

1. Fabrini, F., Fusani, M., Gnesi, S., Lami, G.: Quality evaluation of software requirements. In: Software and Internet Quality Week Conference, pp. 1–18 (2000)
2. Femmer, H.: Requirements engineering artifact quality: definition and control. Ph.D. thesis, Technische Universitat Munchen (2017)
3. Femmer, H., Hauptmann, B., Eder, S., Moser, D.: Quality assurance of requirements artifacts in practice: a case study and a process proposal. In: Abrahamsson, P., Jedlitschka, A., Nguyen Duc, A., Felderer, M., Amasaki, S., Mikkonen, T. (eds.) PROFES 2016. LNCS, vol. 10027, pp. 506–516. Springer, Cham (2016). doi:10. 1007/978-3-319-49094-6_36
4. Femmer, H., Mendez Fernandez, D., Juergens, E., Klose, M., Zimmer, I., Zimmer, J.: Rapid requirements checks with requirements smells: two case studies. In: RCoSE, pp. 10–19. ACM (2014)
5. Femmer, H., Mendez Fernandez, D., Wagner, S., Eder, S.: Rapid quality assurance with requirements smells. J. Syst. Soft. **123**, 190–213 (2017)
6. Femmer, H., Unterkalmsteiner, M., Gorschek, T.: Which requirements artifact quality defects are automatically detectable? A case study. In: AIRE, pp. 1–7. IEEE (2017)
7. Juergens, E., Deissenboeck, F., Feilkas, M., Hummel, B., Schaetz, B., Wagner, S., Domann, C., Streit, J.: Can clone detection support quality assessments of requirements specifications? In: ICSE. ACM (2010)
8. Krisch, J., Houdek, F.: The myth of bad passive voice and weak words: an empirical investigation in the automotive industry. In: RE. IEEE (2015)
9. Lucassen, G., Dalpiaz, F., van der Werf, J.M.E.M., Brinkkemper, S.: Improving agile requirements: the quality user story framework and tool. Requirements Eng. J. **21**(3), 383–403 (2016)
10. Wilson, W.M., Rosenberg, L.H., Hyatt, L.E.: Automated analysis of requirement specifications. In: ICSE, pp. 161–171. ACM (1997)

Need for Speed – Towards Real-Time Business

Janne Järvinen[1(✉)] and Tommi Mikkonen[2]

[1] F-Secure Corporation, Helsinki, Finland
janne.jarvinen@f-secure.com
[2] University of Helsinki, Helsinki, Finland
tommi.mikkonen@helsinki.fi

Abstract. The Finnish software intensive industry has renewed their existing business and organizational ways of working towards a value-driven, adaptive real-time business paradigm. The industry utilizes new technical infrastructures such as data visualization and feedback from product delivery. These new capabilities as well as various sources of data and information help in gaining and applying the deep customer insight. This tutorial has been created and adapted from 100+ concrete N4S consortia results in public domain with several successful examples of adjacency towards the new markets and business areas.

Keywords: Real-time value delivery · Deep customer insight · Mercury business · Lean Startup · Elastic Enterprise

1 Introduction

The Need for Speed (N4S) [7] program was formed to create the foundation for the success of the Finnish software intensive businesses in the new digital economy, in spirit of Lean Startup [9] and Elastic Enterprise [12] ideas. This collaborative, industry driven research program was executed in 2014–2017, and it was at the time the biggest national investment in software-related research with a budget over 50 M€.

In this tutorial, we first discuss today's software development approaches that are commonly applied in Finnish software companies. Then we proceed to N4S building blocks and results that are in the focus of this tutorial. We aim to give participants an overall understanding of N4S and how to utilize its results in practice.

2 Background: Agile and Lean Software Development

Software and software intensive industry have undergone major advances over the last decades. The transition from slow projects lasting years to the rapid cycles of continuous development and deployment have been dramatic (Fig. 1a).

© Springer International Publishing AG 2017
M. Felderer et al. (Eds.): PROFES 2017, LNCS 10611, pp. 621–624, 2017.
https://doi.org/10.1007/978-3-319-69926-4_54

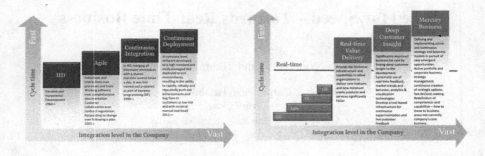

Fig. 1. (a) Agile and lean software development, and (b) real-time value delivery, deep customer insight, and mercury business.

Iterative and incremental development. Ever since (and probably even before) the introduction of the commonly misunderstood Waterfall process [10], iterative and incremental development has been used by software developers to manage risks and uncertainties in software development. By developing software in a piecemeal fashion, where frequent checkpoints can be used to detect anomalies and misinterpretations, the development effort can be more easily managed than by using a big-bang development approach. Consequently, while the rational design process can be used to explain how the development advances [8], in reality it has been customary to conduct at least experiments before advancing too far in the development.

Agile development. Agile software development approaches [3] consist of a wide number of practices where delivering value to a customer is the dominant factor in software development, over following a plan, which once was the prevailing concept in many software projects. Various agile methodologies exist, like Extreme Programming [2], Scrum [11], Kanban [1], and Lean software development, and they more or less share the underlying mindset but implement actual actions differently.

Continuous integration. When numerous developers work on the same project, they commonly make changes in the same software components in their own workspaces. When the changes contradict each other, a conflict arises, which need to be resolved by the developers. The key issue of continuous integration is to minimize such conflicts by merging developer workspaces with a shared mainline [5].

Continuous deployment. While continuous integration is about creating the ability to build a system automatically whenever a change is made, continuous deployment is about creating the ability to deliver the smallest added value to the customers.

To summarize, the evolution of the software development approaches has led towards approaches where the step between the development and deployment is being reduced. Hence, an approach referred to DevOps emerges, where development is treated similarly to operations, and no distinction between the two is made [4]. The promise is that the tighter cooperation results in rapid development and utilization of the software products and services. To reach this target, continuous deployment and/or continuous delivery [6] are commonly used.

3   N4S Building Blocks

The N4S program has been built around three main themes. These are (1) paradigm change from product business to delivering value at real-time; (2) deep customer insight to improve the hit-rate of businesses; and (3) Mercury business which explicitly aims at finding the new money instead of focusing only on the traditional customers. Next, these three goals, which are also illustrated in Fig. 1b, are addressed separately.

Real-time value delivery. The key aspect of the program is to catalyze a paradigm change from the traditional product-based software business to service-based business where value can be delivered at near real time. Achieving this goal requires careful reconsideration of the mode of operation as well as seamless integration of businesses and research and development – the former provides motivation for the latter, whereas the latter enables new forms of business. To reach the above goals, an architecture and technical infrastructure that supports the incremental development, integration and delivery of systems is needed, including introduction and removal of individual features.

Deep customer insight. The goal of deep customer insight is to invent value-creating solutions, and act as a source of inspiration for new products, features, or services that create customer value, which typically stems from the customer contexts and not from the engineering domain. The goal is to quickly gain and assess information regarding the true customer value of potential services, product features, and other possible aspects of user interaction with a service or a product. As a prerequisite, understanding of customer contexts and development opportunities as well as an insight on the ways how customers live and work are needed. The data for deep understanding of the customers is gathered continuously from live use of products, enabling also possible weak signals. Moreover, live experiments enable studying how the users interact with a service or a product. However, successful collection of usage data requires understanding regarding what data to collect. Data that is readily available and simple to collect does not necessarily lend itself to meaningful interpretation in terms of what can be related to the user value of the features or true needs of the user. Therefore, before running the experiments, these experiments should have a defined scope and purpose. To reach the ultimate goal of experimenting and testing ideas and concepts early in the development, there is a thriving demand for automatic and efficient feedback systems, analytics and visualization.

Mercury business. By mercury business, we refer to companies and societies being able to behave like "mercury" finding new grooves where to flow to grow new business. The goal is to enable companies to actively seek new ways to execute their existing businesses, and – perhaps even more importantly – also experiment the options to transform themselves to completely new business areas. The two above goals, real-time value delivery and deep customer insight, are important prerequisites for Mercury business, but there are also other factors that must be considered – like company culture, structure, and leadership for instance – to empower everyone to seek new opportunities. The ways of working may also change dynamically regardless of the existing organizational structures. These changes are possible e.g. in the Finnish individualistic culture, where extremely dynamical changes in the ways of working are possible. Finally, while the Mercury business model may change existing products and portfolios, we believe that its ability to totally convert the company into a new business domain is more important.

4 N4S Experiences and Results: A Summary

In the N4S program, 40 leading Finnish software-intensive companies and research organizations tested real-time business models in practice. The program compiled the results and experience, forming a large-scale collection of advice and tools accessible to everyone. This N4S Treasure Chest located at http://www.n4s.fi/en/treasure-chest-for-business/ helps companies to make use of the possibilities of digitalization and advises upon post-digitalization activities. The program published 3 guide books and a total of 268 scientific articles. As a practical engineering result, the efficiency of the development work of certain N4S program participants has increased up to 250%. The efficiency of infrastructure improved 50% thanks to cloud services. In addition, dependency on maintenance from outside sources decreased 50%. Changing over to software using free source code decreased expenses of licensed products by 30%.

References

1. Anderson, D.: Kanban – Successful Evolutionary Change for Your Technology Business. Blue Hole Press, Sequim (2010)
2. Beck, K.: Extreme Programming Explained, 2nd edn. Addison-Wesley Professional, Boston (1999)
3. Cockburn, A.: Agile Software Development, 1st edn. Addison-Wesley Professional, Boston (2001). 256 pages
4. Debois, P.: DevOps: a software revolution in the making. Cutter IT J. 24(8) (2011). 42 pages
5. Fowler, M.: Continuous integration (2006). http://martinfowler.com/articles/continuous Integration.html
6. Humble, J., Farley, D.: Continuous Delivery: Reliable Software Releases Through Build, Test, and Deployment Automation. Pearson Education, Boston (2010)
7. Huomo, T., Järvinen, J., Kettunen, P., Kuvaja, P., Koivisto, A., Lassenius, C., Lehtovuori, P., Lilja, S., Miettinen, S., Mikkonen, T., Münch, J., Männistö, T., Oivo, M., Partanen, J., Porres, I., Still, J., Tyrväinen, P.: Strategic research agenda for need for speed. ICT SHOK DIGILE, 22 April 2013. http://n4s.fi/articles/SRIA_Need4Speed_V5_0_April_2015.pdf. Accessed Jan 2017
8. Parnas, D.L., Clements, P.C.: A rational design process: how and why to fake it. IEEE Trans. Softw. Eng. 12(2), 251–257 (1986)
9. Ries, E.: The Lean Startup: How Today's Entrepreneurs Use Continuous Innovation to Create Radically Successful Businesses. Crown Publishing Group, New York (2011)
10. Royce, W.: Managing the development of large software systems. In: Proceedings of IEEE WESCON, vol. 26, pp. 1–9, August 1970
11. Schwaber, K.: Scrum development process. In: Workshop Proceedings of Business Object Design and Implementation, OOPSLA 1995, p. 118. The University of Michigan (1995)
12. Vitalari, N., Shaughnessy, H.: The Elastic Enterprise: The New Manifesto for Business Revolution. Telemachus Press, Dublin (2012)

From Zero to Hero: A Process Mining Tutorial

Andrea Janes[1], Fabrizio Maria Maggi[2(✉)], Andrea Marrella[3],
and Marco Montali[1]

[1] Free University of Bozen-Bolzano, Bolzano, Italy
{andrea.janes,marco.montali}@unibz.it
[2] University of Tartu, Tartu, Estonia
f.m.maggi@ut.ee
[3] Sapienza University, Rome, Italy
marrella@diag.uniroma1.it

Abstract. Process mining is an emerging area that synergically combines model-based and data-oriented analysis techniques to obtain useful insights on how business processes are executed within an organization. This tutorial aims at providing an introduction to the key analysis techniques in process mining that allow decision makers to discover process models from data, compare expected and actual behaviors, and enrich models with key information about the actual process executions. In addition, the tutorial will present concrete tools and will provide practical skills for applying process mining in a variety of application domains, including the one of software development.

1 Introduction

Process mining [2] is a recent research discipline that sits between computational intelligence and data mining on the one hand, and process modeling and analysis on the other hand. Through process mining, decision makers can discover process models from data, compare expected and actual behaviors, and enrich models with information retrieved from data. This, in turn, provides the basis for understanding, maintaining, and enhancing processes based on reality.

Since process mining has many applications, this tutorial aims at encouraging participants to apply it in new fields, in which it has not been applied so far. In particular, first, we will introduce the process mining framework, the main process mining techniques and tools, and the different phases of event data analysis through process mining. Second, we will carry out an hands-on session using concrete process mining tools, considering business use cases, as well as the particular scenario of software processes. Finally, we will discuss common pitfalls and critical issues and will give suggestions on how to mitigate them.

2 Process Mining Framework

The reference framework for process mining is depicted in Fig. 1. On the one hand, process mining considers conceptual models describing processes, organizational structures, and the corresponding relevant data. On the other hand,

© Springer International Publishing AG 2017
M. Felderer et al. (Eds.): PROFES 2017, LNCS 10611, pp. 625–629, 2017.
https://doi.org/10.1007/978-3-319-69926-4_55

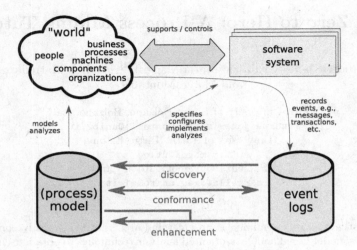

Fig. 1. The reference framework for process mining [1]

it focuses on the real execution of processes, as reflected by the footprint of reality logged and stored by the software systems in use within an enterprise. For process mining to be applicable, such information has to be structured in the form of explicit *event logs*. In fact, all process mining techniques assume that it is possible to record the sequencing of relevant events occurred within an enterprise, such that each event refers to an activity (i.e., a well-defined step in some process) and is related to a particular case [1]. Events may have additional information stored in event logs. In fact, whenever possible, process mining techniques use extra information such as the exact timestamp at which the event has been recorded, the resource (i.e., person or device) that generated the event, the event type in the context of the activity transactional lifecycle (e.g., whether the activity has been started, canceled, or completed), or data elements recorded with the event (e.g., the size of an order).

The three main types of process mining techniques are marked by the three, thick red arrows in the bottom part of Fig. 1. *Discovery* starts from an event log and automatically produces a process model that explains the different behaviors observed in the log, without assuming any prior knowledge on the process. The vast majority of process discovery algorithms focus on the discovery of the process control-flow, towards generating a model that indicates the allowed sequences of activities according to the log. *Conformance checking* compares an existing process model and an event log for the same process, with the aim of understanding the presence and nature of *deviations*. Conformance checking techniques take as inputs an event log and a process model, and return indications related to the adherence of the behaviors contained in the log to the prescriptions contained in the model. *Enhancement* improves an existing process model using information recorded in an event log for that process. The inputs of enhancement techniques are a process model and an event log, and the output is a new process model that incorporates and reflects new information extracted from the data. The first important class of enhancement techniques is that of *extension*, where the input process model is not altered in its structure, but is extended with additional perspectives, using information present in the log. A second important class of enhancement techniques is that of *repair*, where deviations detected by checking the conformance of the input event log to the input process model are resolved by suitably modifying the process model.

The presented tutorial will demonstrate that process mining *can* also be used in the context of software development [9], trying to focus on aspects that occur with a certain regularity and with a finite number of possible activities so that repeating cases within an actual "process" can be discovered. One example will be the *user behavior analysis* [9], i.e., the study on how the users interact with software applications. In particular, we will study an example that can be found in [3], in which the authors applied process mining to study and to improve the user interface of an ERP software.

2.1 Process Mining Tools

A plethora of process mining techniques and technologies have been developed and successfully employed in several application domains[1]. The process mining solutions that will be used in the tutorial are *ProM* (Process Mining framework)[2] and *Disco*[3].

- *ProM* (Process Mining framework) is an Open Source framework for process mining algorithms [10] based on JAVA. It provides a plug-in based integration platform [4] that users and developers can exploit to run and deploy process techniques. This pluggable architecture currently hosts a very large amount of plug-ins covering all the different aspects of process mining, from data import to discovery, conformance checking, and enhancement along different perspectives [2].
- *Disco* is a commercial, stand-alone and lightweight process mining tool. It supports various file formats as input, in particular providing native support for importing CSV files, which can be annotated with case and event information prior to the import. Disco has usability, fidelity, and performance as design priorities, and makes process mining easy and fast [7].

2.2 The XES Standard

In recent years, the *XES (eXtensible Event Stream)* format emerged as the main reference format for the storage, interchange, and analysis of event logs. XES, which is based on XML, appeared for the first time in 2009 [6] as the successor of the MXML format [5]. It quickly became the de-facto standard adopted by

---

[1] http://tinyurl.com/ovedwx4.
[2] http://www.processmining.org/prom/.
[3] https://fluxicon.com/disco/.

the IEEE Task Force on Process Mining[4], eventually becoming an official IEEE standard in 2016 [8]. This standard will be introduced in the tutorial.

3   Agenda

The tutorial is structured as follows:

- Introduction to the process mining framework
- Designing process models and collecting event logs
  - Process modeling: basics of Petri nets and BPMN
  - The XES standard and the OpenXES reference implementation
- Mining event logs, discovering processes
  - ProM, the open-source jack of all trades
  - Choosing a mining algorithm: Alpha, Heuristics miner, Fuzzy miner, or Multi-phase miner?
  - Disco, the user friendly tool
- Interpreting the mined models: discovery, conformance checking, and enhancement
  - Deciding from which perspective to look at the data: choosing a case ID
  - On the representational bias of process mining
- Hands-on session
  - Process mining success stories for business processes and software processes
  - Walk-through of two process mining examples examining a business process and a software process, discussing strategies to collect, filter, analyze, and interpret data
  - Discussion on the differences between mining business and software processes.

References

1. van der Aalst, W., et al.: Process mining manifesto. In: Proceedings of BPM International Workshops, vol. 99, pp. 169–194 (2012)
2. van der Aalst, W.M.P.: Process Mining - Data Science in Action, 2nd edn. Springer, Heidelberg (2016). doi:10.1007/978-3-662-49851-4
3. Astromskis, S., Janes, A., Mairegger, M.: A process mining approach to measure how users interact with software: an industrial case study. In: ICSSP 2015 (2015)
4. van Dongen, B.F., de Medeiros, A.K.A., Verbeek, H.M.W., Weijters, A., van der Aalst, W.M.P.: The ProM framework: a new era in process mining tool support, pp. 444–454 (2005)
5. van Dongen, B.F., van der Aalst, W.M.P.: A meta model for process mining data. In: Proceedings of EMOI - INTEROP, vol. 160. CEUR-WS.org (2005)
6. Gunther, C.W.: XES standard definition version 1.0. Technical report, Fluxicon Process Laboratories. http://www.xes-standard.org

---

[4] http://www.win.tue.nl/ieeetfpm/doku.php.

7. Gunther, C.W., Rozinat, A.: Disco: Discover your processes. In: Proceedings of the Demo Track of BPM, vol. 940, pp. 40–44 (2012)
8. IEEE Computational Intelligence Society: IEEE standard for eXtensible Event Stream (XES) for achieving interoperability in event logs and event streams. IEEE Std. 1849–2016, p. i-50 (2016)
9. Rubin, V.A., Mitsyuk, A.A., Lomazova, I.A., van der Aalst, W.M.P.: Process mining can be applied to software tool. In: Proceedings of the ESEM 2014. ACM (2014)
10. Verbeek, H.M.W., Buijs, J.C.A.M., van Dongen, B.F., van der Aalst, W.M.P.: XES, XESame, and ProM 6. In: Soffer, P., Proper, E. (eds.) CAiSE Forum 2010. LNBIP, vol. 72, pp. 60–75. Springer, Heidelberg (2011). doi:10.1007/978-3-642-17722-4_5

Erratum to: How *Accountability* is Implemented and Understood in Research Tools

A Systematic Mapping Study

Severin Kacianka[1]([⊠]), Kristian Beckers[2], Florian Kelbert[3], and Prachi Kumari[4]

[1] Technical University of Munich, Munich, Germany
kacianka@in.tum.de
[2] Siemens, Munich, Germany
kristian.beckers@siemens.com
[3] Imperial College London, London, England
f.kelbert@imperial.ac.uk
[4] Munich, Germany
prachi.kumari@tum.de

Erratum to:
Chapter "How *Accountability* is Implemented and Understood in Research Tools" in: M. Felderer et al. (Eds.): Product-Focused Software Process Improvement, LNCS 10611, https://doi.org/10.1007/978-3-319-69926-4_15

The presentation of Table 3 was incorrect in the original version of this chapter.

The correct version is given below:

Table 3. Most influential researchers.

Name	Institution	Cit.
Siani Pearson	HP Labs Bristol, UK	16
David L. Chaum	Voting Systems Institute	14
Margo Seltzer	Harvard University, Cambridge, MA, USA	13
Jan Camenisch	IBM Research, Zurich, Switzerland	13
Markus Kirchberg	National University of Singapore, Singapore	11
Kiran Kumar Muniswamy-Reddy	Harvard University, Cambridge, MA, SA	9
Lorrie Faith Cranor	Carnegie Mellon University, Pittsburgh, PA, USA	9

(continued)

The updated online version of this chapter can be found at
https://doi.org/10.1007/978-3-319-69926-4_15

© Springer International Publishing AG 2017
M. Felderer et al. (Eds.): PROFES 2017, LNCS 10611, pp. E1–E2, 2017.
https://doi.org/10.1007/978-3-319-69926-4_56

Table 3. (*continued*)

Name	Institution	Cit.
Elisa Bertino	Purdue University, West Lafayette, Indiana, USA	8
Uri J. Braun	Harvard University, Cambridge, MA, USA	8
Gene Tsudik	University of California, Irvine, California, USA	8
Anna Lysyanskaya	Brown University, Providence, RI, USA	8
Wade Trappe	Rutgers University, Piscataway, New Jersey, USA	7
Ian T. Foster	University of Chicago, Chicago, IL, USA	7
Peter Macko	Harvard University, Cambridge, MA, USA	7
Susan Hohenberger	Johns Hopkins University, Baltimore, MD, USA	7

The original chapter has been corrected.

Author Index